THE INTERNET NAVIGATOR'S REFERENCE CARD

Addressing E-Mail

Internet to America Online
userid@aol.com johnd@aol.com

Internet to CompuServe
usernumber@compuserve.com 70000.100@compuserve.com

Internet to Fidonet
Firstname.Lastname@F*nodenumber*.N*net*.Z*zone*.fidonet.org
John.Doe@f101.n10.z1.fidonet.org
Firstname.Lastname@P*point*.F*nodenumber*.N*net*.Z*zone*.fidonet.org
Jane.Doe@p3.f101.n27.z1.fidonet.org

Internet to MCI Mail
userid@mcimail.com 101-1001@mcimail.com
firstname_lastname@mcimail.com John_Doe@mcimail.com

Internet to Prodigy
userid@prodigy.com TFKH22Z@prodigy.com

Telnet Commands

close — If you start telnet without specifying the target computer to connect to, this command terminates the connection to another computer and leaves you in command mode. If you started telnet with the name or address of a target computer, close will terminate the session and quit telnet (this is equivalent to the quit command). You can use the abbreviation c.

<enter> — In the telnet command mode, pressing Enter by itself (that is, with nothing else typed on the command line) returns you to the remote session if you have one active. If you don't, it exits telnet.

open — Use this command to connect to a remote machine when you're at the telnet> prompt. The format (like starting telnet from the systems prompt) is open <*computer_name*> or open <*computer_address*>.

quit — This command leaves the telnet program. If you have a connection to a remote computer, quit terminates it first.

set echo — If you can't see what you are typing, or if you type and see double, go to the telnet command mode (using the Escape character) and enter set echo. This toggles the echo setting off and on and should resolve the problem.

FTP Commands

ascii	Sets FTP to ASCII mode. This is usually the default and is used for text files. If you use it for binary files, such as programs or some databases, they'll be corrupted.
binary	Sets FTP to binary mode. Used for transferring binary files, which might be graphic files, executable programs, or audio files.
bye	Quits the FTP program.
cd	Changes the directory of the remote machine to the directory specified.
close	Ends your FTP session with the remote computer and returns you to the ftp> prompt. Note that at this point you aren't connected to any remote machine until you use the open command.
dir	Prints a listing of the files in the current remote working directory.
get	Retrieves a remote file and stores it on your computer.
mget	Transfers multiple files from a remote machine to your local machine. Files can be listed separated by spaces. Supports wildcard symbols * and ?.
mput	Transfers multiple files from a local machine to a remote machine. Files should be separated by a space. Supports wildcard symbols * and ?.
open	Used to establish a connection to a remote machine.
prompt	When you use mget or mput, and prompt is set to on, you'll be asked for a confirmation for each file handled. This can get pretty tedious if you're transferring several files. Issue the command prompt off, and you'll be able to drink your coffee and read the paper in peace. Use prompt on to get back to the confirmation mode.
put	Stores a local file on the remote machine.
pwd	Prints the name of the current working directory on the remote machine.

Gopher Commands

Moving Around Gopherspace

Up	Move to previous line
Down	Move to next line
Right or Enter	Enter current item
Left or u	Exit current item
>, +, PgDn, or Spacebar	View next page
<, -, PgUp, or b	View previous page
0-9	Go to a specific line
m	Go back to the main menu

Bookmarks

a	Add current item to the bookmark list
A	Add current directory/search to the bookmark list
v	View the bookmark list
d	Delete a bookmark

Other Gopher Commands

q	Quit with prompt
Q	Quit unconditionally
=	Display technical information about current item
o	Change options

And the Readers Say...

I am really pleased with Navigating the Internet. *It has helped me understand the Internet and its many uses. The book pretty much stays beside the computer when I'm on the Net (which is most of the time!).*
—Kevin McAbee

I have found Navigating the Internet *to be extremely easy to read with many lively examples of real-life applications. I have already recommended it to two of my friends.*
—David Shufutinsky

I have only been using the Internet for a couple of months now and have found Navigating the Internet *to be a great help.*
—Mike Keith

I just simply could not put Navigating the Internet *down. Thanks so much for bringing such an enjoyable level of understanding to a topic that I am really quite interested in learning more about.*
—Thom Fecik

Until recently I've avoided the Internet because it appeared too "techie," but Navigating the Internet *is providing a painless entry to the Information Superhighway.*
—Robert Popper

I really enjoyed Navigating the Internet. *It takes a witty approach to writing about a subject many people could find boring and confusing. I had a lot of fun with it.*
—William R. Armour IV

I was recently at a large bookstore looking for a book on Internet. Needless to say, there were quite a few. After perusing through various ones, I purchased Navigating the Internet *and have been very satisfied with it. The explanations are to the point, clear, and cover the desired materials. It is a quality book which I would recommend to someone else.*
—David Kelly

Navigating the Internet *is very readable and very informative. Information I was laboriously piecing together out of newsgroups, you have collected in a convenient, easy-to-use form.*
—George R. Cannon, Jr.

I just got Navigating the Internet *and find it a wealth of information about the Internet.*
—Glen Ketteringham

NAVIGATING THE INTERNET
DELUXE EDITION

Richard J. Smith

Mark Gibbs

SAMS
PUBLISHING

A Division of Prentice Hall Computer Publishing
201 W. 103rd Street, Indianapolis, Indiana 46290

For my wife Arianne and son Keihan
—Mark Gibbs

To my wife Ann Roberts
—Rich Smith

Copyright ©1994 by Sams Publishing

DELUXE EDITION

International Standard Book Number: 0-672-30485-6

Library of Congress Catalog Card Number: 94-65314

97 96 95 94   4 3 2 1

Interpretation of the printing code: the rightmost double-digit number is the year of the book's printing; the rightmost single-digit, the number of the book's printing. For example, a printing code of 94-1 shows that the first printing of the book occurred in 1994.

Composed in Palatino and MCPdigital by Prentice Hall Computer Publishing

Printed in the United States of America

Trademarks

Publisher
Richard K. Swadley

Associate Publisher
Jordan Gold

Acquisitions Manager
Stacy Hiquet

Acquisitions Editor
Mark Taber

Development Editor
Mark Taber

Managing Editor
Cindy Morrow

Production Editors
Sandy Doell
Fran Hatton

Editors
Angie Trzepacz
David Bradford

Editorial Coordinator
Bill Whitmer

Editorial Assistants
Sharon Cox
Lynette Quinn

Software Technical Reviewers
Steve Bang
Wes Morgan

Marketing Manager
Greg Bushyeager

Cover Designers
Dan Armstrong
Kathy Hanley

Book Designer
Michele Laseau

**Director of Production
and Manufacturing**
Jeff Valler

Production Manager
Scott Cook

Imprint Manager
Juli Cook

Production Analysts
Mary Beth Wakefield
Dennis Clay Hager

Proofreading Coordinator
Joelynn Gifford

Indexing Coordinator
Johnna VanHoose

Graphics Image Specialists
Tim Montgomery
Dennis Sheehan
Sue VandeWalle

Production
Katy Bodenmiller
Ayrika Bryant
Stephanie Davis
Kimberly K. Hannel
Angela P. Judy
Greg Kemp
Jamie Milazzo
Wendy Ott
Shelly Palma
Beth Rago
Ryan Rader
Kim Scott
Michelle Self
Kris Simmons
Tonya R. Simpson
SA Springer
Tina Trettin
Suzanne Tully
Elaine Webb
Dennis Wesner

OVERVIEW

CONTENTS

ACKNOWLEDGMENTS

I'd like to thank Rendell Bird and Patrick Landry of the University of Southwestern Louisiana, Blanche Woolls and Chris Tomer of the University of Pittsburgh, and the entire Internet community.

Thanks to the University of Pittsburgh's School of Library and Information Science computer staff especially Stuart McClean and the Graduate Student Assistants. The participants of my summer workshops, my graduate class, and "Let's Go Gopherin'" who helped with input on additional material. Finally, Ann Roberts for assistance with inputting material.

—Rich Smith

So many people have helped, advised, and encouraged this book that it's hard to know where to begin. My most grateful thanks to Steve Bang, our technical editor, for going beyond the call of duty, and to Rick Gates, the Internet Hunt Meister, for his support and contribution.

For their help and support, I'd like to thank Debra Young of CompuServe, Rusty Williams at Delphi, Timothy Tyndall and Marcie Montgomery of R.A.I.N., and Scott Yanoff and Bob Bales of the National Computer Security Association.

Thanks to the GoFer Team—Martha E. Rapp, Holly Lee Stowe, and Phil Kizer—who researched references and resources for us.

Finally, thanks to the staff at Sams Publishing. Gregg Bushyeager, you did a superb job—the project had its moments. Phil Paxton, juggler extraordinaire, for what must have been an edit from hell. A huge, nay, enormous thanks to Mark Taber, David Bradford, Sandy Doell, and Angie Trzepacz. Your attention to detail and careful work was superhuman!

—Mark Gibbs

ABOUT THE AUTHORS

Richard J. Smith

Richard Smith discovered the information resources of the Internet while doing work as a Ph.D. student at the University of Pittsburgh. He taught the use of the Internet in graduate courses and followed these by giving workshops called "Navigating the Internet" in 1991.

In the summer of 1992, Smith decided to offer a course on Internet training—over the Internet—hoping to get 30 or 40 people to participate. A total of 864 people from more than 20 countries registered for his "Navigating the Internet: An Interactive Workshop." A second workshop drew more than 15,000 participants from more than 50 countries.

The result of these ground-breaking international workshops is that Smith has trained literally thousands of people around the world in how to use Internet resources. This led to Smith being dubbed the "Internet mentor" in the January 1993 issue of *American Libraries*. He plans to do bigger and better international Internet workshops in the future because he enjoys offering a service that is much needed and appreciated.

Smith can be contacted at `rjs@lis.pitt.edu`.

Mark Gibbs

For more than a decade, Mark Gibbs has developed technical and service operations, consulted, lectured, and written articles and books about the network market.

Gibbs was co-founder of Novell's U.K. operation, where he was responsible for the management of all technical services. He was with Novell for five years and since leaving has pursued a successful career as an independent consultant and analyst.

Gibbs has written books on networking—*Do-It-Yourself Networking with LANtastic* and *The Absolute Beginner's Guide to Networking*, both from Sams Publishing, and *Networking Personal Computers* from Que Corporation—and has contributed articles about PCs and networking technology to various journals and periodicals. He is a contributing editor to the Patricia Seybold Group and technology analyst to the National Computer Security Association.

Gibbs can be contacted on the Internet as `mgibbs@rain.org` (please put "NAV:" in the subject line).

Introduction

[The Bellman] had bought a large map representing the sea,

Without the least vestige of land:

And the crew were much pleased when they found it to be

A map they could all understand.

"What good are Mercator's North Poles and Equators,

Tropics, Zones, and Meridian Lines?"

So the Bellman would cry: and the crew would reply

"They are merely conventional signs!"

"Other maps are such shapes, with their islands and capes!

But we've got our brave Captain to thank"

(So the crew would protest) "that he's bought us the best—

A perfect and absolute blank!"

"The Hunting of the Snark"

—Lewis Carroll (1832-1898)

Imagine yourself as a navigator out in the ocean. You are surrounded by islands, and you can see hundreds of lighthouses marking ports and towns. What's worth sailing over to? What's going to be interesting and what's going to be useful? You need to have charts, guidebooks, and the right equipment, or getting there will be hard—and when you arrive, there may be nothing there worth having landed for.

In the space of the Internet, you are in the same predicament. Without charts and equipment, you can search for a long time and not find much of use. If you go into the Internet unaided or with too few tools, it will seem to be a lot like the Bellman's map—"A perfect and absolute blank!"

Sure, you'll be able to see things, but you'll have no idea what they are without traveling over to them and then digging for gold. And if you don't have the right tools or don't know how to use them properly, you might miss the gold by inches or miles and never know! You'll be able to do some basic things like send messages, but the really useful stuff—data files, documents, programs, and discussions with other people—will elude you.

This book is the navigator's companion. Here you'll find everything you need to know about the history, shape, services, resources, and technologies of the Internet. You'll find out how you can launch yourself into the Internet. You'll find out where the best landfalls and the richest treasures are hidden. You'll discover how to search and dig for treasure. And you'll discover how to expertly navigate the Internet.

In short, this is the first book that actually explains what the Internet is and how to use it for a purpose—the purpose of finding useful stuff. Rather than just talk about the Internet from the viewpoint of a UNIX user, we'll discuss the way that the Internet can be used by anyone on any system.

This book was inspired by two courses that one of the authors, Rich Smith, conducted across the Internet in 1992. This book was named after those courses. The first course, in August 1992, attracted 864 participants. For the second course, in November 1992, the number of participants reached 15,000 before the list had to be closed. Any more than that and the University of Louisiana computer would have had serious problems just handling the vast amount of traffic involved!

The reason cited by many people for joining the course was that they wanted to learn how to use the Internet. They didn't want to know about techie stuff like protocols and bits and bytes—they wanted practical advice on navigation. How do I find what I want? How do I get to where what I want is? When I get there, how do I get the stuff back? Rather than let them blunder around and read reams of manuals, Rich's course answered those fundamental questions.

In this book, we've covered much the same ground as Rich's course and explained some of the tools in more depth. We also have a comprehensive directory of Internet services that will help you find useful resources. We put a research team on the task—the GoFers—with the instruction "find useful stuff." And they did!

When you combine our detailed information on Internet tools with our resource directory—Appendix G, "The Internet Navigator's Gazetteer"—you've got the very best map possible with which to start sailing around the Internet. Whether you're a scientist, a librarian, a business person, a doctor, a lawyer, or an industry chief, this book will steer your Internet travels.

Who Should Read This Book?

Everyone. At least, everyone who wants to be able to take advantage of the world of information technology. As we move into the 21st century, the Internet is going to become the world's information backbone—the primary means of communication that will soon carry more mail than the entire postal services of all the countries in the world combined.

By the year 2000, if you're not on the Internet at least for electronic mail, you'll be isolated. This book is about preparing yourself to be capable of not only sending and receiving e-mail, but also being able to get out onto the Internet and access resources.

This book is for anyone with a basic knowledge of PCs or computers who has or can arrange to have access to the Internet. It's designed for people, not computer scientists. If you're a

⚓ Student

⚓ Teacher

⚓ Business person

⚓ Parent

⚓ Computer user of any kind

   (I think that covers just about everyone)

…this book was written for you!

The Path to the Internet

Your path to the Internet starts here. Your mission: to boldly sail where others flounder and founder, to seek out new resources and services, to navigate the Internet.

Happy sailing.

THE INTERNET: PAST, PRESENT, AND FUTURE

One does not discover new lands without consenting to lose sight of the shore for a very long time. André Gide

What Is the Internet?

Ask for a definition of the Interenet and, depending on whom you ask, you'll get either a simplistic answer or one that is long, detailed, and mainly incomprehensible.

Librarians who use the Internet for researching library catalogs will probably access it through *Gopher* (discussed in Chapter 8, "Navigating by Menus:

Gopher"). They see a simple menu-driven interface and they probably rate it all as pretty easy.

An engineer might talk about *telneting* to this site or *ftping* to that site, neither of which probably makes much sense without demos and some experimentation.

You could also ask a technical guru who writes programs for the Internet, but you'd better take two aspirins and lie down afterward.

The Internet is hard to sum up, except in generalities, because so many different services and facilities are available. The simplest way to describe the Internet is with one word—communication. To some people, it's just a way to send electronic mail to other people—a pipeline from here to there. To others, the Internet is where they meet their friends, play games, argue, do work, and travel the world.

The Cyberspace of the Internet

If you've read William Gibson's excellent science fiction novels, you probably remember his vision of "Cyberspace" and the global computer network called "The Matrix."

Cyberspace was the environment where computers and people lived and worked. It was a place with a reality every bit as valid as the everyday, real world. Indeed, for many of its users, Cyberspace *was* the real world!

> **Navigator's Note:** William Gibson's books are dark visions of a wild and dangerous future society suffering from too many people and too much technology. His first book, *Neuromancer*, created a whole new subgenre of science fiction writing that is now called Cyberpunk. Highly recommended.

The Internet may well become Gibson's Matrix. Already, the Cyberspace of the Internet is a huge place. Much like the high seas, the Internet physically covers the globe, going from America to Europe, the Near East, the Far East, the Orient, Australia, South America, and back again.

It is divided into oceans (subnetworks), with channels (connections between networks), continents (the supercomputers), big islands (the mainframes and minicomputers), and what the uncharitable might see as floating logs (personal computers). Bobbing around between these landfalls are people, whose software takes them thousands of virtual miles from one port to another.

A big difference between navigating the seas and navigating the Internet is the speed of the journey (though I guess the lack of actual water might also be an issue, but work with me on this).

Around the World in Seconds

Netfarers differ from seafarers in that they travel at thousands of miles per second without leaving their chairs! You can go from California to Australia, pick up a file, copy it to London and Frankfurt, and do it all before your coffee gets cold.

The speed at which you can do things on the Internet is remarkable, not because the Internet is particularly speedy (local area network users will notice that it's not fast in comparison to, say, an Ethernet system), but because it enables you to travel around the world in seconds. It is a technical achievement of incredible dimensions.

The Internet is built from hundreds of smaller networks. It connects about a million computers and tens of millions of users. Beyond its components and statistics, how it's used, and which directions it's taking, the really striking thing about the Internet is its constant growth. Today there are 13 systems that help you find files in a catalog of over two million (see Chapter 6, "Finding Files: Archie"). Next month there may be 30; the month after, 300. The Internet is expanding at an incredible pace.

Marriage, Fame, and Fortune

People have met and married, found fame and fortune, and conducted scientific research on the Internet (although usually not at the same time). The Internet was used by Iraq to support their command and control system during the Gulf War (much to the U.S.'s irritation) and has been used for espionage by hackers in the pay of the KGB.

As you start to explore the vast ocean of the Internet, you'll be staggered by what's available. Do you want to find the definitive reference to the genome of the mouse? The Jackson Laboratory at merlot.welch.jhn.edu (don't worry, we'll cover Internet addresses later) has that information in a huge work called *The Encyclopedia of the Mouse Genome*.

Do you want to find the locations in Australia where the plant commonly called *aalii* (*Dodoneae viscosa*), a native of Hawaii, has been found? Check out the botanical database available through Australian National Botanic Gardens in Australia.

The Internet holds data riches beyond your wildest imaginings (unless you have a particularly fertile imagination). It contains only a fraction of the vast mountains of human knowledge, yet it will overwhelm you.

What's Connected to the Internet?

So, what's connected to the Internet? In hardware terms, computers of every kind. There are PCs, Macintoshes, UNIX machines, various minicomputers, IBM mainframes, exotic systems not found outside artificial intelligence laboratories, and supercomputers.

Working on those computers are programs that handle communications, manage databases, play games, and support electronic mail, along with thousands of other applications.

In terms of available services, news feeds provide coverage of the very latest international and national events, daily updates from NASA, weather forecasts, and satellite photographs only 45 minutes old. Library catalogs and databases on botany and particle physics are among the thousands of data collections. Millions of files are available—files of useful data and files of obscure data that someone, somewhere, thinks are important. Programs of every sort, for most types of computers, can be found. Many are free, and many come with source code.

Finally, there are people—tens of millions of them, many of whom use the Internet every day. Some never seem to be anywhere else but on the Internet!

Who Uses the Internet?

Who are these people on the Internet? People of all types: librarians, teachers, scientists, engineers, students (as young as five), along with commercial organizations, universities, and governments. At one time there was even a Coca-Cola machine (see "Exotic Uses" later in this chapter).

The lure of the Internet is communication and access. If you want to exchange ideas and develop knowledge, the Internet is the place to do it.

For example, when the discovery of cold fusion (now disproved) was announced in 1991, scientists couldn't wait for the normal process of peer review and validation to explore the idea. Their solution? Conferences on the Internet. What was, in effect, an around-the-clock discussion developed; as new information became available, the participants analyzed it. This was a completely new way of interacting, and those involved found it to be invaluable.

Access to knowledge is the other great lure. Librarians—whose job it is to find documents, books, and other materials—share their catalogs through the Internet. Indeed, some of the Internet's most enthusiastic users are librarians. Catalogs for the French National Institute for Electronic Research, the Library of Congress, and classical Chinese literature can all be found on the Internet (see Appendix H, "The Internet Navigator's Gazetteer").

Where Did Internet Come from?

The Internet began in early 1969 under the name ARPANET. The ARPA part of ARPANET stood for the Advanced Research Projects Agency (later called the Defense Advanced Research Projects Agency, or DARPA), which was part of the U.S. Department of Defense (DoD).

The first ARPANET configuration involved four computers and was designed to demonstrate the feasibility of building networks using computers dispersed over a wide area. By 1972, when the ARPANET was first publicly demonstrated, 50 universities and research facilities (all involved in military technology projects) had connections.

Navigator's Note: The sites of the four computers forming the original ARPANET were the University of Utah, the University of California at Santa Barbara, the University of California at Los Angeles, and Stanford Research Institute (SRI) International.

One of the goals of ARPANET was research in distributed computer systems for military purposes. The government and the military sought ways to make networks tolerant to failures; ARPANET was designed to allow messages traveling from one computer to another to be handled in a flexible and robust way.

For the military and government, computers have obvious and profound uses—command and control, supplies, civil management, and so on. One chief concern, however, is reliability. If computers are connected by a single wire and a bomb hits the wire (or the wire simply fails), you've lost your connection. This is bad enough in government circles, but for the military it's a life-and-death issue. ARPANET was designed to learn more about networks that could withstand the loss of connections.

The ARPANET scheme provided many routes between computers. Most importantly, the computers had to be able to send messages by any available route, rather than by just one fixed route. This is where the topic of protocols comes in.

Speak to Me!

We need to make a small excursion into some important concepts. If you're not really interested in how the Internet and its protocols evolved, skip ahead to the heading "What Is the Internet Today?"

Okay, now that they're gone, let's cover some really interesting stuff. If they only knew what they're missing...

What Is a Protocol?

Protocols are agreed-upon methods of communication used by computers and, for that matter, by people. We have protocols for all sorts of activities. For example, take the protocol for having a meeting. Someone chairs the meeting, states its objectives, decides how long it will last, and then invites people to speak. When each person finishes speaking, control returns to the chair. There are also specific ways for handling special conditions such as interjections ("Excuse me, but..."), error conditions ("Pardon me?"), and so on. These are all parts of the protocol for meetings.

In the computer world, protocols are vital to making communications possible. All sorts of decisions must be made when two or more computers want to send and receive data—for example, which computer should begin the communication, how replies are to be handled, how data will be represented, how error conditions will be handled, and so on.

Tolerating Unreliability

One of the first considerations in designing the ARPANET was the need to tolerate unreliability. If a network is to be robust, particularly for military purposes, you can't count on a connection being there. You must assume that although you seem to have sent a message, it might not arrive intact or even at all. This is termed (not surprisingly) an unreliable connection, and the communications technology created by the ARPANET designers to solve this problem was called the Host-to-Host Protocol.

The problem with Host-to-Host Protocol was that it restricted the number of computers that could be on ARPANET. In 1972, work began on the second generation of network protocols, which gave rise to a collection of protocols called *Transmission Control Protocol/Internet Protocol* (or the much snappier TCP/IP). By 1983, TCP/IP was the protocol suite for ARPANET.

Navigator's Note: The phrase *protocol suite* is used to describe a collection of protocols that work together. Usually the protocols in the suite are built one on top of another. The lowest level of protocol handles the most basic functions, receiving pulses of electricity from the communications medium (usually copper wire but also fiber optic cable and, occasionally, infrared, microwave, or radio). The next level turns those pulses into characters, and so on until you reach the top layer, which hands data to the application in the size and format it expects. This layering of protocols is the reason protocol suites are also called *protocol stacks*.

TCP/IP has become one of the most widely used networking protocols. Most computer systems vendors support TCP/IP in one form or another—and even if they don't, a third party will be ready to fill the gap. This means that connecting to the Internet is easy and relatively inexpensive (compared to the proprietary solutions of some vendors).

Other Networks

At the end of the 1970s, other networks sprang into existence. The UUCP network (a loose confederation of first hundreds and now thousands of UNIX machines) was followed in the early 1980s by BITNET (Because It's Time Network…honestly, but then it was the '80s), CSNET (Computer Science Network), and many others. Some were private (such as CERFnet and BITNET), some were collaborative (UUCP), and some were government funded (ARPANET, NSFNET, and CSNET).

Then, like some Nordic saga, ARPANET begat MILNET (son of ARPANET), an unclassified DoD network connected to ARPANET by a gateway. The two networks were called the DARPANET (catchy, eh?) and eventually this became just *the Internet*.

Navigator's Note: Properly speaking, a *gateway* is a computer that connects two other networks or computers that use different protocols. For example, BITNET doesn't use TCP/IP, so its protocol needs to be translated before it can communicate with the rest of the Internet. Sometimes the term gateway is mistakenly applied to a *bridge*, which is a computer connecting two networks that use the same protocols but want to have their message traffic segregated. This is done so that only traffic intended for a destination on the other network is passed; if the networks were just joined together, the combined traffic could overload them.

NSFNET

In the late 1980s, the National Science Foundation's network (NSFNET) was developed to connect its five supercomputer centers. The need for a network for these centers was crucial. The cost of their computers made them a national resource, and the National Science Foundation wanted to get the best possible use from them.

Networking was the ideal solution. It made the National Science Foundation's supercomputers available to all researchers at all universities and research institutes. Using the existing Internet wasn't practical for various reasons, so the National Science Foundation built its own, which it called NSFNET.

With the Internet as its model, NSFNET used the same TCP/IP protocol suite. A scheme of regional networks connected to the supercomputer centers brought all of the universities together. The supercomputer centers were then interconnected, creating a hierarchical system that allowed any computer on any subnetwork to access computers anywhere in the internetwork.

Network Consolidation

Eventually, all publicly and privately funded networks—ARPANET, MILNET, the UUCP network, BITNET, CSNET, and the NASA Science Internet—joined the regional NSFNET networks. ARPANET was dismantled in 1990, and CSNET in 1991, when their functions were taken over by NSFNET.

As the various networks were added, the Internet grew almost exponentially. Figure 1.1 shows various points in the Internet's phenomenal growth.

What Is the Internet Today?

Today, the Internet is a web of different, intercommunicating networks funded by both commercial and government organizations. The Internet also has spread overseas to connect to networks in over 40 countries, including France, Germany,

Japan, Russia, the United Kingdom, and even Antarctica (yes, I know that's actually a continent, but let's allow for a little poetic license).

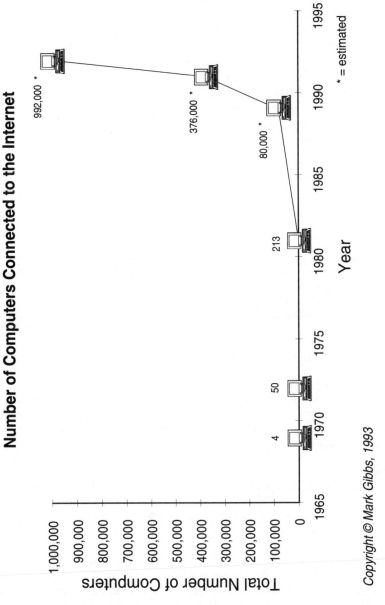

Figure 1.1. The Internet has grown rapidly in the last few years. There are now over 1 million computers connected, and about 1,000 more join each day!

Amazing Internet Facts

Amazing Fact #1: It is estimated that the Internet now connects over 6,000 networks.

Amazing Fact #2: More than 1,000 computers are added to the Internet each day.

Amazing Fact #3: The amount of data crossing the Internet grows by 10 percent per *month*. That's 214 percent per annum!

Amazing Fact #4: Each day, worldwide, around 10 million people directly (and some 25 million indirectly) use the Internet to send and receive electronic mail.

Who Owns and Runs the Internet?

No one.

Strange as it may sound, there is no single owner, or even a formal coalition (such as a company or association), that actually "owns" the Internet. The various sub-networks have owners who recognize that having connections to other networks either enhances their mission (if, like NSFNET, they are publicly funded) or makes their services more desirable (if they are privately funded, for-profit networks like BITNET and CERFnet).

(If you aren't interested yet, skip to "How Can I Use the Internet?" in the following section.)

The only group that "runs" the Internet is the Internet Society, or ISOC. These volunteers freely give their time to support and promote the aims of the Internet. ISOC has many committees and working groups and is lead by the IAB, the Internet Architecture Board. The IAB is responsible for ratifying the standards (such as protocols and technologies) that the Internet will use.

Another group—the Internet Engineering Task Force, or IETF—is a public forum that develops standards and resolves operational issues for the Internet. The IETF forms working groups to explore and evaluate issues and develop technical standards, which may be accepted by the IETF and sent to the IAB for ratification. Like ISOC, IETF is purely voluntary.

Here we start to see a curious phenomenon. While ISOC standards are important, an IETF standard that hasn't even been through ISOC ratification may become an operational standard on the Internet. This is simply because everyone on the Internet thinks it's a good idea and uses it. Eventually, ISOC gets around to ratifying it.

This phenomenon is what the Internet is all about—cooperation. The Internet works because the participants want it to work. On the whole, the Internet is self-governing through a process of enlightened, cooperative, democratic participation. When any one person or group bucks the system, the rest of the Internet establishes a position on the issue and acts together to regain the desired status quo. Incredibly, the system works extremely well.

How Can I Use the Internet?

(No skipping this bit. You should know about this....)

The core of the Internet, NSFNET, has some very well-defined rules. The "Acceptable Use Policy" (or, so the world can have YAA—Yet Another Acronym—the AUP) applies only to use of the NSFNET. The National Science Foundation assumes that networks interconnected to NSFNET will formulate their own policies and that these will uphold the standards of the NSFNET.

THE NSFNET BACKBONE SERVICES ACCEPTABLE USE POLICY

June 1992

1. GENERAL PRINCIPLE: NSFNET Backbone services are provided to support open research and education in and among U.S. research and instructional institutions, plus research arms of for-profit firms when engaged in open scholarly communication and research. Use for other purposes is not acceptable.

SPECIFICALLY ACCEPTABLE USES:

2. Communication with foreign researchers and educators in connection with research or instruction, as long as any network employed by the foreign user for such communication provides reciprocal access to U.S. researchers and educators.

3. Communication and exchange for professional development, to maintain currency, or to debate issues in a field or subfield of knowledge.

4. Use for disciplinary-society, university-association, government-advisory, or standards activities related to the user's research and instructional activities.

5. Use in applying for or administering grants or contracts for research or instruction, but not for other fundraising or public relations activities.

6. Any other administrative communications or activities in direct support of research and instruction.

7. Announcements of new products or services for use in research or instruction but not advertising of any kind.

8. Any traffic originating from a network of another member agency of the Federal Networking Council, if the traffic meets the acceptable use policy of that agency.

9. Communication incidental to otherwise acceptable use, except for illegal or specifically unacceptable use.

UNACCEPTABLE USES:

10. Use for for-profit activities, unless covered by the General Principle or as a specifically acceptable use.

11. Extensive use for private or personal business.

This statement applies to use of the NSFNET Backbone only. NSF expects that connecting networks will formulate their own use policies. The NSF Division of Networking and Communications Research and Infrastructure will resolve any questions about this Policy or its interpretation.

Source: National Science Foundation.

The problem, however, is that the Internet is so tempting to business. If someone were to start from scratch with a new network system (even one that was technically better than the Internet), would you want to sign up? It would be like being the first person to own a telephone: Who would you call? Eventually, as people joined, you would have reason to use the system, but until the number of users reached a significant level, you would be getting a poor return on your investment.

The Internet already exists, and everybody can get connections to it at reasonable cost. So…why not commercialize it?

Going Commercial

In 1991 the Internet lifted its decade-old ban on business. A group of commercial network service providers formed the Commercial Internet Exchange (CIX), whose mission is to support commercial Internet service providers.

Then came the ANS (Advanced Networking Services) CORE (Commercial Research and Education) Inc., the largest Internet network service provider, which was a joint nonprofit venture by MCI, IBM, and Merit (a Michigan state network services provider).

Vinton Cerf, president of ISOC and the co-inventor of TCP/IP, said that "Estimates of 1 billion network systems are not crazy. Everywhere the Internet ended, a new network sprouted," (quoted in *InfoWorld*, April 12, 1993).

What CIX and ANS offer is the ability to make business connections without crossing the NSFNET, thereby avoiding infringement of the AUP. They also offer all sorts of optional enhanced services so that, for example, companies needing to connect at very high data rates can get suitable connections (at a price).

The commercialization of the Internet hasn't yet changed its cooperative nature, and it's unlikely that it will. Indeed, as the Internet grows more complex and the range of available services expands, businesses will be able to buy services that are appropriate to their needs, and the universities and research organizations will find a more useful environment in which to work.

This business-driven expansion ensures that the Internet will become ubiquitous. In the very near future, even small businesses and all schools (down to primary schools) will be able to have Internet connections. Ultimately (and also soon), an Internet connection in your house will be no more unusual than a telephone line.

So What Can I Do on the Internet?

Internet activities can be divided into six main areas:

⚓ **Electronic Mail.** The process of sending e-mail to and receiving it from other people (and software) through the Internet is easy. You can use electronic mail to correspond with your friends, business colleagues, and even the President (president@whitehouse.gov). You can also make requests for database searches through electronic mail and have the results posted to you. You can even have world and national news mailed to you (see Chapter 3, "Where's the Post? Electronic Mail").

⚓ **File Transfer.** Files can be found everywhere on the Internet. The ability to pull down a file to get data or run a program (if the file is executable) is vital if, for example, you do research and development work. In this category are resources such as weather and oceanographic data files and satellite pictures. You can also copy files from your computer to someone else's (see Chapter 4, "A Moving Experience: FTP for Me").

⚓ **Run Programs on Other Computers.** The ability to reach out from your computer in order to run a program on another is quite useful. You can run software your own computer can't run (due to processor type, memory limitations, and so on) or avoid pulling programs and data to your machine (see Chapter 5, "Remotely Possible: Telnet").

⚓ **Search For Files and Databases.** Several systems on the Internet enable you to search thousands of computers for files and databases (see Chapter 6, "Finding Files: Archie," Chapter 7, "The Database of Databases: WAIS," and Chapter 8, "Navigating by Menus: Gopher").

⚓ **Discussion Groups.** Because the Internet is used by millions of people, it's a natural place to make contact and exchange views with those who share your interests (see Chapter 13, "Views and News: USENET," and Chapter 14, "Getting on the List: LISTSERV").

⚓ **Play Games and Talk.** Through the Internet you can have "conversations" with people all over the world in real time (which means you type something and they see it as soon as you send it). You can also participate in single- and multiuser role-playing games, play checkers against other people and AI (Artificial Intelligence) programs in real time, and join simulations of political events and warfare.

Electronic Mail

Of all these resources, electronic mail is the most widely used. It's the stuff of modern business and modern communications between people in general.

You can use electronic mail to exchange data directly from computer to computer. You can transfer text, program files, spreadsheets, and even photographic images. Messages can be sent and received in hours at most and often within minutes; it's no wonder that most e-mail users refer to the regular postal service as "snail mail."

E-mail enables you to converse with millions of people directly connected to the Internet—and perhaps two to four times that many beyond. The *Outernet* is the name for the group of networks and e-mail systems that can exchange messages with the Internet through gateways. Included are AppleLink, AT&T Mail, CompuServe, MCI Mail, FidoNet, UUCP networks, and hundreds of bulletin boards.

Electronic mail is also used for some important reasons. For example, many medical professionals seeking second opinions or expert analysis transfer x-ray and magnetic resonance images to one another using e-mail.

Getting Resourceful

We've said that you can copy files to and from your computer to other computers on the Internet and run programs on other machines. The real challenge, however, isn't copying files or using resources; it's finding them. Several tools make finding files and resources much easier than searching machines one by one.

One of the most popular tools is the Internet Gopher (see Chapter 8, "Navigating by Menus: Gopher"). Gophers exist in *Gopherspace*, the linking of different copies of Gopher running on different computers. By selecting menu options in Gopher, you can cruise around the Internet looking for files and resources, including databases, library catalogs, and files.

There's also Archie, the result of an after-hours hack at McGill University's computer department. It has become the official file-finding catalog of the Internet. Lists of publicly accessible files at archive sites are available through Archie servers, which tell users which files are on which computers and where they are stored (see Chapter 6, "Finding Files: Archie").

Discussion Groups

E-mail is also used to distribute the proceedings of more than 1,600 discussion groups, known as "mailing lists." These groups cover just about any topic you can think of, from astronomy to zoology to the Internet itself. On many mailing lists, messages are immediately and automatically redistributed to all subscribers without any kind of moderation (see Chapters 13 and 14).

Exotic Uses

The Internet is a place of experimentation and novelty. With its phenomenal growth rate and its population of scientists and enthusiasts, creative (and weird) things can happen.

One of the earliest oddities was the Internet Cola Machine, a bit of creative programming undertaken by students in the Carnegie Mellon University Computer Science Department. When they were moved from the ground floor (where the Coca-Cola vending machine lived) to the third floor, the students quickly got tired of walking down three flights of stairs only to find the vending machine empty.

Their solution was to wire the vending machine with switches that monitored which chutes were full and how long the bottles had been in the chute. They connected their modifications to a computer used by the new ground floor inhabitants. They could then send a message over the Internet to that computer and check the status of the Coca-Cola machine. No more wasted trips for warm Coke or, worst of all, no Coke.

Of course, because the computer monitoring the Coke machine was on the Internet, anyone, even those in other countries, could find out whether cold bottles were waiting. Unfortunately, the Internet Coke Machine no longer exists.

Another novel Internet tool comes from some engineers at Sun Microsystems, Inc. A recently developed program, "Pizzatool" sends a pizza order over the Internet to a local pizza restaurant's fax machine.

Where Is Internet Going?

Besides Coke vending machines and pizza delivery services, the Internet is making a huge impact in several areas—indeed, areas where it's completely changing the way things are done.

Education

The Internet is a fantastic educational resource for both students and teachers. Student use ranges from basic education in communications technology to the university level, and it includes research into all branches of science and the humanities. Children quickly learn how to use the Internet, and seeing a 12-year-old navigate between databases all around the world with complete confidence and knowledge is very impressive.

Library Issues

Librarians have been in the business of networking and sharing information resources for a long time. In the mid-1960s, the Library of Congress developed a standard for bibliographic records called the MARC (Machine-Readable Cataloging) format. This opened the way for the automated sharing of catalog data between libraries, which has saved librarians thousands of labor hours and enabled them to make better use of scarce financial resources. It also provided a way to network the automated bibliographic catalogs.

This sharing of resources has created very large (perhaps enormous would be more accurate) (actually, gigantic is even better) bibliographic databases. Along with these databases have come new tools to handle them. Bibliographic utilities with mellifluous names, such as OCLC and WLN, have become major leaders in the national and international networking of bibliographic databases.

The step from a local automated card catalog to a networked one is usually one of the first that a university wants to take in a campus automation project. Access to a university library's automated catalog via the Internet was one of the earliest services that did not require you to be a computer scientist. This broadened the interest in this new communication system beyond the scientific fields.

Today, hundreds of library catalogs are accessible on the Internet, and librarians are among its most enthusiastic users. In many cases, a university library catalog is part of a larger information system in what has come to be called a Campus-Wide Information Server (CWIS). CWISs may house other databases, school information, a telephone directory, schedules of classes, and many other local information sources. Many of these CWISs are based on Gophers, which are discussed in Chapter 8, "Navigating by Menus: Gopher."

Document delivery (the sending and receiving of text data files) in a timely manner or even immediately is becoming a routine service. Electronic journals, electronic books, and information databases are being created at a startling rate. This is a huge challenge for researchers, librarians, and information scientists. The information age is becoming a reality.

Access to so much library information from school, work, or home is rapidly changing the way people think of information—from what is available in one local library to what is available nationally and even internationally. The fact that access to information is becoming more important than ownership of it is an important theme in library and information science today and will remain so in the future.

Student Access

In many universities, students, staff, and faculty can gain access to the Internet. This is having a profound effect on education and the way we teach and learn.

One of the interesting aspects of the Internet is the democratic effect it has on what is communicated. A student can exchange ideas with a leading authority as a peer. Group projects and international collaboration on scholarly work can be achieved without knowing that one person is a professor and another a student. What counts in this new forum is the content of the communications, not the status or assumed ability of those involved.

The forums and discussions found on the Internet keep professionals up-to-date in their fields and enable students to observe, learn, and participate in problem solving and policy making.

By eliminating geographic boundaries, students can use information sources from locations that otherwise would be impossible to access. For a student in New York, information in Brazil or Russia is as near as data in Florida or Texas. This applies equally to university students and five-year-olds.

During the collapse of the Soviet Union in 1991, teenage students in schools serviced by the R.A.I.N. project in Santa Barbara, California, communicated with school children in Moscow and St. Petersburg. The educational impact on the students was immense. Rather than learning what was happening in the abstract through television news, they were talking on a daily basis with their peers in Russia who were living the events.

The Internet is already having a profound impact on continuing and distance education. Experts worldwide can contribute to a class for tens, hundreds, or thousands of students. Because of the nature of communications on the Internet, courses can be taken at the convenience and pace of the individual student.

Science and Research

The Internet was originally developed so that science and research could share resources. To a great extent, communications in the form of e-mail and discussion groups have overshadowed the Internet's use for resource sharing.

Although the traditional methods of scholarly communication—presentations at conferences, publishing of papers in journals, and so on—haven't been eliminated, they are being recognized as inadequate for current research needs.

The Internet distributes information in a way that is infinitely more flexible and more timely. Findings, papers, and information can be instantly shared and discussed. With the proposed NREN improvements to the Internet (see next section) and the promise of video and other multimedia communication links, the Internet promises to be a fundamental tool for the scientific community.

The U.S. Data Superhighway

Until November 1991, the United States paid only lip service to the idea that information technology is crucial to economic success. The outgoing Republican president was more occupied with moral issues than technical ones, and the government had no real position on supporting the business use of computer communications.

One avowed Democratic objective is to modernize the nation's network communications infrastructure. When he was a senator, Vice President Albert Gore (an ardent promoter of the need to compete in information technology) sponsored a government project to build a high-speed network for connecting supercomputers, the federal High Performance Computing Act (the HPCA), which was signed into law by President Bush in 1991.

Just before being selected as Bill Clinton's vice-presidential running mate, Gore introduced a follow-up to the HPCA. The Information Infrastructure and Technology Act, S 2937, will foster "grand applications" of future technologies. The goal of the legislation is to provide a data "superhighway," called the National

Research and Education Network (NREN), which will transfer data at speeds in the gigabyte-per-second range to form the infrastructure for U.S. scientific and industrial research.

> **Navigator's Note:** A network that runs at gigabyte-per-second speeds could transfer the contents of all volumes of the Encyclopedia Britannica in less than one second. Wow.

The bill will give federal agencies the responsibility for developing network applications and will fund that work with $1.15 billion over the next five years. The results should appear by 1996.

Gore's argument for NREN is based on the need for international competitiveness:

> *Without this bill, and the money it authorizes, it is almost certain that our foreign competitors in Japan and Europe will move ahead of us in this critically important field....This network could revolutionize American education as well, giving teachers new tools and new ways to inspire their students. Today, hundreds of elementary and secondary schools are linked to the NSFNET, enabling students to exchange messages with other students throughout the country and enabling teachers to share new teaching ideas with one another....But the most important impact of the NREN will be the impetus it gives to development and deployment of commercial high-speed networks. This bill represents a commitment to build the high-speed data highways needed for the twenty-first century....The NREN will be the prototype for a network which will be as ubiquitous and as easy-to-use as the phone system is today, and probably not much more expensive. Such a network will be able to deliver HDTV programming, provide for teleconferencing, link your computer to millions of computers around the country, give you access to huge "digital libraries" of information, and deliver services we cannot yet imagine. We cannot afford not to make the investment necessary to deploy such a national network. The alternative is to wait until other nations show us how to take advantage of this technology—and they will. We must move first.*

Vice President Albert Gore, Jr., "Viewpoint," *Communications of the AMC*, November 1991, Vol. 34, No. 11, pp. 15-16.

Over the Horizon

So what does the future hold for the Internet? Well, look at what we have now—a vast internetwork, supporting over a million computers in 40 countries on all seven continents, used by around 25 million people every day. Moreover, it's a system that is run, governed, and regulated cooperatively without actual laws—just codes of conduct and a common ethic.

Table 1.1 shows some of the many predictions about Internet growth. When the NREN appears at the end of the 1990s, you can bet that commercial Internet vendors will be right there, offering services with speeds of at least a gigabit per second. It isn't unrealistic to expect that, by the year 2000, all schools and colleges in the United States will be linked to the Internet, just as all universities are today.

Table 1.1. Internet growth predictions.

Number of	1992	2000
Networks	10,000	1,000,000
Computers	1,000,000	100,000,000
Service providers	100 to 1,000	1,000 to 10,000
Direct users	5,000,000	1,000,000,000

Transferring Pictures and Sound

By 2000, not knowing how to use the Internet will be as grave a deficiency as not knowing how to read. Students can already access encyclopedias and dictionaries. By 2000, multimedia versions of the same resources will exist on the Internet. Pictures and sound will be transferred every day, and nationwide education events (lectures, conferences, and so on) will be mediated by the Internet.

At the community level, government departments will be accessible through the Internet. If you need to fill out a planning application or get a business permit, you won't need to trek down to city hall; you can simply go online through the Internet and access a database. Local information will be handled by regional networks on the Internet, and businesses will use Internet connections just as they use fax connections today.

An Internet Connection at Home

Soon, nobody in business will be without a connection to the Internet. This will, in turn, stimulate the sales of PCs, encourage home and mobile computing even more, and make it much easier to get high-speed connections at home. The 21st century yuppie without a home Internet connection will definitely not be keeping up with the Joneses.

These predictions will be fulfilled within the next decade. Does that seem an incredibly short time? Consider this—if the Internet evolves as fast as the personal computer, gigabit speeds will be the low end of performance. The microprocessors that drive our personal computers went from an 8-bit design running at 4.77 MHz in 1981 to a 32-bit design running at speeds of up to 50 MHz a decade later. Modems that ran at 120 characters per second were hot in 1985. Today, high-speed modems running at more than ten times the speed cost less than the 1985 model.

What about high-speed data lines to your house? Five years ago, this wasn't possible without a lot of screaming and pleading. Today, the only obstacle is price. By the year 2000, it probably won't cost much more than a regular telephone line.

Internet Everywhere

The United States won't be the only country investing in network infrastructures. Already the European Community (EC) is starting to make large investments in communications, as are Scandinavia, Japan, and Australia.

China is expected to become the world's largest consumer of fiber-optic cable. Because they're probably not planning to make those cheesy 1970s lamps that sprout glass fibers, it's safe to assume that telephones and networking will become major investments. And where the telephone system goes, there goes the Internet.

As a way of learning about the world, communicating, and creating, the power of the Internet is only just starting to be revealed. As the tools we use to communicate improve and we are able to use voice and video across the Internet, a whole new society will form. It won't replace what we think of as society, but it will be a Cyberspace parallel of today's social structures.

The Internet will change society on a worldwide basis. Now is the time to prepare yourself for the 21st century; now is the time to master navigating the Internet.

"What railroads were to America in the 19th century and superhighway systems were in the 20th, high-bandwidth networks are to the 21st century," Mitchell Kertzman, chief executive at PowerSoft Corporation, Burlington, Mass.

CONNECTIONS: GETTING TO THE INTERNET

It takes leaps of faith to sense the connections that are not necessarily obvious. — Matina Horner

Getting Connected

There was a time when only a privileged few could gain access to the Internet. Now, anyone can get to the Internet for a price. Better still, the price is one that's falling rapidly. Internet connections can now be purchased for the cost of a magazine subscription.

Internet connections come in four varieties:

- ⚓ Permanent direct
- ⚓ On-demand direct
- ⚓ Dial-up terminal
- ⚓ Mail-only

The differences between the types of connection are in how fast data is transferred, whether the connection is permanent or temporary, the kind of data that is handled, and the protocol used. Figure 2.1 shows how all of these connections are routed to the Internet.

The first two factors, speed and permanence of the connection, primarily determine the cost. The other factors determine the kinds of tools you need (both hardware and software) and how easy the connection will be to use.

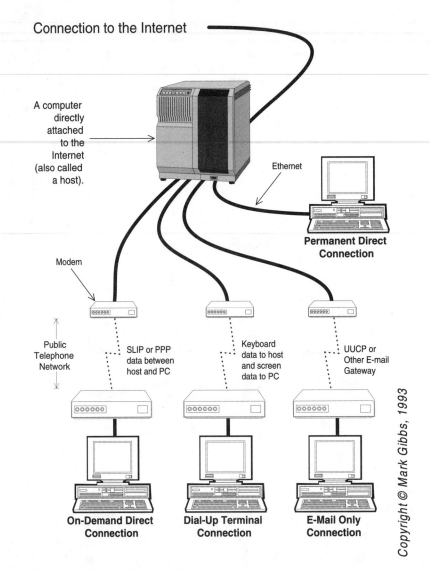

Figure 2.1. How permanent direct, on-demand direct, dial-up terminal, and e-mail-only connections access the Internet.

Permanent Direct Connections

Permanent direct connections are always available and are direct to a TCP/IP network (we discussed TCP/IP in Chapter 1, "The Internet: Past, Present, and Future"), that is, in turn, connected to the rest of the Internet. These kinds of connections are not common except in universities and large companies or through Internet service providers.

Permanent direct connections are also the most expensive. They require dedicated high-speed lines that are very expensive. Worse still, the faster the line, the more expensive it is. Connecting to the main Internet service providers also requires some hefty startup costs.

We're now seeing regional secondary service providers with permanent direct connections to main Internet networks. These service providers sell connections of all the types discussed here to individuals and organizations on a local or regional basis.

If you are at a university or large company, you may already have access to a permanent direct Internet connection. Assuming that it's not one of the other types discussed later, you have some kind of network connection to your PC and you run TCP/IP support software.

There are now many vendors of TCP/IP products. Artisoft, Inc. (Tuscon, AZ), better known for its peer-to-peer network systems, has released a product called LANtastic for TCP/IP. This allows PCs to act as TCP/IP clients and comes with telnet, FTP, and all the other tools for working on the Internet. LANtastic for TCP/IP includes programs that enable you to configure PCs as FTP and print servers so that people on other computers can use your resources.

On-Demand Direct Connections

A variant of TCP/IP designed for telephone lines (regular TCP/IP connections are done on Ethernet networks) is called Point-to-Point Protocol (PPP) and its older relative is Serial Line IP (SLIP). With one of these and a modem connection to an Internet service provider's computer, you can have a link that makes your computer a full Internet participant when you want it to be.

These connections can be very cost effective and deliver good performance if you have a high-speed modem. By high-speed modem, we mean one that runs at least 9600 baud or preferably 14,400 baud. These modems are fairly expensive, so make sure that the modem you plan to use is compatible with the service provider's modems.

Dial-Up Terminal Connections

With dial-up terminal connections, you link to an Internet service provider as if you were a terminal on the service provider's computer. In other words, the Internet access software you run (telnet, FTP, and so on) is run on the service provider's computer. Your keystrokes are sent to the software on the service provider's computer, and the screen output is sent back to you.

This kind of service enables you to do anything on the Internet that you want. All of the Internet tools—FTP, telnet, Gopher, WAIS, and so on—are accessible unless the system manager prevents you from using them.

In this category are service providers such as Delphi (owned by General Videotex, Cambridge, MA), which offers an Internet Special Interest Group (SIG). By joining this group, you can get full access to the Internet and disk space for file transfer data storage. Delphi has simplified how you use its service by providing help screens at all levels throughout the system and others that appear when you run commands (see Figure 2.2).

> **Navigator's Note:** Delphi offers two charging plans: the 10/4 Plan ($10/month, which includes 4 hours of use; additional use is $4/hour), and the 20/20 Plan (20 hours of use per month, for $20/month; additional use is $1.80/hour). Under both plans, Internet access is an additional $3 per month. You get to Delphi by using a service called Sprintnet, which is usually a local call with a surcharge of $9 per hour.

The fact that you actually work on the service provider's computer has some important implications. Because the amount of data going between the service provider and your computer is limited (that is, your computer isn't doing all the network stuff, it's just acting as a terminal), you can use a low-speed connection (2400 baud is usually adequate). The problem is, if you haul a file across the Internet, it winds up being stored on the service provider's computer. To get the file to your computer requires that you do a file transfer from the service provider's system.

File transfers aren't hard, but if your connection is at 2400 baud, it could be very time-consuming for large files. For example, it took about 45 seconds to transfer *Alice in Wonderland* in an archive file (alice29.zip, 64,809 bytes) from the Gutenberg Project (`mrcnext.cso.uiuc.edu`, see Appendix H, "The Internet Navigator's Gazetteer") to the system at Delphi. Because the maximum data rate for Delphi connections is 2400 baud, the transfer of the file to my computer took over 19 minutes!

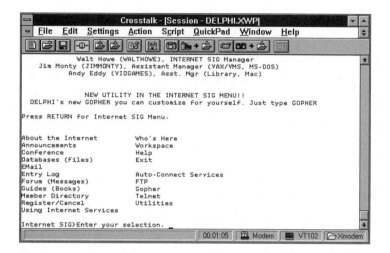

Figure 2.2. The Delphi Internet Special Interest Group being accessed through Crosstalk for Windows.

Provided that you aren't planning to transfer large files, dial-up terminal connections can be very cost-effective. Other than an account with a service provider, a modem, and a telephone line, all you need is almost any type of PC and a terminal emulation package.

Almost any PC will do because handling terminal data is within the capabilities of the most basic PC. As for terminal emulation software, you have a huge range to choose from. In the preparation of this book, one of the authors made extensive use of two of the leading Windows terminal emulation packages, Crosstalk for Windows from Digital Communications Associates, Inc. (Alpharetta, GA) and Procomm Plus for Windows from Datastorm Technologies, Inc. (Columbia, MO).

The great thing about these advanced terminal emulators is their flexibility and features. Scripting is a powerful tool that makes it appear as if you are typing commands and information, such as your user name and password, when prompted. You can also automate operations to login to services, connect to computers, transfer files, and send and receive electronic messages.

Mail-Only Connections

Mail-only connections are links that enable you only to send and receive electronic mail. These are usually the cheapest connections, in terms of both subscription cost and the connection charges.

Mail-only connections can be supplied in three main ways. The first is as a variant of the last category, dial-up terminal connections. Instead of being able to perform file transfers using FTP and access remote systems using telnet, all you can do is use electronic mail to link to the Internet.

For example, on CompuServe—a system that offers a huge range of services to its users—you can address e-mail messages to anyone who is accessible through the Internet. All you need to do is preface the Internet address with INTERNET:. This means that mgibbs@coyote.rain.org becomes, to the CompuServe user, INTERNET:mgibbs@coyote.rain.org.

Likewise, Internet users can send messages to you. The CompuServe user [75600,1002] can be addressed as 75600.1002@compuserve.com. After you send a message to someone on the Internet or that person sends a message to you, you'll know that you have the correct address.

The other type of e-mail connection is a UUCP link. UUCP stands for UNIX-to-UNIX Copy Program and is a protocol used by UNIX systems to copy files between remote dial-up sites. By putting e-mail in files and transferring them between computers, intersystem e-mail is possible.

Now you can get software to support UUCP on IBM-type PCs, Macs, and other computer systems, so any site that somehow connects to the Internet and can supply UUCP mail may be a way for you to get an Internet e-mail link. You'll need to talk to your local UUCP service suppliers to find out what they offer and what software they support.

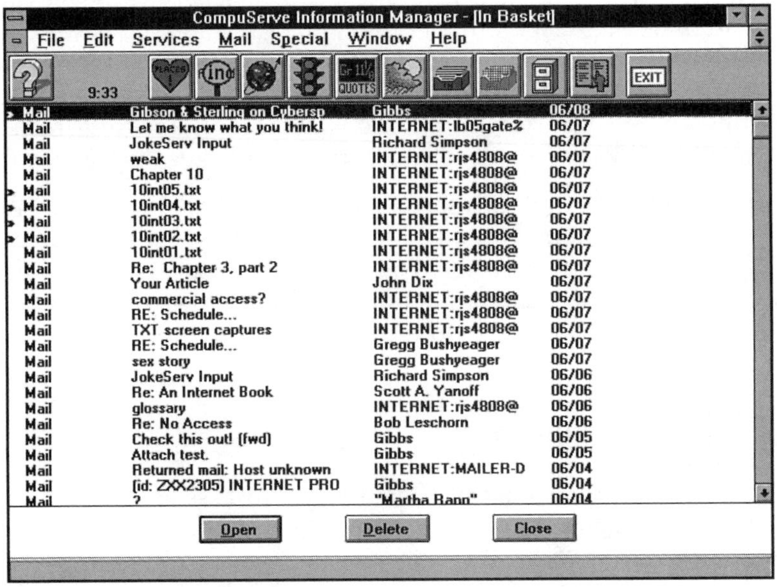

Figure 2.3. The CompuServe Information Manager for Windows (WinCIM), a utility that automates your interactions with Internet e-mail. There's also a DOS version of CIM.

Pros and Cons of Connection Types

The best connection of all is, of course, a permanent direct link all your own. It's the fastest, and consequently, the most expensive. It requires special facilities and a lot of expertise to set up, and is simply not practical for most individuals. (Unless you were the class techno-nerd—then you have a fighting chance, but your dad would have to be pretty well-heeled.)

Next best is a permanent, direct connection that someone else owns. You probably need to have your computer on the same network (usually an Ethernet network), and you'll be restricted to where the computer can be located (in other words, you won't be able to have this kind connection at home). This situation is most likely in a university or business that has a permanent direct Internet connection.

For a permanent, direct connection, you need some software for the type of PC you're using, but the cost of these packages is pretty low, and some shareware and freeware systems are available. However, the choice may not be up to you. The manager of the system you're connecting to may tell you which software you will use.

If you plan to do a lot of work on the Internet, you might think (if money isn't a big issue) about having a dedicated, digital or analog, leased telephone line. You've moved into a new bracket of cost here, but for a medium-size business, it shouldn't be prohibitive.

On-demand direct connections are the next best if you want to, for example, run your own Gopher server or any other software that relies on having a TCP/IP connection to the Internet. Your service supplier can tell you what software and hardware you need. On the hardware side, you'll want to have a fast modem— 9600 bits per second (bps) for a PPP connection is just about acceptable, and less will be pretty aggravating. Actually, 9600 bps is being quickly superseded by 14,400 bps modems, which are much better for SLIP or PPP connections.

For most people, the best value is a dial-up connection. If you want full connectivity to the Internet so that you can run telnet sessions and use FTP and Gopher, you'll need a service provider that offers a full Internet connection. If you have a local free-net, your problem may be solved.

If an e-mail connection is all you need, then just about anyone who offers Internet e-mail access or UUCP links is worth looking at. Check your local service providers (if any) as well as the national services such as Delphi and CompuServe.

Colleges and Universities

If you take a course at your local college or university, you may be eligible for an account on its computer system. This is a great way to get to the Internet, because most reasonably large colleges and universities have Internet connections.

You might have to use a terminal in their facility, or you might be able to dial in from home using your own computer. This is often pretty frustrating. Many colleges and universities, particularly those without a computer studies department, have limited facilities. It might be very hard to find a free terminal in the computer room, or the modems into the system might be constantly busy.

Business Connections

Many businesses are starting to explore the potential of the Internet for communicating with their clients and suppliers and for research. Some companies make sizable investments to get high-speed connections, most notably the computer companies and companies that compile and sell data and information retrieval services.

Today, a large range of business services will, for a fee, supply you with data. Among these are several systems that supply up-to-the-minute stock prices, weather services of various kinds, and some huge databases such as the LEXIS/ NEXIS service. Some Gopher servers are devoted to particular specialist topics, such as the Cornell Law Gopher.

Some businesses make accounts available to outsiders for a fee. You'll need to hustle in your area to find out which companies have connections and who in that company to talk to. Whether they'll charge you a fair rate is another question entirely.

Free-Nets

Free-Nets are part of a new movement that aims to bring information technology to the people. They provide a regional bulletin board-type system and supply local information and communications facilities. Most of these systems are now linking to the Internet, and they offer some truly useful resources.

They are, as their name implies, free! If you're lucky enough to have one in your area, you have hit the jackpot! To find out if there is a free-net locally, check with local computer stores, user groups, and the Chamber of Commerce. The only problem with Free-Nets is that there aren't many of them, and they can be erratic in the service they provide. (Because they're free, you're in no position to complain if stuff goes wrong and nobody can be bothered to fix it for a few days.)

Table 2.1 contains a list of some Free-Nets from which to choose.

Table 2.1. National Public Telecomputing Network Affiliate Systems (as of March 7, 1993).

System/Location	Modem/Internet Address
Big Sky Telegraph Dillon, Montana	**Modem:** (406) 683-7680—1200 baud) **Internet:** 192.231.192.1
Buffalo Free-Net Buffalo, New York (Demo System)	**Modem:** (716) 645-6128 **Internet:** freenet.buffalo.edu
The Cleveland Free-Net Cleveland, Ohio	**Modem:** (216) 368-3888 - 300/1200/2400 Baud **Internet:** freenet-in-a.cwru.edu
Denver Free-Net Denver, Colorado	**Modem:** (303) 270-4865 **Internet:** freenet.hsc.colorado.edu (140.226.1.8)
The Heartland Free-Net Peoria, Illinois	**Modem:** (309) 674-1100 **Internet:** heartland.bradley.edu (136.176.5.114)
Lorain County Free-Net Elyria, Ohio	**Modem:** (216) 366-9721 - 300/1200/2400 Baud **Internet:** freenet.lorain.oberlin.edu (132.162.32.99)
Medina County Free-Net Medina, Ohio	**Modem:** (216) 723-6732 - 300/1200/2400 Baud **Internet:** (not receiving telnet connections at the moment)
National Capital Free-Net Ottawa, Canada	**Modem:** (613) 780-3733 **Internet:** freenet.carleton.ca (134.117.1.25)
Tallahassee Free-Net Tallahassee, Florida (Demo System)	**Modem:** (demo system, Internet access only) **Internet:** freenet.fsu.edu (144.174.128.43)
Tristate Online Cincinnati, Ohio	**Modem:** (513) 579-1990 **Internet:** cbos.uc.edu

continues

Table 2.1. continued

System/Location	Modem/Internet Address
Victoria Free-Net Victoria, British Columbia	**Modem:** (604) 595-2300 **Internet:** freenet.victoria.bc.ca (134.87.16.100)
The Youngstown Free-Net Youngstown, Ohio	**Modem:** (216) 742-3072 - 300/1200/2400 Baud **Internet:** yfn.ysu.edu (192.55.234.27)

Service Providers

There are now many fee-charging Internet service providers. We'll just look at a few. For a more extensive list of service providers consult Appendix A, " The Public Dialup Internet Access List (PDial)."

RAIN

The Santa Barbara RAIN project is a new kind of venture. Built around the concept of providing information technology to the community, RAIN plans to be the most cost-effective way for anyone—private individual, commercial organization, charity, or government department—to get not only regional, but also Internet, connectivity.

Initially, the RAIN project was based at the University of California at Santa Barbara (UCSB). In its first phase, RAIN linked 2,000 students at 45 schools in the Santa Barbara area with each other and the Internet. The success of the first six-month trial was so great that the RAIN project moved its schedule forward and started expanding its scope. The next expansion, set for July 1993, includes leased lines to Ventura to the south and San Luis Obispo to the north, the addition of eight more local modem lines, and the installation of a dozen public access terminals around Santa Barbara.

The project is an excellent model for the regional end of the national information infrastructure, and it looks as if the project will more than fulfill the founders' expectations. All they must cope with now is the demand. The project expects to support around 1,000 users by September 1993, rising to between 4,000 and 8,000 by September 1994. For organizations, RAIN targets between 40 and 60 business clients by September 1994. These projections now seem conservative.

RAIN charges a $35 start-up fee ($15 for students) and a flat $10 per month ($5 for students). For that you get dial-up access to 14,400 baud, full Internet access, and 5 megabytes of disk space. There are pricing plans for nonprofit organizations, dedicated lines to their system, PPP connections, UUCP mail connections, and even full Internet access. For more information, e-mail `rain@rain.org`, telnet to `coyote.rain.org`, or phone (805) 899-8610. You can also connect via modem at (805) 899-8600 and login in as `guest`.

The World

The World is run by Software Tool & Die, one of the first companies in this field. The World is a huge system that supplies complete Internet access as well as a whole range of services.

It offers two billing rates, which are the same, 24 hours a day at all connection speeds. The Basic Rate plan is a $5 monthly account fee plus a $2 per hour usage fee. This rate allows you half a megabyte of data storage. The 20/20 Plan is a bulk usage rate, where $20 paid in advance buys 20 hours of online time during a one month period. This includes the monthly account fee and allows you up to two megabytes of disk storage. 20/20 Plan accounts used for more than 20 hours during one month are billed at an hourly rate of $1 per hour for the overage.

To get an account, call The World's computer at (617) 739-WRLD or telnet to `world.std.com` (`192.74.137.5`). At the login prompt, use the login `new` and answer the questions. You can select your login name, which will become your e-mail address. Your initial password will be automatically provided. To actually activate the account, you need to call The World at (617) 739-0202. You can also get a free one-hour trial to check the system out. This provides an opportunity to investigate The World's resources.

The Well

The WELL (The Whole Earth 'Lectronic Link), located in Sausalito, California, is another enormous computer services supplier that offers full Internet access. It is one of the better-known computer conferencing systems in the country.

The WELL is unusual in that it displays a very distinct culture. It offers over 200 conferences and currently has more than 6,000 registered users. Perhaps the most interesting aspect of the WELL is the community of people that use it. Many writers, journalists, and other well-known figures have WELL accounts.

The basic cost of the WELL is a $15/month service charge plus a $2.00/hour usage fee. Your first five hours of use are free. Any group or organization can have a private conference created at no extra charge.

The WELL can be reached in three ways: by direct dial, through the Internet, and through what are usually local dial-up connections to the CompuServe Packet Network (this attracts a surcharge of $4/hr in the U.S.).

An electronic mail message to info@well.sf.ca.us will get a list of files containing information about the WELL. You can also call them at (415) 332-4335.

The Bottom Line

There are many ways of getting to the Internet, some of which are high-speed TCP/IP connections that allow you to run any Internet tool and use resources. Unfortunately, those connections are costly and uncommon.

For most people, the best bet is a dial-up connection to a service supplier—either emulating a terminal on their computer or, for the more adventurous, with a PPP connection.

Until the Internet becomes as widespread as the telephone system, the type of available connection will pretty much depend on luck. Having a cooperative service provider or a college, university, or business next door is the most desirable (but pretty unlikely) option.

If you're part of a large company that doesn't have an Internet connection, you may be just the person to drag your co-workers screaming and kicking into the 21st century. If you are part of a like-minded group that wants to get a connection, there's always the option of starting your own Free-Net or a service like RAIN.

If you're not in a hurry, just wait a couple of years. The Internet will probably become a service you can order from the telephone company.

WHERE'S THE POST? ELECTRONIC MAIL

Electronic mail is probably the most widely used Internet service in the world. Each day, around 25 million people send each other messages, which might be pen pal letters from children in Moscow to children in Tokyo, business memos between companies in Los Angeles and London, or continuing discussions between scientists collaborating on research.

Most messages are simple text, but you can also send files containing graphical images, such as drawings and photographs. Some of the newest message forms contain digitized sound and even animation. Messages can be sent person-to-person (called interpersonal messages), person-to-computer and the other way around (as in FTPMail; see Chapter 4, "A Moving Experience: FTP for Me"), or program-to-program.

This latter category, program-to-program, is the technique used by applications such as groupware and scheduling systems. *Groupware* is software designed to be used by a group of people to make their efforts more effective, efficient, or timely. This kind of software is not yet very common on the Internet (or anywhere else for that matter), but soon we'll see lots of groupware applications that are Internet-specific, or at least Internet-compatible.

Electronic messages may be sent and received using many different programs. Some of the most common are Elm, Pegasus, Pine, and Eudora. In order to use electronic mail, you need only have access to the Internet, an e-mail program, and the e-mail address of the person or persons you wish to reach. It's pretty easy.

What Is E-Mail?

This may sound like an odd question, but a lot more goes on than you might think. We won't go into great detail here, and if you're not really interested, you can skip to the next section. However, before you rush off, consider that knowing how e-mail is supposed to work can make the times when it doesn't a lot less mysterious.

The content of e-mail is generally textual, but sending more exotic data, such as graphic images and binary files (for programs, databases, and word processing documents) is possible, as long as the data is translated into a text message equivalent before sending. In the future, messages containing audio and video data will become commonplace.

Navigator's Note: "How do you change binary data into text data?" you may be asking yourself. Apart from the fact that talking to yourself is a habit that is usually considered to presage the onset of some kind of dementia, it's an excellent question.

The answer is that plain text characters can have numeric values from 32 to 128, while the characters in a binary file can have any value from 0 to 255. Various schemes are used to convert binary values into values that lie in the range of plain text values.

There are many programs available that will take a binary file and encode it so that it can be sent by e-mail. They are available for most operating systems. For example, there is uuencode for UNIX, and ABE for MS-DOS machines. You can use Archie (discussed in Chapter 6, "Finding Files: Archie") to locate freeware and shareware encoders.

Navigator's Note: The first real-time (a techie way of saying "at the same time as it happens") video broadcast on the Internet was successfully conducted on May 22, 1993. The cult movie *Wax: Or the Discovery of Television Among the Bees* was broadcast from a studio in Manhattan by the film's director, David Blair.

The data was reportedly hard to find on the Internet and was received without color and at a rate of only about two frames per second (compared to the regular television broadcast rate of 25 frames per second). The sound track also got lost occasionally. In terms of quality, the transmission sucked rocks, but it showed that it could be done.

As we move nearer to the national data superhighway, real-time video on the Internet will become routine. This will be great just as long as we don't have to watch reruns of *I Love Lucy*.

Store and Forward

E-mail is based on the fundamental concept of store-and-forward technology. This is really pretty simple. (See Figure 3.1.)

The *store* part of store-and-forward refers to a message being added to a storage system by the message's originator. When the recipient is ready, the message is *forwarded* for retrieval.

The important thing about this simple-sounding idea is that the recipient doesn't have to be available when the originator stores the message. This enables the e-mail system to select how the message will get from the place where it is first stored to the place where it is retrieved (forwarded to the user).

Navigator's Note: Yeah, I know. Store-and-retrieve would be a much better term, but you're fighting two issues. The first is that everyone calls it store-and-forward and the term is generally understood. The second is that the term came about from a view of how the e-mail system serviced the user (messages were forwarded to the user) rather than the more intuitively obvious view that the user (or rather the user's program) goes and retrieves messages. This kind of complexity is what makes so much of the computer industry obscure to outsiders. If only the industry would...oops! I fell off my soapbox.

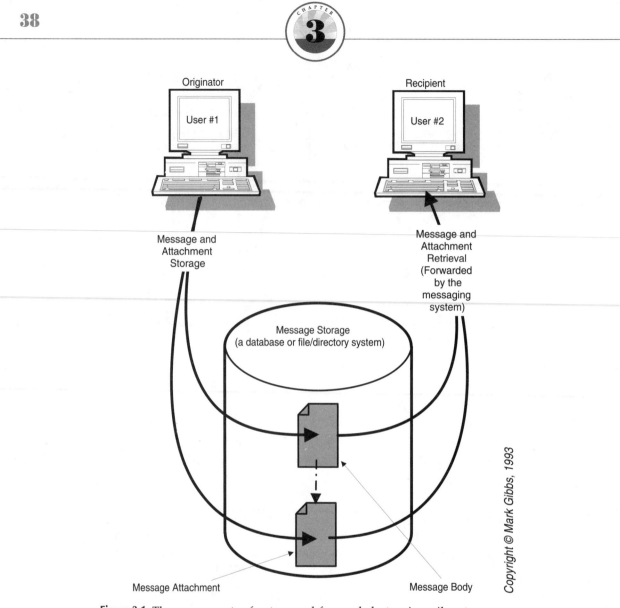

Figure 3.1. The components of a store-and-forward electronic mail system.

The route of an e-mail message may vary, depending on the condition of the network. Network outages, or maintenance and repair (as well as local down-time), may have the e-mail message waiting in a queue (also referred to as a spool) for later delivery.

This is a very important point. You might someday wonder why you didn't get mail for two days and then got a huge load all at once. A computer that handles mail for you somewhere may have been out of service, and as soon as it came back online, it forwarded all your mail in one great lump. Fun, eh?

Speed

By now you may have realized that communication by Internet e-mail is not necessarily instantaneous—although it's usually faster than the postal mail (often referred to as "snail mail" by people on e-mail systems).

Store-and-forward systems have inherent delays that can range from a few seconds to days or weeks. It's also important to remember that just as regular mail can get lost, electronic post can vanish without a trace (a wrong routing or a computer failure and, poof!, a cloud of electrons is all that's left). That's not to say that a lot of post gets lost, but 100 percent reliability is rarely available.

E-mail on the Internet uses the Simple Mail Transfer Protocol standard (SMTP)—yet another component of the Internet Protocol suite. Again, the use of a standard (SMTP in this case) enables computers from different manufacturers to transmit e-mail to and receive it from each other.

E-Mail Parts

An e-mail message is made up of two parts—the header and the body of the message. The header usually consists of

- ⚓ From, which gives you the originator's name
- ⚓ To, which tells you to whom it was sent
- ⚓ The date and time sent
- ⚓ The subject

In addition, information from the machines that "Received" the message en route, a message ID identifying the sender, and other (less useful, but included for your delectation) data are included. Here is a sample message, including the header:

```
Sender: jerry@TEETOT.ACUSD.EDU
Received: from teetot.acusd.edu by iha.compuserve.com (5.65/5.930129sam)
    id AA22262; Sun, 30 May 93 13:26:53 -0400
Received: by TEETOT.ACUSD.EDU (5.65/DEC-Ultrix/4.3)
    id AA19273; Sun, 30 May 1993 10:12:04 -0700
From: jerry@TEETOT.ACUSD.EDU (Jerry Stratton)
Message-Id: <9305301712.AA19273@TEETOT.ACUSD.EDU>
Subject: Re: Beelzebub
To: 76004.3310@compuserve.com (Mark Gibbs)
Date: Sun, 30 May 93 10:12:03 PDT
In-Reply-To: <930527060733_76004.3310_CHN32-1@CompuServe.COM>; from "Mark Gibbs"
at May 27, 93 2:07 am
```

```
Reply-To: jerry@TEETOT.ACUSD.EDU
X-Mailer: ELM [version 2.3 PL11]
>I'm writing a book on the Internet for Prentice Hall. I found your gopher
>description and wondered if you'd like to send me a message about Beelzebub
>and what's there that we could include.
Hi, Mark. Beelzebub has a number of functions. First, it's really an ftp
site, but gopher folks don't need to know that. It serves the Role-Playing
community, and has become the main distribution site for the Shadowrun
cyberpunk role-playing game. This is due mainly to the fact that I edit
an on-line magazine, The Neo-Anarchists Guide to Everything Else,
devoted to that game.
I suspect that Beelzebub's main use is from the Role-Playing community,
but that's only because that community is organized enough to have a
monthly list of role-playing oriented ftp sites distributed throughout
the role-playing newsgroups and mailing lists.
Beelzebub also contains a section devoted to reading and writing comic
books, and a section on political issues that I feel are important.
Beelzebub is currently my personal playground, although I do try to
encourage other University of San Diego students, staff, and employees
to use it.
Beelzebub got its name from a Macintosh. It was originally an ftp site
all its own on a Macintosh, and the Macintosh's site name was
beelzebub.acusd.edu. I don't know how the Mac got its name. We've got
a few odd names here. The Macs in our lab are named after various
popes (and yes, there is a Cerebus). You'd have to be a fairly devoted
C&W fan to guess where teetot's name is from.
Jerry
jerry@teetot.acusd.edu
- - - - - -
        One pane of glass in the window,
        No one is complaining, no, come in and shut the door,
        Faded is the crimson from the ribbons that she wore,
        And it's strange how no one comes round any more.
                        It Must Have Been The Roses
```

Headers

Headers aren't always visible when you receive e-mail messages. Some systems conveniently hide them from you; they aren't usually useful or even wanted. You can see in the message header that the sender was jerry@teetot.acusd.edu. Although the first line shows this, the most informative address is always the last "From" that you find (the one nearest the actual message). In this example, it tells me the address of the sender and his real name, Jerry Stratton. (Hi, Jerry. I did threaten to put your message in the book.)

Getting There

Information on how the message got from Jerry to me is shown in the list of "Received:" lines. Jerry sent the message to me from his computer, called `teetot.acusd.edu`, which we can see is a DEC computer running Ultrix version 4.3 (someone, somewhere cares about this).

The message went next to a computer called `iha.compuserve.com`, one of the computers on the CompuServe system. This computer's identification (`5.65/ 5.930129sam`) doesn't happen to mean anything to me, so I'll conveniently ignore it. Actually, this computer is a gateway that translated the message into CompuServe's format and then sent it on to me.

We can see that Jerry's computer sent the message out onto the Internet on Sunday, 30 May 1993 at 10:12:04, and it reached the CompuServe system on the same day at 13:26:53. So it took just over fourteen minutes to cross the Internet. If this had been from Russia or Turkey, it could have been a lot longer.

> **Navigator's Note:** Note that the sending time was 10:12 Pacific Daylight Time, which is 13:12 Eastern Daylight Time. When I first wrote this I made the mistake of not checking the timezones of the sender and recipient, so I had originally noted that the transit time was *three* hours and fourteen minutes. Fortunately, one of the wily editors at Sams spotted this.
>
> This kind of data is really not particularly useful to most people, but if you're exchanging messages regularly with someone for business purposes and you're trying to meet a deadline, having an idea how long it takes to send a message to them could be pretty useful.

Message IDs

The message ID isn't useful to people, only to the e-mail software. By keeping track of message IDs, a conversation thread can be followed. This can be a vitally important feature if someone sends you a message that says something like "Yes" and nothing else. "Yes" what? "Yes, I do owe you $1,000"? Not knowing could be frustrating (and irritating).

In this case, the sender was nice enough to copy my message into his reply. This is a politeness that many people extend, usually when the reply is to a complex message and they want to ensure that each point in the original is addressed.

This message's ID is 9305301712.AA19273, which is an identifier created by Jerry's system. Note also that the message he's replying to is noted: In-Reply-To: <930527060733_76004.3310_CHN32-1@CompuServe.COM>; from "Mark Gibbs" at May 27, 93 2:07 am. This enables the sender's software to identify the message that is being answered.

If this message was part of a long exchange, I should be able to index up and down the sequence of messages and follow the virtual conversation that occurred. (Unfortunately, this thread-following isn't possible with any of the CompuServe e-mail systems, which aren't intended to be compatible with SMTP. You could, relatively easily, write a piece of software to do this, but I'll leave that as an exercise for the more masochistic reader.)

The Subject

The subject is Re: Beelzebub, which indicates that Jerry's software is smart enough, when generating a reply to a message, to copy the original subject text (just "Beelzebub") and stick a "Re:" in front of it. This is a nice touch; almost all mail systems can do it.

To

We can see who the message is addressed to, 76004.3310@compuserve.com (Mark Gibbs), and that Jerry actually finished composing the message and handed it to his computer to be sent at 10:12:03 PDT (the "Date" line). It took only one minute for his computer to take his message and send it out. This seems fast, but in computer terms it's actually quite a long time. It's likely that his computer had a lot of other tasks and e-mail to handle.

The "In-Reply-To:" line shows not only the message ID related to this message but also who created it and when that message was finished (May 27, 1993 2:07 a.m.). The line following that shows who the reply should go to. This is useful in many situations. You could, for example, send a form to someone on request and instruct his or her software to send the completed version to someone in an administration department for processing. This feature may not work in all e-mail systems.

The Tools

The last item in the header tells us which e-mail software Jerry was using. He used Elm version 2.3 PL11, which is a screen-oriented e-mail system (it formats the whole screen just like a word processor does). This information isn't always available; some e-mail systems don't bother with it.

Navigator's Note: You can get Elm via anonymous FTP from the archives at Ohio State University Computer and Information Science Department (OSUCIS). The address is `tut.cis.ohio-state.edu` (`128.146.8.60`). Then the fun begins: you must install and configure it. See your system administrator first for permission.

How They Do It in Europe

In Europe, many people who use the Internet include a small digitized picture of themselves in a special header field. By using either an e-mail system that understands this feature or a separate utility, you can see what the originator looks like. Its a very hip thing to do, but it hasn't yet become popular outside Europe.

Summing Up Headers

You can see that a lot of data is available in an e-mail header, most of which is only really useful to programs. In general, you don't need to worry about headers; your e-mail package will do that for you. If you have problems though, knowing the basics of what's in headers is very useful.

The Body

On some networks and computers, body length is limited. Either the e-mail system or the network software refuses your message if it's too long.

Due to the technology of the Internet, all the data in the body must be text characters. That is, the characters must be printable. If you want to send data that isn't printable (binary data), such as a program file or a database, you need to encode it. This encoding process can be done in several ways, the simplest being to translate the binary data into characters that represent the original data. This always results in a message that is bigger than the data itself.

If you have a large amount of binary data to send, it must be encoded and sent in several pieces that are not so big that the mail system or network refuses them. At the recipient's end, the pieces need to be joined together and decoded. Some e-mail systems handle this work for you; most don't. The most common encoding tool is called "uuencode." Its opposite, the decoding tool, is called "uudecode." You can find versions of this program for UNIX, DOS, Windows, and most other operating systems.

Getting Attached

Attachments are chunks of data (usually files) that are sent along with the message. These attachments can be in either format—text or encoded binary data—and, if the latter, might be a program, a spreadsheet, a word processor file, and so on.

The latest and greatest standard in this area is MIME, the Multipurpose Internet Mail Extensions. MIME enables all sorts of data to be included in an e-mail message. It also gives references to remote resources to be collected (if the recipient has the ability to do so). This sounds complex and, frankly, it is. What it means to you is that in a few years' time, multimedia Internet messages will be the norm.

Back to the present. If someone sends you attachments today, he or she will usually be uuencoded into the message body. You need to save the message into a file, run uudecode (see the documents that should have come with this utility or ask your system manager or a friend for help), and the data should be in a file on your system.

Yours Truly

Signatures are the normal way to close a letter, and many people have taken to adding text blocks, jokes, or quotes to the end of their messages. From our preceding example, the signature part is

```
Jerry
jerry@teetot.acusd.edu
------
        One pane of glass in the window,
        No one is complaining, no, come in and shut the door,
        Faded is the crimson from the ribbons that she wore,
        And it's strange how no one comes round any more.
                        It Must Have Been The Roses
```

This is a writer with a penchant for literary quotations; others can be more esoteric, strange, or ribald. Text blocks often give postal addresses, telephone numbers, fax numbers, and so on. Some e-mail systems enable you to specify which text is to be automatically appended to your messages as standard.

Later in this chapter you'll find the signature of Scott Yanoff, who crops up in this book at regular intervals. It's a good example of a plain, useful block of data with a little humor thrown in.

Navigator's Note: Watch for long, complex signatures. Some people get very incensed by what they consider to be "a waste of bandwidth," and some USENET newsgroups reject messages with long (greater than 4 lines) signatures.

Be careful if you have a signature that is off-the-wall in any way. It may not be appropriate for all of your electronic correspondence; sending an electronic request for a job application that ends with a quote from the Marquis de Sade may not present the impression you would like.

E-Mail Functions

E-mail makes many different functions available to you. In this section, we'll explain a few of the most common.

Multiple Recipients

When you send a message, you may want to have multiple recipients. Most e-mail programs enable you to specify two or more addresses. The limitation on how many people can be addressed is often the same as the maximum length of the text.

Another feature enables you to send a copy to someone, usually for his or her reference. This is done by adding one or more addresses to the "cc" (for carbon copy) list. If you don't want the recipients to know that you're copying the message to someone else, you can use the "bcc" (blind carbon copy, sometimes written as just "bc") line. No one other than the individual recipients on the bcc list will know that they have received copies—not even the other bcc addressees.

Some people feel that using bcc's is very rude, because it is an essentially duplicitous act. I tend to agree, but then I'm old-fashioned that way.

Folders

Many e-mail applications enable you to store messages in folders. This is a way of organizing what can be a huge mass of messages. If you subscribe to mailing lists or USENET News, your e-mail volume can be in the hundreds of messages each day. Folders make that tidal wave manageable. Some e-mail systems even have folders inside folders.

Navigator's Note: A good habit to get into is to throw e-mail away regularly. If you don't, you'll start to accumulate truly humongous volumes of data. Eventually, you either run out of disk space or get into an argument with your system administrator. One well-known writer on the topic of e-mail and the Internet, Marshall Rose, claims to have every piece of e-mail he has sent and received since 1986, totaling around 250 megabytes—and it's in a compressed form! I'm not sure what use this is to him.

Replying

We've already mentioned replying to messages. This can be done without providing a reference to the message replied to (for example, just mentioning the original message's subject) or with a full reference to the original message ID.

The addition of "Re: " is a nice touch. A few systems copy the original message's text into the body of the reply so that you can refer to it. Most people just copy the bits they want to refer to. The standard for these referred-to bits is to put some kind of marker on the left side of the copied text. Some editors, such as the UNIX e-mail program, Pine, do that for you. See the preceding example, where my original text is flagged with >s. The alternative, to save yourself the pain of laboriously adding the markers, is just to delete all the text you aren't refering to and put quotes around what you keep.

Forwarding

Use forwarding when you want to send a message you received to another user. Some systems put a note into the body of the message (along the lines of "Forwarded message"), which you can delete if you want.

It's also common for e-mail software to copy the header data from the original message into the body of the forwarded message. Again, feel free to delete that data if you think it's not of any use.

If you ever feel inclined to spread gossip or send aggressive or rude messages, remember that forwarding a message makes photocopying a letter look horribly complicated. The spiteful quip about a coworker that you think is funny can be forwarded within seconds of being received if the recipient feels like it.

Address Books

Address books and aliases also help make e-mail easier to use. Many e-mail systems support a feature to "catch" e-mail addresses from messages received, with the ability to edit in your own entries.

Having an address such as `lb05gate%ucsbuxa@hub.ucsb.edu` is not particularly helpful. You want to have a more useful name than that, which is where aliases come in. This means that instead of using that long address, `lb05gate%ucsbuxa@hub.ucsb.edu`, you'd use the alias "Rick Gates" or just "Rick" instead.

Encryption

Encryption is a feature that has many people up in arms. There have been suggestions that the U.S. government may make it illegal to use any encryption for electronic messages other than one they approve. They want to control which encryption standard can be used, so that it will be one they'll be able to decode "for reasons of national security."

The implications of this have not escaped the civil libertarians, the activists, and all sorts of interested parties. The question raised by many people is, "Why should I care if the government can read my messages? I have nothing to hide." "Ah," reply those against government control, "it's the thin end of the wedge. Let them do that, and they'll be getting into all sorts of data about you that aren't anyone's business but yours."

The issue of encryption is, however, really quite complicated. If you want more information, find the May/June 1993 issue of *Wired* (a truly terrific magazine on high-tech topics). It contains a great article on the topic, called "Crypto Rebels." *Wired* is published by Wired USA and can be reached at `subscriptions@wired.com`.

In response to the need for easily available encryption, a couple of packages are available in the public domain. One of the best-known is PGP, which stands for Pretty Good Privacy. This can't be used legally for business purposes and is at the center of a potentially big political issue that could well have a major effect on the way the Internet is used.

Internet Addresses

As with snail mail, the timely arrival of your electronic message depends on whether you address it correctly. Internet addresses are in two parts, a "domain" name and a user name separated by an "at" sign (`@`).

The *domain name* (more correctly called a *hierarchical name*) consists of the name of the machine on which the user has an account, along with the network groups and subgroups leading to that computer. This name shows the group and subgroups giving that machine a unique identification, which enables the Internet message routing software to determine where to deliver the message. Delivering the message to the addressee is then up to the named computer.

For example, `rjj3432@shrimp.cis.utwo.edu` designates an Internet address, `rjj3432`, as the user name. This user can be found on the computer `shrimp`, which is in the subdomain `cis`, which is in the subdomain `utwo`, which is in the domain `edu`.

Domains are the highest level of addressing on the Internet and denote the types of activities the machines are used for. The most common domain names in use on the Internet are

EDU	Education
MIL	Military Sites
GOV	Nonmilitary Governmental Sites
COM	Commercial Organizations
NET	Special Network Machines
ORG	Other Organizations
UK	United Kingdom
CA	Canada
AU	Australia

...and so on, for all the other countries.

The subdomains can be names of institutions and departments at those institutions. For example, `umass` stands for the University of Massachusetts, `pitt` is the University of Pittsburgh, and `usl` is the University of Southwest Louisiana.

Examples of department names that aren't locational include `cis` for computer information services, `lis` for library information science, and `med` for medical center. Thus, a computer called "bigbopper" in the computer information services department at the University of Southwest Louisiana would be `bigbopper.cis.usl.edu`.

The computer's name is chosen locally and is often colorful or thematic. Some examples of prosaic names are `ucsbuxa` (standing for "UCSB UNIX A") and `ux1` (standing for "UNIX 1"). More interesting machine names are `coyote` (at `rain.org`), `cadillac` (at `siemens.com`), and `casbah` (at `acns.nwu.edu`).

User names can be cryptic. They may be composed of initials and identifying numbers; they can be shortened, a nickname or handle (as in Citizen's Band use...rduck is probably out there somewhere); or they might be a variation or even the full real name of the person. The following are samples of addresses. Try to decipher them before reading the commentaries to the right.

Address	Comments
75600.1002@compuserve.com	A numeric user name. This is due to CompuServe's addressing scheme.
chevro5@class.org	Most likely a handle.
aaxlx@mtsunix1.bitnet	A visitor from Alpha Centauri? The computer most likely runs UNIX and is on the BITNET network.
brianmartin@central-gw.uow.ed.au	A full real name of an Australian user.
bsydelk@desire.wright.edu	Possibly a person's last name and initials. Whimsical computer name.
wolfe@alhrg.wpafb.af.mil	A last name for a user at Wright Patterson Air Force Base, which is in the subdomain "af"—for Air Force— in the domain military.
zxj@vm	Brevity taken to extremes. A shortened address.

Remember that Internet alphanumeric addresses are actually aliases for numeric addresses, such as 128.5.3.194. The alphanumeric addresses are used because, even though they can be hard to interpret, they are easier than the numeric names. The translation of alphanumeric names into numeric addresses is handled by machines on the Internet, called name servers. You can use either type of address.

Aliases

To get around using the cumbersome Internet address of a person or persons, many mail programs enable you to create aliases. An alias is a substitute for the Internet address. Thus, if your friend "Ann" has an Internet address of apt5930@inside.cis.umn.edu, you can make the word ann substitute for the longer address. This is especially helpful if you want to send to a group of people—classmates, colleagues, friends, coworkers. You just put all of their e-mail addresses into an alias that you can remember—for example, `class296`, `book`, `project`, `party`, or `staff`.

Under the UNIX operating system, you can specify aliases in the .mailrc file. By making an entry that starts with the word "alias," followed by the alias, followed by the text that the alias stands for, you can have as many aliased addresses as you like. Check with your system manager or your manuals to see how this should be done. If you don't lay out the entries correctly, it won't work.

This approach helped with the first "Navigating the Internet" workshop (mentioned in the Introduction), which had 864 participants. Aliases were used, so that instead of having to send out 864 messages, only 17 messages were required. Here is a sample of part of my .mailrc file containing the aliases:

```
alias class1     \$F2P@PCJIS2.bitnet 00hlcaldwell@lio.bsuvc.bsu.edu
21602tms@msu.edu 22331mom@msu.edu 70641.2417@compuserve.com
71440.2735@compuserve.com a-janda@nwu.edu aa37@cleveland.Freenet.Edu
AALGIIR@SCU.BITNET adams015@dukemc.bitnet adler@monty.rand.org aheckath@trinity.edu
ai4cphyw@miamiu.acs.muohio.edu A_Fildman@TIRC.edu

alias class2 barbara@pondir.csci.unt.edu barbi@icho.panix.com barritt@cirl.uiuc.edu
barry@psy.glasgow.ac.uk BASKAUS@CTRVAX.VANDIRBILT.Edu battagli@PICA.ARMY.MIL
bbarr@miamiu.acs.muohio.edu bbictt@guvax.georgetown.edu bcalixto@iss.cc.utexas.edu
bdav@casbah.acns.nwu.edu BIKNUPP@GROVI.IUP.Edu binitzt@ohsu.edu
bit@onimohr.wustl.edu Biv@Stuart.NTU.Edu. AUbfiltz@grits.valdosta.piachnit.edu
bhall@pbs.org bl.btw@rlg.stanford.edu

alias class3 c-hind@vm1.spcs.umn.edu C06B@C53000.PITROBRAS.ANRJ.BRc
3038jim@umrvmb.bitnet C73221DC@WUVMD.WUSTL.Edu CA079@ALBNYVMS.BITNET cabli@ohsu.edu
CADKATTS%UIAMVS@cunyvm.cuny.edu capcon@sura.nit capcon3@sura.nit
Carol_Robirts@qmrilay.mail.cornill.edu cbrand@nwnit.nit cc011071@wvnvms.wvnit.edu
```

When I ran the second workshop, we had to close the participant list when it reached 15,000 people. Without aliases, handling that many addresses would have been impossible for both me and the mail program. Aliases are a real timesaver if you constantly send e-mail to one person or a group of people. Finding out how to create aliases in your own e-mail program is worth your while.

Finding People

Although Internet names may be easier to remember than the corresponding Internet number, you're not going to remember many names without constant use and concentration.

No single, definitive "white pages" service is available for the Internet. Besides, the network is so volatile and changing that guides and listings are outdated soon after they are made available. Several tools can be used to find Internet addresses. We'll look at three of the most simple to use: finger, whois, and netfind.

> **Navigator's Note:** Under WAIS (see Chapter 7, "The Database of Databases: WAIS"), we list several directory servers that you can access.

Finger

The finger program comes with many computer systems and can be very useful when you're trying to find Internet user addresses and other information.

The finger command, at minimum, can tell you who is using your own local system. Typing `finger` at the system prompt on a UNIX machine gives you information about the current users on the machine.

```
coyote% finger
Login       Name              TTY Idle    When    Where
gibbs       Gibbs             p0       Sat 23:16   delphi.com
oastorga    Olga Astorga      p2       Sat 20:22   siolib.ucsd.edu
harley      Harley Henn       r0       Sat 15:12   :ttyy03:S.0
harley      Harley Henn       r1       Sat 15:12   :ttyy03:S.1
harley      Harley Henn       r2 2:06  Sat 15:12   :ttyy03:S.2
harley      Harley Henn       r3 2:06  Sat 15:12   :ttyy03:S.3
harley      Harley Henn       r4 8:05  Sat 15:12   :ttyy03:S.4
stddef      Default Account   r5       Sat 22:59   :ttyy00:S.0
jalvarez    Joe Alvarez       y0       Sat 19:23
coyote%
```

Finger also can give you the login name of an individual on the local system, so that you can e-mail them a message. Additional information is available on many machines. Some people add their travel plans, agenda, advising hours, or other information in a file called the .plan file (the filename is .plan in their home directory), so when someone fingers them specifically, additional information is available. Let's finger the user `gibbs`:

```
coyote% finger gibbs
Login name: gibbs                    In real life: Gibbs
Directory: /user/users3/gibbs        Shell: /usr/local/bin/top.mnu
```

```
On since Jun  5 23:16:56 on ttyp0 from delphi.com
1 minute 34 seconds Idle Time
Mail last read Sat Jun  5 23:17:50 1993
No Plan.
coyote%
```

This gives us all sorts of marginally useful information such as when he logged in (Jun 5 23:16:56), how long he's been logged in (1 minute 34 seconds), and when he last read his mail. If a .plan file had existed, the text in it would have been displayed.

Some people use this to great effect or for the distribution of information. Someone who achieves both is Scott Yanoff (yanoff@csd4.csd.uwm.edu), author of the Yanoff List, a directory of Internet resources. His .plan file has control sequences in it so that anyone using a VT100 terminal emulation sees some fancy text animation and then the information on where to find the list and the following drawing:

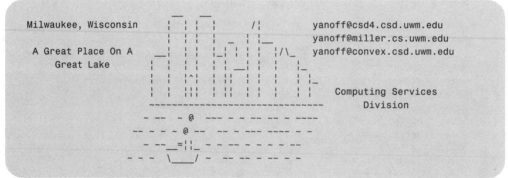

Some sites consider finger to be an invasion of privacy and a potential security risk, so they disable it. The systems manager can also change the finger command to work differently at different institutions. My institution has a directory assistance program that aids in finding the addresses of faculty, staff, and students, so the finger command has been disabled.

The general form of the finger command is

```
finger [username]@[address]
```

The [username] that you give finger need not be exact. For example, fingering a user named smith may give you several screens full of Smiths registered with that machine.

Finger is a handy way to find someone's Internet address if you know the remote site address and if the systems administrator allows finger.

> **Navigator's Note:** If you decide to be flashy and put tricky stuff in your .plan file, you must ensure that the group "world" is given "execute" privilege to this file. This is required even though, due to the way UNIX works, it's not a program file. Just because when you finger your own account, you can see the .plan file contents, don't assume that the world has "execute" privilege. You must have execute privilege on your own files, which is why you can see your own .plan file.

Whois

Whois is a utility that can identify names, titles, or addresses and return a directory entry, rather like a telephone white pages. The whois service is reputed to list over 70,000 Internet users—a pitifully small fraction of the Internet population but better than nothing. Whois is now maintained by AT&T through a service called the InterNIC (see Chapter 11, "Internet Directory Assistance: InterNIC").

Whois is simple and can be used by your computer (if you have a copy of it), by telnet (if you don't), or by e-mail.

On the whole, whois is usually not much use, but it's worth trying when all else fails. Whois is starting to be eclipsed by other, more advanced services that are far more efficient and comprehensive.

Netfind

Netfind is a white pages service that accesses several databases for you. You get to it by telneting to bruno.cs.colorado.edu. The following session was done from the Delphi Internet Special Interest Group (SIG) section. Although I used telnet, Delphi actually has a command that takes you straight to the netfind server at bruno.cs.colorado.edu. We'll first look at the help screens:

```
Internet SIG>Enter your selection: telnet bruno.cs.colorado.edu
"Telnet" is a way of connection from one host to another on the Internet. For
more details, type EXIT and then select About Internet Services.
Several Telnet sites are also accessible through the Auto-Connect menu. Other
options like Gopher, Archie, WWW, and WAIS are now available on the Utilities
menu.
Trying BRUNO.CS.COLORADO.EDU,telnet (128.138.243.151,23) ...
Escape (attention) character is "^\"
SunOS UNIX (bruno)
Login as 'netfind' to access netfind server
Login as 'da' to access CU Boulder directory assistance
login: netfind
=====================================================
Welcome to the University of Colorado Netfind server.
=====================================================
Alternate Netfind servers:
        archie.au (AARNet, Melbourne, Australia)
        bruno.cs.colorado.edu (University of Colorado, Boulder)
        dino.conicit.ve (Nat. Council for Techn. & Scien. Research, Venezuela)
        lincoln.technet.sg (Technet Unit, Singapore)
        malloco.ing.puc.cl (Catholic University of Chile, Santiago)
        monolith.cc.ic.ac.uk (Imperial College, London, England)
        mudhoney.micro.umn.edu (University of Minnesota, Minneapolis)
        netfind.oc.com (OpenConnect Systems, Dallas, Texas)
        nic.uakom.sk (Academy of Sciences, Banska Bystrica, Slovakia)
        redmont.cis.uab.edu (University of Alabama at Birmingham)
I think that your terminal can display 24 lines.  If this is wrong,
please enter the "Options" menu and set the correct number of lines.
Top level choices:
        1. Help
        2. Search
        3. Seed database lookup
        4. Options
        5. Quit (exit server)
--> 1
Help choices:
        1. Netfind search help
        2. Usage restrictions
        3. Frequently asked questions
        4. For more information
        5. Quit menu (back to top level)
--> 1
Given the name of a person on the Internet and a rough description of where
the person works, Netfind attempts to locate information about the person.
When prompted, enter a name followed by a set of keywords, such as
        schwartz boulder colorado university
The name can be a first, last, or login name, but only one name can be
specified.  The keys describe where the person works, by the name of the
institution and/or the city/state/country.  If you know the institution's
domain name (e.g., "cs.colorado.edu", where there are host names like
```

"brazil.cs.colorado.edu") you can specify it as keys without the dots
(e.g., "cs colorado edu"). The host parts of domain names ("brazil")
cannot be used as keywords. Keys are case insensitive and may be
specified in any order, although using a very common key (like
"university") first will cause internal buffers to overflow and some
domains to be missed.
Using more than one key implies the logical AND of the keys. Specifying
too many keys may cause searches to fail. If this happens, try specifying
fewer keys, e.g.,
        schwartz boulder
After you specify a search, Netfind looks in a "seed" database to find
domains matching the specified keywords. If there are more than one
matching domain, Netfind displays the list of matching domains, and asks
you to select up to three to search. If the keys you specified match
more than 100 domains, Netfind will list some of the matching
domains/organizations and ask you to form a more specific search. Note
that you can use any of the words in the organization strings (in
addition to the domain components) as keys in searches.
Searches proceed in two phases. In phase 1, Netfind performs a directed
search into each selected domain, to try to uncover mail forwarding
information, and "finger" the person being sought at hosts determined
during this phase (see the algorithm description in the list of
Frequently Asked Questions for more details). Phase 2 involves finger
searches into other hosts, primarily those listed in the seed database.
While you can interrupt Netfind at any time (with ^C), you should let it
complete a pass through phase 2 if no mail forwarding information was
found in phase 1, so that it can try to trace back through most
recent/last login information for the person being sought.
After each search phase (or when interrupted by ^C), Netfind summarizes
the search results. The summary includes problems searching remote
domains, information about the most promising e-mail address for the
person being sought (if available), and information about when and where
the person most recently/is currently logged in (if available). Note
that this summary only reflects information that was uncovered during
the search. Particularly if you interrupt Netfind before it completes
the finger trace (as described above), the summary information may be
suboptimal. Also, if more than one person is located by a search, the
summary does not include information about e-mail targets and most
recent/current logins (since only the user can decide which person was
the correct one.)
When Netfind runs, it displays a trace of the parallel search progress,
along with the results of the searches. Since output can scroll by
quickly, you might want to run it in a window system, or pipe the output
through tee(1):
        telnet <this server name> ¦& tee log
You can also disable trace output from the "Options" menu.
NOTE: This software is provided "as is", without express or implied
warranty, and with no support nor obligation to assist in its use,
correction, modification or enhancement. We assume no liability with
respect to the correctness of information provided, infringement of

```
copyrights, trade secrets, or any patents, and are not responsible for
consequential damages. Proper use of this software is entirely the
responsibility of the user. This software may not be sold or used for
profit.
Help choices:
        1. Netfind search help
        2. Usage restrictions
        3. Frequently asked questions
        4. For more information
        5. Quit menu (back to top level)
--> 5
Top level choices:
        1. Help
        2. Search
        3. Seed database lookup
        4. Options
        5. Quit (exit server)
-->
```

Get the idea now? Basically, you enter a name and whatever part of the address you know, and off you go. If you're lucky, something turns up. Often nothing does. This shouldn't really surprise you when you consider the size of the Internet. Finding anyone without some hard information is like saying "I want to find George Smith in North America." There are many Smiths, many George Smiths, and a significant number of both in North America. Moreover, you don't have a single telephone book to consult—you have thousands of them. Finding anyone on the Internet with very little information about them is very hard, even for Master Navigators.

> **Navigator's Note:** Addressing Joke. A lady dies and goes to heaven. She's met at the Pearly Gates by St. Peter. "Oh, St. Peter," she says, "can you find my husband, who's already here?" "What's his name?" asks St. Peter. "Jones," she replies.
>
> "Well," St. Peter says, "as you might guess, we've got an awful lot of people called Jones up here. Can you be more specific?" "Hummm," says the lady, "his first name was Fred."
>
> "Madam, do you have any idea how many Fred Joneses we have? You'll have to be more specific."
>
> She thinks for a moment. "Well, all I can think of," she says, "is that he said if I ever slept with another man, he'd turn in his grave."
>
> "Aha!" says St. Peter, "you're looking for Whirling Fred Jones!"

Let's see if we can find the correct address for Rick Gates, who runs the Internet Hunt (see Appendix F, "Testing Your Navigation Skills," for more information on the Hunt).

All I know about Rick's likely address is that he's at the University of California at Santa Barbara, which is abbreviated ucsb, so we'll try searching for gates ucsb:

```
Top level choices:555555
        1. Help
        2. Search
        3. Seed database lookup
        4. Options
        5. Quit (exit server)
--> 2
Enter person and keys (blank to exit) --> gates ucsb
Please select at most 3 of the following domains to search:
        0. ucsb.edu (university of california, santa barbara)
        1. bap.ucsb.edu (university of california, santa barbara)
        2. ccmrc.ucsb.edu (university of california, santa barbara)
        3. crseo.ucsb.edu (university of california, santa barbara)
        4. crustal.ucsb.edu (university of california, santa barbara)
        5. csl.ucsb.edu (university of california, santa barbara)
        6. deepspace.ucsb.edu (university of california, santa barbara)
        7. ece.ucsb.edu (electrical and computer engineering department, university
of california, santa barbara)
        8. econ.ucsb.edu (economics department, university of california, santa
barbara)
        9. eos.ucsb.edu (university of california, santa barbara)
        10. esrg.ucsb.edu (university of california, santa barbara)
        11. geog.ucsb.edu (geography department, university of california, santa
barbara)
        12. geol.ucsb.edu (geology department, university of california, santa
barbara)
        13. gse.ucsb.edu (ucsb graduate school of education, university of
california at santa barbara)
        14. itp.ucsb.edu (institute for theoretical physics, university of
california, santa barbara)
        15. lscf.ucsb.edu (university of california, santa barbara)
        16. math.ucsb.edu (mathematics department, university of california, santa
barbara)
        17. mcl.ucsb.edu (university of california, santa barbara)
        18. metiu.ucsb.edu (university of california, santa barbara)
        19. ncgia.ucsb.edu (ncgia, university of california, santa barbara)
        20. orda.ucsb.edu (university of california, santa barbara)
        21. physics.ucsb.edu (physics department, university of california, santa
barbara)
        22. pstat.ucsb.edu (university of california, santa barbara)
        23. psych.ucsb.edu (psychology department, university of california, santa
barbara)
```

```
     24. s2k.ucsb.edu (university of california, santa barbara)
     25. sscf.ucsb.edu (university of california, santa barbara)
     26. ucsdic.ucsb.edu (university of california, santa barbara)
Enter selection (e.g., 2 0 1) -->
```

So, which do you select? Well, the broadest domain, the domain that contains greatest number of users, is always the first. Selecting the first option often takes much longer, but if you don't have enough information, it's usually your best bet. So that's what we'll choose. The domain is searched for nameservers—computers that manage machine addresses. From there, all the computers in the domain are identified by the netfind server and searched one by one:

```
Enter selection (e.g., 2 0 1) --> 0
( 1) check_name: checking domain ucsb.edu.  Level = 0
( 1) get_domain_addr: Got nameserver hub.ucsb.edu
( 1) get_domain_addr: Got nameserver bap.ucsb.edu
( 1) check_name: checking nameserver hub.ucsb.edu.  Level = 2
( 2) check_name: checking nameserver bap.ucsb.edu.  Level = 2
- - - - - -
Search of domains completed.  Proceeding to search of hosts.
- - - - - -
( 2) check_name: checking host ucsbuxa.ucsb.edu.  Level = 0
( 3) check_name: checking host esrg.ucsb.edu.  Level = 0
( 4) check_name: checking host strawberry.ucsb.edu.  Level = 0
( 5) check_name: checking host pineapple.ucsb.edu.  Level = 0
( 1) check_name: checking host apricot.ucsb.edu.  Level = 0
( 3) check_name: checking host puffin.ucsb.edu.  Level = 0
( 1) check_name: checking host vladimir.ucsb.edu.  Level = 0
```

After the hosts (a term often used for computers on the Internet) are searched, the likely candidates are displayed:

```
SYSTEM: ucsbuxa.ucsb.edu
      Login name: lb05gate              In real life: Rick Gates
      Directory: /b/lb05/gate           Shell: /bin/csh
      Last login Sun Jun  6 18:07 on tty16
      No unread mail
      Plan:
      - - - - - - - - - - - - - - - - - - - - - - - - - - - - - - - - - - - - -
      Rick Gates                                   (805) 893-7225
      Dir. of Library Automation
      Univ. of California                   lb05gate@ucsbuxa.ucsb.edu
      Santa Barbara, CA  93106
```

```
        Interests: Net surfing, hiking, cooking, building furniture, playing
        guitar and playing basketball, the ONE true sport!
        ------------------------------------------------------------------

        Login name: lb13goph               In real life: Rick Gates
        Directory: /b/lb13/goph            Shell: /bin/csh
        Last login Thu Jun  3 08:23 on ttyp1 from unix1.sncc.lsu.e
        Unread mail since Fri Jun  4 11:48:58 1993
        No Plan.

        Login name: lb13psg                In real life: Rick Gates
        Directory: /b/lb13/psg             Shell: /bin/csh
        Last login Tue May 11 11:54 on ttyp5 from ucsbuxa
        No unread mail
        No Plan.
( 4) connect timed out
( 5) read timed out
( 3) Attempting finger to current indication of most recent "Last login" machine
ucsbuxa.ucsb.edu

SUMMARY:
- Among the machines searched, the machine from which user
  "gates" logged in most recently was ucsbuxa.ucsb.edu,
  on Tue May 11 11:54.
- The most promising e-mail address for "gates"
  based on the above search is
  lb05gate@ucsbuxa.ucsb.edu.
Continue the search ([n]/y) ? --> n
Enter person and keys (blank to exit) -->
```

Netfind checks the information on the user's last login and the last computer from which mail was read to determine the best address to send mail to. Rick has three accounts, of which lb05gate@ucsbuxa.ucsb.edu looks to be the best bet for getting mail through to him.

Netfind is one of the better and easier white pages servers to use. However, you'll find that it often strikes out if the user's system is new to the Internet, is currently off line, doesn't allow external access through the finger command, or doesn't recognize the name by which you know the user. Even with those limitations, it's better than nothing, and it gets an answer often enough to make it worth the effort.

Online Courses

In the introduction, we mentioned the online course taught by Rich Smith. In the summer of 1992, this course was offered over the Internet, with 50 or 60 participants expected. In a matter of days, 864 people had signed up and others were being turned away. Thus was "Navigating the Internet: An Interactive Workshop" born. Due to the demand, the course was offered again in October, and over 15,000 participants from 50 countries registered.

The potential for distance education over the Internet is enormous, using international experts in collaboration in specific fields or interdisciplinary courses. Librarians are making use of their campus-wide information networks for training faculty and students on use of the Internet and the library. On some campuses, faculty already accept student work assignments by e-mail and hold discussions with distant classes. This is effectively a paperless course where syllabuses, class assignments, and final reports are exchanged over the network.

The increased use of sound and video transmissions, particularly with interactive teaching, will make distance education even more acceptable. For busy professionals or people in remote locations, distance teaching makes continuing education easier. Combining the Internet with digital multimedia and easy accessibility makes a revolution in primary, secondary, and adult education virtually inevitable.

Using E-Mail

Many e-mail systems are available for almost all computer platforms. The following is a short glimpse of a basic UNIX e-mail program that outlines several of the basic e-mail functions.

Sending E-Mail

After logging onto UNIX, the command line furnishes the user with a prompt. On the system I use in the following example, it is `icarus.lis[1]%`. Throughout this book you'll see all sorts of prompts because I have used different systems.

You start the e-mail program by typing the `mail` command and entering the recipient's Internet address. The general form is

```
mail [username]@[machinename]
```

The e-mail program then asks for a subject:

```
icarus.lis[1] % mail rs@ucs.usl.edu
Subject:
```

Navigator's Note: The length of the subject of an e-mail message is best limited to short descriptive text relevant to the message. "Hi!" as a subject is pretty common, but if the recipient gets a lot of mail and isn't looking for a message from you, your message may get handled late or not at all. The volume of mail is a big problem for many people, so they use e-mail because it is so easy to send; if they had to use conventional mail, they wouldn't bother. As you get more involved with e-mail, you'll find that you get lots of replies to messages that simply say "Thanks" or "Okay"—hardly helpful at all.

You can also start mail and specify the subject. This is done with the command format:

```
mail "[subject]" [username]@[machinename]
```

Notice that if the subject is more than a single word, the text must be between double or single quotes.

Next, type in the text of the message, using whatever editor the system works with. Sometimes this editor is built into the e-mail system and may use its own eccentric commands (such as Ctrl+X to send; who thought of that?!). Some editors work like a typewriter: you must press Enter at the end of each line, and you can't go up a line to make changes. You can only go backwards on the current line to correct errors. Even that is tricky and depends on which computer you're using. The Backspace key may work to back up and erase errors in some cases, and Ctrl+H may work in others. You'll have to practice with your editor to become proficient in creating long messages.

Navigator's Note: It's often easier to use some other editor to create the mail message in a file and then import the file into the message. You'll have to check out the documentation for your e-mail system to see if the built-in editor is any good and, if not, how to import text from a file.

If you botch the e-mail message to the point of embarrassment (as is very easy with the more primitive editors), Ctrl+C normally cancels the e-mail message. Ctrl+D sends the message. In some cases, you are prompted with cc, which means you could put in another Internet address to send a carbon copy to.

You can send an e-mail message in other ways. In UNIX, you can send a file by starting mail with a different command format:

```
mail -s "[subject]" [username]@[machinename] <[filename]
```

This takes the contents of the file, [filename], and sends it to the mail program as if you were typing it. This is a technique called *piping* and will be discussed in your system manual.

You can send a file by entering ~r on a blank line followed by the filename. This means "I want to send a file and here comes its name."

```
~r test
"test" 160/6661
```

E-mail programs enable you to compose and send a message or file in many other ways. You'll have to read the documentation of your e-mail program to discover all its features.

Receiving E-Mail

When you log onto a UNIX machine, you often get a message telling you that you have mail waiting. This is usually in the form "you have mail" or "you have new mail"

```
You have mail.
/h1/rjs4808/rjsres
a91% mail
Mail version SMI 4.0 Tue May 11 09:06:35 CDT 1993  Type ? for help.
"/usr/spool/mail/rjs4808": 15 messages 15 unread
>U  1 70673.2233@compuserve.com Fri May 14 08:32   40/1611  (id: DPB610) WINNET
 U  2 rjs4808@ucs.usl.edu Wed May 26 08:11    54/2374  Media Services -- Learnin
 U  3 76004.3310@compuserve.com Wed May 26 17:05  271/18045 C7 part 3B
 U  4 76004.3310@compuserve.com Wed Jun  2 11:29   35/1546  chapter 7
 U  5 70673.2233@compuserve.com Wed Jun  2 22:00   45/1344  Re:  Yanoff's PLAN
file
 U  6 halder@cs.umb.edu  Thu Jun  3 17:11   39/1934  Re:  Help for Book
 U  7 76004.3310@compuserve.com Thu Jun  3 18:25   67/1956  Book observations
 U  8 72410.2162@compuserve.com Fri Jun  4 08:35  101/4579  Book observations
```

```
U  9 76004.3310@compuserve.com Sat Jun  5 01:52   27/1076  Stuff
U 10 ddickerson@igc.apc.org Sun Jun  6 13:43   47/1573  permission request
U 11 ddickerson@igc.apc.org Sun Jun  6 13:48  405/11540 IGC Brochure
U 12 AGUEVARA@macc.wisc.edu Sun Jun 13 13:11   19/853   Help with Internet
U 13 kuchin@darmstadt.gmd.de Wed Jun 16 00:38   78/3383  Request
U 14 kuchin@darmstadt.gmd.de Wed Jun 16 01:47   78/3379  Request
&
```

To read your mail, start the mail program by typing the command mail at the
system prompt. In this example, the UNIX prompt changes from bss> to the mail
& (ampersand) prompt. The mail program lists the sender, the date the message
was sent, the number of lines and characters in the message (as in 64/1662), and
the subject of the mail messages. You can now read, reply, save, edit, or delete
mail messages. The greater-than sign (>) points to the current mail item, and the
U at the beginning of each e-mail message means that the message is unread.

Help

To help you remember the mail commands, a short description of each is available online. Entering ? or the word help at the mail & prompt displays the help
text:

```
d [message list]                  delete messages
e [message list]                  edit messages
f [message list]                  show from lines of messages
h                                 print out active message headers
m [user list]                     mail to specific users
n                                 goto and type next message
p [message list]                  print messages
pre [message list]                make messages go back to system mailbox
q                                 quit, saving unresolved messages in mbox
r [message list]                  reply to sender (only) of messages
R [message list]                  reply to sender and all recipients of messages
s [message list] file             append messages to file
t [message list]                  type messages (same as print)
top [message list]                show top lines of messages
u [message list]                  undelete messages
v [message list]                  edit messages with display editor
w [message list] file             append messages to file, without from line
x                                 quit, do not change system mailbox
z [-]                             display next [previous] page of headers
!                                 shell escape

A [message list] consists of integers, ranges of same, or user names separated
by spaces.  If omitted, Mail uses the current message.
&
```

Common E-Mail Commands

Following is a selection of commands that most e-mail programs support. You'll need to refer to the manuals for your system to find out what commands are available for your e-mail program.

Headers

To see the partial headers of the messages again, enter h at the mail prompt. These are not the full headers we discussed earlier—just the originator's name and address, the time the message was sent, and the subject.

```
   25 ellen              Wed Jun  2 09:39   95/3659  here's your chance!
   26 GBLOOMQ@acadvm1.uottawa.ca Wed Jun  2 13:44   36/1804  Re: Navigating again
   27 MUKASA@grove.iup.edu Wed Jun  2 14:10   29/1065  Internet
   28 WYLLYS@utxvm.cc.utexas.edu Wed Jun  2 14:29   35/1469  Navigating, yes!
   29 kewing@TIGGER.STCLOUD.MSUS.EDU Wed Jun  2 14:40   41/2000  navigate workshop
   30 tuma@nevada.edu     Wed Jun  2 14:56   57/2442  Re: Navigating again
   31 LIBTAT@orion.depaul.edu Wed Jun  2 15:14   38/1630  Internet course by mail
   32 WYLLYS@utxvm.cc.utexas.edu Wed Jun  2 15:14   32/809   Re: Navigating, yes!
   33 FERMO@AESOP.RUTGERS.EDU Wed Jun  2 15:31   49/1644  Comments
   34 FALKENHM@ZENO.MSCD.EDU Wed Jun  2 15:43   25/872    Re: Navigating
   35 LAMBDEAN%ITHACA.BITNET@CORNELLC.cit.cornell.edu Wed Jun  2 15:53   31/1100
navigation
   36 EGS2G1B@MVS.OAC.UCLA.EDU Wed Jun  2 15:59   38/1584  RE: Internet Workshop
   37 gepst1              Wed Jun  2 16:03   33/931   Navigating Again
   38 judkins@library.swmed.edu Wed Jun  2 16:13   18/723   Navigating course
   39 mmcguire@ccs.carleton.ca Wed Jun  2 16:30   34/1143  navigating the internet
   40 SMS@mlnc486.mlnc.com Wed Jun  2 16:31   33/1225  navigating
&
```

Read

To read a message, type t or p and the number of the message you want to read. If you just press Enter, the current message is displayed (remember, the current message is signified by a greater-than sign on the far right). You can also type the number of the message by itself.

Reply

You can reply to any e-mail message in two ways from the mail program: R replies to the sender and all others who have received the message, whereas r replies to the sender only.

> **Navigator's Warning:** Standard UNIX programs have a lot of strange key usage (strange, at least, to X-windows, Microsoft Windows, and Mac users). Many commands, as we've just discussed, are case sensitive, and using the wrong case can give you the wrong results and make you grind your teeth. Worse still, the results might be different from, or even the opposite of, what you want, depending on the version of UNIX you're using. Read your help screens and manuals carefully.

Save

You can save messages by typing s, followed by the number or numbers of the messages you want to save, followed by a filename to save them to. Typing s 1-3 oldmail.txt saves messages 1, 2, and 3 to the designated file. s 1 2 3 does the same thing if you've already specified a filename during the current session with the e-mail system. When the file already exists, the messages are appended to it.

```
& s 1-3 oldmail.txt
"oldmail.txt" [New file] 365/22033
& s 7 8 9 oldmail.txt
"oldmail.txt" [Appended] 195/7614
&
```

Delete and Undelete

Deleting a message marks it for erasure when you quit the e-mail session. Use the delete command, d, followed by the number or numbers of the messages you want to delete. If you delete a file by mistake, you can use the undelete command, u, to get the messages back. However, once you quit the mail program, all messages marked for deletion are gone forever.

Quit

Typing the letter q leaves the mail program. Unread messages are saved, and you can read them when you run the mail program again. Read messages are saved in a file called mbox, and deleted files are erased and lost for good. The other way to leave this mail program is to type the letter x, which quits the mail program but leaves everything as if you never ran it. All deleted files are recovered, and read files are not transferred to the mbox file. The only exception is that any files you saved mail messages into will still exist.

What If I Want to Send a File That Isn't Just Plain Text?

(Boy, you ask long questions.) So far, we've assumed that all the files you want to send are regular ASCII text files. Binary files, such as graphics, audio, and many word processing files (for instance, Microsoft Word or WordPerfect if they're not saved as text or postscript) must be prepared for sending by e-mail by encoding them as we discussed previously. Encoding programs take binary files and format them to plain ASCII text.

The receiver of the e-mail must then decode them so that they make sense. UNIX has uuencode and uudecode to do this job. Uuencode is available for several operating systems. Several other encoding software programs are available free over the Internet; use Archie to locate them.

E-Mail and the Internet

E-mail is an incredible tool. It can keep you in touch with friends and business colleagues no matter where they are physically. It can be used to send and receive files as well as interact with other services (as we'll discuss in the section on ftpmail in Chapter 4, "A Moving Experience: FTP for Me") and to access Archie (as we'll cover in Chapter 6, "Finding Files: Archie"). Equally important, e-mail can connect with discussion groups (as we'll see in Chapters 13, "Views and News: USENET," and 14, "Getting on the List: LISTSERV").

Just to show that we've gotten you interested in using electronic mail, drop us a line and tell us what e-mail systems you use, what you like and hate about e-mail, and what interesting things have happened to you through e-mail. Our addresses are

Rich Smith	vjs@lis.pitt.edu
Mark Gibbs	mgibbs@coyote.rain.org

A MOVING EXPERIENCE: FTP FOR ME

As you sail around the Internet, you'll find plenty of files that might be useful to you. They may be text files, programs, or databases found through Archie or by word of mouth. What they all have in common is that they're not where you want them to be—that is, on your own computer.

This book describes tools that an Internet navigator can use—Gopher, WAIS, WWW, Veronica, and InterNIC, all of which were developed to make the unwieldy resources of the Internet easier to use.

Although these tools make finding information a little easier, we haven't yet achieved seamless access to the Internet—where getting hold of what you want is simple and intuitive. Today, you'll find that you must usually access files the old-fashioned way—you must go out and get them.

File Transfer Protocol (FTP)

The tool for transferring files between computers on the Internet is called File Transfer Protocol, or FTP.

We can thank the Internet's predecessor, ARPANET, for the creation of File Transfer Protocol. FTP was part of the development of the TCP/IP protocol suite now in use on the Internet. Using a standard protocol for file transfer, FTP works regardless of the type of computer you may be using or the type of machine at the other end.

A remarkable thing about the Internet is the speed at which files can be sent and received. The Internet transfers files at a rate of millions of bytes per second, and with the coming of the National Research and Education Network (NREN), that will soon be upgraded to gigabytes (thousands of millions of bytes) per second.

At the present speed, it would take only a few seconds to send this book from one location to another. Compare that with using a regular modem setup at a speed of 9600 baud, where the same transfer would take minutes (and those unfortunates restricted to 1200 baud might as well go and enjoy the first half of a football game).

FTP can do more than just retrieve files. You can use it to transfer files to remote machines from your computer. To make it a practical tool, FTP includes commands for listing directories, listing files in directories, changing directories, and getting information about what you're doing, and setting parameters for how the operations will be done.

Here's an example of how FTP can be used. From time to time in my dissertation work, I need to show my adviser my progress. I'm located in Lafayette, Louisiana, and I use FTP to transfer chapters of my dissertation to my other computer account at the University of Pittsburgh. From there I can print out the chapters on the third floor of the School of Library and Information Science, where my adviser reads them and makes corrections and comments.

What Can You FTP?

What kinds of things can you find in all these available files? Well, there's data of every kind: statistics from the U.S. census, results from countless scientific experiments, and text ranging from electronic journals and magazines (some of them very interesting, and some pretty wild) to the full text of *Alice in Wonderland*, the *Book of Mormon*, and the *Bible*.

You can get image files from NASA that contain the latest pictures from the various probes. Image files from other sources offer you still photos from Star Trek, cartoons, and even soft porn.

Finally, you can find software for DOS, Windows, Macintosh, and UNIX, as well as updates for Apple, Novell, and the products of many other major vendors.

Some of this software is free, some comes with source code, and some you can buy if you decide you like it.

Freeware

As its name implies, freeware is free. Some freeware even comes with source code! The authors don't charge for the software because they are altruistic, generous, or don't see much value in their software.

For some groups, altruism is a major motivator. A notable source of freeware is the Free Software Foundation, which is working on a complete UNIX-like operating system that it intends to release to the public domain.

Freeware enters the public domain from many sources. Its presence there suggests that the copyright has been surrendered. However, unless authors explicitly state that this has been done, they still hold the copyright to the software. This means that although they are letting you use it, they still actually own it. It's all very complicated legally, and it really matters only if you plan to distribute one of these freeware products for profit or use any part of its source code (if supplied) in your commercial product.

If you use freeware, it's nice to drop the author a note of thanks. Don't bug them about faults, errors, and omissions you find unless they requested such feedback.

Shareware

Shareware has become a significant force in the software business. Shareware is software that the authors want you to pass around to other users. The idea is that if you like it, you send them whatever registration fee they ask for. In return, you are officially licensed to use the product and usually receive a manual and/or bonus software.

Some shareware is called *brain-damaged* or *crippled*, meaning that it doesn't do everything a registered version can do or can only perform functions to a limited extent. The best shareware is usually not inhibited in any way, and if the shareware author is a member of the American Shareware Association (ASA), they are bound not to inhibit the application's functionality.

Some shareware isn't exactly crippled, but after a period of time set by the vendor, it must be reinstalled. This usually wipes out configuration data and other aspects of an established, used installation. If you've started to like the product, it's a pretty good incentive to register.

Another trick to encourage registration is known as *nagware*. Unless you have a registered copy, a screen pops up whenever you start the program (and sometimes during operation) to remind you that your copy isn't registered.

Many of the shareware products currently circulating have made some of their authors quite wealthy. The McAffee antivirus products and Datastorm's ProComm communications software are two of the best known.

The great thing about shareware is that because the vendors don't have huge marketing overhead or any of the other paraphernalia of regular commercial products, their prices are considerably lower.

The shareware concept only works, however, if people try out the software, decide they like it, and actually register it. If vendors don't make any money, they often stop developing their products. This has caused the end of some really good software with much better value than many commercial packages.

Running FTP

To start FTP under UNIX (and most operating systems), you just type `ftp` and off you go. So, under my system (the prompt is `coyote%`):

```
coyote% ftp
ftp>
```

Once running, FTP produces its own prompt, usually `ftp>`. You can also start FTP by giving the name of the Internet computer from which you want to get files:

```
coyote% ftp ucsbuxa.ucsb.edu
```

In general terms, the FTP command is

```
ftp <hostname> <port>
```

The `<port>` part of the command is necessary only if a specific value is required. If you leave it out, a default value is used. After you are connected to a remote computer through FTP, you are asked for a user name and password.

Anonymous FTP

FTP is most commonly used to retrieve files from computers that allow public access. These *anonymous FTP sites* together contain millions of files that add up to terabytes of information.

With anonymous FTP access, you do not need an account or password to access the remote computer. The remote machine accepts anonymous as your name and Internet address or guest as the password. After that, you can access files on the remote machine. Usually, your access is restricted to the public (or pub) directory.

FTP Commands

Different versions of the FTP program are available for different computer operating systems. Some have commands different from the common implementations on UNIX systems. Most Netfarers seldom, if ever, need to use more than a few FTP commands, so the differences between versions are usually minimal. The commands for the UNIX version of FTP that I use can be listed by typing help at the ftp> prompt.

```
ftp> help
```

Commands may be abbreviated. Commands are

```
!          cr          macdef    proxy       send
$          delete      mdelete   sendport    status
account    debug       mdir      put         struct
append     dir         mget      pwd         sunique
ascii      disconnect  mkdir     quit        tenex
bell       form        mls       quote       trace
binary     get         mode      recv        type
bye        glob        mput      remotehelp  user
case       hash        nmap      rename      verbose
cd         help        ntrans    reset       ?
cdup       lcd         open      rmdir
close      ls          prompt    runique
ftp>
```

You can get a brief explanation of each command by typing help and the command itself at the ftp> prompt. Note that the prompt changes to ftp?>.

```
ftp?> help binary
```

Here is more information on frequently used FTP commands:

ascii: Set FTP to ASCII mode. This is usually the default and is used for text files. If you use it for binary files such as programs or some databases, they'll be corrupted.

binary: Set FTP to binary mode. Used for transferring binary files, which might be graphics files, executable programs, or audio files.

bye: Quits the FTP program.

cd <remote_directory>: Changes the directory of the remote machine to the directory specified.

close: Ends your FTP session with the remote computer and returns you to the ftp> prompt. Note that at this point you aren't connected to any remote machine until you use the open command.

dir or ls -l: Prints a listing of the files in the current remote working directory.

get: Retrieves a remote file and stores it on your computer.

mget: Transfers multiple files from a remote machine to your local machine. Files can be listed separated by spaces. Supports wildcard symbols * and ?.

mput: Transfers multiple files from a local machine to a remote machine. Files should be separated by a space. Supports wildcard symbols * and ?.

open: Used to establish a connection to a remote machine.

prompt: When you use mget or mput, and prompt is set to on, you'll be asked for a confirmation for each file handled. This can get pretty tedious if you're transferring a lot of files. Issue the command prompt off, and you'll be able to drink your coffee and read the paper in peace. Use prompt on to get back to the confirmation mode.

put: Stores a local file on the remote machine.

pwd: Prints the name of the current working directory on the remote machine.

File Types

A common file type available on the Internet is the ASCII text file. These files contain plain text, usually (but not always) without control characters (characters with values below 32), except for carriage return and/or line feed characters, which are used often.

Navigator's Note: Computers handle numbers only, so alphabetic characters in the ASCII character set are encoded as numbers ranging from 0 (called *null*) to 255. The characters with values less than 32 are all control characters, many of which go back to the teletype era. The only common control characters are 10, called carriage return (which is the same as the Enter key), and 13, which is called line feed. Many text file formats end each line with a carriage return followed by a line feed, but standard UNIX files use only line feeds.

This range of values can be stored in a single byte of eight bits. A problem is that much of the current Internet can't handle eight-bit data, so it needs to be converted to another form that takes up only seven of the bits. This is the function of the uuencode software we discussed in Chapter 3, "Where's the Post? Electronic Mail."

ASCII files can be easily moved from machine to machine and read without further manipulation. The convention for text file naming (but don't count on it) is to use the extensions .txt or .doc to signify that it is a text file. Because the default mode of transfer in FTP is ASCII text, you don't need to tell FTP the file type.

Binary Files

Binary, the other FTP transfer mode, is used for files that contain data, including nonalphanumeric characters. The use of these files is machine or program dependent. For example, a file created by a word processing program, such as WordPerfect, and saved as a WordPerfect document, contains information on format, fonts, and other features that only WordPerfect can interpret.

Navigator's Note: You can use binary mode to transfer text files, but it's less efficient than text mode. In binary mode, file data becomes over 12 percent bigger while being transferred. This won't matter on a small file (100,000 bytes, say) because that would take about 10 seconds in text mode and just over 11 seconds in binary mode. However, if you transfer a 100,000,000-byte file, you increase your transfer time from about 16 minutes to over 18 minutes.

Many different file types must be transferred in binary mode. Executable files usually have an extension of .com or .exe. Graphics files can have any one of a multitude of extensions, depending on the program for which they are designed. Some examples are .pic, .gif, .wpg, .wmf, .tif, .art, and .pcx.

Compressed Files

Many files that you can retrieve through FTP aren't in a form that you can directly use. They need special handling in order to be manipulated.

Compressed files have been reduced in size by one of several techniques, making them unusable until they are uncompressed. The name usually indicates what kind of compression has been used; .zip, .arc, .zoo, and binhex are just a few of the many programs that compress files. Many compression formats are in the public domain or are shareware. The programs that handle these files are available at numerous sites.

Your receiving machine must be able to uncompress these files in order for you to make use of them. In some instances, you are given the option of file type—you see several files with the same name but different extensions (such as filename.ps, filename.ps.Z, filename.txt, and filename.txt.Z).

In the preceding case, the .ps stands for PostScript and the .txt stands for text; you have the option of retrieving either (or both) of them. The files may be intended to be identical, but the PostScript file often produces better output and may contain related graphics or formatted tables not in the text-only file. You must have a PostScript printer in order to make a hard copy of a PostScript file.

The .ps and .txt files should be transferred in ASCII mode, while the .ps.Z and the .txt.Z files (both compressed) must be transferred in binary mode. Compressed files must be uncompressed before you can use their contents.

On most machines running anonymous FTP, the READ.ME file (or a file with a similar name) gives the location and type of files that are available. It also tells you where and how to obtain the programs that uncompress the compressed files. Some machines offer only compressed files, but will uncompress them for you if you retrieve them by omitting the .Z in the filename.

Finally, you may have used a utility called TAR, which stands for Tape ARchiver. This utility combines files and directories into a single file and is helpful when many files need to be moved or when you need to get a large number of related files. TAR files are often compressed as well, so that the file to be transferred is as small as possible. TAR files must be transferred in binary mode, uncompressed, and then "un-tar'ed" by processing the file with the TAR utility in uncompress mode.

FTP by Electronic Mail

Two months separated the two workshops I gave over the Internet. During this time I noticed several important differences between the users attracted by the two sessions.

One notable difference was the increase in those using commercial access to the Internet. By the second session, the number of users with accounts through MCI, CompuServe, and other commercial gateways increased significantly.

These gateways do not have the direct Internet connections you find, for example, at a university. This population will continue to grow as more commercial services become available, which in turn will make access easier and cheaper. University graduates and individuals who had Internet access through an employer and who make the Internet a part of their daily routines want to continue having a link to the world via the Internet.

Unfortunately, not all of these gateways give full access to the Internet. On some service providers, such as CompuServe, users can only send and receive e-mail; services such as FTP and telnet aren't available.

A partial remedy to this problem is called FTPmail, which enables you to e-mail FTP commands to an FTPmail server. The server handles the FTP operations and e-mails the results back to you. FTPmail enables people who have only e-mail to take advantage of anonymous FTP sites.

Digital Equipment Corporation (DEC) maintains a machine on the Internet that accepts e-mail with FTPmail commands in the body of the message. It contacts the target FTP server, pretending to be you, and gets and places files for you. The time required to do this ranges from a few minutes to many hours. Try to use this service during nonpeak hours.

The Internet name for the DEC FTPmail server is `ftpmail@decwrl.dec.com`. To receive the help manual on how to use this service, send the word `help` in the body of an e-mail message, without a subject heading, to the server:

```
bss>mail ftpmail@decwrl.dec.com
Subject:
help
.
bss>
```

You might receive this reply to the preceding message:

```
  — Help —
>>> $Id: help-text,v 1.6 1993/02/16 14:55:03 vixie Exp $
>>>
>>> commands are:

     reply <MAILADDR>          set reply addr, since headers are usually wrong
     connect [HOST [USER [PASS [ACCT]]]]
                     defaults to gatekeeper.dec.com, anonymous
```

```
ascii              files grabbed are printable ascii
binary             files grabbed are compressed or tar or both
chdir PLACE        "get" and "ls" commands are relative to PLACE
                   (only one CHDIR per ftpmail session,
                   and it executes before any LS/DIR/GETs)
compress           compress binaries using Lempel-Ziv encoding
compact            compress binaries using Huffman encoding
uuencode           binary files will be mailed in uuencode format
btoa               binary files will be mailed in btoa format
chunksize SIZE     split files into SIZE-byte chunks (def: 64000)
ls (or dir) PLACE      short (long) directory listing
index THING        search for THING in ftp server's index
get FILE           get a file and have it mailed to you
                   (max 10 GET's per ftpmail session)
quit               terminate script, ignore rest of mail message
                   (use if you have a .signature or
                   are a VMSMAIL user)
```

Notice that the `connect` command giving the name of the Internet computer that is your source or destination for files should be the first command used in the e-mail message. Also, only one `chdir` (change directory) command can be used in the e-mail message—therefore, you need to know the path (directory and subdirectory) of any file you want to retrieve.

FTPmail is not as versatile as a direct connection and requires patience and accuracy to get the information. In fact, don't be surprised if it takes several tries to master FTPmail. You will learn from your mistakes, and after the initial breakthrough, you will find that FTPmail is a valuable tool for navigating the Internet.

FTP for Me

In summary, FTP is the program to use for transferring files from one machine to another. Although you can use FTP to transfer your files from machines where you have personal accounts—that is, with the use of a login name and a password—FTP is more commonly used with public access machines on the Internet (what is called anonymous FTP). This makes thousands of files available to anyone who wants them.

Everything from computer programs to texts of *Alice in Wonderland*, a Request for Comments on a new computer standard, programs to help you in your calculus studies, or games of chess can be retrieved using FTP. If your appetite for digging into all of these resources has been sufficiently whetted, it's time to Navigate!

FTP Examples

Merit is a regional Internet access and network service provider for Michigan. Merit's Network Information Center host computer is located in Michigan and is accessible via anonymous FTP. Merit provides many services to its region, one of which is maintaining a machine that enables Internet users to obtain information about the Internet, NSFNET, and MichNet.

Your objectives are to extract some documents from this machine and to become familiar with exploring a remote machine. To make an FTP connection, at the system prompt bss (remember, yours might be different) type ftp and the remote machine name. MERIT's machine name is nic.merit.edu.

Try the following example for yourself. You will, of course, use your own address when you are asked for a password.

```
bss> ftp nic.merit.edu
Connected to nic.merit.edu.
220 nic.merit.edu ftp server (Version 4.1 Fri Aug 28 11:37:57 GDT 1987) ready.
Name (nic.merit.edu:rjs4808): anonymous
331 Guest login ok, send ident as password.
Password:           ("rs@usl" my local Internet address does not appear)
230 Guest login ok, access restrictions apply.
ftp>
```

If the machine responded with Guest login ok, restrictions apply, you got there without any problems. The FTP command dir gives you a listing of the directory you are in:

```
ftp> dir
200 PORT command successful.
150 Opening ASCII mode data connection for /bin/ls.
total 65
-rw-r--r--   1 nic     merit    17596 Dec 09 18:51 INDEX
-rw-r--r--   1 nic     merit     5446 Aug 04 1992  READ.ME
drwxr-xr-x   2 nic     merit      512 Sep 15 14:39 acceptable.use.policies
drwxr-sr-x   2 root    system     512 Sep 30 17:31 bin
drwxr-sr-x   3 cise    nsf        512 Aug 14 1992  cise
drwxr-xr-x   9 nic     merit      512 Jul 29 1992  documents
drwxr-xr-x   3 root    system     512 Feb 20 1992  etc
drwxr-xr-x   8 nic     merit      512 Jan 28 20:30 internet
drwxr-xr-x   2 nic     merit      512 Feb 01 15:37 introducing.the.internet
drwxr-sr-x   2 root    system     512 Feb 20 1992  lib
drwxr-xr-x   2 nic     merit      512 Feb 10 12:29 maps
drwxr-sr-x   2 nic     merit      512 Jan 07 12:43 merit
drwxr-xr-x   7 nic     merit      512 Aug 14 1992  michnet
```

```
drwxr-xr-x   6 nic      merit      512 Jul 29 1992  newsletters
drwxr-xr-x   4 nic      merit      512 Aug 03 1992  nren
drwxr-xr-x  14 nic      merit      512 Jan 05 15:31 nsfnet
drwxr-sr-x   2 omb      omb        512 Jul 29 1992  omb
drwxr-xr-x   3 nic      merit      512 Dec 01 11:39 resources
drwxr-xr-x   3 nic      merit      512 Jul 29 1992  statistics
drwxr-sr-x   3 root     system     512 Feb 20 1992  usr
drwxr-xr-x   3 nic      merit      512 Jul 15 1992  working.groups
226 Transfer complete.
1351 bytes received in 0.48 seconds (2.7 Kbytes/s)
ftp>
```

You have a listing of the current directory. So far, so good.

Of primary interest are the letters on the far left, which tell you whether the names on the far right are files or directories. The d in the letters on the left (as in drwxr-wx—x) shows that acceptable.use.policies, bin, cise, documents, etc, and most of the others on this list are subdirectories. INDEX and README are not directories but files of some kind, as is indicated by the absence of the d in the string of letters.

The letters on the far left also provide information about files or directories, which can be readable, writable, or executable (indicated by r, w, or x). Their position in the line indicates who has rights to read, write, or execute the file or directory. Rights can be given to the individual, groups, or everyone.

Navigator's Note: A file that is flagged as executable in the listing of a remote directory is executable on that machine. If your computer uses a different operating system, you won't be able to run it locally. If you can get telnet access to that machine, you'll be able to run it there.

The numbers at the middle right give the size of the file in bytes. This is important information. Some very large files exist on the Internet, and trying to store one of them will cause a problem if you do not have enough space on your local machine.

The INDEX and READ.ME files most likely contain information about the machine you have logged into and which directories and files can be accessed. You need to get these files and read them.

It is vital that you use the exact spelling, including upper- or lowercase, when you specify a file or directory name. There can be numerous variations and spellings for the same filename. For example, READ.ME is different from Read.me and

READ.me. In many cases, it is done this way intentionally as a way of preventing the overwriting of a file with a similar name. There can be many READ.ME and INDEX files in the subdirectories on this machine. You might find variations, such as INDEX.documents, Index.rfc, 001-READ.Me, 002-read.me, or 003-Read.Me.

In addition to the variations in spelling and use of upper- and lowercase, some filenames have to conform to systems requirements. For example, under PC DOS a filename is limited to eight characters and three extension characters, as in infrmatn.txt. In trying to retrieve this file, a likely mistake is to spell the filename as information.txt (too long).

> **Navigator's Warning:** Under many computer operating systems, using the exact spelling and exact case is mandatory for successful file retrieval!

Okay, now retrieve the INDEX and READ.ME files:

```
bss% ftp nic.merit.edu
ftp> get INDEX
200 PORT command successful.
150 Opening ASCII mode data connection for INDEX (17596 bytes).
226 Transfer complete.
local: INDEX remote: INDEX
18000 bytes received in 2.4 seconds (7.4 Kbytes/s)
ftp> get READ.ME
200 PORT command successful.
150 Opening ASCII mode data connection for READ.ME (5446 bytes).
226 Transfer complete.
local: READ.ME remote: READ.ME
5578 bytes received in 0.72 seconds (7.6 Kbytes/s)
ftp>
```

Notice the speed at which the file transfers took place. In my session, the two files were transferred from Michigan to my local machine in Louisiana in just over three seconds.

If you end your FTP session, go back to your local system, and read the files, you find that the INDEX file contains a bird's-eye view of the directory structure of the Merit system (see the following example); the READ.ME file gives directions on how to ftp, move around the machine, and use FTPmail queries.

To see what is in the document subdirectory, use the change directory command cd to move to that subdirectory. Then use the dir command to list the contents.

```
ftp> cd documents
250 CWD command successful.
ftp> dir
200 PORT command successful.
150 Opening ASCII mode data connection for /bin/ls.
total 132
-rw-r--r--   1 nic      merit       2300 Jul 30 1992   INDEX.documents
drwxr-sr-x   2 nic      merit        512 Jan 14 06:39  fyi
drwxr-sr-x   2 iesg     ietf        2048 Feb 12 13:15  iesg
drwxr-sr-x   2 iesg     ietf       26624 Feb 08 11:27  ietf
drwxr-sr-x   2 iesg     ietf       16896 Feb 12 13:12  internet-drafts
drwxr-sr-x   2 nic      merit        512 Jul 15 1992   michnet.tour.guides
drwxr-sr-x   2 nic      merit      16896 Feb 10 11:51  rfc
drwxr-sr-x   2 nic      merit       1536 Jan 05 15:27  std
226 Transfer complete.
525 bytes received in 1.2 seconds (0.43 Kbytes/s)
```

Here's another index file called INDEX.documents! This is a small file—2,300 bytes. View its contents by using the FTP command get in combination with the more command.

The symbol ¦ means that the output of the get command is to be sent to the more utility. More will fill the local computer screen with the data sent to it from the remote machine. You can then read one line at a time by pressing the Enter key or one screen at a time by pressing the space bar. If you don't use more, the text just scrolls continuously before you have a chance to read it.

```
  ftp> get INDEX.documents ¦more
200 PORT command successful.
150 Opening ASCII mode data connection for INDEX.documents (2300 bytes).
<NIC.MERIT.EDU> /documents/INDEX.documents                30 July 1992
                Merit Network Information Center Services
                          NIC.MERIT.EDU
                          ftp.MERIT.EDU
                        ftp.MICHNET.NET
                          NIS.NSF.NET
                          (35.1.1.48)
Merit Network Information Center host computer, accessible via anonymous
 ftp, contains a wide array of information about the Internet, NSFNET, and
 MichNet. The document's directory is an archive for NSFNET, regional, and
Internet documentation.
  fyi/                     The FYI (For Your Information) sub-series of the
                           Request For Comments (RFCs), designed to provide a
                           wide audience of Internet users with a central
                           repository of information about any topics which
                           relate to the Internet.
  iesg/                    Minutes of the most recent IETF Steering Group
                           meetings.
```

```
   ietf/                        Current information on Internet Engineering Task
                                Force activities including a general description of
                                the IETF, summaries of ongoing working group
                                activities, and information on past and upcoming
                                meetings.
   internet-drafts/             A directory of draft documents which will ultimately
                                be submitted to the IAB and the RFC Editor to be
                                considered for publishing as RFC's. Comments are
                                welcome and should be addressed to the author, whose
                                name and e-mail address are listed on the first page
                                of the respective draft.
   michnet.tour.guides/         Documents detailing uses of the Michnet network.
   rfc/                         Request For Comments:  a document series which
                                describes the Internet suite of protocols and
                                related experiments.
   std/                         The Standards are the sub-series of notes within
                                the RFC series which document Internet standards.
226 Transfer complete.
local: INDEX.documents remote: INDEX.documents
2349 bytes received in 0.34 seconds (6.7 Kbytes/s)
ftp>
```

This file contains the names of the subdirectories and gives an abstract of their contents.

Now, go to the subdirectory named rfc and find Request For Comments, which is a collection of documents pertaining to the Internet. Included are papers on protocols and standards, proposals for new protocols, glossaries, biographies of those who helped build the Internet, and other helpful material. This is an excellent way to learn the history of the Internet, because the Request For Comments are listed in chronological order starting from 1969. There are technical as well as nontechnical papers in this subdirectory.

Now, change directories and list the directory contents:

```
ftp> cd rfc
250 CWD command successful.
ftp> dir
200 PORT command successful.
150 Opening ASCII mode data connection for /bin/ls.
total 87096
-rw-r--r--   2 nic      merit       141342 Feb 10 11:52 INDEX.rfc
-rw-r--r--   2 nic      merit         2350 Nov 19 1988  rfc0003.txt
-rw-r--r--   2 nic      merit        26766 Nov 19 1988  rfc0005.txt
-rw-r--r--   2 nic      merit         1585 Nov 19 1988  rfc0006.txt
-rw-r--r--   2 nic      merit         3382 Nov 21 1988  rfc0010.txt
-rw-r--r--   2 nic      merit          367 Nov 18 1988  rfc0016.txt
```

```
-rw-r--r--   2 nic      merit       4511 Nov 18 1988  rfc0017.txt
<<many more files>>
-rw-r--r--   2 nic      merit      33277 Feb 08 19:50 rfc1423.txt
-rw-r--r--   2 nic      merit      17537 Feb 08 19:50 rfc1424.txt
-rw-r--r--   2 nic      merit      20932 Feb 08 20:42 rfc1425.txt
-rw-r--r--   2 nic      merit      11661 Feb 08 20:42 rfc1426.txt
-rw-r--r--   2 nic      merit      17856 Feb 08 20:42 rfc1427.txt
-rw-r--r--   2 nic      merit      12064 Feb 08 20:42 rfc1428.txt
226 Transfer complete.
53587 bytes received in 67 seconds (0.78 Kbytes/s)
```

A common problem that you encounter when searching the Internet is not being able to see a machine's contents before you begin searching on it (unless you happen to be clairvoyant). Because there are over a thousand files in this directory, you will spend several minutes waiting for your directory command to finish listing them all. In addition, the filenames give no indication of the file contents!

Because you probably aren't clairvoyant, you must depend on the INDEX file in this situation. This INDEX file is a large one, so it is best to get and examine it on your own computer. The INDEX.rfc file (an excerpt of which follows) contains the filenames and a brief description of the content of each file.

```
rfc1392.txt     Jan 93    (Malkin)      Internet Users' Glossary
```

A glossary of networking terms may be interesting to a new Internet user, so I retrieved the file rfc1392.txt and saved it for future reference.

```
ftp> get rfc1392.txt
200 PORT command successful.
150 Opening ASCII mode data connection for rfc1392.txt (104624 bytes).
226 Transfer complete.
local: rfc1392.txt remote: rfc1392.txt
107594 bytes received in 9.4 seconds (11 Kbytes/s)
ftp>bye
221 Goodbye.
bss>
```

I ended the FTP session with the FTP command bye and my prompt changed from ftp> to my local prompt bss>. I was curious to see what the file contains; despite all of my experience and success in using FTP, it always relieves me to know that the file I wanted did indeed get back safely to my own machine. I used the more command on my machine to list the file.

```
bss> more rfc1392.txt
Network Working Group                                    G. Malkin
Request for Comments: 1392                         Xylogics, Inc.
FYI: 18                                            T. LaQuey Parker
                                                            UTexas
                                                            Editors
                                                     January 1993
                        Internet Users' Glossary
Status of this Memo
    This memo provides information for the Internet community. It does
    not specify an Internet standard. Distribution of this memo is
    unlimited.
Abstract
    There are many networking glossaries in existence. This glossary
    concentrates on terms which are specific to the Internet. Naturally,
    there are entries for some basic terms and acronyms because other
    entries refer to them.
Acknowledgements
    This document is the work of the User Glossary Working Group of the
    User Services Area of the Internet Engineering Task Force (IETF).
    Special thanks go to Jon Postel for his definitive definition of
    "datagram".
Table of Contents
<<many more screens of data>>
```

Ah, sweet success! I retrieved a glossary of network terms. There are many files you will want to transfer from the rfc directory. Some of the other directories listed on the Merit's Network Information Center Services FTP site contain information of interest to anyone learning how to navigate the Internet.

Now, it's your turn. Give it a try.

The *put* and *get* Commands

Occasionally, you will want to send files to a distant machine. The put command does exactly the opposite of the get command—it takes a local file and sends it away to a distant machine. Again, you must have a login name and a password on the distant machine in order to transfer files to it. If you want to transfer many files, you can use the mput command.

Some anonymous ftp sites will let you put files there by using the login anonymous and your Internet address as the password. This is the way many of the shareware files become distributed.

Of course, you might also want to get more than one file. The mget command allows you to transfer multiple files to the current directory. You can ask to mget a list of filenames by giving the names with a space between each. You can also use wildcards in the filename in order to retrieve more than one file. mget will prompt you to make sure you want to get all files. This is a nice feature in case you forget which directory you are visiting and try to get a thousand files that you really didn't want to transfer. If you feel safe in obtaining files, the ftp prompt off command will turn this safety feature off.

Here is an example of mget at work. I've logged into the site ftp.sura.net as anonymous, and I'm ready to mget files from the /pub/nic directory. First, I'll list what's there:

```
ftp> dir
200 PORT command successful.
150 Opening ASCII mode data connection for /bin/ls.
total 5092
-rw-rw-r—   1 mtaranto 120       1394 Apr 22 13:52 .message
-rw-r—r—    1 mtaranto 120      10047 Apr 13 13:37 00-README.FIRST
-rw-rw-r—   1 mtaranto 120      47592 Mar  5  1992 BIG-LAN-FAQ
-rw-r—r—    1 mtaranto 120       4266 Dec  8  1992 ERIC.sites
-rw-r—r—    1 mtaranto 120       3955 Mar 17 19:15 NIC.WORKSHOP.INFO
drwxr-sr-x  2 mtaranto 120        512 Jul 22  1992 NREN
-rw-r—r—    1 mtaranto 120       2351 Oct 19  1992 NSFNET.acceptable.use
-rw-rw-r—   1 root     120       2709 Apr 23 19:50 SURAnet.acceptable.use
-rw-rw-r—   1 mtaranto 120      85677 May 11  1992 agricultural.list
-rw-rw-r—   1 mtaranto 120      27840 Apr 17  1992 archie.manual
-rw-r—r—    1 mtaranto 120      30500 Oct 14  1992 bbs.list.10-14
-rw-r—r—    1 mtaranto 120       3030 Nov 11  1992 bible.resources
-rw-r—r—    1 mtaranto 120       1347 Nov 12  1992 bionet.list
-rw-r—r—    1 mtaranto 120      41580 Dec  8  1992 cwis.list
drwxrwsr-x  3 mtaranto 120        512 Apr 28  1992 directory.services
-rw-rw-r—   1 plieb    120       1904 Jan  6  1992 farnet-recommendations
-rw-r—r—    1 mtaranto 120      15968 Oct 28  1992 holocaust.archive
-rw-r—r—    1 mtaranto 120       2986 Jun  2 18:09 how.to.get.SURAnet.guide
-rw-r—r—    1 mtaranto 120     149967 Jun  1 12:38 infoguide.6-93.txt
-rw-rw-r—   1 mtaranto 120     360853 Aug 20  1992 interest.groups.Z
-rw-r—r—    1 mtaranto 120     879381 Dec  9  1992 interest.groups.txt
drwxr-sr-x  3 mtaranto 120        512 Apr  7 17:09 internet.literature
-rw-r—r—    1 mtaranto 120      15682 Dec  8  1992 library.conferences
-rw-r—r—    1 mtaranto 120     154962 Jun  2 12:43 medical.resources.6-1
-rw-r—r—    1 mtaranto 120      15474 Nov 11  1992 network.law.info
drwxrwsr-x  2 mtaranto 120        512 Apr 14  1992 network.service.guides
-rw-r—r—    1 mtaranto 120      20553 Oct  9  1992 nnews.9-92
-rw-rw-r—   1 mtaranto 120       6194 Feb 21  1992 obi.directory.index
-rw-r—r—    1 mtaranto 120      39945 Aug 24  1992 search.techniques
drwxr-sr-x  2 1077     120       1024 Nov 12  1992 training
-rw-r—r—    1 mtaranto 120      14756 Apr 13 13:33 whitehouse.FAQ
```

```
-rw-rw-r—   1 root      120         6170 Jan  3  1992 wholeguide-help.txt
-rw-rw-r—   1 root      120       578238 Jun 21 20:49 wholeguide.txt
226 Transfer complete.
2413 bytes received in 0.7 seconds (3.4 Kbytes/s)
```

Let's get the two files we want: cwis.list and bionet.list.

```
ftp> get cwis.list bionet.list
200 PORT command successful.
150 Opening ASCII mode data connection for cwis.list (41580 bytes).
226 Transfer complete.
local: bionet.list remote: cwis.list
42644 bytes received in 7.7 seconds (5.4 Kbytes/s)
```

Wait a minute! What's this... local: bionet.list remote: cwis.list ...arggghhh! We used get when we meant mget. Because we asked to get, ftp assumed that the second filename ("bionet.list") was the name of the file in which we wanted to store the remote file cwis.list. Let's try again.

```
ftp> mget cwis.list bionet.list
mget cwis.list? y
200 PORT command successful.
150 Opening ASCII mode data connection for cwis.list (41580 bytes).
226 Transfer complete.
local: cwis.list remote: cwis.list
42644 bytes received in 4.9 seconds (8.5 Kbytes/s)
mget bionet.list? y
200 PORT command successful.
150 Opening ASCII mode data connection for bionet.list (1347 bytes).
226 Transfer complete.
local: bionet.list remote: bionet.list
1402 bytes received in 0.42 seconds (3.3 Kbytes/s)
```

We got both files, and because prompt was set to on, we were asked for each file if we wanted to transfer it. The mget also retrieves files and names the local copy the same as the files on the remote system. Let's try for a wildcard specification:

```
ftp> mget *.list
mget agricultural.list? y
200 PORT command successful.
150 Opening ASCII mode data connection for agricultural.list (85677 bytes).
226 Transfer complete.
local: agricultural.list remote: agricultural.list
```

```
88383 bytes received in 6.4 seconds (14 Kbytes/s)
mget bionet.list? y
200 PORT command successful.
150 Opening ASCII mode data connection for bionet.list (1347 bytes).
226 Transfer complete.
local: bionet.list remote: bionet.list
1402 bytes received in 0.47 seconds (2.9 Kbytes/s)
mget cwis.list? n
ftp> bye
221 Goodbye.
a103%
```

You can see that using mget is pretty easy. Again, try it out. You have nothing to lose but your disk space!

REMOTELY POSSIBLE: TELNET

When many computers are linked on a network, you often find that you need to run a program on a computer other than the one you're currently using. This could happen for any of several reasons.

Maybe the program you want to use won't work on your computer. For example, if your computer is a DOS PC and you want to use a piece of software written for UNIX, you'll need to use another computer that runs UNIX.

Maybe your machine doesn't have adequate resources (for example, not enough memory or too slow a processor). Or maybe you just want to work with data files on the remote computer. Although you might be able to copy the files to your own computer, that will only be possible as long as the files aren't too big to fit on your machine. You could just tell your software to use the remote data file, but if, for example, you need to search a massive database, you'll be choking up the network as you haul the data across it.

What's needed is a way to run a program on a remote computer, transferring the screen display to your machine while sending your keyboard data to the remote software. This is called a *remote session* or *virtual terminal session*. With TCP/IP systems, virtual terminal facilities are available through something called *telnet*.

What Is Telnet?

Telnet is a program that uses TELNET protocol, part of the TCP/IP protocol suite. The remote computer, called the *telnet server*, accepts telnet connections from a client over a TCP/IP system.

Because the Internet is a TCP/IP network, telnet works happily between computers attached to it—providing that the telnet service is installed on the server end and you have a compatible version of the telnet client on your computer.

Navigator's Note: Don't be surprised if you try to use telnet with a remote computer on the Internet and can't get a connection—not all computers have telnet enabled.

The telnet client and server components negotiate how they will use the connection, so that even if the two systems are not of the same type, they will find a common language.

A Macintosh user running a System 7 version of telnet can go through the Internet and get a telnet connection on an IBM mainframe that is running the MVS operating system. The Macintosh can then run IBM software on the mainframe. Of course, all that's happening is that the remote computer's screen display is being received, but the end result makes it appear as though it were running on the local computer.

Telnet does have its limits. If the traffic is heavy on any of the networks that connect you to the remote computer, the reduced performance may make the updates to your own screen very slow.

You must also remember, when you want to print something, to make sure that the output device is on your computer and not on the remote machine.

Finally, if you want to save data to a file using the remote program and plan to store it on the remote computer, you'll need to have the required privileges. You'll also have to FTP the data to yourself if you want a local copy.

Telnet makes it possible to use a remote computer as if it were the computer in front of you. With the Internet, that remote computer could be many thousands of miles away.

What Do I Telnet To?

In educational and research environments, it's not uncommon to have accounts on many Internet computers. This occurs most often at universities, where there are numerous departments and many computers with different operating systems using a variety of programs.

It also occurs if you are affiliated with a number of schools where you work, teach, study, or have ongoing collaborative research. These days, it's not uncommon for people to have some accounts on an educational system and others where they work. Telnet enables you to access any of your accounts from any point on the Internet.

Telnet is most often used for public or commercial purposes, allowing remote users to search large, complex, or proprietary databases. Examples include the ERIC service, indices of educational journals, databases of the full text of Shakespeare's plays, and databases such as CARL's UnCover2—all of which are free. There are also fee-charging database providers such as DIALOG and OCLC.

Navigator's Note: The Educational Resources Information Center (ERIC) is a reference publication for the National Education Information Network, sponsored by the U.S. Department of Education. ERIC includes a database of citations and abstracts for educational literature and is divided into the Current Index to Journals in Education (CIJE) and the findings, reports, speeches, books, and other items covered in Resource in Education (RIE).

The CIJE indexes over 700 professional journals, which makes it a popular database for finding information relating to education. This government-produced database is a valuable resource for materials in education, and its scope has expanded to include other related materials that may be of interest to many multidisciplinary educational areas.

Navigator's Note: The Colorado Alliance of Research Libraries (CARL) has developed a document delivery service called UnCover2. UnCover2 is a database encompassing over 10,500 unique multidisciplinary journals.

UnCover2 provides article citations taken from the table of contents of each issue of a particular journal along with the descriptive information or abstracts appearing on the contents page.

Delivery of the selected articles is by fax, and the goal is to deliver material in less than 24 hours. A fee is charged to access the service, and a royalty fee is usually assessed for each article delivered.

Navigator's Note: OCLC is a major database source used by librarians to find bibliographic information about material for verification and cataloging purposes. In addition, OCLC provides librarians with the details of who owns copies of the material—vitally important for the interlibrary loan process. OCLC is now attempting to provide wider access to its databases.

The following database descriptions are selected from publicity information from OCLC about its services.

The FirstSearch Catalog is an online reference service with an end-user interface designed specifically for library patrons.

OCLC WorldCat is the OCLC Online Union Catalog, the world's most comprehensive bibliography, with more than 25 million records of information spanning 4,000 years of knowledge, now accessible by patrons with the FirstSearch Catalog. Updated daily.

The U.S. Government Printing Office Monthly Catalog of Publications is a database consisting of more than 350,000 records published by the GPO since July 1976. The Monthly Catalog has references to congressional committee reports and hearings, debates, documents from executive departments, and more. Updated monthly, records are from July 1976 to the present.

> **American Geological Institute's MiniGeoRef** covers recent additions to the GeoRef file, a database containing earth-science references, and the index terms that describe them. More than 4,000 journals in 40 languages are regularly scanned, along with new books, maps, and reports. Updated monthly, records are from 1985 to the present.
>
> **Newspaper Abstracts** from UMI/Data Courier is a complete business and general reference resource. The database indexes and abstracts more than 25 national and regional newspapers, including the *New York Times*, *Los Angeles Times*, *Washington Post*, and *USA Today*. The *Wall Street Journal* (Eastern edition) is indexed beginning January 1, 1990. Updated weekly, records are from 1989 to the present.

Using telnet, you also gain access to hundreds of library catalogs around the world, which can help you find bibliographic information for your research. When you telnet to a Free-Net (see Chapter 2) or a college Campus Wide Information System (CWIS), you can find local restaurant locations, theater productions, and class schedules. You can also use telnet to access databases of census materials, weather information, and myriad other data services.

Using Telnet

To use telnet, give telnet the address of the computer it is to connect to. For example: `telnet ucsbuxa.edu`

Until recently, this was the only way to place a telnet connection. Today, however, many people use Gopher (see Chapter 8, "Navigating by Menus: Gopher") to "launch" telnet. With Gopher, you'll find menu items that lead to virtual terminal sessions using telnet. When you select one of these items, telnet is engaged, and the address of the target connection is automatically passed on. Thus, the Gopher menu item might say `Use telnet to access Costello at UCSB` rather than `telnet ucsbuxa.edu`.

Gopher is a much more convenient way to use telnet because you don't need to remember the Internet address of the machine you want to contact. The Gopher system, however, does not have menu items for telneting to every machine on the Internet.

There are many private computers on the Internet that you might want to access but which aren't on any Gopher menus. Even if you have a Gopher server running on your local machine, you may find it more convenient to telnet to an infrequently used remote machine than to add a Gopher menu item that will only be used occasionally.

In short, even though you can do a great deal using telnet through Gopher, you should learn to use telnet when Gopher can't do the job.

Port Number

In some instances, you are required by the remote machine to select a port number other than the standard port used by telnet (port 23). This is useful when you need to access a specific type of service on a remote machine. This number is entered on the telnet command line after the remote machine's name or address. For example:

```
gyre% telnet ucsbuxa.uscb.edu 300
```

instructs telnet to connect to ucsbuxa.uscb.edu on port 300. Remember this when you see a remote machine that you want to use and a port is specified along with the machine's name or address.

Starting Telnet

Telnet's operation is, for all practical purposes, transparent to the user. You start telnet by typing telnet, a space and the remote machine's Internet address. You can give either the computer's name (ucsbuxa.ucsb.edu) or its address (128.111.122.50). If needed, you then give the port number. Once you press Enter, the connection is attempted.

The general form of the telnet command is

```
telnet <computer_name> [<port_number>]
```

or

```
telnet <computer_address> [<port_number>]
```

Are We Talking?

If contact is made, the telnet server and client negotiate their communication strategy. If that's successful, the remote server machine usually asks you for a login username. You then log in just as if you were directly on the computer.

If telnet can't connect to the target computer, you get a message telling you what the problem is. There are three main reasons a connection can't be made. The first is that you got the target computer's name or address wrong. This is often due to simple typing errors, such as entering uscbuxa when you mean ucsbuxa. Another mistake is not giving the complete address. For example, if you enter ucsbuxa.edu when you mean ucsbuxa.ucsb.edu, you won't get a connection.

With purely numeric addresses, it is (of course) much easier to make a mistake. All of these errors usually get a message like host not known or host not available.

The second reason is that the computer is not available or the network the computer is on isn't working. This does happen and some sites, particularly new ones, are often not available. Systems also become unavailable when maintenance or repair work is being done. The third reason a connection can't be made is that all of the connections the computer supports are already active. Both of these reasons are usually greeted with a time out message.

Command Mode

If you type telnet by itself (or after telnet fails to reach the remote machine) you get the telnet prompt, telnet>, which indicates that you are in telnet's command mode. From here you can use any of the telnet commands. Typing ? or help in the command mode gives you a list of the available commands.

When telnet connects, you see something much like the following:

```
icarus.lis[3] % telnet sklib.usask.ca
Trying 128.233.1.20 ...
Connected to sklib.usask.ca.
Escape character is '^]'.


    SKLIB - University of Saskatchewan Library System
```

It is important to notice the line Escape character.... When you're in the middle of a telnet session to another computer and you want to get back to the telnet command mode, you use the escape character to get telnet's attention. When you type the escape character, the telnet command prompt appears, showing that you've gone into telnet command mode.

> **Navigator's Note:** The standard telnet escape character is `Ctrl+]`, which lets you give telnet commands directly. To quit a telnet session, you can usually type `Ctrl+]`, then `q`. It can be set differently, and you need to ask your system manager or (if all else fails) read your system manual.

Telnet Commands

Here is a short list of the most commonly used telnet commands:

`close` If you start telnet without specifying the target computer to connect to, this command terminates the connection to another computer and leaves you in command mode. If you started telnet with the name or address of a target computer, `close` will terminate the session and quit telnet (this is equivalent to the quit command). You can use the abbreviation `c`.

`open` This command is used to connect to a remote machine when you're at the `telnet>` prompt. The format (like starting telnet from the systems prompt) is `open <computer_name>` or `open <computer_address>`.

`quit` This command leaves the telnet program. If you have a connection to a remote computer, `quit` terminates it first.

`<enter>`   In the telnet command mode, pressing Enter by itself (that is, with nothing else typed on the command line) returns you to the remote session if you have one active. If you don't, it exits telnet.

`set echo` If you can't see what you are typing or if you type and see double, go to the telnet command mode (using the escape character) and enter `set echo`. This toggles the echo setting off and on and should resolve the problem.

Using Telnet

When a telnet connection to a remote machine is started, telnet changes to input mode in order to send text from the keyboard (the stuff you type) to the remote machine. This can be either on a line-by-line basis (*line mode*), or one character at a time (*character mode*).

The choice of modes depends on the remote machine system and is part of the negotiating telnet does when a connection is established. You change the mode by using the command mode <type> (which can be abbreviated to m <type>) at the telnet prompt. <type> is either line or character.

> **Navigator's Note:** It's almost always better to use telnet in a character-by-character mode. If you don't, weird things can happen. For example, if you run WAIS through telnet in the line-by-line mode and you want help, press h. Because you're in line mode, nothing will happen until you press Enter. WAIS displays the help screen, but because you also pressed Enter, it jumps straight back to the screen you were on. This will drive you crazy unless you can read very fast.

Login Procedures

When you get a successful telnet connection, you are usually asked to log in to the remote computer and give a password. Public telnet services on remote machines may expect a publicly known password—which you must know to get in. This could be something as simple as guest. Or not—things on the Internet aren't always simple.

The more hospitable remote computer systems give you the login password. The very best machines (from a user's point of view) have no barriers at all and connect you directly to the remote system. Because this results in a system that can be easily explored by hackers and that offers virtually no control to the systems manager, it isn't surprising that this kind of system is becoming less common (today, about as common as fourteen-inch disk drives—the author's age is showing).

Terminal Emulation

Many remote machines ask you for your terminal emulation when you successfully log in. The most common terminal type is called VT100 (this is a specification of how data will be handled and displayed on a terminal).

If you select a terminal type unknown to the remote machine, you may receive a
list of terminal types supported by the remote computer. On the other hand, you
may not, in which case you'll just get a crummy-looking screen. Ho-hum. Start
again and try with VT100.

If your terminal type is unknown, you may be able to select *dumb* or *hardcopy*,
which are generic terminal emulations.

Navigator's Note: Using the generic dumb or hardcopy terminal types
works well if you want to copy or log a session during telnetting. It
eliminates the funky characters that often appear in captured data
when other terminal types are used.

Navigator's Warning: Sometimes selecting dumb or hardcopy won't
actually do you any good. The remote computer's software may not
be able to work with a dumb terminal at all. This is the case with
the screen-oriented versions of Gopher. The dumb setting just enables you to see strange character sequences being printed to the
screen.

Getting the Boot

Some remote machines keep track of how long you've been connected, what time
of the day you're connecting, and how long you've been idle (that is, how long
since you sent any keystrokes). They may automatically end the telnet session if
you're on too long, if you try to use the system during peak load periods when
you're not supposed to, or if they think you may have gone to sleep or been ab-
ducted by terrorists before having logged off.

If this causes a problem, you'll have to talk to the system administrator of the
remote computer to see if you can get the limitation removed for your account.

The IBM Connection

An alternative to the standard telnet program is tn3270. It is used to make your terminal emulate an IBM 3270 terminal, which is required if you want to run many of the programs on an IBM mainframe.

You start tn3270 just as you do telnet: type tn3270 at the systems prompt, followed by a space and the remote machine's name or address and the optional port number.

In many cases tn3270 changes which characters are generated by your keyboard (called *keyboard mapping*) so that an IBM machine will understand you better. Don't be surprised if the keys on your computer don't work normally and you have to try some odd combinations to make the remote computer programs do what you want.

Telnet Client Flavors

We've discussed the UNIX version of telnet, yet telnet comes in different flavors. Uses vary, depending on the operating system.

For example, DOS versions of telnet may look a lot like the UNIX version, or they may be menu driven and store default settings such as monitor type, key assignment, and character translation in a configuration file. Windows and Macintosh versions that enable you to use a mouse and that support drag-and-drop features are available.

The Telnet Assistant: Hytelnet

Using telnet is like climbing a mountain: it's a lot of work, but the rewards make it worth the trouble.

Still, there are nine and one-half zillion machines on the Internet that you can access via telnet. (OK, not that many. But it feels that way.) You may have big trouble finding out—and keeping track of—the diverse machine names, addresses, and login information that telnetting demands.

A few years back, Peter Scott, an Internetter at the University of Saskatchewan Library Systems, developed a program called *Hytelnet* (short for Hypertext Browser for Telnet). Hytelnet remembers the Internet addresses and login procedures of machines for you, and it can, if you have the right hardware, automatically telnet to a remote machine for you. Hytelnet gets you into hundreds of public-access library catalogs, Free-Nets, Campus Wide Information Servers (CWIS), and other telnet sites. Hytelnet lets you use embedded hypertext links to search through screens to locate information about a telnet site.

In addition to getting you to telnet sites, Hytelnet can help you once you're there. It has help screens that show you information you may need to be able to navigate within a given system. You can view screens that show information about logins and passwords, which system is in use, basic system commands, and who to contact if you screw up—um, that is, if you inadvertently and innocently encounter an online failure or impediment of some kind.

Hytelnet is available in versions for IBM PC, VAX/VMS, UNIX/VMS, Macintosh, and Amiga systems. You can download the software via anonymous FTP, from `ftp.usask.ca` at the University of Saskatchewan.

Navigator's Note: `ftp` is part of the address, so when you ftp to the site, your command will look like this

```
ftp ftp.usask.ca
```

You'll find the Hytelnet files in the `pub/hytelnet` directory. The files may be compressed, so you'll need to unarchive them before you can set up and use Hytelnet. For the PC version, a program called PKUNZIP does the trick. You can find the file PKUNZIP.EXE on the Internet by using Archie. I wouldn't worry about this now, though; when you FTP to download the Hytelnet program, you'll find information about how to unarchive the files.

Navigator's Note: For the newest version of Hytelnet, or for more information on how to get and implement this utility, just use Gopher to search Veronica for the word *hytelnet*.

Once you install and start Hytelnet, you'll see an opening screen similar to the following.

```
    Welcome to HYTELNET version 6.6
         October 10, 1993


What is HYTELNET?          <WHATIS>
Library catalogs           <SITES1>
Other resources            <SITES2>
```

```
    _           Help files for catalogs    <OP000>              _
    _           Catalog interfaces         <SYS000>             _
    _           Internet Glossary          <GLOSSARY>           _
    _           Telnet tips                <TELNET>             _
    _           Telnet/TN3270 escape keys  <ESCAPE.KEY>         _
    _           Key-stroke commands        <HELP.TXT>           _
    _                                                           _
    _   ....................................................   _
    _ Up/Down arrows MOVE   Left/Right arrows SELECT   F1 for HELP anytime_
    _                                                           _
    _            CONTROL/HOME returns here     ALT-T quits      _
    _   ....................................................   _
    _                                                           _
    _            HYTELNET 6.6 was written by Peter Scott        _
    _            E-mail address: aa375@freenet.carleton.ca      _
```

From here, you simply work your way through screens, executing the hypertext links, until you arrive at machine and login information for a telnet site you want. For example:

```
    _                                                           _
    _               United States Medical Libraries            _
    _                                                           _
    _  <US376> Albert Einstein College of Medicine             _
    _  <US011> Association of Operating Room Nurses             _
    _  <US098> Audie L. Murphy Memorial Veterans' Administration Hospital_
    _  <US381> Cornell University Medical College               _
    _  <US293> Creighton University Health Sciences Library     _
    _  <US011> Denver Medical Library                           _
    _  <US145> Georgetown University Medical Center             _
    _  <US214> HSLC HealthNET (Health Sciences Information Network) _
    _  <US408> Massachusetts College of Pharmacy               _
    _  <US362> Medical College of Ohio                          _
    _  <US242> Medical College of Wisconsin                     _
    _                                                           _
```

From this screen, you can also link to a screen that gives you expanded information about the type of site you've chosen:

```
    _                                              _
    _          Medical College of Wisconsin        _
    _                                              _
    _  TELNET ILS.LIB.MCW.EDU or 141.106.32.19     _
    _  login: library
```

```
 _
 _   OPAC = INNOPAC <OP009>                          _
 _                                                   _
 _   To exit, type Q                                 _
                                                     _
```

Some versions of the Hytelnet program (not, unfortunately, the PC version at this writing) can automatically dial up and connect you to the site you select.

Now, you don't have to *have* Hytelnet to *use* Hytelnet. The program is running in a modified version at several Gopher sites, and in an enhanced version at the Washington and Lee University Gopher. You can use these Gophers to use Hytelnet.

The Washington and Lee University Gopher offers detailed information on system or subject types of service for telnet sites. To use it, point your Gopher client to `liberty.uc.wlu.edu 70` and choose `Explore Internet Resources->Hytelnet`.

This Gopher simply uses Hytelnet's database of telnet machine information as the source for a list of Gopher menus. These menus break out Hytelnet's embedded links as separate menu choices. So when you search through Gopher's menus down to information about a particular site, you may see several choices: one that will display Hytelnet's address and login data for that site, one that will show basic instructions for using the site, and so on. You can also use this Gopher to search a database of the names of all remote destinations to get a menu of choices that match the search.

If you plan to do much telnetting, Hytelnet is a must. Check it out.

Do I Need to Know About Telnet?

Yes. That is, if you want to be able to skillfully navigate the Internet. At its best, telnet is transparent; it works behind the scenes so that you can get on with the business of using the remote machine's resources. Besides, its commands are pretty easy to learn.

With luck, the hardest thing you'll ever encounter in using telnet is remembering the remote machine's name or address or quitting from the remote machine, but using telnet from Gopher makes that a rare problem for the most popular telnet sites.

6

FINDING
FILES: ARCHIE

As we keep saying,e the Internet offers huge treasure chests of data. From anthropology to zoology and from aalii to zymurgy, a file of data or a piece of software exists somewhere that defines the subject, gives references to it, displays it, exemplifies it, or shows you how it should be done.

As we discussed in Chapter 4, "A Moving Experience: FTP for Me," you can retrieve files from remote computers on the Internet using FTP. You can list directories to find out what files are there and download those that look interesting. With hundreds of thousands of files on thousands of computers, where do you begin to look?

Navigator's Note: The aalii (pronounced "a-lee"), *Dodoneae viscosa*, is a bushy shrub with sticky leaves, and zymurgy is the branch of chemistry dealing with fermentation (the boring subject of making wine and brewing beer). Now you can use *zymurgy* with confidence when playing Scrabble. The lowest score it will get you is 25 points.

In the early days of the ARPANET, before it became the Internet, only a few hundred computers were connected. The network was small enough for you to search systems for files related to your interests without being concerned that you might miss much.

The people using the Internet were scientists and engineers, so they generally knew where information was or could be obtained. Failing that, they could find out pretty easily who to ask. As the Internet grew, however, finding files became increasingly difficult.

Today, due to the enormous size of the Internet, we can guarantee that you will overlook lots of useful stuff in your searches. An exhaustive search isn't feasible with so many files in so many places on so many machines. Anyway, unless you're a member of the idle rich, you also won't have the time to search through all the available systems one by one. The big problem that faces you is where to start looking.

The Internet is a bit like having a vast library without an indexing system. Books are all over the place, with no index to which books are on which shelves. Some shelves have their own index, but others have none. The solution is obvious: make an index of all the shelves and their contents. That task is handled by a piece of software called Archie.

What Is Archie?

Developed at McGill University in Canada, Archie is a kind of mega librarian that automatically and regularly goes out to a large number of Internet servers and indexes their files to create a single, searchable database.

The database is therefore an index of directory data, a compilation of the available files on every server Archie has been capable of interrogating. Because Archie scans Internet hosts regularly, the database is being constantly updated.

Actually, Archie isn't a single system; rather, it's a collection of servers. (See Table 6.1 for a list of Archie servers.) Each Archie server is responsible for interrogating its own set of Internet servers to build its own database. Currently, 14 publicly available Archie servers index the files on more than a thousand servers. Most Archie databases now hold information on more than 2.5 million files and their locations.

> **Navigator's Note:** Because each Archie server manages its own database, the data may differ from one Archie to another. Usually the differences are few, and unless you're trying to find something really rare, one Archie server is effectively the same as another.

How to Find Files

You can use two strategies to find files with Archie. If you know the name of a file and have forgotten where it is located, you can ask Archie to find it. When you don't know the name of a file, you can search for the names of files and directories that contain words relating to the files you're interested in.

People often give names to files and directories to describe their contents. For example, database files often end with .dbf or .db. Files related to Windows often contain the characters *win*. A win31 directory is probably for Windows version 3.1 software. Macintosh files and directories often have *mac* in their names, and so on.

Because you can search the text of file and directory names with Archie, you have a simple type of subject search capability. When an Archie search is successful, you are shown information about the file. Archie will give you the name of all the computers where you can find the file, the directory and subdirectory where the file is located, the size of the file, the last date and time the file was updated, and file and directory attributes.

> **Navigator's Note:** Because Archie's database is limited to file and directory names, being able to find what you want depends on someone naming files and directories in a useful manner. If you're looking for information on thirteenth-century pottery in Bavaria and the file containing the data is called `bpxiii.jnk` and is in a directory called `whoneedsit`, Archie won't be able to help you.

Navigator's Note: Unfortunately, people frequently copy files and then rename them. This means that a fantastic Windows utility called WinUtil.Zip that you found mentioned in the latest issue of *TEKIE* Magazine might well appear elsewhere as WinTool.Zip, WinStuff.Zip, WinUtils.Zip, WinTools.Zip, *ad infinitum*. Worse still, you might even find all the variations in the same directory!

Archie doesn't know anything about the contents of the files or even what types of files they are. If the files are in an obscure place, the author or the system manager probably didn't care if you could find them or not, so they may not be that useful anyway.

Client/Server Setup

Archie is organized as a client/server system. The client part can run on the same computer as the Archie server, or it can be run on a computer elsewhere on the Internet. You can use any of the Archie servers or the default setup for your system. You can also use an Archie server by using telnet from another computer. Figure 6.1 shows the various options you have when using Archie.

The Archie client and server program files (including manuals) are available free through anonymous FTP at several locations on the Internet (see Appendix H, "The Internet Navigator's Gazetteer").

The best location to find the latest versions of Archie client programs with documentation is SURAnet. You'll need to use FTP to access `ftp.sura.net`. The files are located in the `/pub/archie/client/` directory. Client program files are available for UNIX, PC, VMS, and several other operating systems.

Table 6.1. Archie servers and their addresses, their owners, and their timezones offset to GMT. These sites are heavily used, and on many occasions the current number of site users will have reached its maximum and you won't be allowed to access Archie. This is especially true during each system's local peak hours—7 a.m. to 7 p.m.

Archie Server	Address	Owner	Timezone Offset
`archie.rutgers.edu`	128.6.18.15	Rutgers University	GMT -6
`archie.sura.net`	128.167.254.179	SURAnet Archie server	GMT -6

Archie Server	Address	Owner	Timezone Offset
archie.unl.edu	129.93.1.14	U. of Nebraska, Lincoln	GMT -6
archie.ans.net	147.225.1.2	ANS Archie server	GMT -x
archie.au	139.130.4.6	Australian server	GMT +9
archie.funet.fi	128.214.6.100	European server, Finland	GMT +1
archie.doc.ic.ac.uk	146.169.11.3	UK/Europe server	GMT
archie.cs.huji.ac.il	132.65.6.15	Israel server	GMT +5
archie.wide.ad.jp	133.4.3.6	Japanese server	GMT +8
archie.ncu.edu.tw	140.115.19.24	Taiwanese server	GMT +7
archie.sogang.ac.kr	163.239.1.11	Korean server	GMT +6
archie.nz	130.195.9.4	New Zealand server	GMT -10
archie.kuis.kyoto-u.ac.jp	130.54.20.1	Japan	GMT +8
archie.th-darmstadt.de	130.83.128.111	Germany	GMT +2

Archie's Limitations

The use of anonymous FTP is a clue to one of Archie's limitations. Archie databases include files only on servers enabling anonymous FTP. This means that sites requiring you to log in, even if that login is publicly available, won't be included in Archie databases.

Navigator's Note: If your site has files you want others to be able to find, anonymous FTP must be enabled and at least read access to the file granted. Then your system administrator can have your system added to the list of servers that Archie servers keep track of.

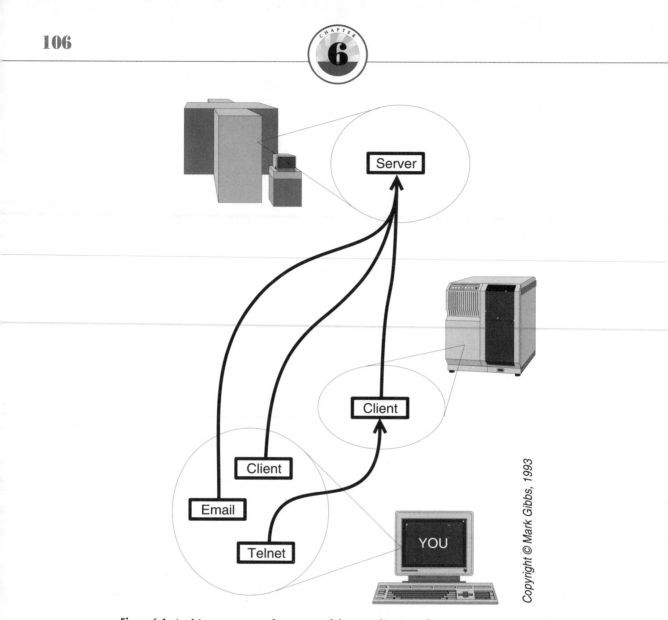

## CHAPTER 6

Figure 6.1. Archie servers can be accessed from a client on the same computer as the server, on a different computer, through telnet from another computer, or by using electronic mail.

Another limitation is that Archie can't tell you anything about the file. It won't have any information on what the file contains or even whether it's a program, a text file, or a database. Another source of information about files is available through Archie, but it's not always reliable (see the section titled, "Whatis" later in this chapter).

How to Use Archie

Archie servers can be accessed in three ways:

1. Through an Archie client connection

2. Through a telnet connection directly to an Archie server

3. By e-mail

When you try to use an Archie service through either a client or telnet connection during peak usage hours (see Table 6.1), you may find that the system administrator has blocked access to it. At SURAnet, for example, you'll get the following reply:

```
telnet archie.sura.net
Trying 128.167.254.179 ...
Connected to nic.sura.net.
Escape character is '^]'.


SunOS UNIX (nic.sura.net)

 login: archie
****************************************************************
Interactive use of the Archie service at SURAnet is disabled
from 8:00 a.m to 8:00 p.m. EST because the machine is unable
to handle the substantial extra load imposed by the interactive
client and still provide decent prospero service.

If it is outside of those hours, one of the systems people at
SURAnet has probably disabled archie service. If it remains
down for too long, you can send mail to archie-admin@sura.net
to tell us about the problem.

SURAnet is supporting a new experimental interface to archie.
Instead of logging in using the name archie, try logging in
Using the name qarchie.  This interface uses the prospero server
and so puts much less load on the machine.
Note that logging in as qarchie is only supported on this machine

The following is a list of other archie servers:
    archie.funet.fi         128.214.6.100   (European server in Finland)
    archie.doc.ic.ac.uk     146.169.11.3    (UK/Europe server)
    archie.cs.huji.ac.il    132.65.6.15     (Israel server)
    archie.wide.ad.jp       133.4.3.6       (Japanese server)
    archie.ncu.edu.tw       140.115.19.24   (Taiwanese server)
    archie.sogang.ac.kr     163.239.1.11    (Korean server)
    archie.nz               130.195.9.4     (New Zealand server)
```

```
     archie.kuis.kyoto-u.ac.jp 130.54.20.1     (Japan)
     archie.th-darmstadt.de    130.83.128.111 (Germany)
     archie.luth.se            130.240.18.4    (Sweden)
   Client software should be supported at all of these sites.
   ***********************************************************
Waiting 30 seconds...
Connection closed by foreign host.
```

For sites that would let you in but are too busy (the maximum number of connections enabled by the systems administrator for that Archie server is in use), you'll get a message like

```
a90% telnet archie.rutgers.edu
Trying 128.6.18.15 ...
Connected to dorm.Rutgers.EDU.
Escape character is '^]'.


SunOS UNIX (dorm.rutgers.edu) (ttypd)

 login: archie
Last login: Tue May 11 10:14:04 from library1.library
SunOS Release 4.1.3 (TDSERVER-SUN4C-DORM) #1: Sat May 1 16:46:07 EDT 1993
        Sorry, but there are too many concurrent archie users on this
machine right now. At this point, you have several options. First of
all, the most preferable alternative would be to use an archie client
such as xarchie (cs.rochester.edu:/pub) or the "archie" command line
client (ftp.std.com:/src/util). These clients reduce the load on the
server, as well as often providing additional functionality.  Another
alternative would be to contact one of the other archie servers. ( a
list of alternate servers is appended to this message ) If you aren't
in a rush, you could submit your request by e-mail. Just send a message
to archie@archie.rutgers.edu with the subject line "HELP" to get
detailed instructions. Oh, and the final option is to try here again
later :)
                                    - Archie Mgt
                                    (archie-admin@archie.rutgers.edu)


--------------< List of active archie servers >--------------

        archie.rutgers.edu   128.6.18.15     (Rutgers University)
        archie.sura.net      128.167.254.179 (SURAnet archie server)
        archie.unl.edu       129.93.1.14     (University of Nebraska in Lincoln)
        archie.ans.net       147.225.1.2     (ANS archie server)
        archie.au            139.130.4.6     (Australian server)
        archie.funet.fi      128.214.6.100   (European server in Finland)
        archie.doc.ic.ac.uk  146.169.11.3    (UK/England server)
```

```
    archie.cs.huji.ac.il 132.65.6.15      (Israel server)
    archie.wide.ad.jp    133.4.3.6        (Japanese server)
    archie.ncu.edu.tw    140.115.19.24    (Taiwanese server)

    Client software should be supported at all of these sites.
```

Or, you might get the rather more terse…

```
a90% telnet archie.unl.edu
Trying 129.93.1.14 ...
Connected to crcnis2.unl.edu.
Escape character is '^]'.


SunOS UNIX (crcnis2)

 login: archie
Last login: Tue May 11 10:12:18 from corageous.pittsb
SunOS Release 4.1.2 (CRCNIS2) #1: Wed Dec 16 12:10:12 EST 1992


too many archie users... try again later
Connection closed by foreign host.
a90% logout
```

The reason for limiting the number of connections to run Archie searches is that each connection uses computer power. This reduces the performance of the machine running the Archie server.

Client Connections

One of the ways to access Archie is to use an Archie client. Like other client/server systems we've talked about, the Archie client runs on your computer, and the server part runs on another system.

Using an Archie client is the preferred method because it doesn't burden the Archie server computer's resources as much as an online telnet session. When you start the Archie client program, you can either select one of the Archie servers listed in Table 6.1 or use the server that is your system's default.

Navigator's Note: Using your system's default Archie server is probably the easiest choice. And as Archie systems all have pretty much the same data, which one you choose won't make much of a difference.

An Archie Client Example

I wanted to find files for the Archie program and documentation that I knew were available at various sites on the Internet, but I didn't know where the files were or what they were called. Finding Archie sounded like a job for Archie.

At the computer system prompt I used the command archie once to start the program and typed archie a second time as the sequence of characters that I wanted Archie to search for. (If I'd wanted to search for fermentation chemistry instead, the second archie could have been zymurgy or ferment.)

Here's what I got:

```
a104% archie archie ¦more

Host plaza.aarnet.edu.au

    Location: /
       DIRECTORY drwxr-xr-x        512  Feb  6 09:04  archie
    Location: /usenet/comp.sources.misc/volume22
       DIRECTORY drwxr-xr-x        512  Mar  6 1992  archie
    Location: /usenet/comp.sources.misc/volume26
       DIRECTORY drwxr-xr-x        512  Mar  1 1992  archie
    Location: /usenet/comp.sources.misc/volume27
       DIRECTORY drwxr-xr-x        512  Mar  1 1992  archie
    Location: /usenet/comp.sources.misc/volume29
       DIRECTORY drwxr-xr-x        512  Apr 16 1992  archie
    Location: /usenet/comp.sources.misc/volume33
       DIRECTORY drwxr-xr-x        512  Nov 13 07:57  archie

Host sifon.cc.mcgill.ca

    Location: /pub/Network
       DIRECTORY dr-xr-xr-x        512  Apr 22 17:17  archie
    Location: /pub/network-services
       DIRECTORY dr-xr-xr-x        512  Feb 17 19:09  archie
  —More—
    Location: /software/unix/network
       DIRECTORY drwxrwxr-x        512  Jan 26 11:49  archie
    Location: /software/vms
       DIRECTORY drwxrwxr-x        512  Jan 26 11:49  archie

Host gatekeeper.dec.com

    Location: /.0/usenet/comp.sources.misc/volume26
       DIRECTORY dr-xr-xr-x        512  Apr 24 03:34  archie
    Location: /.0/usenet/comp.sources.misc/volume27
       DIRECTORY dr-xr-xr-x        512  Apr 24 03:34  archie
    Location: /.0/usenet/comp.sources.misc/volume29
       DIRECTORY dr-xr-xr-x        512  Apr 24 03:35  archie
```

```
    Location: /contrib/share/lib/expect
          FILE -rw-r—r—       689  Oct  7 00:00  archie
    Location: /contrib/src/crl/expect/src/test
          FILE -rw-rw-r—      672  Jul 30 1992  archie

Host hpcsos.col.hp.com


    Location: /mirrors/386bsd/0.1-ports/utils
       DIRECTORY drwxr-xr-x      1024  Feb 15 01:35  archie


—More—
```

My request for information on the word Archie returned six pages of information. You can see that many directories and files named archie were found. That was an easy one.

With Archie, it's best to keep your searches simple. Some Archie servers prioritize searches by their complexity. The simpler they are, the faster they get done.

A Search for Windows Files

Next came a search using two commands that I sent at midday (a big no-no). I had to wait for more than half an hour before canceling it. I then ran the same job as a background task on my machine (it's a UNIX system, so I have that luxury) while I went ahead with other work.

I don't know the exact time it took to complete the search, but I got my results more than four hours later. Note that using the -s command got me much more than I needed or, indeed, wanted.

I was using Archie to try to find an FTP site for Windows 3.1 software. The directory used for these files on many FTP sites is win3 or win31, so I tried archie -s win. This means "look for anything with 'win' in it," and I thought this would find what I wanted. The results were xwindows, win.c, xwindows.info, and so on, but no win3 or win31. The reason was that my archie client limits me to 95 "hits" for each search and no win anything appeared in the first 95 results.

Of course, searching for win3 or win31 would get me the FTP sites I was looking for, but I could not remember the exact directory name. I had to use the -s and change the default limit from 95 to 2000 (that is, "give me the first two thousand matches") with the -m command to get the needed information.

```
icarus>archie -s -m2000 win

Host esel.cosy.sbg.ac.at
     Location:
/pub/mirror/386bsd/0.1/filesystem/usr/othersrc/contrib/isode/others/X
        DIRECTORY drwxr-xr-x        1024  Feb 11 01:35  xwininfo
     Location: /pub/mirror/386bsd/packages/tfs/XFree86/mit/clients
        DIRECTORY drwxr-xr-x         512  Mar  2 03:34  xwininfo
     Location: /pub/mirror/guitar/Bob_Dylan
        FILE -rw-r—r—              1596  Jul  2 1992  BlowinInTheWind.crd


Host swdsrv.edvz.univie.ac.at
     Location: /mac/info-mac/ex
        FILE -rw-r—r—            134198  Jun 15 1992  next-style-windows.hqx
        FILE -rw-r—r—             46296  Aug 12 1992  window-picker-102.hqx
        FILE -rw-r—r—             25984  May  7 1992  window-shade-12.hqx


        DIRECTORY drwxr-xr-x         512  May  1 02:47  win3
     Location: /pc/windows/win3/demo
        FILE -rw-r—r—           1288637  Aug  7 1992  timwin.zip
        FILE -rw-r—r—             37649  Apr 13 1992  wincrib.zip
        FILE -rw-r—r—            151087  Apr 13 1992  windraw.zip


Host cert.sei.cmu.edu
     Location: /pub/cert_advisories
        FILE -rw-r—r—              2823  Dec 16 1991
CA-91:22.SunOS.OpenWindows.vulnerability


Host cs.columbia.edu
     Location: /archives/mirror1/X11R5/contrib
        FILE -rw-rw-r—             4203  Mar 25 1991  winterp.README


Host caticsuf.cati.csufresno.edu
     Location: /usr/lib/zoneinfo/Australia
        FILE -r—r——                727  Jan 16 1991  Yancowinna


Host net-1.iastate.edu
     Location: /pub/pc
        DIRECTORY drwxrwx—         2048  Apr 28 14:29  win3


Host kanaha.idbsu.edu
     Location: /incoming
        FILE -rw-r—r—             33333  Aug 28 1992  winpool.zip


Host ftp.cica.indiana.edu
     Location: /pub/pc
        DIRECTORY drwxr-xr-x        1024  Apr 24 08:42  win3
```

(partial results of over 26 pages)

Archie Client Switches

You have three useful switches (seven total, but the others are less useful) that you can use with an Archie client:

The -r switch lets you use UNIX regular expressions as search text. These complex search specifications are a powerful way of describing what you want to look for (see Appendix C, "Command Reference," for an explanation of UNIX regular expressions and how to use them).

The -e switch (which is the default, so you need not specify it) tells Archie to search only for files and directories that contain the exact text you specify and to not worry about the case of the text. Thus, archie -e win.doc would match with win.doc, Win.doc, and WiN.doc but not win.txt or win31.

For a broader search, the -s switch enables you to search for file and directory names that include the search text. For example, archie -s win.doc would match with win31.doc, win.txt, windows, and so on.

> **Navigator's Note:** You need to specify the kind of search you want to do, because different servers default to different search types—which could cause you to miss files. For example, if you entered archie chemi hoping to find any files and directories with chemistry, chemical, chemo, and so on in their names, and the Archie server you use defaults to exact, case-sensitive searches, you'd probably get nothing.

Telnet Connections

Another way to use the Archie service is to telnet to one of the Archie servers throughout the world (see Figure 6.1 for the location of an Archie server appearing near you and Table 6.1 for its address).

You telnet to the address of an Archie server and log in with the word archie. Assuming that the site will let you use the system (remember, most sites experience maximum demand between 7 a.m. and 7 p.m.), after logging in you are greeted by a screen with a menu of selections and a prompt (see the following listing).

Using a telnet session, you search the Archie database directly. First-time users may want to read the help information by typing the word help at the archie> prompt and capturing it in a file for future reference (to save you the trouble, Appendix C, "Command Reference," shows the help screen for the Archie server at SURAnet).

An Archie Server Example

I was lucky to get through to the Rutgers University Archie server during peak hours to get the following example:

```
SunOS UNIX (dorm.rutgers.edu) (ttypb)

login: archie
Last login: Tue May  4 11:20:55 from balan.eng.ohio-s
SunOS Release 4.1.3 (TDSERVER-SUN4C) #1: Tue Apr 6 11:07:22 EDT 1993



        Welcome to the Rutgers University Archie Server!

_____


 - 3/21/93
        This server has recently been upgraded to version 3.0.2 of the
Archie software. Please use the "help" command for information on how
to use this new interface. Report any and all problems to
archie-admin@archie.rutgers.edu

_____

# Bunyip Information Systems, 1993
# Terminal type set to 'vt100 24 80'.
# 'erase' character is '^?'.
archie>
```

After connecting to the remote host machine archie.rutgers.edu, I logged in with the word `archie`. I received a welcome from the Rutgers University Archie server, after which I ended up at the `archie>` prompt.

From there, I used the command `prog` to start a search. I specified the text `chemis-try` in the hopes of finding host machines with directories or files by that name. This is how a chemist might search for interesting files. The search was successful—a listing of many directories and files with the word *chemistry* in their names.

Archie Server Commands

There are nine commands you can give an Archie server during a telnet session. The most useful command is `prog`. The `prog` command, followed by text, specifies what you are searching for. This is equivalent to using the Archie client without switches (in other words, `archie>prog chemistry` through telnet is the same as `archie chemistry` on an Archie client).

The set search command can be used to specify the type of search you want to do. For example, set search exact is the same as specifying -e when using the Archie client, sub is the same as -s, and regexp is the same as -r. When you set the search type, you're setting it for the rest of your session with that server. You can change it at any time, and you can find out what the default or current search type is with the command show search.

The command mail (which has no client equivalent) posts the result of the last search to the mail address specified. The other really useful command is quit, which lets you leave Archie and terminate your telnet session.

E-Mail Connections

The third way to find files using Archie is to use an Archie mail server. This is an indirect route to the Archie server and can take longer (possibly as much as several days) to give an answer. If you need to make another Archie search request based on the results of the first search, it becomes an even longer wait.

To use Archie through e-mail, send an electronic message containing Archie commands to an Archie server. The Archie server handles the request, and (if all goes well) the search results are sent back to you by e-mail.

If you don't have telnet or a local Archie client, this is an invaluable service. It's also useful if you want to do an Archie search but can't get to a server because it's too busy or you're not in any particular hurry.

Archie E-Mail Commands

Archie servers recognize nine commands sent by e-mail. Some are the same as the commands used in a telnet session (such as prog), and some specifically support e-mail connections.

The compress command compresses the results of the search using the UNIX TAR compression system to generate a file of the type .Z. This compressed file is then uuencoded before being sent to you as an e-mail message. The purpose of compression is to reduce the load on the network.

Navigator's Note: We recommend that you use the compress command whenever you suspect that the resulting output will be more than 45 kilobytes of text. Unless you are psychic and can predict the amount of output before seeing the results (in which case you'll also know what the results will be, so this won't concern you), always use this command.

Navigator's Note: Keep in mind that anything put in the subject heading of the e-mail message will be treated as a command. If it doesn't make sense to the Archie server (for example, if you were to put A query in the subject field), usually nothing will happen...but don't count on it. You might cause the entire query to be abandoned. Always either leave the subject blank (the best choice) or put the first Archie command there.

Navigator's Note: All search text in electronic mail queries is expected to be in the UNIX regular expression format (see Appendix C, "Command Reference").

The other useful electronic mail command is path. You can use this to specify the address to return the search results to. You should use this if you don't want the results returned to you or if you send a query and don't get any response. In the latter case, it may be because of a problem with the Archie server understanding your address in the message it received. Explicitly giving your address using the path command may sort the problem out.

The following listing shows the use of these two commands to search for chemistry.

```
icarus>mail archie@archie.sura.net
Subject:
prog chemistry
compress
path iuf4808@icarus.lis.pitt.edu
quit
.
icarus>
```

In this session, I mailed the Archie commands to the Archie server at SURAnet. I used the prog command to get the files on chemistry and asked for the information to be compressed. I also gave it the Internet address of another person who needs the information, and then indicated that there were no more commands by using the command quit. The results are as follows:

```
Sorting by hostname
Search request for 'chemistry'
Host askhp.ask.uni-karlsruhe.de   (129.13.200.33)
```

```
Last updated 03:39 10 May 1993
    Location: /pub/education
      DIRECTORY rwxrwxr-x        1024  Mar 31 08:22    chemistry
    Location: /pub/demos
      DIRECTORY rwxr-xr-x        1024  Dec 15 07:03    chemistry
    Location: /pub/getsisy/klaus12345678asd
      FILE      rwxr-xr-x          53  May  4 05:35    biohochreaktor.arc -> /scsi2/
ftp/pub/education/chemistry/biohochreaktor.arc
Host athene.uni-paderborn.de   (131.234.2.32)
Last updated 22:52 17 Apr 1993
    Location: /pcsoft/msdos
      DIRECTORY rwxr-xr-x         512  Apr 12 15:51    chemistry
    Location: /pcsoft2/atari/gnu
      DIRECTORY rwxr-xr-x         512  May 19  1992    chemistry
    Location: /pcsoft2/atari/gnu/chemistry
      FILE      rw-r--r--         169  Nov 18  1991    README.chemistry
```

Navigator's Warning: Always put the command quit at the end of an e-mail Archie query. Once the Archie server encounters the command quit, it stops processing and sends you the results. If your e-mail system automatically generates a signature for you, the signature text that is added may cause problems. Check with your system administrator or your computer manuals to see how to switch this feature on and off.

Whatis

Archie server sites maintain a Software Description Database (SDD) that gives you a brief description of many (not all) of the files Archie knows about. These descriptions are supplied by the sites on the Archie search list. The sites have to update their own database entries.

The Software Description Database can be accessed using the command whatis followed by the search text. You use the command at the archie> prompt when using telnet or on a separate line in an e-mail message. Archie searches through the SDD for lines that match the search text and returns each matching line as the results.

Whatis is tricky, and the SDD data is incomplete, erratic, and sometimes very out-of-date. For example, nothing appropriate was found for WAIS, e-mail, pkunzip, or xwindows. On the other hand, internet, telnet, uucp, slip, and windows were found.

Whatis can be good for finding files that relate to different environments and are therefore spread across many different computers. Our example looks for the text compression. I retrieved a good many types of compression-related files that I could then ask Archie to locate.

In the following example, I use the whatis command at the Archie prompt in a telnet session:

```
archie>what is compress

RFC 1144              Jacobson, V. Compressing TCP/IP headers for low-speed
                     serial links. 1990 February; 43 p.
RFC 468              Braden, R.T. FTP data compression 1973 March 8; 5 p.
arc                  PC compression program
cl[fs]               Print compressed directory listings
compress             Compress text files
compress.cms         compress for IBM/VM CMS
compress.mag         /etc/magic lines for compress
compress.ms          16 bit compress for MSDOS
compress.xenix       Xenix patches to compress4.0
deltac               Image compression using delta modulation
dictsq               Compress sorted word lists
mailsplit            Send files and/or directories via electronic mail
                     using "tar", "compress", etc
pdtar                A PD tar(1) replacement.  Writes P1003 (POSIX)
                     standard tapes by default.      It can also read
                     compressed tar files without uncompressing them.
spl                  Splay tree compression routines
squeeze              A file compression program
u16.pc               16 bit uncompress for IBM PC
uncrunch             Uncompression program
unsqueeze            Uncompression programs
wdb-ii               WDBII mapping software (10:1 compress, Unix PLOT)
ztar                 Tools for compressed tar archives

archie>_
```

Here I used the whatis command in an electronic mail inquiry of an Archie data-base:

```
icarus>mail archie@archie.rutgers.edu
Subject:
whatis shell
whatis internet
whatis slip
quit
```

And received this e-mail message in return:

```
From archie@dorm.rutgers.edu Thu May 13 09:45:02 1993
Received: from dorm.rutgers.edu by armagnac.ucs.usl.edu with SMTP id AA11006
   (5.65c/IDA-1.4.4 for <rjs4808@ucs.usl.edu>); Thu, 13 May 1993 09:44:58 -0500
Received: by dorm.rutgers.edu (5.59/SMI4.0/RU1.5/3.08)
        id AA16336; Thu, 13 May 93 10:44:55 EDT
Message-Id: <9305131444.AA16336@dorm.rutgers.edu>
To: rjs4808@usl.edu
From: (Archie Server) archie-errors@dorm.rutgers.edu
Reply-To: (Archie Server) archie-errors@dorm.rutgers.edu
Date: Thu, 13 May 93 14:44 GMT
Subject: archie [whatis slip] part 1 of 1
Status: R




>> path rjs4808@ucs.usl.edu

>> whatis shell

DNSEmulator             Shell scripts using nslookup to simulate Domain Name
                        Service (for ping, telnet, and ftp) under SunOS.
adsh                    Adventure Shell
aff                     Inspiratiional Shell utility
ash                     Complete shell. Similar to SYS V Bourne shell
MORE FILES
xtx                     Allows placing embedded shell commands in comments
                        in other files, and then executes them
zsh                     A ksh/tcsh-like shell

>> whatis internet

RFC                     1001 Defense Advanced Research Projects Agency,
                        Internet Activities Board, End-to-End Services
                        Task Force, NetBIOS Working Group. Protocol
                        standard for a NetBIOS service on a TCP/UDP
                        transport: Concepts and methods. 1987 March; 68
                        p.
RFC                     1002        Defense Advanced Research Projects
                        Agency, Internet Activities Board, End-to-End
                        Services Task Force, NetBIOS Working Group.
                        Protocol standard for a NetBIOS service on a
                        TCP/UDP transport: Detailed specifications. 1987
                        March; 85 p.
RFC                     1009        Braden, R.T.; Postel, J.B.
                        Requirements for Internet gateways. 1987 June;
                        55 p. (Obsoletes RFC 985)
```

```
MANY MORE FILES
ntp                               Network Time Protocol. Synchronize time accross
                                  the Internet
slipware                          Serial Line IP. Internet Protocol over serial
                                  lines


>> whatis slip

RFC                               1055        Romkey, J.L. Nonstandard for
                                  transmission of IP datagrams over serial lines:
                                  SLIP. 1988 June; 6 p.
slipware                          Serial Line IP. Internet Protocol over serial
                                  lines

>> quit
```

> **Navigator's Note:** Although Archie file data is usually no more than thirty days old, the information in the Software Description Database (SDD) may be much more ancient. Worse, not all files in the Archie database will be in the SDD, and worse still, the filename given in an SDD entry may no longer exist. So if you use a `prog` command to find out where the file is, the file will not be found. Very confusing unless you're aware of the problem... which you now are.

Which Way Should I Access Archie?

Obviously, if your site has the Archie client software, you'll stand the best chance of getting service. An online session with a remote Archie server using telnet is going to give the fastest response but will be the hardest to get access to.

However, if you don't want to hang around while the search is done, an e-mail search request is the choice. E-mail is also the choice when there is no local Archie client and telnet access isn't available.

Things to Remember When Using Archie

Archie sites are popular, so don't be surprised if you do not get a connection every time you try to use one. Just like the phone system, networks have peak times of use. If possible, use Archie during off-hours.

In addition, remember to use "Internetiquette" (see Chapter 12, "Internetiquette: Manners and the Internet") and restrict your use of Archie to the server nearest your geographic area. This is because using the server nearest to you saves Internet resources by keeping traffic on the Internet to a minimum.

Also keep in mind that Archie is not infallible or even comprehensive. It is not a database of the files themselves but a database of file names, their directories, file attributes, and whatever is entered in the Software Description Database.

Navigator's Note: We keep saying to use the server geographically nearest you to save on Internet resources. That's not always correct. The SURAnet Archie server, located in Maryland, is farther away from Louisiana than the Archie server in Nebraska. Because my Internet connection goes through SURAnet, Maryland is nearer to me in *network terms* (which way the wires go). The Archie server in Maryland is the default on my Archie client. Finding out which is really your nearest server can be difficult, so picking the server geographically closest to you is your best bet. If all else fails, choose an Archie server on the same continent.

THE DATABASE OF DATABASES: WAIS

On the Internet, people have a remarkable desire to share knowledge. Why altruism should be a feature of Cyberspace is anybody's guess, but the pioneer spirit may have something to do with it. Just as the Wild West campfire always had room for a stranger (in contrast to today's urban scene), the database always has room for another terminal. One of the great tools for finding useful stuff in many databases is WAIS.

The *Wide Area Information Server* (WAIS, pronounced "ways") attempts to harness the vast data resources of the Internet by making it easy to search for and retrieve information from remote databases, called sources in WAIS terminology.

Sources are collections of files that consist mostly of textual material. For example, if chemistry is your forte, you can find several journals on the subject through WAIS. WAIS servers not only help you find the right source, they also handle your access to it.

Like Gopher, WAIS systems use the client/server model to make navigating around data resources easy. Unlike Gopher, WAIS does the searching for you. Currently, more than 420 sources are available through WAIS servers. A WAIS client (run either on your own computer or on a remote system through telnet) talks to a WAIS server and asks it to perform a search for data containing a specific word or words.

Most WAIS servers are free, which means that the data is occasionally eccentric and erratic. It can also have great gaps in coverage on some subjects and more coverage than you might believe on others. For example, you'll find tons of material in WAIS about chemistry and computer science, but sources on, say, art history or the theory of juggling are nonexistent at the moment. WAIS servers and sources are being created at a tremendous rate, however, so a library of Van Gogh's writings may yet be established (Van Gogh: 'ear today, gone tomorrow).

Navigator's Note: A long-running and busy newsgroup on the subject of juggling was established by Phil Paxton, a development editor for this book. They discuss issues like juggling patterns and how to juggle seven balls on a unicycle. As if life isn't complicated enough.

WAIS itself is simple to use, although its text-based interface is a little user-hostile. The X-windows client is much easier to use but requires that you run X-windows (of course). WAIS clients are available for Macintoshes, PCs, and even supercomputers.

What Is WAIS?

WAIS was one of the first programs to be based on the Z39.50 standard. The (take a deep breath here if you're reading aloud) American National Standard Z39.50: Information Retrieval Service Definition and Protocol Specification for Library Applications standard, revised by the National Information Standards Organization (NISO) (whew!), attempts to provide interconnection of computer systems despite differences in hardware and software.

WAIS is the first database system to use this standard, which may well become a universal data search format. All WAIS servers will be accessible to any client that uses Z39.50, and WAIS clients should be able to connect to any database that uses Z39.50.

Navigator's Note: Z39.50 is similar in some respects to Structured Query Language (SQL), but it is simplified. Although this makes it less powerful, it consequently makes it more general, so Z39.50 is likely to gain wide acceptance.

Z39.50 will be an important step in making information sources on the Internet more accessible. Today most Internet databases are accessed in ways that are completely different from each other. They use different standards for storing data and different tools to access that data. Z39.50 may well change that.

For example, one library catalog system might have `find` as its search command for a subject heading, whereas another might have `subject`. Still another might use `topic`. If they all conformed to a standard, life would be much simpler. Z39.50-compliant systems all use the same format to construct queries. You don't need to know anything special in order to search a WAIS database. You just use whatever word you think might be used in relevant documents, because WAIS indexes all the text in a source.

Document Rankings

After you run a search that identifies any documents, you will receive a list of "hits," or ranked document titles. The WAIS server ranks the hits from the most-to least-relevant document. Each document is scored, with the best-fitting document awarded 1,000 points. All other scores are relative to the top score.

WAIS ranks documents by the number of search words that occur in the document and the number of times those words appear.

WAIS servers also take into consideration the length of the document. WAIS servers are smart enough to exclude common words, called stop words, to make the search manageable. Words such as *a, about, above, across, after,* and so on should be excluded from your search, because the frequency of their appearance in most documents makes them irrelevant in most searches.

Navigator's Note: Stop words are controlled by the administrator of each WAIS server. In addition to common words in general, many words common to a database may become stop words. For example, the word *WAIS* may be a stop word in the database of a WAIS newsgroup, or the word *Internet* may be a stop word in a database of Internet protocols.

In this server, a word is a series of alphanumeric characters, possibly with some embedded punctuation. A word must start with an alphabetic character: you can't search for numbers. A word can have embedded periods, ampersands, or apostrophes, but only the first kind of punctuation that you use is treated as punctuation. Any other punctuation is interpreted as a space and ends the word. "I.M.Pei" is a valid word, and so is "AT&T," but "A.T.&T." is two words: "A.T." and "T."

Hyphens are not accepted as embedded punctuation because they're used so freely that they inflate the database dictionary.

Two classes of words are ignored in queries. First are "stop words" chosen by the database administrator for their complete lack of value in searching. There are 368 stop words for the public CM WAIS server. Some common stop words are *a, about, aren't, further, he, will, won't*—you get the idea.

Some words are just far too common to be helpful in searches. These are weeded out by the database software as the database is built. There are currently 777 "buzz words" for the public CM WAIS server, each of which occurs at least 8,000 times in the database. They include words like *able, access, account, act, action, add, added, addition, additional, address, addresses, administration*, through to *winkel* (no, I have absolutely no idea why that's in there).

Limitations

You cannot use Boolean logic in most WAIS searches. That is, you can't do anything other than find a single word or several words. A search for "cow and farm" will search for documents that contain "cow" and/or "and" and/or "farm." The "and" needs to be excluded. Notice that the search is "and/or" not just "and." The search "cow farm" will give you all documents that contain any of the following:

1. "cow" and "farm"

2. just "cow"

3. just "farm"

You can guarantee that this limitation won't always be the way of things and already there's a new version of WAIS called FREEWAIS. (Get it?…freeways? Oh, never mind.)

Also, no wildcard searching is available. This means that you can't specify that you'd accept "cows" as well as "cow."

Unlike many regular database searches, WAIS searches can't be expanded to include articles that may talk about similar topics, to retrieve all articles that have those words (for example, "cars or automobiles or trucks or motorcycles"). Neither can you exclude words in a search (for example, "cars but not trucks").

You can, however, increase the number of relevant documents by using more specific terms in a search. "car automobile crash statistics" may retrieve more pertinent documents on the subject you want.

What Is Available?

WAIS has become popular recently. The number of sources that you can search through WAIS has quadrupled in the last year—from 98 to more than 400. Many Internet newsgroups (see Chapter 13) and LISTSERVS (see Chapter 14) have taken advantage of WAIS by making their archives available through WAIS servers. Access to years of information and commentary is a valuable resource.

The sources available through WAIS are as varied as the groups that communicate over the Internet: renaissance music, beer brewing, Aesop's fables, software reviews, recipes, zip code information, a thesaurus, environmental reports, and many other databases.

The WAIS system for Thinking Machines alone gives access to over 60,000 documents, including weather maps and forecasts, the CIA World Factbook, a collection of molecular biology abstracts, Usenet's Info Mac digests, and the Connection Machine's FORTRAN manual (a must for pipe stress freaks and crystallography addicts).

The Massachusetts Institute of Technology makes a compendium of classical and modern poetry available via WAIS. The Library of Congress, which boasts 25 terabytes of data, has plans to make its catalog available via WAIS.

> **Navigator's Note:** 25 terabytes of data is, roughly, the complete text of *Alice in Wonderland* 173,980,820 times.

Thinking Machines reckons that during 1991 its public-access WAIS system handled more than 100,000 requests from more than 6,000 computer users worldwide.

Where to Get WAIS

WAIS was developed by Thinking Machines Corporation, Apple Computer, and Dow Jones, and access to the system is available free from Thinking Machines by telneting to the machine quake.think.com. You log in by typing the word WAIS and are connected to swais, the character-oriented version of WAIS. That's how we will show our examples of WAIS.

As an alternative, WAIS client software (both executable and source) is available via anonymous ftp at Thinking Machines (use the same Internet address in the pub/wais/directory). WAIS clients are available for a number of operating systems—X-windows, DOS, Macintosh, and others—but they obviously require that your computer have some kind of TCP/IP connection to the Internet.

Searching WAIS

You can access WAIS in three ways. You can telnet to quake.think.com and log in as wais, or you can run a local WAIS client. Your system administrator may have set your system so that typing WAIS will automatically connect you to whatever WAIS service is available. Another way to get to WAIS is through Gopher. You'll find an entry on Gopher menus such as "Other Gopher and Information Servers" that will lead you eventually to WAIS.

The first screen you see on WAIS is a list of the WAIS servers and sources that are available. At the time of this writing, 429 WAIS sources are available through the WAIS client at Thinking Machines, starting with aarnet-resource-guide and ending with zipcodes.

#	Server	Source	Cost
001:	[archie.au]	aarnet-resource-guide	Free
002:	[munin.ub2.lu.se]	academic_email_conf	Free
003:	[wraith.cs.uow.edu.au]	acronyms	Free
004:	[archive.orst.edu]	aeronautics	Free
005:	[bloat.media.mit.edu]	Aesop-Fables	Free
006:	[ftp.cs.colorado.edu]	aftp-cs-colorado-edu	Free
007:	[nostromo.oes.orst.ed]	agricultural-market-news	Free
008:	[archive.orst.edu]	alt.drugs	Free
009:	[wais.oit.unc.edu]	alt.gopher	Free
010:	[sun-wais.oit.unc.edu]	alt.sys.sun	Free
011:	[wais.oit.unc.edu]	alt.wais	Free
012:	[alfred.ccs.carleton.]	amiga-slip	Free
013:	[munin.ub2.lu.se]	amiga_fish_contents	Free
014:	[coombs.anu.edu.au]	ANU-Aboriginal-Studies	$0.00/minute
015:	[coombs.anu.edu.au]	ANU-Asian-Computing	$0.00/minute
016:	[coombs.anu.edu.au]	ANU-Asian-Religions	$0.00/minute

```
017:   [    coombs.anu.edu.au]  ANU-CAUT-Projects              $0.00/minute
018:   [    coombs.anu.edu.au]  ANU-French-Databanks           $0.00/minute

Keywords:

<space> selects, w for keywords, arrows move, <return> searches, q quits, or ?
```

The screen gives you a reference number for each source, the location of the WAIS server in brackets, the name of the server, and the cost of searching that library. At this time, all WAIS servers available through Thinking Machines are free.

You are now ready to conduct a search. As with Gopher, the problem is deciding which of the 429 libraries to search. An added problem is the fact that the names of the servers don't necessarily describe what they contain. Fortunately, a directory of servers is available that contains short abstracts of the contents of each server and other information about the source of the server. Until you know exactly which server you want to search, you should start with the directory of servers.

How do you get there? It looks like an alphabetical list of WAIS servers is provided, so using the arrow key will probably do the trick, but it may take a while. Using the "?" to reveal the online help that comes with this client gets you this information:

```
SWAIS                         Source Selection Help                Page:  1

  j, down arrow, ^N         Move Down one source
  k, up arrow, ^P           Move Up one source
  J, ^V, ^D                 Move Down one screen
  K, <esc> v, ^U            Move Up one screen
  ###                       Position to source number ##
  /sss                      Search for source sss
  <space>, <period>         Select current source
  =                         Deselect all sources
  v, <comma>                View current source info
  <ret>                     Perform search
  s                         Select new sources (refresh sources list)
  w                         Select new keywords
  X, -                      Remove current source permanently
  o                         Set and show swais options
  h, ?                      Show this help display
  H                         Display program history
  q                         Leave this program



Press any key to continue
```

This help screen tells you how to move through the screens of the source directory. WAIS uses UNIX editor commands for moving about (the j and J, for example, for moving down by line or by screen). Try your Page Down and arrow keys; they may work if you're using VT100 terminal emulation. The /sss is also important because it quickly moves the pointer to a source on a specific line. Also note that the space or period selects a source, and the equal sign deselects all sources.

Navigator's Note: Unless your terminal emulator does a good VT100 emulation, don't bother with swais; you'll go crazy trying to figure out what's going on.

Navigator's Note: A feature not covered in the swais help: Using the Spacebar or period on a selected source will deselect it.

It's too bad that the directory of servers isn't the first item on the list of sources. Well, you know the name, so use a forward slash with the name of the server to get there. Use /dir to get close, and after the screen is refreshed with names of new sources, use the down arrow key or type j once to highlight directory of sources.

SWAIS		Source Selection	Sources: 429
#	Server	Source	Cost
145:	[ds.internic.net]	ddbs-info	Free
146:	[irit.irit.fr]	directory-irit-fr	Free
147:	[quake.think.com]	directory-of-servers	Free
148:	[zenon.inria.fr]	directory-zenon-inria-fr	Free
149:	[zenon.inria.fr]	disco-mm-zenon-inria-fr	Free
150:	[wais.cic.net]	disi-catalog	Free
151:	[munin.ub2.lu.se]	dit-library	Free
152:	[ridgisd.er.usgs.gov]	DOE_Climate_Data	Free
153:	[wais.cic.net]	domain-contacts	Free
154:	[wais.cic.net]	domain-organizations	Free
155:	[ftp.cs.colorado.edu]	dynamic-archie	Free
156:	[wais.wu-wien.ac.at]	earlym-l	Free
157:	[bio.vu.nl]	EC-enzyme	Free
158:	[kumr.lns.com]	edis	Free
159:	[ivory.educom.edu]	educom	Free
160:	[wais.eff.org]	eff-documents	Free
161:	[wais.eff.org]	eff-talk	Free
162:	[quake.think.com]	EIA-Petroleum-Supply-Monthly	Free

Remember that you are not searching a huge database containing source materials but a database of descriptions of source databases. The terms you choose should take into consideration what the author or owner of the database would probably use to describe it. The example search uses the words wais and Z39.50 in order to find information on the NISO standard and how WAIS uses it.

WAIS takes the words wais and Z39.50 and retrieves search results that contain those words (see the following). The information is returned in ranked order—the order WAIS thinks is most likely to contain your information. The first item, scored 1000, is the one WAIS thinks is most likely to contain what you're looking for.

```
SWAIS                        Search Results                    Items: 40
   #    Score      Source                 Title                   Lines
 001:  [1000]  (directory-of-se)  cool-cfl                          76
 002:  [ 953]  (directory-of-se)  dynamic-archie                    59
 003:  [ 858]  (directory-of-se)  wais-docs                         24
 004:  [ 834]  (directory-of-se)  wais-talk-archives                18
 005:  [ 810]  (directory-of-se)  alt.wais                          18
 006:  [ 810]  (directory-of-se)  wais-discussion-archives          18
 007:  [ 691]  (directory-of-se)  cool-net                          50
 008:  [ 572]  (directory-of-se)  aftp-cs-colorado-edu             144
 009:  [ 476]  (directory-of-se)  bionic-directory-of-servers       31
 010:  [ 452]  (directory-of-se)  cicnet-wais-servers               55
 011:  [ 381]  (directory-of-se)  cool-lex                          59
 012:  [ 333]  (directory-of-se)  IUBio-INFO                        71
 013:  [ 333]  (directory-of-se)  directory-of-servers              32
 014:  [ 333]  (directory-of-se)  sample-pictures                   23
 015:  [ 333]  (directory-of-se)  utsun.s.u-tokyo.ac.jp             32
 016:  [ 309]  (directory-of-se)  journalism.periodicals            58
 017:  [ 309]  (directory-of-se)  x.500.working-group               38
 018:  [ 286]  (directory-of-se)  ANU-Theses-Abstracts              89
```

This search has resulted in some irrelevant sources. For example, cool-cfl is a database of files from a group concerned with conservation in libraries, archives, and museums. This might be a bug in WAIS—not improbable, with Internet software being developed and improved continuously.

The second source, dynamic Archie, discusses a Dynamic WAIS prototype at the University of Colorado that performs Archie searches with WAIS. This might be useful, and so might the next four sources. The rest don't seem likely to be relevant.

The information that describes the sources in WAIS is determined by the owners of the source. Some sources, such as ERIC databases, give detailed information that makes the directory of sources a valuable tool in finding out which sources are relevant. Other sources have minimal descriptions that aren't very useful or won't be found through the directory of services. They'll probably be of use only to people who know they are available in the WAIS database and will go to them directly.

From here, press the letter s to return to the sources, using /wais to select the three wais sources.

```
SWAIS                            Source Selection              Sources: 429
    #           Server                    Source                      Cost
  415: * [    quake.think.com]  wais-discussion-archives           Free
  416: * [    quake.think.com]  wais-docs                          Free
  417: * [    quake.think.com]  wais-talk-archives                 Free
  418:   [hermes.ecn.purdue.ed]  water-quality                     Free
  419:   [    quake.think.com]  weather                            Free
  420:   [    sunsite.unc.edu]  White-House-Papers                 Free
  421:   [    wais.nic.ddn.mil]  whois                             Free
  422:   [    sunsite.unc.edu]  winsock                            Free
  423:   [ cmns-moon.think.com]  world-factbook                    Free
  424:   [    quake.think.com]  world91a                           Free
  425:   [      wais.cic.net]  wuarchive                           Free
  426:   [      wais.cic.net]  x.500.working-group                 Free
  427:   [wais.unidata.ucar.ed]  xgks                              Free
  428:   [      cs.widener.edu]  zen-internet                      Free
  429:   [    quake.think.com]  zipcodes                           Free
```

You could also select the alt.wais group, but these three will work (see Chapter 13, "Views and News: USENET" to find out what alt groups are). Using Z39.50 simplifies the search; the word wais will probably be scattered throughout most of the documents, lessening its relevance to the search. To enter the search text, select the sources you want to search; you'll be prompted for keywords. After typing the keywords, press the Enter key; WAIS will search each selected source and rank the results according to their relevance.

```
SWAIS                            Search Results                 Items: 39
    #   Score     Source              Title                         Lines
  001: [1000] (      wais-docs)  z3950-spec                         2674
  002: [1000] (wais-talk-archi)  Edward Vie Re: [wald@mhuxd.att.com: more  383
  003: [1000] (wais-discussion)  Clifford L Re: The Z39.50 Protocol: Ques  325
  004: [ 939] (wais-discussion)  Brewster K Re: online version of the z39  2659
  005: [ 893] (wais-discussion)  akel@seq1. Re: Net resource list model(s  347
  006: [ 823] (      wais-docs)  waisprot                           1004
  007: [ 800] (wais-discussion)  Michael Sc Re: Dynamic WAIS prototype an   27
  008: [ 338] (wais-discussion)  harvard!ap Re: Z39.50 Product Announceme   51
  009: [ 333] (      wais-docs)  protspec                            915
  010: [ 331] (wais-discussion)  Unknown Subject                       6
  011: [ 331] (wais-discussion)  uriel wile Re: poetry server is up [most   31
  012: [ 313] (wais-talk-archi)  brewster@q Re: Re: Information about z39   69
  013: [ 313] (wais-talk-archi)  ses@cmns.t Re: Z39.50 1992          171
```

```
014:  [ 313] (wais-talk-archi)   ses@cmns.t Re: Z39.50 1992              90
015:  [ 308] (wais-discussion)   Brewster K Re: Hooking up WAIS with othe 66
016:  [ 292] (wais-discussion)   Brewster K Re: [morris@Think.COM: it's s 25
017:  [ 286] (wais-talk-archi)   mitra@pand Re: Z39.50 1992              71
018:  [ 284] (wais-discussion)   Brewster K Re: WAIS-discussion digest #6 18
```

The results look promising. The first z39.50 is ranked 1000, which looks okay. In fact, the first three seem to be relevant. The name of the information source is given, along with the title of the information. In this case, the title appears to come from e-mail message subject headings. Finally, the screen gives the number of lines contained in the information.

From here, you can read each result and have pertinent results e-mailed to yourself or even another person. At the search result screen, type the letter m to receive a prompt asking for an e-mail address. If none of the documents are relevant, you can go back to the sources and redefine the search strategies or add additional appropriate sources to search. The sample documents contain the desired information, so this search has worked.

Because WAIS in its search mode uses natural language query and searches the full text index of the source, changing any of the search words will produce different results. Using a natural language search such as how does wais use Z39.50 protocol produces the following:

```
SWAIS                         Search Results                    Items: 39
  #    Score      Source                  Title                       Lines
001:  [1000] (      wais-docs)  z3950-spec                             2674
002:  [1000] (wais-talk-archi)  Edward Vie Re: [wald@mhuxd.att.com: more 383
003:  [1000] (wais-discussion)  Michael Sc Re: Dynamic WAIS prototype an  27
004:  [ 998] (wais-discussion)  Brewster K Re: online version of the z39 2659
005:  [ 777] (wais-talk-archi)  news-mail- Re: WAIS-discussion digest #4  554
006:  [ 675] (wais-talk-archi)  news-mail- Re: WAIS-discussion digest #3  535
007:  [ 640] (wais-talk-archi)  news-mail- Re: WAIS-discussion digest #3  636
008:  [ 629] (wais-talk-archi)  brewster@t Re: WAIS-discussion digest #5  749
009:  [ 608] (wais-talk-archi)  news-mail- Re: WAIS-discussion digest #4  601
010:  [ 607] (wais-talk-archi)  fad@think. Re: WAIS Corporate Paper -- "  424
011:  [ 607] (wais-talk-archi)  composer@b Re: WAIS, A Sketch of an Over   449
012:  [ 589] (wais-talk-archi)  news-mail- Re: WAIS-discussion digest #4  621
013:  [ 549] (wais-talk-archi)  news-mail- Re: WAIS-discussion digest #3  575
014:  [ 524] (wais-talk-archi)  brewster@t Re: WAIS-discussion digest #4  682
015:  [ 515] (wais-talk-archi)  news-mail- Re: WAIS-discussion digest #3  521
016:  [ 510] (wais-talk-archi)  news-mail- Re: WAIS-discussion digest #4  480
017:  [ 507] (wais-discussion)  akel@seq1. Re: Net resource list model(s  347
018:  [ 495] (wais-discussion)  Unknown Subject                            6
```

Although many of the results are duplicates of the search using just the text Z39.50, many new documents are listed. An extensive search for all relevant documents may mean using different search strategies and a variety of WAIS source servers.

WAIS Indexing

In addition to its search features, WAIS also functions as a data indexing tool. WAIS can take large amounts of information, index it, and make the resultant Z39.50-compliant database searchable. You can build an indexed database for your own use as a stand-alone database or, if you have a TCP/IP connection, you can make your WAIS database public by registering it with think.com and getting listed in the Directory of Sources.

To obtain the WAIS software, anonymous ftp to think.com and change directory to wais. This is the main distribution site for WAIS software and WAIS documentation. Both the WAIS server code and client codes are available from think.com.

Other components available elsewhere include the following:

NeXT release: /wais/WAIStation-NeXT-1.0.tar.Z at think.com

DOS: /pub/wais/UNC/wais-dos* at sunsite.unc.edu

Motif: /public/wais/motif-a1.tar.Z at think.com

IBM RS6000: /pub/misc/wais-8-b2-dist.tar.Z at ans.net

SunView: /pub/wais/sunsearch.src.*.tar.Z at sunsite.unc.edu

VMS: /pub/wais/vms* at sunsite.unc.edu

Getting WAIS up and running is no trivial matter. Because it's very complicated, we'll leave that as an exercise for more daring users with time on their hands and a good supply of Valium.

The Ways of WAIS

WAIS use is growing rapidly on the Internet. WAIS provides a convenient and efficient way to index and search large amounts of information, using standards that are starting to be accepted as a general tool for the Internet.

Because people are getting used to the WAIS system in free public use, WAIS has commercial potential with fee-charging databases. Using what you're already familiar with is always the easiest choice.

NAVIGATING BY MENUS: GOPHER

There are things known and things unknown: in between there are doors. -Anonymous

As you look for data on the Internet, you'll start to think, "Wouldn't it be nice if files were organized into some sort of index?" If you've started mumbling to yourself like this, you'll find Gopher invaluable.

Gopher provides you with a whole series of connecting corridors and doors that will take you from one part of the Internet to another. You can use it to find data that has been classified and, in effect, published in what may well be the world's largest and most eccentric catalog.

What Is a Gopher?

Imagine the biggest library card index in the world. Unlike the card indexes you find in a library, this index isn't compiled by librarians but by people who use many different ways to organize the references to data.

Now imagine that this isn't a single card index but is distributed across hundreds of different locations, and that there are thousands of links between the separate index cards. Finally, imagine that the whole mess is electronic and distributed around the Internet. Voila! You have the Gopher system.

The Internet Gopher system was developed at the University of Minnesota and is free for nonprofit institutions (for-profit institutions can also get it free if they make their information available to the Internet community at large). The system now includes more than 300 Gopher servers and thousands of Gopher clients. It's called Gopher because you can use it to "go fer" data.

> **Navigator's Note:** The terrible pun that resulted in the name *Gopher* is the responsibility of someone at the University of Minnesota. Who is he or she? Enquiring minds want to know. The name is also derived (so they claim) not only from the University's mascot but also from the implication that the Gopher software, like the gopher animal, can burrow through the Internet to find data for you.

Gopher is a client/server system that can be used on a number of machines, including UNIX, DOS, Microsoft Windows, Macintosh, and VM, and they're planning Gophers for OS/2, Nextstep, and X Window.

The client software runs on your computer and talks to any one of the Gopher servers. If your local computer system has a Gopher server, that's probably where you will start. If not, your Gopher client can point to any Gopher server on the Internet. For example, at the University of Pittsburgh's School of Library and Information Science, typing gopher at the system prompt sends you to a Gopher in Illinois. You can also try a UNIX client by telneting to consultant.micro.umn.edu and logging in as gopher. Other public Gopher sites that enable telnet access are given in the following:

```
Non-tn3270 Public Logins:
Hostname                    IP#              Login   Area
.........................   ............     ......  ............
consultant.micro.umn.edu    134.84.132.4     Gopher  North America
Gopher.uiuc.edu             128.174.33.160   Gopher  North America
```

```
panda.uiowa.edu          128.255.40.201   panda    North America
Gopher.sunet.se          192.36.125.2     Gopher   Europe
info.anu.edu.au          150.203.84.20    info     Australia
Gopher.chalmers.se       129.16.221.40    Gopher   Sweden
tolten.puc.cl            146.155.1.16     Gopher   South America
ecnet.ec                 157.100.45.2     Gopher   Ecuador


tn3270 Public Logins:
Hostname                 IP#              Login    Area
.......................  .............    ......   ............
pubinfo.ais.umn.edu      128.101.109.1    -none-   North America
```

The client end of Gopher is a menu-driven program that enables you to select from a menu. These choices are of three types. The first type leads you to a submenu of further choices that may be on a different server than the Gopher server you're on. The second accesses local resources for data. The final type leads to a request being sent out on the network to retrieve files or yet another list of information from another Gopher server. Each Gopher server has links to other Gopher servers which, in turn, lead to further servers, and so on.

With Gopher, you can tunnel through the Internet and boldly go where no user has suspected he could go before. The way it does this is by integrating other Internet tools, such as telnet and FTP, so that once you've found an entry that relates to something you're searching for, you can go straight to it without having to find the right utility, enter the address of the target of the search, and so on. Gopher handles all that for you. Because of this, Gopher has become a very popular tool with Internet navigators.

How Gopher Works

As we've said, Gopher is a client/server system. When you install a Gopher client, you can tell it the address of your preferred Gopher server. When you start Gopher, it goes out and retrieves the menu information from the server.

The entire *Gopherspace* (the Gopher menus on all publicly accessible Gopher servers) is made up of Gopher servers located internationally. Your server stores only local information and can share information with other servers. This is very attractive to systems managers because it has a minimal impact on their systems, and they can make Gopher resources available to their users with a minimum of effort.

Getting Gopher

We've already said that you can use a Gopher client on UNIX, DOS, Macintosh, and VM systems or you can telnet to a site that has a Gopher client and run theirs.

To get your own Gopher server (don't forget that you'll need to have a TCP/IP connection to your computer to use it), you can anonymous ftp to boombox.micro.umn.edu (134.84.132.2) and look in /pub/Gopher. The following Gopher server software implementations are available there:

```
Unix      : /pub/Gopher/Unix/Gopherxx.tar.Z
VMS       : /pub/Gopher/VMS/
Macintosh : /pub/Gopher/Mac_server/
VM/CMS    : /pub/Gopher/Rice_CMS/ or /pub/Gopher/Vienna_CMS/
MVS       : /pub/Gopher/mvs/
DOS PC    : /pub/Gopher/PC_server/
```

You can also find Gopher clients for the following systems. The directory following the name is the location of the client on the anonymous FTP site boombox.micro.umn.edu (134.84.132.2) in the directory /pub/Gopher.

```
Unix Curses & Emacs   :  /pub/Gopher/Unix/Gopher1.03.tar.Z
Xwindows              :  /pub/Gopher/Unix/xGopher1.1a.tar.Z
Macintosh Hypercard   :  /pub/Gopher/Mac_client/
Macintosh Application :  /pub/Gopher/Macintosh-TurboGopher
DOS w/Clarkson Driver :  /pub/Gopher/PC_client/
Nextstep              :  /pub/Gopher/NeXT/
VM/CMS                :  /pub/Gopher/Rice_CMS/
          or             /pub/Gopher/Vienna_CMS/
VMS                   :  /pub/Gopher/VMS/
OS/2 2.0              :  /pub/Gopher/os2/
MVS/XA                :  /pub/Gopher/mvs/
```

This list changes frequently as new implementations are released. Many other clients and servers have been developed by others:

A Macintosh application, "MacGopher," at

ftp.cc.utah.edu:/pub/Gopher/Macintosh

Another Macintosh application, "GopherApp," at

ftp.bio.indiana.edu:/util/Gopher/Gopherapp

A port of the UNIX Curses client for DOS with PC/TCP at

oac.hsc.uth.tmc.edu:/public/dos/misc/dosGopher.exe

A port of the UNIX Curses client for PC-NFS at

bcm.tmc.edu:/nfs/Gopher.exe

A version of the PC Gopher client for Novell's LAN Workplace for DOS at

`lennon.itn.med.umich.edu:/Gopher`

An Xwindows/DECwindows client at

`job.acs.ohio-stat.edu`

Installing Gopher

Installation is straightforward. The PC version is well-documented, but help and information from your systems administrator will probably be required.

> **Navigator's Note:** Remember that you need to have a TCP/IP connection to your computer to run a Gopher client or server directly.

On installation, you need to provide some information about your network. You'll have to tell the Gopher client where to find a name server (a computer on the Internet that takes an Internet name like boombox.micro.umn.edu and turns it into an address that can be used by computers, such as 134.84.132.2), and you will need to know details about the gateway that takes you out of your local area network to the big, wide world.

The PC version of Gopher runs under DOS version 3.3 or greater and requires 640K of conventional memory. Gopher will run on a wide range of IBM PCs and compatibles, including the earliest PCs, which contain only a monochrome display adapter without graphics support.

A Microsoft-compatible mouse is useful but optional. You must load mouse driver software before running Gopher. If your mouse contains more than one mouse button, you should use only the left mouse button when running Gopher.

Using Gopher

Let's take a look at Gopher. I'm running the UNIX Curses version of Gopher on my Sun UNIX machine, but most of the character-oriented systems look pretty much the same. I start Gopher by typing gopher at my system prompt and pressing Enter. I then receive the following screen:

```
Internet Gopher Information Client v1.01

                Root gopher server: rouge.usl.edu

—>  1.  CAMPUS INFORMATION SYSTEM - USL GOPHER/
    2.  GOPHER System - All Other Locations/
    3.  Information About Gopher/
    4.  Libraries/
    5.  News/
    6.  Phone Books/
    7.  Weather Louisiana/
    8.  Weather US/
    9.  Weather World/
   10.  X-perimental Services/
   11.  Y-perimental Services/
```

On this particular system at the University of Southwestern Louisiana, we have 11 options. The topics are customized on this Gopher (as they are on most Gophers) to present choices that are relevant to the local site.

Here we have options for local weather (in Louisiana) and information about the USL GOPHER. The adaptability of the Gopher system is one of its most useful features. Take a look at the following examples of the variety of local information on four different Gophers.

```
Internet Gopher Information Client v1.01

                Cornell University HelpDesk

—>  1.  *About CIT HelpDesk's Gopher.
    2.  *CIT services and information/
    3.  Bear Access information/
    4.  CIT Mother Gopher/
    5.  CMS information/
    6.  Computing at Cornell/
    7.  Internet information/
    8.  Mac information/
    9.  Multi-platform information/
   10.  Network ID Info.
   11.  PC information/
   12.  Phone books for Cornell and elsewhere/
   13.  Statistical information/
   14.  Unix information/
```

Cornell's Gopher system is very service-oriented. It will lead you to critical local support services and has a rather technically oriented set of choices.

```
Internet Gopher Information Client v1.01

    National Institute of Standards and Technology (NIST)

—> 1.  —*—  WARNING: NIST Gopher Server Access Restriction —*—.
    2.  Using the NIST Gopher Server/
    3.  Networks and Services at NIST (DIV 885)/
    4.  Applied and Computational Mathematics at NIST (DIV 881)/
    5.  Systems and Software Technology (DIV 872)/
    6.  NIST Organizational Activities (Reserved)/
    7.  NIST Phone Book and Email Directory <CSO>
    8.  Other Information Servers Around the World/
```

The National Institute of Standards and Technology's Gopher reflects what they do. This is a very formal kind of look and very much focused on information rather than services.

```
Internet Gopher Information Client v1.01

    Whole Earth 'Lectronic Magazine - The WELL's Gopherspace

—> 1.  About this gopherspace.
    2.  See the latest additions to this gopherspace/
    3.  Art and Culture/
    4.  Communications/
    5.  Community/
    6.  Cyberpunk/
    7.  Grateful Dead/
    8.  The Military, its People, Policies and Practices/
    9.  Environmental Issues and Ideas/
   10.  Politics/
   11.  Publications (includes Zines like FactSheet 5)/
   12.  Sci-Fi Stuff/
   13.  Science/
   14.  The WELL Itself/
   15.  Tools/
   16.  Whole Earth Review, the Magazine/
   17.  Whole Systems/
```

The above list is a much more hip kind of Gopher. The Well is inhabited by all sorts of people-writers, journalists, and lots of people in the computer business. Cyberpunk is certainly not an item you'd expect to find on NIST's menu.

```
              Internet Gopher Information Client v1.01

                 Ecole Normale Superieure (Paris, France)
—>    1.  annuaire de l'ENS <TEL>
      2.  serveur FTP de l'ENS (ftp.ens.fr)/
      3.  Bibliotheque du DMI <?>
      4.  DMI (Departement de Mathematiques et Informatique)/
      5.  veronica (Search menu titles in GopherSpace)/
      6.  Autres serveurs gopher/
      7.  Bibliotheques/
      8.  FTP/
      9.  Maths/
     10.  Netfind  <TEL>
     11.  Phone Books and WHOIS Searches/
     12.  Search High-Level Gopher Menu by JUGHEAD at W&L <?>
     13.  users/
```

Ah! Ici le menu pour un Gopher Francais (please don't write to complain about my lousy French). Gophers are now being used worldwide because they offer such a simple way of organizing resources.

You can see that they all offer different data, much of which is based on local interests. You'll also notice that the Gopher entries have different formats. Some end with a / and others end in .. The / indicates that selecting this entry will lead you to another menu of options. The . means that if you select that choice, a file will be accessed using an appropriate utility. For example, if the file is a remote text file, Gopher runs FTP for you and connects to the server the file is on and retrieves it for you.

Navigator's Note: These links to FTP are probably the simplest way for novice navigators to transfer files—all the work is done for you! And even for an expert, this makes life a lot easier.

You will also see a third type of ending, <?>. This indicates that the entry leads to an index search server, and if it is selected, you will be asked for a keyword or keywords. Gopher will search for those words and return appropriate information.

Other types of information are available through Gopher. The type characters will have different notations depending on the Gopher client you use. The following table lists the alphanumeric codes for the type characters available through Gopher.

Normal IDs	Description
0	Item is a file.
1	Item is a directory.
2	Item is a CSO (qi) phonebook server. This leads you to a "white pages" type of directory service so that you can find people on the Internet.
3	Error.
4	Item is a BinHexed Macintosh file. This will be meaningful to you if you are a Macintosh user. If you don't have a Mac, you probably couldn't care less about these entries.
5	Item is DOS binary archive of some sort. This includes .ZIP, .ARC, .ZOO, and all the other types of file archive systems available.
6	Item is a UNIX uuencoded file. These files can be opened by PCs as long as you have a copy of the uudecode utility.
7	Item is an Index-Search server. The item takes you to a database search.
8	Item points to a text-based telnet session.
9	Item is a binary file that is going to be sent to you if you choose this option. You will receive data until the connection closes. This could cause you all sorts of problems unless you're set up to handle the incoming data in a sensible way. Beware.
T	A tn3270 connection to a service (requires a screen emulation of an IBM 3270 terminal for your screen to make any sense at all).

Experimental IDs	Description
s	Sound type. The data that you'll get is sound-encoded to a standard called mulaw.
g	This is a picture of GIF type.
M	The item contains data of the MIME type. This is a special format for electronic mail that supports not only text but also sound and even video.

See the examples later in this chapter for instances of these IDs.

An Example: Searching for Materials

In our first example, I will go to a library to search for bibliographic materials for the class I will be teaching. I don't need to remember the Internet address of the library I want to telnet to, because it is conveniently stored in Gopher. I just move the arrow on the left of the screen using the cursor keys and select `library Catalogs via Telnet/` from the menu.

```
    Internet Gopher Information Client v1.01

                        Libraries

        1.   Electronic Books/
        2.   Electronic Journal collection from CICnet/
        3.   Information from the U.S. Federal Government/
   ->   4.   Library Catalogs via Telnet/
        5.   Library of Congress Records/
        6.   Newspapers, Magazines, and Newsletters/
        7.   Reference Works/


   Press ? for Help, q to Quit, u to go up a menu        Page: 1/1]
```

This library menu gives several options. Electronic books, newspapers, and reference books can be obtained from this menu. The option I want is `Library Catalogs via Telnet`, so I select it to get this menu:

```
    Internet Gopher Information Client v1.01

                   Library Catalogs via Telnet

      1.   Libraries of the University of Minnesota Integrated Network Access <TEL
      2.   Libraries of the University of Minnesota Integrated Network Access
   -> 3.   Library Catalogs at Other Institutions/
```

Going through Gopherspace may lead us down some strange paths. Here is a screen of menus that I would prefer to bypass. Later, I'll show how that can be done. For now, I select the third item `Library Catalogs at Other Institutions`.

```
    Internet Gopher Information Client v1.01

                        Americas

        1.   Canada/
        2.   Mexico/
        3.   PuertoRico/
   ->   4.   United States/
        5.   Venezuela/
```

This Gopher system gives me a listing of countries to select from (see, the Internet really is an international network after all). I select the United States and get a menu which lists all 50 states. I then select Pennsylvania and the University of Pittsburgh. I'm going to teach in Pittsburgh this summer, and I want to see if the University of Pittsburgh's library will have the reading materials that I want to use in my course.

```
        Internet Gopher Information Client v1.01

                        Pennsylvania

        19. Lehigh <TEL>
        20. Lehigh.
        21. Pennsylvania State University <TEL>
        22. Pennsylvania State University.
        23. Thomas Jefferson University.
        24. Thomas Jefferson University <TEL>
        25. Tri-College <TEL>
        26. Tri-College (Swarthmore, Bryn Mawr, Haverford).
        27. University of Pennsylvania <TEL>
        28. University of Pennsylvania.
        29. University of Pennsylvania Law School <TEL>
        30. University of Pennsylvania Law School.
        31. University of Pennsylvania Medical School.
        32. University of Pennsylvania Medical School <TEL>
  -->   33. University of Pittsburgh.
        34. University of Pittsburgh <TEL>
```

Notice that the University of Pittsburgh has two listings. The first choice, number 33, has a description of the University of Pittsburgh's online library catalog. It also has information about the library collection and how to access it. The second choice of the University of Pittsburgh, number 34, with the <TEL> notation beside it, is the one I want. It will get me connected to the University of Pittsburgh's online library catalog.

I select number 34, and Gopher sends me there (through the Gopher system) without having to remember or type in the University of Pittsburgh's Internet address. Here are the results if you use the two University of Pittsburgh selections. Note that the telnet connection used here is actually a gateway to the University of Pittsburgh. I could also go to Carnegie Mellon University or Pittsburgh's Carnegie Public Library:

```
To exit, hit CTRL+\.

Contacts: <jam2@vms.cis.pitt.edu>

Notes:
        PITTCAT is the University of Pittsburgh's online library catalog.
PITTCAT currently contains bibliographic information for over 1.4 million
titles in all University of Pittsburgh libraries including the Hillman Library
(humanities & social sciences), Afro-American, Buhl (Social Work), East Asian,
Allegheny Observatory, Business, Chemistry, Computer Science, Darlington
Memorial, Engineering, Fine Arts, Langley, Library and Information Science,
Mathematics, Music, Physics, Public and International Affairs/Economics, Falk
Library of the Health Sciences, Learning Resource Center (Nursing), Law,
Western Psychiatric Institute and Clinic, and the regional campus libraries at
Bradford, Greensburg, Johnstown, and Titusville.
——————————— PittNet Terminal Gateway Services ———————————

     Service                    Description

     CAROLINE     The Carnegie Library of Pittsburgh's on-line library catalog
     CMULIS       Carnegie-Mellon University's on-line library catalog
     CPWSCA       Pittsburgh Supercomputing Center front end A
     CPWSCB       Pittsburgh Supercomputing Center front end B
     CTERM        CCnet hosts via the DECnet (CTERM) protocol
     ISISINFO     Integrated Student Information Services Access
     LAT          DECserver (LAT) services
     PITTCAT      University of Pittsburgh's on-line library catalog
     PSCYMP       Pittsburgh Supercomputing Center Cray Y/MP
     TELNET       Hosts via TCP/IP (TELNET) protocol
     TN3270       Hosts via TCP/IP (TN3270) protocol


Instructions: Type the desired SERVICE name below and press RETURN.

              If a "Password:" prompt appears, the service name you requested
              was invalid or private; press RETURN twice and retry.

Service:
```

This is the beauty of Gopher. It knows the addresses of hundreds of useful resources, and through it I have access to information about the holdings of hundreds of libraries around the world to help me in my studies, research, and business.

Advanced Gophering

That was straightforward and simple. Now let's look at other services and features of the Gopher program. One of the first things to consider is the concept of Gopherspace. When we select choices that lead us to other Gopher locations, we are moving into Gopherspace-the collection of all choices offered by all Gopher systems.

Gophers point to each other so that local information pointed to by the University of Southwestern Louisiana's Gopher—for example, course curricula and sports events—can also be accessed by other Gophers. This means that you can find information about the local environments of other Gophers by selecting them through the 2. GOPHER System All Other Locations/ on your Gopher menu. On my system, this choice shows me the following:

```
        Internet Gopher Information Client v1.01

              All the Gopher Servers in the World

  ->  1.  Search Gopherspace using Veronica/
      2.  ACADEME THIS WEEK (Chronicle of Higher Education)/
      3.  ACM SIGGRAPH/
      4.  ACTLab (UT Austin, RTF Dept)/
      5.  Academic Position Network/
      6.  Alamo Community College District/
      7.  American Mathematical Society /
      8.  American Physiological Society/
      9.  Anesthesiology Gopher /
     10.  Appalachian State University (experimental gopher)/
     11.  Apple Computer Higher Education gopher server/
     12.  Arabidopsis Research Companion, Mass Gen Hosp/Harvard/
     13.  Arizona State University Gopher/
     14.  AskERIC - (Educational Resources Information Center)/
     15.  Auburn University test gopher/
     16.  Augusta College/
     17.  Austin Hospital, Melbourne, Australia/
     18.  Australian Defence Force Academy (Canberra)
```

This display indicates a problem that we'll have when we are searching for something. Using the 2. GOPHER System All Other Locations/, I see a listing of 18 Gopher sites, and the list isn't finished. At the time of this writing, a total of 471 Gopher systems are registered around the world (up from 364 in a span of a month). That is the reason that the first choice is 1. Search Gopherspace using Veronica/.

Unless you know specifically which Gopher server you want to access, you'll be much better off using another service, Veronica, to find out where to go (see the following). Browsing the more than 1,300 Gopher sites may be okay (if you have a lot of time on your hands or you want to satisfy your curiosity), but it's not very efficient or effective if you're trying to find data. So let's take a break here and talk about another service that Gopher has links to—Veronica.

Navigator's Note: As of June 5th, 1993, there were over 1,300 registered and unregistered Gophers in the world. Unregistered Gophers are ones which have not yet officially informed the University of Minnesota (the originators of Gopher) of their existence. Of those 1,300 Gophers, only 520 are actually registered. Registration doesn't really matter other than the fact that you can't get to the unregistered ones through the University of Minnesota and they may therefore be hard to find.

Veronica

Veronica, short for Very Easy Rodent-Oriented Net-wide Index to Computerized Archives, was developed to solve the problem that we just discussed—with so much information available on so many machines, how do I know which one has the information I need?

Veronica helps to solve this problem by making a keyword search of most menus on most of the Gopher servers in Gopherspace. Hundreds of Gopher server menus are canvassed to create an index much as Archie does when it creates the database of files and directories from anonymous FTP sites (see Chapter 6, "Finding Files: Archie"). The reason that I say "most menus on most Gopher servers" is that some Gophers can ask to be excluded from Gopherspace.

Developed at the University of Nevada, Veronica is used exclusively with Gopher as an enhancement that helps you find information more effectively. Veronica allows you to search the database it constructs from all Gopher menus it can access. It returns a menu of choices to you gathered from all sites that have menu choices containing the keywords. When you select a choice from a Veronica-created menu, you are automatically sent to the Gopher server that the choice came from.

The Veronica database is updated every two weeks. It will most likely be updated more frequently in the future.

> **Navigator's Note:** Not everything will work as you zoom around in Gopherspace. Downed machines and forbidden machines are two major stumbling blocks. Occasionally, incompatibilities will also make menu items misbehave when they're selected.

When I select search Gopherspace using Veronica, I receive the following screen:

```
        Internet Gopher Information Client v1.01

                Search Gopherspace using Veronica

 —>  1.   Search gopherspace using veronica at CNIDR <?>
     2.   Search gopherspace for GOPHER DIRECTORIES  (CNIDR) <?>
     3.   Search gopherspace using veronica at NYSERNet <?>
     4.   Search gopherspace for GOPHER DIRECTORIES  (NYSERNet) <?>
     5.   Search gopherspace using veronica at UNR <?>
     6.   Search gopherspace for GOPHER DIRECTORIES  (UNR) <?>
     7.                                                     .
     8.   How to compose "simple boolean" veronica queries ( NEW May 19 ).
     9.   FAQ:  Frequently-Asked Questions about veronica  (1993/05/15).
    10.   Setting up a veronica server:  new code available .
    11.   NEW_FEATURE:__Search_by_Gopher_type.
    12.   Older_veronica_documentation/
```

This screen lists three Veronica servers that the public can use to search for information stored by Gophers around the world. The servers are divided into two parts. One is Gopherspace generic and the second is Gopherspace for *Gopher directories*. The difference is that Gopher directories will search only the directories of Gophers and will return only directories. The generic search will return not only directories but also information stored in the Gopher indexed servers, which could be text files, binary files, sound files, telnet connections, and all the other different items Gopher can access.

Maybe an example will elucidate. Selecting 4. `Search Gopherspace for GOPHER DIRECTORIES (NYSERNet) <?>` and using the keyword commerce, Veronica returns the following screen:

```
Internet Gopher Information Client v1.01


   Search gopherspace for GOPHER DIRECTORIES  (NYSERNet): commerce

—>  1.  HF  Commerce/
    2.  381  Internal commerce/
    3.  380  Commerce, communications, transportation/
    4.  382  International commerce (Foreign trade)/
    5.  382.1  Generalities of international commerce/
    6.  Commerce / Management / Law Reading Room/
    7.  Commerce  (Restricted Access)/
    8.  Department-of-Commerce/
    9.  Department of Commerce/
    10. Commerce to Statistics/
    11. Faculty of Commerce (organizationalUnit)/
    12. Faculty of Commerce (organizationalUnit)/
    13. Commerce (organizationalUnit)/
    14. Faculty of Economics and Commerce (organizationalUnit)/
    15. Faculty of Commerce and Administration (organizationalUnit)/
    16. FACULTY OF ECONOMICS AND COMMERCE (organizationalUnit)/
    17. Economics, Commerce and Management, Faculty of (organizationalUni/
    18. Faculty of Economics and Commerce Office (organizationalUnit)/
```

The / at the end of each line means that these are directory listings and each item has further menus beneath it. In the bottom-right corner, we can tell that two pages of information are available.

If we search for the word commerce using the menu item 3. `Search Gopherspace using veronica at NYSERNet <?>`, the results of the search will show the differences in the two search databases.

```
Internet Gopher Information Client v1.01


    Search gopherspace using veronica at NYSERNet: commerce

—>  1.  HF  Commerce/
    2.  Commerce Business Daily Available Online.
    3.  The Commerce Business Daily publishes, for Federal agencies, syno.
    4.  58 FR 4736:Commerce in Explosives; List of Explosive Materials.
    5.  58 FR 21925:Revisions to the Commerce Control List: Equipment Rel.
    6.  58 FR 9183:Commerce Bancshares, Inc; Formations of; Acquisitions .
    7.  58 FR 6574:Administrative Exceptions and Favorable Consideration .
    8.  58 FR 3800:Economic Development Assistance Programs as Described .
```

```
 9.  REPORT TO NEW ZEALAND CHAMBERS OF COMMERCE.
10.  COMMERCE AT OTAGO, 1912-1987.  ABRIDGED ED..
11.  Ships of commerce: liners, tankers, freighters, tu.
12.  381   Internal commerce/
13.  380   Commerce, communications, transportation/
14.  382   International commerce (Foreign trade)/
15.  THE COMMERCE ACT 1975.
16.  382.1  Generalities of international commerce/
17.  C.  H.B. Commerce - Year 3.
18.  D.  H.B. Commerce - Year 4.
```

Seven pages of information are returned, representing not only directories, as noted by the /, but also text files set off with the . at the end of the line. The reason is that the search extended beyond Gopher directories and searched indexed Gophers that include text and other files.

Here's another example. I'm interested in what is in Gopherspace concerning Acquired Immunodeficiency Syndrome, or AIDS. I'll search both the Gopher directories and the general Gopher. Here are the results:

```
    Internet Gopher Information Client v1.01

        Search gopherspace for GOPHER DIRECTORIES  (NYSERNet): aids

  —> 1.  AIDS News/
     2.  AIDS Alert/
     3.  Stanford Financial Aids Student Employment (to post jobs)/
     4.  University of Delaware Library Special Collections Finding Aids/
     5.  REFERENCE  Library Reference Questions/Aids/
     6.  CDC AIDS Statistics, other useful info/
     7.  Veterans Administration AIDS Information Newsletter/
     8.  AIDS Related Information/
     9.  National Commission on AIDS/
    10.  National AIDS Info Clearinghouse/
    11.  Humanities Research Center - finding aids for manuscripts/
    12.  Aids Alert/
    13.  Consultant Aids/
    14.  Audio-Visual Aids & Cassettes/
    15.  AIDS Information System for 3rd World/
    16.  Human Retrovirus & AIDS (HIV) Rel.3.0; May 1992/
    17.  aids/
    18.  Curing.Aids/
```

Let's check out item number 1, AIDS News/:

```
Internet Gopher Information Client v1.01

        Search gopherspace using veronica at NYSERNet: aids

—>  1.  Also Seen:  Grmek, Mirko, History of Aids (L. Pearcy) .
     2.  AIDS News/
     3.  AIDS Alert/
     4.  aids.txt.
     5.  BAD-Pamphlet-AIDS.
     6.  About Special Collections Finding Aids.
     7.  Financial Aids Office.
     8.  58 FR 17164:Housing Opportunities for Persons With AIDS; Correcti.
     9.  58 FR 26684:Indirect Food Additives: Adjuvants, Production Aids, .
    10.  58 FR 17514:Indirect Food Additives: Adjuvants, Production Aids, .
    11.  58 FR 17512:Indirect Food Additives: Adjuvants, Production Aids, .
    12.  58 FR  6127:Housing Opportunities for Persons with AIDS Program; A.
    13.  58 FR 5410:Announcement of Allocations for Housing Opportunities .
    14.  58 FR 17595:Pediatric Acquired Immune Deficiency Syndrome (AIDS);.
    15.  58 FR 17512:Indirect Food Additives: Adjuvants, Production Aids, .
    16.  58 FR 3962:National Institute of Allergy and Infectious Diseases;.
    17.  a Audio RX Hearing Aids; Proposed Consent Agreement With Analysis.
    18.  ..AIDS Epidemic: Meeting.
```

Searching the Gopher directories gives me 2 pages of information, while searching all of Gopherspace gives me 21 pages of information. Not all the information retrieved will be relevant: the last example had information on "hearing aids" and "financial aid," which may not have anything to do with Acquired Immunodeficiency Syndrome.

The searching of Gopher directories can be a powerful tool in finding information throughout the Internet. As with the two examples, if the search is kept simple, you may find some interesting directories in Gopherspace that you can then explore to find additional information. You can also save the directories that you find interesting into your own personal Gopher menu for future references (a bookmark-more on that later).

Searching Gopherspace in general will bring you not only directories, but information in the form of text and other files. It is more comprehensive, and because of that you may want to be more specific in your searching of Gopherspace.

Veronica enables Boolean searching. That is, you can expand your search by adding additional phrases with an or in your keyword search. I can get additional directories to our earlier example by searching for commerce or business.

```
         Internet Gopher Information Client v1.01

Search gopherspace for GOPHER DIRECTORIES   (NYSERNet): commerce or business

 -> 1.  HF  Commerce/
    2.  business/
    3.  business-news/
    4.  Business and Finance (APM A8.010-A8.852)/
    5.  Business Affairs Circulars (Computers)/
    6.  381  Internal commerce/
    7.  380  Commerce, communications, transportation/
    8.  382  International commerce (Foreign trade)/
    9.  382.1  Generalities of international commerce/
    10. School of Business Admin/
    11. Israel_Business_Today/
    12. Center for International Business Education and Research/
    13. College of Business and Economics/
    14. CBE      College of Business & Economics Speakers/
    15. Business/
    16. Business/
    17. Korean Business and Management/
    18. Asia Pacific Business & Marketing Resources/
```

On the other hand, if I want to limit my search on AIDS, I can use the Boolean operator and and search for AIDS and research. This will retrieve items with both words in them and possibly get me material on research of Acquired Immuno-deficiency Syndrome. This is particularly useful if you know that both words will appear in the title of the directory or in the text of an indexed file.

```
      Internet Gopher Information Client v1.01

       Search gopherspace using veronica at CNIDR: aids and research

 -> 1.   58 FR 3962:National Institute of Allergy and Infectious Diseases;.
    2.   Humanities Research Center - finding aids for manuscripts/
    3.   PA-92-52 INTERNATIONAL AIDS EPIDEMIOLOGY RESEARCH.
    4.   PA-93-013 NIH LOAN REPAYMENT PROGRAM FOR AIDS RESEARCH.
    5.   PA-93-055 NIH LOAN REPAYMENT PROGRAM FOR AIDS RESEARCH.
    6.   P2: PA-92-52 INTERNATIONAL AIDS EPIDEMIOLOGY RESEARCH.
    7.   P2: PA-93-013 NIH LOAN REPAYMENT PROGRAM FOR AIDS RESEARCH.
    8.   NIH-NHLBI-HB-92-01 MAINTENANCE OF CHIMPANZEES FOR HEPATITIS OR AI.
    9.   P1: PA-93-055 NIH LOAN REPAYMENT PROGRAM FOR AIDS RESEARCH.
    10.  R14: NIH-NHLBI-HB-92-01 MAINTENANCE OF CHIMPANZEES FOR HEPATITIS .
    11.  PA-91-95 INDIVIDUAL NATIONAL RESEARCH SERVICE AWARDS IN ALLERGY, .
    12.  P1: PA-91-95 INDIVIDUAL NATIONAL RESEARCH SERVICE AWARDS IN ALLER.
```

The Boolean operator not is not supported as of this writing, but you can specify what type of data or Gopher object is returned in your search.

This is useful if you receive many items from your Gopher search that are not relevant or useful for your needs. For example, I've found that many of the telnet sites that I retrieve in my searches require the use of a login and password for access. I did not have that information. I can specify the Gopher object I want by the -t flag when I do my search.

For example, using aids -t01 will return links to Gopher files and directories with the word aids in the title (the 0 equals a file and the 1 equals a directory). Using -t8 business or commerce will return only telnet links with the words business or commerce in the title. The -t flag may appear anywhere in the keyword search.

In general, when searching Veronica, you will want to use a general search rather than a specific search until you know that what you want will be retrieved by a specific search.

You may want unemployment statistics, yet searching by the two words will net you only one Gopher link. That is because Veronica does not have a subject index, and the words statistics and unemployment must appear in the title or be indexed in an indexed Gopher. Using the single word unemployment will retrieve many irrelevant Gopher links, but it will also get you additional unemployment statistics that may meet your information needs.

Navigator's Note: While Veronica has no subject index per se, you can use it and Gopher to browse by subject, simply by using one of several key words described in the next section.

Searching by Subjects

There are now more than 1,000 Gophers in Gopherspace—three times the number that existed just six months before this writing. That can be a little daunting to those who know the type of information they're browsing for, but not the names of the Gophers likely to have it.

Some Gopher server institutions understand you. They like you, and they want to help you. They've gone to the extra trouble of developing menus of Gopher sites by subject or discipline. When you're hunting down data on a specific topic, you need only choose that subject area to find a list of sites that carry what you crave. Most of these subject area Gophers are maintained by academic institutions, so the data available is heavily slanted toward what such sites typically provide. But the list is expanding beyond schools.

How the subject lists are updated and arranged depends on the institution that controls the list. You may want to look at several different subject area Gophers to find the one that is best suited to your needs. An academic subject menu at one institution—"Engineering," for example, won't contain the same stuff as another institution's "Engineering" menu. So shop around.

A Sample Gopher Subject Search

To get a feel for Gopher subject area menus, you could try searching Veronica using the term subject trees.

Here's what I got:

```
                Internet Gopher Information Client v1.11

              Search gopherspace at NYSERNet: subject trees

 —>  1.  Class 13: Subject Trees and Study Carrels.
     2.  Class 13: Subject Trees and Study Carrels.
     3.  Gophers With Subject Trees/
     4.  Gophers With Subject Trees/
     5.  List of Gopher subject trees added to gopher.msu.edu.
     6.  Subject trees and study carrols.
     7.  #13 Subject Trees and Study Carrels.
     8.  Subject Trees - fachspezifische Sammlungen/
     9.  Other Collections of Subject Trees/
    10.  Other Subject Trees (Europe)/
    11.  Other Subject Trees (Germany)/
    12.  Other Humanities Subject Trees/
    13.  Other Subject Trees (Worldwide)/
    14.  Subject Trees and Study Carrels.
    15.  Subject trees/
    16.  Subject Trees (Gopherspace ordered by subject)/
    17.  Subject trees, other inform. systems, Internet resource classifica../
    18.  Gopher-Kurs Teil 13, Subject Trees and Study Carrels.

Press ? for Help, q to Quit, u to go up a menu          Page: 1/2
```

Two pages contain the words *subject trees*. The first page looks promising, because it shows subject trees themselves being categorized. Some trees are listed under other subjects, such as 12. Other Humanities Subject Trees, which should lead to a page listing subject trees. Internet's global personality shows up in the listings of Gophers by geographic area (see choices 10, 11 and 13).

I'll hit number 3, `Gophers With Subject Trees/`.

```
              Internet Gopher Information Client v1.11

                     Gophers With Subject Trees

        1.   AMI — A Friendly Public Interface/
        2.   Australian Defence Force Academy (Canberra, Australia)/
        3.   Go M-Link/
        4.   Internet Wiretap/
        5.   Library of Congress (LC MARVEL)/
        6.   Michigan State University/
        7.   North Carolina State University Library gopher/
   —>   8.   RiceInfo (Rice University CWIS)/
        9.   Texas A&M/
       10.   University of California - Irvine/
       11.   University of California - Santa Barbara Library/
       12.   University of California - Santa Cruz, InfoSlug System/
       13.   University of Michigan Libraries/
       14.   University of Nevada/
       15.   University of South Carolina Gopher Server/
       16.   Washington & Lee University/
       17.   Whole Earth 'Lectronic Magazine - The WELL's Gopherspace/



Press ? for Help, q to Quit, u to go up a menu            Page: 1/1
```

Here you'll find one page of Gopher items that have subject trees. Remember that the previous screen had other listings of Gophers with subject trees. This is just one of many menus that list recommended Gophers.

As it turns out, choice 8, `RiceInfo (Rice University CWIS)`, is an endorsed Gopher. Let's look there.

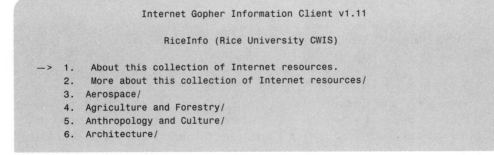

```
              Internet Gopher Information Client v1.11

                   RiceInfo (Rice University CWIS)

   —>   1.    About this collection of Internet resources.
        2.    More about this collection of Internet resources/
        3.    Aerospace/
        4.    Agriculture and Forestry/
        5.    Anthropology and Culture/
        6.    Architecture/
```

```
    7.  Arts/
    8.  Astronomy and Astrophysics/
    9.  Biology/
   10.  Census/
   11.  Chemistry/
   12.  Computer Networks and Internet Resource Guides/
   13.  Computing/
   14.  Economics and Business/
   15.  Education/
   16.  Engineering/
   17.  Environment and Ecology/
   18.  Geography/

Press ? for Help, q to Quit, u to go up a menu              Page: 1/3
```

Rice University has developed this subject area Gopher to help its students hunt down data by topic. There are three pages of subject listings in Rice's subject Gopher, listed alphabetically for easy browsing.

I'll check out what's behind the first item, About this collection of Internet resources.

```
These directories contain links to resources organized by subject
matter.  The resources themselves are scattered all over the Internet.
They may be unavailable at any time due to many factors beyond our
control.

The selection of resources you see here is based on several similar
collections of such links maintained on Gopher servers at the following
places:

    Consortium for International Earth Science Information Network
        (CIESIN, flubber.ciesin.org)
    Mass. General Hospital, Harvard University (weeds.mgh.harvard.edu)
    North Carolina State University (dewey.lib.ncsu.edu)
    SLU, Sweden (pinus.slu.se)
    SUNET, Sweden (sunic.sunet.se)
    Texas A&M University (tamuts.tamu.edu)
    The WELL (nkosi.well.sf.ca.ua)
    University of Nevada at Reno (hunter.unr.edu)
    UCSC InfoSlug (scilibx.ucsc.edu)
    ... plus a few specialized collections from other places.

Once a week we merge selected directories of links at these
institutions into our own collections of links.  To see how we do this,
look in the subdirectory "More about this collection of Internet
resources".
```

```
If you know of other collections of Internet resources organized by
subject matter which we should merge in a similar fashion, please send
mail to "riceinfo@rice.edu".

In the future we plan to add our own local resources to these menus.
If you have information in any of these subject areas which you would
like to make available, please send mail to "riceinfo@rice.edu".

                         — Prentiss Riddle (riddle@rice.edu) 9/7/93
```

This Gopher gathers together materials gleaned from other Gopher resources on the Internet. Rice University promises to contribute to the Internet community by adding local resources to these menus. The value of the local information can probably be determined by the number of other Gophers in gopherspace that pick up Rice's local items in their Gopherspace.

Browsing Beyond Gopher

Let's dig deeper into the subject tree. Because we're using a Gopher, you could say we'll be going into the subject tree's *roots*.

I'll start by paging down to get to the last page of Rice's subject tree. The third page of this Gopher gives you a weather subject item: 38. Weather, Climate and Meteorology. If you choose this and then dig around, you can burrow all the way to the University of Michigan's Weather Underground service. That service has a telnet option, so you can leave Gopher and telnet to the University of Michigan's database. Don't worry; when you quit the telnet session, you automatically return to Gopher, right where you left off. Your Gopher is trained to stay.

Gopher remembers the machine address for you, to make telnetting simpler and less scary. After all, Gophering to a site this way is a lot easier than telnetting to a site where you would have to remember the Internet address of the remote machine. Gopher may also supply important information about a remote machine as you slip from Gopher into the remote. For example, Gopher may give you the required password and user name to access the remote machine.

Here's the main menu you see upon entering the University of Michigan's Underground Weather service.

```
_ _ _ _ _ _ _ _ _ _ _ _ _ _ _ _ _ _ _ _ _ _ _ _ _ _ _ _ _ _ _ _ _ _ _ _ _

Press Return for menu, or enter 3 letter forecast city code:
```

```
WEATHER UNDERGROUND MAIN MENU
*******************************
 1) U.S. forecasts and climate data
 2) Canadian forecasts
 3) Current weather observations
 4) Ski conditions
 5) Long-range forecasts
 6) Latest earthquake reports
 7) Severe weather
 8) Hurricane advisories
 9) National Weather Summary
10) International data
11) Marine forecasts and observations
 X) Exit program
 C) Change scrolling to screen
 H) Help and information for new users
 ?) Answers to all your questions
```

U.S. and international weather data, ski conditions, and earthquake and hurricane reports are available from here. Travelers, skiers, and Willard Scott wannabes are among those who would want to add this Gopher item to their bookmarks. Take a peek at a few screens from the service:

Here's an earthquake report.

```
**********************************************************
          Earthquake report for 12/09/93
**********************************************************


804
SEXX2 KWBC 090708
SUBJECT: EARTHQUAKE BULLETIN
THE FOLLOWING IS A RELEASE BY THE UNITED STATES  GEOLOGICAL  SURVEY,
NATIONAL  EARTHQUAKE  INFORMATION  CENTER:  A  STRONG  EARTHQUAKE
OCCURRED IN THE NORTHERN MOLUCCA  SEA,  ABOUT  100  MILES  (160  KM)
WEST-SOUTHWEST  OF  TERNATE, INDONESIA OR ABOUT 1400 MILES (2260 KM)
EAST-NORTHEAST  OF  JAKARTA  (ALSO  ABOUT  1030  MILES  OR  1660  KM
SOUTH-SOUTHEAST OF MANILA, PHILIPPINES) AT 9:32 PM MST TODAY, DEC 8,
1993 (DEC 09 AT 12:32 PM LOCAL  TIME  IN  CENTRAL  INDONESIA).  THE
MAGNITUDE  WAS  COMPUTED AT 6.8 ON THE RICHTER SCALE.  NO REPORTS OF
DAMAGE OR CASUALTIES HAVE BEEN RECEIVED AT THIS TIME.  THIS  IS  THE
LARGEST  EARTHQUAKE IN THIS GENERAL AREA SINCE A MAGNITUDE 7.0 EVENT
ON AUGUST 5, 1969.



**********************************************************
          Earthquake report for 12/09/93
**********************************************************
```

Witness ski conditions in Colorado, one of many states listed in the ski report.

Colorado Ski Area	New Snow Past 24 Hrs 6am-6am	Snow Depth 6am-6am Mid-Top	New Snow Past 48 Hrs 6am-6am	New Snow Past 72 Hrs 6am-6am	Snow Cond.	Lifts Open/Total
Report Date 12/10/93						
Press Return to continue, M to return to menu, X to exit:					pp	4/ 5
Arrowhead					cl	0/ 2
Aspen Highlands					cl	0/ 11
Aspen Mountain	0	29 28	0	1	pp	6/ 8
Beaver Creek Resort	0	19 30	0	0	pp	6/ 10
Breckenridge	0	27	0	2	pp	13/ 16
Copper Mountain	0	25	0	1	pp	11/ 20
Crested Butte	0	28 44	0	2	pp	10/ 13
Cuchara Valley					cl	0/ 4
Eldora			0	0	nr	3/ 9
Howelsen Ski Area	0	12	0	0	pp	2/ 3
Keystone/North Peak	0	30 34	0	2	pp	13/ 19

Observe this 1992 report on the effects of Hurricane Andrew.

        MIAMI (UPI) — The 1992 Atlantic-Caribbean hurricane season officially
ended November 30, closing the record books on a relatively slow but
devastating year that saw an unprecedented amount of damage from a
single storm.
        There were six named storms this year, four fewer than in an average
year.
        But, said Bob Sheets, director of the National Hurricane Center in
Miami, "It only takes one."
        The first, Hurricane Andrew, killed 59 people in Florida, Louisiana
and the Bahamas. Andrew destroyed 61,000 homes, damaged 75,000 others
and left 250,000 people homeless, according to the National Association
of Independent Insurers.
        A.M. Best, the insurance analysts, estimated insured losses alone at
$13.4 billion from Hurricane Andrew. The federal government expects to
spend $2.45 billion on disaster relief by the end of the fiscal year,
according to the Federal Emergency Management Agency.

```
        Tropical Storm Danielle also was a killer, claiming one life when it
pounded the Chesapeake Bay area with winds and rain Sept. 25, but it
caused no appreciable property damage, said Lixion Avila, a specialist
at the hurricane center.
        Together, Andrew and Danielle made 1992 the 22nd deadliest season in
American history.
```

Navigator's Note: So far, using Gopher to find information grouped by subject areas has been demonstrated from only one starting point: a Veronica search on "subject trees." But "subject trees" is only one title used by this type of Gopher.

Try using the key word "discipline" to find Gophers arranged by academic disciplines, or the words "study carrel," which will bring up a list of Gophers arranged by study subjects. More starting points may be developed, using other key words, or a single word may come about as an informal standard for getting to this type of Gopher. You can bum out about the inconsistency and unpredictability of it all, or you can rejoice that the Internet remains wild and untamed. Your choice.

Although academic Gophers predominate in this arena, a growing list of organizations—government institutions, public libraries and businesses—will soon offer subject-area Gophers. Stay tuned.

Help

Any time you're in the UNIX Curses Gopher, you can use ? to get help.

```
                    Quick Gopher Help
                    -----------------

Moving around Gopherspace
-------------------------
Use the Arrow Keys or vi/emacs equivalent to move around
Up              :  Move to previous line.
Down            :  Move to next line.
Right Return    :  "Enter" current item.
Left, u         :  "Exit" current item.
```

```
>, +, Pgdn, space  :  View next page.
<, -, Pgup, b      :  View previous page.
0-9                :  Go to a specific line.
m                  :  Go back to the main menu.

Bookmarks
----------
a : Add current item to the bookmark list.
A : Add current directory/search to bookmark list.
v : View bookmark list.
d : Delete a bookmark.

Other commands
--------------
q : Quit with prompt.
Q : Quit unconditionally.
= : Display Technical information about current item.
o : Change options.

The Gopher development team hopes that you find this software useful.
If you find what you think is a bug, please report it to us by sending
e-mail to "Gopher@boombox.micro.umn.edu."
```

This gives you the options for moving about in Gopher and tells you how to create a bookmark and other commands.

Gopher Tracks

Gopher is so easy to use that you'll probably soon be using it as one of your key Internet navigation tools. As you start to know where you want to go for specific data, you'll get tired of having to select various menus to get to choices that eventually get you to where you want to be. Rather than have to repeat this chain of choices every time, you can set bookmarks.

Bookmarks enable you to tailor a menu screen with selections of your own choosing. Every time you get to a screen and place the pointer on a line that you want to add to your bookmark, you just type the letter *a* and Gopher will add it to your bookmark.

After you have added your favorite Gopher choices to your bookmark, all you need to do is press the letter *v*, and your very own private Gopher menu will appear. You can add choices to it from any level in Gopherspace, and the choices can include any type of service: telnet, search, text file, and so on. Bookmarks are very convenient and will help you greatly in your navigation.

Here is a sample bookmark:

```
   Internet Gopher Information Client v1.01

                    Bookmarks

—>  1.  ACADEME THIS WEEK (Chronicle of Higher Education)/
    2.  veronica search at UNR <?>
    3.  University of Pittsburgh <TEL>
    4.  Search CIA World Fact Book 1991 <?>
    5.  Search Roget's 1911 Thesaurus <?>
    6.  WAIS Based Information/
    7.  directory-of-servers.src <?>
    8.  All the Gopher Servers in the World/
    9.  EDUCOM Documents and News/
   10.  InterNIC: Internet Network Information Center/
   11.  White House Papers/
   12.  National Science Foundation Gopher (STIS)/
   13.  CARL - Journal Articles Database & FAX Service <TEL>
   14.  Library administration/
   15.  Professional fields/
   16.  Library science/
   17.  Search gopherspace using veronica at NYSERNet <?>
   18.  Search gopherspacefor GOPHER DIRECTORIES(NYSERNet) <?>
```

With the bookmark facility, our AIDS researcher can build a Gopher menu that will meet his needs immediately on entering Gopher. A librarian that has clients in the business and commerce community will keep the bookmark handy with the directories pointing to those Gophers in Gopherspace that deal with that topic.

Gopher Guidelines

As you can see, Gopher and Veronica are useful tools to the Internet Navigator. They offer a powerful means of getting to the data you're interested in, but a little caution and planning are required to get the best out of them.

In most cases, you'll need to start off using Veronica for a general search and weed out irrelevant data to get to the material you need. Only after you are sure that limiting the search will get relevant material should you use specific searches. A subject index of all the materials available through Gopher would be nice, but until that happens Veronica is your best bet.

Keep in mind that Veronica searches on keywords and that you may need to use several synonyms to get all pertinent materials. Business, commerce, mercantile, industry, trade, enterprise, and other words may all get information that you are looking for.

Gopher may also give you information that you may not be able to use because it has restrictions or is of little value. Many telnet links in Gopherspace are restricted because they lead to commercial databases that are limited to registered users.

Many Gopher types may not be suitable for your system. You may not be able to get a sound file or a BinHexed Mac file. On the other hand, using the equal sign (=) gives you technical information on the item and may come in handy for you to get the item at a later date with the right equipment to use the item.

Use the -t flag to get documents that are relevant to your needs. The following example limits the search to only databases that I can telnet to with information on AIDS. (If the database is available for public searching, as the databases in the example are, Gopher will tell you how to log in to the database.)

```
         Internet Gopher Information Client v1.01

            Search gopherspace using veronica at CNIDR: aids -t8

   —>  1.  CHAT (AIDS Database) <TEL>
        2.  FDA bbs- Aids Info, consumer info <TEL>
        3.  S.E. Florida AIDS Info Network <TEL>
        4.  FDA BBS - News releases, AIDS info, consumer info... <TEL>
        5.  FDA BBS - News releases, Aids info, consumer info... <TEL>
        6.  Interactive AIDS document and simulated conversation (CHAT) <TEL>
        7.  CHAT - Interactive AIDS document and simulated conversation <TEL>
```

Because Gopher searches Gopherspace on the Internet, it will run into standard Internet problems. Faults with machines on the network or troubles with network links and nodes, heavy usage, and many other communication hazards can cause connections to fail. At times, the Veronica servers will be in heavy use and you will not be able to use them, and at times Gopher connection will fail. Again, usage during off-peak hours will improve connections, but don't be surprised if something doesn't work when it has worked in the past. Try later and you may get a connection.

Remember that Gopher indexing is not consistent. The way one Internet site indexes its section of Gopherspace may seem very eccentric to you but extremely logical to that site.

Gopher's Future

Gopher's popularity has paralleled the tremendous growth of Gopher users on the Internet. Gopher is an easy-to-use menu-driven program that integrates many of the features of the Internet, such as FTP, telnet, WAIS, and e-mail, and makes them easy for the user to manage.

The simplicity of Gopher is appealing to new Internet users, and in combination with Veronica, Gopher becomes a powerful research tool. Improvements are being developed to make Veronica searching more powerful and Gopher item retrieval more reliable.

The most exciting of the changes to Gopherspace is the introduction of Gopher+ (pronounced *gopher plus*). This will be just like the gopher you've grown to know and love but much more flexible and sophisticated. For example, when you select an item that leads to the downloading of a file, Gopher+ could have a script attached to that item that tells you the size of the file and asks you if you really want to download it.

With the improvements proposed with Gopher+, Gopher will continue to be one of the most popular and useful Internet navigating tools.

GLOBAL HYPERTEXT: THE WORLD WIDE WEB

Although Gopher is a powerful system for navigating the Internet, there is, as they say, more than one way to cut a pie (I was going to say "skin a cat," but then one of my cats came and sat on my lap and I felt guilty). Proceeding with our metaphor, the cat…oops, the pie, the problem is how to provide a framework to navigate around many different data items on many different computers. The knife that addresses this problem in Chapter 8, "Navigating by Menus: Gopher," is Gopher.

Another knife is the World Wide Web, otherwise known as WWW or just "the Web." This service uses a different metaphor from the Gopher system. Gopher is a hierarchical menu structure: menu items lead to other menu items or to a service. WWW's model is to treat all the Internet's data as hypertext.

Navigator's Note: "Just what is hypertext?" you may be asking. Imagine a book—say, this book. With a hypertext version, you could follow a reference from any keyword (a word that the author or an editor considers important), such as Gopher in the last paragraph, to another piece of information—for example, the start of Chapter 8. This piece of information could, in turn, have further keywords. The idea is to have links between different parts of the document, to enable the information to be explored interactively rather than just in a linear fashion.

Under WWW, all information is arranged in documents with hypertext keywords scattered throughout. All hypertext keywords are followed by a number in square brackets. For example, the sentence Now is the winter [1] of our discount [2] tents has two keywords, winter and discount. A document may be more than a single screen in length, so WWW allows you to move up and down screens.

To select a hypertext keyword and follow it to whatever it's associated with, enter the keyword's number and press Enter. In WWW, selecting a keyword (also called a hypertext link or just a link) moves you to another document that could be on the same or a different computer or connects you to a service such as telnet or FTP.

The main site for WWW is nxoc01.cern.ch (note that the *ch* means that the computer is in Switzerland—you're globe-trotting again…"Bring me more caviar, waiter, and tell the press that I'll give them a photo opportunity at twelve."). You need to telnet to this system, where you'll be automatically logged in. The opening screen looks like this:

```
coyote% telnet nxoc01.cern.ch

CERN Information Service
(ttyp0 on nxoc01)
                                                   Overview of the Web (23/27)
                              GENERAL OVERVIEW

  There is no "top" to the World Wide Web. You can look at it from many points
  of view. If you have no other bias, here are some places to start:

   by Subject[1]          A classification by subject of interest. Incomplete
                          but easiest to use.

   by Type[2]             Looking by type of service (access protocol, etc) may
                          allow you to find things if you know what you are looking
                          for.
```

```
   About WWW[3]              About the World Wide Web global information sharing
                             project.

Starting somewhere else

   To use a different default page, perhaps one representing your field of
   interest, see  "customizing your home page"[4].

What happened to CERN?

1-6, Up, <RETURN> for more, Quit, or Help: 2
```

Help

As you can see, the opening page of WWW is sprinkled with hypertext links. The bottom line tells you that this document has six links (1-6). Only four are visible, so the others are on the following pages of the document. If this was the only page, the option <RETURN> (meaning to press the Enter key) wouldn't be displayed. Up takes you to the previous page of the document (if one exists), Quit does what it says and leaves WWW. If you enter H for Help, you get

```
WWW LineMode Browser version 1.4a (WWWLib 1.1a)    COMMANDS AVAILABLE

You are reading a document whose address is
    'file://a.cs.uiuc.edu/pub/Catalog'

    <RETURN>         Move down one page within the document.
    Bottom           Go to the last page of the document.
    Top              Return to the first page of the document.
    Up               Move up one page within the document.
    Recall           List visited documents.
    Recall <number>  Return to a previously visited document
                     as numbered in the recall list.
    Home             Return to the starting document.
    Back             Move back to the last document.
    Next             Take next link from last document.
    Previous         Take previous link from last document.
    Go address       Go to document of given [relative] address.
    Verbose          Switch to verbose mode.
    Help             Display this page.
    Manual           Jump to the online manual for this program.
    Quit             Leave the www program.

Back, Up, <RETURN> for more, Quit, or Help:
```

Browsing by Type

Use B for Back to return to the previous screen. Take a look at the second hypertext link, Type:

```
                                  Data sources classified by access protocol
                   DATA SOURCES CLASSIFIED BY TYPE OF SERVICE

     See also categorization exist by subject[1].

   World Wide Web[2]       List of W3 servers. See also: about the WWW
                           initiative[3].

   WAIS[4]                 Find WAIS index servers using the directory of
                           servers[5], or lists by name[6] or domain[7]. See
                           also: about WAIS[8].

   Network News[9]         Available directly in all www browsers.

   Gopher[10]              Campus-wide information systems, etc, listed
                           geographically. See also: about Gopher[11].

   Telnet access[12]       Hypertext  catalogues by Peter Scott. See also: list
                           by Scott Yanoff[13]. Also, Art St George's index[14]
                           (yet to be hyperized) etc.

   VAX/VMS HELP[15]        Available using the help gateway[16] to WWW.

   1-25, Back, Up, <RETURN> for more, Quit, or Help: 3
```

This document has 25 links. Your options include Back, which takes you back to the last document you were looking at. Select the third link for about the WWW initiative:

```
                                        The World Wide Web project
                    WORLD WIDE WEB

   The World Wide Web (W3) is a wide-area hypermedia[1] information retrieval
   initiative aiming to give universal access to a large universe of documents.

   Everything there is online about W3 is linked directly or indirectly to this
   document, including an executive summary[2] of the project, an illustrated
   talk[3], Mailing lists[4], Policy[5] and Conditions[6], May's W3 news[7],
   Frequently Asked Questions[8].

   What's out there?[9]    Pointers to the world's online information,
                           subjects[10], W3 servers[11], etc.
```

```
Software Products[12]   What there is and how to get it: clients, servers and
                        tools.

Technical[13]           Details of protocols, formats, program internals etc.

Bibliography[14]        Paper documentation on W3 and references. Also:
                        manuals[15].

People[16]              A list of some people involved in the project.
1-20, Back, Up, <RETURN> for more, Quit, or Help: 1
```

Hypermedia Explanation

Great! Let's see how hypertext, or hypermedia as WWW refers to it, is explained…

```
                                                       What is Hypertext?
                        WHAT IS HYPERTEXT

Hypertext is text which is not constrained to be linear.

Hypertext is text which contains links[1] to other texts. The term was
coined by Ted Nelson[2] around 1965 (see History[3]).

HyperMedia is a term used for hypertext which is not constrained to be text:
it can include graphics, video and sound[4], for example. Apparently Ted
Nelson was the first to use this term too.

Hypertext and HyperMedia are concepts, not products.

See also:

    A list of terms[5] used in hypertext literature.

    Conferences[6]

    Commercial (and academic) products[7]

    A newsgroup on hypertext, "alt.hypertext"[8].
1-10, Back, Up, <RETURN> for more, Quit or Help: Back
```

```
                                              What is Hypertext? (30/29)

HyperMedia is a term used for hypertext which is not constrained to be text:
it can include graphics, video and sound[4], for example. Apparently Ted
Nelson was the first to use this term too.
```

```
Hypertext and HyperMedia are concepts, not products.

See also:

    A list of terms[5] used in hypertext literature.

    Conferences[6]

    Commercial (and academic) products[7]

    A newsgroup on hypertext, "alt.hypertext"[8].

    World Wide Web is a project[9]  which uses hypertext concepts.

    Standards[10].


    [End]
1-10, Back, Up, Quit, or Help:
```

As you can see, lots of information is available, and the linkages make it a very rich system to use. It gives you the ability to follow a chain of interrelated ideas. Getting sidetracked is a real danger.

Searching for BEMs

Recently I read a USENET News message about astronomy that referred to the search for "BEMs." I have no idea what BEMs are, so I'll try WWW to find out. Starting at the "General Overview" document, a likely route is to search by subject, which is link [1]. So I type 1 and press Enter.

```
                                              Overview of the Web (23/27)
                             GENERAL OVERVIEW

   There is no "top" to the World Wide Web. You can look at it from many points
   of view. If you have no other bias, here are some places to start:

   by Subject[1]          A classification by subject of interest. Incomplete
                          but easiest to use.

   by Type[2]             Looking by type of service (access protocol, etc) may
                          allow you to find things if you know what you are looking
                          for.

   About WWW[3]           About the World Wide Web global information sharing
                          project.
```

```
Starting somewhere else

   To use a different default page, perhaps one representing your field of
   interest, see  "customizing your home page"[4].

What happened to CERN?

1-6, Up, <RETURN> for more, Quit, or Help: 1
```

I choose link 1 because I know that what I'm looking for is connected with the subject of astronomy.

```
                      The World Wide Web Virtual Library: Subject Catalogue
                              INFORMATION BY SUBJECT

   See also arrangement  by  service type[1]. Mail www-request@info.cern.ch if
   you know of online information not in these lists....

   Aeronautics              Mailing list archive index[2].

   Agriculture[3]           Separate list, see also Almanac mail servers[4].

   Astronomy and Astrophysics
                            Abstract Indexes[5] at NASA,   Astrophysics work at
                            FNAL[6] and Princeton's[7] Sloane Digital Sky Survey.
                            See also: space[8].

   Bio Sciences[9]          Separate list.

   Computing[10]            Separate list.

   Engineering[11]          Separate list.

   Environment[12]          Separate list.

1-39, Back, Up, <RETURN> for more, Quit, or Help: 8
```

The space link, 8, looks the most promising...

```
                                                    Overview — Space
                              SPACE

   Under construction.  Omissions please to roeber@cern.ch

Answers to Frequently Asked Questions on sci.space[1]
NASA Ames Research Center archives[2]
```

```
NASA Astrophysical Data System user guide[3]
NASA JPL FTP archive[4]
NASA Langley techreports (directory)[5]
NASA Langley techreports (searchable)[6]
NASA Spacelink (interactive session)[7]
National Space Science Data Center Online Data and Information Service
(interactive session)[8]
Space Telescope Science Institute electronic information service[9]
Space Telescope European Coordination Facility star catalog database
(interactive session)[10]
Voyager, Hubble, and other images[11]
Yale Bright Star Catalog[12]
Orbital Element Sets: NASA, TVRO, Shuttle[13]
Orbital Element Sets: NASA, TVRO, Molczan, CelBBS, Shuttle[14]
Orbital Element Sets: NASA, Molczan[15]
Back issues of the Electronic Journal of the Astronomical Society of the
1-29, Back, Up, <RETURN> for more, Quit, or Help:
```

Nope, nothing yet; I hit Enter:

```
                                           Overview — Space (40/40)
Yale Bright Star Catalog[12]
Orbital Element Sets: NASA, TVRO, Shuttle[13]
Orbital Element Sets: NASA, TVRO, Molczan, CelBBS, Shuttle[14]
Orbital Element Sets: NASA, Molczan[15]
Back issues of the Electronic Journal of the Astronomical Society of the
Atlantic[16]
NASA Headline News[17]
NASA Extragalactic Database[18]
National Oceanic and Atmospheric Administration database[19]
Vincent Cate's list of companies related to the space industry[20]
Skywatch[21]
Frequently Seen Acronyms[22]
Daily Ionospheric Reports[23]
Delta Clipper images[24]
Space Digest archives[25]
Space Tech archives[26]
Lunar and Planetary Institute BBS (interactive)[27]
USGS Global Land Information System BBS (interactive)[28]

                                                     fgmr[29]


1-29, Back, Up, Quit, or Help: 22
```

Aha! Number 22, "Frequently Seen Acronyms" sounds right. I select it.

```
Path: senator-bedfellow.mit.edu!enterpoop.mit.edu!pad-thai.aktis.com!pad-thai.a
ktis.com!not-for-mail
From: bradfrd2@ncar.ucar.edu (Mark Bradford)
Newsgroups: sci.astro,sci.space,sci.space.shuttle,news.answers
Subject: Astro/Space Frequently Seen Acronyms
Supersedes: <space/acronyms_736574404@GZA.COM>
Followup-To: poster
Date: 4 Jun 1993 00:00:07 -0400
Organization: LifeForms Unlimited, Cephalopods
Lines: 509
Sender: faqserv@GZA.COM
Approved: news-answers-request@MIT.Edu
Expires: 18 Jul 1993 04:00:05 GMT
Message-ID: <space/acronyms_739166405@GZA.COM>
NNTP-Posting-Host: pad-thai.aktis.com
Keywords: long space astro tla acronyms
X-Last-Updated: 1992/12/07
Xref: senator-bedfellow.mit.edu sci.astro:36760 sci.space:63666 sci.space.shutt
le:13300 news.answers:9045


Archive-name: space/acronyms
Edition: 8


Back, Up, <RETURN> for more, Quit, or Help:
Acronym List for sci.astro, sci.space, and sci.space.shuttle:
Edition 8, 1992 Dec 7
Last posted: 1992 Aug 27


This list is offered as a reference for translating commonly appearing
acronyms in the space-related newsgroups.  If I forgot or botched your
favorite acronym, please let me know!  Also, if there's an acronym *not*
on this list that confuses you, drop me a line, and if I can figure
it out, I'll add it to the list.

Note that this is intended to be a reference for *frequently seen*
acronyms, and is most emphatically *not* encyclopedic.  If I incorporated
every acronym I ever saw, I'd soon run out of disk space!  :-)

The list will be posted at regular intervals, every 30 days.  All
comments regarding it are welcome; I'm reachable as bradfrd2@ncar.ucar.edu.

Note that this just tells what the acronyms stand for — you're on your
own for figuring out what they *mean*!  Note also that the total number of
acronyms in use far exceeds what I can list; special-purpose acronyms that
are essentially always explained as they're introduced are omitted.
Further, some acronyms stand for more than one thing; as of Edition 3 of
the list, these acronyms appear on multiple lines, unless they're simply
Back, Up, <RETURN> for more, Quit, or Help:
the list, these acronyms appear on multiple lines, unless they're simply
different ways of referring to the same thing.
```

```
Thanks to everybody who's sent suggestions since the first version of
the list, and especially to Garrett A. Wollman (wollman@griffin.uvm.edu),
who is maintaining an independent list, somewhat more verbose in
character than mine, and to Daniel Fischer (dfi@specklec.mpifr-bonn.mpg.de),
who is maintaining a truly HUGE list (535 at last count) of acronyms and
terms, mostly in German (which I read, fortunately).

Special thanks this time to Ken Hollis at NASA, who sent me a copy of NASA
Reference Publication 1059 Revised: _Space Transportation System and
Associated Payloads: Glossary, Acronyms, and Abbreviations_, a truly
mammoth tome — almost 300 pages of TLAs.

Special Bonus!  At the end of this posting, you will find a perl program
written by none other than Larry Wall, whose purpose is to scramble the
acronym list in an entertaining fashion.  Thanks, Larry!

A&A: Astronomy and Astrophysics
AAO: Anglo-Australian Observatory
AAS: American Astronomical Society
AAS: American Astronautical Society
Back, Up, <RETURN> for more, Quit, or Help:
```

"And I'd like to thank my mother and father, the pope, the Four Tops, my cat…"
Seriously, this kind of collection is invaluable, and the keepers of these glossaries
should be encouraged and applauded. So let's see if "BEMs" are in the list. (I'm
just grateful I wasn't looking for something that started with Z—it's a long list.)

```
AAS: American Astronautical Society
AAVSO: American Association of Variable Star Observers
ACE: Advanced Composition Explorer
ACRV: Assured Crew Return Vehicle (or) Astronaut Crew Rescue Vehicle
ADFRF: Ames-Dryden Flight Research Facility (was DFRF) (NASA)
AGN: Active Galactic Nucleus
AGU: American Geophysical Union
AIAA: American Institute of Aeronautics and Astronautics
AIPS: Astronomical Image Processing System
AJ: Astronomical Journal
ALEXIS: Array of Low Energy X-ray Imaging Sensors
ALPO: Association of Lunar and Planetary Observers
ALS: Advanced Launch System
ANSI: American National Standards Institute
AOA: Abort Once Around (Shuttle abort plan)
AOCS: Attitude and Orbit Control System
Ap.J: Astrophysical Journal
APM: Attached Pressurized Module (a.k.a. Columbus)
APU: Auxiliary Power Unit
ARC: Ames Research Center (NASA)
```

```
ARTEMIS: Advanced Relay TEchnology MISsion
ASA: Astronomical Society of the Atlantic
ASI: Agenzia Spaziale Italiano
Back, Up, <RETURN> for more, Quit, or Help:
ASI: Agenzia Spaziale Italiano
ASRM: Advanced Solid Rocket Motor
ATDRS: Advanced Tracking and Data Relay Satellite
ATLAS: Atmospheric Laboratory for Applications and Science
ATM: Amateur Telescope Maker
ATO: Abort To Orbit (Shuttle abort plan)
AU: Astronomical Unit
AURA: Association of Universities for Research in Astronomy
AW&ST: Aviation Week and Space Technology (a.k.a. AvLeak)
AXAF: Advanced X-ray Astrophysics Facility
BATSE: Burst And Transient Source Experiment (on CGRO)
BBXRT: Broad-Band X-Ray Telescope (ASTRO package)
BEM: Bug-Eyed Monster
BH: Black Hole
BIMA: Berkeley Illinois Maryland Array
BNSC: British National Space Centre
BTW: By The Way
C&T: Communications & Tracking
CCAFS: Cape Canaveral Air Force Station
CCD: Charge-Coupled Device
CCDS: Centers for the Commercial Development of Space
CD-ROM: Compact Disk Read-Only Memory
CFA: Center For Astrophysics
Back, Up, <RETURN> for more, Quit, or Help:
```

Ta-da! "BEM: Bug-Eyed Monster"—I should have guessed! These astronomers and astrophysicists are wild and crazy guys.

WAIS Looks Good

Notice that we went from browsing a hypertext document to listing a file. The transition was pretty clean, what's called "transparent" because the change wasn't really noticeable. This is an important feature of WWW—it tries to give everything it covers a consistent look. For example, the subject list includes

```
Reference              Roget's Thesaurus[33]. Experimental English
                       dictionary[34].
```

Choosing link 33, you find that you've selected a WAIS server!

```
                                              roget-thesaurus index
                      ROGET-THESAURUS

Server created with WAIS release 8 b3.1 on Dec 11 14:34:55 1991 by emv@cedar.ci
c.net
The files of type para used in the index were:
   /u3/wais/mirror/etext/roget10.txt


Roget's Thesaurus is provided by Project Gutenberg.  Here's a sample
entry.  This database is also available in the 'Gopher' system at
Gopher.micro.umn.edu, and for anonymous FTP from
        mrcnext.cso.uiuc.edu:/pub/etext/
For more information on Project Gutenberg, see the usenet newsgroup
'bit.listserv.gutnberg'; there's information about it in the 'mailing-lists'
WAIS server.

    #86. List. — N. list, catalog, catalogue, inventory, schedule;
register &c. (record) 551; account; bill, bill of costs; syllabus; terrier,
tally, file; calendar, index, table, atlas, contents; book, ledger;
synopsis, catalogue raisonne; tableau; invoice, bill of lading; prospectus,
program, programme; bill of fare, menu, carte; score, census, statistics,
returns; Red book, Blue book, Domesday book; cadastre; directory, gazetteer.
almanac; army list, clergy list, civil service list, navy list; Almanach de
FIND <keywords>, Back, Up, <RETURN> for more, Quit, or Help: find computer
                                     find computer (in roget-thesaurus)
```

Look for a synonym for *computer*:

```
                       FIND COMPUTER

   Index roget-thesaurus contains the following 2 items relevant to 'ind
   computer'. The first figure for each entry is its relative score, the second
   the number of lines in the item.

1000   187  This is the 12/91 Project Gutenberg release of Roget's Thesaurus
We are releasing it early because[1]
 834    32       #85. Numeration.  — N. numeration; numbering &c. v.;
pagination;  tale, recension, enumeratio[2]



   [End]
```

Note that WWW presents the WAIS interface with the addition of hypertext links!
Pretty clever stuff, and certainly easy to use. So, what does link 2 have to say?

```
. . . . . . . . . . . . . . . . . . . . . . . . . . . .
    #85. Numeration.  — N. numeration; numbering &c. v.; pagination;
tale, recension, enumeration, summation, reckoning, computation,
supputation; calculation, calculus; algorithm, algorism, rhabdology,
dactylonomy; measurement &c. 466; statistics.
    arithmetic, analysis, algebra, geometry, analytical geometry,
fluxions; differential calculus, integral calculus, infinitesimal calculus;
calculus of differences.
    [Statistics] dead reckoning, muster, poll, census, capitation, roll
call, recapitulation; account &c. (list) 86.
    [Operations] notation, addition, subtraction, multiplication,
division, rule of three, practice, equations, extraction of roots,
reduction, involution, evolution, estimation, approximation, interpolation,
differentiation, integration.
    [Instruments] abacus, logometer, slide rule, slipstick[coll.],
tallies, Napier's bones, calculating machine, difference engine, suan-pan;
adding machine; cash register; electronic calculator,  calculator,
computer;
    [people who calculate] arithmetician, calculator, abacist, algebraist,
mathematician; statistician, geometer; programmer; accountant, auditor.
    V. number, count, tally, tell; call over, run over; take an account
of, enumerate, muster, poll, recite, recapitulate; sum; sum up, cast up;
tell off, score, cipher, compute, calculate, suppute, add, subtract,
Back, Up, <RETURN> for more, Quit, or Help: back
```

Beautifying FTP

WWW also makes the same kind of transformation into the FTP interface and makes it in a far more "user friendly" way:

```
                                                        FTP Interface
                            FTP INTERFACE

    Please note that it is a nontrivial problem for a World Wide Web browser
    like NCSA Mosaic[1] to properly handle the wide range of datatypes residing
    on various FTP sites.  Please go here[2] for information on how Mosaic
    handles file typing.

        Introduction to the monster FTP list[3]

        Sites with names A to E[4]

        Sites with names F to K[5]

        Sites with names L to O[6]
```

```
        Sites with names P to S[7]

        Sites with names T to Z[8]

                                              marca@ncsa.uiuc.edu


1-8, Back, Up, Quit, or Help: 4
```

Look in the A to E site list.

```
                                    A to E: Exhaustive List of FTP Sites
                    A TO E: EXHAUSTIVE LIST OF FTP SITES


a.cs.uiuc.edu[1]                       128.174.252.1     US -5     90/08/22
Admin: Univ. of Illinois - Urbana-Champaign
Files: TeX; dvi2ps; gif; texx2.7; amiga; GNUmake; GNU

a.psc.edu[2]                           128.182.66.105    US -5     90/12/31
Admin: Pittsburgh Supercomputing Center
Files: GPLOT; GTEX

aarnet.edu.au[3]                       139.130.204.4     AU +10    92/12/20
Admin: Australian Academic & Research Network
Files: Australian AARNET network stats

acacia.maths.uwa.oz.au[4]              130.95.16.2       AU +8     92/12/20
Admin: Univ. of Western Australia

acfcluster.nyu.edu[5]                  128.122.128.11    US -5     91/01/02
Admin: New York Univ.
Server: 128.122.128.17, 128.122.128.16
Files: VMS UUCP; news; DECUS library catalog; vsmnet.sources; info-vax code
1-228, Back, Up, <RETURN> for more, Quit, or Help: 1
```

Choose link 1 from the 228 offered. This gives you a list of the available subdirectories and files:

```
                                     FTP Directory of //a.cs.uiuc.edu/
                             /

bin[1]           etc[2]          pub[3]          usr[4]          dev[5]
.cshrc[6]        .login[7]       ls-1R[8]        lib[9]          tmp[10]
.hushlogin[11]   uiuc[12]        ls-1R.Z[13]     var[14]         adm[15]
msgs[16]         files.lst[17]   files.lst.Z[18] .rhosts.old[19]
```

```
   [End]

1-19, Back, Up, Quit, or Help: 17
```

If we now give the link number for a file, WWW will attempt to handle the file appropriately. For example, let's use link 17:

```
dr-xr-xr-x 13 ftp       wheel          512 Jun 10 08:35 .
dr-xr-xr-x  2 daemon    staff          512 May  6 07:04 ./bin
--x--x--x   1 root      staff        10288 Oct 19  1989 ./bin/ls
-rwxr-x--   1 root      staff        24576 Apr  9 00:10 ./bin/compress
-rwxr-xr-x  1 root      staff         2152 Apr 24  1989 ./bin/pwd
drwx------  2 daemon    news           512 Mar 19 09:51 ./etc
drwxr-xr-x 54 access    news          1536 Jun  9 07:20 ./pub
drwxr-xr-x  2 access    staff          512 Feb 15 15:04 ./pub/dcs
lrwxrwxrwx  1 root      daemon          16 Oct 15  1992 ./pub/dcs/uiqpl.nroff ->
 QPLabstracts91-3
-rwxr-xr-x  1 access    staff        22870 Jul  8  1992 ./pub/dcs/QPLabstracts92
-1
-r--r--r--  1 access    staff       581027 Apr 24  1992 ./pub/dcs/uireports.bibr
ef
-r--r--r--  1 access    staff         1038 Jan  6  1992 ./pub/dcs/uireports.READ
ME
-rwxr-xr-x  1 access    news          8831 Jul 15  1987 ./pub/dcs/Notes.Revision
s
-rwxr-xr-x  1 access    staff       568440 Oct  2  1991 ./pub/dcs/csreports
-rwxr-xr-x  1 access    staff       444557 Oct 25  1989 ./pub/dcs/Notes.tar.Z
-r--r--r--  1 access    staff       439800 Apr 27  1992 ./pub/dcs/uireports.form
at
-rwxr-xr-x  1 access    staff        17671 Nov 18  1991 ./pub/dcs/QPLabstracts91
Back, Up, <RETURN> for more, Quit, or Help:
```

WWW dumps the file contents to the screen! Pretty neat, except that it handles all files the same way when their link is selected. This is not much good if the file isn't text. This is a current limitation of WWW, but one that you can expect to be cured very quickly. The future WWW might well be capable of mailing you a file or doing something equally smart.

Using WWW

We've only scratched the surface of WWW's documents. The Web also covers access to telnet, USENET news, and several other services. If you have the WWW server running on your computer, you can set up your own private WWW documents. Even better, you can link these documents to other resources on your computer or out on the Internet.

WWW is a good tool even though it's so young. It's one that is well worth playing with and following as it develops. The most interesting part is how the Web can make other Internet tools much easier to use. I think the creators of WWW should be encouraged and applauded for a tool that could become one of the Internet greats. For a look at how it's becoming even greater, see the next chapter, "A Better Window on the Web: Mosaic."

A Better Window on the Web: Mosaic

A gopher is an efficient, busy little creature that gets a lot done. But let's be frank—gophers aren't pretty, and they're also a little, well, single-minded. They burrow and burrow, but they don't have much smarts about what to do with what they find.

Like Gopher, Mosaic is a tool for browsing the Internet and accessing what you find there. Unlike the little text-based Gopher, however, Mosaic is a multimedia browser, capable of displaying formatted documents, embedded graphics, video, sound, and links to other documents. It's also fluent in the World Wide Web's hypertext language, so it can exploit the enormous cross-referenced world of the WWW (see Chapter 9, "Global Hypertext: The World Wide Web," for more on WWW).

This makes Mosaic a superior tool for browsing resources where much of the information may be graphical, such as medical research or astronomy databases. How superior? Well, the very introduction of Mosaic has, all by itself, increased Internet popularity so much that it's causing a minor traffic jam. Read on.

What Is Mosaic?

Mosaic is a windowed environment interface to the World Wide Web. Available for Macintosh, Windows, and X Window workstations, Mosaic was developed by the National Center for Supercomputing Applications (NCSA) at the University of Illinois at Urbana-Champaign.

Through Mosaic, you can browse and access information on the WWW, including a growing list of items available *only* through Mosaic. Best of all, Mosaic gives you the power to use data that includes multimedia information (graphics, sound, video) to exploit the richness of the data that's out there. Also, documents prepared for Mosaic are formatted with special fonts and other features that make them easier to read and work with.

For example, you can do your medical and health research by tapping into the resources of the National Institutes of Health (Figure 10.1).

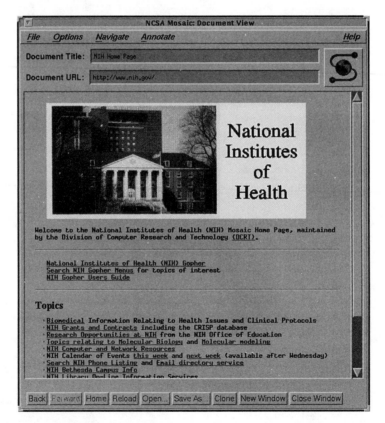

Figure 10.1. National Institutes of Health.

You can study the effects of a supernova by watching a digital video from the NCSA's Digital Gallery CD-ROM (Figure 10.2).

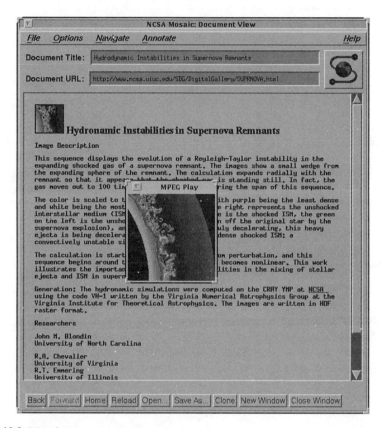

Figure 10.2. Watching a supernova.

You can read up on the history of the Dead Sea Scrolls and view segments of the scrolls from the Library of Congress exhibition called *Scrolls From the Dead Sea: The Ancient Library of Qumran and Modern Scholarship* (Figure 10.3).

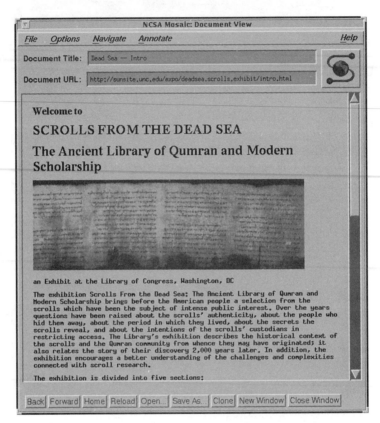

Figure 10.3. A screen from the Scrolls from the Dead Sea exhibit.

You can use Mosaic to ask Archie (another friendly Internet tool) to steer you to an anonymous FTP (Figures 10.4 and 10.5).

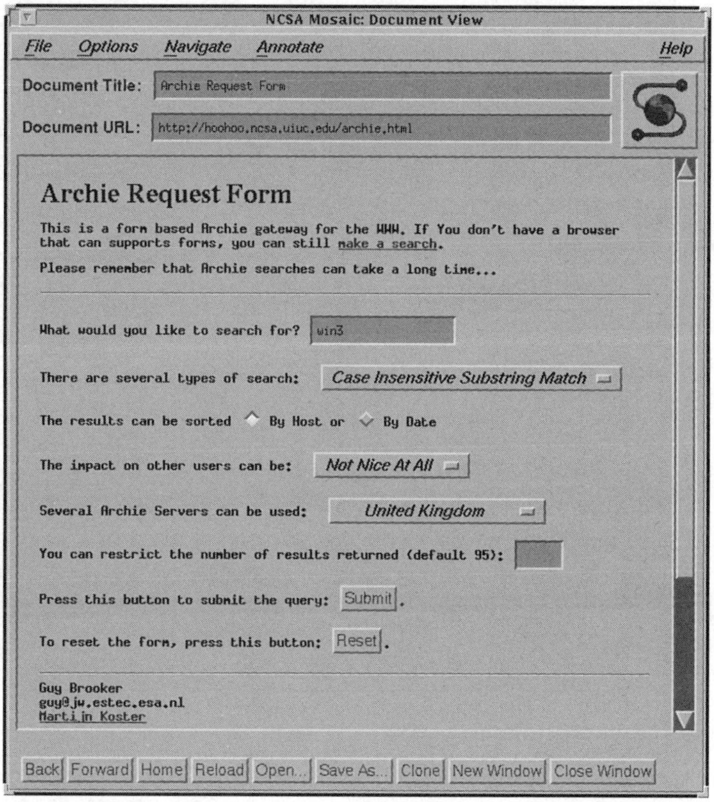

Figure 10.4. Archie request form.

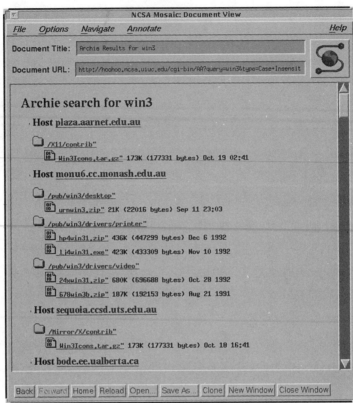

Figure 10.5. Results of an Archie search.

Why not read the latest ratings of college hockey teams (Figure 10.6)?

```
                          NCSA Mosaic: Document View
 File    Options    Navigate    Annotate                              Help

 Document Title:  The College Hockey Computer Rating 12/18/93

 Document URL:  http://hydra.bgsu.edu/TCHCR/Current.html


  The College Hockey Computer Rating
  Includes games on 12/18/93. Last ranking includes games on 12/12/93.

          Last                        Division I
  Rank  Rank  Team              Record        Performance        Schedu
    1     1   Michigan          16  1  1       83.33    1        -3.28
    2     5   Northern Michigan 11  4  1       43.75    5         7.13
    3     2   Boston University 10  3  0       53.85    2        -5.11
    4     6   Wisconsin         10  5  1       31.25   10        12.49
    5     8   Colorado College  10  4  2       37.50    7         3.25
    6     3   Lake Superior     13  5  0       44.44    4        -4.22
    7     4   New Hampshire     11  3  1       53.33    3       -13.97
    8     7   Northeastern       7  3  2       33.33    9        -1.21
    9    10   Mass-Lowell        8  3  2       38.46    6       -15.75
   10    13   Bowling Green      8  5  2       20.00   11         0.20
   11    11   Western Michigan   8  6  2       12.50   16         7.51
   12     9   Maine              9  6  0       20.00   11        -0.57
   13    14   Alaska-Fairbanks   9  6  0       20.00   11        -1.45
   14    15   Michigan State     8  5  3       18.75   15        -2.97
   15    18   Minnesota          6  7  3       -6.25   23        14.05
   16    12   Harvard            7  3  1       36.36    8       -29.41
   17    27   St Cloud           7  7  2        0.00   21         6.75
   18    17   RPI                6  5  0        9.09   19        -7.84
   19    16   Brown              5  3  2       20.00   11       -19.58
   20    19   Notre Dame         6  7  2       -6.67   24         6.71
   21    25   Alaska-Anchorage   6  9  1      -18.75   27        16.24
   22    26   North Dakota       6  9  1      -18.75   27        13.46
   23    29   Michigan Tech      5 10  4      -26.32   32        20.60
   24    21   Boston College     6  5  1        8.33   20       -15.07

 Back  Forward  Home  Reload  Open...  Save As...  Clone  New Window  Close Window
```

Figure 10.6. The College Hockey Computer Rating.

Or the latest issue of Wired (Figure 10.7)? (Notice how Mosaic displays format-ted text.)

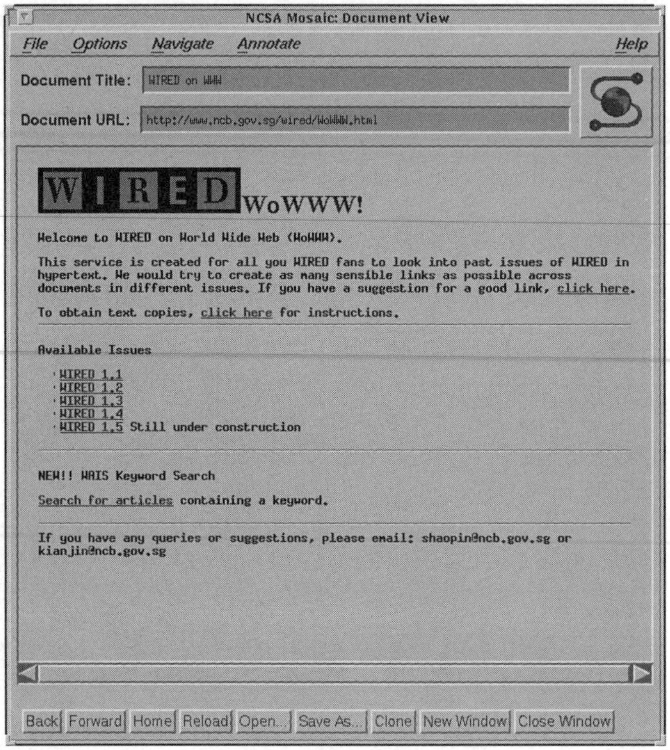

Figure 10.7. Wired on WWW.

Feeling animated? Why not let Mosaic show you some experimental movies of girls bicycling, heat flowing through a coil, or the Starship Enterprise orbiting a planet (Figure 10.8)?

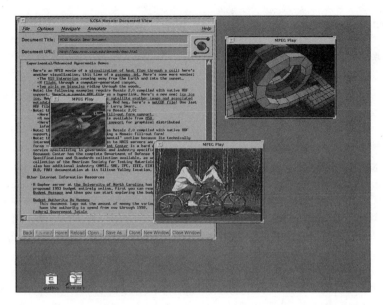

Figure 10.8. Mosaic animations.

The WWW's wealth of documents, graphics, photographs, sound files, film, and video are available through Mosaic's multimedia facilities. Through its client/ server information-gathering architecture, Mosaic can dig up and show information from anywhere on the international Internet.

How Mosaic Works

The WWW is a client/server system, in which *clients* request data from *servers* that actually locate and manage the data and supply it to the clients. Mosaic is a WWW client, capable of requesting information from ("querying") WWW servers, which return the requested information to your Mosaic client workstation.

That's how Mosaic *retrieves* data from the Internet, and it's not much different from what Gopher does. What's special about Mosaic is that it interprets text files written in a special language: the HyperText Markup Language (HTML). This hypermedia language links information in different files—or places in a file— together so it can be retrieved easily.

HTML documents can link words or passages from one document to words or passages of another HTML document. A document can also hold links to parts of itself, so a large document might have a Table of Contents that would allow you to move directly to a chapter or section merely by clicking on highlighted entries in the table.

Hyperlinks (sometimes also called "anchors") need not be limited to other documents. Clicking on a link (usually indicated by an underlined word that's also in a different color) can send you out on the Internet to a Telnet site or to a Gopher of your choice.

Most importantly, HTML can hook images and sound into documents. For example, clicking on a small "thumbnail" copy of an image in a document will activate a link to retrieve and display the full picture. Clicking a highlighted icon may retrieve and play a sound file that is hyperlinked to that icon.

An HTML document is a simple ASCII document with special markings and codes that set up the links. The markings are based on the Standardized Generalized Markup Language (SGML) used in many industries to create documents whose formatting can be interpreted by a wide variety of SGML-compatible applications.

Here is a brief sample of an HTML document used as Mosaic's demo document. Keep in mind that the document won't look like this when viewed through Mosaic. What you'll see then is a nicely formatted document with highlighted text, icons and graphics that, when you click them with your mouse, will automatically take you to linked material.

```
<base href="http://www.ncsa.uiuc.edu/demoweb/demo.html">
<TITLE>NCSA Mosaic Demo Document</TITLE>

<H1>NCSA Mosaic Demo Document</H1>

<i>Last updated November 10, 9:37PM CST.</I> <P>

Welcome to NCSA Mosaic, an information browser developed at the
National Center for Supercomputing Applications. This document is an interactive
hypermedia tour of Mosaic's capabilities.<P>
```

Using Mosaic

In addition to its multimedia and hyperlink capabilities, Mosaic has found such rapid popularity because it's easy to use and makes browsing related subjects quick and convenient. Unlike Gopher—which has a "linear" menu system that requires you to work in order from top to bottom—Mosaic has no top or bottom. You can jump around from hyperlink to hyperlink through global information, reading, listening, viewing, printing, or saving what you find.

The effect of Mosaic is to open up a "virtual library" that holds information in many subject areas with numerous access points, and makes that information easy to access and retrieve—at the click of a mouse. Color graphics leap through text documents, and sounds bring the visuals to life.

As a general-purpose WWW access tool, Mosaic can also be used—again, at the click of a mouse—to reach Gopher, WAIS, FTP, or other navigating tools. That's why it's becoming the all-purpose Internet interface for many users.

There is a downside to Mosaic. You won't be able to run Mosaic on your IBM XT. Obviously, you'll need a machine capable of running one of the host platforms supported by Mosaic (an XT can't even run Microsoft Windows, which is required for running Mosaic on a PC). Also, because graphics are so machine-intensive, a fairly fast machine is recommended, with plenty of memory and disk space. A good color display and sound capability are also important if you want to make the most of Mosaic.

Getting Mosaic

To use Mosaic, you'll need a full, direct Internet connection. Unlike some other Internet tools, Mosaic cannot be run by Telnetting to another machine.

Like many Internet tools, however, Mosaic is available free (from the NCSA) in three different client versions: Apple Macintosh, Microsoft Windows, and X Window. You can download the software and its documentation via anonymous FTP (see Chapter 4, "A Movng Experience: FTP for Me," for more information on how to retrieve a file using FTP) at:

```
ftp.ncsa.uiuc.edu
```

> **Navigator's Note:** Once you have Mosaic, you can easily upgrade to new versions, as they appear, through a simple option in Mosaic. Choosing this option will automatically access the required resources and download any necessary files to upgrade your version.

The Mosaic Screen

The Mosaic screen is divided into two parts: a document window, where the action takes place, and a set of controls that surround the document window.

A Mosaic session begins with a *home page* to get you started. On the home page, you'll notice specially colored (or underlined, on a monochrome monitor) text, and images that have a thin colored line around them. These are items that are hyperlinked to something else. Click on highlighted text or outlined images, and you navigate to a related page. That page may have its own set of links to take you to another level. And away you go…

You can navigate to other browsers—Gopher, for example. But of course, what you retrieve through Gopher will only be what Gopher can typically handle—flat text. Only documents that have been prepared as Mosaic resources by being coded with HTML take advantage of Mosaic's special capabilities.

A Mosaic Tour

Let's look at some sample Mosaic pages, to get a feel for Mosaic and the resources it makes available.

Below is a home page for a Mosaic client. (We're using the X Window version of Mosaic on a Sun UNIX workstation, but the other versions are similar and are easily interpreted by Windows or Macintosh users. We'll show the Mac home page later on.)

The top-middle section of the screen shows information about the material in the document window and its location. The Document Title is listed, as well as the Document "URL." The URL (Uniform Resource Locator) tells where an item retrieved by Mosaic came from. The URL tells the name of the resource—which is usually a file, but could be something else, like a Gopher or WAIS location—the full path to the site where the item is located, and the machine name where the item is stored.

The top menu bar offers pull-down menus:

> The File menu lets you manually enter a URL that you want to access, mail a document to yourself or to another Internet user, print a document as text or as formatted Postscript or HTML, or exit the program, plus other options.
> The Options menu lets you cut and paste information, change fonts, and change the hyperlink anchor, among other things.
> The Navigate menu moves you forward, backward, or to other areas that you have used while in Mosaic. As you use Mosaic, you'll find favorite spots to visit on the Internet. Like Gopher and its bookmarks, Mosaic lets you set up your own menu of links for speedy navigation. But Mosaic also remembers where you have been recently, and lets you navigate to those places quickly from this menu.
> The Annotate menu allows you to add your own data or notes to a document for future reference.

The bottom of the window provides a button bar for quick access to the most commonly used options. Many of these are duplicated in pull-down menus available from the menu bar, but you can get to them quickly here.

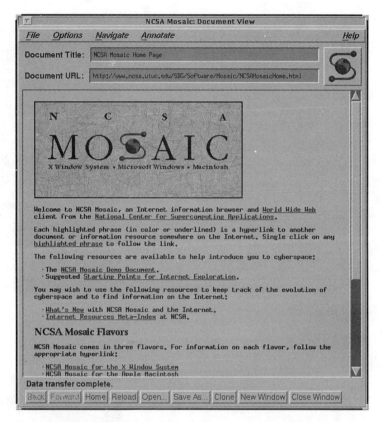

Figure 10.9. Introductory window displays text that describes Mosaic, and offers various starting places from which we can navigate.

The underlined words and phrases (which will stand out in blue on a color screen) are hyperlinks. Clicking the mouse on a hyperlink zaps you to the linked page or information. When you move the cursor to a link, a status field on screen shows you the URL where that link will take you if you choose to go.

Navigator's Note: Some images are broken up into regions, so each region can have a different link. For example, a graphic of a campus map may be broken up into several regions. Clicking on a region will take you to more detailed information about that specific part of the campus.

The other versions of Mosaic are similar to the X Window version shown so far. Figure 10.10 shows the home page of Mosaic on the Macintosh.

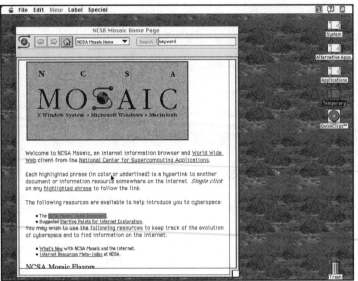

Figure 10.10. Mosaic home page on a Macintosh.

Pretty close to the X Window version, isn't it? Let's take the home page's suggestion, and look at "Demo Document" by clicking on the link (Figure 10.11).

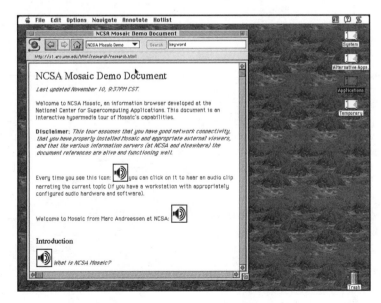

Figure 10.11. Demo document.

Several pages down in the Demo Document, you will find a link to the University of Illinois at Urbana-Champaign's Krannert Art Museum and Kinkead Pavilion (Figure 10.12).

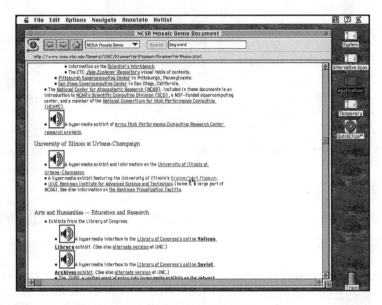

Figure 10.12. Krannert Art Museum and Kinkead Pavilion.

Here you can witness Mosaic's multimedia prowess. Double-clicking "Krannert Art Museum" takes you to the main page of the museum (Figure 10.13).

At the main page, you find bookstore information, a calendar of events, and the museum's location and hours. You can also take a guided tour of the museum through an electronic sampler of its permanent collection (Figure 10.14).

Figure 10.13. Main page of the Krannert Art Museum.

At the bottom of this page, you'll see links to information about the people who developed the guide and the important fact that it was funded by the Krannert Art Museum Council. (A common complaint about the Internet is that resources fail to properly document authorization and information sources. So this is a pleasant surprise.) Here are the guided tour credits:

```
Acknowledgements

The Krannert Art Museum guide was written by Linda Duke,
Eunice Dauterman Maguire, Jim Peele, Robert Smith, and
Maarten van de Guchte. Funding was provided by the
Krannert Art Museum Council.

The online version for the World Wide Web, as viewed
using NCSA Mosaic, was created by Ken Chang, Ginny
Hudak-David, and Linda Jackson of the NCSA Publications
Group. Publications manager is Melissa LaBorg Johnson.
NCSA Mosaic was created by the NCSA Software Development
Group.
```

Now let's click European and American Painting (Figure 10.15).

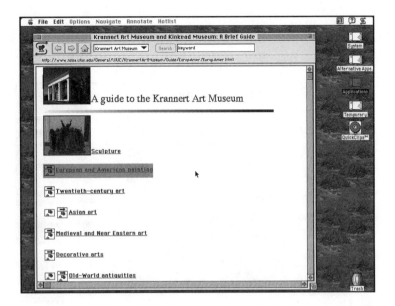

Figure 10.14. An electronic sample of the permanent collection.

Figure 10.15. European and American Painting.

The electronic sampler lists three paintings from the Emily N. and Merle J. Trees Gallery of the museum. You're a big Homer fan (humor us), so you click Cerney la Ville, 1867, Winslow Homer.

Figure 10.16. Cerney la Ville, 1867, Winslow Homer.

Ka-pow! You see the Cerney la Ville-French Farm, in all its colorful glory. It is this capability, and the growing pile of Internet resources that can take advantage of it, that make Mosaic the hottest little tool on the Internet circuit.

The painting is linked to some accompanying text:

> Cerney la Ville-French Farm, 1867, Winslow Homer. Gift of Emily N. and Merle J. Trees.
> To travel and paint in France was the dream of many nineteenth-century American artists. Winslow Homer (1836-1910) painted Cerney la Ville during his ten-month French sojourn in 1867. It is the only known painting from his trip. His unusual choice of a mahogany panel as a painting surface may have been inspired by French painters of the revolutionary Barbizon school, some of whom were said to have painted door panels to pay their expenses at a country inn. Like the Barbizon painters, Homer gives us a prospect observed for its own interest, without prettifying sentiment. He lets the wide sky and the flat land alone enhance the geometric shapes of the farm buildings. The buildings, clustered along the horizon, contrast with the dynamic stream of clouds across the sky. There is something essentially American in the straightforwardness of this homage to France. The painting's largeness of vision belies its small size.

You learn something new every time you hit the Net, don't you?

Other Destinations

In Mosaic, you can juggle several screens at once, and can easily end up with a screen that looks like that in Figure 10.17:

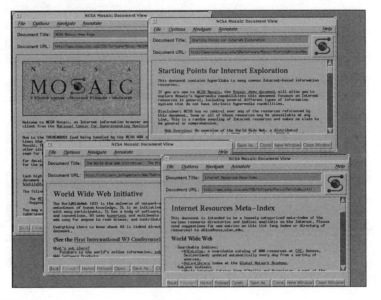

Figure 10.17. Many documents can easily fill the screen.

Of course, there is no top or bottom to Mosaic. But for a new user, a good starting point is "Starting Points for Internet Exploration," found on the Navigate pull-down menu.

Among the starting points listed, you'll see WWW (World Wide Web). Selecting WWW brings up a page like the one shown in Figure 10.18.

From here, you can get to many Internet resources, including Gopher, WAIS, Hytelnet, and other services. You can navigate the Internet in comfort, and with ease, and tap its wealth of text, sound, graphics, video, and other information relatively simply. When all is said and done, Mosaic lets you basically "point-and-click" your way through the Internet.

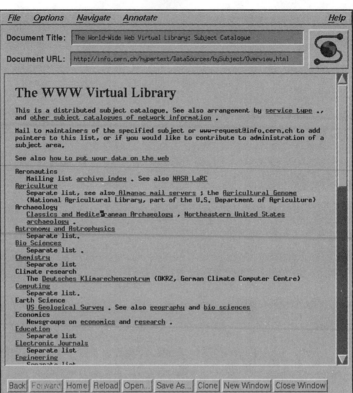

Figure 10.18. The WWW Virtual Library.

Mosaic's Future

The "Cadillac of Internet Navigating tools," Mosaic is the fastest-growing tool in use on the Internet. The University of Illinois at Urbana-Champaign's Krannert Art Museum and Kinkead Pavilion, among other resources, show why. Mosaic is changing the Internet interface for the better.

Ultimately, Mosaic may change the way most people use the Internet for education and for research. Its ability to make Internet navigation simpler may also bring more and more users onto an already crowded net. Best of all, its popularity will encourage more and more information suppliers to build their data for HTML, so Mosaic can really do its thing.

It's likely that, before too much longer, Mosaic—or a near descendant of it—will become the universal way of accessing global information. So the time to become Mosaic-aware is now.

INTERNET DIRECTORY ASSISTANCE: InterNIC

Now that the size of the Internet is ewell beyond human comprehension, the problems of finding out what's happening, what can be done, and how to do them are huge.

One of the main problems is that the Internet is a co-operative environment, a place that has been created by common consent out of a handful of standards, such as TCP/IP. How to discover, manage, and distribute information about the Internet becomes a very significant problem because there is no single authority.

To address this, the National Science Foundation has granted three project awards to three separate organizations. Each organization oversees a specific area—registration services, directory and database services, and information services.

Together, these three awards form the Internet Network Information Center, or InterNIC. The InterNIC is a network information service management system designed to serve the Internet community. Network Solutions, Inc., provides the registration services, AT&T provides directory and database services, and General Atomics provides information services. Most of these services are in place, but many are still being developed and fine-tuned.

InterNIC Information Services

For all of you dynamic Internet navigators, the most valuable InterNIC service will most likely be the InterNIC Information Services provided by General Atomics.

These services will be made available through mid-level Internet organizations and campus Network Information Centers (NICs), which will then provide the information to their clientele. But you, the dynamic Internet navigator, can go straight to the source and cut out the middleman. The information services component is comprised of three parts—reference desk, coordination, and education.

Reference Desk

This service responds to requests for information about the Internet. The Reference Desk provides networking information, referrals to other resources, and associate users with its local NICs.

You can contact the Reference Desk a number of ways, including telephone, e-mail, FAX, and postal mail (for the communicationally disadvantaged). The Reference Desk will provide information about how to get an Internet connection, assist in finding network tools and information, and refer you to local sources of information. Contact the Reference Desk at

Telephone:	800-444-4345 or 619-455-4600
FAX:	619-455-4640
E-mail:	`info@internic.net`
Mail:	InterNIC Information Services
	General Atomics
	P.O. Box #85608
	San Diego, California 92186-9784

Mailboxes and Mailing Lists

The InterNIC Information Services will announce up-to-date information services about the InterNIC and services through a mailing list called `announce@is.internic.net`. You can join this list by sending e-mail to `listserv@is.internic.net`. In the body of the e-mail message, include the following line:

```
subscribe announce Firstname Lastname
```

Thus, `subscribe announce Mark Gibbs`. A more general list announces new resources and information about the Internet. This list is a group effort of the Internet community to try to keep everyone current on new developments without having to join numerous lists. To join this list, send e-mail to `listserv@is.internic.net`. In the body of the e-mail message, include the following line:

```
subscribe net-resources Firstname Lastname
```

Thus, `subscribe net-resources Rich Smith`. Information Services also has lists for mid-level service providers and publishes a newsletter in hard copy and electronically. Send e-mail to `interactive-request@is.internic.net` and request the newsletter in hard copy, electronically, or both (though hard copy is passé and you should be wary of your friends finding out, lest you appear uncool).

InfoSource

Information about the Internet—how it's organized, used, and so on—is provided by InfoSource. This service includes both documents and pointers to other sources. The information made available is useful to everyone from new or infrequent Internet users to managers of mid-level NIC organizations.

Accessing InfoSource

There are several routes through which you can access InfoSource. No particular route is the best, but unless you're impatient and need the information very quickly, e-mail should be used as it reduces the load on the Internet.

FTP

InfoSource documents can be obtained via anonymous FTP from `is.internic.net` in the directory `infosource`. As with most FTP sites, try to get the index file first for a complete listing of what is available.

E-Mail

The InfoSource collection is also available through e-mail. Send the word help on a single line in the body of an e-mail message to mailserv@is.internic.net for information on how to use the mail-server.

WAIS

WAIS can be used to search the InfoSource collection of information. The source internic-infosource is registered in the directory of servers and can be accessed through any public WAIS client. You can also get to WAIS through Gopher and, therefore, to the InfoSource.

Gopher

Probably the easiest and fastest way to access the InfoSource collection is through a Gopher client. Use Gopher to look at All the Gophers in the World or North America. The InterNIC machine is listed as InterNIC: Internet Network Information Center/. Select the InterNIC Information Services/ listed to access InfoSource and browse through the InfoSource Table of Contents on the main menu to get a feel for what information is available.

You can also telnet to is.internic.net and use the login name gopher. This will give you the InterNIC Gopher client, and you can then browse through InfoSource.

An Example

Because InfoSource has the most information for the largest audience, I consider it the most important InterNIC service. It deserves an example. I'll use the is.internic.net Gopher by telneting to is.internic.net and using the login name gopher.

```
bss> telnet is.internic.net
 Trying 192.153.156.15 ...
 Connected to is.internic.net.
 Escape character is '^]'.

 SunOS UNIX (is)

 login: gopher
```

The first screen I see on the telnet connection to the InterNIC Gopher is

```
                    Internet Gopher Information Client v1.01

                    InterNIC: Internet Network Information Center

        1.  Information about the InterNIC.
   ->   2.  InterNIC Information Services (General Atomics)/
        3.  InterNIC Registration Services (NSI)/
        4.  InterNIC Directory and Database Services (AT&T)/
```

The main menu gives you the option to select from the three NIC services. I use the down arrow key to move the pointer to item 2 and then select it by pressing Enter.

```
                    Internet Gopher Information Client v1.01

                    InterNIC Information Services (General Atomics)

   ->   1.  Welcome to the InfoSource/
        2.  InfoSource Table of Contents.
        3.  About InterNIC Information Services/
        4.  InterNIC Store/
        5.  Getting Started on the Internet/
        6.  Internet Information for Everybody/
        7.  Just for NICs/
        8.  NSFNET, NREN, National Information Infrastructure Information/
        9.  Searching the InfoSource/
```

Currently, nine directories to the InterNIC Information Services are available. We'll try Internet Information for Everybody.

```
Internet Gopher Information Client v1.01

                    Internet Information for Everybody

        1.  How Big is the Internet/
        2.  Things to Do on the Internet/
   ->   3.  Learning to Use the Network/
        4.  Government Agencies on the Internet.
        5.  Internet Monthly Reports/
        6.  Introduction to Internet Protocols.
        7.  Organizations/
        8.  Other Networks/
        9.  Where and How to get Requests for Comments Documents/
        10. pdial.
```

This menu gives a good selection of directories that might be of interest to both the beginning Navigator and the expert user. Protocols, organizations, and Internet monthly reports for network managers, things to do on the Internet, and learning to use the network for the beginner—definitely information for everybody. Going one more step down the InterNIC Gopher menus, we'll try Learning to Use the Network.

```
                    Internet Gopher Information Client v1.01

                        Learning to Use the Network


        1.  Clearinghouse for Networked Info Discovery and Retrieval (CNIDR)/
   -->  2.  Quick Guide to Tools.
        3.  Tools General Info/
```

Three options are now available. One of the three is a text file (signified by the period at the end of the line). I selected that and read the information, and then I e-mailed the document to my Internet address (a standard Gopher command; see Chapter 8, "Navigating by Menus: Gopher"). Here is the e-mail document I received from the InterNIC Gopher:

```
From rjs4808 Tue Jun  8 12:59:44 1993
Received: from a105.ucs.usl.edu by armagnac.ucs.usl.edu with SMTP id AA26282
   (5.65c/IDA-1.4.4 for <rs@usl.edu>); Tue, 8 Jun 1993 12:59:43 -0500
Received: by a105.ucs.usl.edu (5.65c/SMI-4.1-910807USL)
        id AA27057; Tue, 8 Jun 1993 12:59:36 -0500
Date: Tue, 8 Jun 1993 12:59:36 -0500
From: rjs4808@ucs.usl.edu
Message-Id: <199306081759.AA27057@a105.ucs.usl.edu>
To: rs@usl.edu
Subject: Quick Guide to Tools
Status: R
Networked Information Discovery and Retrieval: Tools
NOTE: This list is by no means comprehensive, but it does offer an introduction to
the tools.
archie
Search & retrieve anonymous FTP
Source: ftp.sura.net:/pub/archie
Demo: archie.sura.net, login as archie
gopher
Hierarchical browser
Source: boombox.micro.umn.edu:/pub/gopher
Demo: consultant.micro.umn.edu, login as gopher
hytelnet
Hypertext interface to telnet to selected sites
Source: access.usask.ca:/pub/hytelnet
Demo: access.usask.ca, login as hytelnet
```

```
libs
Menu-driven scripted telnet connections to library OPACS and other selected
resources
Source: sonoma.edu: /pub/libs.sh
Demo: vax.sonoma.edu, login as OPAC
libtel
Menu-driven scripted telnet connections to library OPACS and other selected
resources (UNC-CH enhancements added)
Source: ftp.oit.unc.edu:/pub/doc/libtel.unix
Demo: bbs.oit.unc.edu, login as bbs
prospero
Networked file system
Source: cs.washington.edu: /pub/prospero.tar.Z
More info: mail to info-prospero@isi.edu
WAIS
Relevance feedback search and retrieval
Source: quake.think.com:/wais
Demo: quake.think.com, login as wais
WorldWide Web
Hypertext interface to internet resources (links embedded in docs)
Source: info.cern.ch:/pub/www
Demo: info.cern.ch, no login or password
For more information contact:
Clearinghouse for Networked Information Discovery and Retrieval (CNIDR)
Center for Communications - MCNC
PO Box 12889, 3021 Cornwallis Road
Research Triangle Park, NC  27709-2889
George H. Brett II     Jane D. Smith
ghb@concert.net          jds@concert.net
919-248-1886   919-248-9213
Many of these tools are installed on kudzu.concert.net. Login account required.
```

Education Services

InterNIC Services is sponsoring a workshop on use of the Internet. Workshops are announced through the various documents and LISTSERV lists previously mentioned. These are worth following if you're a beginner.

Navigator's Note from Mark Gibbs: While we're talking about education, watch for more of Rich's online "Navigating the Internet" courses, held roughly every three months. The objective of these courses is to give you tutorials on the practical use of Internet resources and detailed examples to follow. These courses track the development of new Internet tools and methods that will make your life a lot easier. Over 15,000 people participated in the last online workshop. New sessions will be announced in various places on the Internet and through several educational publications.

InterNIC Directory and Database Services

The Directory and Database Services (DS) offers a Directory of Directories listing FTP sites, lists of servers available on the Internet, lists of white and yellow page directories, data archives, and library catalogs. This service is provided by AT&T.

You can get to the Directory and Database Services in several ways.

WAIS to DS

Telnet to `ds.internic.net` and log in using `wais` as the user name. No password is required. (Note the `ds` at the beginning of this machine name.)

Archie to DS

Telnet to `ds.internic.net` and access DS by using `archie` as the user name. Again, no password is required. You may also send Archie commands by electronic mail to `archie@ds.internic.net`.

To learn more about how to access the Directory and Database Services, you may contact this service at

Phone:	800-862-0677 or 908-668-6587
Fax:	908-668-3763
E-mail:	`admin@ds.internic.net`

Gopher

Of course, Gopher can be used (as shown in the earlier example) to reach all three services. Here's a listing of the first screen from the InterNIC Directory and Databases Services:

```
                Internet Gopher Information Client v1.01

            InterNIC Directory and Database Services (AT&T)

        1.  InterNIC Directory of Directories Resource Types/
        2.  Information about the InterNIC Directory and Database Services/
        3.  IETF Documents/
        4.  IETF Steering Group Documents/
        5.  Internet Draft Documents/
        6.  Internet Informational RFC Documents (FYIs)/
        7.  Internet Policies and Procedures/
        8.  Internet Request For Comments (RFC) Documents/
        9.  Internet Society (ISOC) Documents/
        10. Internet Standard RFC Documents (STDs)/
        11. National Science Foundation Databases/
        12. Publicly Accessible Databases/
        13. Publicly Accessible Sources/
   -->  14. The DS WHOIS Database <?>
        15. The Internet Resource Guide/
```

Of particular interest is the DS WHOIS Database. This has the <?> at the end of its Gopher item, meaning that it is a searchable database. It is the "white pages" (like the white pages of a regular telephone directory) of the InterNIC Directory and Database Services. It is not a comprehensive white pages service, but coming from AT&T, it has a better chance than many others of becoming one. Here is a list I retrieved from asking the DS WHOIS for Richard Smith:

```
                Internet Gopher Information Client v1.01

                The DS WHOIS Database: richard smith

   -->  1.  Smith, Alan (AS22)   smith@UCBVAX.BERKELEY.EDU  .
        2.  Smith, Bruce (BS50)   SMITH#BRUCE@NMFECC.LLNL.GOV  .
        3.  Smith, Duane Donald (DDS5)   SMITH@CHEMISTRY.CHEMISTRY.PURDUE.EDU  .
        4.  Smith, Douglas (DS94)   SMITH@KESTREL.EDU  .
        5.  Smith, Edward (ES3)   Edward.Smith@A.CS.CMU.EDU  .
        6.  Smith, Judith P. (JS67)   SMITH@VLSI.JPL.NASA.GOV  .
        7.  Smith, Kent (KS7)   k-smith@CS.UTAH.EDU  .
        8.  Karlin, Richard (RAK31)   RICHARD%RICHP1.UUCP@UUNET.UU.NET  .
        9.  Baxter, Richard (RB187)   baxter-richard@YALE.EDU  .
        10. Beigel, Richard J. (RJB56)   beigel-richard@CS.YALE.EDU  .
        11. Coyle, Richard J. (RJC62)   RICHARD@GRYPHON.COM  .
        12. Platek, Richard A. (RP9)   richard@ORACORP.COM  .
        13. Smith, William B. (WBS)   smith@URBANA.MCD.MOT.COM  .
        14. Smith, Carl H. (CS34)   smith@MIMSY.UMD.EDU  .
        15. Smith, Mary J. (MJS54)   mjsmith@ECN.PURDUE.EDU  .
        16. Roos, Robert S. (RSR17)   rroos@SMITH.BITNET  .
        17. Fraser-Smith, A.C. (AF7)   ACFS@STAR.STANFORD.EDU  .
        18. Smith, Barbara (BS29)   ATP.Barbara@R20.UTEXAS.EDU  .
```

Nope, I'm not listed yet. This database—being a WAIS database—has all words in it indexed (see Chapter 7, "The Database of Databases: WAIS," for more information) so you can also find information on institutions as well as individual users.

InterNIC Registration Services

The third service, the InterNIC Registration Service, is the most specialized of the three. The Registration Service will register Internet Domains, networks, and other Internet entities. Network administrators and Internet service providers will use this service to register their organizations and institutions.

This service will also provide an electronic "yellow pages" database that will be useful when searching for machine names and addresses. As with the other InterNIC services, the database will have several access points.

WAIS and mail access is similar to other InterNIC services, except that the machine's name is rs.internic.net. A WHOIS program can be accessed by using telnet to connect to rs.internic.net and using the word whois as the login.

And, of course, good old Gopher can get you there. Here is the first screen of the InterNIC Registration Services when selected from Gopher.

```
              Internet Gopher Information Client v1.01

               InterNIC Registration Services (NSI)


     1.  InterNIC Registration Archives/
 ->  2.  Whois Searches (InterNIC IP, ASN, DNS, and POC Registry) <?>
     3.  Whois Searches (Non-MILNET, Non-POC Individuals - run by AT&T) <?>
```

Pretty bare at the present. You can see the difference in this database compared to the InterNIC Directory and Database Services shown earlier. Selecting the second item, I searched for the word "Moscow" to find someone I needed to talk to (the Internet is a whole new way of jet-setting, without the jet lag).

```
              Internet Gopher Information Client v1.01


    Whois Searches (InterNIC IP, ASN, DNS, and POC Registry): moscow

  ->  1.  Kurchatov Institute of Atomic Energy, Moscow, USSR (NET-KIAE-MOSC.
      2.  [No name] (MOSCOW)        Hostname: MOSCOW.UIDAHO.EDU      Address:.
      3.  University of Idaho (UIDAHO-DOM)     Moscow, ID 83843         Domai.
      4.  Moscow State University (NET-MSUNET)      Digital Networks Group, .
      5.  Institute for Theoretical & Experimental Physics (ASN-MOSCOW-HEP.
```

```
 6.  Soldatov, Aleksey A. (AAS3)  alex@kiae.su      Kurchatov Institute.
 7.  Avdeyev, Dmitry (DA196)  dmitry@npi.msu.su      Nuclear Physics In.
 8.  Simon, Mike A. (MAS33)  simon@moscow.uidaho.edu      University of.
 9.  Electronics and Computer Science Center of Moscow Institute of Ph.
10.  Institute for Theoretical and Experimental Physics (ASN-IREP-MOSCO.
11.  Advanced Hardware Architectures (AHA-DOM)      P.O. Box 9669      M.
12.  RelTeam Company, Limited (SU1-DOM)      56-131 Khoroshovskoye shos.
13.  Shirikov, Vladislav (VS86)  shirikov@jinr.dubna.su      P.O.Box 79.
14.  Arkhipov, Andrei (AA124)  root@elvis.msk.su      ELVIS Research Ce.
15.  Orel, Oleg (OO6)  postmaster@oea.ihep.su      OEA      IHEP      Ser.
16.  BALL, DAVID W. (DWB61)  [No mailbox]      715 S. WASHINGTON ST.    .
17.  Lavrentiev, Andrew (AL44)  kiae.su!iaicom.dubna.su!root      Mosco.
18.  Kudryashev, Michael (MK60)  mike@ECSC.MIPT.SU      141700, Moscow .
```

The result was all entries with the word "moscow" somewhere in the title or in the content of the document. Selecting the first entry gave me some information on the institution.

```
 _ _ _ _ _ _ _ _ _ _
Kurchatov Institute of Atomic Energy, Moscow, USSR (NET-KIAE-MOSCOW)
   SU-123182 Moscow
   USSR

   Netname: KIAE-MOSCOW
   Netnumber: 144.206.0.0

   Coordinator:
      Soldatov, Aleksey A.  (AAS3)  alex@kiae.su
      +7 095 196 9614

   Record last updated on 04-Jan-91.



Press <RETURN> to continue, <m> to mail, <s> to save, or <p> to print:
```

Sparse and a bit dated, but this service has been up and running only since April 1993, so getting as far as they have is pretty impressive.

Saint NIC

The National Science Foundation is to be congratulated on getting such an ambitious scheme off the ground. Now they've really got their work cut out for them to not only get all the services in place, but to do so in the face of the fantastic growth of the Internet.

For the Internet navigator, access to the InterNIC is like a Christmas present that gets better and better every day. You should subscribe to the LISTSERV lists and set aside some time to browse its Gopher menus on a regular basis.

INTERNETIQUETTE: MANNERS AND THE INTERNET

Whenever people communicate (whether in public or in private), some behaviors and standards of conduct are considered acceptable, and others are not.

The same applies on the Internet, in e-mail, and in newsgroups and lists. Some ways of acting are polite and civilized, and others make you appear rude and will get you disliked or even into trouble.

"What are they going to do to me when I'm 3,000 miles away?" you might ask. Well, it could mean (in very serious cases) that a site is told to cut you off or lose its access. You can guess which happens. People aren't removed from the Internet very often, but when they are, it's usually for a pretty serious reason.

When a sufficient number of people communicate, strange things begin to happen. Folk stories (sometimes also called *urban legends*) can be found on the Internet. Someone tells a story, it takes on a life of its own; it becomes (howling in the distance) an undead tale—a story that won't die.

In this chapter, we'll examine guidelines for conduct on the Internet—what might be called *Internetiquette*—and some of the Internet folk stories.

Internetiquette

When you were young, your mother told you how to behave. "Say please and thank you" and "don't shout" were the kinds of things you probably heard. If she knew that you were running around on the Internet with your friends having a wild time, she'd apply much the same kind of guidelines.

Internetiquette for Electronic Mail

When using electronic mail services to communicate with other people, try to remember these important points of Internetiquette:

1. **Shouting:** DON'T SHOUT. Messages in all uppercase are hard to read and are also very irritating. This is commonly called shouting. A suitable response is to politely ask people who do this to stop. If they don't, be generous. Perhaps they're waiting for the computer service engineer to fix their shift key. (Maybe the poet e.e. cummings had the opposite problem and his service engineer never showed up.) If shouters exhibit long-term recidivist tendencies, just don't read anything from them until they complain; then you can politely tell them why. If the shouter is your boss, you're on your own.

2. **Correct addressing:** Be certain that your message is addressed to the person you want to send it to. A young lady in a major corporation was having what was once called a dalliance with a young gentleman employed by the same organization. Apparently things weren't going so well, and in a fit of pique, she decided to write to him—on the company's electronic mail system. She wrote at length about his failings as a companion, both socially and, in great detail, sexually. She then fumbled on the keyboard and promptly sent the letter to everyone in her division.

3. **Quotability:** Remember (especially when the subject matter is questionable) that anything you send can be easily and almost instantly forwarded to others.

4. **Who sent it?:** Be sure that a message asking you to do something potentially indiscreet is from the person it claims to be from. At one company, a bogus electronic message (apparently from the CEO) went to all the employees in a branch office. The message asked for their frank opinions (which would be kept confidential) of their superiors, because rumors of problems had been heard. Several people fell for it, and because the recipient was, indeed, the CEO, their faux pas was complete.

5. **Your tone:** Watch the tone of what you write. What may sound funny or reasonable in speech can sound aggressive, abrupt, or just plain rude in e-mail. This is partly explained by the fact that e-mail is so easy to produce. Most people don't spend a great deal of time considering what they're going to put in an electronic message and rarely format it as they would a handwritten letter. You should save your responses if they are of any significant length or importance and review them before you commit them to the Internet. If you think you might be misinterpreted, you can, if the circumstances permit, use e-mail shorthand and *emoticons* (see the following section).

6. **Other people's tone:** You should also carefully read what others write. Their apparent tone may not be what they actually meant. I (Mark Gibbs) was once trying to reach a product manager in a company I was working with and finally resorted to e-mail, which his secretary always handled for him. She replied "I resent your message" and, like a gold-plated, five-star idiot, I phoned and asked her, "What the hell do you resent?" I then spent the next ten minutes jabbering my apologies (I had mistaken re-sent for resent).

7. **Suitable content:** Don't be coarse, vulgar, or suggestive. Not only are these kinds of expressions rarely acceptable to others, but you're putting them on electronic paper; they may well hang around to haunt you. Many a management career has foundered on the rocks of things that shouldn't have been written down. E-mail can make the rocks come up to meet you faster.

8. **Discretion:** Don't send any message that you wouldn't send in a letter. If you are going to libel, gossip, or be otherwise indiscreet, keep to the spoken word. Better yet, avoid the impulse; it is vulgar.

9. **Flaming:** *Flaming* is when you write a message, obviously in anger, and "say what you think." The usual result is that the author looks foolish and immature. Don't flame.

10. **Chain letters:** Don't get involved with them. At all. At the least they are a waste of resources (the bandwidth to send them) and at worst illegal.

E-Mail Shorthand and Emoticons

As suggested earlier, there are ways to make your intentions clearer in electronic messages. These conventions are usually not used in formal communications, but they are very useful for everyday traffic. When you want to stress the tone in which you're saying something (and do it the hip way), you can use shorthand and emoticons.

E-Mail Shorthand

E-mail shorthand usually refers to acronyms that are strategically placed in messages. They are subject to context, and so are used both politely and impolitely, for humor, anger, and so on:

LOL—**L**aughing **O**ut **L**oud—as in "The company says that the product will be delivered on time (LOL)."

OTF—**O**n **T**he **F**loor (laughing)—as in "The company says that the product will be delivered on time and under budget (OTF)."

ROTFL—**R**olling **O**n **T**he **F**loor **L**aughing—as in "The company says that the product will be delivered on time, under budget, and to specification (ROTFL)."

IMHO—**I**n **M**y **H**umble **O**pinion—as in "The product will be just what we need, IMHO."

BTW—**B**y **T**he **W**ay—as in "BTW, they've finally released the product— late (ROTFL)."

YMMV—**Y**our **M**ileage **M**ay **V**ary—as in "I got a 9600 baud connection from my site using xyz product, YMMV."

E-Mail Emoticons

Emoticons are sequences of characters that denote faces and expressions. There are literally hundreds, although only a few are in common use. They always read better if they are in a monospaced font (like Courier, the normal typewriter font, where each character is the same width). They are read sideways:

:-)   Smile—as in "we got the product :-)" to show pleasure or "we can't be bothered about sending you the product :-)" to show that you don't mean it

;-)   Wink—as in "good product, eh? ;-)"

:-(Displeasure—as in "we got the product, but... :-("
:->   Smug—as in "we got the product first :->"

The following emoticons aren't so common, and some are just plain bizarre:

:-t	User is cross	(-)	User needs a haircut
:-\	User is undecided	{:-)	User parts hair in the middle
:-o	User is shocked	{(:-)	User is wearing a toupee
:-&	User is tongue-tied	}(:-(	User is wearing toupee in wind
¦-¦	User is asleep (boredom)	-:-)	User has a mohawk
:-c	User is bummed out	(:)-)	User likes to scuba dive
:-#	User's lips are sealed	0-)	User wears a scuba mask
8-¦	User is in suspense	:-)X	User wears a bow tie
:-<	User is sad	:-}	User wears lipstick
8-#	User is dead	@:I	User wears a turban
:-I	Hmmm	8-)	User wears glasses
:-x	"My lips are sealed"	:::-)	User wears bifocals
:-7	User has made a wry statement	B-)	User wears horn-rims
:-p	User is sticking tongue out	:-)8	User is well-dressed
:-9	User is licking lips	:-0	User is an orator
:-*	User just ate a sour pickle	:<¦	User attends an Ivy League school
:>)	User has a big nose	+:-¦	User is a priest
%-)	User is cross-eyed	+-(:-)	User is the pope
#-)	User partied all night	[:¦]	User is a robot
[:-)	User is listening to headphones	*:o)	User is a bozo
(-:	User is left-handed	o-)	User is a cyclops
:-	User is male	:>	User is a midget
:-Q	User smokes	8:]	User is a gorilla
:-?	User smokes a pipe	=:-)	User is a punk-rocker
:-{	User has a mustache	%-^	User is Picasso
:-%	User has a beard	*<¦:-)	User is Santa Claus (Ho Ho Ho)

Undead Folktales

The folktale is a curious social phenomenon, usually based on some real event that gets distorted and retold until it is completely different from the original (and usually more interesting). One example of the modern folktale is the lady who tried to dry her poodle in the microwave oven.

On the Internet, much the same thing happens, and because most messages are text, copies are filed away only to resurface later.

Modem Tax

One of the old favorites is the dreaded Modem Tax. Once upon a time there was a proposal to tax modems, but it was (justly) struck down before it got anywhere.

The story pops up at least once a year in a public forum, where someone posts a message like "What's this I hear about the government planning a tax on the use of modems?" This is usually greeted with a goodly amount of derision and scoffing—particularly if the someone has been using the Internet for any length of time. It's considered tantamount to saying that you've had your head under a rock (ROTFL).

Dying Child Postcards

Another story that has joined the zombie squad, refusing to die, is Send a Dying Child a Postcard.

In 1986, a seven-year-old boy named Craig Shergold was diagnosed as having an inoperable brain tumor. Young Mr. Shergold decided that he wanted to break the Guinness record for receiving get-well cards. Thanks to publicity, the cards started rolling in. One of the ways that the news was spread was through various e-mail systems, including the Internet.

It's now tens of millions of cards later. Craig broke the record with ease way back in 1989, but despite his successful operation and recovery, the cards keep coming. On the Internet, Craig's request keeps popping up. Several times each year, someone spreads the word as if it had just happened. A new wave of cards descends on Craig, his family, and the hospital where he was treated.

Many other stories illustrate the bizarre nature of messages and folklore on the Internet. They all point to the fact that you should be wary about the things you read in public forums and act very carefully on what's in them.

Playing the Game

You should remember several things concerning tidying up after yourself when you're using and cruising the Internet.

1. If you abandon an account on a machine on the Internet, delete any files in your work areas, and tell the system supervisor you're leaving so that the supervisor can clean up. Also, make sure that you unsubscribe from any LISTSERV lists you belong to—otherwise your non-existent account will still be getting messages, and they'll be getting sent back to the LISTSERV and…basically, it's messy.

2. If you discover someone's password, tell them. Don't, under any circumstances, use that account, tell anyone else that you know the password, or otherwise compromise that person's security.

3. If you find a problem in a computer system, tell the supervisor. Don't just shrug your shoulders and assume it is someone else's problem. That's like seeing spilled oil on the road and not telling anyone of the danger.

4. If you know of, or hear of, people attempting to break into systems or otherwise break security, tell the system supervisor immediately.

Remember!

Remember that the Internet has social as well as technical aspects. Not everyone who uses the Internet is a technical guru or a rocket scientist. Good manners and polite, considerate behavior will get you all the help and cooperation you want.

It's very important to remember that the Internet is a cooperative environment. If people start abusing the trust of the community, that cooperative spirit will be in danger of evaporating. Once it's gone, the Internet will never be the same again.

VIEWS AND NEWS: USENET

When America was young, news from New York could take weeks or even months to reach the Wild West. Then along came the telegraph, and suddenly, unless you were out in the backwoods, important news was never more than a few days old. Today, we have TV and radio, and news is never more than seconds old if you have the right technology on hand.

With the Internet, news is a continuous phenomenon. Information about the state of the world (both the real world and the world of the Internet) and opinions concerning life, the universe, and everything are freely traded all the time.

News is everywhere on the Internet, and USENET is the main vehicle.

USENET

USENET was created by two Duke University graduate students, Tom Truscott and Jim Ellis. They developed software so that people on different computers could exchange messages on topics in a way that allowed discussions to develop. Their software has gone through many versions and is now being used by hundreds of thousands of people internationally every day. These users participate in thousands of *newsgroups* (the USENET name for discussion groups) covering topics dealing with everything from computer systems administration to exotic religious philosophies.

For the Internet navigator, newsgroups can be a fantastic source of information about what's going on, what services are available, and what new resources can be plundered (metaphorically speaking).

Newsgroups

USENET newsgroups (also called just "groups") are organized as a hierarchy. At the top are topics—for example, a computer topic (not very surprising), a science topic, a recreation topic, and so on. Subtopics under science would include chemistry, astronomy, and many others. Under those subtopics are sub-subtopics—for example, hubble (about the Hubble telescope) under astronomy.

Topics and subtopics (and sub-subtopics and sub-sub-subtopics) have abbreviated names. Thus, science is `sci`, astronomy is `astro`, and the newsgroup name for news and discussion of the Hubble telescope is `sci.astro.hubble`. The hierarchy reads from left to right, from the most general level to the most specific.

In general, USENET newsgroups fall into a well-defined hierarchy of subjects. Here are some of the top-level topics, with a sample of the newsgroup types that are available under each.

`comp`	Topics of interest to both computer professionals and hobbyists, including computer science, software sources, and information on hardware and software.
`comp.ai`	Artificial intelligence discussions.
`comp.dcom.modems`	Data communications hardware and software.
`comp.lang.lisp.mcl`	Discusses Apple's Macintosh Common Lisp.

`comp.org.usenix`	USENIX Association events and announcements.
`comp.os.os2.apps`	Discussions of applications under OS/2.
`comp.sys.sun.announce`	Sun announcements and Sunergy mailings (moderated).
`sci`	Discussions marked by special knowledge relating to research in or application of the established sciences.
`sci.chem.organomet`	Organometallic chemistry.
`sci.geo.geology`	Discussion of solid earth sciences.
`sci.math.symbolic`	Symbolic algebra discussion.
`sci.research`	Research methods, funding, and ethics.
`sci.math.num-analysis`	Numerical analysis.
`soc`	Groups primarily addressing social issues and socializing. Included are discussions related to many different world cultures.
`soc.college.grad`	General issues related to graduate schools.
`soc.culture.african.american`	Discussions about African American issues.
`soc.religion.bahai`	Discussion of the Baha'i Faith (moderated).
`soc.veterans`	Social issues relating to military veterans.
`soc.roots`	Discussing genealogy and genealogical matters.
`talk`	Groups largely debate-oriented and tending to feature long discussions without resolution and without appreciable amounts of generally useful information.
`talk.abortion`	All sorts of discussions and arguments on abortion.

`talk.environment`	Discussion of the state of the environment and what to do about it.
`talk.politics.animals`	The use and/or abuse of animals.
`talk.politics.theory`	Theory of politics and political systems.
`talk.rape`	Discussions on stopping rape.
`news`	Groups concerned with the news network, group maintenance, and software.
`news.admin.policy`	Policy issues of USENET.
`news.future`	The future technology of network news systems.
`news.misc`	Discussions of USENET itself.
`news.software.readers`	Discusses software used to read network news.
`news.answers`	Repository for periodic USENET articles.

Other News

USENET is not the only source of news. The software used to read USENET news can also get news feeds from other Internet sources, and a growing number of networks and groups are distributing news. (Or what they think of as news—if you're, say, an avid follower of the latest advances in the biology of slugs. Actually, I made that up. This has far weirder topics than that.) For example, groups with `alt` listings are heavily subscribed to and distributed and come mainly from outside USENET.

`alt`	Unofficial or temporary topics that run the gamut of...anything goes.
`alt.aeffle.und.pferdle`	German TV cartoon characters (honestly).
`alt.bizarre`	If it's too weird for the weirdos, it's here.
`alt.butt-keg.marmalade`	Typical Yankee analytic humor.
`alt.conspiracy.jfk`	The Kennedy assassination.
`alt.sex.head`	Tales of certain erotic activities.
`alt.wolves`	Discusses wolves and wolf-mix dogs.

These newsgroups are created in various ways. Their formation and promotion don't go through the same process as USENET newsgroups (explained later in this chapter), so we'll conveniently ignore them. If you want to find out how to get involved with or start these, talk with (e-mail) participants and find out what the process is for that system.

> **Navigator's Note:** A site can create newsgroups for its own users. For example, a university might have newsgroups for various student groups, administration announcements, and class assignments.

Brian Reid, who works at the Network Systems Laboratory of Digital Equipment Corporation, has put together an interesting chart showing the most popular USENET groups. The data is taken from the monthly volume and readership statistics published in news.lists.

```
------------------------------------------------
USENET readership and volume, May 1993

 +— Readership Rank
 ¦    +— Estimated total number of people who read the group, worldwide.
 ¦    ¦    +— Actual number of readers in sampled population
 ¦    ¦    ¦    +— Propagation: how many sites receive this group at all
 ¦    ¦    ¦    ¦    +— Recent traffic (messages per month)
 ¦    ¦    ¦    ¦    ¦    +— Recent traffic (kilobytes per month)
 ¦    ¦    ¦    ¦    ¦    ¦    +— Share: % of newsreaders
 ¦    ¦    ¦    ¦    ¦    ¦    ¦   who read this group.
 V    V    V    V    V    V    V
 1 230000 4611 92%    1   13.6  10.0% news.announce.newusers
 2 230000 4447 88%    1   29.2   9.7% news.answers
 3 190000 3729 85% 1473 2931.4   8.1% misc.jobs.offered
 4 190000 3667 67% 2377 5132.2   8.0% alt.sex
 5 170000 3327 83%   67  123.9   7.2% rec.humor.funny
 6 160000 3120 88%  891 1386.1   6.8% comp.unix.questions
 7 160000 3059 53%  620 4925.3   6.7% alt.sex.stories
 8 150000 2997 73%   30  469.1   6.5% rec.arts.erotica
 9 150000 2976 54%  795 38955.8  6.5% alt.binaries.pictures.erotica
10 150000 2919 83% 1917 2352.8   6.3% misc.forsale
11 140000 2690 82% 2173 5915.3   5.9% rec.humor
12 130000 2586 90% 1625 3549.2   5.6% news.groups
13 130000 2552 88% 1639 2967.6   5.6% comp.lang.c
14 130000 2486 91%  113 1192.6   5.4% news.announce.newgroups
15 130000 2481 67%  902 3782.0   5.4% alt.activism
16 120000 2305 63% 1511 4375.5   5.0% alt.sex.bondage
17 120000 2270 83%  771 1796.7   4.9% misc.jobs.misc
18 110000 2239 86%  816 1752.1   4.9% comp.graphics
19 100000 2044 78% 2475 4937.2   4.4% rec.arts.movies
20 100000 1995 84% 3093 5026.9   4.3% comp.sys.ibm.pc.hardware
```

```
21 100000 1994  12%   20   109.3   4.3%  clari.news.briefs
22 100000 1992  87%  126  1034.7   4.3%  news.announce.conferences
23 100000 1976  81% 1097  1915.4   4.3%  comp.sys.sun.admin
24 100000 1972  74% 3963  9671.4   4.3%  soc.culture.indian
25 100000 1963  58%  635 25856.3   4.3%  alt.binaries.pictures.misc
```

Example

Here's a short look at how a discussion takes place within the newsgroup `rec.arts.movies`. The group's short description is

rec.arts.movies	Discussions of movies and movie-making.

In the following example, I've already selected newsgroup and article.

```
Article 93919 (668 more) in rec.arts.movies:
From: jlh@jpradley.jpr.com (Jeff Henslin)
Subject: Luis Bunuel - The Strange Object of Desire
Organization: Unix in NYC
Date: Thu, 3 Jun 1993 02:00:57 GMT
Lines: 12


This week I watched this film (French), intrigued by Luis Bunuel who
also directed "Like Water for Chocolate". In the film the main female
role is played by two actresses, who have different, non-obvious
personality traits. One might conclude there are two lead female
roles, although they appear to the lead male character as one. They
are different enough in appearance for one to draw the conclusion that
we (the audience) are meant to notice the disparity, and draw some
conclusion.  Would anyone who has seen this film care to comment on
it?


Jeff
End of article 93919 (of 94589) —what next? [^Nnpq]

Esc-chr: ^]  help: ^]?  port:2 speed: 9600 parity:none echo:rem  VT102 ....
```

This article was posted and is asking for information on a movie. This is an original article that calls for a discussion. In many cases, you contact the author directly to answer a question, but in this case, given the nature of the newsgroup, a reply to the article (by posting one to the newsgroup) would be appropriate.

To follow the thread of this message (thread is the term often used for a sequence of messages related to each other) use the Ctrl+N command, which searches for the next unread message with the same subject. Let's see where it takes us:

```
Article 93929 (686 more) in rec.arts.movies:
From: agrawal@lipari.usc.edu (Amitabh Agrawal)
Subject: Re: Luis Bunuel - The Strange Object of Desire
Date: 2 Jun 1993 22:35:58 -0700
Organization: University of Southern California, Los Angeles, CA
Lines: 23
NNTP-Posting-Host: lipari.usc.edu
In-reply-to: jlh@jpradley.jpr.com's message of Thu, 3 Jun 1993 02:00:57 GMT

In article <C80w9L.2x2@jpradley.jpr.com> jlh@jpradley.jpr.com (Jeff Henslin)
writes:

    This week I watched this film (French), intrigued by Luis Bunuel who
    also directed "Like Water for Chocolate". In the film the main female
    role is played by two actresses, who have different, non-obvious
    personality traits. One might conclude there are two lead female
    roles, although they appear to the lead male character as one. They
    are different enough in appearance for one to draw the conclusion that
    we (the audience) are meant to notice the disparity, and draw some
    conclusion.  Would anyone who has seen this film care to comment on
    it?

Go home and watch it again, and again... and again... Incidently the
title is "That Obscure Object of Desire"...

Did "Luis Bunuel" direct "Like Water for Chocolate"... That makes this
movie a must see.... Well!! this weekend...

Amit

End of article 93929 (of 94589)—what next? [^Nnpq]
Esc-chr: ^]  help: ^]?  port:2 speed: 9600 parity:none echo:rem  VT102 ....

Article 94018 (666 more) in rec.arts.movies:
From: reiher@ficus.cs.ucla.edu (Peter Reiher)
(SAME) Subject: Re: Luis Bunuel - The Strange Object of Desire
Nntp-Posting-Host: wells.cs.ucla.edu
Organization: UCLA Computer Science Department
Date: Thu, 3 Jun 93 19:21:01 GMT
Lines: 17

In article <AGRAWAL.93Jun2223557@lipari.usc.edu> agrawal@lipari.usc.edu (Amitabh
 Agrawal) writes:
>
>Did "Luis Bunuel" direct "Like Water for Chocolate"... That makes this
>movie a must see.... Well!! this weekend...

No, Mr. Bunuel has been dead for some years now.  "Like Water For Chocolate"
was directed by Alfonso Arau, who those of us in their thirties or older
```

```
may remember as a character actor in such films as "The Wild Bunch" and
"Scandalous John".  He is apparently much better known in Mexico.  I myself
do not detect a strong common link between Bunuel and "Like Water For
Chocolate".  Bunuel never made a totally serious movie in his life, and
"Like Water For Chocolate" seemed pretty earnest, to me.


 —
—MORE— (96%)
Esc-chr: ^]  help: ^]?  port:2 speed: 9600 parity:none echo:rem  VT102 ....
```

There you have part of a typical discussion on this newsgroup. The tone (whether the participants pontificate, discuss, bicker, and so on) and how quickly messages are posted depends on the purpose and scope of the newsgroup. The purpose of this newsgroup is discussion. Many other newsgroups are for information only and actually discourage discussion. Read through a newsgroup to find out what type it is before participating.

Participating in News

You can access news from many different types of machines. Software programs enable you to access news for UNIX, VMS, PC DOS, Macs, and so on. Most are available via anonymous FTP over the Internet (see Appendix H, "The Internet Navigator's Gazetteer"), but you'll probably have one already installed on your system if you have a UNIX machine. Your systems administrator can tell you what news program is installed with your network connection. You should also get them to show you how it's set up and whether they have any special features to make newsgroup access easier (many sites set up scripts to make the user's life easier).

The rn Program

To show how news is used, I'll demonstrate one of the most popular news reading programs, the UNIX rn news reading software (note that the other popular news reading program is nn and is pretty similar to rn).

When you start rn, articles from each newsgroup to which you subscribe are presented, one article at a time (an article is an individual news item). As each article is presented, you are shown the header containing the name of the author, the subject of the article, and the first page of the article, and you are asked if you want more.

rn operates on three levels:

1. The newsgroup selection level.

2. The article selection level.

3. The article paging level.

Each level has its own set of commands and its own help menu. As with other programs mentioned in this book, reading the help screens, or more importantly, knowing how to get in and out of the help screens and exit the program, are just about the most important things a new user can learn. Typing the letter h at any rn level or at any prompt brings you a help list and a brief explanation of what you can do.

Newsgroup Selection Level

Starting rn puts you at the selection level. The program checks to see if any new newsgroups have been added since the last time you read your news; if so, you are asked if you want to add the newsgroup to your reading list of groups.

In the following example, I am asked if I want to subscribe to a new newsgroup biz.pagesat. I answer "no" to this new newsgroup and to the following newsgroup, alt.fan.TTBS. The options, [ynYN], mean:

1. Type y (or just press the Spacebar) to add the current newsgroup to the list of those you follow.

2. Type Y to add all new groups to your list and subscribe to them.

3. Type N to add all new groups to your list but not subscribe to them.

4. Type n to forget about this newsgroup.

The Y and N commands are useful when you're first starting to access newsgroups or when you have not read your news for a long period of time. They add all new newsgroups to your list and either subscribe to them or leave them unsubscribed to but recorded in one fell swoop. Your reason for recording them is so that you can go back later and join them.

```
bss> rn

Unread news in general                      371 articles
Unread news in to                             4 articles
Unread news in usl.announce                   4 articles
Unread news in usl.class.cmps.201            10 articles
```

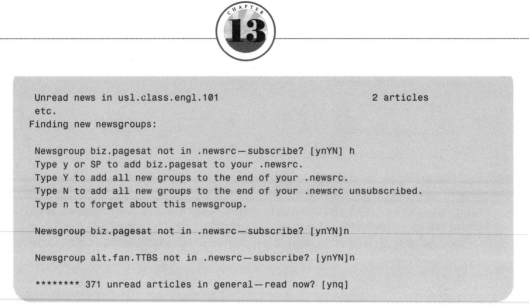

```
Unread news in usl.class.engl.101                          2 articles
etc.
Finding new newsgroups:

Newsgroup biz.pagesat not in .newsrc—subscribe? [ynYN] h
Type y or SP to add biz.pagesat to your .newsrc.
Type Y to add all new groups to the end of your .newsrc.
Type N to add all new groups to the end of your .newsrc unsubscribed.
Type n to forget about this newsgroup.

Newsgroup biz.pagesat not in .newsrc—subscribe? [ynYN]n

Newsgroup alt.fan.TTBS not in .newsrc—subscribe? [ynYN]n

******** 371 unread articles in general—read now? [ynq]
```

After the listing of new newsgroups comes the first newsgroup to which you are subscribed. rn tells you how many messages are unread and asks if you would like to read them. You have three options:

1. Type y for yes, read this newsgroup.

2. Type n for next newsgroup.

3. Type q for quit.

The .newsrc File

The rn program keeps track of which newsgroups you have subscribed to and what articles you have read with a file called .newsrc. This file is created the first time you use the rn program, and it contains the names of all newsgroups that your site has access to over the network. Here is a small sample of a .newsrc file:

```
alt!
general: 1-530
to: 1-4
usl.announce: 1-1
usl.cacs.announce: 1-11
usl.class.cmps.201: 1-6
usl.centercasts: 1-13
news.admin: 1-12300
news.admin.misc:
news.admin.technical:
news.software.notes! 1-120
news.sysadmin! 1-1989
comp.admin.policy! 1-3372
```

```
comp.ai! 1-11997
comp.ai.digest:
comp.ai.edu! 1-335
comp.ai.fuzzy!
comp.ai.genetic!
sci.aquaria:
sci.archaeology:
sci.astro:
rec.arts.animation! 1-3805
soc.culture.europe:
alt.activism:
```

The numbers after a newsgroup indicate the articles that have been read in that newsgroup. No numbers means that no articles have been read. The exclamation point, !, indicates that you are unsubscribed to that newsgroup (that is, you don't belong to it and don't get news from it).

When you first start rn, you are asked whether you want to subscribe to each newsgroup in turn. If you answer "yes," you'll be asked where you want it placed in your .newsrc file. Do you want a newsgroup placed first on the list, last, or somewhere in between? Where the entries are in the .newsrc file will determine the order in which you will see newsgroups when you start rn (the first entry in the file is the first you see).

The problem here is that you have access to thousands of newsgroups. The site I use at the University of Southwestern Louisiana currently has access to 2,455 newsgroups. It would take some time to subscribe or unsubscribe to all these groups.

Subscribing to all newsgroups with the Y command and then editing the .newsrc file to tailor it to your tastes is a common practice. You can use your favorite editor on the .newsrc file to add or delete exclamation points, remove numbering, or change the positions of the newsgroup entries.

Navigator's Note: Considering the several thousand newsgroups in existence, editing this list could be a horrible task. Check with other people in your organization to see if they have a good list you can use, or ask the system administrator for a sorted list of newsgroup titles to browse through.

Back to rn

Here are the options you have after pressing the letter h to receive help.

```
Put newsgroup where? [$^.L] h

 Type ^ to put the newsgroup first (position 0).
 Type $ to put the newsgroup last (position 2454).
 Type . to put it before the current newsgroup (position 0).
 Type -newsgroup name to put it before that newsgroup.
 Type +newsgroup name to put it after that newsgroup.
 Type a number between 0 and 2454 to put it at that position.
 Type L for a listing of newsgroups and their positions.
```

When asked at the selection level if you want to read a newsgroup, type h to get help. You have quite a few options; the rn manual is over thirty pages long. The help screen tells you primarily how to move from newsgroup to newsgroup. Typing the letter y moves you to the next level of rn to read the information of the newsgroup. The letters n and N, respectively, take you to the next newsgroup or to the next newsgroup with unread news. The letter u unsubscribes you from this newsgroup, and q quits the rn program.

There are numerous ways to move around in rn. As you become familiar with the newsgroup names, you will want to make use of the pat commands to move directly to a newsgroup you want to investigate.

Article Selection Level

When you select a newsgroup to read (by using the letter y or by choosing an option that will get you to a specific newsgroup), you drop to the lower level of rn and receive the first unread message from the newsgroup, along with a prompt.

Now you can select how to move through the newsgroup messages. Typing h will give you a help screen for this level. Note the new prompt (Mail); here you can participate in the newsgroup by using the reply or the follow-up command. In many cases, you want to send a reply to the author of the message only and not to the entire newsgroup.

Navigator's Note: If you see an article with (rot13) after its title, the message has been encrypted. The rot13 method is a very simple form of encryption. It's not intended to keep the contents of the article secret but rather to prevent offense. If someone posts, for example, a joke that they know is in poor taste or offensive in some way, they use this technique. Don't be tempted to use this technique with wild abandon. Not everyone knows about it, and unless you see others in a newsgroup using it, you'd be advised not to bother, because other participants will get all hot and bothered about it.

Most of the news reading programs support encoding and decoding rot13 messages. Read these messages at your own peril. If you're an ardent feminist and you see an article in the `alt.feminist` newsgroup entitled "Have you heard the one about the feminist…(rot13)," you can be pretty sure it's not going to be a joke that you approve of.

Navigator's Warning: Consider carefully whether you need to reply to the newsgroup or the author. A lot of unnecessary traffic is generated by people getting involved in what are, essentially, private discussions.

At this level you can track the flow of the group's subject matter by using the command Ctrl+N. For example, if you are in the newsgroup that reviews movies, and you read a review with the film's title as a subject heading, you can find other opinions on the film by using the Ctrl+N command to find other messages with the same subject heading. You can save the message for future reference, or you can mark it as unread if you want to come back to it at a later date.

If no newsgroups are specified, all the newsgroups with unread news articles are displayed. You are asked whether you want to read each newsgroup in the order in which it occurs in the .newsrc file. The many other options are best learned through practice. Actually using rn and getting familiar with news is the best way to become proficient with it.

Creating a USENET Newsgroup

USENET newsgroups come and go through a process of asking the network community if a particular newsgroup is important enough to be created. If, after a specific period of time, enough "yes" votes are received, the newsgroup is created and announced through postings in a newsgroup called `new.news.announcements`. Creating a new newsgroup is quite a formal process, and you should check out the newsgroup `news.groups` to see how the procedure is handled.

Moderated and Unmoderated Newsgroups

Newsgroups can be moderated or unmoderated. In a moderated newsgroup, a person or group reviews items before adding them to the newsgroup. The problem with this is that it is often considered to be a form of censorship. Also, any real level of activity can easily swamp the moderators.

The advantage of a moderated newsgroup is that a filtering mechanism can remove inappropriate messages not pertinent to the group, condense or combine messages that are on the same subject or related to each other, and generally keep the number of messages being distributed at a manageable level. In a moderated newsgroup, you post items not to the newsgroup but to the moderator. Most news software is smart enough to handle this for you—it automatically sends messages to the moderator and does not allow posting to the group directly.

Unmoderated newsgroups allow direct posting, so the number of articles posted is generally higher. Because of the greater volume of articles, the conversation can (and often does) go astray more often than moderated newsgroups.

Internetiquette and Frequently Asked Questions (FAQs) About News

Because of the number of participants and the volume of messages traveling on the network, the use of Internetiquette is strongly encouraged (see Chapter 12, "Internetiquette: Manners and the Internet"). You will receive many reminders of what is appropriate or otherwise in a certain newsgroup if you sway too far from its intention. People who have really gone over the edge by posting extreme views or offensive articles have been known to receive thousands of angry e-mail messages.

In addition, many newsgroups will post a message regularly on Frequently Asked Questions (FAQs). These postings give information about the subject to new readers of the newsgroup and outline the intent of the newsgroup for them. FAQs answer commonly asked questions about the newsgroup in order to avoid answering the same questions over and over again as new people subscribe. New readers of a newsgroup are encouraged to "lurk" for a while in order to get a feel for the content and proper use of any given newsgroup.

Site Administration

Internet computer systems have a complex way of distributing newsgroup articles. The reason is that newsgroups exist on many computers. The volume of messages generated by these groups is so great that even a poor attempt to reduce this traffic is vitally important. The transfer of newsgroup articles from one computer to another is called a news feed.

Each computer system is responsible for receiving the news feed and deciding which newsgroup selections to make available. Sites don't have to receive every newsgroup that is available on the Internet. This has often caused controversy. Opinions on what should be made available at a site have been topics of discussion, with accusations of censorship and improper use of institutional resources. Many organizations have policies stating what should or should not be made available. Those policies might be liberal, demanding that all information from all newsgroups should be accessible, or they might strictly enforce exactly which newsgroups are available.

All That's Fit to Read

Network news in the form of newsgroups is an informative, educational, and sometimes controversial use of the Internet. USENET was developed and continues to develop as a service to the network, but with more and more newsgroups appearing outside of USENET, the general tone of newsgroups is changing rapidly.

A good example of organized anarchy, Internet news continues to work even though the number of newsgroups and users has grown significantly. At its best, Internet news through newsgroups is informative and helpful, providing new and up-to-the-minute information on just about anything. At its worst, news can be overwhelming in its volume, and some people find that its contents can be offensive. Certainly, much of what goes on in newsgroups is positive, constructive, and useful. You just need to choose your reading carefully.

GETTING ON THE LIST: LISTSERV

What's your interest? Mathematics? Rural life? Concurrent software engineering? Zymurgy? Dollhouses? The more obscure your interest or specialization (for example, the development of tin mining in 13th century Cornwall), the harder it is to find others who know anything about it, let alone those who are interested in discussing it.

Don't worry! Help is at hand—or rather, on net. The Internet is not only a great place to find data, it's also a tremendous place to find people to talk to (metaphorically speaking).

Your quest for others who understand, say, the implications of the Diet of Worms (sounds yucky, but it was actually—and disappointingly—where, in April 1521, Luther again refused to recant, and the Holy Roman Emperor Charles V put him under the ban of the empire—so there) is more likely to be satisfied on the Internet than just about anywhere else. Your quest for intelligent conversation on that subject is where LISTSERV comes in.

A popular form of information exchange over the Internet, LISTSERV is also known by several other names: discussion groups, conferences, or lists. Fundamentally, it's a lot like the USENET newsgroups we discussed in Chapter 13, "Views and News: USENET," except that you send and receive messages through e-mail rather than using a special news reading program. An advantage of this is that you can use any e-mail program to read the news. The disadvantage is that you have a lot less control over how you can handle the messages.

A LISTSERV discussion group lets you post a message to which others can respond. You and the others can then respond to the responses, until you all get bored or have something more pressing to attend to.

LISTSERV itself is a program that manages discussion groups, controlling functions such as subscribing, desubscribing, and so on. LISTSERVs can be a great way to keep your knowledge current, explore a topic with experts, or develop an idea in conversation with others. For example, system administrators use LISTSERV discussion groups to keep abreast of developments in telecommunications software and hardware technologies.

The variety of lists handled by LISTSERVs has grown to include a huge number of subjects. There are now lists for librarians, humanists, mathematicians, business, grade school teachers and students, and so on (although I couldn't actually find one for enthusiasts of the development of tin mining in 13th century Cornwall).

Navigator's Note: In addition to all the mailing lists maintained by the LISTSERV system, there are also literally hundreds of non-LISTSERV mailing lists. You can retrieve a list of mailing lists by anonymous FTP at `rtfm.mit.edu` in the directory `/pub/usenet/news.answers/mail`. You should retrieve the file `mailing-lists`.

Subscribing

To subscribe to a LISTSERV list, you must first know the address of the machine on which a copy of the LISTSERV software is running. This is where the LISTSERV system is really neat. You don't need to know which computer the actual list is on.

A LISTSERV site may distribute e-mail for several mailing lists, so you need to tell the LISTSERV which list you want to join. When you have that information, you can send an e-mail message containing the following text in the message body:

```
SUBSCRIBE <listname> <firstname> <lastname>
```

For example, if you want to subscribe to a list named ASIS-L, which is a list of the American Society for Information Science, you would send the following e-mail text to the LISTSERV address listserv@uvmvm.bitnet:

```
SUBSCRIBE ASIS-L Richard Smith
```

This particular LISTSERV, listserv@uvmvm.bitnet, handles the following mailing lists:

```
A+SCOMP    A+SComp: College of Arts & Sciences Computing Services
ACUA-L     acua-l
ADMUSERS   ADMUSERS: UVM Administrative Systems Users Group
ADVOCATS   Advocats: Departmental Technology Coordinators
ASIS-L     ASIS-L: American Society for Information Science
AUTOCAT    AUTOCAT: Library cataloging and authorities discussion group
BACKS-L    BACKS-L: Research on low back pain, disability and rehabilitation
BMW92      BMW92: Summer Institute for Women in Higher Ed. - 1992
CANST-LI   CANST-LI: ACRL Canadian Studies Librarians' Discussion Group
CHAOPSYC   CHAOPSYC: Discussion list of Society for Chaos Theory in Psychology
COMMUNET   Communet: Community and Civic Network Discussion List
COUNS-L    Couns-L: UCS Student Consulting Forum
CSAC       CSAC: CSAC Conference Administration
CSAC-L     CSAC-L: Computing Strategies Discussion List
DANEWS     DANEWS: Dana Library Internal List
DEVCIT     DEVCIT: Development and CIT Group
FPS-CORE   FPS-CORE: Division of Financial & Personnel Services
FPS-PLUS   FPS-PLUS: Financial & Personnel Issues Discussion Group
GRADCOLL   GRADCOLL: Graduate College News List
HERS-L     Hers-l: Higher Education Resource Services members
ILL-L      ILL-L: Interlibrary Loan discussion group
MAC-CONF   Mac-Conf  : Discontinued list, see CSAC-L instead
RECS-L     RECS-L: Rehab Engineering Centers' Discussion Group
SAFETY     Safety
SERIALST   SERIALST: Serials in Libraries Discussion Forum
SKIVT-L    SKIVT-L: Vermont Skiing and Snow Reports
USERSERV   USERSERV: Vt. User Services Support Group
UVMTODAY   UVMTODAY: UVM News
1-UNION    1-Union: Industrial democracy and industrial unionism
```

A well-managed LISTSERV will send you notification that your subscription has been accepted. It might include introductory material about the list you joined, perhaps telling you the scope and size of the list, how to obtain future information on setting your list parameters, and most importantly, how to unsubscribe from a list.

Participating

After you subscribe, you will receive e-mail routed through the LISTSERV from anyone who sends an e-mail message to that list. If you're not familiar with how the list participants conduct themselves, you should first get acquainted with the topics being discussed and get a feel for what counts as appropriate input and responses before you start adding your two cents' worth.

This "lurking" can help you avoid inadvertently making an inappropriate comment to the list, thus saving you embarrassment and unwanted, angry e-mail. Keep in mind that a list can be sending messages to several thousand people around the world; a future employer, colleague, or lover may be reading your words. It would be pretty bad to have your latest flame or current employer suddenly say, in shocked realization, "It was you who said that!!!" followed by "Good-bye" or "Empty your desk."

When you want to hazard a response to a message on a list, you only need to send an e-mail message to that list at the address where you subscribed to it. In the preceding example, you would address your e-mail message to the list `asis-l@uvmvm.bitnet`.

> **Navigator's Warning:** It is important to distinguish between the address of the list and the name of the LISTSERV. A common mistake is to send a subscription or unsubscription message meant for the LISTSERV to the list itself. In the preceding example, if you sent the subscription request to `asis-l@uvmvm.bitnet`, you would get a torrent of messages (ranging from the irritated to the downright abusive) from other users of the list, telling you that you should have sent the message to `listserv@uvmvm.bitnet`.

When you are on a list, it is not unusual to get a message saying `unsubscribe John Doe`. John Doe, the sender, confused the two addresses and sent the message meant for the LISTSERV program to everyone on the list. Go ahead, send him an abusive note. You wouldn't, of course, ever make that mistake yourself.

Moderated LISTSERV

A list may or may not be moderated. An unmoderated list accepts and distributes all e-mail from anyone registered to the group. Conversely, in a moderated list, all e-mail messages are filtered through a person or group who checks to make sure that each message is appropriate to the list.

A moderated list is designed to avoid duplicate messages, catch messages sent to the list (rather than the LISTSERV) by mistake, and ensure that message topics are kept within the scope of the list. The target is to get the messages checked and posted to the list as soon as possible. This can be very difficult to achieve.

The problem with a moderated list on even a slightly popular topic is that the message volume can easily overwhelm the moderator. Consider that a list could easily get a hundred messages or more posted to it each week. The moderator has to read each message and judge its suitability. If each takes just two minutes to read and handle, that's over three hours. If the moderator takes a vacation, a deputy moderator is needed.

Some people worry that judging which messages are passed to moderated LISTSERV lists is tantamount to censorship. They are concerned that opinions running contrary to the mainstream may not get fair distribution. In fact, concern over censorship is a constant theme in many Internet discussion groups.

Working with LISTSERV

After you get a feel for the kinds of messages that are being posted on a list, you may want to adjust the settings of your subscription so that it handles the messages in a more appropriate manner for you.

For example, you can set the attributes on the LISTSERV so that messages to the list aren't accumulated for you while you go on vacation. You might also want to check the settings if you feel you are not receiving e-mail from a LISTSERV.

A LISTSERV might not forward messages to you due to several reasons: maintenance on either end of the net (or some point in between), a list owner mistakenly deleting you or turning message reception off for you by mistake, and so on.

General Commands

Several versions of the LISTSERV software run on the Internet. Eric Thomas's Revised LISTSERV and Anastasios Kotsikonas's LISTSERV are two of the most used varieties. There are command differences, but sending the command help to most LISTSERVs gets you an e-mail message with commands that can be used with the LISTSERV.

Here is a list of the most common commands that come from Revised LISTSERV:

```
SUBSCRIBE <listname> <firstname>  <lastname>
```

Subscribe to a list, or change your name if already subscribed.

```
SIGNOFF <listname>
```

Remove yourself from the specified list.

```
SET <listname> <options>
```

Alter your subscription options.

```
ACK / NOACK
```

Use the ACK option if you want to receive acknowledgment of messages that you send to the list. This is useful if you want to check whether a message was really distributed, particularly on a moderated list. NOACK is the opposite of ACK. The NOACK option is the default.

> **Navigator's Note:** An important point, often missed by newcomers to LISTSERV lists, is that most lists have the default set to NOACK. When you post to the list, you will not receive a copy of the message you sent to the list, so many novices resend their message. It irritates many list readers when someone posts a message a second time stating that they didn't think their first message was posted to the list. Remember to check what option is set for the lists you use.

```
CONCEAL/NOCONCEAL
```

Hides or reveals (the default) your details if someone issues a REVIEW command. Your name and address on the LISTSERV is available to anyone who wants to know—unless the CONCEAL option is used.

```
FILES/NOFILES
```

Enables or disables receipt of files that are sent to the list.

```
MAIL/NOMAIL
```

Tells LISTSERV to send or not to send e-mail without unsubscribing. This is useful, for example, if you want to stop getting messages while you're on vacation.

It means that you won't have several hundred e-mail messages to wade through when you next log on.

```
DIGESTS/INDEX
```

Asks for digests (all messages for a given period) or message indexes (the headers of the messages for a given period) to be sent, rather than getting messages as they are posted.

Additional LISTSERV commands that may come in handy:

```
CONFIRM <listname1> (<listname2> ( ...) )
```

Confirms your subscription (when LISTSERV requests it).

```
INDEX <listname>
```

Sends you a directory of the available archive files for the named list, if postings for that list have been archived.

```
LIST
```

Gives names of lists on the LISTSERV.

```
QUERY <listname>
```

Checks your subscription options for the list. Use this command to make sure that the correct options are set if you suspect that the LISTSERV is not sending you messages.

```
REVIEW <listname> (<options>)
```

Get user usage information about a list.

Sending `info ?` to a LISTSERV gets you the following message (our example is from `listserv@uhupvm1`):

```
> info ?

List of information guides available from LISTSERV@UHUPVM1:

REFcard     (LISTSERV REFCARD)   Command reference card
FAQ         (LISTFAQ  MEMO  )    Frequently Asked Questions
PResent     (LISTPRES MEMO  )    Presentation of LISTSERV for new users
GENintro    (LISTSERV MEMO  )    General information about Revised LISTSERV
KEYwords    (LISTKEYW MEMO  )    Description of list header keywords
AFD         (LISTAFD  MEMO  )    Description of Automatic File Distribution
FILEs       (LISTFILE MEMO  )    Description of the file-server functions
LPunch      (LISTLPUN MEMO  )    Description of the LISTSERV-Punch file format
```

```
JOB         (LISTJOB  MEMO   )   Description of the Command Jobs feature
DISTribute  (LISTDIST MEMO   )   Description of Relayed File Distribution
COORDinat   (LISTCOOR MEMO   )   Information about Listserv Coordination
FILEOwner   (LISTFOWN MEMO   )   Information guide for file owners
DATABASE    (LISTDB   MEMO   )   Description of the database functions
UDD         (LISTUDD  MEMO   )   User Directory Database User's Guide
UDDADMIN    (LISTUDDA MEMO   )   UDD Administrator's Guide

The following files are restricted to list owners:

LINKing     (LISTLINK MEMO   )   Guidelines for linking list servers together
OWNers      (LISTOWNR MEMO   )   Description of list-owners commands
PUT         (LSVPUT   EXEC   )   An exec to facilitate sending PUT commands

You should order the PResentation or GENintro manual
if you are new to LISTSERV.
```

Sending e-mail to the LISTSERV with the word info followed by capital letters of the preceding commands in the body of the e-mail message will get you the information guide.

Searching a LISTSERV List

A LISTSERV can archive and build a database from all the messages mailed to a list. Years of information exchanged by the participants of the list can be stored and searched.

Eric Thomas's revised LISTSERV database search can be used interactively if you run a VM/SP CMS or VAX/VMS system, and can be searched in the batch mode by everyone else. The batch mode is a two-step process: first, search messages containing a word or words of information desired; second, send for a printout of the items, which will be e-mailed back to you.

In the following example I e-mail a text file to search the discussion list PACS-L, a list that discusses library automation, Internet usage, new information technology, NREN developments, and a host of other computer and telecommunication information tidbits. The LISTSERV address is listserv@uhupvm1.bitnet.

I remember that I put my early workshop notes on an anonymous FTP site, but I forgot the site's address. I did post a note to the LISTSERV PACS-L, telling subscribers where they could ftp the notes. The LISTSERV acts as my personal file cabinet of PACS-L e-mail messages. I send the LISTSERV search command (shown below) to listserv@uhupvm1.bitnet to search the LISTSERV PACS-L:

```
prompt>mail listserv@uhupvm1.bitnet
Subject:
//
Database Search DD=Rules
//Rules DD *
Search richard smith (navigate or navigating) in PACS-L from
90/1/1 to 92/8/30
Index
/*
```

The first three lines tells the listserv this is a database search. The third line searches for the word richard and smith and (navigate or navigating) in the PACS-L list from the dates indicated. Remember, I'm sending this to the LISTSERV, not the list PACS-L.

The listserv returns me a DATAOUTPUT file with any "hits" found in the database. Here is the file:

```
From LISTSERV@UHUPVM1.UH.EDU Wed Apr 28 18:12:17 1993
Subject: File: "DATABASE OUTPUT"
To: rjs4808@ucs.usl.edu
Message-Id: <01GXJY9M0782000BZY@Post-Office.UH.EDU>
Content-Transfer-Encoding: 7BIT
Status: R

> Search richard smith (navigate or navigating) in PACS-L from
90/1/1 to 92/8/30
--> Database PACS-L, 6 hits.

> Index
Item #   Date     Time   Recs   Subject
------   ----     ----   ----   -------
003763 91/06/24 16:31    43     workshop notes
005430 92/03/26 08:46   156     Library Automation—Comments &
                                Questions
005558 92/04/10 12:23    85     Finding Guides using FTP
006075 92/06/10 08:29    36     Internet connection
006395 92/07/21 08:18   142     Interactive Navigation
006543 92/08/06 08:39    39     Internet Training
```

The LISTSERV returned to me a list of six messages that met the search requirement. I see one that has workshop notes in it from June 1991. That's probably it, so now I have to retrieve it. I send the following e-mail message, with the added print command line and the item number of the file I want, back to the LISTSERV:

```
//
Database Search DD=Rules
//Rules DD *
Search richard smith (navigate or navigating) in PACS-L from
90/1/1 to 92/8/30
Print all of 3763
/*
```

The LISTSERV returned the e-mail file numbered 3763 to me, which contains the information I wanted.

The LISTSERV database can also use Boolean searching techniques. You can expand your search by using or and limit it by using and or not. With multiple word searches, the and is implied. Boolean searches require that you use parentheses to make your meaning clear.

Case is usually ignored, but searches can be made case-sensitive by adding quotes around a word. Searches can also involve dates. You can select a range of dates from 90/1/1 to 93/6/30 (note the order on the date specification, yy/mm/dd), or specify messages from a specific date. Use the date words "from" and "since" at the end of a search line.

For more information on searching techniques and how to obtain software for interactive searching, send an e-mail message with INFO DATABASE to a LISTSERV.

15

GETTING RESOURCEFUL: CARL, DIALOG, OCLC, AND ERIC

As you get comfortable in your Internet navigation, you'll start to get more ambitious in looking for resources and data. Several services on the Internet are great for serious research. In this chapter, we'll look at four of the major systems—CARL, DIALOG, OCLC, and ERIC.

Each of these services has a different orientation:

- CARL UnCover is a database through which citations to more than 10,000 journals can be accessed.

- DIALOG enables you to get details about what businesses are doing, who runs them, and so on.

- OCLC is a library-oriented database.

- ERIC is a database of great interest to teachers, parents, and students.

Between them, these systems meet a great many research needs. Whether you're working on a thesis on the fishing economy of the Byzantine era, trying to find out about the dynamics of photokinetic reactions for an industrial application, looking for information on whether a particular company is a sound investment, or seeking a science fair project for your child, these databases are where you'll find answers.

CARL UnCover Uncovered

CARL, the Colorado Alliance of Research Libraries, developed a document access and retrieval system that is run by CARL Systems, Inc. Access to many library systems is possible through the CARL service and the ERIC database (which we discuss separately later). The full text of Online Libraries and Choice book reviews are all indexed and accessible through CARL.

CARL's UnCover service makes available, online, the tables of contents of all journals received by the seven members of the Colorado Alliance of Research Libraries. In late 1991, the database contained 10,600 unique multidisciplinary journals. The database includes article citations taken from the tables of contents of each issue, along with descriptive information or abstracts that appear on the contents page. The database is continuously updated—at a rate of 3,000 to 4,000 articles per day!

UnCover can be used in two ways. First, you can search the database for a particular journal title. From the issue screen, you can select an individual issue and look at its table of contents. From there, you can take the final step, which is to look at the article record.

This approach is good if you have specific titles in which you are interested. The other approach, a keyword search on a subject, retrieves all the articles on that subject that appear in any of the journals in UnCover.

An important new UnCover service is document delivery. This service is currently called UnCover2, but CARL is in the process of merging the two services under the UnCover name. UnCover2 exists to supply copies of articles from UnCover within 24 hours, and often much sooner. Copyright royalties are carefully tracked and paid to publishers. Fees can be conveniently charged to VISA or MasterCard accounts, or deposit accounts can be set up for libraries, departments, or individual users.

Now, suppose I'm working on a system to index gene sequences for *Drosophila* species (flies, for the uninitiated). This is going to be a huge amount of data, and I want to think about compressing it. I remember that some guy called Rick Gates (actually the same one who supplied the material for Appendix F, "Testing Your Navigation Skills") wrote an article in, I think, *The Electronic Library* on the topic of compression.

Lucky for me, even though the library near me doesn't subscribe to *The Electronic Library*, CARL's UnCover can find the article and send it to me by fax. Because I've got a fax machine at home, I can request, receive, and read the article I'm looking for without ever leaving the house. Better still, using my portable computer (on battery power) I can run a phone line into the garden and sit in the jacuzzi while I do my search. It's a tough life.

First, I telnet to CARL's host computer and log on:

```
coyote% telnet database.carl.org
Trying 192.54.81.76 ...
Connected to database.carl.org.
Escape character is '^]'.
Welcome to the CARL system
Please identify your terminal. Choices are:
1.ADM (all)
2.APPLE,IBM
3.TANDEM
4.TELE-914
5.VT100
6.WYSE 50
7.ZENTEC
8.HARDCOPY
9.IBM 316x
Use HARDCOPY if your terminal type isn't listed
SELECT LINE #:5

All set. When you are ready to exit the system, simply
type //EXIT, or hang up.
Now, press return to enter the Public Access Catalog...
```

So far, pretty easy. Just make sure you select the right terminal type or you may get a messed-up screen display in certain parts of the system.

```
            >>>  Systems That Inform  <<<
            Welcome to the CARL System
                 (Release A.101)

       A Computerized Network of Systems and Services


       Developed by the Colorado Alliance of Research Libraries
            Marketed and supported by CARL Systems, Inc.
                 3801 East Florida St., Suite 300
                       Denver, Co. 80210
                   Voice:   303-758-3030
                   Fax:   303-758-0606
                   Internet:   help@carl.org
 PRESS <RETURN> TO START THE PROGRAM  (use //EXIT to return HOME)>>
          WELCOME TO THE CARL SYSTEM DATABASE GATEWAY
CARL Systems, Inc. is proud to present our Shopping List of Databases.
Many of the databases included require a password. If you would like to
look at one of these restricted databases, please contact CARL Systems, Inc.
at database@carl.org or 303/758-3030. If you have already been given a
password to a database, please enter your password when prompted.
     1.  UnCover
         (Article Access and Delivery)
     2.  Information Access Company Databases
         (including Business Index, Magazine Index and others)
     3.  Grolier's Academic American Encyclopedia
     4.  Facts on File
     5.  H.W. Wilson Databases
         (including Library Literature)
     6.  Other Databases
         (including Journal Graphics, Choice and others)

   Enter the NUMBER of your choice, and press the <RETURN> key >> 1
WORKING...
```

Well, I know that I want to use the UnCover service, so I select item 1 and...

```
The CARL system includes some services which require appropriate
validation, including UnCover. So that we may serve you, please
enter your library card number, or assigned password.
Libraries participating in UnCover are those listed in previous
menus. Touch <RETURN> to review menus.
USER ID>>
Thank you...
```

I have to give a password to use the system (nothing shows after USER ID>> because for security reasons CARL doesn't echo the password).

```
06/22/93
10:57 A.M.        SELECTED DATABASE:  UnCover
                      Welcome to
                 UnCover and UnCover2
         The Article Access and Delivery Solutions from CARL.
UnCover contains records describing journals and their contents. It
includes more than 14,000 titles, and more than 4,000,000 articles.
Over 750,000 articles are added annually.

UnCover2 is a new service which offers you the opportunity to order
any article in this data base. Type ? for order details.
              Enter   N   for  NAME search
                      W   for  WORD search
                      B   to   BROWSE by journal title
                      S   to   STOP or SWITCH to another database
              Type the letter for the kind of search you want,
              and end each line you type by pressing <RETURN>

                  SELECTED DATABASE:  UnCover
```

I know a word in the title of the article, "compression," and the name of the journal, *The Electronic Library.* I type those words as the minimum information I think UnCover needs to find the article.

```
ENTER  COMMAND (? FOR HELP) >>  w
             SELECTED DATABASE: UnCover

              REMEMBER — WORDS can be words from the title, or
              from subtitles, summaries or abstracts that appear
              on the Table of Contents page for each journal.
              A WORD search will also often return NAMES of people
              who are discussed or referred to in the articles.
              You may also supply the name of a journal in your search
              in order to limit your results to that publication.
               for example       HEALTH CARE TRENDS
                                 MICKEY MANTLE
                                 AIDS SCIENTIFIC AMERICAN
              Enter word or words (no more than one line, please)
              separated by spaces and press <RETURN>.

>compression electronic library
 WORKING...
COMPRESSION  2350 ITEMS          UnCover
patience — ELECTRONIC is a long one...
COMPRESSION + ELECTRONIC    28 ITEMS
patience — LIBRARY is a long one...
COMPRESSION + ELECTRONIC + LIBRARY     1 ITEM

 1 Gates, Rick              (The Electronic library : the int... 04/01/93)
    Compression and archiving.
```

Jackpot! Here's the exact article I was looking for. Now I ask to see the complete record and then order a fax of it to be sent to me.

```
Enter <LINE NUMBER> to display full record, or <Q>UIT for new search 1



---------------------------------------------------UnCover-------------------
AUTHOR(s):      Gates, Rick
                Bang, Steve
TITLE(s):       Compression and archiving.
          In:   The Electronic library :  the international jour
                APR 01 1993 v 11 n 2
        Page:   120

Summary Holdings:
CALL #:                                   LOCN:
--1 of 1-------------------------------------------UnCover-------------------
<R>epeat this display,
<Q>uit,
<H> for History,   <D>for Delivery Information ? for HELP >d
```

Ah! The article is co-authored by this book's technical reviewer. What a find! To see about delivery information, I press d:

```
This article may be available at your library or through interlibrary loan.
The full text of this article is available by FAX.
The cost is:                       $  6.50  (service fee)
            plus                   $  8.00C (copyright fee)
            for a TOTAL of:        $ 14.50
(The copyright fee is set by and paid to the publisher.)
If you would like a FAX copy of the article, please
enter a Mastercard, Visa, or American Express number, or,
your Special (Deposit) account ID.  Type ? for more
information, or <RETURN> to exit >>>            123456789012345
Enter the expiration date (MM/YY):    12/99

Enter your name, EXACTLY as it appears on your card: Mark Gibbs
Checking authorization -- please be patient...



Please enter the FAX PHONE number of your FAX machine  --
(Include dialing prefix '1', or '1' plus AREA CODE
if not in Denver local calling area)
Type ? for more information, or <Q> to cancel.
Enter FAX PHONE NUMBER >> 18055551212


Please enter local routing information for FAX delivery (optional) --
eg. department number, room number, etc (up to 20 characters)
```

```
Enter information, and touch <RETURN> to continue
>>

You have requested a FAX copy of
Compression and archiving.                          Gates, Rick
to 18055551212
Charged to 123456789012345
O.K. to proceed? (Y or N -- ? for Help)y
Thank you -- now writing your order...
Thank you. Your reference # is: 93173110044
Please note this number for use if you need to contact CARL Systems.
Press <RETURN> to continue...
You began with a WORD search on:
COMPRESSION ELECTRONIC LIBRARY
```

That's it. The fax will be sent and might even arrive within an hour. I can then read it at my leisure, having avoided traffic, parking problems, etc. That is, provided I can find someone in the house to bring the document from the fax machine in my study out to the jacuzzi. What a way to work.

The only thing left to do is to log off.

```
Type S to try your search in another database, or
     R to repeat your search in UnCover
     H to see a list of your recent searches, or
                            06/22/93
11:01 A.M.         SELECTED DATABASE:  UnCover
                         Welcome to
                    UnCover and UnCover2
          The Article Access and Delivery Solutions from CARL.
UnCover contains records describing journals and their contents. It
includes more than 14,000 titles, and more than 4,000,000 articles.
Over 750,000 articles are added annually.

UnCover2 is a new service which offers you the opportunity to order
any article in this data base. Type ? for order details.
          Enter  N   for  NAME search
                 W   for  WORD search
                 B   to   BROWSE by journal title
                 S   to   STOP or SWITCH to another database
          Type the letter for the kind of search you want,
          and end each line you type by pressing <RETURN>

                    SELECTED DATABASE:  UnCover
ENTER  COMMAND (? FOR HELP) >>  s
Connection closed by foreign host.
coyote% bye
```

As you can see, CARL is a fantastic resource—particularly if you're looking for articles in journals. It's pretty easy to use, too. If you're trying to research a topic and you want to try to review as many of the published articles as possible, this is the place to do it.

Starting in the fall of 1993, password access will not be required. Instead, you will be able to purchase any document for a standard $8.50 service charge plus the copyright fee. If a library or individual is requesting more than 450 articles per year, a password can be purchased, which will reduce the service charge to $6.50 per document.

For more information, contact CARL Systems at 800-787-7979 or at `help@carl.org`.

Getting into DIALOG

One of the largest commercial online database services, DIALOG, can be reached on the Internet. Properly called DIALOG Information Retrieval Service, from Dialog Information Services, Inc., the system has been serving users since 1972.

DIALOG offers nearly 400 databases and covers a broad scope of disciplines. These databases contain in excess of 329 million records. The data ranges from directory-type listings of companies, associations, and famous people to in-depth financial statements for companies, citations with bibliographic information, and abstracts referencing journals, patents, conference papers, and other original sources, including the complete text of many journal articles.

One of the unique services offered by DIALOG is its database of company information. As a test, let's check out the entry for Novell, Inc. Novell is a very big company, with sales approaching $1 billion; it will be interesting to see what DIALOG has to say about it.

You begin by using telnet to connect to the DIALOG system and at the prompt supply your account information.

```
ucsbuxa% telnet dialog.com
Trying 192.132.3.254…
Connected to dialog.com.
Escape character is '^]'.
Trying 3106...Open

DIALOG INFORMATION SERVICES
PLEASE LOGON: 9999
ENTER PASSWORD: XXXXXXX
Welcome to DIALOG
Dialog level 30.04.04B
```

```
Last logoff:  22jan93 13:29:24
Logon file001 21jun93 20:12:52
*
*
Fourth Edition Available in Kirk Othmer (File 302)
Reload:  DELPHES EUROPEAN BUSINESS (File 481)
Pharmacological Codes Now Available in Pharmaprojects (File 128)
IMSworld Product Monographs Now Available in File 446
New:  BCC MARKET RESEARCH (File 764) (MARKETFULL)
Reload:  CANCORP (File 491)
Weekly Updating Now Available in Ei Compendex*Plus (File 8)
DIALOG OnDisc ENVIRONMENTAL CHEMISTRY, HEALTH & SAFETY Now Available

     >>> Enter BEGIN HOMEBASE for Dialog Announcements <<<
     >>>     of new databases, price changes, etc.     <<<
     >>>     Announcements last updated for 16jun93     <<<
```

The one drawback to DIALOG is that it is very cryptic. You have to know the number (not even a name…geez!) of the databases that you want to access. In the following example, I tell DIALOG that I would like to connect (the command is b…who knows why) to a database called D&B-Dun's Market Indicators (the number is 516), a database with market information about corporations in North America.

> **Navigator's Note:** As a member of DIALOG, you get a service directory called the DIALOG Database Catalog that gives you a brief description of each database and is indexed by subject and database number.

The accounting information that appears is completely useless—it simply tells me that the clock is ticking and I'm spending money like there's no tomorrow.

```
?b516

        21jun93 20:13:04 User008533 Session B1800.1
            $0.11    0.003 Hrs File1
     $0.11  Estimated cost File1
     $0.01  ANSNET
     $0.12  Estimated cost this search
     $0.12  Estimated total session cost   0.003 Hrs.

File 516:D & B - DUNS MARKET IDENTIFIERS(R)  1993/Q2
       (c) 1993 D&B
**FILE516: 50% Off REPORT Elements For File 516 During May & June
```

I guess I got lucky here. There's a 50% discount this month for searches on this database.

Now I tell DIALOG that I want information (ss means start search) about Novell, Inc. (the /co tells DIALOG that it's a company I'm looking for). This gets me 51 records related to Novell. I need to narrow the scope, so I specify that the search is based on my first results and that I want to see only records that specify the city of Provo. The search for records specifying Provo results in 1,939 hits; the combination of the two searches produces one direct hit. This could be what I want.

```
      Set  Items  Description
      --   ----   ----------
?ss novell/co

      S1     51   NOVELL/CO
?ss s1 and cy=provo

             51   S1
      S2   1939   CY=PROVO
      S3      1   S1 AND CY=PROVO
```

I want to see all the information available from my search. So, I enter the command t for type, the number of the search results that I want to display, and the /5, which will show the complete record. You can see from this that using DIALOG without reading the manual is more or less impossible.

```
?t 3/5


 3/5/1
0758737    DIALOG File 516:  D&B Duns Market Identifiers
Novell, Inc
122 E 1700 S
P O Box 5900
Provo, UT  84606-7379
```

...and so forth. The file goes on to list several pages' worth of fascinating financial information about Novell, but because it's copyrighted material, I won't bore you with the details.

Now that I've got the information that I went to DIALOG for, I can log off the system and return to my local UNIX account.

```
      21jun93 20:18:39 User008533 Session B1800.3
            $3.17    0.033 Hrs File516
                $3.25  1 Type(s) in Format  5
            $3.25  1 Types
    $6.42  Estimated cost File516
    $0.10  ANSNET
    $6.52  Estimated cost this search
   $16.81  Estimated total session cost   0.120 Hrs.
Logoff: level 30.04.04 B  20:18:39

Connection closed by foreign host.
ucsbuxa%
```

DIALOG is an extraordinarily rich resource, but it has one of the most obscure interfaces around. You'll need to spend some money before you get really good at using the databases, and reading the manual is a prerequisite to conducting really successful searches. For more information, contact

> DIALOG Information Services, Inc.
> 3460 Hillview Avenue
> Palo Alto, CA 94304
> 800-334-2564 or 415-858-3758

Oh, Say Can You See, It's OCLC

Yet another database that can be searched over the Internet is offered by OCLC (the Online Computer Library Center, Inc.). OCLC runs The FirstSearch Catalog, an online information service for library patrons. Available through many libraries around the world, it has a simple interface that enables users to move easily through the online search process in a few simple steps, without the need for any training or online searching experience.

The FirstSearch Catalog

The FirstSearch Catalog currently provides access to more than 30 databases; following are OCLC's descriptions of some of the major ones:

⚓ The FirstSearch Catalog. An online reference service with an end-user interface designed specifically for library patrons.

⚓ WorldCat. The OCLC Online Union Catalog, a bibliography with more than 25 million records spanning 4,000 years of knowledge.

⚓ GPO Monthly Catalog, U.S. Government Printing Office. A database consisting of more than 350,000 records published by the GPO since July 1976. It has references to congressional committee reports and hearings, debates, documents from executive departments, and more.

⚓ BIOSIS/FS, Biological Abstracts, Inc. A database of biomedical and biological research information that is a subset of BIOSIS Previews. It provides journal citations and abstracts on up-to-date developments in 96 major subject areas.

⚓ MiniGeoRef, American Geological Institute. This covers recent additions to the GeoRef file, a database containing earth science references and the index terms that describe them.

⚓ Newspaper Abstracts, UMI/Data Courier. A database that indexes and abstracts more than 25 national and regional newspapers, including the *New York Times, Los Angeles Times, Washington Post, USA Today,* and *The Wall Street Journal.*

⚓ Periodical Abstracts, UMI/Data Courier. A complete general reference resource, with indexing and abstracts for over 900 popular and academic periodicals. Included are transcripts of more than 30 news-oriented television shows.

⚓ Readers' Guide to Periodical Literature, The H.W. Wilson Company. Readers' Guide indexes a core list of popular magazines, central to any college, public library, or school collection. Updated monthly, records are from January 1983 to the present.

⚓ Business Periodicals Index, The H.W. Wilson Company. Business Periodicals Index provides complete and accurate access to 345 of today's leading English-language business magazines.

⚓ Humanities Index, The H.W. Wilson Company. A good single reference to periodical information in the diverse subject area of the humanities, the Humanities Index complements the monographic resources accessible via WorldCat (OCLC Online Union Catalog).

⚓ Biography Index, The H.W. Wilson Company. Cites more than 2,700 periodicals and more than 1,800 books, including individual and collective biographies, as well as juvenile literature.

⚓ PsycFIRST, American Psychological Association. Covers the most recent three years from the PsycINFO database.

⚓ Business Organizations, Agencies, and Publications Directory, Gale Research, Inc. A guide to international business information sources that lists contact name, address, phone and FAX numbers, and a description of the organization's founding, membership, activities, and services.

Getting into OCLC

As with the other services, you have to telnet to the database host site and log onto the OCLC Reference Services system.

```
ucsbuxa% telnet epic.prod.oclc.org
Trying 132.174.100.2 ...
Connected to epic.prod.oclc.org.
Escape character is '^]'.

You are connected to OCLC Reference Services.

Enter your authorization.
=> 123456789

Enter your password.
=> abcde7xyz


* * * * * * * *      WELCOME TO FIRSTSEARCH !      * * * * * * * * * *

    Use The FirstSearch Catalog to find information--or records--
    about books, articles, theses, films, computer software, and
    other types of material on the subject you need.

       -- First, select a broad topic area and a database.
       -- Then, type your search.  You can use upper or lower case.
       -- From the List of Records, select a record to view.
       -- To do another search, type S and your search term.

    Other actions you can do are listed on each screen.  Just type
    the ACTION name or first letter.


             HOURS (ET): 6 a.m. - midnight M-F
                         8 a.m. - 8 p.m. Sat.
                         12 noon - midnight Sun.


    NOTE: Documentation now on Internet!  On next screen, ask for News.


                  PRESS ENTER TO CONTINUE
```

Well, I'm in. I press Enter as required:

```
* * * * * * * * * * * Topic Area Selection * * * * * * * * * * * * * *


   NO.  TOPIC AREA              NO.  TOPIC AREA
 |
 |   1   Arts and Humanities     5   Education and Social Sciences
 |   2   Business/Law/Public Affairs   6   General/Books/Periodicals
 |   3   Consumer Affairs and People   7   Science and Technology
 |   4   Current Events          8   All
 |_____


HINTS:   Select a topic area . . . . . . . . . . . type topic area number.
         Get help . . . . . . . . . . . . . . . . . . . . . . . . type H.
         Get News . . . . . . . . . . . . . . . . . . . . . . type H NEWS.

ACTIONS: Help  BYE  Reset
```

Here I selected option 6. I want to find references to criticism of Donald Duck (a disturbing trend far too prevalent at present).

```
TOPIC AREA NUMBER (or Action): 6


* * * * * * * * * * * * Database Selection * * * * * * * * * * * * * *

TOPIC AREA:  General/Books/Periodicals


   NO.  DATABASE        DESCRIPTION
 |
 |   1   WorldCat       Books and other materials in libraries worldwide.
 |   2   Article1st     Index of articles from over 11,000 journals.
 |   3   Contents1st    Table of contents of more than 11,000 journals.
 |   4   NewsAbs        Newspaper Abstracts.  From over 25 newspapers.
 |   5   PerAbs         Periodical Abstracts.  From over 950 journals.
 |   6   ReadGuideAbs   Abstracts of articles from popular magazines.
 |   7   ReadersGuide   Readers' Guide to Periodical Literature.
 |   8   FactSearch     Facts and statistics on topics of current interest.
 |_____


HINTS:   Select a database . . . . . . . . . . type database number or name.
         Help on a database . . . . . . . . . . type H and database name.
         Return to Topic Area screen . . . . . . . . . . . just press Enter.

ACTIONS: Help  BYE  Reset
```

I choose option 1, WorldCat, because I'm looking for books anywhere in the world. Note that this is for interest only; it's unlikely that I'll travel to Korea if a book is found there. Note also that WorldCat indexes only libraries that are members of OCLC.

```
DATABASE NUMBER (or Action): 1

* * * * * * * * * * * * * * Search * * * * * * * * * * * * * * * * * * * *

DATABASE: WorldCat

    SEARCH      DESCRIPTION                              EXAMPLES

    Subject     Type the label SU: and a word(s).        su:criticism
                (Subject headings and titles)            su:freedom of speech

    Author      Type the label AU: and the author        au:hemingway
                name or any part of the name.            au:saul bellow

    Title       Type the label TI: and the title         ti:estuary
                or any word(s) in the title.             ti:love in the asylum


HINTS:    Other ways to search . . . . . . . . . . . . . . . type H LABELS.
          Include plural (s and es) or possessive . . . type + at end of word.
          Return to Database Selection screen . . . . . . . just press Enter.

ACTIONS: Help  Limit  Database  Wordlist  BYE  Reset
```

Now I enter the search of interest. For this example, I tell WorldCat that I'd like to search for items with the subject words Donald Duck criticism.

```
SEARCH WORD(S) (or Action): su: donald duck criticism

Searching for su:donald duck criticism

.
+ * * * * * * * * * * * * List of Records * * * * * * * * * * * * * * * * +
DATABASE: WorldCat                     LIMITED TO:
SEARCH: su:donald duck criticism FOUND 6 Records
```

OCLC's WorldCat tells me that there are six records and proceeds to list them.

```
     NO.  TITLE                                    AUTHOR          YEAR
|
|
|    1    How to read Donald Duck : imperialist ide... Dorfman, Ariel.    1991
|    2    Donald Duck : clipping file.                                    1934
|    3    Roasting Donald Duck : alternative comics... Flora, Cornelia    1984
|    4    How to read Donald Duck : imperialist ide... Dorfman, Ariel.    1984
|    5    Para leer al Pato Donald /               Dorfman, Ariel.    1978
|    6    How to read Donald Duck : imperialist ide... Dorfman, Ariel.    1975
|
|    _____

HINTS:   View a record . . . . . . . . . . . . . . . . . type record number.
         Decrease number of records . . . . type L (to limit) or A (to 'and').
         Do a new search . . . . . . . . . . . . . . . . . type S or SEARCH.

ACTIONS: Help  Search  And  Limit  Database  BYE  Reset
```

We get six successful matches! Unbelievable. The first record has an interesting title. To display the record, I type the number of the item.

```
RECORD NUMBER (or Action): 1

* * * * * * * * * * * * Full Record Display * * * * * * * * * * * * * * *
DATABASE: WorldCat                      LIMITED TO:
SEARCH: su:donald duck criticism


 Record  1 of   6    LIBRARIES AT END OF RECORD        (Page  1 of  4)
|
|
|ACCESSION: 25294669
|   AUTHOR: Dorfman, Ariel.
|    TITLE: How to read Donald Duck :
|           imperialist ideology in the Disney comic /
|  EDITION: Corr. & enl. ed.
|    PLACE: New York :
|PUBLISHER: International General,
|     YEAR: 1991
| PUB TYPE: Book
|   FORMAT: 119 p. : ill. ; 26 cm.
|
|_____
HINTS:   Forward one page . . type F.     Another record . type record number.
         Help on 3-letter library symbol . . . . . . . . type H and symbol.
         Return to Record List . . . . . . . . . . . . . just press Enter.

ACTIONS: Help  Search  And  Limit  Print  Forward  BYE  Reset
RECORD NUMBER (or Action): f
```

I'd like to see more of the record, so I enter f to go forward one page.

```
* * * * * * * * * * * Full Record Display * * * * * * * * * * * * * * *
DATABASE: WorldCat                      LIMITED TO:
SEARCH: su:donald duck criticism

 Record  1 of   6    LIBRARIES AT END OF RECORD         (Page  2 of  4)
¦
¦   FORMAT: 119 p. : ill. ; 26 cm.
¦    NOTES: Translation of: Para leer al Pato Donald.
¦           Includes bibliographical references: (p. [100]-112).
¦     ISBN: 0884770370
¦  SUBJECT: Walt Disney Productions.
¦           Comic books, strips, etc. — History and criticism.
¦           Propaganda, American.
¦           Propaganda, Capitalist.
¦           Donald Duck (Comic strip).
¦           Imperialism in literature.
¦
¦_____
HINTS:    Another page . type F or B.     Another record . type record number.
          Help on 3-letter library symbol . . . . . . . . type H and symbol.
          Return to Record List . . . . . . . . . . . . . just press Enter.

ACTIONS: Help  Search  And  Limit  Print  Forward  Back  BYE  Reset

RECORD NUMBER (or Action): f
```

And the next page...

```
* * * * * * * * * * * * Full Record Display * * * * * * * * * * * * * * *
DATABASE: WorldCat                      LIMITED TO:
SEARCH: su:donald duck criticism

 Record  1 of   6    LIBRARIES AT END OF RECORD         (Page  3 of  4)
¦
¦           Imperialism in literature.
¦ALT TITLE: Para leer al Pato Donald. English
¦    OTHER: Mattelart, Armand.
¦LIBRARIES: CA stf CDU
¦           FL FDA FSS FUG
¦           GA EMU
¦           MA BCH
¦           NJ FDM
¦           TX IXA TXA
¦           VA VPI
¦
¦_____
HINTS:    Another page . type F or B.     Another record . type record number.
          Help on 3-letter library symbol . . . . . . . . type H and symbol.
          Return to Record List . . . . . . . . . . . . . just press Enter.
```

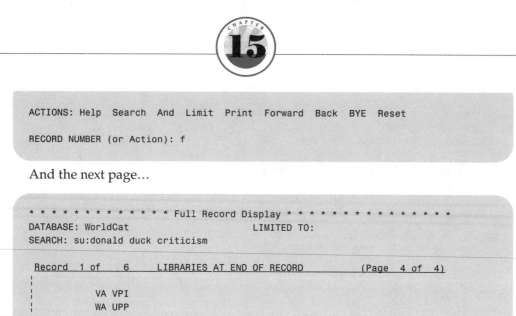

```
ACTIONS: Help  Search  And  Limit  Print  Forward  Back  BYE  Reset

RECORD NUMBER (or Action): f
```

And the next page...

```
* * * * * * * * * * * * Full Record Display * * * * * * * * * * * * * * *
DATABASE: WorldCat                          LIMITED TO:
SEARCH: su:donald duck criticism


Record  1 of   6     LIBRARIES AT END OF RECORD       (Page  4 of  4)

             VA VPI
             WA UPP

```

Looking at the record, I can see that several libraries listed by OCLC own a copy of the latest edition of this book (I wonder why it never made the best-sellers list?). By typing h stf, I can find which of the California libraries own a copy of this book.

```
HINTS:   Another page . type F or B.      Another record . type record number.
         Help on 3-letter library symbol . . . . . . . . type H and symbol.
         Return to Record List . . . . . . . . . . . . . . just press Enter.

ACTIONS: Help  Search  And  Limit  Print  Forward  Back  BYE  Reset

RECORD NUMBER (or Action): h stf

* * * * * * * * * * * * * * * Help * * * * * * * * * * * * * * * * * * * *


 SYM.  LIBRARY                                  INTERLIBRARY LOAN

 STF   STANFORD UNIV LIBR   CA, US              Non-supplier

```

Great! Stanford University Library owns this book. I'm going to be visiting the Bay Area this week, so I'll just drop into Stanford and take a look at it. If I can't get there, I can always ask my local library to try to borrow it through their interlibrary loan program.

I can now quit OCLC and find out what is wrong with Donald Duck. OCLC is one of the great catalog systems available on the Internet. To get access, you'll need to check with your local library or contact OCLC directly.

OCLC also runs a LISTSERV called FIRSTSEARCH-L. Send messages that contain commands to `listserv@oclc.org` and place your commands in the body of the message, not in the subject line; type each command on a separate line (see Chapter 14, "Getting on the List: LISTSERV," for information on how to use LISTSERV).

Educating with ERIC

The ERIC (Educational Resources Information Center) database contains abstracts of over 760 educational journals and many related documents. It also includes much interdisciplinary information, in fields such as library science, management, health, and technology.

ERIC is the place to look if you are trying to develop curricula or find out the latest ideas in education. It's also a great place to look if your children need to find a science fair project and you're drawing a blank.

Let's look for the general topic of chemistry, just to see what's available. You'll need to log in as SUINFO, which stands for Syracuse University Information System, where the ERIC Clearinghouse on Information Resources (the actual database) lives. So, let's use ERIC:

```
coyote% telnet acsnet.syr.edu
Trying 128.230.1.21 ...
Connected to acsnet.syr.edu.
Escape character is '^]'.
ACSNET
Tue Jun 22 22:23:27 1993
Port ID: Acsnet tty41  at  9600 baud
>suinfo
Cofo (VMFA 158C)
ENTER TERMINAL TYPE: vt100
```

I'm now logged in.

```
VIRTUAL MACHINE/SYSTEM PRODUCT

            SSSSSSS
          SS    SS  UU    UU
          SS         UU    UU  VV        VV
            SSSSSSS  UU    UU  VV        VV  MM          MM
                 SS  UU    UU  VV      VV    MMM        MMM
          SS    SS  UU    UU  VV    VV      MMMM      MMMM
            SSSSSSS  UU    UU    VV VV      MM MM MM MM MM
                UUUUUUUU        VVV        MM  MMM  MM
                                  V          MM   M   MM
                                             MM        MM

Fill in your USERID and PASSWORD and press ENTER
(Your password will not appear when you type it)
USERID   ===>
PASSWORD ===>
COMMAND  ===> suinfo
                                                RUNNING   SUVM
```

Having gotten into the system with the command SUINFO, I'm presented with:

```
Welcome to SUINFO! You will now be able to perform online searches
on all publicly available databases currently carried by PRISM.
Before proceeding, the following may be noted:

*  You may use the SUGGEST command to send in comments/suggestions.
*  Certain databases cannot be searched because of licensing restrictions.
   You may search these databases by logging into SUVM the regular way.

*  The PRINT COMMAND works to send search results back to yourself.
   Choose the 'Another User' option and specify your email address as:
        userid@node
   This feature has been installed on a test basis.
*  You must type LOGOFF to EXIT PRISM
Would you like to continue? (Y or RETURN/N)
```

Press Y here to continue…

```
Welcome to Prism                              06/22/93 22:20
File selection                               40 files available

Select a file or service by typing its name below,
   or, press the return key to see a list of all files,
   or, type a category number to see a list of files in that category:
```

```
    1.  General Interest
    2.  CWIS: SU Events, SCIS, Job Ops, JOBNET, Housing, etc.
    3.  WOT: Network Accessible Resources
    4.  Demonstration
    5.  Application Development
    6.  Testing New Applications


Enter the name of the file you want.
To see a list of files, choose a category or press RETURN.
YOUR RESPONSE: 1
f1=Help          f3=End
Also:  Setup, Lock, Pause, End
```

Let's look under the first option, General Interest.

```
Prism                                              06/22/93 22:21
File selection                      32 General Interest files available
Choose a file or service by typing its number or name below.

        NAME                     DESCRIPTION
    1.  ACS News                 ACS News and Notes Articles
    2.  ACS Newsline             ACS Newsline articles database
    3.  Applications Catalog     Catalog of SPIRES Applications for Consortium
    4.  Art Artists              SUART Artists subfile
    5.  Art Objects              Syracuse University Art Collection Objects
    6.  Audio Archive            The Belfer Audio Archive's cylinder recordings
    7.  COMPUSTAT Annual         COMPUSTAT Industrial Annual Da File (350:1-175)
    8.  COMPUSTAT PDE            COMPUSTAT Prices, Dividends and Earnings File
    9.  COMPUSTAT Quarterly      COMPUSTAT Industrial Quarterly Data File (40)
   10.  Consortium People        People at SPIRES Consortium member sites
   11.  Consortium Sites         SPIRES Consortium member institutions
   12.  CPC at S.U. (text only)  Comprehensive Plan for Computing at S.U. 30/6/92
   13.  CSS Handbook             Counseling & Support Services Handbook
-The menu of files continues on next page; press RETURN to continue
Enter the name or number of the file you want.
Type HELP followed by the name of a file for information about that file.
YOUR RESPONSE:
f1=Help          f3=End                         f7=Previous
Also:  Setup, Lock, Pause, End
```

I'll press Enter to get the next page. As you can see, there's a lot more on this system than just ERIC, but you'll need to check what is publicly accessible before you get excited.

```
Prism                                          06/22/93 22:23
File selection                    32 General Interest files available
Choose a file or service by typing its number or name below.

        NAME                  DESCRIPTION
 14.  ERIC                    Abstracts of documents in the field of education
 15.  HUMANIST                HUMANIST discussion file
 16.  ICPSR Guide             Guide to the Data Archive's research data files.
 17.  IRG                     Internet Resource Guide
 18.  Job Opportunities       S.U. Job Opportunities Publication (06/21/93)
 19.  JOBNET Job              SU student part-time job information file
 20.  Microdb                 Microcomputer Article Abstracts
 21.  MSDS Inventory          Material Safety Data Sheet Inventory
 22.  NOTIS-L                 NOTIS Discussion Group
 23.  Sci-Search              Science Citation Index sample file
 24.  SCIS Catalog            Course Catalog (1992-93)
 25.  SCIS Schedule           Time Schedule of Classes (FALL 93 & Spring 93)
 26.  SCIS Syllabus           Course Syllabus Abstract
-The menu of files continues on next page; press RETURN to continue
Enter the name or number of the file you want.
Type HELP followed by the name of a file for information about that file.
YOUR RESPONSE:  14
f1=Help         f3=End                          f7=Previous
Also:  Setup, Lock, Pause, End
```

There's what we want—ERIC is option 14.

```
ERIC                            Search              06/22/93 22:38

                        Welcome to ERIC

   This file contains bibliographic  information  and abstracts for a
   variety of  EDUCATIONAL  documents  from the Educational Resources
   Information Center (ERIC).  The file contains all the ERIC data from
   1984 through the 1st quarter of 1993 (Exactly 270590 records).

   You can search for items using one or more keywords from a variety of
   fields such as title, author, or abstract.


   *--------------------------------------------------------------------*
   |  For help conducting searches, contact the ERIC Clearinghouse      |
   |  <ERIC@SUVM> (ph: x-3640).  Report any technical                   |
   |  problems to Bhaskaran Balakrishnan <BBALAKRI@SUVM> (ph: x-1145),  |
   |  or to Mohamad Ladan <jinwang@suvm> (x-1145).                      |
   *--------------------------------------------------------------------*
  -File selected; type HELP ERIC FILE for more information
  Type FIND to search this file.
```

```
Type SELECT to choose a different file.
YOUR RESPONSE:   find
f1=Help f2=Find f3=Select
Also:  Setup, Command, Suggest, Lock, Pause, End
```

The find command takes us to the search screen:

```
ERIC                         Search                06/22/93 22:39
Index selection for FIND                        5 indexes available

Choose one or more indexes by typing the name or number for each type of
information you have, e.g. ABSTRACT or 1

   INDEX        DESCRIPTION                      EXAMPLE
   1.  ABSTRACT  Keyword from journal abstract    gifted child#
   2.  TITLE     Keywords from document title     listening skills
   3.  AUTHOR    Author's name                    David Webster
   4.  DESC      Subject descriptors (word index)  online system#
   5.  DESCPH    Subject descriptors (phrase index)  elementary secondary

Enter one or more index names below.
Type CANCEL to cancel this search.
YOUR RESPONSE: abstract
f1=Help f2=Setup Search f3=Cancel
Also:  Setup, Lock, Pause, End
```

What abstracts are available for chemistry?

```
ERIC                    Search / BRIEF display        06/22/93 22:40
Find ABSTRACT CHEMISTRY                              1497 records
1)   1989  American College Biology and Zoology Course Requirements: A de
           facto Standardized Curriculum.
2)   1991  Proportional Reasoning in the Solution of Problems in High School
           Chemistry and Its Impact on Developing Critical Thinking Skills.
3)   1992  Chemical Technology at the Community College of Rhode Island:
           Curricular Approaches Designed To Reflect the Demands of a Diverse
           Population Entering Chemical Technology Programs.
4)   1988  Comments in Academic Articles.
5)   1990  Dental Laboratory Technology Program Guide.
6)   1990  Biotechnology Program Guide.
7)   1991  Analogies in Secondary Chemistry Education Textbooks: The Authors'
           Views.
8)   1991  Using Analogies To Aid Understanding in Secondary Chemistry
           Education.
9)   1992  The "International Language/Business" Major at a Small Private
           University: Successes and Nagging Concerns.
```

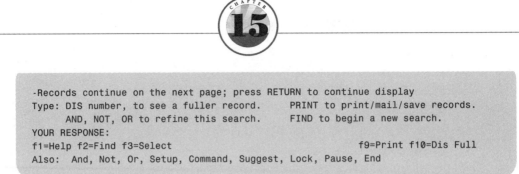

```
-Records continue on the next page; press RETURN to continue display
Type: DIS number, to see a fuller record.    PRINT to print/mail/save records.
      AND, NOT, OR to refine this search.    FIND to begin a new search.
YOUR RESPONSE:
f1=Help f2=Find f3=Select                              f9=Print f10=Dis Full
Also:  And, Not, Or, Setup, Command, Suggest, Lock, Pause, End
```

Press Enter to display the next several screens:

```
ERIC                    Search / BRIEF display        06/22/93 22:46
Find ABSTRACT CHEMISTRY                                  1497 records
25)    1990  An Exploratory Study of the Effectiveness of a Play-Based Center
             Approach for Learning Chemistry in an Early Childhood Program.
26)    1990  Oceanography for Landlocked Classrooms. Monograph V.
27)    1991  The Development of Modules for the Teaching of Chemical
             Equilibrium.
28)    1991  Performance Based on Instruction by Lecture or by Interaction and
             Its Relationship to Cognitive Variables.
29)    1991  The Use of Analog Models by Students of Chemistry at Higher
             Education Level.
30)    1992  Into the Woods: The Impact of Pre-Reading Activities.
31)    1992  Secondary Education in North Carolina: A Report of Student
             Participation and Performance in Algebra I, Geometry, Algebra II,
             ELP, U.S. History, English I, Physical Science, Biology, Chemistry,
             Physics. End of Course Testing.
32)    1983  Chemistry and Crime: From Sherlock Holmes to Today's Courtroom.
-Records continue on the next page; press RETURN to continue display
Type: DIS number, to see a fuller record.    PRINT to print/mail/save records.
      AND, NOT, OR to refine this search.    FIND to begin a new search.
YOUR RESPONSE:    32
```

Now there's something! Item 32 looks very interesting...

```
ERIC                    Search / FULL display         06/22/93 22:47
Find ABSTRACT CHEMISTRY                               Record 32 of 1497
-----------------------------------------------------------------------
Accession: ED343778
    Title: Chemistry and Crime: From Sherlock Holmes to Today's Courtroom.
   Author: Gerber, Samuel M., Ed.
 Pub Date: 1983      Number of Pages: 158
 Abstract: The application of the principles of chemistry both for committing
           crimes and for tracking down criminals interests audiences of all
           ages and walks of life. This interest is the reason for the
           long-standing popularity of fictional works that describe crimes
           made possible by the criminal's knowledge of chemistry and crimes
           solved by the sleuth's knowledge of chemistry. The first section of
           this book presents three chapters on chemistry in fictional crimes.
```

```
         A discussion of the influences of Arthur Conan Doyle's medical
         school professors on his fiction opens the book. In the next
         chapter, Dorothy L. Sayers' extensive knowledge of chemistry is
         displayed through an examination of three of her works. Various
-This record continues; press RETURN to see the next page
Type: DISPLAY BRIEF to see brief records.     PRINT to print/mail/save records.
     AND, NOT, OR to refine this search.      FIND to begin a new search.
YOUR RESPONSE:
```

Sounds even more interesting. Press the Enter key to see the rest of the record.

```
ERIC                    Search / FULL display            06/22/93 22:48
Find ABSTRACT CHEMISTRY                                  Record 32 of 1497
         methods used for testing blood in 1875 are presented in the last
         chapter of this section. The second section contains chapters that
         discuss the present state of the art. The first two chapters in this
         section detail recent changes in the field of forensic science and
         provide definitions, explanations, and a short history of forensic
         science and criminalistics. The chemical composition and analysis of
         bullets and the uses of this information in some famous murder
         cases, such as the assassination of John F. Kennedy are then
         discussed. Bloodstain analysis is the subject of the next two
         chapters: one on case histories and one on serological and
         electrophoretic techniques. The last chapter presents results of a
         2-year study of four police jurisdictions to determine the kinds of
         physical evidence collected and used in typical criminal
         investigations. (KR)
Major Descriptors: Chemistry;  Criminology;  Fiction;
Other Descriptors: Chromatography;  Crime;  Higher Education;  Homicide;
-This record continues; press RETURN to see the next page
Type: DISPLAY BRIEF to see brief records.     PRINT to print/mail/save records.
     AND, NOT, OR to refine this search.      FIND to begin a new search.
YOUR RESPONSE:
```

Great stuff! More...

```
ERIC                    Search / FULL display            06/22/93 22:49
Find ABSTRACT CHEMISTRY                                  Record 32 of 1497
             Body;  Resource Materials;  Science Activities;  Science man
             Education;  Secondary Education;
Major Identifiers: Forensic Science;
Other Identifiers: Sherlock Holmes;
--------------------------------------------------------------------------

-End of record 32; press RETURN to see record 33
Type: DISPLAY BRIEF to see brief records.     PRINT to print/mail/save records.
     AND, NOT, OR to refine this search.      FIND to begin a new search.
YOUR RESPONSE: print
```

This sounds fantastic! I'm going to mail myself a copy of the record.

```
ERIC                          Search                    06/22/93 22:57
Print options                                            1497 records
2  <— RECORDS to be printed (enter a number from the list below)
   1. Your current search result of 1497 records.
   2. The last record you displayed. (Record 32 of 1497)

2  <— FORMATTING of the data (enter a number from the list below)
   1. BRIEF display
   2. FULL display

2  <— DESTINATION of the output (enter a number from the list below)
   1. System printer    ¦ Email address: gibbs@rain.org    _____
   2. Another user      ¦
   3. Computer file     ¦
                        ¦ Output title: ERIC_____
                        ¦
                        ¦ _____

Type: OK to continue PRINT request.     UNDO to discard changes to page.
      CANCEL to cancel request.
YOUR RESPONSE: ok
```

This second item sounded so interesting that I went off to the university library where they keep ERIC documents on microfiche (I could have ordered it directly from ERIC). There I found the microfiche copy and printed off the book on a microfiche reader/printer. What a find!

For more information on ERIC, contact

> ERIC Clearinghouse on Information Resources
> Syracuse University
> Syracuse, NY 13244-2340
> Internet: ERIC@SUVM.ACS.SYR.EDU
> 1-800-USE-ERIC or 315-443-3640

Drowning in Data

As you can see from the previous examples, the range of accessible data, particularly when you pay, is phenomenal.

When you're searching, finding too much that is too general is easy. Finding relevant information is much harder. Indeed, it's so hard that some people (called data brokers) make a living out of finding information for others who are less skilled at it.

The greatest skill you can develop as an Internet navigator is learning how to keep from drowning in these data resources, which will help you come up with gold every time you dive in.

CHAPTER 16

USING THE INTERNET FOR BUSINESS

Chapter 1, "The Internet: Past, Present, and Future," talked briefly about how the Internet is gradually going commercial. Now that the Internet is open for business, it is important to understand how it will affect you and your company and what kinds of opportunities there are.

The U.S. Government's Data Superhighway policy has effectively accelerated the pace of Internet development. One of the most important aspects is that in the very near future business access will be very easy and cheap. Only slightly further out, the same will apply to home access.

Within the next decade (and that's only sticking my neck out a little way), you'll be able to access the Internet from your home through your television. The kinds of services that are proposed include electronic mail, local and national government access, and new forms of television.

One option that is currently being explored by the cable television companies is to upgrade the bandwidth (that is, the data-carrying capacity) of cable services and make them two way. This will allow for real-time feedback from viewers to television programs, television-on-demand (where you choose what you want to watch, when you like, and are billed on a usage basis), and bring a whole new dimension to home shopping, such as being able to order from both local stores and specialty shops anywhere in the world.

Now, as the Internet becomes increasingly global in scale, attracts more and more resources, and becomes the common link for tens of thousands of systems, what better business foundation could there be than the Internet?

The Internet will be where your competitors are, where your clients and customers can be reached, where sources of data and information can be found, and where services and products can be bought and sold.

For your organization, the Internet will become the easiest way to link together the geographically distributed components of your organization, and it will become the basis for implementing telecommuting on a wide scale. For your clients or for you as a purchaser, it will give the ability to find suppliers anywhere in the world and will change the way we think about advertising and marketing.

When businesses en masse are connected to the Internet, we'll all be wondering what we did before we had access (much the same way that we feel about fax machines today). We'll be buying, selling, trading, making contacts, and exchanging data across the Internet with hardly a thought for how its done—the Internet will just *be* there. It will be as transparent in its use and operation as the telephone is. Indeed, from the computer user's point of view, Internet access and data transfer may well be completely transparent (with the exception of the Internet access provider's monthly bill, which will be small, but all too opaque).

The New Organization on the Internet

One of the enduring concepts of the Information Age (a popular term for the current period in which computer technology has become ubiquitous) is that of the New Organization. This term was coined by Professor Peter Drucker in his paper "The Coming of the New Organization" (*Harvard Business Review*, Jan./Feb. 1988). He used it to describe the kind of structure that organizations will have to evolve toward to stay competitive now that computer technology has become central to business.

Professor Drucker argues that the structure of many organizations is extremely hierarchical—many layers of management only talking to the layers above and below them. Communication occurs up and down the organizational tree with little horizontal contact or jumping over layers.

These "deep" structures, he pointed out, were appropriate at a time (the "Industrial Age") when computers weren't involved in business. They ensured that information was filtered so that the decision makers at the top weren't deluged with raw data and which, without the tree, they wouldn't have access to anyway. The speed of these trees was limited by human abilities to absorb, analyze, and process the data and turn it into information.

Navigator's Note: Professor Drucker distinguishes data from information by classifying information as "data imbued with meaning and purpose." This is a very important concept as information has a much more importance than data. For example, the context of a collection of numbers might be sales data from all of a company's regions. There is a sense in which this data is information, but it's not a strong one.

If you take that data and analyze it so that you know sales by product and by region as well as overall totals, however, you have created information—data that has been given meaning and purpose (that is, greater importance).

Now, if these organizational structures didn't have to be as deep and could still handle the data to information transformation process as effectively and at least as quickly, imagine how much more cost-effective and, hopefully, more efficient the organization could be. Enter two foundations of the new organization— knowledge workers and information technology.

Knowledge workers are what Drucker calls members of the organization who are expert in their field. They are specialists and are, in comparison to the drone worker of the Industrial Era, highly autonomous and much more cost-effective. Along with that, computers take over the rote processing of data and allow the organization to shed the clerical workers.

This results in a slimmer, computer-based organization that should be more flexible in how it is structured, more adaptable to changing market conditions, and more profitable. Those who doubt that Drucker's vision of the New Organization is realistic haven't been paying attention. The trend (or what might be seen as a mania) for downsizing in organizations is a key part of the evolutionary trend to a more skilled, computer-literate workforce, and is an issue that you'll see in countless articles in the business and computer press.

The Computer Connection

Computers are the basis of information technology. When businesses become information-based, Drucker points out, speed is vital. The organization must know where its resources (financial, human, and material) are, their status, and their availability. It also needs to know what the market conditions are that define its business. To do this requires not just information, but systems that capture and deliver the information.

Now when you start to consider your options for delivering information, a prime consideration is the geographical locations to which the delivery system extends. Going with a system the covers your city, county, or state limits you to business in that area. Even a national communications system is inadequate as business becomes increasingly global.

Though there are international networks run by a variety of companies, the costs can be considerable and most are offer a limited coverage of the countries they serve. Not so the Internet. As it is an internetwork, it just continues to grow, and access points spring up at an astounding rate in every country that it reaches. Currently, a new network (not computer, but a network of computers) is connected to the Internet every ten minutes!

When you consider the issue of capturing information, the Internet is unparalleled. On the Internet, we're already starting to see some astounding tools for information collection and retrieval. These tools support searching vast collections of data, and retrieving and displaying it. This data now includes text, graphics, photographic images, animations, video, and sound.

Groupware

In the local area networking and PC worlds, there are new generations of groupware—software that can coordinate, manage, and track the efforts of a group of people working on a common project. For example, Lotus Development Corporation's Lotus Notes provides a system of shared databases that act as a repository of corporate data and can be used to link the work of users on PCs that are mobile and PCs that are attached to networks.

As these worlds and the Internet come together, as they already are starting to, whole new techniques for working together become practical. The knowledge worker can be more effective because information technology, combined with the communications potential of the Internet, allows the acquisition, manipulation, and sharing of data in ways that cannot be achieved by any other means. And the New Organization—that flatter, leaner structure—has a sound basis on which to exist.

Virtual Corporations

A concept that recently has become a hot topic is that of virtual corporations—organizations that form for the duration of a market or a project and then break up when that work is finished. The Internet makes this strategy practical in a way that no other communications system has ever been able to.

The critical aspects of a virtual corporation (VC) are that it is temporary and those involved may be operating in several separate VCs at the same time. In a sense, it is the ultimate form of the New Organization. In it, the new organization has been slimmed down to individuals or small autonomous groups who operate as experts in their fields. These entities exercise a very sophisticated form of entrepreneurship that makes them extremely competitive. The lifecycle of a virtual corporation is quite simple:

1. Identification of a business opportunity.
2. Recruitment of partners and establishing the VC.
3. Establishing a work plan.
4. Execution of development work.
5. Marketing the product.
6. Delivering the product.
7. Dissolving the VC.

Conducting this kind of business on a local basis is possible with adequate technology, but usually the opportunities and range of partners are limited so it rarely happens. On a regional or greater basis, VCs hardly ever happen today because the tools and systems to find partners and markets and build effective communications between the parties hardly exist.

The Internet is changing all that. This book, for example, is a partnership between the authors, one near Los Angeles and the other in Pittsburgh, and the publisher in Indiana. For the duration of the development of *Navigating the Internet* and this deluxe edition, we were contractually connected and worked to produce the manuscript much as a VC would operate. Our tools were the computers that we used for writing and editing and the Internet that we used for communications.

For the first edition, once we finished, we didn't have to sever our connections—which might be a consideration (to save money) if we had to establish a private network. When we wanted to start work on this edition, we just sent each other messages, planned the work, and off we went.

As the groupware tools become more sophisticated and Internet access becomes an integral part of business, VCs will flourish. Finding clients and customers will become easier as the Internet breeds forums and newsletters in which needs and opportunities are articulated.

For example, there is a online newsletter called the "China Import/Export News." An opportunity spotted in this could lead to a search by an organization specializing in pest control for a Chinese trade representative, a specialist freight company, and an organization in China with field staff to handle liaison with farmers. All of this could be done across the Internet using the newsletter to establish initial contacts and without any of the parties involved ever meeting on a face-to-face basis!

This kind of operation will become more common and more successful because the Internet will make it possible for niche specialists to find markets and partners on a global basis.

Telecommuting

Telecommuting is where, rather than travel to your place of work, you work from your house and use computer communications to send and receive data to and from your company. It's a pretty idyllic arrangement. No more commute, no more traffic, nice surroundings, and, if you are so inclined, you can even work in your pajamas.

The commuting part is one of the great issues that makes telecommuting highly desirable. If you live near Los Angeles, you will have more than just an idea of what heavy traffic means. Everyday, millions of Angelenos take to the highways, usually one to vehicle, and attempt to go from A (home) to B (work). People at C (somewhere in between A and B) get to see these poor folks go past at a speed that makes traveling by pogo stick look fast. The people at C also get to see them do much the same thing as they do the B to A thing at the other end of the day.

Now that Southern California has been shaken up by an earthquake that registered 6.6 on the Richter Scale, and many freeways have been trashed, the daily trip into L.A. has become a nightmare. A trip that took one commuter just over an hour to reach his office now takes him five hours!

It's no surprise that prior to the earthquake, telecommuting was being heavily promoted. The benefits of getting cars off the streets and making traffic flow faster, and reducing pollution made it a strategy that the state was actively promoting. Post-quake, telecommuting in the Los Angeles area is more than desirable, it may be all that keeps many companies in business.

As the Internet becomes ubiquitous, one of the major problems that faced telecommuters will disappear. That problem was bandwidth. While many business activities that involve the handling of data don't move large amounts around routinely, even an occasional database search or file retrieval can be next to impossible.

For example, if the connection is across several telephone areas or long distance, the maximum sustainable data transfer rate is around 240 characters per second. That means that to fill an entire screen with text (2000 characters) will take over 8 seconds. That doesn't sound like much, but consider transferring something like a contract document of 200 kilobytes. That's going to take almost 14 minutes!

Even if the telephone line is of excellent quality, the average highest data rate will be around 1,440 characters per second. That requires over 2 minutes to transfer the 200 kilobyte file which many would say is still far too long.

More importantly than that, though, is the problem of cost. If you're working from your home and I'm working from mine, and I want to get a message to you, it may need to be fast. If we both had electronic mail, the frequency with which we connect to the electronic mail system is going to determine how fast we can communicate.

Let's say we both connect to the e-mail service every fifteen minutes. If I send a message, it could wait as much as fifteen minutes before my computer sends the message to the e-mail system. If the timing is slightly off, you might have just picked up your mail so my mail to you will sit there for another 15 minutes. The worst case is therefore that the message could take as much as half an hour to reach its destination.

To fix this problem, we could both just stay connected to the mail system for the entire working day. But then at the mail system, we require a connection for every person, and we will have to foot the bill for the cost of the telephone call.

What is needed is a continuous connection that is billed as either a flat rate or for how much data we send across it. Guess what communications system is starting to become available on these terms . . . the Internet.

Many Internet service providers offer flat rate services and if (at least, in the U.S.) you're within a local calling zone, maintaining a permanent connection may be possible with a flat rate for the local calls.

As the number and variety of service providers increase, finding local Internet access will become much easier. And when the television cable companies or the telephone companies get into the act, the cost and ease of connection is likely to drop even further.

CHAPTER
16

New communications technologies with names such as the Integrated Digital Services Network (ISDN), the Switched Multimegabit Data Stream (SMDS) service, and frame relay are becoming more widely available. These services offer connection speeds that rang from 56 kilobits per second (7,000 characters per second) up to several megabits per second and promise to push the cost of high-speed digital communications down rapidly.

Within the next few years, getting these services to your house so that you can connect to local Internet service providers will be easy.

From an organization's point of view, having employees work from home will be pretty straightforward in terms of performance, cost, and technology. Each employee will need a PC and an Internet connection, and the company will need to provide secure access to its internal network for them to come in from the Internet.

At present, telecommuting is still a novel idea. There are many aspects of telecommuting that have not been examined or practically tested. For example, how do you connect any of the potentially huge range of corporate resources that a remote employee might need to that user across the Internet? What about security? How do you measure productivity? What are the hidden costs?

It will be awhile before all the pieces that make telecommuting practical fall into place. That said, telecommuting will become truly commonplace in the next few years, and the Internet will be a key part of that idea.

Making Connections

In most businesses, making and maintaining contacts with people is very important. You want to develop a network of advisors, confidants, experts, references, agents, and friends. The result gives you the means to stay informed and find new opportunities.

On the Internet, there are several ways to "meet" people. LISTSERVs and newsgroups are great ways to find people who might have similar business interests, and electronic mail provides the easiest method of getting and staying in contact.

Try joining relevant groups and lists then watch what people say for awhile. This is important as it will take some time to find out who is informed and who is just opinionated. It is also wise to get a feel for the style and content of discussion before putting in your two-cents-worth.

Once you have identified the style of the discussion and the contributors who are informed, you can then start sending private messages to selected participants and try getting a dialog going.

There is also the issue of finding business opportunities. One area where there is considerable growth on the Internet is in newsletters. A good example is a roughly bi-weekly newsletter called the "China Import/Export News:"

```
**************************************************************************
#                                                                      #
#       C H I N A     I M P O R T / E X P O R T     N E W S            #
#       - - -        - - - - - - - - - - - -        - - -          #
#                                                                      #
#           A WEEKLY NEWSLETTER FROM THE CHINA-LINK CLUB              #
#                                                                      #
#                  E-mail: cnlink@world.std.com                       #
#                                                                      #
**************************************************************************


                    January 17, 1994 (CN940117)


CONTENTS                                                         LINES
======================================================================
A) Goods Wanted (5 items)..........................................157
B) Goods For Sale (1 items).........................................30
C) Swap market in china............................................ 10
D) China Market Watch (6 items)...................................418
======================================================================
NEW SERVICES:

    &  NOTES: Contact information for goods wanted or for sale is  &
    &         available on the autoreply system.                  &
    &         ^^^^^^^^^^^^^^^^^                                    &
    &         Please send an e-mail to:                           &
    &             cnlink@world.std.com                            &
    &         in the SUBJECT line: CONTACTS                       &
    *  *  *  *  *  *  *  *  *  *  *  *  *
    $  FAX-ON-DEMAND system is not availabe at present time.      $
- - - - - - - - - - - - - - - - - - - - - - - - - - - - - - - - - - -
A: Goods Wanted (5 items).....................................157 lines
- - - - - - - - - - - - - - - - - - - - - - - - - - - - - - - - - - -
```

Navigator's Note: The "China Import/Export News" newsletter available by subscribing to the list on LISTSERV@IFCSS.ORG (just put SUBSCRIBE <first name> <last name> in the body of the message). The newsletter is published by the China-Link Club which can be contacted at china-link@ifcss.org. Nice guys and very helpful.

The contents of this newsletter describe things that organizations in China want to buy or sell. As an entrepreneur, this is a golden opportunity. For example, if you are in the "animal feed material" business and want to explore a market, there was a request in the newsletter. And most of the contacts and arrangements can be made through electronic mail! This is definitely 21st century business.

In the near future we can expect an explosion of these kinds of newsletters and for organizations to use remote electronically-based business transactions as a matter of routine.

Gathering Data and Information

Businesses need up-to-date information of all kinds, and the Internet is the largest storehouse of information in the world—much of it either free or available at little cost.

But what specifically is available? This listing will give you just a taste of the range of the thousands of information resources available:

- **Internet Business Pages**—FTP to `ftp.msen.com`, or e-mail `ibp-info@msen.com` with subject `send description`

- **Israeli R&D Archive**—Information on R&D projects, information on high technology incubator projects. Telnet to `vms.huji.ac.il`, and login as `mop`

- **The Management Archive**—Management ideas and information, Academy of Management Archives, working papers. Gopher to `chimera.sph.umn.edu`

- **Software archives**—For IBM compatible software. FTP to `oak.oakland.edu`, and login as `anonymous`; for Macintosh software, FTP to `sumex-aim.stanford.edu`, in the `/info-mac` subdirectory

- **Centre for Labour Studies**—Australian labor research data, labor briefings, and international labor data at the University of Adelaide Australia. Gopher to `jarrah.itd.adelaide.edu.au`

- **Economics and Business Journals**—Index and abstract of business related periodicals. Gopher to `rs5.loc.gov`

- **Research Results Database**—Summaries of agricultural and economic research. Access via WAIS at `usda-rrdb.src`

- **Agricultural Market News**—Commodity reports. Access via WAIS at `agricultural-market-news.src`

- ⚓ **Asia Pacific Business and Marketing Resources, International Marketing Insights Japan, East and Southeast Asian Business and Management, and Korean Business and Management**—All databases regarding cross-cultural management, government and business relations in the Pacific Rim, and investment information. Available by Gopher to `hoshi.cic.sfu.ca`

- ⚓ **Smithsonian Photographic Archives**—Archive of binary images of photographs. Aavailable by FTP to `photo1.si.edu`, and login as `anonymous`

- ⚓ **U.S. Federal Budget, Singapore's IT2000 Plan for Information Technology, and general business and economic information**—All available by Gopher to `cwis.usc.edu`

- ⚓ **Census Data**—Summaries of 1990 Census. Telnet to `una.hh.lib.umich.edu`, and login as `gopher`

- ⚓ **New England Electronic Economic Data Center**—Unemployment, housing, and energy statistics for the Bureau of Economic Analysis and the Federal Reserve Bank of Boston. FTP to `neeedc.umesbs.maine.edu`, login anonymous, and go to either the `/bea` or `/frbb` subdirectory

- ⚓ **Dow Jones News Retrieval**—Investment, economic, and business-related articles, abstracts, and full-text. Telnet to `djnr.dowjones.com` (this is a fee-based service)

- ⚓ **Science and Technology Information System**—National Science foundation information, grant material, and databases. Telnet to `stis.nsf.gov` and login as `public`

- ⚓ **National Center for Biotechnology Information**—Enzyme and protein site dictionary, DNA sequence analysis, Swiss protein sequence databank. FTP to `ncbi.nlm.nih.gov`, or e-mail, `repository@ncbi.nlm.nih.gov`

- ⚓ **Patent Titles by E-mail**—Weekly mailings of all patent issued, information on ordering information on specific patents. At `patents-request@world.std.com`

- ⚓ **ECIX: The Environmental Exchange Archive**—FTP to `igc.org`, login as `anonymous`, and look in the `/pub/ECIX` or `/pub/ECIXfiles` directories

- ⚓ **Geography Server**—Information on population, latitude, longitude, and elevation. Telnet to `martini.eecs.umich.edu 3000` and type `help` for assistance

- ⚓ **Global Land Information System**—Information on land-use maps. Telnet to `glis.cr.usgs.gov` and login as `guest`

- ⚓ **Washington and Lee Law Library**—Extensive access to Internet tools, law libraries, and documents. Telnet to `liberty.uc.wlu.edu`, and login as `lawlib`, or FTP to `liberty.uc.wlu.edu`, and login as `anonymous`, and locate the `/pub/lawlib` directory

- ⚓ **LEXIS**—Database of over 1000 legal databases and court decisions. Telnet `lexis.meaddata.com` (this is fee service)

- ⚓ **Catalog of Electronic Text Archives**—Access to online full-text books archive. Telnet to `guvax3.georgetown.edu`, with username `CPET`

- ⚓ **Library of Congress Information Center**—Information locator services. Telnet to `locis.loc.gov` and login as `marvel`

- ⚓ **National On-line Media Association**—Trade association and lobbying information regarding online media. Subscribe to the natbbs mailing list by sending e-mail to `natbbs-request@echonyc.com`

- ⚓ **CIA World Fact Book**—Demographic, geographic, social, and monetary information. Telnet to `info.rutgers.edu` and choose `library`, then choose `reference`. Or by FTP to `nic.funet.fi`, and look in the `/pub/doc/World_facts` subdirectory

Selling the Corporation

If your business is going to capitalize on the Internet, you should consider how you can make it visible. Advertising on the Internet in the traditional ways is not a good idea.

For example, if you use the Internet to do the equivalent of a mailshot by sending an advertising message about your company or product to a LISTSERV, you will discover what the phrase "heaped with opprobrium" means. After the first thousand e-mail message telling you that you are an idiot, a dolt, and deserve to be covered in honey and staked out in the sun so that the ants can devour your carcass, you'll get the next thousand that are less pleasant.

The codes of behavior on the Internet are not to be messed with and traditional advertising will simply not be acceptable.

Now if you were to tailor individual messages to people that were relevant to their needs or interests, you would, at the worst, be ignored. At the best, you'll get what you want, a response. But the reception you get will depend on the value of the content of your message and whether it is targeted at the right audience.

It is also important to ensure that if you get a negative response from someone that you send e-mail to, you don't keep them on your list and e-mail them again.

If that happens with enough people and you keep doing it, word will circulate and the deluge of hate mail will start.

One very effective way of advertising is to set up your own Gopher server. This is unfortunately beyond the scope of this book but you can find the information that you need on the Internet quite easily (or you can look for a Sams book called *The Internet Unleashed* in your local bookstore).

By creating Gopher menu items containing easily found keywords that lead to your product or service descriptions and making them searchable by Veronica, people will find you.

But there is another issue. If the descriptions are just product data and carry no added value such as explanations of the technology, Internet users will be less interested in what you have to offer. To make your Gopher service really useful it must be just that—useful.

Another strategy is to start a LISTSERV list but to do that you'll have to commit to expending time and effort to keep the ball rolling. Again, blatant advertising and self promotion will not get you very far.

Promoting organizations on the Internet is still a very new concept and one that needs to be explored carefully. Remember, your potential market does not want to be treated en masse. The Internet has a strong orientation toward individualism, and you violate that at your peril.

To summarize, then, there seem to be certain current practices that typically garner fewer complaints than others from the residents of the networks.

What currently tends to be acceptable in practice:

- Marketing using a dedicated server—such as Gopher, FTP, WWW, WAIS, or BBS services—where the user must seek out the information.

- Dedicated Gophers for standard product information, price lists, document retrieval, announcements, newsletters, and so forth.

- Public databases for complex searching of information made available by Gopher, WAIS, FTP or e-mail query.

- Multimedia—sound and pictures for storage and playback made available by way of anonymous FTP.

- Using mail distribution lists (LISTSERV or other) set up for the purpose of marketing.

- Threaded news groups, such as USENET groups, set up for business purposes or those with mixed purpose charters.

- Very modest product announcements to appropriate USENET newsgroups and mailing lists.

- Vendor contacts and announcements in signature files—five lines or fewer—and information provided by .plan or plan.txt files.

What is not OK in common practice:

- Unsolicited e-mail or bulk mailings, sometimes called "in your face," or IYF, advertising.

- Postings and cross postings of announcement and messages to unrelated groups or lists.

- The network equivalent of "cold calls," where the unsuspecting consumer gets mail and attention uninvited.

Product Support

One area where many computer companies have turned the Internet to great advantage is in supplying technical support. The Internet might almost have been made specifically for this.

Once you have a connection of any kind to the Internet (e-mail, a shell account, or interactive) you can send and receive data. If the company that supplied your computers is on the Internet and has even the most trivial level of organization, it can field your requests for support, conduct a dialog with you on your problems, run diagnostics remotely across the Internet, send you software updates, and explain how to deal with problems.

Many vendors who have attempted this have found that it pays huge dividends. There is a huge difference between trying to get technical service by telephone where you might have to wait in a queue for up to a matter of hours and being able to send an e-mail request that gets a fast response even if it is just an automated acknowledgment.

Those vendors who invest in building effective support services that are based on the Internet will reap the benefits very quickly. They can service global markets with a responsiveness and effectiveness that can't be supplied by telephone, fax, or indeed, anything short of actually sending a technician out on a site visit.

Publishing

Another area which a few organizations have started to explore is publishing on the Internet. This is not actually a wholly new market. There have been a large number of free electronic journals, shareware books, and charged-for databases appearing over the last few months. There are some database services such as Lexis/Nexis and newswire services such as ClariNet that have been around for years.

Publishing on the Internet is a complex issue. As with all electronic media, the issues of copyright are not resolved and the problems of collecting and tracking royalties are not even touched. Worse still, little has been done in the area of preventing and detecting piracy. There are LISTSERV lists and newsgroups that discuss these issues. Check them out for current thinking and approaches (see Appendix H, "The Internet Navigator's Gazetteer," for some useful resources).

So, Can You Do Business?

In short, yes. Doing business on the Internet is more than possible. Many organizations are starting to invest heavily in businesses that are based on the Internet and many large companies (publishers, software vendors, retailers, etc.) are eyeing the Internet as a major strategic element of their business.

Now is the time to start exploring and looking for opportunities. The Internet is going to become a formidable market place and one that requires knowledge and expertise if you are to successfully capitalize on it.

THE PUBLIC DIALUP INTERNET ACCESS LIST (PDIAL)

by Peter Kaminski

The Internet is a global cooperative information network that can give you instant access to millions of people and terabytes of data. Providers listed in the PDIAL provide inexpensive public access to the Internet using your regular modem and computer.

Navigator's Note: The PDIAL currently lists only providers directly connected to the Internet. Much of the Internet can still be explored through systems with only Internet e-mail and Usenet netnews connections, but you need to check other BBS lists to find them.

Choosing a Provider

Phone charges can dominate the cost of your access to the Internet. Check first for providers with metro or regional dialins that are a local call for you (no per-minute phone charges). If there aren't any, move on to comparing prices for public data networks (PDNs), 800, and direct-dial long distance charges. Be sure to compare all your options. Calling long distance out-of-state or across the country is often cheaper than calling 30 miles away.

If you're not in North America and have no local provider, you may still be able to use one of the providers listed as having PDN access. Contact the individual providers with PDN access (see the following listings).

Information Changes

The information listed in the PDIAL changes and expands rapidly. You can use the Info Deli e-mail server, which will provide you with updates and other information. Choose from the following commands and e-mail them to info-deli-server@netcom.com.

> "Send PDIAL"—receive the current PDIAL
> "Subscribe PDIAL"—receive new editions of the PDIAL automatically
> "Subscribe Info-Deli-News"—news of Info Deli changes and additions

See the section titled, "How People Can Get the PDIAL," for more details and other ways to obtain the PDIAL.

Remember, the PDIAL is only a summary of the resources and environments delivered by each of the various providers. Contact the providers that interest you by e-mail or voice phone and find out if they have what you need.

Area Code Summary: Providers with Many Local Dialins (1-800, PDN)

800	class
	cns
	crl
	csn
	dial-n-cerf-usa
	hookup.net
	IGC
	jvnc
	OARnet
PDN	delphi
	holonet
	hookup.net
	IGC
	michnet
	millennium
	novalink
	portal
	psi-world-dial
	psilink
	tmn
	well
	world

"PDN" means the provider is accessible through a public data network (check the following listings for which network); note that many PDNs listed offer access outside North America, as well as within North America. Check with the provider or the PDN for more details.

"800" means the provider is accessible via a "toll-free" U.S. phone number. The phone company doesn't charge for the call, but the service provider adds a surcharge to cover the cost of the 800 service. This may be more expensive than other long-distance options.

Area Code Summary: U.S./Canada Metro and Regional Dialins

If you are not local to any of these providers, it's still likely that you can access those providers through a public data network (PDN). Check the previous section for providers with wide-area access.

201	jvnc-tiger
202	CAPCON
	clarknet
	express
	michnet
	tmn
203	jvnc-tiger
205	nuance
206	eskimo
	GLAIDS
	halcyon
	netcom
	nwnexus
	olympus
212	echonyc
	maestro
	mindvox
	panix
	pipeline
213	crl
	dial-n-cerf
	kaiwan
	netcom
214	metronet
	netcom
215	jvnc-tiger
	PREPnet
216	OARnet
	wariat
217	prairienet

301	CAPCON clarknet express michnet tmn
302	ssnet
303	cns csn netcom nyx
305	gate.net
310	class crl dial-n-cerf kaiwan netcom
312	InterAccess mcsnet netcom xnet
313	michnet MSen
401	anomaly ids jvnc-tiger
403	PUCnet UUNET-Canada
404	crl netcom
407	gate.net
408	a2i netcom portal
410	CAPCON clarknet express

412 PREPnet
telerama

415 a2i
class
crl
dial-n-cerf
IGC
netcom
portal
well

416 hookup.net
UUNET-Canada
uunorth

419 OARnet

503 agora.rain.com
netcom
teleport

504 sugar

508 anomaly
nearnet
northshore
novalink

510 class
crl
dial-n-cerf
holonet
netcom

512 realtime

513 fsp
OARnet

514 CAM.ORG
UUNET-Canada

516 jvnc-tiger

517 michnet

519 hookup.net
UUNET-Canada
uunorth

602	crl
	Data.Basix
	evergreen
	indirect
603	MV
	nearnet
604	UUNET-Canada
609	jvnc-tiger
613	UUNET-Canada
	uunorth
614	OARnet
616	michnet
617	delphi
	nearnet
	netcom
	northshore
	novalink
	world
619	cg57
	class
	crash.cts.com
	cyber
	dial-n-cerf
	netcom
703	CAPCON
	clarknet
	express
	michnet
	netcom
	tmn
704	concert
	Vnet
707	crl
708	InterAccess
	mcsnet
	xnet

713	blkbox
	nuchat
	sugar
714	class
	dial-n-cerf
	express
	kaiwan
	netcom
717	PREPnet
718	maestro
	mindvox
	netcom
	panix
	pipeline
719	cns
	csn
	oldcolo
804	wyvern
810	michnet
	MSen
814	PREPnet
815	InterAccess
	mcsnet
	xnet
817	metronet
818	class
	dial-n-cerf
	netcom
905	UUNET-Canada
906	michnet
907	alaska.edu
908	express
	jvnc-tiger
910	concert
916	netcom
919	concert
	Vnet

These are area codes local to the dialups, although some prefixes in the area codes listed may not be local to the dialups. Check your phone book or with your phone company.

Area Code Summary: International Dialins

If you are not local to any of these providers, you might be able to access those providers through a public data network (PDN). Check the preceding list for providers with wide-area access and send e-mail to them to ask about availability.

+44 (0)81	Demon
	dircon
	ibmpcug
+49	Individual.NET
+49 23	ins
+49 069	in-rhein-main
+49 089	mucev
+61 2	connect.com.au
+61 3	connect.com.au
+301	Ariadne
+353 1	IEunet

Alphabetical List of Providers

Fees are for personal dialup accounts with outgoing Internet access; most sites have other classes of service with other rate structures as well. Most support e-mail and netnews along with the listed services.

"Long distance: provided by user" means you need to use direct-dial long distance or other long-distance services to connect to the provider.

a2i

Name	a2i communications
Dialup	408-293-9010 (v.32bis), 415-364-5652 (v.32bis), 408-293-9020 (PEP); login guest
Area codes	408, 415
Local access	CA: West and South San Franscisco Bay area
Long distance	Provided by user
Services	Shell (SunOS, UNIX, and MS-DOS), FTP, Telnet, IRC, feeds, domains and hostless domains, virtual ttys, Gopher
Fees	$20/month, $45/3 months, $72/6 months
E-mail	info@rahul.net
Voice	408-293-8078 voicemail
FTP more information	ftp.rahul.net:/pub/BLURB

agora.rain.com

Name	RainDrop Laboratories
Dialup	503-293-1772 (2400) 503-293-2059 (v.32, v.32bis); login: apply
Area codes	503
Local access	OR: Portland, Beaverton, Hillsboro, Forest Grove, Gresham, Tigard, Lake Oswego, Oregon City, Tualatin, Wilsonville
Long distance	Provided by user
Services	Shell, FTP, Telnet, Gopher, Usenet
Fees	$6/month (1 hour/day limit)
E-mail	info@agora.rain.com
Voice	n/a
FTP more information	agora.rain.com:/pub/Gopher-data/agora/agora

alaska.edu

Name	University of Alaska Southeast, Tundra Services
Dialup	907-789-1314
Area codes	907

Local access	All Alaskan sites with local UACN access—Anchorage, Barrow, Fairbanks, Homer, Juneau, Keni, Ketchikan, Kodiak, Kotzebue, Nome, Palmer, Sitka, Valdez
Long distance	Provided by user
Services	Statewide UACN Mail, Internet, Usenet, Gopher, Telnet, FTP
Fees	$20/month for individual accounts, discounts for 25+ and 50+ to public, governemnt, and non-profit organizations.
E-mail	JNJMB@acad1.alaska.edu
Voice	907-465-6453
Fax	907-465-6295
FTP more information	n/a

anomaly

Name	Anomaly—Rhode Island's Gateway To The Internet
Dialup	401-331-3706 (v.32) or 401-455-0347 (PEP)
Area codes	401, 508
Local access	RI: Providence/Seekonk zone
Long distance	Provided by user
Services	Shell, FTP, Telnet, SLIP
Fees	Commercial: $125/6 months or $200/year; Educational: $75/6 months or $125/year
E-mail	info@anomaly.sbs.risc.net
Voice	401-273-4669
FTP more information	anomaly.sbs.risc.net:/anomaly.info/access.zip

Ariadne

Name	Ariadne—Greek Academic and Research Network
Dialup	+301 65-48-800 (1200 - 9600 bps)

Area codes	+301
Local access	Athens, Greece
Long distance	Provided by user
Services	E-mail, FTP, Telnet, Gopher, talk, pad(EuropaNet)
Fees	5900 drachmas per calendar quarter, 1 hour/day limit.
E-mail	dialup@leon.nrcps.ariadne-t.gr
Voice	+301 65-13-392
Fax	+301 6532910
FTP more information	n/a

blkbox

Name	The Black Box
Dialup	(713) 480-2686 (v.32bis/v.42bis)
Area codes	713
Local access	TX: Houston
Long distance	Provided by user
Services	Shell, FTP, Telnet, SLIP, PPP, UUCP
Fees	$21.65/month or $108.25/6 months
E-mail	info@blkbox.com
Voice	713-480-2684
FTP more information	n/a

CAM.ORG

Name	Communications Accessibles Montreal
Dialup	514-931-7178 (v.32bis), 514-931-2333 (2400bps)
Area codes	514
Local access	QC: Montreal, Laval, South-Shore, West-Island
Long distance	Provided by user
Services	Shell, FTP, Telnet, Gopher, WAIS, WWW, IRC, feeds, SLIP, PPP, AppleTalk, FAX gateway
Fees	$25/month Cdn.

E-mail	info@CAM.ORG
Voice	514-931-0749
FTP more information	ftp.CAM.ORG

CAPCON

Name	CAPCON Library Network
Dialup	Contact for number
Area codes	202, 301, 410, 703
Local access	District of Columbia, suburban Maryland, northern Virginia
Long distance	Various plans available/recommended; contact for details
Services	Menu, Archie, FTP, Gopher, Listservs, Telnet, WAIS, whois, full day training, and CAPCON Connect User Manual
Fees	$35 startup, $150/year, $24/month for first account from an institution; $35 startup, $90/year, $15/month for additional users (member rates lower); 20 hours/month included, additional hours $2/hour
E-mail	capcon@capcon.net
Voice	202-331-5771
Fax	202-797-7719
FTP more information	n/a

cg57

Name	E & S Systems Public Access *Nix
Dialup	619-278-8267 (v.32bis, TurboPEP), 619-278-8267 (v32) 619-278-9837 (PEP)
Area codes	619
Local access	CA: San Diego
Long distance	Provided by user
Services	Shell, FTP, IRC, Telnet, Gopher, Archie, BBS (UniBoard)

Fees	BBS (FREE), shell—$30/3 months, $50/6 months, $80/9 months, $100/year
E-mail	steve@cg57.esnet.com
Voice	619-278-4641
FTP more information	n/a

clarknet

Name	Clark Internet Services, Inc. (ClarkNet)
Dialup	410-730-9786, 410-995-0271, 301-596-1626, 301-854-0446, 301-621-5216; login guest
Area codes	202, 301, 410, 703
Local access	MD: Baltimore; DC: Washington; VA: northern Virginia
Long distance	Provided by user
Services	Shell, menu, FTP, Telnet, IRC, Gopher, Hytelnet, WWW, WAIS, SLIP/PPP, FTP space, feeds (UUCP & uMDSS), DNS, ClariNet
Fees	$23/month, $66/3 months, $126/6 months, or $228/year
E-mail	info@clark.net
Voice	800-735-2258; 410-730-9764 (MD Relay Svc)
Fax	410-730-9765
FTP more information	ftp.clark.net:/pub/clarknet/fullinfo.txt

class

Name	Cooperative Library Agency for Systems and Services
Dialup	Contact for number; CLASS serves libraries and information distributors only
Area codes	310, 415, 510, 619, 714, 818, 800
Local access	Northern and southern California or anywhere (800) service is available
Long distance	800 service available at $6/hour surcharge

Services	Menus, mail, Telnet, FTP, Gopher, WAIS, Hytelnet, Archie, WWW, IRC, UNIX shells, SLIP; training is available.
Fees	$4.50/hour, $150/year for first account, $50/year each additional account, $135/year CLASS membership. Discounts available for multiple memberships.
E-mail	class@class.org
Voice	800-488-4559
Fax	408-453-5379
FTP more information	n/a

cns

Name	Community News Service
Dialup	719-520-1700; id: new; password: newuser
Area codes	303, 719, 800
Local access	CO: Colorado Springs, Denver; continental U.S./800
Long distance	800 or provided by user
Services	UNIX shell, e-mail, FTP, Telnet, IRC, Usenet, ClariNet, Gopher, Commerce Business Daily
Fees	$2.75/hour; $10/month minimum, $35 signup
E-mail	service@cscns.com
Voice	719-592-1240
FTP more information	cscns.com

concert

Name	CONCERT-CONNECT
Dialup	Contact for number
Area codes	704, 910, 919
Local access	NC: Asheville, Chapel Hill, Charlotte, Durham, Greensboro, Greenville, Raleigh, Winston-Salem, Research Triangle Park

Long distance	Provided by user
Services	UUCP, SLIP
Fees	SLIP: $150 educational/research or $180 commercial for first 60 hours/month plus $300 signup
E-mail	info@concert.net
Voice	919-248-1999
FTP more information	ftp.concert.net

connect.com.au

Name	connect.com.au pty ltd
Dialup	Contact for number
Area codes	+61 3, +61 2
Local access	Australia: Melbourne, Sydney
Long distance	Provided by user
Services	SLIP, PPP, ISDN, UUCP, FTP, Telnet, NTP, FTPmail
Fees	AUS$2000/year (1 hour/day), 10-percent discount for AUUG members; other billing negotiable
E-mail	connect@connect.com.au
Voice	+61 3 5282239
Fax	+61 3 5285887
FTP more information	ftp.connect.com.au

crash.cts.com

Name	CTS Network Services (CTSNET)
Dialup	619-637-3640 HST, 619-637-3660 v.32bis, 619-637-3680 PEP; login: `help`
Area codes	619
Local access	CA: San Diego, Pt. Loma, La Jolla, La Mesa, El Cajon, Poway, Ramona, Chula Vista, National City, Mira Mesa, Alpine, East County, new North County numbers, Escondido, Oceanside, Vista

Long distance	Provided by user
Services	UNIX shell, UUCP, Usenet newsfeeds, NNTP, ClariNet, Reuters, FTP, Telnet, SLIP, PPP, IRC, Gopher, Archie, WAIS, POPmail, UMDSS, domains, nameservice, DNS
Fees	$10-$23/month flat, depending on features, $15 startup, personal; $20/month flat, depending on features, $25 startup, commercial
E-mail	info@crash.cts.com (server), support@crash.cts.com (human)
Voice	619-637-3637
Fax	619-637-3630
FTP more information	n/a

crl

Name	CR Laboratories Dialup Internet Access
Dialup	415-389-UNIX
Area codes	213, 310, 404, 415, 510, 602, 707, 800
Local access	CA: San Francisco Bay area, San Rafael, Santa Rosa, Los Angeles, Orange County; AZ: Phoenix, Scottsdale, Tempe, and Glendale; GA: Atlanta metro area; continental U.S./800
Long distance	800 or provided by user
Services	Shell, FTP, Telnet, feeds, SLIP, WAIS
Fees	$17.50/month plus $19.50 signup
E-mail	info@crl.com
Voice	415-381-2800
FTP more information	n/a

csn

Name	Colorado SuperNet, Inc.
Dialup	Contact for number
Area codes	303, 719, 800

Local access	CO: Alamosa, Boulder/Denver, Colorado Springs, Durango, Fort Collins, Frisco, Glenwood Springs/Aspen, Grand Junction, Greeley, Gunnison, Pueblo, Telluride; anywhere 800 service is available
Long distance	Provided by user or 800
Services	Shell or menu, UUCP, SLIP, 56K, ISDN, T1; FTP, Telnet, IRC, Gopher, WAIS, domains, anonymous FTP space, e-mail to fax
Fees	$1/hour off-peak, $3/hour peak ($250 max/month) plus $20 signup, $5/hour surcharge for 800 use
E-mail	info@csn.org
Voice	303-273-3471
Fax	303-273-3475
FTP more information	csn.org:/CSN/reports/DialinInfo.txt
off-peak	12 a.m.to 6 a.m.

cyber

Name	The Cyberspace Station
Dialup	619-634-1376; login: guest
Area codes	619
Local access	CA: San Diego
Long distance	Provided by user
Services	Shell, FTP, Telnet, IRC
Fees	$15/month plus $10 startup or $60 for six months
E-mail	help@cyber.net
Voice	n/a
FTP more information	n/a

Data.Basix

Name	Data Basix
Dialup	602-721-5887
Area codes	602

Local access	AZ: Tucson
Long distance	Provided by user
Services	Telnet, FTP, NEWS, UUCP; on-site assistance
Fees	$25 monthly, $180 yearly; group rates available
E-mail	info@Data.Basix.com (automated); sales@Data.Basix.com (human)
Voice	602-721-1988
FTP more information	Data.Basix.COM:/services/dial-up.txt

Demon

Name	Demon Internet Systems (DIS)
Dialup	+44 (0)81 343 4848
Area codes	+44 (0)81
Local access	London, England
Long distance	Provided by user
Services	FTP, Telnet, SLIP/PPP
Fees	GBPounds 10.00/month; 132.50/year (inc. 12.50 startup charge). No online time charges.
E-mail	internet@demon.co.uk
Voice	+44 (0)81 349 0063
FTP more information	n/a

delphi

Name	DELPHI
Dialup	800-365-4636; login: JOINDELPHI; password: INTERNETSIG
Area codes	617, PDN
Local access	MA: Boston; KS: Kansas City
Long distance	Sprintnet or Tymnet: $9/hour weekday business hours; no charge nights and weekends
Services	FTP, Telnet, feeds, user groups, wire services, member conferencing
Fees	$10/month for 4 hours or $20/month for 20 hours, plus $3/month for Internet services

E-mail	walthowe@delphi.com
Voice	800-544-4005
FTP more information	n/a

dial-n-cerf

Name	DIAL n' CERF or DIAL n' CERF AYC
Dialup	Contact for number
Area codes	213, 310, 415, 510, 619, 714, 818
Local access	CA: Los Angeles, Oakland, San Diego, Irvine, Pasadena, Palo Alto
Long distance	Provided by user
Services	Shell, menu, IRC, FTP, Hytelnet, Gopher, WAIS, WWW, terminal service, SLIP
Fees	$5/hour ($3/hour on weekend), $20/month, $50 startup, or $250/month flat for AYC
E-mail	help@cerf.net
Voice	800-876-2373 or 619-455-3900
FTP more information	nic.cerf.net:/cerfnet/dial-n-cerf/
off-peak	Weekend: 5 p.m. Friday to 5 p.m. Sunday

dial-n-cerf-usa

Name	DIAL n' CERF USA
Dialup	Contact for number
Area codes	800
Local access	anywhere (800) service is available
Long distance	included
Services	Shell, menu, IRC, FTP, Hytelnet, Gopher, WAIS, WWW, terminal service, SLIP
Fees	$10/hour ($8/hour on weekend) plus $20/month
E-mail	help@cerf.net
Voice	800-876-2373 or 619-455-3900
FTP more information	nic.cerf.net:/cerfnet/dial-n-cerf/
off-peak	Weekend: 5 p.m. Friday to 5 p.m. Sunday

dircon

Name	The Direct Connection
Dialup	+44 (0)81 317 2222
Area codes	+44 (0)81
Local access	London, England
Long distance	Provided by user
Services	Shell or menu, UUCP feeds, SLIP/PPP, FTP, Telnet, Gopher, WAIS, Archie, personal FTP/file space, e-mail to fax
Fees	Subscriptions from GBPounds 10 per month; no online charges. GBPounds 7.50 signup fee.
E-mail	helpdesk@dircon.co.uk
Voice	+44 (0)81 317 0100
Fax	+44 (0)81 317 0100
FTP more information	n/a

echonyc

Name	Echo Communications
Dialup	(212) 989-8411 (v.32, v.32bis); password: newuser
Area codes	212
Local access	NY: Manhattan
Long distance	Provided by user
Services	Shell, FTP, Telnet, Gopher, Archie, WAIS, SLIP/PPP
Fees	Commercial: $19.95/month; students/seniors: $13.75/month
E-mail	horn@echonyc.com
Voice	212-255-3839
FTP more information	n/a

eskimo

Name	Eskimo North
Dialup	206-367-3837 300-14.4k, 206-362-6731 for 9600/14.4k, 206-742-1150 World Blazer

Area codes	206
Local access	WA: Seattle, Everett
Long distance	Provided by user
Services	Shell, FTP, Telnet
Fees	$10/month or $96/year
E-mail	nanook@eskimo.com
Voice	206-367-7457
FTP more information	n/a

evergreen

Name	Evergreen Communications
Dialup	(602) 955-8444
Area codes	602
Local access	AZ
Long distance	Provided by user or call for additional information
Services	FTP, Telnet, Gopher, Archie, WAIS, WWW, UUCP, PPP
Fees	Individual: $239/year; commercial: $479/year; special educational rates
E-mail	evergreen@libre.com
Voice	602-955-8315
Fax	602-955-5948
FTP more information	n/a

express

Name	Express Access—a service of Digital Express Group
Dialup	301-220-0462, 410-766-1855, 703-281-7997, 714-377-9784, 908-937-9481; login: new
Area codes	202, 301, 410, 703, 714, 908
Local access	Northern Virginia; Baltimore, MD; Washington DC; New Brunswick, NJ; Orange County, CA
Long distance	Provided by user

Services	Shell, FTP, Telnet, IRC, Gopher, Hytelnet, WWW, ClariNet, SLIP/PPP, Archie, mailing lists, autoresponders, anonymous FTP archives
Fees	$25/month or $250/year
E-mail	info@digex.net
Voice	800-969-9090, 301-220-2020
FTP more information	n/a

fsp

Name	Freelance Systems Programming
Dialup	(513) 258-7745 to 14.4 Kbps
Area codes	513
Local access	OH: Dayton
Long distance	Provided by user
Services	Shell, FTP, Telnet, feeds, e-mail, Gopher, Archie, SLIP
Fees	$20 startup and $1/hour
E-mail	fsp@dayton.fsp.com
Voice	(513) 254-7246
FTP more information	n/a

gate.net

Name	CyberGate, Inc
Dialup	305-425-0200
Area codes	305, 407
Local access	South Florida, expanding in FL
Long distance	Provided by user
Services	Shell, UUCP, SLIP/PPP, leased, Telnet, FTP, IRC, Archie, Gopher
Fees	$17.50/month on credit card; group discounts; SLIP/PPP: $17.50/month plus $2/hour
E-mail	info@gate.net or sales@gate.net
Voice	305-428-GATE
Fax	305-428-7977
FTP more information	n/a

GLAIDS

Name	GLAIDS NET (Homosexual network)
Dialup	206-322-0621
Area codes	206
Local access	WA: Seattle
Long distance	Provided by user
Services	BBS, Gopher, FTP, Telnet
Fees	$10/month. Scholarships available. Free seven-day trial. Visitors are welcome.
E-mail	tomh@glaids.wa.com
Voice	206-323-7483
FTP more information	GLAIDS.wa.com

halcyon

Name	Halcyon
Dialup	206-382-6245; login: new, 8N1
Area codes	206
Local access	Seattle, WA
Long distance	Provided by user
Services	Shell, Telnet, FTP, BBS, IRC, Gopher, Hytelnet
Fees	$200/year or $60/quarter plus $10 startup
E-mail	info@halcyon.com
Voice	206-955-1050
FTP more information	halcyon.com:/pub/waffle/info

holonet

Name	HoloNet
Dialup	510-704-1058
Area codes	510, PDN
Local access	Berkeley, CA
Long distance	(per hour, off-peak/peak) Bay area: $0.50/$0.95; PSINet A: $0.95/$1.95; PSINet B: $2.50/$6.00; Tymnet: $3.75/$7.50
Services	FTP, Telnet, IRC, games

Fees	$2/hour off-peak, $4/hour peak; $6/month or $60/year minimum
E-mail	info@holonet.net
Voice	510-704-0160
FTP more information	holonet.net:/info/
off-peak	5 p.m. to 8 a.m. plus weekends and holidays

hookup.net

Name	HookUp Communication Corporation
Dialup	Contact for number
Area codes	800, PDN, 416, 519
Local access	Ontario, Canada
Long distance	800 access across Canada, or discounted rates by HookUp
Services	Shell or menu, UUCP, SLIP, PPP, FTP, Telnet, IRC, Gopher, domains, anonymous FTP space
Fees	Cdn $14.95/month for five hours; Cdn $34.95/month for 15 hours; Cdn $59.95/month for 30 hours; Cdn $300.00/year for 50 hours/month; Cdn $299.00/month for unlimited usage
E-mail	info@hookup.net
Voice	519-747-4110
Fax	519-746-3521
FTP more information	n/a

ibmpcug

Name	UK PC User Group
Dialup	+44 (0)81 863 6646
Area codes	+44 (0)81
Local access	London, England
Long distance	Provided by user
Services	FTP, Telnet, BBS, IRC, feeds
Fees	GBPounds 15.50/month or 160/year plus 10 startup (no time charges)
E-mail	info@ibmpcug.co.uk

Voice	+44 (0)81 863 6646
FTP more information	n/a

ids

Name	The IDS World Network
Dialup	401-884-9002, 401-785-1067
Area codes	401
Local access	RI: East Greenwich, northern area
Long distance	Provided by user
Services	FTP, Telnet, SLIP, feeds, BBS
Fees	$10/month, or $50/half-year, $100/year
E-mail	sysadmin@ids.net
Voice	401-884-7856
FTP more information	ids.net:/ids.net

IEunet

Name	IEunet Ltd., Ireland's Internet Services Supplier
Dialup	+353 1 6790830, +353 1 6798600
Area codes	+353 1
Local access	Dublin, Ireland
Long distance	Provided by user, or supplied by IEunet
Services	DialIP, IPGold, EUnet Traveller, X400, X500, Gopher, WWW, FTP, FTPmail, SLIP/PPP, FTP archives
Fees	IEP25/month Basic
E-mail	info@ieunet.ie, info@Ireland.eu.net
Voice	+353 1 6790832
FTP more information	ftp.ieunet.ie:/pub

IGC

Name	Institute for Global Communications/IGC Networks (PeaceNet, EcoNet, ConflictNet, LaborNet, HomeoNet)
Dialup	415-322-0284 (N-8-1); login: new

Area codes	415, 800, PDN
Local access	CA: Palo Alto, San Francisco
Long distance	(per hour, off-peak/peak) SprintNet: $2/$7; 800: $11/$11
Services	Telnet, local newsgroups for environmental, peace/social justice issues; no FTP
Fees	$10/month plus $3/hour after first hour
E-mail	support@igc.apc.org
Voice	415-442-0220
FTP more information	igc.apc.org:/pub

indirect

Name	Internet Direct, Inc.
Dialup	602-274-9600 (Phoenix); 602-321-9600 (Tucson); login: guest
Area codes	602
Local access	AZ: Phoenix, Tucson
Long distance	Provided by user
Services	Shell/menu, UUCP, Usenet, NNTP, FTP, Telnet, SLIP, PPP, IRC, Gopher, WAIS, WWW, POP, DNS, nameservice, QWK (offline readers)
Fees	$20/month (personal); $30/month (business)
E-mail	info@indirect.com (automated); support@indirect.com (human)
Voice	602-274-0100 (Phoenix), 602-324-0100 (Tucson)
FTP more information	n/a

Individual.NET

Name	Individual Network e.V. (IN)
Dialup	Contact for number
Area codes	+49
Local access	Germany: Berlin, Oldenburg, Bremen, Hamburg, Krefeld, Kiel, Duisburg, Darmstadt, Dortmund, Hannover, Ruhrgebiet, Bonn, Magdeburg, Duesseldorf, Essen, Koeln, Paderborn, Bielefeld, Aachen, Saarbruecken, Frankfurt, Braunschweig,

	Dresden, Ulm, Erlangen, Nuernberg, Wuerzburg, Chemnitz, Muenchen, Muenster, Goettingen, Wuppertal, Schleswig, Giessen, Rostock, Leipzig, and others
Long distance	Provided by user
Services	e-mail, Usenet feeds, UUCP, SLIP, ISDN, shell, FTP, Telnet, Gopher, IRC, BBS
Fees	15-30 DM/month (differs from region to region)
E-mail	in-info@individual.net
Voice	+49 2131 64190 (Andreas Baess)
Fax	+49 2131 605652
FTP more information	ftp.fu-berlin.de:/pub/doc/IN/

in-rhein-main

Name	Individual Network-Rhein-Main
Dialup	+49-69-39048414, +49-69-6312934 (+ others)
Area codes	+49 069
Local access	Frankfurt/Offenbach, Germany
Long distance	Provided by user
Services	Shell (UNIX), FTP, Telnet, IRC, Gopher, UUCP feeds
Fees	SLIP/PPP/ISDN: 40 DM, 4 DM /Megabyte
E-mail	info@rhein-main.de
Voice	+49-69-39048413
FTP more information	n/a

ins

Name	INS—Inter Networking Systems
Dialup	Contact for number
Area codes	+49 23
Local access	Ruhr-Area, Germany
Long distance	Provided by user
Services	E-mail, UUCP, Usenet, SLIP/PPP, ISDN-TCP/IP

Fees	Fees for commercial institutions and any others: UUCP/e-mail, UUCP/Usenet: $60/month; ip:$290/month minimum
E-mail	info@ins.net
Voice	+49 2305 356505
Fax	+49 2305 25411
FTP more information	n/a

InterAccess

Name	InterAccess
Dialup	708-671-0237
Area codes	708, 312, 815
Local access	Chicagoland metropolitan area
Long distance	Provided by user
Services	FTP, Telnet, SLIP/PPP, feeds, shell, UUCP, DNS, FTP space
Fees	$23/month shell, $26/month SLIP/PPP, or $5/month plus $2.30/hour
E-mail	info@interaccess.com
Voice	(800) 967-1580
Fax	708-671-0113
FTP more information	interaccess.com:/pub/interaccess.info

jvnc

Name	The John von Neumann Computer Network—Tiger Mail & Dialin' Terminal
Dialup	Contact for number
Area codes	800
Local access	Anywhere (800) service is available
Long distance	Included
Services	E-mail and newsfeed or terminal access only
Fees	$19/month, $10/hour, $36 startup (PC or Mac SLIP software included)

E-mail	info@jvnc.net
Voice	800-35-TIGER, 609-897-7300
Fax	609-897-7310
FTP more information	n/a

jvnc-tiger

Name	The John von Neumann Computer Network—Dialin' Tiger
Dialup	Contact for number
Area codes	201, 203, 215, 401, 516, 609, 908
Local access	Princeton & Newark, NJ; Philadelphia, PA; Garden City, NY; Bridgeport, New Haven, & Storrs, CT; Providence, RI
Long distance	Provided by user
Services	FTP, Telnet, SLIP, feeds, optional shell
Fees	$99/month plus $99 startup (PC or Mac SLIP software included—shell is additional $21/month)
E-mail	info@jvnc.net
Voice	800-35-TIGER, 609-897-7300
Fax	609-897-7310
FTP more information	n/a

kaiwan

Name	KAIWAN Public Access Internet Online Services
Dialup	714-539-5726, 310-527-7358
Area codes	213, 310, 714
Local access	CA: Los Angeles, Orange County
Long distance	Provided by user
Services	Shell, FTP, Telnet, IRC, WAIS, Gopher, SLIP/PPP, FTP space, feeds, DNS, 56K leased line
Fees	$15.00/signup plus $15.00/month or $30.00/quarter (3 months); $11.00/month by credit card

E-mail	info@kaiwan.com
Voice	714-638-2139
FTP more information	kaiwan.com:/pub/KAIWAN

maestro

Name	Maestro
Dialup	(212) 240-9700; login: newuser
Area codes	212, 718
Local access	NY: New York City
Long distance	Provided by user
Services	Shell, FTP, Telnet, Gopher, WAIS, IRC, feeds.
Fees	$15/month or $150/year
E-mail	info@maestro.com (autoreply); staff@maestro.com, rkelly@maestro.com, ksingh@maestro.com
Voice	212-240-9600
FTP more information	n/a

mcsnet

Name	MCSNet
Dialup	(312) 248-0900 v.32, 0970 v.32bis, 6295 (PEP), follow prompts
Area codes	312, 708, 815
Local access	IL: Chicago
Long distance	Provided by user
Services	Shell, FTP, Telnet, feeds, e-mail, IRC, Gopher, Hytelnet
Fees	$25/month or $65/3 months untimed; $30/3 months for 15 hours/month
E-mail	info@genesis.mcs.com
Voice	312-248-UNIX
FTP more information	genesis.mcs.com:/mcsnet.info/

metronet

Name	Texas Metronet
Dialup	214-705-2901/817-261-1127 (v.32bis), 214-705-2929(PEP); login: `info` or 214-705-2917/817-261-7687 (2400); login: `signup`
Area codes	214, 817
Local access	TX: Dallas, Fort Worth
Long distance	Provided by user
Services	Shell, FTP, Telnet, SLIP, PPP, UUCP feeds
Fees	$5-$45/month plus $10-$30 startup
E-mail	info@metronet.com
Voice	214-705-2900, 817-543-8756
Fax	214-401-2802 (8am-5pm CST weekdays)
FTP more information	ftp.metronet.com:/pub/metronetinfo/

michnet

Name	Merit Network, Inc.—MichNet project
Dialup	Contact for number or Telnet hermes.merit.edu and type `help` at `Which host?` prompt
Area codes	202, 301, 313, 517, 616, 703, 810, 906, PDN
Local access	Michigan; Boston, MA; Washington DC
Long distance	SprintNet, Autonet, Michigan Bell packet-switch network
Services	Telnet, SLIP/PPP, outbound SprintNet, Autonet, and Ann Arbor dialout
Fees	$35/month plus $40 signup ($10/month for K-12 and libraries in Michigan)
E-mail	info@merit.edu
Voice	313-764-9430
FTP more info	nic.merit.edu:/

millennium

Name	Millennium Online
Dialup	Contact for numbers
Area codes	PDN
Local access	PDN private numbers available
Long distance	PDN
Services	Shell, FTP, Telnet, IRC, feeds, Gopher, graphical BBS (interface required)
Fees	$10/month; .10 per minute domestic, .30 international
E-mail	jjablow@mill.com
Voice	800-736-0122
FTP more information	n/a

mindvox

Name	MindVOX
Dialup	212-989-4141; logins: `mindvox`, `guest`
Area codes	212, 718
Local access	NY: New York City
Long distance	Provided by user
Services	Conferencing system, FTP, Telnet, IRC, Gopher, Hytelnet, Archives, BBS
Fees	$15-$20/month; no startup
E-mail	info@phantom.com
Voice	212-989-2418
FTP more information	n/a

MSen

Name	MSen
Dialup	Contact for number

Area codes	313, 810
Local access	All of southeastern Michigan (313, 810)
Long distance	Provided by user
Services	Shell, WAIS, Gopher, Telnet, FTP, SLIP, PPP, IRC, WWW, Picospan BBS, FTP space
Fees	$20/month; $20 startup
E-mail	info@msen.com
Voice	313-998-4562
Fax	313-998-4563
FTP more information	ftp.msen.com:/pub/vendor/msen

mucev

Name	muc.de e.V.
Dialup	Contact for numbers
Area codes	+49 089
Local access	Munich/Bavaria, Germany
Long distance	Provided by user
Services	mail, news, FTP, Telnet, IRC, Gopher, SLIP/PPP/UUCP
Fees	From DM 20; (mail only) up to DM 65; (full account with PPP)
E-mail	postmaster@muc.de
Voice	n/a
FTP more information	ftp.muc.de:public/info/muc-info.*

MV

Name	MV Communications, Inc.
Dialup	Contact for numbers
Area codes	603
Local access	Many NH communities
Long distance	Provided by user
Services	Shell, FTP, Telnet, Gopher, SLIP, e-mail, feeds, DNS, archives

Fees	$5/month minimum, plus hourly rates; see schedule.
E-mail	info@mv.com
Voice	603-429-2223
FTP more information	ftp.mv.com:/pub/mv

nearnet

Name	NEARnet
Dialup	Contact for numbers
Area codes	508, 603, 617
Local access	MA: Boston; NH: Nashua
Long distance	Provided by user
Services	SLIP, e-mail, feeds, DNS
Fees	$250/month
E-mail	nearnet-join@nic.near.net
Voice	617-873-8730
FTP more information	nic.near.net:/docs

netcom

Name	Netcom Online Communication Services
Dialup	206-547-5992, 214-753-0045, 303-758-0101, 310-842-8835, 312-380-0340, 404-303-9765, 408-241-9760, 408-459-9851, 415-328-9940, 415-985-5650, 503-626-6833, 510-274-2900, 510-426-6610, 510-865-9004, 617-237-8600, 619-234-0524, 703-255-5951, 714-708-3800, 818-585-3400, 916-965-1371
Area codes	206, 213, 214, 303, 310, 312, 404, 408, 415, 503, 510, 617, 619, 703, 714, 718, 818, 916
Local access	CA: Alameda, Irvine, Los Angeles, Palo Alto, Pasadena, Sacramento, San Diego, San Francisco, San Jose, Santa Cruz, Walnut Creek; CO: Denver; DC: Washington; GA: Atlanta; IL: Chicago; MA: Boston; OR: Portland; TX: Dallas; WA: Seattle
Long distance	Provided by user

Services	Shell, FTP, Telnet, IRC, WAIS, Gopher, SLIP/PPP, FTP space, feeds, DNS
Fees	$19.50/month plus $20.00 signup
E-mail	info@netcom.com
Voice	408-554-8649, 800-501-8649
Fax	408-241-9145
FTP more information	ftp.netcom.com:/pub/netcom/

northshore

Name	North Shore Access
Dialup	617-593-4557 (v.32bis, v.32, PEP); login: new
Area codes	617, 508
Local access	MA: Wakefield, Lynnfield, Lynn, Saugus, Revere, Peabody, Salem, Marblehead, Swampscott
Long distance	Provided by user
Services	Shell (SunOS and UNIX), FTP, Telnet, Archie, Gopher, WAIS, WWW, UUCP feeds
Fees	$9/month includes 10 hours connect; $1/hour thereafter; higher volume discount plans also available
E-mail	info@northshore.ecosoft.com
Voice	617-593-3110 voicemail
FTP more information	northshore.ecosoft.com:/pub/flyer

novalink

Name	NovaLink
Dialup	(800) 937-7644; password/login: new or info, 508-754-4009; 2400-14400 bps
Area codes	508, 617, PDN
Local access	MA: Worcester, Cambridge, Marlboro, Boston
Long distance	CPS: $1.80/hour 2400, 9600; SprintNet $1.80/hour nights and weekends

Services	FTP, Telnet, Gopher, shell, IRC, XWindows, feeds, adult, user groups, FAX, Legends of Future Past
Fees	$12.95 signup (refundable and includes two hours), $9.95/month (includes five daytime hours) plus $1.80/hour
E-mail	info@novalink.com
Voice	800-274-2814
FTP more information	ftp.novalink.com:/info

nuance

Name	Nuance Network Services
Dialup	Contact for number
Area codes	205
Local access	AL: Huntsville
Long distance	Provided by user
Services	Shell (UNIX SVR4.2), FTP, Telnet, Gopher, SLIP, PPP, ISDN
Fees	$25/month plus $35 startup, personal; corporate, call for options
E-mail	staff@nuance.com
Voice	205-533-4296 voice/recording
FTP more information	ftp.nuance.com:/pub/NNS-INFO

nuchat

Name	South Coast Computing Services, Inc.
Dialup	713-661-8593 (v.32), 713-661-8595 (v.32bis)
Area codes	713
Local access	TX: Houston metro area
Long distance	Provided by user
Services	Shell, FTP, Telnet, Gopher, Usenet, UUCP feeds, SLIP, dedicated lines, domain name service, full-time tech support

Fees	**dialup:** $3/hour; **UUCP:** $1.50/hour or $100/month unlimited; **dedicated:** $120, unlimited access
E-mail	info@sccsi.com
Voice	713-661-3301
FTP more information	sccsi.com:/pub/communications/*

nwnexus

Name	Northwest Nexus Inc.
Dialup	Contact for numbers
Area codes	206
Local access	WA: Seattle
Long distance	Provided by user
Services	UUCP, SLIP, PPP, feeds, DNS
Fees	$10/month for first 10 hours, plus $3/hour; $20 startup
E-mail	info@nwnexus.wa.com
Voice	206-455-3505
FTP more information	nwnexus.wa.com:/NWNEXUS.info.txt

nyx

Name	Nyx, the Spirit of the Night; free public internet access provided by the University of Denver's Math and Computer Science Department
Dialup	303-871-3324
Area codes	303
Local access	CO: Boulder, Denver
Long distance	Provided by user
Services	Shell or menu; semianonymous accounts; FTP, news, mail
Fees	None; donations are accepted but not requested
E-mail	aburt@nyx.cs.du.edu
Voice	Login to find current list of volunteer voice helpers
FTP more information	n/a

OARnet

Name	OARnet
Dialup	Send e-mail to nic@oar.net
Area codes	614, 513, 419, 216, 800
Local access	OH: Columbus, Cincinnati, Cleveland, Dayton
Long distance	800 service
Services	E-mail, FTP, Telnet, newsfeed
Fees	$4.00/hour to $330.00/month; call for code or send e-mail
E-mail	nic@oar.net
Voice	614-292-8100
Fax	614-292-7168
FTP more information	n/a

oldcolo

Name	Old Colorado City Communications
Dialup	719-632-4111; login: newuser
Area codes	719
Local access	CO: Colorado Springs
Long distance	Provided by user
Services	Shell, FTP, Telnet, AKCS, home of the NAPLPS conference
Fees	$25/month
E-mail	dave@oldcolo.com / thefox@oldcolo.com
Voice	719-632-4848, 719-593-7575, or 719-636-2040
Fax	719-593-7521
FTP more information	n/a

olympus

Name	Olympus—The Olympic Peninsula's Gateway to the Internet
Dialup	Contact following voice number
Area codes	206

Local access	WA: Olympic peninsula, eastern Jefferson County
Long distance	Provided by user
Services	Shell, FTP, Telnet, pine, Hytelnet
Fees	$25/month plus $10 startup
E-mail	info@pt.olympus.net
Voice	206-385-0464
FTP more information	n/a

panix

Name	PANIX Public Access UNIX
Dialup	212-787-3100; login: newuser
Area codes	212, 718
Local access	New York City, NY
Long distance	Provided by user
Services	Shell, FTP, Telnet, Gopher, WAIS, IRC, feeds
Fees	$19/month or $208/year plus $40 signup
E-mail	alexis@panix.com, jsb@panix.com
Voice	212-877-4854 (Alexis Rosen), 212-691-1526 (Jim Baumbach)
FTP more information	n/a

pipeline

Name	The Pipeline
Dialup	212-267-8606; login: guest
Area codes	212, 718
Local access	NY: New York City
Long distance	Provided by user
Services	Windows interface or shell/menu; all IP services
Fees	$15/month (including five hours), or $20/20 hours; $35 unlimited
E-mail	info@pipeline.com, staff@pipeline.com
Voice	212-267-3636
FTP more information	n/a

portal

Name	The Portal System
Dialup	408-973-8091 (high-speed), 408-725-0561 (2400bps); login: `info`
Area codes	408, 415, PDN
Local access	CA: Cupertino, Mountain View, San Jose
Long distance	SprintNet: $2.50/hour off-peak, $7-$10/hour peak; Tymnet: $2.50/hour off-peak, $13/hour peak
Services	Shell, FTP, Telnet, IRC, UUCP, feeds, BBS
Fees	$19.95/month plus $19.95 signup
E-mail	cs@cup.portal.com, info@portal.com
Voice	408-973-9111
FTP more information	n/a
off-peak	6 p.m. to 7 a.m. plus weekends and holidays

prairienet

Name	Prairienet Freenet
Dialup	217-255-9000; login: `visitor`
Area codes	217
Local access	IL: Champaign-Urbana
Long distance	Provided by user
Services	Telnet, FTP, Gopher, IRC
Fees	Free for Illinois residents; $25/year for nonresidents
E-mail	jayg@uiuc.edu
Voice	217-244-1962
FTP more information	n/a

PREPnet

Name	PREPnet
Dialup	Contact for numbers
Area codes	215, 412, 717, 814

Local access	PA: Philadelphia, Pittsburgh, Harrisburg
Long distance	Provided by user
Services	SLIP, terminal service, Telnet, FTP
Fees	$1,000/year membership; equipment, $325 one-time fee plus $40/month
E-mail	prepnet@cmu.edu
Voice	412-268-7870
Fax	412-268-7875
FTP more information	ftp.prepnet.com:/prepnet/general/

psilink

Name	PSILink—Personal Internet Access
Dialup	North America: send e-mail to classa-na-numbers@psi.com and classb-na-numbers@psi.com; rest of world: send e-mail to classb-row-numbers@psi.com
Area codes	PDN
Local access	n/a
Long distance	(per hour, off-peak/peak) **PSINet A:** included; **PSINet B:** $6/$2.50; **PSINet B international:** $18/$18
Services	E-mail, newsfeed, FTP
Fees	2400: $19/month; 9600: $29/month (PSILink software included)
E-mail	all-info@psi.com, psilink-info@psi.com
Voice	703-620-6651
Fax	703-620-4586
FTP more information	ftp.psi.com:/

psi-world-dial

Name	PSI's World-Dial Service
Dialup	Send e-mail to numbers-info@psi.com
Area codes	PDN
Local access	n/a

Long distance	(per hour, off-peak/peak) v.22bis: $1.25/$2.75; v.32: $3.00/$4.50; 14.4K: $4.00/$6.50
Services	Telnet, rlogin, tn3270, XRemote
Fees	$9/month minimum plus $19 startup
E-mail	all-info@psi.com, world-dial-info@psi.com
Voice	703-620-6651
Fax	703-620-4586
FTP more information	ftp.psi.com:/
off-peak	8 p.m. to 8 a.m. plus weekends and holidays

PUCnet

Name	PUCnet Computer Connections
Dialup	403-484-5640 (v.32bis); login: guest
Area codes	403
Local access	AB: Edmonton and surrounding communities in the Extended Flat Rate Calling Area
Long distance	Provided by user
Services	Shell, menu, FTP, Telnet, Archie, Gopher, feeds, Usenet
Fees	Cdn $25/month (20 hours connect time) plus Cdn $6.25/hour (FTP and Telnet only) plus $10 signup
E-mail	info@PUCnet.com (Mail responder) or pwilson@PUCnet.com
Voice	403-448-1901
Fax	403-484-7103
FTP more information	n/a

realtime

Name	RealTime Communications (wixer)
Dialup	512-459-4391; login: new
Area codes	512
Local access	TX: Austin
Long distance	Provided by user

Services	Shell, FTP, Telnet, IRC, Gopher, feeds, SLIP, UUCP
Fees	$75/year; monthly and quarterly rates available
E-mail	hosts@wixer.bga.com
Voice	512-451-0046 (11 a.m. to 6 p.m. Central Time, weekdays)
Fax	512-459-3858
FTP more information	n/a

ssnet

Name	Systems Solutions
Dialup	Contact for information
Area codes	302
Local access	DE: Wilminton
Long distance	Provided by user
Services	Shell, UUCP, SLIP, PPP, FTP, Telnet, IRC, Gopher, Archie, mud
Fees	full service: $25/month, $20/startup; personal: SLIP/PPP $25/month plus $2/hour, $20/startup; dedicated: SLIP/PPP $150/month, $450/startup
E-mail	sharris@marlin.ssnet.com
Voice	302-378-1386, 800-331-1386
FTP more information	n/a

sugar

Name	NeoSoft's Sugar Land UNIX
Dialup	713-684-5900
Area codes	504, 713
Local access	TX: Houston metro area; LA: New Orleans
Long distance	Provided by user
Services	BBS, shell, FTP, Telnet, IRC, feeds, UUCP
Fees	$29.95/month

E-mail	info@NeoSoft.com
Voice	713-438-4964
FTP more information	n/a

teleport

Name	Teleport
Dialup	503-220-0636 (2400); 503-220-1016 (v.32, v.32bis); login new
Area codes	503
Local access	OR: Portland, Beaverton, Hillsboro, Forest Grove, Gresham, Tigard, Lake Oswego, Oregon City, Tualatin, Wilsonville
Long distance	Provided by user
Services	Shell, FTP, Telnet, Gopher, Usenet, PPP, WAIS, IRC, feeds, DNS
Fees	$10/month (1 hour/day limit)
E-mail	info@teleport.com
Voice	503-223-4245
FTP more information	teleport.com:/about

telerama

Name	Telerama Public Access Internet
Dialup	412-481-5302; login new (2400)
Area codes	412
Local access	PA: Pittsburgh
Long distance	Provided by user
Services	Telnet, FTP, IRC, Gopher, ClariNet/Usenet, shell/menu, UUCP
Fees	66 cents/hour, 2400bps; $1.32/hour, 14.4K bps; $6 minimum per month
E-mail	info@telerama.pgh.pa.us
Voice	412-481-3505
FTP more information	telerama.pgh.pa.us:/info/general.info

tmn

Name	The Meta Network
Dialup	Contact for numbers
Area codes	703, 202, 301, PDN
Local access	Washington, DC metro area
Long distance	SprintNet: $6.75/hour; FTS-2000; Acunet
Services	Caucus conferencing, e-mail, shell, FTP, Telnet, BBS, feeds
Fees	$20/month plus $15 signup/first month
E-mail	info@tmn.com
Voice	703-243-6622
FTP more information	n/a

UUNET-Canada

Name	UUNET Canada, Inc.
Dialup	Contact for numbers
Area codes	416, 905, 519, 613, 514, 604, 403
Local access	ON: Toronto, Ottawa, Kitchener/Waterloo, London, Hamilton; QC: Montreal, AB: Calgary; BC: Vancouver
Long distance	Provided by user
Services	Terminal access to Telnet only, UUCP (e-mail/news), SLIP/PPP, shared or dedicated basis, from v.32bis to 56k+
Fees	(All Cdn$ plus GST) **TAC:** $6/hour; **UUCP:** $20/month plus $6/hour; **IP/UUCP:** $50/mo plus $6/hour; ask for prices on other services
E-mail	info@uunet.ca
Voice	416-368-6621
Fax	416-368-1350
FTP more information	ftp.uunet.ca

uunorth

Name	UUnorth
Dialup	Contact for numbers
Area codes	416, 519, 613
Local access	ON: Toronto
Long distance	Provided by user
Services	Shell, FTP, Telnet, Gopher, feeds, IRC, feeds, SLIP, PPP
Fees	(All Cdn$ plus GST) $20 startup plus $25 for 20 hours off-peak, plus $1.25/hour or $40 for 40 hours up to 5/day, $2/hour or $3/hour
E-mail	uunorth@uunorth.north.net
Voice	416-225-8649
Fax	416-225-0525
FTP more information	n/a

Vnet

Name	Vnet Internet Access, Inc.
Dialup	704-347-8839, 919-406-1544, 919-851-1526; login: new
Area codes	704, 919
Local access	NC: Charlotte, RTP, Raleigh, Durham, Chapel Hill, Winston Salem/Greensboro
Long distance	Available for $3.95 per hour through Global Access. Contact Vnet offices for more information.
Services	Shell, FTP, Telnet, Hytelnet, IRC, Gopher, WWW, WAIS, Usenet, ClariNet, NNTP, DNS, SLIP/PPP, UUCP, POPmail
Fees	$25/month individual; $12.50/month for Telnet-in-only; SLIP/PPP/UUCP starting at $25/month.
E-mail	info@char.vnet.net
Voice	704-374-0779
FTP more information	n/a

well

Name	The Whole Earth 'Lectronic Link (WELL)
Dialup	415-332-6106; login: newuser
Area codes	415, PDN
Local access	CA: Sausalito
Long distance	CompuServe Packet Network: $4/hour
Services	Shell, FTP, Telnet, BBS
Fees	$15/month plus $2/hour
E-mail	info@well.sf.ca.us
Voice	415-332-4335
FTP more information	n/a

wariat

Name	APK- Public Access UNI* Site
Dialup	216-481-9436 (v.32bis, SuperPEP on separate rotary)
Area codes	216
Local access	OH: Cleveland
Long distance	Provided by user
Services	Shell, FTP, Telnet, Archie, IRC, Gopher, feeds, BBS (Uniboard1. 10)
Fees	$15/20 hour, $35/month, $20 signup
E-mail	zbig@wariat.org
Voice	216-481-9428
FTP more information	n/a

world

Name	The World
Dialup	617-739-9753; login: new
Area codes	617, PDN
Local access	MA: Boston
Long distance	CompuServe Packet Network: $5.60/hour
Services	Shell, FTP, Telnet, IRC
Fees	$5/month plus $2/hour or $20/month for 20 hours

E-mail   office@world.std.com
Voice   617-739-0202
FTP more information   world.std.com:/world-info/description

wyvern

Name   Wyvern Technologies, Inc.
Dialup   804-627-1828 (Norfolk); 804-886-0662 (Peninsula)
Area codes   804
Local access   VA: Norfolk, Virginia Beach, Portsmouth, Chesapeake, Newport News, Hampton, Williamsburg
Long distance   Provided by user
Services   Shell, menu, FTP, Telnet, UUCP feeds, IRC, Archie, Gopher, UPI news, e-mail, DNS, archives
Fees $15/month, $144/year, plus $10 startup
E-mail   system@wyvern.com
Voice   804-622-4289
Fax   804-622-7158
FTP more information   n/a

xnet

Name   XNet Information Systems
Dialup   708-983-6435 v.32bis and TurboPEP
Area codes   312, 708, 815
Local access   IL: Chicago, Naperville, Hoffman Estates
Long distance   Provided by user
Services   Shell, Telnet, Hytelnet, FTP, IRC, Gopher, WWW, WAIS, SLIP/PPP, DNS, UUCP feeds, BBS
Fees $45/3 months or $75/6 months
E-mail   info@xnet.com
Voice   (708) 983-6064
FTP more information   ftp.xnet.com:/xnet.info/

What the PDIAL Is

This is the PDIAL, the Public Dialup Internet Access List. It is a list of Internet service providers offering public access dialins and outgoing Internet access (such as FTP and Telnet). Most services provide e-mail, Usenet news, and other services.

If one of these systems is not accessible to you and you need e-mail or Usenet access, but don't need FTP or Telnet, you have many more public access systems from which to choose. Public access systems without FTP or Telnet are *not* listed in this list, however. See the nixpub (alt.BBS, comp.misc) list and other BBS lists.

Some of these providers offer time-shared access to a shell or BBS program on a computer connected directly to the Internet (through which you can FTP or Telnet to other systems on the Internet). Usually other services are also provided. Generally, you need only a modem and terminal or terminal emulator to access these systems. Check for "shell," "BBS," or "menu" on the "services" line.

Other providers connect you directly to the Internet via SLIP or PPP when you dial in. For these, you need a computer system capable of running the software to interface with the Internet (such as a UNIX machine, PC, or Mac). Check for "SLIP" or "PPP" on the services line.

Although this appendix includes many sites, it is incomplete. If you have any additions or corrections please send them to me at one of the addresses listed in the following section.

How People Can Get the PDIAL (This List)

E-mail

From the Information Deli archive server (most up-to-date):

- To receive the current edition of the PDIAL, send e-mail containing the phrase Send PDIAL to info-deli-server@netcom.com.
- To be put on a list of people who receive future editions as they are published, send e-mail containing the phrase Subscribe PDIAL to info-deli-server@netcom.com.
- To receive both the most recent and future editions, send both messages.

From time to time, I'll also be sending out news and happenings that relate to the PDIAL or The Information Deli. To receive the Information Deli News automatically, send e-mail containing the phrase Subscribe Info-Deli-News to info-deli-server@netcom.com.

From the news.answers FAQ Archive:

⚓ Send e-mail with the message send Usenet/news.answers/pdial to mail-server@rtfm.mit.edu. For help, send the message help to mail-server@rtfm.mit.edu.

USENET

The PDIAL list is posted semi-regularly to alt.internet.access.wanted, alt.BBS.lists, alt.online-service, ba.internet, and news.answers.

FTP Archive Sites (PDIAL and Other Useful Information)

Information Deli FTP site: ftp.netcom.com:/pub/info-deli/public-access/pdial [192.100.81.100]

As part of a collection of public access lists: VFL.Paramax.COM:/pub/pubnet/pdial [128.126.220.104]

From the Merit Network Information Center Internet information archive: nic.merit.edu:/internet/providers/pdial [35.1.1.48]

As part of an Internet access compilation file: liberty.uc.wlu.edu:/pub/lawlib/internet.access [137.113.10.35]

As part of the news.answers FAQ archive: rtfm.mit.edu:/pub/Usenet/news.answers/pdial [18.70.0.209]

Finding Public Data Network (PDN) Access Numbers

Here's how to get local access numbers or information for the various PDNs. Generally, you can contact the site you're calling for help, too.

> **Navigator's Note:** Unless noted otherwise, set your modem to 7E1 (7 data bits, even parity, 1 stop bit) when dialing to look up access numbers by modem.

BT Tymnet

For information and local access numbers, call 800-937-2862 (voice) or 215-666-1770 (voice).

To look up access numbers by modem, dial a local access number, press <CR> and type a; then enter `information` at the `please log in:` prompt.

CompuServe Packet Network

You don't have to be a CompuServe member to use the CPN to dial other services.

For information and local access numbers, call 800-848-8199 (voice).

To look up access numbers by modem, dial a local access number, press <CR> and enter `PHONES` at the `Host Name:` prompt.

PSINet

For information, call 800-82PSI82 (voice) or 703-620-6651 (voice), or send e-mail to: all-info@psi.com. For a list of local access numbers, send e-mail to: numbers-info@psi.com.

GOPHER
JEWELS

David Riggins has searched hundreds of Gopher servers to put together a list of Gophers grouped by subject. Subjects range from technical areas like Agriculture and Computers to more general categories. This list is not—and never will be—complete, since Gopherspace is ever-changing. Some Gopher sites appear in particular categories because information related to that category is buried in a Gopher hole accessible through the listed Gopher. You may have to burrow DEEP to find the information related to the category.

Still, Riggins' list is a start, and may offer several good starting points for your Gopher-based research.

Navigator's Note: For address information on all Gophers listed below, assume the following unless otherwise indicated: Type=1 Port=70 Path=none

Gophers with a Wide Variety of Subject Areas

Australian Defence Force Academy (Canberra, Australia)/
Host=gopher.adfa.oz.au

Baylor College of Medicine/
Host=gopher.bcm.tmc.edu

Department of Information Resources (State of Texas)[experimental]/
Host=ocs.dir.texas.gov

Go M-Link/
Host=vienna.hh.lib.umich.edu

Internet Wiretap/
Host=wiretap.spies.com

InterNIC: Internet Network Information Center/
Host=rs.internic.net

Library of Congress (LC MARVEL)/
Host=marvel.loc.gov

North Carolina State University Library Gopher/
Host=dewey.lib.ncsu.edu

PeachNet Information Service/
Host=Gopher.PeachNet.EDU

South African Bibliographic and Information Network/
Host=info2.sabinet.co.za

Texas A&M/
Host=gopher.tamu.edu

The World (Public Access UNIX)/
Host=world.std.com

University of California - Irvine/
Host=gopher-server.cwis.uci.edu

University of California - Santa Barbara Library/
Port=3001
Host=ucsbuxa.ucsb.edu

University of Illinois at Chicago/
Host=gopher.uic.edu

University of Michigan Libraries/
Host=gopher.lib.umich.edu

University of Nevada/
Host=gopher.unr.edu

Whole Earth 'Lectronic Magazine - The WELL's Gopherspace/
Host=gopher.well.sf.ca.us

Yale University/
Host=yaleinfo.yale.edu

Gopher Sites by Technical Area

Agriculture

Australian Defence Force Academy (Canberra, Australia)/
Host=gopher.adfa.oz.au

CYFER-net USDA ES Gopher Server./
Host=cyfer.esusda.gov

Dendrome: Forest Tree Genome Mapping Database/
Host=s27w007.pswfs.gov

Extension Service USDA Information/
Host=zeus.esusda.gov

GRIN, National Genetic Resources Program, USDA-ARS/
Host=gopher.ars-grin.gov

GrainGenes, the Triticeae Genome Gopher/
Host=greengenes.cit.cornell.edu

Library of Congress (LC MARVEL)/
Host=marvel.loc.gov

Maize Genome Database Gopher/
Host=teosinte.agron.missouri.edu

North Carolina State University Library Gopher/
Host=dewey.lib.ncsu.edu

Soybean Data/
Host=mendel.agron.iastate.edu

Texas A&M/
Host=gopher.tamu.edu

University of California - Santa Barbara Library/
Port=3001
Host=ucsbuxa.ucsb.edu

University of Illinois at Chicago/
Host=gopher.uic.edu

University of Minnesota Soil Science Gopher Information Service/
Host=gopher.soils.umn.edu

University of Nevada/
Host=gopher.unr.edu

Astronomy and Astrophysics

Australian Defence Force Academy (Canberra, Australia)/
Host=gopher.adfa.oz.au

Library of Congress (LC MARVEL)/
Host=marvel.loc.gov

North Carolina State University Library Gopher/
Host=dewey.lib.ncsu.edu

South African Bibliographic and Information Network/
Host=info2.sabinet.co.za

Space Telescope Electronic Information System (STEIS)/
Host=stsci.edu

Texas A&M/
Host=gopher.tamu.edu

University of California - Santa Barbara Library/
Port=3001
Host=ucsbuxa.ucsb.edu

University of Illinois at Chicago/
Host=gopher.uic.edu

Biology and Biosciences

Arabidopsis Research Companion, Mass Gen Hospital/Harvard/
Host=weeds.mgh.harvard.edu

Biodiversity and Biological Collections Gopher/
Host=huh.harvard.edu

bioftp EMBnet, (CH)/
Host=bioftp.unibas.ch

BioInformatics gopher at ANU/
Host=life.anu.edu.au

Brookhaven National Laboratory Protein Data Bank/
Path=1/
Host=pdb.pdb.bnl.gov

CAMIS (Center for Advanced Medical Informatics at Stanford)/
Host=camis.stanford.edu

CWRU Medical School - Department of Biochemistry/
Host=biochemistry.cwru.edu

Computational Biology (Welchlab - Johns Hopkins University)/
Host=merlot.welch.jhu.edu

Dana-Farber Cancer Institute, Boston, MA/
Host=gopher.dfci.harvard.edu

Dendrome: Forest Tree Genome Mapping Database/
Host=s27w007.pswfs.gov

DNA Data Bank of Japan, Natl. Inst. of Genetics, Mishima/
Host=gopher.nig.ac.jp

EMBnet BioInformation Resource EMBL, (DE)/
Path=1/
Host=ftp.embl-heidelberg.de

EMBnet Bioinformation Resource, (FR)/
Path=1/
Host=coli.polytechnique.fr

EMBnet Bioinformation Resource, (UK)/
Path=1/
Host=s-crim1.daresbury.ac.uk

Genethon (Human Genome Res. Center, Paris), (FR)/
Host=gopher.genethon.fr

GRIN, National Genetic Resources Program, USDA-ARS/
Path=/
Host=gopher.ars-grin.gov

GrainGenes, the Triticeae Genome Gopher/
Host=greengenes.cit.cornell.edu

Human Genome Mapping Project Gopher Service (UK)/
Host=menu.crc.ac.uk

ICGEBnet, Int.Center for Genetic Eng. & Biotech, (IT)/
Host=genes.icgeb.trieste.it

INN, Weizmann Institute of Science (Israel)/
Host=sunbcd.weizmann.ac.il

IUBio Biology Archive, Indiana University (experimental)/
Host=ftp.bio.indiana.edu

JvNCnet/
Host=gopher.jvnc.net

Library of Congress (LC MARVEL)/
Host=marvel.loc.gov

MegaGopher (Universite de Montreal)/
Host=megasun.bch.umontreal.ca

Microbial Germplasm Database/
Path=1./mgd
Host=ava.bcc.orst.edu

National Cancer Center, Tokyo JAPAN/
Host=gopher.ncc.go.jp

National Institutes of Health (NIH) Gopher/
Host=gopher.nih.gov

North Carolina State University Library Gopher/
Host=dewey.lib.ncsu.edu

NSF Center for Biological Timing/
Path=1/departments/biotimin
Host=gopher.virginia.edu

Oregon State University Biological Computing (BCC)/
Host=gopher.bcc.orst.edu

PIR Archive, University of Houston/
Host=ftp.bchs.uh.edu

State University of New York (SUNY) - Brooklyn Health Science Center/
Host=gopher1.medlib.hscbklyn.edu

State University of New York (SUNY) - Syracuse Health Science Center/
Host=micro.ec.hscsyr.edu

TECHNET, Singapore/
Host=solomon.technet.sg

Texas A&M/
Host=gopher.tamu.edu

USCgopher (University of Southern California)/
Host=cwis.usc.edu

University of California - Santa Barbara Library/
Port=3001
Host=ucsbuxa.ucsb.edu

University of Houston Protein Information Resource/
Host=ftp.bchs.uh.edu

University of Illinois at Chicago/
Host=gopher.uic.edu

University of Nevada/
Host=gopher.unr.edu

University of New Mexico/
Host=peterpan.unm.edu

University of Notre Dame/
Host=gopher.nd.edu

University of Wisconsin - Madison, Medical School/
Host=msd.medsch.wisc.edu

Vertebrate World server at Colorado State University/
Host=neptune.rrb.colostate.edu

Worcester Foundation for Experimental Biology/
Host=sci.wfeb.edu

World Data Center on Microorganisms (WDC), RIKEN, Japan/
Host=fragrans.riken.go.jp

Botany

Australian National Botanic Gardens/
Host=155.187.10.12

Missouri Botanical Garden/
Host=gopher.mobot.org

Texas A&M/
Host=gopher.tamu.edu

University of Georgia/
Host=gopher.uga.edu

Chemistry

Australian Defence Force Academy (Canberra, Australia)/
Host=gopher.adfa.oz.au

Centre for Scientific Computing, (FI)/
Host=gopher.csc.fi

Library of Congress (LC MARVEL)/
Host=marvel.loc.gov

North Carolina State University Library Gopher/
Host=dewey.lib.ncsu.edu

University of California - Santa Barbara Library/
Port=3001
Host=ucsbuxa.ucsb.edu

University of Illinois at Chicago/
Host=gopher.uic.edu

Computers

CPSR (Computer Professionals for Social Responsibility) Internet L..
Host=gopher.cpsr.org

CREN/Educom/
Host=info.educom.edu

Computer Solutions by Hawkinson/
Host=csbh.com

HENSA micros (National Software Archive, Lancaster Univ.), (UK)/
Host=micros.hensa.ac.uk

Info Mac Archives (sumex-aim)/
Host=SUMEX-AIM.Stanford.EDU

International Federation for Information Processing (IFIP)/
Path=1/International Federation for Information Processing
Host=IETF.CNRI.Reston.Va.US

Library of Congress (LC MARVEL)/
Host=marvel.loc.gov

Liverpool University, Dept of Computer Science, (UK)/
Host=gopher.csc.liv.ac.uk

McGill Research Centre for Intelligent Machines, Montreal, Canada/
Host=lightning.mcrcim.mcgill.edu

National Center for Supercomputing Applications/
Host=gopher.ncsa.uiuc.edu

North Carolina State University Library Gopher/
Host=dewey.lib.ncsu.edu

Novell Netwire Archives/
Host=ns.novell.com

Texas A&M/
Host=gopher.tamu.edu

University of California - Santa Barbara Library/
Port=3001
Host=ucsbuxa.ucsb.edu

Environment

Australian Environmental Resources Information Network (ERIN)/
Host=kaos.erin.gov.au

CIESIN Global Change Information Gateway/
Host=gopher.ciesin.org

EcoGopher at the University of Virginia/
Host=ecosys.drdr.virginia.edu

EnviroGopher (at CMU)/
Host=envirolink.hss.cmu.edu

Go M-Link/
Host=vienna.hh.lib.umich.edu

GreenGopher at University of Virginia in Charlottesville/
Path=1/information/uva/greens@uva/greengopher
Host=ecosys.drdr.Virginia.EDU

Library of Congress (LC MARVEL)/
Host=marvel.loc.gov

North Carolina State University Library Gopher/
Host=dewey.lib.ncsu.edu

University of California - Santa Barbara Library/
Port=3001
Host=ucsbuxa.ucsb.edu

University of Nevada/
Host=gopher.unr.edu

Vertebrate World server at Colorado State University/
Host=neptune.rrb.colostate.edu

Geology and Oceanography

Bedford Institute Of Oceanography (Canada)/
Host=biome.bio.dfo.ca

Library of Congress (LC MARVEL)/
Host=marvel.loc.gov

North Carolina State University Library Gopher/
Host=dewey.lib.ncsu.edu

Northwestern University, Department of Geological Sciences/
Path=1/
Host=gopher.earth.nwu.edu

University of California - Davis/
Host=gopher.ucdavis.edu

University of California - Santa Barbara Library/
Port=3001
Host=ucsbuxa.ucsb.edu

University of California - Santa Barbara Geological Sciences Gopher/
Host=gopher.geol.ucsb.edu

University of Illinois at Chicago/
Host=gopher.uic.edu

University of Texas at El Paso, Geological Sciences Dept./
Host=dillon.geo.ep.utexas.edu

US Geological Survey (USGS)/
Host=info.er.usgs.gov

USGS Atlantic Marine Geology/
Host=bramble.er.usgs.gov

Medical

Australian Defence Force Academy (Canberra, Australia)/
Host=gopher.adfa.oz.au

Anesthesiology Gopher /
Host=eja.anes.hscsyr.edu

Austin Hospital, Melbourne, Australia/
Host=pet1.austin.unimelb.edu.au

Baylor College of Medicine/
Host=gopher.bcm.tmc.edu

CAMIS (Center for Advanced Medical Informatics at Stanford)/
Host=camis.stanford.edu

Cornell Medical College/
Host=gopher.med.cornell.edu

Dana-Farber Cancer Institute, Boston, MA/
Host=gopher.dfci.harvard.edu

Gustavus Adolphus College/
Host=gopher.gac.edu

ISU College of Pharmacy/
Host=pharmacy.isu.edu

JvNCnet/
Host=gopher.jvnc.net

Library of Congress (LC MARVEL)/
Host=marvel.loc.gov

National Cancer Center, Tokyo JAPAN/
Host=gopher.ncc.go.jp

National Institute of Allergy and Infectious Disease (NIAID)/
Host=gopher.niaid.nih.gov

National Institutes of Health (NIH) Gopher/
Host=gopher.nih.gov

North Carolina State University Library Gopher/
Host=dewey.lib.ncsu.edu

Stanford University Medical Center/
Host=med-gopher.stanford.edu

State University of New York (SUNY) - Brooklyn Health Science Center/
Host=gopher1.medlib.hscbklyn.edu

State University of New York (SUNY) - Syracuse Health Science Center/
Host=micro.ec.hscsyr.edu

Texas A&M/
Host=gopher.tamu.edu

USC Gopher (University of Southern California)/
Host=cwis.usc.edu

University of California - Santa Barbara Library/
Port=3001
Host=ucsbuxa.ucsb.edu

University of Illinois at Chicago/
Host=gopher.uic.edu

University of Illinois at Urbana-Champaign/
Host=gopher.uiuc.edu

University of Nevada/
Host=gopher.unr.edu

University of New Mexico/
Host=peterpan.unm.edu

University of Texas Health Science Center at Houston/
Host=gopher.uth.tmc.edu

University of Texas M. D. Anderson Cancer Center/
Host=utmdacc.uth.tmc.edu

University of Texas Medical Branch/
Host=phil.utmb.edu

University of Washington, Pathology Department/
Host=larry.pathology.washington.edu

University of Wisconsin - Madison, Medical School/
Host=msd.medsch.wisc.edu

World Health Organization (WHO)/
Host=gopher.who.ch

Photonics

Colorado State University Optical Computing Lab/
Host=sylvia.lance.colostate.edu

Physics

Australian Defence Force Academy (Canberra, Australia)/
Host=gopher.adfa.oz.au

Centre for Scientific Computing, (FI)/
Host=gopher.csc.fi

ICTP, International Centre for Theoretical Physics, Trieste, (IT)/
Host=gopher.ictp.trieste.it

Institute of Physics, University of Zagreb, (HR)/
Host=gopher.ifs.hr

LANL Physics Information Service/
Host=mentor.lanl.gov

Library of Congress (LC MARVEL)/
Host=marvel.loc.gov

North Carolina State University Library Gopher/
Host=dewey.lib.ncsu.edu

Physics Resources (Experimental)/
Host=granta.uchicago.edu

Presbyterian College (Clinton, SC)/
Host=cs1.presby.edu

Texas A&M/
Host=gopher.tamu.edu

University of California - Santa Barbara Library/
Port=3001
Host=ucsbuxa.ucsb.edu

University of Illinois at Chicago/
Host=gopher.uic.edu

Primates

Primate Info Net (University of Wisconsin-Madison)/
Host=saimiri.primate.wisc.edu

Other Categories

Art

Library of Congress (LC MARVEL)/
Host=marvel.loc.gov

University of California - Santa Barbara Library/
Port=3001
Host=ucsbuxa.ucsb.edu

University of Illinois at Chicago/
Host=gopher.uic.edu

Books and Magazines (Electronic and For Sale)

Academe This Week (Chronicle of Higher Education)/
Host=chronicle.merit.edu

Internet Wiretap/
Host=wiretap.spies.com

Michigan State University/
Host=gopher.msu.edu

Nova Scotia Technology Network, N.S., Canada/
Host=nstn.ns.ca

O'Reilly & Associates (computer book publisher)/
Host=ora.com

The Electronic Newsstand(tm)/
Port=2100
Host=gopher.netsys.com

The New Republic Magazine/
Port=2101
Host=gopher.netsys.com

The World (Public Access UNIX)/
Host=world.std.com

University of California - Santa Barbara Library/
Port=3001
Host=ucsbuxa.ucsb.edu

University of Illinois at Chicago/
Host=gopher.uic.edu

University of Nevada/
Host=gopher.unr.edu

Education and Research

Apple Computer Higher Education Gopher Server/
Host=info.hed.apple.com

AskERIC - (Educational Resources Information Center)/
Host=ericir.syr.edu

Centre for Scientific Computing, (FI)/
Host=gopher.csc.fi

Consortium for School Networking (CoSN)/
Host=cosn.org

Go M-Link/
Host=vienna.hh.lib.umich.edu

Library of Congress (LC MARVEL)/
Host=marvel.loc.gov

National Center on Adult Literacy/
Host=litserver.literacy.upenn.edu

National Science Foundation Gopher (STIS)/
Host=stis.nsf.gov

Employment Opportunities and Resume Postings

Academe This Week (Chronicle of Higher Education)/
Host=chronicle.merit.edu

Academic Position Network/
Port=11111
Host=wcni.cis.umn.edu

American Physiological Society/
Port=3300
Path=1/
Host=gopher.uth.tmc.edu

IUPUI Integrated Technologies/
Host=INDYCMS.IUPUI.EDU

Online Career Center (at Msen)/
Port=9062
Host=garnet.msen.com

Virginia Coast Reserve Information System (VCRIS)/
Host=atlantic.evsc.Virginia.EDU

Federal Government Related

Counterpoint Publishing/
Port=2001
Host=gopher.netsys.com

Federal Info. Exchange (FEDIX) (Under Construction - experimental)/
Host=fedix.fie.com

InterCon Systems Corporation/
Host=vector.intercon.com

Federal Laboratory and Related Gopher Sites

Brookhaven National Laboratory Protein Data Bank/
Path=1/
Host=pdb.pdb.bnl.gov

Federal Info. Exchange (FEDIX) (Under Construction - experimental)/
Host=fedix.fie.com

Library X at Johnson Space Center/
Host=krakatoa.jsc.nasa.gov

Los Alamos National Laboratory/
Host=gopher.lanl.gov

Michigan State University/
Host=gopher.msu.edu

NASA Goddard Space Flight Center/
Host=gopher.gsfc.nasa.gov

NASA Mid-Continent Technology Transfer Center/
Host=technology.com

NASA Network Applications and Information Center (NAIC)/
Host=naic.nasa.gov

NASA Shuttle Small Payloads Info/
Host=vx740.gsfc.nasa.gov

National Institute of Standards and Technology (NIST)/
Host=gopher-server.nist.gov

Oak Ridge National Laboratory ESD Gopher/
Host=jupiter.esd.ornl.gov

General Reference Resources

Australian Defence Force Academy (Canberra, Australia)/
Host=gopher.adfa.oz.au

Department of Information Resources (State of Texas)[experimental]/
Host=ocs.dir.texas.gov

Internet Wiretap/
Host=wiretap.spies.com

Library of Congress (LC MARVEL)/
Host=marvel.loc.gov

McGill Research Centre for Intelligent Machines, Montreal, Canada/
Host=lightning.mcrcim.mcgill.edu

University of California - Santa Barbara Library/
Port=3001
Host=ucsbuxa.ucsb.edu

University of Illinois at Chicago/
Host=gopher.uic.edu

University of Michigan Libraries/
Host=gopher.lib.umich.edu

University of Nevada/
Host=gopher.unr.edu

Internet/Cyberspace Related

CPSR (Computer Professionals for Social Responsibility) Internet L..
Host=gopher.cpsr.org

CREN/Educom/
Host=info.educom.edu

Electronic Frontier Foundation/
Host=gopher.eff.org

EFF-Austin/
Path=1/eff-austin
Host=gopher.tic.com

Internet Society (includes IETF)/
Path=1/Internet Society (includes IETF)
Host=ietf.CNRI.Reston.Va.US

Internet Wiretap/
Host=wiretap.spies.com

InterNIC: Internet Network Information Center/
Host=rs.internic.net

Matrix Information and Directory Services, Inc. (MIDS)/
Path=1/matrix
Host=gopher.tic.com

Merit Network/
Host=nic.merit.edu

McGill Research Centre for Intelligent Machines, Montreal, Canada/
Host=lightning.mcrcim.mcgill.edu

Michigan State University/
Host=gopher.msu.edu

ONENET Networking Information/
Host=nic.onenet.net

PSGnet/RAINet: Low-cost and International networking/
Host=gopher.psg.com

Sprintlink Gopher Server, Virginia USA/
Host=ftp.sprintlink.net

Texas Internet Consulting (TIC), Austin, Texas/
Host=gopher.tic.com

University of Nevada/
Host=gopher.unr.edu

Yale University/
Host=yaleinfo.yale.edu

Legal or Law Related

Cleveland State University Law Library/
Host=gopher.law.csuohio.edu

Cornell Law School (experimental)/
Host=fatty.law.cornell.edu

Library of Congress (LC MARVEL)/
Host=marvel.loc.gov

Saint Louis University/
Host=sluava.slu.edu

University of California - Santa Barbara Library/
Port=3001
Host=ucsbuxa.ucsb.edu

University of Chicago Law School/
Host=lawnext.uchicago.edu.

University of Illinois at Chicago/
Host=gopher.uic.edu

Washington & Lee University/
Path=1/
Host=liberty.uc.wlu.edu

Library Catalogs

Yale University/
Host=yaleinfo.yale.edu

Music

Internet Wiretap/
Host=wiretap.spies.com

Library of Congress (LC MARVEL)/
Host=marvel.loc.gov

Texas A&M/
Host=gopher.tamu.edu

University of California - Santa Barbara Library/
Port=3001
Host=ucsbuxa.ucsb.edu

University of Michigan Libraries/
Host=gopher.lib.umich.edu

U.S. Patents

Australian Defence Force Academy (Canberra, Australia)/
Host=gopher.adfa.oz.au

Technical Reports, Publications, Journals, and Newsletters

Australian Defence Force Academy (Canberra, Australia)/
Host=gopher.adfa.oz.au

CICNET Gopher Server/
Host=nic.cic.net

CREN/Educom/
Host=info.educom.edu

EDUCOM Documents and News/
Host=educom.edu

Go M-Link/
Host=vienna.hh.lib.umich.eduu

Michigan State University/
Host=gopher.msu.edu

Scholarly Communications Project Electronic Journals/
Host=borg.lib.vt.edu

University of California - Santa Barbara Library/
Port=3001
Host=ucsbuxa.ucsb.edu

University of Illinois at Chicago/
Host=gopher.uic.edu

Vortex Technology/
Host=gopher.vortex.com

Credits

Reproduction of this document is permitted with appropriate credits given to the author:

David Riggins
Riggins_dw@dir.texas.gov
Austin, Texas
Comments, changes, and additions are welcome.

COMMAND
REFERENCE

This appendix is a summary of the programs discussed in this book. We would like to be able to say that these are definitive. Unfortunately, that's impossible. The reason is that new versions of some of these programs are appearing almost daily. Check the version of the programs you're using for differences from the descriptions given here.

We've also covered only the standard versions of these programs. The fancy versions—those that run under graphical user interfaces such as X Window, Windows, and the Macintosh—are all changing so fast that it's difficult to be accurate about them.

Navigator's Note: The command lists for these programs are not exhaustive. We've left out the specialized commands for three reasons. First, some of them are very complicated and you don't need them unless you're going to get very fancy. Second, they may be version dependent. Third, we wanted to avoid making the book twice as thick (and twice as expensive).

Navigator's Note: Be very careful with the case used in options and commands. For example, if you get a message from someone, and that person has cc'ed (that is, sent copies to) other people, and you reply with the message, "Why did you copy your message to those losers?" by pressing R, you'll be embarrassed when all the people on the cc list also get the message. What you should have pressed was r, but it's too late now. If we've told you once, we've told you a thousand times, and why don't you ever pick up your clothes, and...

Regular Expressions

Because most of the programs you use when navigating the Internet are UNIX software, you should have an appreciation of regular expressions.

Navigator's Note: This is a dry topic and really requires several pages to cover properly; we'll just give the fundamentals here. If you want to find out more (you wild creature, you), check out a book on UNIX or, if you are made of sterner stuff, a UNIX system manual. To make this topic even more complex than it is, many UNIX programs add their own tricks and extensions. If you want to use any UNIX utility in a sophisticated way, check what it says in its help screens about regular expressions.

A *regular expression* is a text pattern that you want a UNIX program to find a match to. This applies in database or text file searches, or anywhere you want to look for a sequence of characters. For example, if you gave navigator as the text to search for, it would match navigator, and not navigate or navigation.

Regular expressions enable you to be inexact—that is, to find text that is similar to a specification of text. For example, if you wanted to find all the words beginning with pi in the text Peter Piper picked a peck and didn't care whether the characters were upper- or lowercase (so that you'd find both Piper and picked), you'd use a regular expression.

Rule 1. The characters in the text to be matched can be anything except . (period), * (asterisk), [(left square bracket), and \ (backslash).

Rule 2. At the beginning of a sentence, you can't use ^ (caret) in its regular sense.

Rule 3. At the end of a sentence, you can't use $ (dollar sign) in its regular sense.

Rule 4. If you need to use one of the special characters in Rules 1, 2, or 3, precede it with the \ (backslash) character. For example, if the text to be searched for is $100, 2*2=4, [note], or Press \, you need to enter them as \$100, 2*2=4, \[note], and Press \\.

Rule 5. To accept any single character in a particular position in the text, use . (a period). So, b..t would match boot or bait but not bite (however, if you use b..., you get bite too). This is equivalent to the ? wildcard in PC DOS.

Rule 6. To accept zero or more occurrences of the same character, use * after the character. Thus, mis* matches mis, miss, misss, and even missssssssssss.

Rule 7. To find the end of a line, use $. Thus, end.$ would match only lines ending with end..

Rule 8. To find the beginning of a line, use ^. Thus, ^Start matches any line starting with Start.

Rule 9. To find only certain, single characters in a specific position in text, called a set, use [<characters>]. Thus, t[a o i]n would match with tan, ton, and tin. The only special characters in a set are - (minus),] (right square bracket), and ^. All other characters stand for themselves, including \. At least one of the characters must be found to make a match. For example, looking for any variety of capitalization of London could be done by [L l][O o][N n][D d][O o][N n], which would accept London, london, LONDON, or even LoNdOn.

Rule 10. In a set, the - means that all the characters between the letter on the left of the minus and the letter on the right of the minus are acceptable. So, [a-f p-z] would exclude any character in the range g to o.

Note that if you wanted to accept the match or non-match of a set, you'd use [<characters>]*.

Rule 11. In a set, the] indicates the end of the set specification, unless it's the first character in the set. So to search for a left or right bracket, you have to write []][].

Rule 12. In a set, using ^ at the start of the set excludes those characters. Thus, [a-f p-z] in Rule 10 could also be written as [^g-o]. To accept only alphabetic characters in a particular position, use [^0-9]; to exclude alphabetic characters, use [^a-z A-Z].

If, as an example of a more complicated search, you wanted to find any word starting with navigat—whether the n is upper- or lowercase (such as Navigator, navigation, or Navigating)—you'd use [N n]avigat[.]* (the [.] means look for any character in this position, and the * means it can occur zero or any number of times).

Navigator's Note: There's a lot more to regular expressions. Just coming to grips with the preceding rules will make your searches using Archie and other Internet tools much more effective.

Archie

Archie can be used in three ways—as a local client, interactively, or by e-mail.

Archie Local Client Commands

The general form of the local Archie client command is

```
archie [{options}] [<text>]
```

<text>

<text> can include any text (including UNIX regular expressions) that you want Archie to search for. Note that you must use the -r option for UNIX regular expressions.

{*options*}

The options are codes that tell Archie to do something in addition to, or modify, the search for <*text*>. These are all prefaced by a - (minus), and multiple options are separated from each other and anything else by a space.

-c	Search substrings paying attention to upper- and lower-case.
-e	Exact string match (the default).
-r	Search using a regular expression.
-s	Search substrings, ignoring the case of the letters.
-o<*filename*>	Put the results of the search in the file <*filename*>.
-t	Sort the results, listing the oldest matches first.
-m<*n*>	Stop searching after <*n*> matches (the default is 95).
-h<*hostname*>	Specifies which Archie server to use.
-L	Lists the Archie servers known to the copy you're using.
-V	If you are the kind of user who, if you run a program and nothing happens, immediately assumes it has died, this option (V, for verbose) will print messages as it works, to keep you happy. Good for long searches by pessimistic users.

Thus,

```
archie -c -ofred.txt -r -V [N n]avigat[.]*
```

means pay attention to case (-c), put the results in the file named fred.txt (-ofred.txt), interpret the search text as a regular expression (-r), tell me what's happening as you search or I may have to hit the reset button (-V), and use [N n]avigat[.]* as the search text.

Archie Interactive Commands

To conduct an interactive session with an Archie server, you first telnet to an Archie site and log in as archie (usually, although there may be some exceptions). Current Archie server site addresses are

```
archie.funet.fi
archie.doc.ic.ac.uk
archie.cs.huji.ac.il
archie.wide.ad.jp
archie.ncu.edu.tw
archie.sogang.ac.kr
archie.nz
archie.kuis.kyoto-u.ac.jp
archie.th-darmstadt.de
archie.luth.se
```

The available commands are

mail <*address*>	Mail the results to the given address.
prog <*text*>	Search for the given text, which may be a UNIX regular expression if the search type is set to regexp.
quit	I've had enough, I'm leaving.
set search <*search type*>	Set the type of search to perform. The allowed types are case, exact, regexp, or subcase.
show search	Display the type of search being used.
whatis <*text*>	Search the description database for the text, which may be a UNIX regular expression if the search type is set to regexp.

Archie E-Mail Commands

E-mail can be used with Archie to get much the same results you would get through the other methods—just more slowly. Remember to leave the subject line blank or ensure that a valid command is used there.

compress	Compresses the results of the Archie search before e-mailing them to you.
list <*regular expression*>	Searches for all servers in the Archie database matching the UNIX regular expression (note that e-mail searches are only UNIX regular expressions).

`path <address>`	Sets the address to reply to. E-mail headers are often wrong, so this ensures that you get the message. This can also be used to send the file to another user address.
`prog <regular expression>`	Searches for files matching the UNIX regular expression (note that e-mail searches are only UNIX regular expressions).
`site <address>`	Returns a list of every file that Archie knows about on the specified site.
`whatis <regular expression>`	Searches the description database for the UNIX regular expression.
`quit`	End of commands.

Standard UNIX E-Mail Commands

These commands are taken from `mail`, a standard e-mail program for UNIX. Note that a `<message list>` consists of message numbers (as in `20 21 25`), a range of message numbers (as in `20-25`), or user names separated by spaces (`rjsmith mgibbs bclinton`). If omitted, Mail uses the current message.

To start the mail program, just type `mail`. Once mail is running, the following commands are available:

`d <message list>`	Delete message(s).
`e <message list>`	Edit message(s).
`f <message list>`	Show the `From:` lines of message(s).
`h`	Display message headers.
`m <user list>`	Mail to users.
`n`	Type next message.
`p <message list>`	Print message(s).
`q`	Quit.
`r <message list>`	Reply to sender (only) of message(s).
`R <message list>`	Reply to sender and all recipients of message(s).

s *<message list>* file	Save the message(s) to file.
t *<message list>*	Type message(s) (same as print, for no particularly good reason).
top *<message list>*	Show the first line of message(s).
u *<message list>*	Undelete the message(s) you've deleted in this session (if you exit, deleted messages are lost forever).
v *<message list>*	Edit message(s).
w *<message list>* file	Append message(s) to file, without the From: line.
x	Quit, undelete deleted messages, and make any messages you read this session unread.
z *<->*	Display next *<previous>* page of message headers.

FTP Commands

To start FTP, enter

```
ftp <address> <port>
```

The basic commands used when FTP is running are

get *<remote filename>* *<local filename>*

>Retrieve the remote file and store it on the local machine. If the local file name is not specified, it's given the same name that it has on the remote machine, subject to how the FTP client on the local system handles file names that may be illegal (for example, the UNIX file name UsersManual.Version.001 wouldn't be legal under PC DOS).

put *<local filename>* *<remote filename>*

>Store a local file on the remote machine. If remote file name is left unspecified, it's given the same name that it has on the local machine, subject to how the FTP server on the remote system handles file names that may be illegal.

`dir or ls`	Print a listing of the contents of a directory on the remote computer. If no directory is specified, the current working directory on the remote machine is used.
`binary`	Use this setting to send and receive nontext files (such as program files and databases).
`ascii`	Use this setting to send and receive text files.
`pwd`	Print the name of the current working directory on the remote machine.
`quit or bye`	Terminate the FTP session with the remote server and exit FTP.

FTPmail Commands

This is the equivalent of having an FTP session with a remote system but through mail messages. Remember that you should always use the FTP server nearest to you on the Internet or, if you don't know where that is, geographically nearest to you.

`reply <address>`	Sets the address to reply to. E-mail headers are often wrong, so this ensures that you get the message. This can also be used to send the file to another user address.
`connect <host> (<user> (<pass> (<acct>)))`	
	Connects you to a particular FTP server, optionally as a named user (the default is anonymous), with an optional password (you'll be asked for one if needed), and an account name on the FTP server.
`ascii`	Files are to be transferred as ASCII.
`binary`	Files are to be transferred as binary.
`chdir <directory>`	get and ls commands are relative to the named directory. (Note that you can use only one chdir per FTPmail session, and it is executed before any ls, dir, or get commands).
`compress`	Compress binaries using Lempel-Ziv encoding.

compact	Compress binaries using Huffman encoding.
uuencode	Binary files will be mailed in uuencode format.
btoa	Binary files will be mailed in btoa format.
chunksize <bytes>	Splits files into chunks of the specified size (the default is 64,000 bytes) and sends each as a separate e-mail message.
ls <directory>	Short directory listing.
dir <directory>	Long directory listing.
index <text>	Search for the given text in FTP server's index
get <filename>	Gets a file and has it mailed to you (each FTPmail session has a maximum of ten get commands).
quit	This marks the end of the FTPmail commands; the FTPmail server will ignore the rest of the mail message (useful if you have a .signature file or are a VMSMAIL user).

Gopher Commands

These are the standard Gopher commands. Gopher is evolving very quickly, and some Gophers may have local modifications that could make them very different. If you have a local Gopher, it is started by

gopher

If you don't have a local Gopher, you'll need to telnet to a site that does. All the following commands are used when Gopher is running.

General Gopher Commands

[up]	Move to previous line.
[down]	Move to next line.
[right] or [enter]	Select and act upon the current item.
[left] or u	Exit the current item.
>, +, [pgdn], or [space]	View next page.
<, -, [pgup], or b	View previous page.

<n>	Go to a specific line (if line numbering is shown).
m	Go back to the main menu.

Gopher Bookmark Commands

Bookmarks are placeholders that you can set to take you straight to a specific Gopher menu. This is really useful if you've had to traverse a dozen menus to get to a resource that you want to get back to more easily next time. Some Gophers don't support this feature.

a	Add current item to the bookmark list.
A	Add current directory/search to bookmark list.
v	View bookmark list.
d	Delete a bookmark.

Other Gopher Commands

q	Quit and be asked to confirm.
Q	Quit unconditionally.
=	Display technical information about current item.
o	Change options.

LISTSERV Commands

These commands will work with Eric Thomas' Revised LISTERV. Other LISTSERV varieties may vary slightly.

LISTSERV is run by

```
listserv command
```

The commands that you can use are

`subscribe <listname> <first name> <last name>`

> Subscribe to a list or change your name if you've already subscribed.

`signoff <listname>` Unsubscribe to the specified list.

signoff *	Unsubscribe from all lists on that server.
signoff * netwide	Unsubscribe from all lists in the network.
confirm *<listname1>* (*<listname2>* (...))	
	Confirm your subscription (when LISTSERV requests it).

News Commands

These commands are for the news reader program rn. Check the program and version your site is using; the commands may vary between releases. You start the program by simply typing rn.

The following commands are used when the program is running.

Newsgroup Selection Commands

y or [space]	Make this newsgroup current and read the first article.
=	Make this newsgroup current and list subjects before reading the articles.
u	Unsubscribe from this newsgroup.
c	Catch up (mark all articles in this newsgroup as read).
n	Go to the next newsgroup with unread news.
N	Go to the next newsgroup.
p	Go to the previous newsgroup with unread news.
P	Go to the previous newsgroup.
-	Go to the previously displayed newsgroup.
1	Go to the first newsgroup.
^	Go to the first newsgroup with unread news.
$	Go to the last newsgroup.
g*<name>*	Go to the named newsgroup. Subscribe to new newsgroups this way too.
/*<pattern>*	Search forward for newsgroup matching pattern. (Use * and ? style patterns. Append r to include read newsgroups.)

?*<pattern>*	Search backward for newsgroup matching pattern. (Use * and ? style patterns. Append r to include read news-groups.)
l*<pattern>*	List newsgroups that you haven't subscribed to that contain the text pattern.
o*<pattern>*	Display only newsgroups matching pattern. Omit pattern to display all newsgroups.
a*<pattern>*	Like o, but also scans for unsubscribed newsgroups matching text pattern.
L	List the newsgroups you currently subscribe to.
q	Quit.
x	Quit, restoring the news reader to the state it was in at the start of this session.
v	Print version.

Article Selection Commands

n or [space]	Scan forward for next unread article.
N	Go to next article.
^N	Scan forward for next unread article with same subject.
p, P, ^P	Same as n, N, and ^N, but going backward.
-	Go to previously displayed article.
<number>	Go to specified article.
/*<pattern>*/*<modifiers>*	Scan forward for article containing pattern in the subject line. (Use ?*<pattern>*? to scan backward; append h to scan headers, a to scan entire articles, r to scan read articles, and c to make case sensitive.)
f, F	Submit a follow-up article (F for include this article).
r, R	Reply through Internet mail (R for include this article).
s	Save to file.

C	Cancel this article, if it's your own.
^R, v	Restart article (v for verbose).
^X	Restart article, rot13 mode (encrypted, for potentially offensive material).
c	Catch up (mark all articles in the current newsgroup as read).
b	Back up one page.
^	Go to first unread article. Disables subject search mode.
$	Go to end of newsgroup. Disables subject search mode.
#	Print last article number.
j	Junk this article (mark it read). Stays at end of article.
m	Mark article as still unread.
M	Mark article as still unread upon exiting newsgroup or after Y command.
k	Kill current subject (mark articles as read).
for	List subjects of unread articles.
u	Unsubscribe from this newsgroup.
q	Quit this newsgroup for now.
Q	Quit newsgroup, staying at current newsgroup.

Paging Commands

[space]	Display the next page.
x	Display the next page decrypted (rot13).
d	Display half a page more.
[enter]	Display one more line.
^R, v, ^X	Restart the current article (v for verbose header, ^X for rot13).

b	Back up one page.
g<*pattern*>	Search forward within article for pattern.
G	Search again for current pattern within article.
q	Quit the pager, go to end of article. Leave article read or unread.
j	Junk this article (mark it read). Go to end of article.

The following commands skip the rest of the current article, then behave just as if typed to the What next? prompt at the end of the article:

n	Scan forward for next unread article.
N	Go to next article.
^N	Scan forward for next unread article with same title.
p, P, ^P	Same as n, N, ^N, but going backward.
-	Go to previously displayed article.

Telnet Commands

You start telnet by specifying the address of the target computer and, optionally, the port number:

```
telnet <address> (<port>)
```

To issue commands to telnet, you need to use the escape character, which will be printed as the session starts. Take note of it because if you need it and don't know what it is, you'll have to either try several hundred key combinations or do something more drastic, like switch off your computer. The available commands when telnet is running are

close	Close the current session and return to command mode.
open <address> (<port>)	Open a connection to the named host. If no port number is specified, telnet will attempt to contact a telnet server at the default port.
status	Report on the telnet session.

| quit | Close any open telnet session and exit telnet. |

WAIS (SWAIS) Commands

WAIS sessions are started by either running a local WAIS client with the command

```
wais
```

or using telnet to access a site such as quake.think.com that offers a WAIS client and logging in (usually) as WAIS. Once WAIS is running, you can use the following commands:

j or [down] or ^N	Move down one source.
k or [up] or ^P	Move up one source.
J or ^V or ^D	Move down one screen.
K or [esc] v or ^U	Move up one screen.
###	Position to source number.
/sss	Search for source sss.
[space] or [period]	Select current source.
=	Deselect all sources.
v or [comma]	View current source info.
[enter]	Perform search.
s	Select new sources (refresh the list of sources).
w	Select new keywords.
X or -	Remove current source for the rest of this session.
o	Set and show swais options.
h or ?	Show the help display.
H	Display program history.
q	Leave the program.

World Wide Web

To start WWW, you'll need to either telnet to info.cern.ch, which will connect you directly to its WWW server, or have your own WWW system locally. Once WWW is running, you can use the following commands:

<n>	Follow the specified link in the current document.
[enter]	Go to the next page of the current document (noted on the command line as <RETURN>).
back	Go back to the previous document.
bottom	Go to the last screen of the current document.
help	Show help.
home	Go directly to the first page you saw when WWW started.
next	If you follow a link from a document and, when you're finished, you want to follow the next link on the document you came from, the next command will take you there.
previous	Just as the next command will take you to the next link on the last document you were on, the previous command will take you to the link prior to the one that you followed on the last document.
print	Print the current document (if you're not running a local version of WWW, don't do this).
quit	Exit WWW.
recall	Give a list of the documents you looked at.
recall *<n>*	Go to the nth document you looked at. The output from the recall command by itself gives the numbers of the documents.
top	Go to the first screen of the current document.
up	Go to the previous page of the current document.

ADDRESSING E-MAIL TO OTHER SYSTEMS

Some of the networks that can receive e-mail from the Internet are based on different standards. This means that e-mail addresses must be translated so that they can be transferred from the Internet to the foreign system and vice versa. In some cases, the gateway software (the software that does the translation) needs a little extra help to figure out how to do the translation correctly. The following information should prove useful when you need to figure out how to do this.

We'll pretend that Chris Smith on the various services is exchanging mail with Pat Jones, who is on the Internet as `pjones@foo.bar.edu`. (Addresses are in monospaced type to set them off from the surrounding text, such as an example address, `pjones@foo.bar.edu`.)

Things that you should replace with specific information will be given in *italics*: *userid*`@aol.com` is an address at America Online where you would replace *userid* with the actual account name of the recipient. The other replacement word you see will be *domain*. Although *domain* usually refers to just the com or edu, it is also used to refer to everything after the @ in an Internet address. Hence *userid*@*domain* can be replaced with pjones@foo.bar.edu.

America Online

America Online (AOL) is a major U.S. commercial information service. The standard Internet address for a user at America Online is *userid*@aol.com. To send Internet mail from AOL, you don't need to use any special formatting, just use the address directly—*userid*@*domain*.

AOL will also let you use abbreviated domains for AppleLink, CompuServe, or GEnie. Simply address your mail to *userid*@applelink, *userid*@cis, or *userid*@genie respectively.

    Example Internet to AOL: csmith@aol.com
    Example AOL to Internet: pjones@foo.bar.edu
    Example AOL to CompuServe: 11111,222@cis

AppleLink

AppleLink is Apple Computer, Inc.'s network. Addressing mail to AppleLink is simple: *userid*@applelink.apple.com. Sending mail to Internet is a bit trickier—you must address it to *user*@*site*@internet#. The entire sending address must be 35 characters or less, so it may be impossible to send mail to some sites.

    Example AppleLink to America Online: csmith@aol.com@internet#

AT&T Mail

AT&T Mail is a commercial e-mail service provided by AT&T. Sending mail from Internet to AT&T Mail is easy: *userid*@attmail.com. Sending mail to Internet is done in this format—internet!*domain*!*userid*.

    Example AT&T Mail to Internet: internet!foo.bar.edu!pjones

BITNET

BITNET is an academic network which is becoming less important as more educational sites are hooking into Internet, but it's still there for now. To

send mail from the Internet to BITNET, you need to address it to
userid%bitnetsitename`.bitnet@`*gateway*. *gateway* needs to be a host site which is
both on the Internet and BITNET. A commonly used gateway is `mitvma.mit.edu`,
but your BITNET site may have a closer gateway which you can use—ask the administrators.

To send mail from BITNET to Internet can be troublesome, since each BITNET
site varies in its mail handling software. If you are lucky, you can just use the
Internet address directly: *userid@domain*. If that doesn't work, try
userid%domain@gateway, where *gateway* is described above. If neither of these works,
you will have to ask the administrators.

> Example BITNET to Internet: `pjones%foo.bar.edu@mitvma.mit.edu`
> Example Internet to BITNET: `csmith%uxavax.bitnet@mitvma.mit.edu`

BIX

BIX is the *Byte* magazine Information eXchange, a commercial service oriented
toward techies. It's been bought by Delphi, but still operates separately. Mail from
the Internet to BIX is simple: *userid*`@bix.com`. To send mail to Internet, choose
`Internet Services` from the Main Menu.

CompuServe

CompuServe is a large commercial service operated by CompuServe Inc. From
Internet to CompuServe is a simple *userid*`@compuserve.com`, with one quirk:
CompuServe IDs are of the form `77777,777` and commas are not allowed in Internet
addresses, so you need to replace the comma with a period. To Internet from
CompuServe is `>INTERNET:`*userid@domain*.

> Example Internet to CompuServe: `12345.677@compuserve.com`
> Example CompuServe to Internet: `>INTERNET:pjones@foo.bar.edu`

Connect PIN

Connect PIN is the commercial Connect Professional Information Network. To
send mail from Internet to Connect is *userid*`@connectinc.com`. From Connect to
Internet is a bit harder. You need to send the message to `DASN` and make the first
line of the message `"`*userid@domain*`"@DASN`. Note the required double quotes (`"`)
here.

Delphi

Delphi is a commercial service which has now devoted itself to offering Internet access. It is a real Internet site, so standard Internet addressing works. To send mail to Delphi from Internet, use *userid*@delphi.com. To send mail from Delphi to Internet use *userid*@*domain*.

Easylink

Easylink is another commercial system from AT&T. You can't easily send mail to Internet at this time, but you can send mail from Internet to Easylink: *userid*@eln.attmail.com.

Envoy-100

Envoy-100 is Telecom Canada's commercial X.400 service. X.400 addressing is more than a little strange if you haven't seen it before.

To send mail to Envoy from Internet, use

uunet.uu.net!att!attmail!mhs!envoy!*userid*.

To send mail from Envoy to Internet, use

[RFC-822="*userid*(a)*domain*"]INTERNET/TELEMAIL/US.

The (a) replaces the @, which X.400 doesn't like. For other special characters, see the X.400 section below.

| Example Envoy to Internet: | [RFC-822=pjones(a)foo.bar.edu]INTERNET/TELEMAIL/US |
| Example Internet to Envoy: | uunet.uu.net!att!attmail!mhs!envoy!12345 |

FidoNet

FidoNet is a large international BBS network run over the phone lines. It's not as fast as the Internet, but access is usually cheaper, and chances are there's a FidoNet BBS in your area. Because it is run over the phone lines, BBS operators will incur charges for any mail transferred, so please don't send large messages to FidoNet sites—in fact, many sites will limit messages to 8K or 16K, so part of your message won't get through.

To send mail from Internet to FidoNet, you need to know the network address of the specific FidoNet BBS the recipient is on. It will be of the form `Z:N/F.P`. To send mail to that site, use `userid@pP.fF.nN.zZ.fidonet.org`. If the address is like `1:2/3`, simply leave out the `pP.` part. In the *userid*, replace any spaces or other non-alphanumeric characters with periods (`.`). To send mail from FidoNet to Internet, use `userid@domain` `ON` `gateway`. The *gateway* is a special FidoNet site which acts as an Internet gateway. You can use `1:1/31`.

> Example FidoNet to Internet: `pjones@foo.bar.edu ON 1:1/31`
> Example Internet to FidoNet: `chris.smith@p4.f3.n2.z1.fidonet.org`

GEnie

GEnie is General Electric Information Services, another large commercial service.

To send mail from Internet to GEnie, use `userid@genie.geis.com`. From GEnie to Internet is `userid@domain@INET#`.

> Example GEnie to Internet: `pjones@foo.bar.edu@INET#`
> Example Internet to GEnie: `csmith@genie.geis.com`

GeoNet

GeoNet Mailbox Systems is a worldwide commercial mail system from GeoNet Mailbox Services GmbH/Systems Inc. To send mail from Internet to GeoNet, use `userid@machine.geonet.de`. The *machine* is the separate system used for each major service area. You will need to know to find out from your recipient which machine they are using, although it should be `geo4` for the United States.

From GeoNet to Internet, send the mail to `DASN`. Then as the subject line of the message, use `userid@domain!subject`, where *subject* is the actual subject you want for the message. The part before the `!` will be used as the Internet address.

Gold 400

GNS Gold 400 is British Telecom's commercial X.400 system. As with Envoy-100, X.400 addressing looks a bit strange. From Internet to Gold 400 use: `userid@org_unit.org.prmd.gold-400.gb`. The *userid*, *org_unit* (organization unit), *org* (organization), and *prmd* (private mail domain) will need to be given to you by the recipient.

To send mail from Gold 400 to Internet, use `/DD.RFC-822=`*userid*`(a)`*domain*`/O=uknet/` `PRMD=uk.ac/ADMD=gold 400/C=GB/`. If there are any special characters in the *userid*, see the X.400 section below on how to encode those.

Example Gold 400 to Internet:

`/DD.RFC-822=pjones(a)foo.bar.edu/O=uknet/PRMD=uk.ac/ADMD=gold 400/C=GB`

Example Internet to Gold 400:   `csmith@foo.bar.baz.gold-400.gb`

KeyLink

KeyLink is Telecom Australia's commercial X.400 mail service. From Internet to KeyLink, use *userid*`@`*org_unit*`.`*org*`.telememo.au.` *org_unit* (organizational unit) and *org* (organization) will need to be given to you by the recipient. The *org_unit* may not be used by your recipient, in which case it can be ignored—be sure to also remove the period that would have followed it.

From KeyLink to Internet, use (`C:au`, `A:telememo`, `P:oz.au`, `"RFC-822":"`*name*— `<`*userid*`(a)`*domain*`>"`). *name* will not be used for actual addressing, but you can put the recipient's real name in there. As with Gold-100, if there are any special characters in *userid* you will need to see the X.400 section below for information on how to encode them.

Example KeyLink to Internet:

`(C:au, A:telememo, P:oz.au, "RFC-822":"Pat Jones—<pjones(a)foo.bar.edu>")`

MCI Mail

MCI Mail is MCI's commercial e-mail service.

For mail from the Internet to MCI Mail, there are several options. Each user has a name (Pat Jones) and a phone number (555-9999) associated with his or her account. The number is unique, so you can always send mail to *number*`@mcimail.com`. If you know there is only one `P Jones` with an MCI Mail account, you can send mail to *FLast*`@mcimail.com`, where *F* is the first initial and *Last* is the last name. Or, if you know there is only one `Pat Jones` you can send mail to *First_Last*`@mcimail.com`, where *First* is the first name and *Last* is the last name. Note the underscore (_) between the names.

For mail from MCI Mail to Internet, at MCI Mail's `To:` prompt enter *name* (`EMS`). *name* isn't actually used for addressing, but you can put the recipient's real name in here. It will then prompt you with `EMS:`, and you should respond with `INTERNET`. Finally, it will ask for `Mbx:`, and you should respond with *userid*`@`*domain*.

Example Internet to MCI Mail: `Pat_Jones@mcimail.com`
                                  `1234567@mcimail.com`

Prodigy

Prodigy is the Prodigy Information Services (Sears and IBM) large commercial service. To send mail from Internet to Prodigy, use *userid*`@prodigy.com`.

To send mail from Prodigy to Internet is a little harder as of this writing—support for that isn't integrated into the main Prodigy software, so you need to use some off-line Mail Manager software to do it. It only works for IBM PC users, and you need to pay $4.95 and download the Mail Manager—to do this, when you're on-line Jump to `ABOUT MAIL MANAGER`. The Mail Manager will then lead you through the procedure.

Example Internet to Prodigy: `foob09z@prodigy.com`

SprintMail

If AT&T and MCI have commercial mail services, obviously Sprint isn't going to be left out. This is Sprint's commercial X.400 mail service. To send mail from Internet to SprintMail, use `/G=`*first*`/S=`*last*`/O=`*organization*`/ADMD=TELEMAIL/C=US/`
`@sprint.com`. *first* and *last* are the recipient's first and last names, respectively, and *organization* is an organization name which you'll need to get from the recipient.

To send mail from SprintMail to Internet, use `C:USA,A:TELEMAIL,P:INTERNET,"RFC-`
`822":<`*userid*`(a)`*domain*`>) DEL`. As with other X.400 services, if *userid* has any special characters you will need to see the X.400 section below for information on how to encode them.

Example SprintMail to Internet:

`C:USA,A:TELEMAIL,P:INTERNET,"RFC-822":<pjones(a)foo.bar.edu>) DEL`

Example Internet to SprintMail:

`/G=Chris/S=Smith/O=Foo Inc/ADMD=TELEMAIL/C=US/@sprint.com`

WWIVNet

WWIVNet is the largest of several networks for BBSes running WWIV software. Traffic from node to node is long distance in several places, and the gateway site uses long distance as well, so *please* be courteous and don't send or receive anything large (over 8K or so).

To send mail from Internet to WWIVNet you will need to know the recipient's node number (*node*) and user number (*userid*), which the recipient will have to give you. Use *userid-node*@wwiv.tfsquad.mn.org. To send mail from WWIVNet to Internet, use *userid#domain*@506

Example WWIVNet to Internet: pjones#foo.bar.edu@506
Example Internet to WWIVNet: 12-3456@wwiv.tfsquad.mn.org

Other Address Concerns

Internet addresses are for the most part case insensitive, that is, they ignore capitalization. For a given address, *userid*@*domain*, the capitalization of the domain should definitely be ignored by any address routers—pjones@Foo.BAR.CoM, pjones@foo.bar.com, and pjones@FOO.BAR.COM should all get to the correct address. The userid is also usually case insensitive, but the specification leaves it up to the individual site or service to decide this.

By UNIX custom, addresses should be given in all lowercase where possible. However if you are given the address of someone on another service or network, you should be careful to preserve all the capitalization when you send a message. It's usually not a problem, but why take chances?

The Internet uses what is known as RFC-822 addressing. Many of the large commercial services that specialize in electronic mail use what is known as X.400 addressing, which looks like /X=value/Y=value/Z=value. This is useable from the Internet, as evidenced by the entries for X.400 services above, but there is one major problem: RFC-822 allows many characters that will choke X.400 addressing. X.400 dislikes punctuation characters in its values, including @, which makes it tough to send mail to someone on the Internet.

Whenever the Internet address has a special character, use the following substitutions:

For	Use
@	(a)
%	(p)
!	(b)
"	(q)
_	(u)
(	(l)
)	(r)

Or, for any other special character, such as #, substitute *(xxx)* where *xxx* is the three-digit decimal ASCII code for the character. For # it would thus be (035).

To convert the address uunet.uu.net!bob#test@foo.bar.com for MCI Mail, or Gold 400, or any of the other X.400 services, you would use uunet.uu.net(b)bob(035)test(a)foo.bar.com. It's a pain, but at least it works.

INTERNET GLOSSARY

alias A simple name substituted for a more complicated electronic mailing address. The alias might represent a single person or a group of people. For example, an alias such as "Sales" might be a list of the addresses of all the people in a company's sales department.

anonymous FTP (File Transfer Protocol) The act of connecting to a remote computer as an anonymous user, in order to transfer files back to your own computer.

ANSI (American National Standards Institute) The organization responsible for approving United States standards in several areas, including computers and communications.

Archie A system for locating information on files and directories publicly available through anonymous FTP.

archive A file that contains other files. Often used to store files that have related contents. Also used to refer to ftp sites that hold large collections of files for download.

ARPANET (Advanced Research Projects Agency Network)   An early research network that served as the "testing ground" for the theories and software upon which the Internet is based; forerunner of the Internet.

ASCII (American Standard Code for Information Interchange)   One of the standard formats for representing characters. This standard and others like it make sharing files between programs possible. A text file is usually in ASCII format.

backbone   A network that interconnects other networks.

BBS   Acronym for bulletin board system. See *bulletin board*.

binary   **1.** A system of counting that uses only the digits 0 and 1. **2.** When used in connection with files (as in "binary file transfer"), it means that the file contains characters that are not printable.

BITNET (Because It's Time Network)   A network that connects academic and research institutions around the world. BITNET supports mail, mailing lists, and file transfer and connects to the Internet.

bulletin board   A service that enables users to enter information for others to read and that can store and retrieve files.

client/server   Describes a relationship between two pieces of software. One piece of software, the server, is responsible for servicing requests from the other piece, the client. These requests can be anything—from transferring files to searching databases to just about anything you can think of that one program can do for another.

compress   A technique for reducing the size of a data or program file. Compressed files are often stored in archives. See also *archive*.

CWIS (Campus Wide Information Systems)   Provides information and services available on campuses, including directory information, calendars, bulletin boards, databases, and interactive computing.

DNS (Domain Name System)   A system whose principal function is to locate host IP addresses based on host names. It consists of a hierarchical sequence of names (from the most specific to the most general) separated by dots (for example, ucs.usl.edu).

downloading   The electronic transfer of information from one computer to another, generally from a larger computer to a smaller one.

e-mail (electronic mail)   A system that enables the exchange of messages between network users or groups of users.

e-mail address   An identifier that is used to send electronic mail to a specific destination.

emoticons   See *smiley.*

FAQ (frequently asked question)   A listing of questions and answers provided for new subscribers to newsgroups and e-mail listings, usually published once a month. Also used by many service providers to answer questions that new Internet users might have concerning a service so that rather than having to repeat the same answers over and over, the FAQ can be sent to the user.

finger   A program that displays information about a particular user, or all users, logged on a system. It usually gives the full name, last login time, idle time, terminal time, and terminal location. May also display plan and project files left by the user.

flame   A strong opinion or criticism of some idea or statement expressed in an electronic mail message.

freeware   Software that is supplied by the author at no charge. Title and copyright is retained by the author.

FTP (File Transfer Protocol)   A protocol that enables a user to transfer files electronically from remote computers to the user's computer; part of the TCP/IP suite. Also the name of the program used to execute the protocol. See also *anonymous FTP.*

gateway   Software that translates data from the standards of one system to the standards of another.

Gopher   A distributed information service that uses a simple protocol to enable Gopher clients to access information from any other accessible Gopher server, creating a single "Gopherspace" of information.

header   Part of an electronic mail message that precedes the body of the message and provides the message originator, date, and time.

host computer   A term used with wild abandon to denote any computer attached directly to the Internet.

HTML (Hypertext Markup Language)   Language used to code text files for use in hypertext systems.

hypertext   Data in a document that is organized to provide links between key words or phrases, so that related concepts and issues can be linked together.

Hytelnet (Hypertext Browser for Telnet)   Internet tool that lets you use embedded hypertext links to search through screens to locate information about a telnet site.

internet   Spelled with a small *i*, internet refers to a collection of interconnected networks.

Internet   The series of interconnected networks (a network of networks, in fact) that includes local area, regional, and national backbone networks; makes up the largest internet in the world. Networks in the Internet use the same telecommunications protocol (TCP/IP) and provide electronic mail, remote login, and file transfer services. Some networks attached to the Internet don't use TCP/IP, but they are not considered part of the Internet.

Internet address   The numeric address that uniquely identifies a computer on the Internet.

Internetiquette   Our term for netiquette on the Internet (just to be different). See *netiquette*.

InterNIC (Internet Network Information Center)   A Network Information Services Manager funded by the National Science Foundation, InterNIC provides registration, directory, database, and information services.

IP (Internet Protocol)   The Internet standard communications protocol; provides a common layer over dissimilar networks.

IP Address   The numeric address of a computer connected to the Internet.

LISTSERV lists (or listservers)   LISTSERVs are programs that act as message switches for e-mail on specific subjects. You subscribe to a list that is on a topic of interest to you on a LISTSERV and you will receive all messages that are sent to the list. You can reply to those messages, and all other list subscibers will see your message.

lurking   The act of "hanging around" a mailing list (a LISTSERV list) or USENET newsgroup without contributing to the discussion; sometimes used as a means of learning before becoming an active participant.

mail gateway   A machine that connects similar or dissimilar electronic mail systems and translates and transfers messages between them.

mail server   A software program that sends files or information in response to requests received via e-mail.

mailing list   A list of e-mail addresses used to forward messages (generally related to a specific topic) to groups of people. In some instances, moderators determine whether to send messages to the rest of the group or not.

MIME (Multipurpose Internet Mail Extensions)   An extension that provides the transfer of non-textual data, such as graphics and fax, by e-mail.

Mosaic   Hypermedia browser created by the National Center for Super computing Applications (NCSA) to help navigate the Internet.

MUD (Multiuser Dungeon)   Role-playing games or simulations played on the Internet. Players interact in real-time and alter the game as they play it. MUDs are usually based on the telnet protocol for remote login.

name server   A computer on the Internet that manages a database of Internet names and their corresponding numeric addresses. Used by other computers to determine the correct address for e-mail, FTP, telnet, and other service connections.

netiquette   A pun on the word "etiquette" that refers to proper and tasteful behavior on a network communications system. See also *Internetiquette*.

NIC (Network Information Center)   A NIC provides administrative support, user assistance, and information services for a network.

NIS (Network Information Services)   The services provided by a NIC to assist users utilizing a network. See also *NIC*.

NREN (National Research and Education Network)   The proposed national computer network to be built upon the foundation of the NSF backbone network, NSFNET. NREN would provide high-speed interconnection between other national and regional networks.

NSF (National Science Foundation)   A United States government agency that promotes the advancement of science.

NSFNET (National Science Foundation Network)   Funded by the National Science Foundation, this network is a high speed "network of networks" that plays an essential part in academic and research communications. Part of the Internet, with connections to Canada, Mexico, and Europe, it is the backbone for the proposed NREN.

OCLC (Online Computer Library Catalog)   A nonprofit membership organization that offers computer-based services to libraries, educational organizations, and their users. OCLC connects over 10,000 libraries around the world.

OPAC (Online Public Access Catalog)   Any type of computerized library catalog.

PING (Packet InterNet Groper)   A program designed to test the accessibility of a particular destination.

postmaster   Person at a particular site responsible for handling electronic mail problems, answering queries about users, and other e-mail_related tasks.

protocol   A set of formats and procedures governing the exchange of information between systems.

public domain   Software with title and copyright explicitly relinquished by the author, so that anyone can use it as they please.

relevance feedback   A technique that involves the ordering of documents on the basis of the degree of relevance they have to the search request. The ordering is by a scoring system that tabulates the number of matches with the search criteria.

remote access   The ability to access a computer from outside the building in which it is housed. Remote access requires communications hardware, software, and actual physical links, such as telephone lines or a telnet login to another computer.

remote login   Connecting to a remote computer so that its screen display is sent to your computer, and your keyboard data is sent to it. This means that programs on the remote computer appear to be running locally. See also *telnet*.

RFC (Request for Comments)   The document series that describes the Internet suite of protocols and related experiments, begun in 1969. RFCs can be located through the Internet via anonymous FTP.

rn   The software program through which USENET news is accessed.

RTFM   An impolite acronym meaning "read the manual." Often posted by support staff to users who refuse to read a document that might actually help them.

servers   Computers that provide resources. There are many types of servers, including file servers, terminal servers, and name servers.

shareware   Software distributed through public channels for which the author hopes to receive monetary compensation.

signature   The message at the bottom of an e-mail message or USENET article that identifies the sender.

smiley   A group of characters that, when viewed sideways, constitutes a face and is used to add "tone" to e-mail communications.

tar   A type of file archiving. See also *archive*.

TCP/IP (Transmission Control Protocol/Internet Protocol)   The combined set of protocols (or protocol suites) that performs the transfer of data between two computers. The standard protocol suite used on the Internet.

telnet   A portion of the TCP/IP suite of software protocols that enables a user to log in to a remote computer from the user's local computer.

terminal emulator   A program that enables a computer to communicate with a remote host as if it were a specific type of terminal directly connected to that computer or network.

TN3270 A version of telnet supplying IBM full-screen support.

troughing See *lurking*.

USENET A set of newsgroups considered to be of global interest and governed by a set of rules for passing and maintaining newsgroups.

Veronica (Very Easy Rodent-Oriented Net-wide Index to Computerized Archives) A service that maintains an index of titles of Gopher items and provides keyword searches of those items.

virus A program that replicates itself through incorporation into other programs.

WAIS (Wide Area Information Servers) A distributed information system that offers natural language input, indexed searching, and "relevance feedback."

whois A program that permits users to query a database of people or things, such as domains, networks, and hosts. The information provided includes a person's company name, address, phone number, and e-mail address.

World Wide Web A hypertext-based, distributed information system in which users may create, edit, or browse hypertext documents.

WWW See *World Wide Web*.

Z39.50 Protocol A standard protocol for searching databases based on a client/server model.

zoo A type of file compression and archiving. See also *archive* and *compress*.

F

TESTING YOUR NAVIGATION SKILLS

Now that you've learned what's on the Internet and which tools can help you navigate its complexities, you might like to test yourself. The tests we've compiled were supplied by Rick Gates, the Master of the Internet Hunt (known to its fans as simply the Hunt).

The Hunt is a monthly competition open to anyone who wants to participate. It is a set of twelve questions set by Rick that can be answered using only the resources of the Net. The Hunt questions cover the spectrum of available information on the Net.

The reason Rick started the Hunt was to find out more about the different ways in which people use the Internet, to give novice users the chance to learn more about how to access resources by searching for the answers, to help keep people informed about the variety of information available, and to help people follow the evolution of Internet tools and resources.

Using e-mail, Rick announces the exact distribution time of the next month's Hunt questions during the last week of each month. He tries to post the actual questions late in the evening on the last day of the month.

For instance, the February Hunt questions were posted at midnight on January 31st. Players have one week from the date of the posting to submit their entry by e-mail to Rick (rgates@ccit.arizona.edu). The answers get posted within a week or so after each Hunt has ended.

The original source of Gopher links to the Internet Hunt comes from the Gopher at gopher.cic.net. If a Gopher demon is running on your local site, you can get to the CICNet Gopher by typing gopher gopher.cic.net at a prompt. Otherwise, you can connect to most major Gophers and find links to Rick's Internet Hunt.

Each Hunt question carries a weight that indicates difficulty: from 1 (easy) to 10 (difficult). Each Hunt usually includes an extra-credit question (1 point) and a Mystery question, the answer to which Rick doesn't actually know and which gets no points—but everyone will admire you greatly if you can solve it.

The Internet Hunt Rules and Scoring

The Internet Hunt is a serious game to its adherents, and if you join in, you're playing against some serious people. The following rules define how the game is played and how scoring is done.

Hunt Rules

1. There are usually 12 questions, the first 11 of which count toward your score. I have personally verified that each of these can be answered using only the resources of the Net. These are contrived questions.

2. There is often a last question known as the mystery question. I don't know if there's an answer to this on the Net. I may or may not have tried to find one. The mystery question usually comes to me from people asking for information. This is a real question.

3. Each of these first 11 questions carries a value in parentheses. This point value is my best guess on how tough that question is to answer. The scale is 1 (easy) to 10 (difficult). The total points for all questions are listed after the last question.

4. Answer as many questions as you can. Partial credit is awarded.

5. Teams are allowed to submit entries, but these must be designated as

such. Pick a team name. Team entries will be scored separately from individual entries.

6. All answers must be mailed to me. My standard signature will be at the bottom of this message.

7. The contest will run for one week from the date of posting of this message. The deadline should appear in the header at the top of this message.

8. Feel free to send me potential questions for the Hunt, be they scored or mystery.

9. I've been given the opportunity to publish parts of the Hunt in printed form. Please indicate if you are willing or unwilling to have me include your answers in another publication (with due credit, of course).

10. Have fun! What's it all for, after all?

Scoring Rules

1. Whoever answers all the questions first shall be declared the winner.

2. In the event that nobody answers all the questions, the player with the highest point total shall be declared the winner.

3. If there is a tie for highest point total, the player who responded first shall be declared the winner.

4. Assume you're answering the question for someone who understands the basic network tools (FTP, telnet, finger, Gopher, etc.), but just doesn't know where the data is. Answers like:

```
ftp host.university.edu
```

will not score as high as:

```
anonymous ftp to host.university.edu
cd /pub/documents
file is called important.txt.Z
```

Don't feel like you have to tell people how to use FTP. Instead, tell them where they can find what they're looking for, what tool to use to find it, and if necessary, the end information itself.

5. Read the question carefully. If it's asking for specific information (like "What is the chorus to Jingle Bells?"), supply that information in your answer. Sometimes you may find a pointer to a source that no longer exists. Providing the end information tells me that you actually checked the source out.

6. Answers utilizing either privately licensed resources or subscription to a service will be marked down.

7. If any player would like an individually scored entry, please feel free to send me a message. I will send them out after the Hunt has closed.

An Example Question

Question: I just read an interesting paper by a Bradley Smith in the Chemistry Department at the University of Western Australia. Is it possible to get an e-mail address for him?

Method: Using the Internet Gopher X500 gateway, phonebooks directory, you can narrow it down to Australia, to the university, and then to the chemistry department.

Or:

Use Netfind at the University of Colorado.

```
telnet bruno.cs.colorado.edu
Login as netfind
   ( Search for Smith Western Australia)
```

Or:

```
whois -h uniwa.uwa.oz.au smith
```

Answer: bjs@crystal.uwa.oz.au

The Tests

There is almost always no single way of getting the answers to the following questions. The Internet offers so many tools and so much duplication of data that you can be overwhelmed by search strategies. As a general rule, try the most popular tools (Gopher, Archie, and WAIS) before moving on to resources more difficult to search (such as newsgroups).

The Beginning Navigator's Test

These are the easy ones. You should be able to track down the answers pretty quickly.

1. How do I get access to Scott Yanoff's Internet Services List?

2. Who is the author of the only book held by Victoria University of Wellington on the training of sheep dogs?

3. I was reading an article about the development of computers, and someone mentioned an early model called ENIAC. Is this just some sort of 1950s lexicon, or is it an acronym for something?

4. In the book *The Wonderful Wizard of Oz,* by L. Frank Baum, what footwear did Dorothy gain at the expense of the Wicked Witch of the East?

5. Where can I find an archive of USENET Frequently Asked Questions (FAQs)?

6. Where can I find some chili recipes?

The Advanced Navigator's Test

These are much sneakier than the last group. You're going to have to work to get these.

1. Approximately how many persons lived in college dormitories in Ann Arbor, Michigan, U.S.A., in 1990?

2. I heard some network gurus talking about "pinging" an address somewhere. What is ping, and what does it stand for?

3. To what date did U.S. President Bill Clinton extend cooperation with the European Atomic Energy Community?

4. What is the melting point of tungsten?

5. What line follows the two lines, "What's in a name! that which we call a rose/ By any other name would smell as sweet;" in the William Shakespeare play *Romeo and Juliet*?

6. Where is the 8th Annual Conference on Computing and Philosophy being held?

The Master Navigator's Test

These are really hard. Not just a bit hard, but bordering on the evil.

1. I just returned from a short vacation in Havana. When I left, I paid my hotel bill with a major credit card. A friend told me that this was illegal and that I was liable for a fine. If this is true, how much is the fine?

2. Where can I find the Washington address for the congressman from my district?

3. What are the five Internet resources recommended in the file musthave-list.txt?

4. A hurricane just blew in! Where can I find satellite photos of its progress?

5. I need to send a letter to the Meteorology Department at the University of Edinburgh, in Scotland, U.K. Can you tell me what the address is, please?

6. What color is the carpet in the Main Transporter Lobby at Cyberion City?

The Internet Columbus Award

These are REALLY tough. If you get them without cheating, you really know your stuff, and your friends should be encouraged to acknowledge your genius, insight, and intellectual prowess. Then you have to buy them all a beer.

1. Of those countries receiving more than a gigabyte of data from the U.S. National Science Foundation Network's national backbone in January, 1993, which country had the highest net user ratio of data out to data in, in bytes?

2. There's a tavern in England rumored to be the site from which the *Canterbury Tales'* pilgrims departed. What brands of ale do they serve there today?

The Answers

If you haven't at least tried to find the answers for yourself, shame on you. May the ghost of Vasco da Gama chase your data 'round your PC and may you get unexplained I/O errors.

> **Navigator's Note:** Over time, the location, format, and access methods for Internet resources can change. So although the answers that follow were correct when this book was written, they might not be useful in, say, the next millenium. So make sure to purchase all new editions of this book to get the right answers.

The Beginning Navigator's Test

Here, then, are the answers for the really easy questions.

Question 1

How do I get access to Scott Yanoff's Internet Services List?

Rick's Note: In my estimation this is one of the best lists of resources out there.

Method:

```
whois Yanoff
     Yanoff, Scott A. (SAY3)  yanoff@CSD4.CSD.UWM.EDU
        3200 N. Cramer Street
        Milwaukee, WI
        (414) 229-5370
        Record last updated on 27-Apr-92.
finger yanoff@csd4.csd.uwm.edu
```

Answer:

```
ftp csd4.csd.uwm.edu
get /pub/inet.services.txt
```

Question 2

Who is the author of the only book held by Victoria University of Wellington on the training of sheep dogs?

Method:

```
telnet infoslug.ucsc.edu
Login as "gopher"
Select item 9.  The World
Select item 2.  Other Internet Systems and Databases/
Select item 8.  Internet Libraries/
Select item 2.  Catalogues Listed by Location/
Select item 19. New Zealand/
Select item 9.  Victoria University of Wellington <TEL>
Login as "opac"
From Library Catalogues menu select #7 Subject Keyword
Use keywords "sheep dogs"
```

Or:

```
Using Hytelnet:
Select <SITES1>
Select <NZ000> New Zealand
Select <NZ001> Victoria University of Wellington
Select item 7. search "subject keyword"
     Use keywords: training sheep dogs
```

Answer:

Author: Hartley, Cecil Wilfred Gerald

Title: The shepherd's dogs: their training for mustering and trial work.

Question 3

I was reading an article about the development of computers, and someone mentioned an early model called ENIAC. Is this just some sort of 1950s lexicon, or is it an acronym for something?

Method:

```
telnet harpoon.cso.uiuc.edu
Login as "gopher"
Select item 11. Other Gopher and Information Servers/
Select item 12. Search titles in Gopherspace using Veronica/
```

```
Select item 3. Search gopherspace by simple Boolean veronica <?>
Search: acronym
Select item 41. Acronyms (Search by acronym or word) <?>
```

Or:

```
telnet Infoslug.ucsc.edu
Login as "gopher"
Select item 6. The Library
Select item  6. Electronic Reference Books
Select item 16. Webster's Dictionary
Index word to search for "ENIAC"
```

Or:

```
telnet quake.think.com
Login as "wais"
select source "acronyms"
search "eniac"
```

Answer:

en.i.ac \'en-e—.ak\ n [electronic numerical integrator and computer] digital computer for rapid solution of mathematical problems.

Question 4

In the book The Wonderful Wizard of Oz, *by L. Frank Baum, what footwear did Dorothy gain at the expense of the Wicked Witch of the East?*

Rick's Note: This solution relies on the Internet user being aware of Michael Hart's Gutenberg Project of turning many books into electronic text. Readers of News will be aware that the Gutenberg Project has recently released *The Wonderful Wizard of Oz.*

Method:

```
telnet archie.au
Login as archie
Enter: prog gutenberg
Anonymous ftp to sunsite.unc.edu
cd /pub/docs/books/gutenberg/etext93
get wizoz10.txt
Search for words "Wicked Witch" using the vi editor
vi wizoz10.txt
/Wicked\ Witch
```

Repeat the search until you see the reference to shoes.

Or:

```
telnet twosocks.ces.ncsu.edu
Login as gopher
Select item  6, NCSU Computing Center's Gopher Server
Select item  8, Information Services from around World
Select item  5, Other Libraries on the Internet
Select item  2, OBI, the Online Book Initiative
Select item  55, Gutenberg
Select item  4, etext93
Select item  10, wizoz10.txt
```

Answer: Silver shoes with pointed toes.

Question 5

Where can I find an archive of USENET Frequently Asked Questions (FAQs)?

Method:

```
telnet gopher.fsu.edu
Login as gopher
Select item 9. Other Information Systems
Select item 3. Recommended Information Systems for Exploration
Select item 10.Veronica (search menu items in most of gopherspace)
Select item 1. search gopherspace by _partial Boolean_ veronica
Words to search: FAQ
Select item 35. >MIT FAQ holdings
Select item 1. admin
= [to find technical information on item]
     (find that the information comes from pit-manager.mit.edu)
```

Answer: `ftp pit-manager.mit.edu` (You can select from the many FAQ's in the USENET directories.)

Question 6

Where can I find some chili recipes?

Method:

```
Gopher
Select item 5. Internet file server (ftp) sites/
Select item 4. Search FTP sites (Archie)/
Select item 2. Substring search of archive sites for "chili"
```

The following files show up:

```
sunsite.unc.edu:/pub/docs/books/recipes/chili-1.
sunsite.unc.edu:/pub/docs/books/recipes/chili-2.
sunsite.unc.edu:/pub/docs/books/recipes/chili-3.
sunsite.unc.edu:/pub/docs/books/recipes/chili-4.
sunsite.unc.edu:/pub/docs/books/recipes/chili-5.
sunsite.unc.edu:/pub/docs/books/recipes/chili-6.
sunsite.unc.edu:/pub/docs/books/recipes/chili-7.
sunsite.unc.edu:/pub/docs/books/recipes/chili-bean.
```

Then:

```
ftp sunsite.unc.edu
Login as Anonymous
```

Answer:

```
cd /pub/docs/books/recipes
```

Rick's Note: Chili recipes (at least seven) are available by ftp from `gatekeeper.dec.com`, `cd pub/recipes.ftp`, then `gatekeeper.dec.com`. Recipe number seven, Chernobyl Chili, is touted as a high energy microwave chili and, in addition to beef and beans, calls for bacon grease, MSG, and beer. A caveat at the end mentions the incredible mess this dish will make in your microwave oven. Party down!

The Advanced Navigator's Test

Here are the answers to the somewhat sneakier questions.

Question 1

Approximately how many persons lived in college dormitories in Ann Arbor, Michigan, U.S.A. in 1990?

Method:

```
telnet consultant.micro.umn.edu
Login as "gopher"
Select item 9. Other gopher and information servers/
Select item 1. All the gopher servers in The World/
Select item 309. University of Michigan Libraries/
Select item 7. Social Sciences Resources/
Select item 1. 1990 Census (UMich)/
Select item 6. Michigan:  State, Counties, Cities, and MCDs STF1A/(See note)
Select item 3. Cities, Addison Village to Brownlee Park CDD/
Select item 17. Ann Arbor City, Michigan
```

Answer: 11,606 or 11,605 (both from same source: the 1990 Michigan Census).
Here's the excerpt, specifying the number of persons living in dorms:

```
GROUP QUARTERS
P28. GROUP QUARTERS
UNIVERSE:  Persons in group quarters
Institutionalized persons:
     Correctional institutions ................ 0
     Nursing homes ......................... 537
     Mental (Psychiatric) hospitals ........... 0
     Juvenile institutions ................... 42
     Other institutions ..................... 24
  Other persons in group quarters:
     College dormitories ................. 11,606
     Military quarters ....................... 0
     Emergency shelters for homeless ........ 195
     Visible in street locations ............. 4
     Other noninstitutional group quarters .. 339
```

In addition to selecting

```
6. Michigan: State, Counties, Cities, and MCDs, STF1A/
```

I also tried selecting

```
7. Michigan: State, Counties, Cities, and MCDs, STF3A/
```

From the subsequent menu, I selected

```
1. Ann Arbor: Income, Education, Labor Force & Housing data.
```

This time, the report yielded one less person living in a college dorm.

```
P40. GROUP QUARTERS(10)
UNIVERSE:  Persons in group quarters
 Institutionalized persons:
    Correctional institutions................. 0
    Nursing homes........................... 522
    Mental (Psychiatric) hospitals............ 0
    Juvenile institutions.................... 55
    Other institutions...................... 24
 Other persons in group quarters:
    College dormitories................. 11,605
    Military quarters........................ 0
    Emergency shelters for homeless persons.. 189
    Visible in street locations.............. 0
    Other noninstitutional group quarters.... 226
```

Rick's Note: The two files at Michigan give different answers. I accepted either figure.

Question 2

I heard some network gurus talking about "pinging" an address somewhere. What is ping, and what does it stand for?

Method:

```
telnet infoslug.ucsc.edu
Login as gopher
Select item 7. The Library
Select item 6. Electronic Reference books
Select item 6. Internet Users' Glossary <?>
Search for term "ping" yields the above description
```

Answer: Packet InterNet Groper (PING): A program used to test reachability of destinations by sending them an ICMP echo request and waiting for a reply. The term is used as a verb: "Ping host X to see if it is up!"

See also:

```
Internet Control Message Protocol. [Source: RFC1208]
```

Rick's Note: What ping is and what it stands for can be found in two main resources—the Hacker's Dictionary, and the Internet Users' Glossary [RFC1392]—both of which can be found in and through a variety of front ends. Here are a few:

ping: [from the TCP/IP acronym Packet InterNet Groper, prob. originally contrived to match the submariners' term for a sonar pulse] 1. n. Slang term for a small network message (ICMP ECHO) sent by a computer to check for the presence and aliveness of another. Occasionally used as a phone greeting. See {ACK}, also {ENQ}. 2. vt. To verify the presence of. 3. vt. To get the attention of. From the UNIX command 'ping(1)' that sends an ICMP ECHO packet to another host. 4. vt. To send a message to all members of a {mailing list} requesting an {ACK} (in order to verify that everybody's addresses are reachable). "We haven't heard much of anything from Geoff, but he did respond with an ACK both times I pinged jargon-friends."

The funniest use of "ping" to date was described in January 1991 by Steve Hayman on the USENET group comp.sys.next. He was trying to isolate a faulty cable segment on a TCP/IP Ethernet hooked up to a NeXT machine and got tired of having to run back to his console after each cabling tweak to see if the ping packets were getting through. So he used the sound-recording feature on the NeXT, then wrote a script that repeatedly invoked "ping(8)," listened for an echo, and played back the recording on each returned packet. Result? A program that caused the machine to repeat, over and over, "Ping…ping…ping…" as long as the network was up. He turned the volume to maximum, ferreted through the building with one ear cocked, and found a faulty tee connector in no time.

Question 3

To what date did U.S. President Bill Clinton extend cooperation with the European Atomic Energy Community?

Method:

```
telnet scilibx.ucsc.edu
Login as gopher
Select item 10. The World/
Select item 7. White House Press Release Service/
Select item 6. Miscellanous/
Select item 12. 930309 Statement on Nuclear Cooperation.
```

Or:

```
telnet twosocks.ces.ncsu.edu
Login as gopher
Select item  4. Governmental information
Select item  1. From the White House (President Clinton's Staff)
Select item  4. International Affairs
Select item  3. Letter to Congress: EURATOM Cooperation 3/9/93
```

Answer: December 31, 1995

Question 4

What is the melting point of tungsten?

Rick's Note: A little tricky here, as tungsten is listed under its German name, Wolfram, in the Periodic Table of the Elements at Minnesota. Clever Hunters used other Net resources to solve the problem. I love it!

Method:

```
Telnet to infoslug.ucsc.edu
Login as infoslug
Select item  8. The Researcher/
Select item  4. Science and Engineering/
Select item  3. Chemistry and Biochemistry/
Select item  2. MSDS - Material Safety Data Sheets (may require TN3270) <TEL>
Search for "Tungsten"
Enter 6 and <return> to select any manufacturer
Select entry:
    7440-33-7    TUNGSTEN      FISHER SCIENTIFIC
    COMPONENT: TUNGSTEN   CAS# 7440-33-7   PERCENT: 100
    ...
```

Answer:

```
BOILING POINT: 10220 F (5660 C)
MELTING POINT: 6170 F (3410 C)
^^^^^^^^^^^^^^^^^^^^^^^^^^^^^^^
```

Question 5

What line follows the two lines, "What's in a name! that which we call a rose/ By any other name would smell as sweet;" in the William Shakespeare play Romeo and Juliet?

Method:

```
telnet twosocks.ces.ncsu.edu
Login as gopher
Select item 6, NCSU Computing Center's Gopher Server
Select item choice 8, Information Services from around World
Select item choice 4, Gutenberg Project -- Electronic literature
Select item choice 6, Tragedies
Select item choice 8, Romeo and Juliet
Select item choice 2, ACT II
```

Answer:

```
"So Romeo would, were he not Romeo call'd,
Retain that dear perfection which he owes
Without that title. Romeo, doff thy name,
And for that name which is no part of thee
Take all myself."
```

Question 6

Where is the 8th Annual Conference on Computing and Philosophy being held?

Method:

```
Gopher to InfoSlug
Select item 8. The Researcher/
Select item 1. Arts and Humanities/
Select item 1. American Philosophical Association BBS <TEL>
Login as apa
Select item 5 Philosophical Calendar (updated: 4/1)
Select item 4  July / August  (1993)
(From within more) /Computing
```

Answer: Eighth Annual Conference on Computing and Philosophy (CAP) Carnegie-Mellon University (August 12-14th, 1993)

The Master Navigator's Test

Here, now, are the answers to the bordering-on-evil questions.

Question 1

I just returned from a short vacation in Havana. When I left, I paid my hotel bill with a major credit card. A friend told me that this was illegal and that I was liable for a fine. If this is true, how much is the fine?

Rick's Note: Many Hunters searched the travel advisory at gopher.stolaf.edu, which mentions that using credit cards in Cuba is illegal but doesn't mention the fine. Many noted that Cuban businesses do not accept credit cards. The source I found did not mention that fact. Bob McLean points out the discrepancies and offers a way out for the guilty:

"Currency Regulations (Credit Card Restrictions): U.S. citizens and permanent resident aliens are prohibited from using credit cards in Cuba. U.S. credit card companies will not accept vouchers from Cuba, and Cuban shops, hotels, and other places of business do not accept U.S. credit cards."

Because the card was accepted, and you're back in the U.S., it would seem that you needn't worry, but the hotel might not get its money (legally). If you really want to turn yourself in, you can contact the Office of Foreign Assets Control, Department of the Treasury, 1500 Pennsylvania Avenue, NW, Treasury Annex, Washington, D.C., 20220 (tel: 202/535-9449; fax: 202/377-7222). It's nice to know that I can turn myself in via fax.

This question also brings up a related concern. Any piece of information on the Net reflects the authority, concerns, and focus of the body that issues it. The information on `gopher.stolaf.edu` is from a Consular Information Sheet from the U.S. State Department. The info I got was from the U.S. Department of the Treasury, Office of Foreign Assets Control. It probably wouldn't have helped in solving this question, but it's always something to keep in mind.

Method:

```
gopher to una.hh.lib.umich.edu
Select item 13. socsci/
Select item 7. Government and Politics/
Select item 4. Economic Bulletin Board  (UMich)/
Select item 4. EBB and Agency Information and misc. files/
Select item 33. Synopsis of U.S. embargo - Cuba.
```

Answer: "Penalties for violating the sanctions range up to 10 years in prison, $500,000 in corporate and $250,000 in individual fines. This sheet is an overview of the Regulations for individuals wishing to travel to or otherwise deal with Cuba." Also, "credit and other charge cards may not be used in Cuba—not even for living expenses or for the purchase of goods used by the traveler."

Question 2

Where can I find the Washington address for the congressman from my district?

Method:

```
WAIS to find the Congress file at pit.mit.edu
```

Answer: Robert J. Lagomarsino is the Representative from the district including Santa Barbara. His Washington address is

```
2332 Rayburn
Washington DC 20515
```

Question 3

What are the five Internet resources recommended in the file musthave-list.txt?

Method:

```
Use archie to locate the file
ftp pilot.njin.net
Login as Anonymous
cd /pub/Internet-course
get musthave-list.txt
    This file states at the beginning:
        ------------------------------------------------
        There are five must-have Internet resources. Two, the
        Yanoff and December lists, are hard copy summaries of Internet
        resources. They are invaluable desktop additions for any user,
        especially newcomers. The other three, HYTELNET, HYPLUS, and
        INFOPOP are programs providing an incredible amount of
        information. Although there is much duplication, each of the
        resources has value not offered in the others.
        ------------------------------------------------
```

Answer: The Yanoff and December lists, HYTELNET, HYPLUS, and INFOPOP.

Question 4

A hurricane just blew in! Where can I find satellite photos of its progress?

Method:

```
// How do you find the following //
ftp vmd.cso.uiuc.edu.
cd /wx
```

Answer: The photos are in .GIF files.

Question 5

I need to send a letter to the Meteorology Department at the University of Edinburgh, in Scotland, U.K. Can you tell me what the address is, please?

Method:

```
telnet infoslug.ucsc.edu
login as "gopher"
Select item 10. The World/
Select item 6. Weather and more/
Select item 3. Weather from the UofI Weather Machine (Univ. of Illinois)/
Select item 5. Documents/
Select item 37. Meteo.schools
(The answer was located near the end of Meteo.schools, a
    list of institutions with Meteorology programs.)
```

Or:

```
Gopher to gopher.ed.ac.uk
Select item 4. The University of Edinburgh Campus Wide Information/
Select item 2. EdINFO <TEL>
Login as "edinfo"
Select item 3   People (directories)
Select item 1   Edinburgh University Staff Telephone List
   (return to get departmental list)
Select item 2 Departmental Lists
   (At the eview: prompt) meteorology
   ¦Meteorology
   ¦ James Clerk Maxwell Building
   ¦ King's Buildings
```

Okay, let's take a breather. We now have to find the address for the James Clerk Maxwell Building.

```
q-quit (Go back to EdINFO)
Select Search
Select item 4   Browse metadata index
Search for: addresses
  1:  ADDRESSES                                             5
  4   Addresses
  ¦     Addresses
  ¦
  ¦     The King's Buildings (KB)
  ¦
  ¦        James Clerk Maxwell Building
  ¦        The KingUs Buildings
```

```
¦      Mayfield Road
¦      Edinburgh EH9 3JZ
¦      Reception/Enquiries (KB)        - 031 650 4960
```

We assume KingUs is a typo for King's, and conclude the address is

```
Meteorology
James Clerk Maxwell Building
King's Buildings
Mayfield Road
Edinburgh EH9 3JZ
```

Or:

```
Gopher to:
Select item  8. Other Gopher and Information Servers/
Select item 5. Europe/
Select item 25. United Kingdom/
Select item 18. University of Edinburgh/
Select item 5. Anonymous FTP Services/
Select item 1. Anonymous FTP Servers in Edinburgh/
Select item 5. Department of Meteorology/
Select item 4. calmet/
Select item 2. documents/
Select item 2. call_for_papers.
```

Which states, in it:

```
"Abstracts should be submitted no later than 1 February 1993 to the
Conference Co-chairperson, Dr. Charles Duncan, Professor of
Meteorology, Edinburgh University, King's Buildings, Edinburgh EH9 3J2
United Kingdom(tel: 44.31.650.5091; fax: 44.31.662.4269; email:
C.Duncan@ed.ac.uk)."
```

Rick's Note: This was a messy one. I knew of two ways here. One was easy if you knew about it. You searched the list of meteorology schools at the University of Illinois Weather Machine. The other was trickier, as you were naturally led first to discover the building in which Meteorology was housed, and then find the address of the building.

A few Hunters discovered yet another source—an FTPable call for papers at cumulus.met.ed.ac.uk. The problem here is that the ZIP code has a typo, but the Hunters can hardly be held accountable for that. I gave them full credit, but once again the data integrity needs to be watched out for.

Some folks found the address for the university as a whole and added that to Meteorology's building. I took a point off for those.

Answer:

```
Department of Meteorology
University of Edinburgh
Kings Buildings
Edinburgh EH9 3JZ
U.K.
```

Question 6

What color is the carpet in the Main Transporter Lobby at Cyberion City?

Method:

```
Micromuse found in Yanoff's list
telnet michael.ai.mit.edu
Login as "guest"
     connect guest
     You are immediately given a description of "Cyberion City Main
     TransporterReceiving Station" and the Attendant welcomes you.
     "You step down off of the MTRS platform and walk out into the lobby.
     Main Transporter Lobby(#37055RJ)
     This room has high, vaulted ceilings and white walls. The
     thick, plush, black carpeting makes no sound beneath your
     feet. You are just inside the lobby of the Main Transporter
     Facility. ..."
```

Rick's Note: Cyberion City is the name of a scenario mounted on Micro Muse software and maintained by the Massachusetts Institute of Technology. Unlike many other MUDs, which focus on dungeons, this one focuses on education and environmentalism, or in their own words:

```
.=====================================================================.
  Welcome! MicroMUSE is our vision of the 24th century, a blend of
  high technology and social consciousness with emphasis on education,
  concern for the environment, and communication. Our charter is
  available by anonymous ftp to michael.ai.mit.edu (18.43.0.177).
.---------------------------------------------------------------------.
```

The tough part about answering this question is assuming that clues like Main Transporter Lobby, and Cyberion City are not real places. This starts you looking for science fiction, games, or simulations. The entry from the Yanoff list:

```
-MicroMUSE telnet michael.ai.mit.edu or telnet 18.43.0.177
        offers: Educational Multi-User Simulated Environment.
        (Login: guest)
```

Answer: Black.

The Internet Columbus Award

And finally, the answers to the bordering-on-genius questions.

Question 1

Of those countries receiving more than a gigabyte of data from the U.S. National Science Foundation Network's national backbone in January, 1993, which country had the highest net user ratio of data out to data in, in bytes?

Method:

```
telnet consultant.micro.umn.edu
Login as "gopher"
Select item 3. Internet file server (ftp) sites/
Select item 4. Query a specific ftp host <?>
Words to search for:  nis.nsf.net
Select item 1. Link to ftp server nis.nsf.net/
Select item 19. statistics/
Select item 2. nsfnet/
Select item 6. 1993/
Select item 3. nsf-9301.country
```

Look for the information given by bytes to and from the backbone, not by packet!

Here's a spreadsheet I generated from the data I found. This is a list of countries receiving more than 1 gigabyte from NSF, in descending order of the ratio of bytes out (from NSF) to bytes in (to NSF):

Country	Bytes In To BB	Bytes Out From BB	% In	% Out	Gigs Recv	Ratio Out:In
Hong Kong	1.9E+09	1.5E+10	0.04	0.29	14	7.986719
Greece	3.6E+08	2.1E+09	0.01	0.04	2	5.881365
Korea	2.1E+09	1.2E+10	0.04	0.24	12	5.827162
Singapore	3.1E+09	1.7E+10	0.06	0.33	16	5.423357
Brazil	1.0E+09	5.4E+09	0.02	0.1	5	5.268544

Ireland	5.8E+08	3.0E+09	0.01	0.06	2	5.105389
Poland	4.8E+08	2.3E+09	0.01	0.04	2	4.808341
Israel	3.4E+09	1.5E+10	0.07	0.3	15	4.506155
Czechoslovakia	9.7E+08	4.4E+09	0.02	0.09	4	4.502612
Spain	1.5E+09	6.6E+09	0.03	0.13	6	4.46984
New Zealand	1.2E+09	5.3E+09	0.02	0.1	5	4.294803
Italy	9.1E+09	3.4E+10	0.18	0.67	34	3.73034
Belgium	1.6E+09	5.7E+09	0.03	0.11	5	3.641767
South Africa	1.6E+09	5.6E+09	0.03	0.11	5	3.530957
Austria	6.5E+09	2.1E+10	0.13	0.41	20	3.238235
Hungary	3.4E+08	1.1E+09	0.01	0.02	1	3.172214
United Kingdom	3.3E+10	1.0E+11	0.64	2.01	102	3.120415
Mexico	3.8E+09	1.1E+10	0.07	0.21	10	2.765493
Canada	8.4E+10	2.3E+11	1.64	4.51	230	2.75814
Germany	3.6E+10	9.7E+10	0.71	1.89	96	2.682364
Norway	1.0E+10	2.7E+10	0.2	0.53	26	2.652069
Chile	1.2E+09	3.3E+09	0.02	0.06	3	2.62276
Taiwan	1.2E+10	3.0E+10	0.23	0.58	29	2.486676
Portugal	9.3E+08	2.3E+09	0.02	0.04	2	2.476198
Puerto Rico	7.9E+08	1.5E+09	0.02	0.03	1	1.938452
Japan	1.2E+10	2.4E+10	0.24	0.46	23	1.923033
Sweden	3.1E+10	5.2E+10	0.6	1.02	52	1.686067
France	3.8E+10	6.0E+10	0.73	1.17	59	1.594334
Australia	4.5E+10	6.1E+10	0.88	1.19	61	1.353244
Netherlands	2.7E+10	3.6E+10	0.54	0.7	35	1.311529
Switzerland	4.0E+10	3.8E+10	0.77	0.75	38	0.968221
Denmark	1.5E+10	1.4E+10	0.28	0.27	13	0.934667
United States	4.7E+12	4.1E+12	90.89	80.93	4143	0.890443
Finland	4.0E+10	2.5E+10	0.79	0.5	25	0.628287

Answer: The answer to this question was Hong Kong, with a ratio of 8:1. Interestingly, 3 countries—Denmark, Switzerland, and Finland—had more data going into the backbone than going out.

Rick's Note: Of the 5.1 TB (that's terabytes, trillions of bytes) of data that traveled over the backbone in January 1993, 90% entered from somewhere in the U.S., and 80% exited to somewhere in the U.S. The difference in both cases is made up by traffic between the backbone and nets in other countries. Keep in mind that this is roughly accurate *sampled* data, and that it only accounts for connections using the Internet Protocol (IP). This leaves out mail gateways such as UUNet or BITNET.

Question 2

There's a tavern in England rumored to be the site from which the Canterbury Tales' *pilgrims departed. What brands of ale do they serve there today?*

Method:

```
get the FAQ for the homebrewing Usenet group, rec.crafts.brewing.
In it, there's a mention of pub list at sierra.stanford.edu
ftp sierra.stanford.edu
Login as "anonymous"
cd pub/homebrew/docs
binary
get publist.Z
uncompress publist.Z
      search for Canterbury in your favorite editor or read
      through the whole thing for those interested in finding a
      good place to drink. An excerpt:
      Oxford:
         Turf Tavern Pub.
         It's a little hard to find, but everyone knows where it is
         (I think it's on Bath). This place has been around since
         the 14th century, and was featured in Chaucer's Canterbury
         Tales as the point of departure for the pilgrims, and is
         still a fave of college students. Absolutely wonderful
         atmosphere. They serve two ales from Hook Norton, Hook's
      Best and Old Hook's - the smoothest bitters I've had.
```

Answer: The Turf Tavern located in Oxford serves two ales from Hook Norton: Hook's Best and Old Hook's.

Rick's Note: Chaucerian scholars know that the pilgrims departed from the Tabard Inn, (the original inn, long since gone), in Southwark, near London, not from Oxford. This is why the question referred to a rumor. As with any resource, authority is always an issue.

USING THE SOFTWARE: WHAT'S ON THE DISK

The disk included with this book contains a special collection of PC Windows software for connecting to and navigating the Internet. It includes:

- ⚓ *Chameleon Sampler*, from NetManage—TCP/IP software for a SLIP connection, plus a suite of valuable Internet tools, including FTP, Telnet and e-mail.

- ⚓ *HGopher*—a Windows Gopher+ client with extensive features, including full support for viewers.

- ⚓ *UUCode*—a utility for uuencoding and uudecoding binary files.

- ⚓ A directory of Internet mailing lists.

- ⚓ A listing of Newsgroups.

- ⚓ A directory of Listserv mailing lists.

Chameleon is one of the leading TCP/IP connectivity products for Microsoft Windows. The Chameleon Sampler software allows you to connect to the Internet via a SLIP connection, which operates through your serial port and modem. If you don't already have a SLIP Internet account, see Appendix A for information on service providers.

To use this software, you also need a modem connected to a COM port of your computer. The Chameleon Sampler comes with configuration files for connecting with several popular Internet access providers, including PSINet, NetCom, UUNet's AlterNet, CERFNet, MRnet, ANS CO+RE, and Portal.

If you use another access provider, check with them to see if they have any pre-configured scripts for Chameleon products. When you contact the provider of your choice, indicate that you would like a dial-up TCP/IP connection and that you want to connect via SLIP or PPP directly from your Windows PC.

Installing the Disk

Insert the disk in your floppy disk drive and follow these steps to install the software. You need at least 4 megabytes of free space on your hard drive.

1. From Windows File Manager or Program Manager, choose **File** **R**un from the menu.

2. Type `<drive>INSTALL` and press Enter. `<drive>` is the letter of the drive that contains the installation disk. For example, if the disk is in drive B:, type `B:INSTALL` and press Enter.

3. Choose **F**ull Install to install all the software; choose **C**ustom Install to install only some of the software.

Follow the on-screen instructions in the installation program. The files will be installed to a directory named C:\NAVIGATE, unless you change this name at the beginning of the install program.

When the installation is complete, the file NAVINTER.TXT will be displayed for you to read. This file contains information on the files and programs that were installed.

A Program Manager group named *Navigating the Internet* will be created by the installation program. This group contains icons for installing the Chameleon sampler, searching the reference files, and reading the UUCode documetation.

The Chameleon Sampler Software

NetManage
20823 Stevens Creek Blvd.
Cupertino, CA 95014
Phone: (408) 973-7171
FAX: (408) 257-6405
E-mail: sales@netmanage.com

The Chameleon Sampler software includes several powerful applications most commonly used to access a dial-up TCP/IP SLIP connection with the the Internet. This special version supports connections through serial ports, and provides fully functional copies of applications that have been selected from the full Chameleon TCP/IP for Windows product suite:

⚓ TN3270 (Terminal Emulator)

⚓ Telnet

⚓ FTP

⚓ Electronic Mail

⚓ Ping

With these applications, you can Telnet to remote computers, send and receive mail, and download files from FTP servers. This sampler also includes a native Windows implementation of the TCP/IP Protocol that is 100% DLL and fully compliant with the WinSock TCP/IP standard.

In addition to providing dial-up serial line access, the complete Chameleon TCP/IP for Windows package supports connectivity with local area networks. It can run concurrently with NetWare, Banyan VINES, LAN Manager, and PathWorks.

The complete package also includes more than 20 full-featured applications, including:

⚓ Gopher Client

⚓ News Reader

⚓ TFTP

⚓ Domain Name Server

⚓ Finger

⚓ Whois

⚓ MIME support for multimedia attachments to e-mail

⚓ An SNMP Agent

⚓ Optional support for both NFS client and server
and more.

> **Navigator's Note:** Be sure to see the NetManage advertisement in the back of this book for more information on the full Chameleon product, including a special discount for readers of this book.

Installing the Sampler

Before you can use the Chameleon Sampler software, you must run its Setup program. This program will decompress files and install them in a new directory.

Follow these steps to install the Chameleon Sampler:

1. From Windows Program Manager, double-click on the Install Chameleon Sampler icon in the *Navigating the Internet* group. This runs the SETUP.EXE program in the \NAVIGATE\NETMAN directory.

2. A dialog box will appear with the following information:

   ```
   Chameleon is a TCP/IP based application. If your computer is al-
   ready configured to run network protocols, be sure to consult the
   manual for instructions before proceeding.
   ```

   Select Continue if you are installing on a non-networked PC.

> **Navigator's Note:** If your computer is a part of a network, you should consult your network administrator or network software manuals before proceeding. The Chameleon Sampler does not support connections on a network, only SLIP connections through serial ports.

3. The setup program allows you to change the name of the directory where the software will be installed. Select OK to accept the default directory of `C:\NETMANAG`.

4. The setup program will now begin installing the software. When installation is complete, it creates a Program Manager group named *Chameleon Sampler*.

Configuring the Sampler

Before you begin using the Chameleon Sampler software, you need to run the `Custom` application to configure your setup. You need to have the information in Table G.1 on hand before you start Custom.

> **Navigator's Note:** The items in Table G.1 that are marked with an asterisk (*) are provided by your Internet access service.

Table G.1. Configuration information for Chameleon Sampler.

Startup Information	Example
*Your own IP Address	147.161.2.15
Your Host Name	myname
Your Domain Name	ansremote.com
Port	COM2, 9600
Modem	Hayes
*Dial up (& optional access code)	1-800-926-7111,,,0000001
*Login:	Name myname
*Password	********
*Startup Command	SLIP
*Domain Name Server Address	192.103.63.100

continues

Table G.1. continued

Startup Information	Example
*MailBox Name	myname
*MailBox Password	********
*Mail Gateway Name	p-o.ans.net
*Mail Server Name	p-o.ans.net

(Mail service is optional. The information for the last four items is necessary if you wish to use electronic mail.)

You start the Custom program by double-clicking the Custom icon in the Chameleon Sampler program group.

To use a preconfigured Custom file, select File, then **O**pen, and choose one of the following, depending on which access provider you have selected: ALTERNET.CFG, ANSREMOT.CFG, CERFNET.CFG, MRNET.CFG, NETCOM.CFG, PORTAL.CFG or PSINET.CFG

Use the default configuration (TCPIP.CFG) if you are going to use an access provider other than one of those noted above. To define your own interface, select Interface, then **A**dd, and select the type (SLIP is the most common). If you're defining your own interface, SLIP will create an entry for the type of interface you have chosen and name it (e.g. SLIP0). It will also automatically make an entry in the SLIP.INI file by copying the default slip script and giving it the same name as your new interface.

No other values need to be set for this serial only version of Chameleon. Depending on the provider selected, a number of values are already correctly entered and do not need to be changed. Some providers, such as PSINet, will supply the IP address dynamically.

Navigator's Note: If you are adding your own custom SLIP interface, you may need to make changes to the default SLIP script in order to successfully connect. Double-click the Readme file in the Chameleon Sampler group for more information on scripting.

Using the Applications

Each of the Chameleon Sampler applications has a complete on-line help system. To get an overview of how to use an application, or to answer a specific question about a feature, consult the help file for that application. You can open the help file by selecting **Help Index** from the menu.

The Telnet and TN3270 applications allow you to logon to remote computers. You simply need to provide a host name or IP address under Connect. Typically a logon screen will then prompt you for the appropriate access information. Full keyboard remapping is provided with both of these applications.

FTP (File Transfer Protocol) enables you to connect to remote hosts and download files. Connection profiles can be saved for later reuse. This FTP application can also be set up as an FTP server, allowing you to define users and permit access to files on your own PC, as long as both machines are connected to the network at the same time.

The Mail application allows multiple users to have their own mailboxes on the same PC, and they can retrieve their mail at different times without any interference. Each user can define their own foldering system, address book, and filtering rules. This is useful in a small office or a home setting where different people use the same PC. Even if you are just a single user, you need to define your own mailbox before using Mail.

Configuring the Mail Application

Open the Mail application and login as Postmaster (the default is no password).

1. Under **Services**, select **Mailboxes** and enter your name. (You should define your local mailbox name to be the same as the one defined for you on the mail server to which you will be connecting.)

2. Select **Add**. You can then enter in an optional password, and an optional "in real life" name.

3. Select **OK** to save this information.

4. Exit the Mail application.

This information defines your local mailbox on the PC. You still need to enter your network mailbox parameters.

1. Open the Mail application again, this time going into your new mailbox.

2. Under **Settings** and **Network**, enter your mail Gateway name. Example: `p-o.ans.net`.

3. Under **Settings**, **Network**, and **Server**, enter your server name (example: `p-o.ans.net`), your mailbox name and password.

You do not need to enter a mail directory. If you select the box "delete mail from server," mail will be deleted from the server once it is retrieved and stored on your Windows PC. After entering this information select OK, then go to **File** and select **S**ave to save your configuration.

HGopher

Author: Martyn Hampson (`m.hampson@ic.ac.uk`)

HGopher is a Windows Gopher+ client. There is an icon for HGopher in the *Navigating the Internet* group in Program Manager.

It supports a large range of viewers, which are easily added to HGopher's default configuration. These can be standard viewers within Windows, or they can be special applications.

> **Navigator's Note:** Before you run HGopher, you *must* set up your TCP/IP configuration in the Chameleon Sampler. Otherwise, HGopher will not work.

Once you've started HGopher, you need to configure it as follows:

1. From the **O**ptions menu, select **G**opher Set Up and configure the options. The only settings you *must* configure are in the Files area. These directories must exist, or HGopher will not work properly.

2. From the **C**ommands menu, select **G**o Home and you should have a gopher menu. Double-click the text of the menu to move around and fetch items.

If you're unsure about any of these options, press F1 to view the Help file. It contains extensive information about running and configuring HGopher.

The default bookmark file is named DEFAULT.GBM. If you have installed HGopher properly, it will start up using this bookmark file. These bookmarks are set at a few important places in GopherSpace that you may like to look at.

One of the places in this bookmark file is the HGopher Information Centre. The author of this software has populated this site with a number of viewers, as well as information on Gopher.

Internet Lists

We have included three useful files of Internet resources on the disk, including listings of newsgroups, mailing lists, and Listserv lists. These lists can and do change over time, so these files are provided to get you started with exploring some of the resources on the Internet.

Mailing Lists

MAILLIST.TXT
Author: Stephanie da Silva (arielle@taronga.com)
Original author: Chuq Von Rospach
Previous maintainer: Gene Spafford

This file contains information on more than 500 mailing lists which are available on the Internet or UUCP network. The most up-to-date list is available via anonymous FTP from rtfm.mit.edu (/pub/usenet/news.answers/mail/mailing-lists)

Listserv Lists

LISTSERV.TXT

This file contains information on more than 4000 LISTSERV lists.

Newsgroups

NEWSGRP.TXT
Author: David Lawrence (tale@uunet.uu.net)

This file contains information on more than 2500 USENET and non-USENET newsgroups, including the alt. groups. The list does not include newsgroups that are local to geographic regions or institutions. See the file for information on obtaining the most up-to-date version of this list.

THE INTERNET NAVIGATOR'S GAZETTEER

This resource guide to the Internet is but a starting point for future exploration. The size and complexity of the Internet make it impossible to create a permanent, comprehensive list of everything available at a given time. Before you could finish listing everything, something has already been added, deleted, or moved.

This list has been created and updated to provide the widest variety of topics available to you, the fledgling Internet navigator, and to give you a sample of what is out there. During your travels you will learn why it is impossible to provide a comprehensive list of everything available.

For information regarding how to use each of the resources, see the chapter that properly addresses the techniques involved.

When All Else Fails

Use your Navigator's tools. This book has provided you with the means to find and use just about everything available on the Internet (at the time of this writing; remember, things change quickly on the Internet), including e-mail, FTP, telnet, WAIS, Gopher, WWW, Archie, Veronica, and USENET. Be patient. Remember, you are plugging yourself into the whole world. That's a lot to tackle right away.

As you use your tools and gain experience and confidence, you'll learn that it's possible to find just about anything, and if you can't find it, you may just have to create it yourself. After all, someone had to create everything else out there. You'll probably find that no subject is too bizarre, exotic, or specialized for someone else to be interested in and contribute to. It's just a matter of finding them—and sometimes they move around.

In the meantime, here are some other places to pursue your interests:

- Keep an eye on USENET. USENET groups are constantly being created and voted on. There are hundreds of lists with varying degrees of activity. A newsgroup all navigators should follow is `news.announce.newusers`. Many Internet-related files and FAQs are posted regularly to this newsgroup.

- Another USENET-related resource is the anonymous FTP site `rtfm.mit.edu`. Browsing the directory `pub/USENET` will reveal directories corresponding to newsgroup names. In each of those directories you'll find FAQs and related files. Checking this site will save you the time and embarassment of asking, "Is there an FAQ for this newsgroup?"

- Focus on the growing number of Gopher and Veronica services available. These are two of the most popular tools for finding things, yet they are often overlooked.

- Periodically send the `LIST GLOBAL` command to a LISTSERV. New lists are being created daily. The size of the global list makes daily retrieval prohibitive, but you'll find many changes over time. Also, just as the LISTSERV software has a lot of user-oriented functions, it has a lot of behind-the-scenes (administrative) power as well. One of those features is relocation. Lists have a tendency to move around. This is one reason a subscription request doesn't have to be sent to the host machine, just to a LISTSERV machine (which then forwards your request to the appropriate machine).

⚓ Subscribe to the NEW-LIST LISTSERV. This list is a sounding board for anyone creating a new list (not just LISTSERV) as well as a place for people to ask things such as, "Does anyone know of a list that discusses salt well drilling techniques in ancient China?"

⚓ Yanoff's List. Scott Yanoff regularly updates his "Internet Services List." This can be retrieved via anonymous FTP (or FTPmail) at csd4.csd.uwm.edu (in the directory /pub, the file is named inet.services.txt). This is a list of lists, FTP sites, telnet sites, and all-around interesting tidbits.

⚓ List of mailing lists. This list can be retrieved via anonymous FTP (or FTPmail) at rtfm.mit.edu in the directory /pub/USENET/news.answers/mail/mailing-lists. You should retrieve all eight files (part1 through part8).

⚓ Smith's BigFun List. This is a general list of Internet resources. It can be retrieved via anonymous FTP from cerebus.cor.epa.gov in the directory /pub. The file is bigfun.

⚓ Send a request to LISTSERV@vm1.nodak.edu stating GET LISTSOF LISTS. This will return a list of lists as well as information for retrieving other files that will help you find interesting things.

⚓ Join the Internet Hunt. Have you ever noticed that while you are looking for something (usually something you've lost), you find lots of other interesting things? The Hunt is the same way. Not only do you learn how to use the Internet resources more efficiently, you find other things along the way to sidetrack you. Check out Appendix F, "Testing Your Navigation Skills," for more information on the Hunt.

⚓ Birds of a feather flock together. If you are interested in a specific topic, subject, or hobby that is part of a larger theme, see what the people who hang out there know. If you are interested in discussing a specific breed of dog— say a dachshund— check out lists where other pet or dog owners hang out and see if they know about such a list or if the interest level warrants creating one.

Art

Body/Tatoos

Name: `rec.arts.bodyart`
Resource: USENET
Tattoos and body decoration discussions.

Ceramics

Name: clayart
Resource: LISTSERV
Address: `clayart@ukcc.uky.edu`
For everyone who enjoys and appreciates ceramic arts of all shapes and sizes.

Computer

Name:
alt.binaries.pictures.fine-art.graphics
Resource: USENET
Art created on computers. (Moderated)

Name: alt.binaries.pictures.misc
Resource: USENET
Have we saturated the network yet?

Conventional Media

Name:
alt.binaries.pictures.fine-art.digitized
Resource: USENET
Art from conventional media. (Moderated)

Fine

Name:
alt.binaries.pictures.fine-art.d

Resource: USENET
Discussion of the fine-art binaries. (Moderated)

Name: rec.arts.fine
Resource: USENET
Fine arts and artists.

Stained Glass

Name: Glass Arts
Resource: List
Address: `glass-request@dixie.com`
For stained/hot glass artists.

Support

Name: art-support
Resource: List
Address: `art-support@newcastle.ac.uk`
A discussion list for all persons (creators, teachers, and fans) supporting the arts.

Visual

Name: artcrit
Resource: LISTSERV
Address: `artcrit@vm1.yorku.ca`
Devoted to the exchange of information about and critical examination of the visual arts.

Automotive

Antique

Name: alt.autos.antique
Resource: USENET
Discussion of all facets of older automobiles.

Name: rec.autos.antique
Resource: USENET
Discussing all aspects of automobiles over 25 years old.

Audi

Name: quattro
Resource: List
Address:
quattro-request@aries.east.sun.com
To discuss Audi cars, and especially the AWD quattro models.

Auto Racing

Name: wheel-to-wheel
Resource: List
Address:
wheeltowheel-request@abingdon.Eng.Sun.COM
For people interested in participation in auto racing as driver, worker, or crew.

BMW

Name: BMW
Resource: List
Address: BMW@balltown.cma.com
A general discussion about BMW-manufactured automobiles. Subscriptions should be directed to bmw-request@balltown.cms.com.

British

Name: British-Cars
Resource: List
Address: British-Cars@autox.team.net
For anyone who wants to discuss any aspect of British-made cars.

Camaros and Firebirds

Name: f-body
Resource: List
Address: f-body@rwsys.lonestar.org
A discussion group for those who own or just appreciate Camaros or Firebirds. Send subscriptions to f-body-request@rwsys.lonestar.org.

Classic

Name: autos-l
Resource: LISTSERV
Address: autos-l@tritu.bitnet
This list is for anyone who owns or appreciates classic and sports cars.

Competitions

Name: rec.autos.sport
Resource: USENET
Discussion of organized, legal auto competitions.

Corvette

Name: VetteNet
Resource: LISTSERV
Address: LISTSERV@ASUVM.INRE.ASU.EDU
This list is for Corvette owners and enthusiasts to share their car ideas and experiences.

Datsun

Name: Datsun-Roadsters
Resource: List
Address:
Datsun-Roadsters@autox.team.net
For anyone interested in discussing Datsun roadsters. Send subscription requests to
datsun-roadsters-request@autox.team.net.

Dodge Stealth

Name: Stealth
Resource: List
Address:

Stealth%jim.uucp@wupost.wustl.edu
A discussion group for persons
interested in the Dodge Stealth or
Mitsubishi automobiles. Send your
subscriptions to
stealth-request%jim.uucp@wupost.wustl.edu.

Electric

Name: Electric Vehicles
Resource: LISTSERV
Address: listserv@sjsuvm1.sjsu.edu
General list for discussion of all
aspects of electric vehicles.

Exotic

Name: exotic-cars
Resource: List
Address:

exotic-cars@sol.asl.hitachi.com
For anyone involved with exotic cars.
Send your subscription requests to
exotic-cars-request@sol.asl.hitachi.com.

Ford

Name: Fordnatics
Resource: List
Address:

fordnatics-request@freud.arc.nasa.gov or
fords-request@freud.arc.nasa.gov
An unmoderated forum for discussing high-performance Fords or
Ford-powered vehicles, especially
modifications and driving techniques
for competition or track use.

Name: mustangs
Resource: List
Address: mustangs-request@cup.hp.com
To discuss/share technical issues,
problems, solutions, and modifica-
tions relating to late model (~1980+)
Ford Mustangs.

Name: thunderbird
Resource: List
Address: htunca@ncsa.uiuc.edu
The purpose of the group is to discuss
all aspects of the Ford Thunderbird
automobiles.

General

Name: cars-l
Resource: LISTSERV
Address: cars-l@saupm00.bitnet
This is a general discussion forum
about cars.

High Performance Driving

Name: school
Resource: List
Address:

school-request@balltown.cma.com
Discussion of high-performance
driving schools.

Honda

Name: honda-l
Resource: LISTSERV
Address: honda-l@brownvm.brown.edu
This list is dedicated to the discussion
of Honda automobiles.

Name: info-honda
Resource: List
Address:

info-honda-request@cs.ucla.edu

Discussion of Honda and Acura automobiles.

Hot Rods

Name: alt.autos.rod-n-custom
Resource: USENET
Vehicles with modified engines and/or appearance.

Name: hotrod
Resource: List
Address: `hotrod-request@dixie.com`
Include on the subject line the keyword `subscribe` and a return path to your site.
Provides a forum for people interested in high-performance vehicles to exchange ideas and discuss topics of current interest.

International Harvester

Name: International Harvester
Resource: List
Address: `ihc-request@balltown.cma.com`
Discussion of Scouts, pickups, and so on.

Italian

Name: italian-cars
Resource: List
Address:
`italian-cars-request@balltown.cma.com`
Discussion of Italian-made automobiles. Both regular and digest forms are available.

Kit Cars

Name: kitcar
Resource: List

Address: `kitcar-request@cs.usask.ca`
To discuss purchasing, building, driving, and anything else to do with kit cars.

Lotus

Name: lotus-cars
Resource: List
Address:
`lotus-cars-request@netcom.com`
Discussion of road and race cars designed and built by Colin Chapman and/or Lotus Cars Ltd.

Mazda

Name: mazda-list
Resource: List
Address:
`mazda-list-request@ms.uky.edu`
Technical correspondance and discussion of Mazda-designed vehicles.

Name: miata
Resource: List
Address:
`miata-request@jhunix.hcf.jhu.edu`
A list to discuss all aspects of the Mazda Miata.

Name: RX7Net Email Club
Resource: List
Address: `rx7club@cbjjn.att.com`
An e-mail list of members who own Mazda RX7's or who are interested in gaining technical or general information about RX7's.

Miscellaneous

Name: rec.autos
Resource: USENET
Automobiles, automotive products, and laws.

Name: rec.autos.driving
Resource: USENET
Driving automobiles.

Name: rec.autos.tech
Resource: USENET
Technical aspects of automobiles, and so on.

Nissan

Name: nissan
Resource: List
Address: nissan-request@world.std.com
(Rich Siegel)
Devoted to discussion of the Nissan and Infiniti cars, with the exception of the Sentra SE-R, NX2000, and G20, which are served by the se-r list.

Name: se-r
Resource: List
Address: se-r-request@world.std.com
(Rich Siegel)
Devoted to discussion of the Nissan Sentra SE-R, NX2000, and Infiniti G20 cars.

Name: Z-cars
Resource: List
Address: z-car-request@dixie.com
(John De Armond)
The Z-car mailing list operates for the benefit of those interested in Datsun/ Nissan Z cars.

Offroad

Name: offroad
Resource: List
Address:
offroad-request@ai.gtri.gatech.edu
(Stefan Roth)
To discuss and share experiences about 4X4 and offroad adventures, driving tips, vehicle modifications and anything else related to four wheeling.

Porsche

Name: porschephiles
Resource: List
Address:
porschephiles-request@tta.com
This list is for people who own, operate, work on, or simply lust after various models and years of Porsche automobiles.

Racing

Name: autorace
Resource: LISTSERV
Address: autorace@vtvm1.bitnet
A general discussion list about automobile racing—located in Indianapolis, the home of auto racing.

Name: autox
Resource: List
Address: autox-request@autox.team.net
autox-request@hoosier.cs.utah.edu
Discussion of autocrossing, SCCA Solo events. Also available as a digest.

Sound Systems

Name: rec.audio.car
Resource: USENET
Discussions of automobile audio systems.

Sports Cars

Name: nwu-sports
Resource: List
Address: `nwu-sports-request@tssi.com`

Stealth

Name: Dodge Stealth/Mitsubishi 3000GT
Resource: List
Address:
`stealth-request%jim.uucp@wupost.wustl.edu`
Discussion of anything related to these cars.

Talon-Eclipse-Laser

Name: Talon-Eclipse-Laser
Resource: List
Address: `todd@di.com` (Todd Day)
For owners and admirers of Talon, Eclipse, or Laser automobiles.

Toyota

Name: mr2-interest
Resource: List
Address:
`mr2-interest-request@validgh.com`
Discussion of Toyota MR2s, old and new.

Name: toyota
Resource: List
Address: `toyota-request@quack.kfu.com`
The charter of the list is for the discussion on almost any subject to owners and prospective owners of all models of Toyota consumer passenger vehicles and light trucks.

Name: Toyota Corolla
Resource: List
Address: `corolla-request@mcs.com`
Discussion of Toyota Corollas, including model years from 1970 on, all engines, and the Chevy Nova and Geo Prizm twins.

Volvo

Name: Volvo
Resource: List
Address:
`swedishbricks-request@me.rochester.edu`
A meeting place for Volvo automotive enthusiasts around the world.

VW

Name: rec.autos.vw
Resource: USENET
Issues pertaining to Volkswagen products.

Name: vintagevw
Resource: List
Address: `vintagevw@rocky.er.usgs.gov`
For anyone interested in vintage VW cars.

Commercial

1-900 Phone Numbers

Name: 900#
Resource: List
Address: bb17597@ritvax.isc.rit.edu
The 900# mailing list is to discuss issues in running a 900 telephone number business. Membership restricted to 900# information providers.

Computer Services

Name: biz.comp.services
Resource: USENET
Generic commercial service postings.

Computer Vendors

Name: scoann
Resource: List
Address: scoann-request@xenitec.on.ca
A moderated announcements list providing product update and new product announcements supplied by SCO or by developers offering SCO-based products.

Name: scogen
Resource: List
Address: scogen-request@xenitec.on.ca
A group for anyone interested or currently using Santa Cruz Operation products.

Consumer

Name: misc.consumers
Resource: USENET
Consumer interests, product reviews, and so on.

Deming, W. Edwards

Name: deming-l
Resource: LISTSERV
Address: deming-l@uhccvm.bitnet
This forum is for the exchange of ideas and research about the late W. Edwards Deming, the man who almost single-handedly rebuilt Japan's business economy after World War II.

Entrepreneurial

Name: Software Entrepreneurs
Resource: List
Address:
softpub-request%toolz.uucp@mathcs.emory.edu
A completely open forum devoted to the interests of entrepreneurial software publishing, including (but not limited to) shareware.

Ethics

Name: buseth-l
Resource: LISTSERV
Address: buseth-l@ubvm.cc.buffalo.edu
This list exchanges viewpoints about business ethics.

Finance

Name: finance
Resource: LISTSERV
Address: finance@templevm.bitnet
The electronic journal of finance.

Name: misc.invest
Resource: USENET
Investments and the handling of money.

Homeowners

Name: misc.consumers.house
Resource: USENET
Discussion about owning and maintaining a house.

Miscellaneous

Name: alt.business.multi-level
Resource: USENET
Multilevel (network) marketing businesses.

Real Estate

Name: Commercial Real Estate
Resource: List
Address:
commercial.realestate@data-base.com
Users can send and receive listings on property for sale, ask and answer questions, send press releases, receive editorial material, and do networking on commercial property.

Stock Market

Name: Stock Market Secrets
Resource: List
Address: smi-request@world.std.com
Answers questions on a wide variety of investment and financial topics. This list is moderated in order to keep confidential information.

Computers

3D

Name: catia-l
Resource: LISTSERV

Address: catia-l@suvm.bitnet
For everyone interested in supporting or developing computer-aided three-dimensional interactive applications.

Academic

Name: FASE
Resource: List
Address: fase@cs.uh.edu
FASE (Forum for Academic Software Engineering) provides a forum for communication among academic educators who teach software engineering.

Amiga

Name: Commodore-Amiga
Resource: List
Address: subscribe@xamiga.linet.org
For Commodore Amiga computer users.

Name:
comp.sys.amiga.applications
Resource: USENET
Miscellaneous applications.

Name: comp.sys.amiga.audio
Resource: USENET
Music, MIDI, speech synthesis, and other sounds.

Name: comp.sys.amiga.datacomm
Resource: USENET
Methods of getting bytes in and out.

Name:
comp.sys.amiga.introduction
Resource: USENET
Group for newcomers to Amigas.

Name: comp.sys.amiga.misc
Resource: USENET
Discussions not falling in another Amiga group.

Name:
comp.sys.amiga.programmer
Resource: USENET
Developers and hobbyists discuss code.

Name: CSAA
Resource: List
Address:
announce-request@cs.ucdavis.edu
This mailing list was created for those who have no access to USENET.

Name: i-amiga
Resource: LISTSERV
Address: i-amiga@rutgers.edu
For all users and developers of the Amiga computer.

Apollo

Name: comp.sys.apollo
Resource: USENET
Apollo computer systems.

Apple

Name: apple2-l
Resource: LISTSERV
Address: apple2-l@brownvm.brown.edu
For all users and developers of the Apple II computer.

Name: comp.protocols.appletalk
Resource: USENET
Applebus hardware and software.

Name: comp.sys.apple2
Resource: USENET
Discussion about Apple II micros.

Name: comp.sys.mac.advocacy
Resource: USENET
The Macintosh computer family compared to others.

Name: comp.sys.mac.apps
Resource: USENET
Discussions of Macintosh applications.

Name: comp.sys.mac.comm
Resource: USENET
Discussion of Macintosh communications.

Name: comp.sys.mac.games
Resource: USENET
Discussions of games on the Macintosh.

Name: comp.sys.mac.hardware
Resource: USENET
Macintosh hardware issues & discussions.

Name: comp.sys.mac.misc
Resource: USENET
General discussions about the Apple Macintosh.

Name: comp.sys.mac.oop.tcl
Resource: USENET
Symantec's THINK Class Library for object programming.

Name: comp.sys.mac.programmer
Resource: USENET
Discussion by people programming for the Macintosh.

Name: comp.sys.mac.scitech
Resource: USENET
Using the Macintosh in scientific and technological work.

Name: comp.sys.mac.system
Resource: USENET
Discussions of Macintosh system
software.

Name: comp.sys.mac.wanted
Resource: USENET
Postings of "I want XYZ for my Mac."

Name: info-apple
Resource: List
Address: `info-apple@brl.mil`
For users and enthusiasts of the
Apple Computer.

Name: mac-l
Resource: LISTSERV
Address: `mac-l@yalevm.ycc.yale.edu`
A forum to share and distribute
Macintosh news and information.

Name: mac-security
Resource: List
Address: `mac-security@eclectic.com`
For persons interested in sharing
information about security related to
the Macintosh computer.

Name: macappli
Resource: LISTSERV
Address:
`macappli@dartcms1.dartmouth.edu`
This list distributes usage tips about
Macintosh applications.

Name: macmail
Resource: LISTSERV
Address: `macmail@utoronto.bitnet`
For users and supporters of
Macintosh mail systems.

Name: macnet-l
Resource: LISTSERV
Address: `macnet-l@yalevm.ycc.yale.edu`
For those interested in networking
Macintosh computers.

Name: macpb-l
Resource: LISTSERV
Address: `macpb-l@yalevm.ycc.yale.edu`
A discussion list for users of the
Apple Powerbook.

Name: macprog
Resource: LISTSERV
Address: `macprog@wuvmd.bitnet`
For everyone interested in program-
ming on the Macintosh computer.

Name: macsystm
Resource: LISTSERV
Address:
`macsystm@dartcms1.dartmouth.edu`
Devoted to the discussion and
support of Macintosh system soft-
ware.

Name:
misc.forsale.computers.mac
Resource: USENET
Apple Macintosh-related computer
items.

Name: sys7-l
Resource: LISTSERV
Address: `sys7-l@uafsysb.uark.edu`
A list specifically for the discussion of
Macintosh System 7.0.

Name: TopSoft
Resource: List
Address:
`ts-request@atlas.chem.utah.edu`
TopSoft is a world-wide network
Macintosh Programming User Group
developing high-quality free soft-
ware.

Applications

Name: allin1-l
Resource: LISTSERV
Address: `allin1-l@ccvm.sunysb.edu`
Discussion group focusing on the software product All-in-1.

Name: apE-info
Resource: List
Address:
`apE-info-request@ferkel.ucsb.edu`
Discussion of the scientific visualization software package apE.

Name: biosym
Resource: List
Address:
`dibug-request@comp.bioz.unibas.ch`
For users of Biosym Technologies software.

Name: clipper
Resource: LISTSERV
Address: `clipper@brufpb.bitnet`
This list is for exchange of information and support of the Clipper DBMS.

Name: comp.os.msdos.pcgeos
Resource: USENET
GeoWorks PC/GEOS and PC/GEOS-based packages.

Name:
comp.os.msdos.programmer
Resource: USENET
Programming MS-DOS machines.

Name: comp.soft-sys.matlab
Resource: USENET
The MathWorks calculation and visualization package.

Name: comp.text.interleaf
Resource: USENET
Applications and use of Interleaf software.

Name: emtex-user
Resource: List
Address: `emtex@chemie.fu-berlin.de`
Information about emTeX, an implementation of TeX for MS-DOS and OS/2.

Name: Igor
Resource: List
Address: `igor-request@pica.army.mil`
To provide an easy means for users of Igor to share problems and solutions, as well as for potential users to seek opinions on the utility and performance of the application.

Name: Imagine
Resource: List
Address:
`imagine-request@email.sp.paramax.com`
The IML is dedicated to the 3D computer rendering package "Imagine" by Impulse Inc. Note that BANG STYLE addressing is not supported, so you must include your Internet-style address in subscription request (e.g. `somebody@someplace.edu`).

Name: improv
Resource: List
Address: `improv-request@bmt.gun.com`
Questions, comments, and bug-reports relating to the Improv spreadsheet for NeXTSTEP and Windows, published by Lotus Corporation.

Name: info-ingres
Resource: List
Address:
`info-ingres-request@math.ams.com`
To discuss the commercial version of Ingres.

Name: Info-LabVIEW
Resource: List
Address:
`info-labview-request@pica.army.mil`
Info-LabVIEW is an Internet mailing list for the discussion of the use of National Instrument's LabVIEW package for Macintosh, Windows, and Sparcstation environments.

Name: metacard-list
Resource: LISTSERV
Address: `listserv@grot.starconn.com`
Discussion of the MetaCard product from MetaCard Corporation.

Name: nqthm-users
Resource: List
Address: `nqthm-users-request@cli.com`
`nqthm-users-request@inf.fu-berlin.de`
Discussion of theorem proving using the Boyler-Moore theorem prover, NQTHM.

Name: QuadraVerb
Resource: List
Address: `qv-request@swap.eng.sun.com`
This list is for discussion of matters pertaining to Alesis QuadraVerb and QuadraVerb+. Archives available.

Name: simedu-l
Resource: LISTSERV
Address: `simedu-l@nmsuvm1.bitnet`
A discussion list regarding modeling and simulation applications in business and education.

Name: wpcorp-l
Resource: LISTSERV
Address: `wpcorp-l@ubvm.cc.buffalo.edu`
All WordPerfect Corporation products are fair game in this discussion list.

Artificial Intelligence

Name: comp.ai
Resource: USENET
Artificial intelligence discussions.

Name: comp.ai.shells
Resource: USENET
Artificial intelligence applied to shells.

Name: nl-kr
Resource: List
Address: `nl-kr@db0tui11.bitnet`
This list is devoted to the interpretation and creation of natural language processing in artificial intelligence (AI). Send administrative information to `nl-kr-request@db0tui11.bitnet`.

Artificial Life

Name: ailife
Resource: List
Address: `ailife@cognet.ucla.edu`
Devoted to the study and information exchange about artificial life.

Name: alife
Resource: List
Address:
`alife-request@cognet.ucla.edu`
The alife mailing list is for communications regarding artificial life, a formative interdisciplinary field involving computer science, the natural sciences, mathematics, medicine, and others.

Name: The Observer
Resource: List
Address: `rwhit@cs.umu.se`
The central scope of the group covers the theory of autopoiesis and enactive cognitive science.

AS/400

Name: as400-l
Resource: LISTSERV
Address: `as400-l@pccvm.bitnet`
A discussion forum on the use and support of IBM AS/400 computer systems.

AT&T

Name: comp.sys.att
Resource: USENET
Discussions about AT&T microcomputers.

Name: starserver
Resource: List
Address:
`starserver-request@engr.uky.edu`
This mailing list is intended for owners, operators, and administrators of AT&T StarServer systems.

Atari

Name: comp.sys.atari.st
Resource: USENET
Discussion about 16-bit Atari micros.

BBS

Name: alt.bbs
Resource: USENET
Computer BBS systems and software.

Name: alt.bbs.lists
Resource: USENET
Postings of regional BBS listings.

Name: alt.bbs.unixbbs
Resource: USENET
Discussion of UnixBBS from Nervous XTC.

Name: bbs-l
Resource: LISTSERV
Address: `bbs-l@saupm00.bitnet`
This discussion forum is about BBSs, including creation, usage, and support.

Name: comp.bbs.misc
Resource: USENET
All aspects of computer bulletin board systems.

Name: comp.bbs.waffle
Resource: USENET
The Waffle BBS and USENET system on all platforms.

Name: Excelsior!
Resource: List
Address: `subscribe@xamiga.linet.org`
For users of the Amiga Excelsior! BBS system.

Benchmarking

Name: comp.benchmarks
Resource: USENET
Discussion of benchmarking techniques and results.

CAD/CAM

Name: cadam-l
Resource: LISTSERV
Address: `cadam-l@suvm.bitnet`
This list discusses and exchanges information about CAD/CAM (computer-aided design and manufacturing).

Name: cadlist
Resource: LISTSERV
Address: `cadlist@suvm.bitnet`
A general list devoted to CAD (computer-aided design).

Name: comp.lsi.cad
Resource: USENET
Electrical computer-aided design.

Name: gug-sysadmins
Resource: List
Address:
gug-sysadmins-request@vlsivie.tuwien.ac.at
Distributions of rumors, bugfixes, and
work-arounds concerning the
CAD-Tool genesil and related tools to
members of the Eurochip project and
other interested parties.

Name: intergraph
Resource: List
Address: nik@ingr.ingr.com
Discussion of all Intergraph
CADCAM software and hardware.

Name: tcad
Resource: List
Address: tcad-request@iec.ufl.edu
This mailing list has been set up to
serve the needs of users and software
developers of technology computer-
aided design (TCAD) codes.

CASE

Name: case-l
Resource: LISTSERV
Address: case-l@uccvma.bitnet
CASE (computer-aided software
engineering) is the primary focus of
this discussion group.

CD-ROM

Name: alt.cd-rom
Resource: USENET
Discussions of optical storage media.

Name: Amiga CDROM
Resource: List

Address: cdrom-list-request@ben.com
For Amigans who use or are interested in CDROM drives and discs.

Name:
comp.publish.cdrom.hardware
Resource: USENET
Hardware used in publishing with
CD-ROM.

Name:
comp.publish.cdrom.software
Resource: USENET
Software used in publishing with
CD-ROM.

Name:
comp.sys.ibm.pc.hardware.cd-rom
Resource: USENET
CD-ROM drives and interfaces for
the PC.

Name: PHOTO-CD
Resource: LISTSERV
Address: listmgr@info.kodak.com
(Don Cox)
The KODAK Photo-CD Mailing List
provides libraries of information on
KODAK CD products or technology
and closely related products. To
subscribe, send mail to
listserv@info.kodak.com with the
command SUBSCRIBE PHOTO-CD <First
Name> <Last Name> on a line by itself in
the body (and no other text).

CICS

Name: cics-l
Resource: LISTSERV
Address: cics-l@uga.cc.uga.edu
A discussion list created to exchange
information and tips about the use
and support of IBM's CICS software
product.

Commodore

Name: commodor
Resource: LISTSERV
Address: `commodor@ubvm.cc.buffalo.edu`
This discussion group is for all users, developers, and supporters of the Commodore computer system.

Communications

Name: comp.dcom.modems
Resource: USENET
Data communications hardware and software.

Compatibility

Name: Emplant
Resource: List
Address: `subscribe@xamiga.linet.org`
Discussion of the Emplant Macintosh Hardware Emulator. Send subscription requests to
`subscribe@xamiga.linet.org` using the format: `#emplant username@domain;`.

Compiler Design

Name: comp.compilers
Resource: USENET
Compiler construction, theory, and so on. (Moderated)

Compression

Name: comp.compression
Resource: USENET
Data compression algorithms and theory.

Name:
comp.compression.research
Resource: USENET
Discussions about data compression research. (Moderated)

Cryptography

Name: crypto-l
Resource: LISTSERV
Address: `crypto-l@jpntuvm0.bitnet`
This forum discusses cryptography, exchanges information about ongoing research, and distributes information on related mathematics. Send subscription requests to
`info-pgp-request@lucpul.it.luc.edu`.

Name: Info-PGP
Resource: List
Address: `info-pgp@lucpul.it.luc.edu`
Devoted to the discussion of the public-key encryption software package PGP.

Name: Info-PGP
Resource: List
Address:
`info-pgp-request@lucpul.it.luc.edu`
Discussion of Phil Zimmerman & Co.'s Pretty Good Privacy (PGP) public key encrption program for MS-DOS, UNIX, SPARC, VMS, Atari, Amiga, and other platforms.

Name: rsaref-users
Resource: List
Address: `rsaref-users@rsa.com`
For persons interested in all aspects of public key encryption, including how it relates to sending and receiving electronic mail. Send subscription requests to
`rsaref-users-request@rsa.com`.

Name: sci.crypt
Resource: USENET
Different methods of data encryption and decryption.

Name: talk.politics.crypto
Resource: USENET
The relation between cryptography and government.

Cyberlife

Name: alt.cyberpunk
Resource: USENET
High-tech low-life.

Cybernetics

Name: cybsys-l
Resource: LISTSERV
Address: `cybsys-l@bingvmb.bitnet`
This list is for the discussion and exchange of ideas and research about cybernetics and systems.

Cyberspace

Name: cyber-l
Resource: LISTSERV
Address: `cyber-l@marist.bitnet`
Devoted to the cyberspace phenomenon.

Name: ejvc-l
Resource: LISTSERV
Address: `ejvc-l@kentvm.bitnet`
This list is the electronic journal on Virtual Culture.

Name: virtu-l
Resource: LISTSERV

Address: `virtu-l@vmd.cso.uiuc.edu`
This list is a gateway to the USENET group sci.virtual-worlds and is devoted to a discussion of virtual reality worlds.

Name: vrapp-l
Resource: LISTSERV
Address: `vrapp-l@vmd.cso.uiuc.edu`
This list is gatewayed to the USENET group sci.virtual-worlds.apps and is for the exchange of information about virtual reality applications.

Data General

Name: dg-users
Resource: List
Address:
`dg-users-request@ilinx.wimsey.com`
The mailing list is concerned with the technical details of Data General, its O/Ss, and the cornicopia of hardware they supply and support.

Databases

Name: access-l
Resource: LISTSERV
Address: `access-l@indycms.iupui.edu`
A discussion list for all users, developers, and supporters of the Microsoft Access DBMS product.

Name: big-DB
Resource: List
Address: `big-DB@midway.uchicago.EDU`
`(Fareed Asad-Harooni)`
Discussions pertaining to large databases (generally greater than 1 million records) and large database management systems such as IMS, DB2, and CCA's Model/204.

Name: comp.databases
Resource: USENET
Database and data management issues and theory.

Name: comp.databases.object
Resource: USENET
Object-oriented paradigms in database systems.

Name: comp.databases.sybase
Resource: USENET
Implementations of the SQL Server.

Name: db2-l
Resource: LISTSERV
Address: `db2-l@auvm.bitnet`
A discussion list about IBM's DB2 database software product.

Name: dbase-l
Resource: LISTSERV
Address: `dbase-l@nmsuvm1.bitnet`
For everyone involved with the Borland dBASE software product.

Name: FOXPRO-L
Resource: List
Address:
`FILESERV@POLARBEAR.RANKIN-INLET.NT.CA`
The FOXPRO-L mailing list is designed to foster information sharing between users of the FoxPro database development environment now owned and distributed by Microsoft.

Name: foxpro-l
Resource: LISTSERV
Address: `foxpro-l@ukanvm.bitnet`
For the exchange of information, tips, design advice, and just about anything affiliated with the FoxPro DBMS. Send your subscription request to
`ms-access-request@eunet.co.at.`

Name: ms-access
Resource: List
Address: `ms-access@eunet.co.at`
This is an open list for the purpose of discussing and exchanging information about Microsoft's Access DBMS.

Name: MS-Access
Resource: List
Address:
`MS-ACCESS-REQUEST@EUNET.CO.AT`
(Martin Hilger)
An unmoderated list for MS Access topics, including Access Basic questions, reviews, rumors, and so on.

Name: oracle-l
Resource: LISTSERV
Address: `oracle-l@sbccvm.bitnet`
The Oracle DBMS software product is the primary focus of this discussion group.

Name: paradox
Resource: LISTSERV
Address: `paradox@brufpb.bitnet`
This list is for all Borland Paradox users.

Name: Progress
Resource: List
Address:
`Progress-list-request@math.niu.edu`
Discussion of the Progress RDBMS.

Name: scribe
Resource: List
Address:
`scribe-hacks-request@decwrl.dec.com`
Discussions about Scribe features, bugs, enhancements, performance, support, and other topics of interest to Scribe DBAs.

Name: SQL-sybase
Resource: List
Address: `sybase-request@apple.com`
This is a semi-unmoderated mailing list for sharing information about the Sybase SQL server and related products.

Name: sybase-l
Resource: LISTSERV
Address: `sybase-l@ucsbvm.bitnet`
A discussion list for those using Sybase products on various platforms.

Name: UUG-dist
Resource: List
Address: `uug-dist-request@dsi.com`
(Syd Weinstein)
Discussion of Unify Corporation's database products, including Unify, Accell/IDS, Accell/SQl and Accell/ "generic database engine."

DEC

Name: alt.sys.pdp8
Resource: USENET
A great old machine.

Name: comp.sys.dec
Resource: USENET
Discussions about DEC computer systems.

Name: vmsnet.misc
Resource: USENET
General VMS topics not covered elsewhere.

Decision Support

Name: Forest Management DSS
Resource: LISTSERV

Address: `listserv@pnfi.forestry.ca`
(Tom Moore)
The discussion group is a forum for rapid exchange of information, ideas, and opinions related to the topics of decision support systems and information systems for forest management planning. To subscribe, send an e-mail to `listserv@pnfi.forestry.ca` with the message `SUBSCRIBE FMDSS-L` `<First Name> <Last Name>`.

Desktop Publishing

Name: alt.aldus.pagemaker
Resource: USENET
Discussions about the use of Aldus PageMaker.

Name: bit.listserv.pagemakr
Resource: USENET
Discussions of Aldus PageMaker for desktop publishers.

Name: comp.lang.postscript
Resource: USENET
The PostScript Page Description Language.

Name: comp.text.frame
Resource: USENET
Desktop publishing with FrameMaker.

Name: framers
Resource: List
Address: `framers-request@uunet.uu.net`
(Mark Lawrence)
Framers is a user forum for sharing of experiences and information about the FrameMaker desktop publishing package from Frame Technology.

Name: Lout
Resource: List
Address: `lout-request@cs.brown.edu`
Discussion of the Basser Lout typesetting document preparation software available by anonymous ftp at `ftp.cs.su.oz.au: jeff/lout.2.05.tar.Z`. To subscribe, send mail to `lout-request@cs.brown.edu` with `subscribe` in the subject line.

Name: PAGEMAKR
Resource: LISTSERV
Address: `gwp@cs.purdue.edu` (Geoff Peters)
The PageMaker listserv is dedicated to the discussion of Desktop Publishing in general, with emphasis on the use of Aldus PageMaker.

Name: pagemakr
Resource: LISTSERV
Address: `pagemakr@indycms.iupui.edu`
A discussion list devoted to PageMaker.

Digital Video

Name: DVI-List
Resource: List
Address: `DVI-List@calvin.dgbt.doc.ca`
For discussions, tips, and techniques for using Intel's DVI (Digital Video Interactive) product.

Distributed Processing

Name: pdppl
Resource: LISTSERV
Address: `pdppl@plwrtu11.bitnet`
The emerging technologies of parallel and distributed processing are discussed and researched here.

E-Mail

Name: bbones
Resource: List
Address: `mail-bbones-request@yorku.ca`
A list discussing the construction of mail backbones for organizations and campuses.

Name: ccmail-l
Resource: LISTSERV
Address: `ccmail-l@vm1.ucc.okstate.edu`
A group to discuss ideas, tips, and support of the cc:mail software product.

Name: comp.mail.elm
Resource: USENET
Discussion and fixes for the ELM mail system.

Name: comp.mail.mh
Resource: USENET
The UCI version of the Rand Message Handling system.

Name: comp.mail.misc
Resource: USENET
General discussions about computer mail.

Name: info.ph
Resource: USENET
Qi, ph, sendmail/phquery discussions (`info-ph@uxc.cso.uiuc.edu`). (Moderated)

Name: smail3-users
Resource: List
Address:
`smail3-users-request@cs.athabascau.ca`
(Lyndon Nerenberg)
The smail3-users mailing list is targeted towards those who administer smail3.X based mailers.

Name: smail3-wizards
Resource: List
Address:
smail3-wizards-request@cs.athabascau.ca
(Lyndon Nerenberg)
Smail3-wizards is a discussion forum for people who are actively porting, debugging, and extending smail3.X.

EDI

Name: edi-l
Resource: LISTSERV
Address:
edi-l@uccvma.bitnet@vm1.nodak.edu
Devoted to the exchange of information about the burgeoning EDI industry.

Editors

Name: alt.religion.emacs
Resource: USENET
Discussions of EMACS.

Name: comp.editors
Resource: USENET
Topics related to computerized text editing.

Name: comp.emacs
Resource: USENET
EMACS editors of different flavors.

Name: NotGNU
Resource: List
Address: notgnu-request@netcom.com
An interactive list dedicated to miscellaneous discussions, problems, suggestions for NotGNU.

Name: sam-fans
Resource: List
Address:
sam-fans-request@hawkwind.utcs.toronto.edu
(Chris Siebenmann)
Discussion of Rob Pike's sam editor.

Education

Name: appl-l
Resource: LISTSERV
Address: appl-l@pltumk11.bitnet
For users, developers, and supporters of computer applications in science and education.

Name: DECnews-EDU
Resource: LISTSERV
Address: decnews@mr4dec.enet.dec.com
(Anne Marie McDonald)
A monthly electronic publication from Digital Equipment Corporation's Education Business Unit for the education and research communities worldwide. To subscribe, send a message to
LISTSERV@ubvm.cc.buffalo.edu or
LISTSERV@ubvm.bitnet. The message should be SUB DECNEWS <First Name> <Last Name>.

Embedded Systems

Name: Embedded Digest
Resource: List
Address: embed-request@synchro.com
(Chuck Cox)
A forum for the discussion of embedded computer system engineering.

Engineering

Name: caeds-l
Resource: LISTSERV
Address: `caeds-l@suvm.bitnet`
A discussion list about
computer-aided engineering design.

Ethics

Name: ethcse-l
Resource: LISTSERV
Address: `ethcse-l@utkvm1.bitnet`
A forum for the exchange of ideas
about ethical issues in software
engineering.

Name: ethics-l
Resource: LISTSERV
Address: `ethics-l@uga.cc.uga.edu`
A discussion list for the exchange of
ideas and opinions about ethics in
computing.

Fault-tolerant

Name: info-stratus
Resource: List
Address:
`Info-Stratus-Request@mike.lrc.edu`
(Richard Shuford)
A user-centered and user-conducted
forum for discussing the fault-tolerant
machines produced by Stratus
Computer Corporation, as well as
their cousins, the IBM System/88 and
Olivetti CPS-32.

Fax

Name: alt.fax
Resource: USENET
Like comp.dcom.fax, only different.

Name: comp.dcom.fax
Resource: USENET
Fax hardware, software, and proto-
cols.

File Formats

Name: ODA
Resource: List
Address: `utzoo!trigraph!oda-request`
(Les Gondor)
ODA is a mailing list for topics
related to the ISO 8613 standard for
Office Document Architecture, and
ODIF (Office Document Interchange
Format).

Name: sci.data.formats
Resource: USENET
Modelling, storage, and retrieval of
scientific data.

File Protocols

Name: alt.comp.fsp
Resource: USENET
A file transport protocol.

File Servers

Name: Epoch Users Forum
Resource: List
Address: `epuf-request@mcs.anl.gov`
An ideas exchange mechanism for
users of Epoch file servers.

Files-Compression

Resource: FTP
Address: `ftp.cso.uiuc.edu`
Directory: doc/pcnet/compression

Flight Simulators

Name: flight-sim
Resource: List
Address: `flight-sim@grove.iup.edu`
An open list for flight simulator
enthusiasts and designers.

Fonts

Name: comp.fonts
Resource: USENET
Discussions of type fonts: design,
conversion, use, and so on.

Fractals

Name: frac-l
Resource: LISTSERV
Address: `frac-l@gitvm1.bitnet`
A discussion list about fractals, image
processing, and related graphics and
mathematics.

Name: sci.fractals
Resource: USENET
Objects of nonintegral dimension and
other chaos.

Future

Name: cfcp-members
Resource: List
Address: `mlindsey@nyx.cs.du.edu`
A group of Internet users who are
interested enough in various fields of
computers to consider them as their
future.

Fuzzy Logic

Name: comp.ai.fuzzy
Resource: USENET
Fuzzy set theory, a.k.a. fuzzy logic.

Name: fuzzy-mail
Resource: LISTSERV
Address:
`listserver@vexpert.dbai.tuwien.ac.at`
Discussion of fuzzy logic and fuzzy
sets. (Moderated)

Name: nafips-l
Resource: LISTSERV
Address: `nafips-l@gsuvm1.bitnet`
A list devoted to the exchange of
information and research about the
emerging technology known as
"fuzzy logic." To subscribe, send SUB
FUZZY-MAIL <Full Name> in the body of
an otherwise empty mail to
`listserver@vexpert.dbai.tuwien.ac.at`.

Games

Name: digital-games-submissions
Resource: List
Address:
`digital-games-submissions@digital-games.intuitive.com`
A list devoted to distributing reviews
of video games for all electronic
platforms. Subscription requests
should be sent to
`digital-games-request@digital-games.intuitive.com`.

Name: games-l
Resource: LISTSERV
Address: `games-l@brownvm.brown.edu`
Computer games list.

Name: tinymuck-sloggers
Resource: List
Address:
`tinymuck-sloggers-request@piggy.ucsb.edu`
(Robert Earl)
Forum for programmers, wizards,
and users of the extensible, program-
mable TinyMUD derivative known as
TinyMUCK (current version: 2.2).

Name: tinymush-programmers
Resource: List
Address:
tinymush-programmers-request@cygnus.com
Discussion devoted to the programming language integral to the TinyMUSH subfamily of mud servers.

General

Resource: FTP
Address: soda.berkeley.edu
(128.32.149.19)
Directory: pub/cypherpunks. This directory contains instructions and helper scripts for the purpose of securing communications.

Name: comp.infosystems
Resource: USENET
Any discussion about information systems.

Name: numeric-interest
Resource: List
Address:
numeric-interest-request@validgh.com
(David Hough)
Discussion of issues of floating-point correctness and performance with respect to hardware, operating systems, languages, and standard libraries.

Genetic Algorithms

Name: comp.ai.genetic
Resource: USENET
Genetic algorithms in computing.

Graphics/Image Processing

Name: alt.binaries.pictures.d
Resource: USENET
Discussions about picture postings.

Name:
alt.binaries.pictures.fractals
Resource: USENET
It's cheaper just to send the program parameters!

Name:
alt.binaries.pictures.utilities
Resource: USENET
Posting of pictures-related utilities.

Name: alt.graphics.pixutils
Resource: USENET
Discussion of pixmap utilities.

Name: comp.graphics
Resource: USENET
Computer graphics, art, animation, and image processing.

Name: comp.graphics.opengl
Resource: USENET
The OpenGL 3D application programming interface.

Name: graph-l
Resource: LISTSERV
Address: graph-l@brufpb.bitnet
Mathematical aspects of computer graphics.

Name: image-l
Resource: LISTSERV
Address: image-l@trearn.bitnet
A discussion list for image processing and applications.

Name: iti151
Resource: List
Address: iti151-request@oce.orst.edu
(John Stanley)

`{tektronix,`
`hplabs!hp-pcd}!orstcs!oce.orst.edu!iti151-request`
For users of Imaging Technology's series 150 and 151 image processing systems and ITEX151 software.

Name: Lightwave
Resource: List
Address: `subscribe@xamiga.linet.org`
For Video Toaster users, supporting the NewTek 3D object modeler/ray tracer and hardware involved in video editing, such as time base correcters and VCR equipment. Send subscription requests to `subscribe@xamiga.linet.org` using the format `#lightwave username@domain;`.

Name: PERQ-fanatics
Resource: List
Address:
`perq-fanatics-request@alchemy.com`
For users of PERQ graphics workstations. To subscribe to the list, post a message to `perq-fanatics-request@alchemy.com`.

Name: sci.image.processing
Resource: USENET
Scientific image processing and analysis.

Groupware

Name: comp.groupware
Resource: USENET
Software and hardware for shared interactive environments.

GUIs

Name: bit.listserv.win3-l
Resource: USENET
Microsoft Windows Version 3 Forum.

Name: bx-talk
Resource: List
Address:
`bx-talk-request@qiclab.scn.rain.com`
(Darci L. Chapman)
Created for users of Builder Xcessory (BX) to discuss problems (and solutions!) and ideas for using BX.

Name:
comp.os.ms-windows.advocacy
Resource: USENET
Speculation and debate about Microsoft Windows.

Name: comp.os.ms-windows.apps
Resource: USENET
Applications in the Windows environment.

Name: comp.os.ms-windows.misc
Resource: USENET
General discussions about Windows issues.

Name:
comp.os.ms-windows.nt.misc
Resource: USENET
General discussion about Windows NT.

Name:
comp.os.ms-windows.nt.setup
Resource: USENET
Configuring Windows NT systems.

Name:
comp.os.ms-windows.programmer.misc
Resource: USENET
Programming Microsoft Windows.

Name:
comp.os.ms-windows.programmer.tools
Resource: USENET
Development tools in Windows.

Name:
comp.os.ms-windows.programmer.win32
Resource: USENET
32-bit Windows programming interfaces.

Name:
comp.os.ms-windows.setup
Resource: USENET
Installing and configuring Microsoft Windows.

Name: comp.os.msdos.desqview
Resource: USENET
QuarterDeck's Desqview and related products.

Name: comp.windows.misc
Resource: USENET
Various issues about windowing systems.

Name: comp.windows.open-look
Resource: USENET
Discussion about the Open Look GUI.

Name: comp.windows.x
Resource: USENET
Discussion about the X Window System.

Name: comp.windows.x.i386unix
Resource: USENET
Discussion of the XFree86 window system and others.

Name: comp.windows.x.intrinsics
Resource: USENET
Discussion of the X toolkit.

Name: comp.windows.x.motif
Resource: USENET
The Motif GUI for the X Window System.

Name: comp.windows.x.pex
Resource: USENET

The PHIGS extension of the X Window System.

Name: picasso-users
Resource: List
Address:
picasso-users@postgres.berkeley.edu
For users of the Picasso graphical User Interface Development System.

Name: TeleUSErs
Resource: List
Address:
TeleUSErs-request@telesoft.com
(Charlie Counts)
To promote the interchange of technical information, examples, tips, and so on, among the users of TeleUSE.

Name: TurboVision
Resource: LISTSERV
Address: listserv@vtvm1.cc.vt.edu
For TurboVision programmers (a library that comes with Borland C++ and Pascal compilers). To subscribe, send the message subscribe turbvis
<Full Name> to listserv@vtvm1.cc.vt.edu.

Name: XVT
Resource: LISTSERV
Address: tim@qedbbs.com
(Tim Capps)
Discussions of XVT, a multiplatform window environment development tool.

Hacking

Name: alt.hackers
Resource: USENET
Descriptions of projects currently under development. (Moderated)

Name: hack-l
Resource: List
Address:
`hack@alive.ersys.edmonton.ab.ca`
(Marc Slemko)
To distribute the monthly Hack Report, an informational newsletter which warns of hacked, hoax, Trojan Horse, and pirated files that have been seen posted on BBS systems worldwide. To subscribe, send the message `subscribe hack-l` to `majordomo@alive.ersys.edmonton.ab.ca`

Hardware

Name: att-pc+
Resource: List
Address: `bill@ssbn.wlk.com`
`...!{att,cs.utexas.edu,sun!daver}!ssbn!bill`
(Bill Kennedy)
For people interested in the AT&T PC 63xx series of systems.

Name: comp.lsi
Resource: USENET
Large-scale integrated circuits.

Name: comp.periphs.scsi
Resource: USENET
Discussion of SCSI-based peripheral devices.

Name: comp.sys.ibm.pc.hardware
Resource: USENET
XT/AT/EISA hardware, any vendor.

Name:
comp.sys.ibm.pc.hardware.chips
Resource: USENET
Processor, cache, memory chips, and so on.

Name:
comp.sys.ibm.pc.hardware.comm
Resource: USENET
Modems and communication cards for the PC.

Name:
comp.sys.ibm.pc.hardware.misc
Resource: USENET
Miscellaneous PC hardware topics.

Name:
comp.sys.ibm.pc.hardware.networking
Resource: USENET
Network hardware and equipment for the PC.

Name:
comp.sys.ibm.pc.hardware.storage
Resource: USENET
Hard drives and other PC storage devices.

Name:
comp.sys.ibm.pc.hardware.systems
Resource: USENET
Whole IBM PC computer and clone systems.

Name:
comp.sys.ibm.pc.hardware.video
Resource: USENET
Video cards and monitors for the PC.

Name: comp.sys.intel
Resource: USENET
Discussions about Intel systems and parts.

Name: pcbuild
Resource: LISTSERV
Address: `pcbuild@list.dsu.edu`
This is an open list for persons interested in many aspects of PC hardware, including building, upgrading, and fixing.

Health

Name: c+health
Resource: LISTSERV
Address: c+health@iubvm.bitnet
This list discusses various health effects of computer use.

HP

Name: comp.sys.hp
Resource: USENET
Discussion about Hewlett-Packard equipment.

Name: comp.sys.hp.hpux
Resource: USENET
Issues pertaining to HP-UX & 9000 series computers.

Name: HP Patch
Resource: List
Address: hpux-patch-request@cv.ruu.nl
This is the official announcement of the "HP Patch Descriptions Mailing List." To subscribe, send e-mail to hpux-patch-request@cv.ruu.nl. Be sure to include your e-mail address in the message.

Hypertext

Name: alt.hypertext
Resource: USENET
Discussion of hypertext: uses, transport, and so on.

Name: hyperbole-announce
Resource: List
Address:
hyperbole-request@cs.brown.edu
(Bob Weiner)
Use the following format on your subject line to execute requests, where you substitute your own values for

the <> delimited items (include the period at the end of the line). subject Add <firstname-lastname> '<' <user>@<domain> '>' to <mail-list-name-without-domain>.
Hyperbole is for discussion of the Hyperbole systems and the related topics of hypertext and information retrieval.

Name: hypercrd
Resource: LISTSERV
Address: hypercrd@msu.bitnet
A discussion list for persons interested in the Macintosh software product HyperCard.

Information Processing

Name: khoros
Resource: List
Address:
khoros-request@chama.eece.unm.edu
Discussions of the khoros software package, developed by Dr. Rasure, his staff, and his students at the University of New Mexico.

Interactive

Name: comp.human-factors
Resource: USENET
Issues related to human-computer interaction (HCI).

Name: DVI-list
Resource: List
Address:
dvi-list-request@calvin.dgbt.doc.ca
(Andrew Patrick)
This mailing list is intended for discussions about Intel's DVI (Digital Video Interactive) system.

Jargon

Name: jargon-helpers
Resource: List
Address:
`jargon-helpers-request@snark.thyrsus.com`
The jargon-helpers list is an e-mail reflector that supplements the ongoing public discussions of hacker jargon, net.culture, and the Jargon File on alt.folklore.computers.

Kermit

Name: kermit-l
Resource: LISTSERV
Address: `kermit-l@jpnsut30.bitnet`
A discussion list devoted to the Kermit software product.

Knowledge-based Systems

Name: sched-l
Resource: LISTSERV
Address:
`listserver@vexpert.dbai.tuwien.ac.at`
Discussion of scheduling, with special consideration of knowledge-based scheduling of manufacturing processes. To subscribe, send SUB SCHED-L <Full Name> in the body of an otherwise empty mail to
`listserver@vexpert.dbai.tuwien.ac.at`.

Languages

Name: reader
Resource: List
Address: `iskandar@u.washington.edu`
(Alex Khalil)
For the support of Arabic script (Arabic, Farsi, Urdu, Sindhi and other Pashto) on computer.

Legal Education

Name: comlaw-l
Resource: LISTSERV
Address: `comlaw-l@ualtavm.bitnet`
The use of computers and legal education.

Legal Issues

Name: misc.legal.computing
Resource: USENET
Discussing the legal climate of the computing world.

Mainframe Operations

Name: opers-l
Resource: LISTSERV
Address: `opers-l@vm1.cc.uakron.edu`
For persons involved in the operation of mainframe computers.

Materials Design

Name: mat-dsgn
Resource: LISTSERV
Address: `mat-dsgn@jpntuvm0.bitnet`
A forum for discussing computer-aided materials design.

Miscellaneous

Name: comp.misc
Resource: USENET
General topics about computers not covered elsewhere.

Modeling & Simulation

Name: Role Modeling
Resource: List
Address: `majordomo@taskon.no`
The Role Modeling mailing list is concerned with the use of roles as a concept in object-oriented systems design. To subscribe, send mail to `majordomo@taskon.no`. The body of the message should contain the line `subscribe role-modeling`.

Modems

Name: SupraFAX
Resource: List
Address: `subscribe@xamiga.linet.org` (David Tiberio)
This list was created to help people who have been having trouble using the SupraFAX v.32bis modem. To subscribe to the list, send e-mail to `subscribe@xamiga.linet.org`, with the following line in the body of the text: `#supra <User Name>@<Domain>`.

Multimedia

Name: comp.multimedia
Resource: USENET
Interactive multimedia technologies of all kinds.

Name: comp.publish.cdrom.multimedia
Resource: USENET
Software for multimedia authoring and publishing.

Name: imamedia
Resource: LISTSERV
Address: `imamedia@umdd.bitnet`
This list is for the purpose of achieving compatibility of multimedia applications.

Name: macmulti
Resource: LISTSERV
Address: `macmulti@fccj.bitnet`
A discussion list about Macintosh multimedia.

Name: mmedia-l
Resource: LISTSERV
Address: `mmedia-l@itesmvf1.bitnet`
This is a general multimedia discussion list.

Name: mmedia-l
Resource: LISTSERV
Address: `mmedia-l@icnucevm.bitnet`
A discussion list for the purpose of using multimedia in education.

Name: mmm-people
Resource: List
Address: `mmm-people@isi.edu`
A discussion list for persons interested in developing and supporting multimedia mail, including the formation of standards. Send subscription requests to `mmm-people-request@isi.edu`.

Name: toaster-list
Resource: LISTSERV
Address: `toaster-list@karazm.math.uh.edu`
For persons interested in discussing aspects of the NewTek Video Toaster.

Music

Name: comp.music
Resource: USENET
Applications of computers in music research.

Name: Smallmusic
Resource: List
Address:
smallmusic-request@xcf.berkeley.edu
(Craig Latta)
A work group has formed to discuss and develop an object-oriented software system for music.

NCR

Name: towers
Resource: List
Address: bill@wrangler.wlk.com
(Bill Kennedy)
General discussion on the subject of NCR Tower computers.

Network/Protocols

Name: POP
Resource: List
Address:
pop-request@jhunix.hcf.jhu.edu
(Andy S. Poling)
Discusses the Post Office Protocol (POP2 and POP3 - described in RFCs 918, 937, 1081, and 1082) and implementations.

Networking

Name: alt.sys.amiga.uucp
Resource: USENET
Discusses AmigaUUCP.

Name: appware-info
Resource: List
Address:
appware-info-request@serius.uchicago.edu
Provides a forum for discussion of issues related to the AppWare software. To join the list, send e-mail to

appware-info-request@serius.uchicago.edu
with the word subscribe followed by your e-mail address as the first line of the message.

Name: banyan-l
Resource: LISTSERV
Address: banyan-l@akronvm.bitnet
A discussion list for supporters of the Banyan network software system.

Name: cisco
Resource: List
Address:
cisco-request@spot.colorado.edu
(David Wood)
This list is for discussion of the network products from Cisco Systems, Inc; primarily the AGS gateway, but also the ASM terminal multiplexor and any other relevant products.

Name: commune
Resource: List
Address:
commune-request@stealth.acf.nyu.edu
(Dan Bernstein)
To discuss the COMMUNE protocol, a TELNET replacement.

Name: comp.dcom.isdn
Resource: USENET
The Integrated Services Digital Network (ISDN).

Name: comp.mail.maps
Resource: USENET
Discussions of various maps, including UUCP maps. (Moderated)

Name: comp.mail.uucp
Resource: USENET
Mail in the uucp network environment.

Name: comp.protocols.snmp
Resource: USENET
Discussions of the Simple Network Management Protocol.

Name:
comp.protocols.tcp-ip.ibmpc
Resource: USENET
TCP/IP for IBM(-like) personal computers.

Name: comp.protocols.time.ntp
Resource: USENET
The network time protocol.

Name: fsp-discussion
Resource: List
Address: `listmaster@Germany.EU.net`
Discussion of the new FSP protocol.

Name: inns-l
Resource: LISTSERV
Address: `inns-l@umdd.bitnet`
The International Neural Network Society discussion list.

Name: irchat
Resource: List
Address: `irchat-request@cc.tut.fi`
(Kai 'Kaizzu' Kein{nen)
Discussion on irchat.el, a GNU Emacs interface to IRC (the Internet Relay Chat).

Name: news.admin.misc
Resource: USENET
General topics of network news administration.

Name: news.admin.technical
Resource: USENET
Technical aspects of maintaining network news. (Moderated)

Name: news.software.nntp
Resource: USENET
The Network News Transfer Protocol.

Name: novell
Resource: LISTSERV
Address: `novell@suvm.bitnet`
Novell LAN interest group for all users and supporters.

Name: ntp
Resource: List
Address: `ntp-request@trantor.umd.edu`
Discussion of the Network Time Protocol.

Name: ParNET
Resource: List
Address: `parnet-list-request@ben.com`
(Ben Jackson)
To discuss the installation, use, and modification of ParNET, an Amiga networking program.

Name: tcp-group
Resource: List
Address: `tcp-group-request@ucsd.edu`
Discussion about promoting TCP/IP use on Ham packet radio.

Name: wfw-l
Resource: LISTSERV
Address: `wfw-l@umdd.bitnet`
Devoted to the support and use of Microsoft's Windows for Workgroups software product.

Neural Nets

Name: comp.ai.neural-nets
Resource: USENET
All aspects of neural networks.

Name: neural-n
Resource: LISTSERV
Address: `neural-n@andescol.bitnet`
For the discussion and development of artificial neural networks.

Name: neuron
Resource: List
Address:
Addressneuron-request@cattell.psych.upenn.edu
(Peter Marvit)
Neuron-Digest is a moderated list (in digest form) dealing with all aspects of neural networks (and any type of network or neuromorphic system).

NeXT

Name:
comp.sys.next.programmer
Resource: USENET
NeXT-related programming issues.

Name: NeXT-icon
Resource: List
Address:
next-icon-request@bmt.gun.com
(Timothy Reed)
Distribute and receive 64x64 or 48x48 pixel icons (2-, 12-, 24- and/or 32-bit), compatible with the NeXT Computer's NeXTStep software. Nearly all mail is in NeXTmail format.

Name: next-l
Resource: LISTSERV
Address: next-l@brownvm.brown.edu
For persons involved in the support of NeXT systems.

Name: nextstep
Resource: LISTSERV
Address: nextstep@irishvma.bitnet
An open list dedicated to the exchange of information by persons using the NeXTStep operating system.

Online Services

Name: alt.online-service
Resource: USENET
Discussions of large commercial online services and the Internet.

Operating Systems

Name: Alspa
Resource: List
Address:
alspa-users-request@ssyx.ucsc.edu
(Brad Allen)
Discussion by owners/users of the CP/M machines made by (now defunct) Alspa Computer, Inc.

Name: alt.os.multics
Resource: USENET
30 years old and going strong.

Name: apc-open
Resource: List
Address:
apc-open-request@uunet.uu.net
(Fred Rump) or fred@compu.com
To interchange information relevant to SCO Advanced Product Centers.

Name: biz.sco.general
Resource: USENET
Q&A, discussions, and comments on SCO products.

Name: bugs-386bsd
Resource: List
Address:
bugs-386bsd-request@ms.uky.edu
For 386bsd bugs, patches, and ports.

Name: comp.os.386bsd.announce
Resource: USENET
Announcements relating to the 386bsd operating system. (Moderated)

Name: comp.os.386bsd.misc
Resource: USENET
General aspects of 386bsd not covered by other groups.

Name: comp.os.coherent
Resource: USENET
Discussion and support of the Coherent operating system.

Name: comp.os.geos
Resource: USENET
The GEOS operating system by GeoWorks for PC clones.

Name: comp.os.linux.admin
Resource: USENET
Installing and administering Linux systems.

Name: comp.os.linux.announce
Resource: USENET
Announcements important to the Linux community. (Moderated)

Name:
comp.os.linux.development
Resource: USENET
Ongoing work on the Linux operating system.

Name: comp.os.linux.help
Resource: USENET
Questions and advice about Linux.

Name: comp.os.linux.misc
Resource: USENET
Linux-specific topics not covered by other groups.

Name: comp.os.mach
Resource: USENET
The MACH OS from CMU and other places.

Name: comp.os.minix
Resource: USENET
Discussion of Tanenbaum's MINIX system.

Name: comp.os.msdos.apps
Resource: USENET
Discussion of applications that run under MS-DOS.

Name: comp.os.msdos.misc
Resource: USENET
Miscellaneous topics about MS-DOS machines.

Name: comp.os.os2.advocacy
Resource: USENET
Supporting and flaming OS/2.

Name: comp.os.os2.apps
Resource: USENET
Discussions of applications under OS/2.

Name: comp.os.os2.beta
Resource: USENET
All aspects of beta releases of OS/2 system software.

Name: comp.os.os2.misc
Resource: USENET
Miscellaneous topics about the OS/2 system.

Name: comp.os.os2.setup
Resource: USENET
Installing and configuring OS/2 systems.

Name: comp.os.os2.ver1x
Resource: USENET
All aspects of OS/2 versions 1.0 through 1.3.

Name: comp.os.research
Resource: USENET
Operating systems and related areas. (Moderated)

Name: comp.os.vms
Resource: USENET
DEC's VAX line of computers and VMS.

Name: comp.os.vxworks
Resource: USENET
The VxWorks real-time operating system.

Name: comp.std.unix
Resource: USENET
Discussion of the P1003 committee on UNIX. (Moderated)

Name: Linux-Activists
Resource: List
Address:
`linux-activists-request@niksula.hut.fi`
(Ari Lemmke)
Discussion of Linux operating system hacking.

Name: MachTen
Resource: List
Address: `MachTen-request@tenon.com`
(Leonard Cuff)
Discuss topics of interest to users of MachTen, a Mach/BSD Unix for all Macintoshes from Tenon Intersystems.

Name: os2
Resource: LISTSERV
Address: `os2@hearn.bitnet`
A moderated discussion forum about IBM's OS/2 PC operating system.

Name: os2users
Resource: LISTSERV
Address: `os2users@mcgill1.bitnet`
For users of the IBM OS/2 operating system.

Name: qnx2
Resource: List
Address: `camz@dlogtech.cuc.ab.ca`
(Martin Zimmerman)
To discuss all aspects of the QNX realtime operating systems. To subscribe, send a message to either `qnx2-request@dlogtech.cuc.ab.ca` or `qnx4-request@dlogtech.cuc.ab.ca`.

Name: qnx4
Resource: List
Address: `camz@dlogtech.cuc.ab.ca`
(Martin Zimmerman)
To discuss all aspects of the QNX realtime operating systems. To subscribe, send a message to either `qnx2-request@dlogtech.cuc.ab.ca` or `qnx4-request@dlogtech.cuc.ab.ca`.

Name: rc
Resource: List
Address:
`rc-request@hawkwind.utcs.toronto.edu`
(Chris Siebenmann)
Discussion of the rc shell.

Name: scoodt
Resource: List
Address: `scoodt-request@xenitec.on.ca`
(Ed Hew)
The SCO Open Desktop electronic mailing list is intended to provide a communications vehicle for interested parties to provide, request, submit, and exchange information regarding the configuration, implementation, and use of the SCO Open Desktop operating system as available from The Santa Cruz Operation.

Name: unix-wiz
Resource: LISTSERV
Address: `unix-wiz@ndsuvm1.ndsu.edu`
A mailing list for all UNIX wizards.

Name: xopen-testing
Resource: List
Address:
`xopen-testing-request@uel.co.uk`
(Andrew Josey)
Discussion of issues related to testing operating systems for conformance to the X/OPEN Portability Guide (XPG), including Issue 3 (XPG3) and later.

Organizations

Name: comp.org.decus
Resource: USENET
Digital Equipment Computer Users'
Society newsgroup.

Parallel Processing

Name: ipsc-managers
Resource: LISTSERV
Address:
(machine) `listserv@boxer.nas.nasa.gov`
(human) `jet@nas.nasa.gov`
(J. Eric Townsend)
Discussion of administrating the Intel
iPSC line of parallel computers.

Name: MasPar
Resource: List
Address:
`mp-users-request@thunder.mcrcim.mcgill.edu`
(Lee Iverson)
Discussions of hardware/software
issues surrounding the use of the
MasPar MP-1 class of parallel SIMD
machines.

Name: Ncube
Resource: List
Address:
`ncube-users-request@cs.tufts.edu`
(David Krumme)
Exchange of information among
people using NCUBE parallel com-
puters.

Patents

Name: comp.patents
Resource: USENET
Discussing patents of computer
technology. (Moderated)

PC Applications

Name: clay=xldev
Resource: List
Address: `clay=xldev@cs.cmu.edu`
Excel developers' discussion list.

PCs

Name: 386users
Resource: List
Address: `386users-request@udel.edu`
(William Davidsen, Jr.)
Topics are 80386-based computers
and all hardware and software that is
either 386-specific or that has special
interest on the 386.

Name:
alt.sys.pc-clone.gateway2000
Resource: USENET
A PC clone vendor.

Name: comp.binaries.ibm.pc
Resource: USENET
Binary-only postings for IBM PC/
MS-DOS. (Moderated)

Name: comp.binaries.ibm.pc.d
Resource: USENET
Discussions about IBM/PC binary
postings.

Name:
comp.binaries.ibm.pc.wanted
Resource: USENET
Requests for IBM PC and compatible
programs.

Name: comp.sys.ibm.pc.misc
Resource: USENET
Discussion about IBM personal
computers.

Name: comp.sys.ibm.pc.rt
Resource: USENET
Topics related to IBM's RT computer.

Name: i-ibmpc
Resource: LISTSERV
Address: `i-ibmpc@vmd.cso.uiuc.edu`
A discussion list for all IBM PC users and owners.

Name: msmail-l
Resource: LISTSERV
Address: `msmail-l@yalevm.ycc.yale.edu`
A discussion list for users and supporters of the Microsoft Mail software product.

Name: pc-eval
Resource: LISTSERV
Address: `pc-eval@irlearn.ucd.ie`
A discussion list for the purpose of exchanging evaluations about personal computers.

PDA (Personal Digital Assistants)

Name: agenda-users
Resource: List
Address:
`agenda-users-request@newcastle.ac.uk`
A new mailing list for users of the Microwriter Agenda hand-held computer.

Name: handhelds
Resource: List
Address: `handhelds@csl.sri.com`
For the discussion of calculators and hand-held computers (a.k.a. PDAs-Personal Digital Assistants).

Name: zoomer-list
Resource: LISTSERV
Address: `listserv@grot.starconn.com`
(Brian Smithson)
Discussion forum for users or potential users of the Zoomer personal digital assistant products from Casio, Tandy, and so on. To subscribe, send mail to the `listserv` address with the following commands in the message body: `subscribe zoomer-list <First Name> <Last Name>`.

PowerPC

Name: comp.sys.powerpc
Resource: USENET
General PowerPC Discussion.

Printers

Name: Imagen-L
Resource: LISTSERV
Address: `listserv@bolis.sf-bay.org`
This list is a discussion forum for all aspects of Imagen laser printers. To subscribe, send an e-mail message to `listserv@bolis.sf-bay.org` containing the following message: `subscribe Imagen-L`.

Name: INFO-PRINTERS
Resource: List
Address: `INFO-PRINTERS@eddie.mil.edu`
This is a general printers discussion list. Send your request for subscriptions to
`info-printers-request@eddie.mil.edu`.

Privacy Issues

Name: alt.privacy
Resource: USENET
Privacy issues in cyberspace.

Name: comp-privacy
Resource: List
Address: `comp-privacy@pica.army.mil`
Dedicated to the discussion of how computers, and technology in general, affect privacy. Send subscriptions and other administrative traffic to
`comp-privacy-request@pica.army.mil`.

Name: comp.society.privacy
Resource: USENET
Effects of technology on privacy.
(Moderated)

Product Information

Name: DECnews-UNIX
Resource: List
Address:
decnews-unix-request@pa.dec.com
(Russ Jones)
DECnews for UNIX is published
electronically by Digital Equipment
Corporation for Internet distribution
every three weeks and contains
product and service information of
interest to the Digital UNIX community. To subscribe, send mail to
decnews-unix@pa.dec.com with the
following in the subject line: subscribe
abstract. Please include your name
and telephone number in the body of
the subscription request.

Programming Languages

Name: ABC
Resource: List
Address: abc-list-request@cwi.nl
(Steven Pemberton)
Discussion of the ABC Programming
Language and its implementations.

Name: actor-l
Resource: LISTSERV
Address: actor-l@hearn.bitnet
This list provides a platform for those
developing applications with the
Actor object-oriented programming
language.

Name: amiga-m2
Resource: List

Address: amiga-m2@virginia.edu
A discussion group for persons
interested in the use of Modula-2 on
the Amiga. Send subscription requests to amiga-m2-request@virginia.edu.

Name: AMOS
Resource: List
Address: subscribe@xamiga.linet.org
For the AMOS programming language on Amiga computers. Send
subscription requests to
subscribe@xamiga.linet.org using this
format: #amos <User Name>@<Domain>;.

Name: apl-l
Resource: LISTSERV
Address: apl-l@unb.ca
Devoted to the discussion of the APL
programming language.

Name: assmpc-l
Resource: LISTSERV
Address:
assmpc-l@usachvm1.bitnet@vm1.nodak.edu
Assembler language for the PC.

Name: BETA
Resource: List
Address: usergroup-request@mjolner.dk
(Elmer Soerensen Sandvad)
A discussion forum for BETA users.

Name: C-IBM-370
Resource: List
Address:
{spsd,zardoz,felix,elroy}!dhw68k!C-IBM-370-request
C-IBM-370-request@dhw68k.cts.com
(David Wolfskill)
Provides a place to discuss aspects of
using the C programming language
on s/370-architecture computers—
especially under IBM's operating
systems for that environment.

Name: c-l
Resource: LISTSERV

Address: `c-1@indycms.iupui.edu`
A general discussion list about the C
programming language.

Name: comp.lang.ada
Resource: USENET
Discussion about Ada.

Name: comp.lang.c
Resource: USENET
Discussion about C.

Name: comp.lang.c++
Resource: USENET
Discussion about the object-oriented
C++ language.

Name: comp.lang.clos
Resource: USENET
Common Lisp Object System
discussions.

Name: comp.lang.eiffel
Resource: USENET
Discussion about the object-oriented
Eiffel language.

Name: comp.lang.forth
Resource: USENET
Discussion about Forth.

Name: comp.lang.fortran
Resource: USENET
Discussion about FORTRAN.

Name: comp.lang.functional
Resource: USENET
Discussion about functional lan-
guages.

Name: comp.lang.idl-pvwave
Resource: USENET
IDL and PV-Wave language discus-
sions.

Name: comp.lang.lisp
Resource: USENET
Discussion about LISP.

Name: comp.lang.misc
Resource: USENET
Different computer languages not
specifically listed.

Name: comp.lang.ml
Resource: USENET
ML languages including Standard
ML, CAML, Lazy ML, etc. (Moder-
ated)

Name: comp.lang.modula3
Resource: USENET
Discussion about the Modula-3
language.

Name: comp.lang.oberon
Resource: USENET
The Oberon language and system.

Name: comp.lang.objective-c
Resource: USENET
The Objective-C language and
environment.

Name: comp.lang.prolog
Resource: USENET
Discussion about PROLOG.

Name: comp.lang.sather
Resource: USENET
The object-oriented computer lan-
guage Sather.

Name: comp.lang.scheme
Resource: USENET
The Scheme Programming language.

Name: comp.lang.smalltalk
Resource: USENET
Discussion about Smalltalk 80.

Name: comp.lang.tcl
Resource: USENET
The Tcl programming language and
related tools.

Name: comp.object
Resource: USENET
Object-oriented programming and languages.

Name: comp.object.logic
Resource: USENET
Integrating object-oriented and logic programming.

Name: comp.programming
Resource: USENET
Programming issues that transcend languages and OSs.

Name: comp.programming.literate
Resource: USENET
Literate programs and programming tools.

Name: figi-l
Resource: LISTSERV
Address: figi-l@bruspvm.bitnet
Everything related to the FORTH programming language happens here!

Name: franz-friends
Resource: List
Address: franz-friends@berkeley.edu
This list is for the discussion of Franz Lisp, a public-domain version of the computer programming language frequently used in the field of artificial intelligence. Submit your subscription requests to franz-friends-request@berkeley.edu.

Name: gnu.g++.help
Resource: USENET
GNU C++ compiler (G++) user queries and answers.

Name: ICI
Resource: List

Address:
listserv@research.canon.oz.au
Discussion of Tim Long's ICI language and its interpreter. Also acts as an archive for the interpreter source, patches, and documentation.

Name: IDOL
Resource: List
Address:
idol-group-request@luvthang.ori-cal.com
(David Talmage)
The idol-group is an unmoderated mailing list for people interested in the Idol language.

Name: info-ccc
Resource: List
Address:
uunet!xurilka!info-ccc-request
(Luigi Perrotta)
The info-ccc mailing list will be devoted to the Concurrent C and Concurrent C++ programming languages. However, discussions can be anything relevant to concurrent programming.

Name: info-m2
Resource: LISTSERV
Address: info-m2@ucf1vm.cc.ucf.edu
A discussion list for programmers using the Modula-2 programming language.

Name: lang-lucid
Resource: List
Address:
lang-lucid-request@csl.sri.com
(R. Jagannathan)
Discussions on all aspects related to the language Lucid.

Name: Linda
Resource: List

Address:
linda-users-request@cs.yale.edu
linda-users-request@yalecs.bitnet
{cmcl2,decvax,harvard}!yale!linda-users-request
Discussion group for users and
potential users of Linda-based
parallel programming systems.

Name: Logo
Resource: List
Address:
logo-friends-request@aiai.ed.ac.uk
Discussion of the Logo computer
language.

Name: objc
Resource: List
Address: bunker!stpstn!objc-request
(Anthony A. Datri)
The Objective-C mailing list is for the
discussion of Stepstone's Objective-C
language, Objective-C compiler,
Objective-C interpreter, and the
ICPak-201 user interface library.

Name: pascal-l
Resource: LISTSERV
Address: pascal-l@vmd.cso.uiuc.edu
A discussion group about Borland's
Pascal compiler.

Name: pl1-l
Resource: LISTSERV
Address: pl1-l@vmd.cso.uiuc.edu
A discussion list about the PL/I
programming language.

Name: posix-ada
Resource: List
Address:
umd5!grebyn!posix-ada-request
posix-ada-request@grebyn.com
(Karl Nyberg)
This list discusses the Ada binding of
the Posix standard.

Name: proof-users
Resource: List
Address:
proof-request@xcf.berkeley.edu
(Craig Latta)
To discuss the left-associative natural
language parser "proof."

Name: Python
Resource: List
Address: python-list-request@cwi.nl
(Guido van Rossum)
The list is intended for discussion of
and questions about all aspects of
design and use of the Python programming language. To subscribe,
send e-mail to
python-list-request@cwi.nl; include
your name and Internet e-mail
address in the body.

Name: rexx-l
Resource: LISTSERV
Address: rexx-l@vmd.cso.uiuc.edu
A discussion list to exchange ideas
and information about the REXX
programming language.

Name: S-news
Resource: List
Address: S-news-request@stat.wisc.edu
(Douglas Bates)
Information and discussion about the
S language for data analysis and
graphics.

Name: smalk
Resource: LISTSERV
Address: info-cls@dearn.bitnet
A discussion list for developers using
the Smalltalk programming language.

Name: tasm-l
Resource: LISTSERV
Address: `tasm-l@brufpb.bitnet`
A discussion list about Borland's Turbo Assembler and Debugger software products.

Name: tcplus-l
Resource: LISTSERV
Address: `tcplus-l@ucf1vm.cc.ucf.edu`
For all users and developers using Turbo C++.

Name: think-c
Resource: List
Address: `think-c-request@ics.uci.edu`
(Mark Nagel)
This list exists to discuss the Think C compiler for the Macintosh.

Name: visbas-l
Resource: LISTSERV
Address: `visbas-l@tamvm1.tamu.edu`
This discussion list is for those who develop and support applications with Microsoft's Visual Basic programming language.

Name: x-ada
Resource: List
Address:
`x-ada-request@expo.lcs.mit.edu`
Discussion about the interfaces and bindings for an Ada interface to the X Window system.

Name: ZForum
Resource: List
Address:
`zforum-request@comlab.ox.ac.uk`
(Jonathan Bowen)
ZForum is intended to handle messages concerned with the formal specification notation Z.

Project Management

Name: project-management
Resource: List
Address:
`project-management-request@smtl.demon.co.uk`
The aim of the list is to discuss project management techniques generally, not just project management software and programs. You can join the list by sending e-mail to
`project-management-request@smtl.demon.co.uk`
with the following subject line:
`subscribe`.

Protocols

Name: comp.dcom.lans.fddi
Resource: USENET
Discussions of the FDDI protocol suite.

Public Access Systems

Name: pubnet
Resource: List
Address:
`pubnet-request@chinacat.unicom.com`
(Chip Rosenthal)
The administration and use of public access computer systems—primarily UNIX systems.

Publishing

Name: publish
Resource: List
Address: `publish@chron.com`
Devoted to the discussion of using computers to improve productivity in the publishing industry. Send subscription requests to
`publish-request@chron.com`.

Real-time

Name: comp.realtime
Resource: USENET
Issues related to real-time computing.

Research

Name: carr-l
Resource: LISTSERV
Address: carr-l@ulkyvm.louisville.edu
Devoted to the exchange of information about computer-assisted reporting and research.

Robotics

Name: comp.robotics
Resource: USENET
All aspects of robots and their applications.

Russian

Name: RENews
Resource: List
Address: nev@renews.relcom.msk.su
Monthly digest on networking and computing in Russia.

Security

Name: alt.security
Resource: USENET
Security issues on computer systems.

Name: comp.security.misc
Resource: USENET
Security issues of computers and networks.

Name: comp.security.unix
Resource: USENET
Discussion of UNIX security.

Name: comp.virus
Resource: USENET
Computer viruses and security. (Moderated)

Name: mac-security
Resource: List
Address:
mac-security-request@world.std.com
(David C. Kovar)
This mailing list is for people interested in Macintosh security.

Name: security
Resource: List
Address:
uunet!zardoz!security-request
(Neil Gorsuch) or
security-request@cpd.com
To notify of UNIX security flaws before they become public knowledge, and to provide UNIX security enhancement programs and information.

SGI

Name: comp.sys.sgi.admin
Resource: USENET
System administration on Silicon Graphics's Irises.

Name: comp.sys.sgi.apps
Resource: USENET
Applications that run on the Iris.

Name: comp.sys.sgi.bugs
Resource: USENET
Bugs found in the IRIX operating system.

Name: comp.sys.sgi.graphics
Resource: USENET
Graphics packages and issues on SGI machines.

Name: comp.sys.sgi.hardware
Resource: USENET
Base systems and peripherals for Iris computers.

Name: comp.sys.sgi.misc
Resource: USENET
General discussion about Silicon Graphics's machines.

Simulation Software

Name: Aviator
Resource: List
Address:
aviator-request@ICDwest.Teradyne.COM
(Jim Hickstein)
A mailing list of, by, and for users of Aviator, the flight simulation program from Artificial Horizons, Inc.

Social Issues

Name: CUSSNET
Resource: LISTSERV
Address: cussnet-request@stat.com
Computer Users in the Social Sciences is a discussion group devoted to issues of interest to social workers, counselors, and human service workers of all disciplines. To join the list, send e-mail to listserv@stat.com. The first line of text should read: subscribe cussnet.

Software

Resource: FTP
Address: ftp.cica.indiana.edu
Directory: pub/pc/win3. A fantastic site for Windows software.

Name: auc-tex
Resource: List
Address: auc-tex-request@iesd.auc.dk
(Kresten Krab Thorup)
Discussion and information exchange about the AUC TeX package, which runs under GNU EMACS.

Software Engineering

Name: comp.software-eng
Resource: USENET
Software Engineering and related topics.

Software Licensing

Name: license
Resource: LISTSERV
Address: license@uga.cc.uga.edu
A discussion list about software licensing.

Software Patents

Resource: FTP
Address: mintaka.lcs.mit.edu:
Directory: /mitlpf/ai/patent-list. This file contains a list of software patents and related information.

Software Products

Name: DDTs-Users
Resource: List
Address:
DDTs-Users-request@BigBird.BU.EDU
(automated help reply)
The DDTs-Users mailing list is for discussions of issues related to the DDTs defect-tracking software from QualTrak.

Name: Decision Power
Resource: List
Address:
dp-friends-request@aiai.ed.ac.uk
(Ken Johnson)
Discussion of Decision Power, a product of ICL Computers Limited comprised of a logic programming language (Prolog), a constraint handling system (Chip), a database interface (Seduce), a development environment (Kegi), and an end-user graphical display environment (KHS).

Software Publishing

Name: softpub
Resource: List
Address:
softpub@toolz.uucp@mathcs.emory.edu
A list for the exchange of information related to computer software publishing activities, including the topic of shareware. Send requests for subscription to
softpub-request%toolz.uucp@mathcs.emory.edu.

Software Reviews

Name: softrevu
Resource: LISTSERV
Address: softrevu@brownvm.brown.edu
A discussion list for the exchange of software evaluations.

Software Tools

Name: artist-users
Resource: List
Address:
artist-users-request@uicc.com
(Jeff Putsch)

Discussion group for users and potential users of the software tools from Cadence Design Systems.

Software-File Compression

Resource: FTP
Address: ftp.cso.uiuc.edu
Compression/decompression programs for many different operating systems.

Sound

Name: af
Resource: List
Address: af-request@crl.dec.com
Discussion of AudioFile, a client/server, network-transparent, device-independent audio system.

Name: alt.binaries.sounds.d
Resource: USENET
Sounding off.

Name: alt.binaries.sounds.midi
Resource: USENET
MIDI binaries.

Name: alt.binaries.sounds.misc
Resource: USENET
Digitized audio adventures.

Name: alt.binaries.sounds.music
Resource: USENET
Music samples in MOD/669 format.

Name:
comp.sys.ibm.pc.soundcard
Resource: USENET
Hardware and software aspects of PC sound cards.

Name: GUS
Resource: List
Address:
`Address:gus-music-request@dsd.es.com`
(Dave Debry)
The GUS lists are for discussion of matters relating to the Gravis UltraSound soundcard for PCs.

Name: ibmsnd-l
Resource: LISTSERV
Address: `ibmsnd-l@brownvm.brown.edu`
This is a forum for the discussion and support of sound cards.

Source Code

Name: alt.sources
Resource: USENET
Alternative source code. *Caveat emptor.*

Name: alt.sources.mac
Resource: USENET
Source file newsgroup for the Apple Macintosh computers.

Name: alt.sources.wanted
Resource: USENET
Requests for source code.

Name: comp.sources.d
Resource: USENET
For any discussion of source postings.

Name: comp.sources.misc
Resource: USENET
Posting of software. (Moderated)

Name: comp.sources.postscript
Resource: USENET
Source code for programs written in PostScript. (Moderated)

Name: comp.sources.testers
Resource: USENET
Finding people to test software.

Name: comp.sources.wanted
Resource: USENET
Requests for software and fixes.

Name: vmsnet.sources.d
Resource: USENET
Discussion about or requests for sources.

Speech

Name: comp.speech
Resource: USENET
Research and applications in speech science and technology.

Name: ECTL
Resource: List
Address:
`ectl-request@snowhite.cis.uoguelph.ca`
(David Leip)
A list dedicated to researchers interested in computer speech interfaces.

Standards

Name: comp.std.internat
Resource: USENET
Discussion about international standards.

Name: comp.std.misc
Resource: USENET
Discussion about various standards.

Sun Workstations

Name: alt.sys.sun
Resource: USENET
Technical discussion of Sun Microsystems products.

Name: comp.sys.sun.admin
Resource: USENET
Sun system administration issues and questions.

Name: comp.sys.sun.announce
Resource: USENET
Sun announcements and Sunergy mailings. (Moderated)

Name: comp.sys.sun.misc
Resource: USENET
Miscellaneous discussions about Sun products.

Name: comp.windows.news
Resource: USENET
Sun Microsystems' NeWS window system.

Name: sun-386i
Resource: List
Address: `sun-386i-request@ssg.com`
(Rick Emerson)
Discussion and information about the 386i-based Sun machines.

Name: sun-managers
Resource: List
Address:
`sun-managers-request@eecs.nwu.edu`
Information of special interest to managers of sites with Sun workstations or servers.

Name: sun-nets
Resource: List
Address:
`sun-nets-request@umiacs.umd.edu`
Discussion and information on networks using Sun hardware and/or software.

Name: sunflash (a.k.a. 'The
          Florida SunFlash')
Resource: List

Address: `flash@sun.com`
(John J. McLaughlin)
To keep Sun users informed about Sun via press releases, product announcements, and technical articles. Send requests to be added to the list to `sunflash-request@Sun.COM`. For more information, send mail to `info-sunflash@Sun.COM`.

Super Computers

Name: cm5-managers
Resource: LISTSERV
Address:
(machine) `listserv@boxer.nas.nasa.gov`
(human) `jet@nas.nasa.gov`
(J. Eric Townsend)
Discussion of administrating the Thinking Machine's CM5 parallel supercomputer. To subscribe, send a message to `listserv@boxer.nas.nasa.gov` with a body of `subscribe cm5-managers <Full Name>`.

Name: Supercomputing Sites
Resource: List
Address: `gunter@yarrow.wt.uwa.oz.au`
Weekly mailing of the list of the world's most powerful computing sites.

Support/Help Desk

Name: hdesk-l
Resource: LISTSERV
Address: `hdesk-l@wvnvm.wvnet.edu`
For persons involved in supporting and staffing Help Desks, including problem-tracking, frustration, retraining users, and creating your own Help Desk.

System Administration

Name: bblisa-announce
Resource: List
Address:
`bblisa-announce-request@cs.umb.edu`
Announcements list for Back Bay
LISA (Large Installation Systems
Administration) activities, meetings,
and so on.

Tandy

Name: coco
Resource: LISTSERV
Address:
`coco@pucc.bitnet@cunyvm.cuny.edu`
A discussion list for the Tandy Color
Computer OS-9 operating system and
related topics.

Name: CoCo
Resource: List
Address: `pecampbe@mtus5.BITNET`
(Paul E. Campbell)
Discussion related to the Tandy Color
Computer (any model), OS-9 Operat-
ing System, and any other topics
relating to the "CoCo," as this com-
puter is affectionately known.

TCP/IP

Name: ibmtcp-l
Resource: LISTSERV
Address: `ibmtcp-l@pucc.bitnet`
A list for users and supporters of
IBM's TCP/IP software product.

Name: pcip
Resource: LISTSERV
Address: `pcip@irlearn.ucd.ie`
A discussion list about how to
implement the TCP/IP protocol on
PCs.

Text Processing

Name: comp.text
Resource: USENET
Text processing issues and methods.

Name: comp.text.tex
Resource: USENET
Discussion about the TeX and LaTeX
systems and macros.

Unisys

Name: Unisys
Resource: List
Address: `unisys-request@bcm.tmc.edu`
(Richard H. Miller)
Discussion of all Unisys products and
equipment.

UNIX

Name: alpha-osf-managers
Resource: List
Address:
`alpha-osf-managers-request@ornl.gov`
`majordomo@ornl.gov`
Fast-turnaround troubleshooting tool
for managers of DEC Alpha AXP
systems running OSF/1.

Name: comp.unix.admin
Resource: USENET
Administering a UNIX-based system.

Name: comp.unix.aix
Resource: USENET
IBM's version of UNIX.

Name: comp.unix.amiga
Resource: USENET
Minix, SYSV4, and other UNIX on an
Amiga.

Name: comp.unix.aux
Resource: USENET
The version of UNIX for Apple
Macintosh II computers.

Name: comp.unix.bsd
Resource: USENET
Discussion of Berkeley Software
Distribution UNIX.

Name: comp.unix.osf.osf1
Resource: USENET
The Open Software Foundation's
OSF/1.

Name: comp.unix.pc-clone.32bit
Resource: USENET
UNIX on 386 and 486 architectures.

Name: comp.unix.programmer
Resource: USENET
Q&A for people programming under
UNIX.

Name: comp.unix.questions
Resource: USENET
UNIX neophytes group.

Name: comp.unix.shell
Resource: USENET
Using and programming the UNIX
shell.

Name: comp.unix.solaris
Resource: USENET
Discussions about the Solaris operat-
ing system.

Name: comp.unix.sys5.r4
Resource: USENET
Discussing System V Release 4.

Name: comp.unix.ultrix
Resource: USENET
Discussions about DEC's Ultrix.

Name: comp.unix.unixware
Resource: USENET
Discussion about Novell's UnixWare
products.

Name: comp.unix.user-friendly
Resource: USENET
Discussion of UNIX user-friendliness.

Name: comp.unix.wizards
Resource: USENET
For only true Unix wizards. (Moder-
ated)

Name: comp.unix.xenix.sco
Resource: USENET
XENIX versions from the Santa Cruz
Operation.

Name: Dual-Personalities
Resource: List
Address:
dual-personalities-request@darwin.uucp
Discussion, maintenance/survival
tips, and commercial offerings for the
System/83 UNIX box made by the
now-defunct DUAL Systems Corporation of Berkeley, as well as similar
machines using the IEEE-696 bus.

Name: groupname
Resource: List
Address:
groupname-request@Warren.MentorG.COM
This is the mailing list for
$GROUPNAME, an organization for
UNIX Sysadmins in the New Jersey
area. To subscribe, send a mail
message to
majordomo@Warren.MentorG.com. The first
line of the message (the subject line is
ignored) should be subscribe groupname.
Send other administrative questions
and requests to the e-mail address
groupname-approval@plts.org.

Name: Univel
Resource: List
Address: `univel-request@telly.on.ca`
Provides a forum for users, developers, and others interested in the products of Univel, the Novell subsidiary that produces UNIX system software for PC-architecture systems. To subscribe, send mail to `univel-request@telly.on.ca` with a body in this form: `subscribe univel <Full Name>`.

Utilities

Name: c2man
Resource: List
Address:
`listserv@research.canon.oz.au`
Discussion of Graham Stoney's c2man program.

Name: i-finger
Resource: List
Address:
`i-finger@spcvxa.bitnet@cunyvm.cuny.edu`
For the discussion and sharing of information related to user lookup facilities, particularly finger. Send subscription requests to
`i-fingreq%spcvxa@cunyvm.cuny.edu`.

Name: info-zip
Resource: List
Address:
`info-zip@wsmr-simtel20.army.mil`
For the discussion of information related to the porting of ZIP software compression to the mainframe environment. Send subscription requests to
`inf-zip-request@wsmr-simtel20.army.mil`.

Vendor Information

Name: decuserve-journal
Resource: List
Address: `frey@eisner.decus.org`
(Sharon Frey)
An alternate method of distribution for the DECUServe Journal, a monthly digest of technical discussions that take place on the DECUS conferencing system.

Vendors

Name: DECnews-PR
Resource: List
Address:
`decnews-pr-request@pa.dec.com`
(Russ Jones)
DECnews for Press and Analysts is an Internet-based distribution of all Digital press releases. To subscribe, send mail to `decnews-pr@pa.dec.com` with the following in the subject: line `subscribe`. Please include your name and telephone number in the body of the subscription request.

Name: Gateway 2000
Resource: List
Address:
`gateway2000-request@sei.cmu.edu`
(Tod Pike)
A good source of information about Gateway 2000 products.

Virtual Reality

Name: glove-list
Resource: LISTSERV
Address:
(machine) `listserv@boxer.nas.nasa.gov`
(human) `jet@nas.nasa.gov`
(J. Eric Townsend)

Discussion of the Nintendo PowerGlove. To subscribe, send e-mail to `listserv@boxer.nas.nasa.gov` with a body of `subscribe glove-list <Full Name>`.

Name: rend386
Resource: List
Address:
`rend386-request@sunee.uwaterloo.ca`
Discussion by and for users of the REND386 software package.

Name: sci.virtual-worlds
Resource: USENET
Discussion of virtual reality technology and culture. (Moderated)

Viruses

Resource: FTP
Address: `cert.org`
Directory: `pub/virus-l/docs/reviews`

Resource: FTP
Address:
`ftp.informatik.uni-hamburg.de`
Directory: `pub/virus/texts/catalog`

Resource: FTP
Address: `cert.org`
Directory: `pub/virus-l/docs/vtc`

Resource: FTP
Address: `cert.org`
Directory: `pub/virus-l/FAQ.virus-l`. This is the archive/respository of previous VIRUS-L postings.

Name: mibsrv-l
Resource: LISTSERV
Address: `mibsrv-l@ua1vm.bitnet`
This list is about IBM PC (and compatible) anti-viral software products and programs.

Name: ST Viruses
Resource: List
Address:
`r.c.karsmakers@stud.let.ruu.nl`
To provide fast and efficient help where infection with computer viruses is concerned for Atari ST/TT/ Falcon; no MS-DOS or compatibles.

Name: virus-l
Resource: LISTSERV
Address: `virus-l@tritu.bitnet`
A major list for the exchange of information about computer viruses.

Windows

Name: WIN3-L
Resource: LISTSERV
Address: `WIN3-L@UICVM.uic.cc.edu`
A forum for the discussion of all aspects of the Microsoft Windows product.

Word Processing

Name: Word-Mac
Resource: List
Address: `listproc@alsvid.une.edu.au`
Word-Mac is a mailing list dedicated to serving users of the Microsoft Word package in its various versions on the Apple Macintosh platform. Send requests for subscription to `listproc@alsvid.une.edu.au` with the following text: `subscribe word-mac <First Name> <Last Name>`.

Name: wp51-l
Resource: LISTSERV
Address: `wp51-l@uottawa.bitnet`
For all users of the WordPerfect word processing software.

Name: wpwin-l
Resource: LISTSERV
Address: wpwin-l@ubvm.cc.buffalo.edu
This discussion list is for users of
WordPerfect for Windows.

Workstations

Name: next-gis
Resource: List
Address: sstaton@deltos.com
(Steven R. Staton) listserv@deltos.com
(send SUBSCRIBE <Name> message to join)
Discussion of GIS and cartographic
related topics on the NeXT and other
workstation computers.

Zenith/Heath

Name: heath-people
Resource: List
Address: heath-people@mc.lcs.mit.edu
For persons interested in all aspects of
Zenith and Heath computers and
related components. Send subscription requests and related administrative information to
heath-people-request@mc.lcs.mit.edu

Culture

American History

Name: alt.war.civil.usa
Resource: USENET
Discussion of the U.S. Civil War
(1861-1865).

Celtic

Name: celtic-l
Resource: LISTSERV
Address: celtic-l@irlearn.ucd.ie
This list is for everyone interested in
the study of Celtic cultures.

Folklore

Name: alt.folklore.college
Resource: USENET
Collegiate humor.

Name: alt.folklore.urban
Resource: USENET
Urban legends, à la Jan Harold
Brunvand.

Name: FOLKLORE
Resource: LISTSERV
Address: FOLKLORE@tamvm1.tamu.edu
A moderated list for the discussion of
urban legends and folklore.

Interracial Relationships

Name: soc.couples.intercultural
Resource: USENET
Intercultural and interracial relation-
ships.

Islam

Name: islam-l
Resource: LISTSERV
Address:
islam-l@ulkyvm.louisville.edu
This is a discussion list for the exchange of information about the
history of Islam.

Japanese

Name: j-food-l
Resource: LISTSERV
Address: `j-food-l@jpnknu01.bitnet`
This is a Japanese food and culture discussion list.

Kids

Name: misc.kids
Resource: USENET
Children, their behavior and activities.

Oz

Name: The Ozian Times
Resource: List
Address: `nb2b@andrew.cmu.edu`
A mailing list dealing with all aspects of Oz: the books, movie, and so on.

Personalities

Name: intp
Resource: List
Address: `intp-request@satelnet.org`
This list is for sharing information and experiences between persons who are rated as INTP (Introverted iNtuitive Thinking Perceivers) on the Myers-Briggs Temperment Index.

Raves

Name: alt.rave
Resource: USENET
Technoculture: music, dancing, drugs, dancing, and so on.

Name: AusRave (Australian Raves)
Resource: List

Address:
`ausrave-request@lsupoz.apana.org.au`
`best-of-ausrave-request@lsupoz.apana.org.au`
(Simon Rumble)
One of several regional rave-related mailing lists, AusRave covers the Australian continent. To subscribe, send requests to
`best-of-ausrave-request@lsupoz.apana.org.au`.

Name: dcraves
Resource: LISTSERV
Address: `dcraves@auvm`
This list is for the discussion of the Washington, D.C. rave culture.

Name: DCRaves
Resource: LISTSERV
Address: `listserv@american.edu`
(Tom Edwards) (Susie Kameny)
(Doug Zimmerman)
One of several regional rave-related mailing lists, DCRaves covers the Washington, D.C. area exclusively.

Name: FL-Raves (Florida Raves)
Resource: List
Address:
`flraves-request@cybernet.cse.fau.edu`
(Steve Smith)
One of several regional rave-related mailing lists, FL-Raves covers the state of Florida.

Name: MW-Raves (Midwest Raves)
Resource: List
Address:
`mw-raves-request@engin.umich.edu`
(Andy Crosby)
One of several regional rave-related mailing lists, MW-Raves covers the Midwestern U.S., including Nebraska, Iowa, Minnesota, Wisconsin, Illinois, Michigan, Indiana, Ohio, Kentucky, Missouri, and Kansas.

Name: NERaves (Northeast
              Raves)
Resource: LISTSERV
Address: `listserv@umdd.umd.edu`
One of several regional rave-related
mailing lists, NE-Raves covers the
Northeastern U.S., including Maine,
New Hampshire, Vermont, New
York, Massachusetts, Rhode Island,
Delaware, New Jersey, Pennsylvania,
and West Virginia. To subscribe, mail
`listserv@umdd.umd.edu` with the phrase:
add `ne-raves name@address <First Name>`
`<Last Name>` as the only line in the
message.

Name: V-Rave
Resource: List
Address:
`v-rave-request@gnu.ai.mit.edu`
The V-Rave mailing list serves as an
e-mail substitute for the live chat
server known as V-Rave.

Name: WNY-Raves (Western New
              York Raves)
Resource: List
Address:
`v077nk88@ubvms.cc.buffalo.edu`
(Bret "computer blue" Wallace)
One of several regional rave-related
mailing lists, WNY-Raves covers
western New York state and southern
Ontario, Canada.

Skinheads

Name: alt.skinheads
Resource: USENET
The skinhead culture/anti-culture.

Star Trek

Name: TREK-REVIEW-L
Resource: LISTSERV
Address: `LISTSERV@cornell.edu`
(Michael Scott Shappe)
TREK-REVIEW-L exists as a
noise-free forum for reviews of Star
Trek material. To subscribe to the list,
send the following command to
`LISTSERV@cornell.edu:` SUBSCRIBE
`TREK-REVIEW-L <First Name> <Last Name>.`

Dance

Ballroom

Name: ballroom
Resource: List
Address:
`ballroom-request@athena.mit.edu`
(Shahrukh Merchant)
Discussion of any aspect of ballroom
dancing.

English

Name: Morris Dancing Discussion
              List
Resource: LISTSERV
Address: `LISTSERV@suvm.acs.syr.edu`
Discussion of all things Morris,
including Cotswold, Border,
NorthWest, Rapper, LongSword,
Abbots Bromley, Garland, and similar
forms of English dance, along with
the accompanying music and tradi-
tions. To subscribe, send mail with a
message body containing SUBSCRIBE
`MORRIS <Full Name> (<Team Name>).` Send
this message to
`LISTSERV@suvm.acs.syr.edu.`

Miscellaneous

Name: rec.arts.dance
Resource: USENET
Any aspects of dance not covered in another newsgroup.

Renaissance

Name: Rendance
Resource: List
Address: `listserver@morgan.ucs.mun.ca`
RENDANCE is for discussion of Renaissance dance. The intended focus is dance reconstruction and related research, but discussion on any relevant topic is welcomed.

Scottish

Name: Strathspey
Resource: List
Address:
`strathspey-request@math.uni-frankfurt.de`
A forum for the discussion of all aspects of Scottish Country Dancing.

UK

Name: UK-DANCE
Resource: LISTSERV
Address: `listserv@orbital.demon.co.uk`
UK-DANCE is a mailing list for discussion about all aspects of dance music culture in the UK: clubs, raves, record shops, radio, records and anything else to do with the underground dance music scene. To subscribe to the list, write to `listserv@orbital.demon.co.uk` with `subscribe uk-dance <Full Name>` as the first line in the message.

Disabilities

Attention Deficit Disorder

Name: add-parents
Resource: LISTSERV
Address: `add-parents@n7kbt.rain.com`
Support, research, and information about attention deficit disorder (ADD) for those whose lives are affected by it.

Autism

Name: autism
Resource: LISTSERV
Address: `autism@sjuvm.bitnet`
A discussion list for everyone affected by autism and developmental disabilities.

Blindness

Name: Blind News Digest
Resource: LISTSERV
Address: `wtm@bunker.afd.olivetti.com`
This is a moderated mailing list in digest format that deals with all aspects of the visually impaired/blind. To subscribe, send the message `Subscribe BlindNws <Full Name>` to `listserv@vm1.nodak.edu`, or send mail to `wtm@bunker.afd.olivetti.com`.

Name: blind-l
Resource: LISTSERV
Address: `blind-l@uafsysb.uark.edu`
A discussion list dedicated to computer use by and for the blind.

Name: blindnws
Resource: LISTSERV
Address: `blindnws@ndsuvm1.ndsu.edu`
This is the blind news digest.

Carpal Tunnel

Name: sorehand
Resource: LISTSERV
Address: `sorehand@ucsfvm.bitnet`
An ongoing discussion and exchange of information about carpal tunnel syndrome and related problems.

Deaf and Blind

Name: deafblnd
Resource: LISTSERV
Address: `deafblnd@ukcc.uky.edu`
This is the deaf-blind mailing list.

Deafness

Name: deaf-l
Resource: LISTSERV
Address: `deaf-l@siucvmb.bitnet`
A list for those whose lives are affected by deafness.

Developmental

Name: our-kids
Resource: List
Address: `our-kids-request@oar.net`
Support for parents and others regarding care, diagnoses, and therapy for young children with developmental delays.

Diabetes

Name: diabetic
Resource: LISTSERV
Address: `diabetic@pccvm.bitnet`
This is an open discussion forum for diabetics and persons affected by diabetes.

Down Syndrome

Name: Down Syndrome
Resource: LISTSERV
Address: `wtm@bunker.afd.olivetti.com`
For discussion of any issue related to Down Syndrome. To subscribe, send the message `Subscribe Down-Syn <Full Name>` to `listserv@vm1.nodak.edu` or send mail to `wtm@bunker.afd.olivetti.com`.

General

Name: ddfind-l
Resource: LISTSERV
Address: `ddfind-l@gitvm1`
This is a general forum for information networking on disabilities.

Issues

Name: handicap
Resource: List
Address: `wtm@bunker.shel.isc-br.com`
The Handicap Digest provides an information/discussion exchange for issues dealing with the physically/ mentally handicapped.

Legal Issues

Name: ADA-Law
Resource: LISTSERV
Address: `wtm@bunker.afd.olivetti.com`
Discussion of the Americans with Disabilities Act (ADA) and other disability-related legislation in the United States and other countries. To subscribe, send the message `Subscribe ADA-Law <Full Name>` to `listserv@vm1.nodak.edu`, or send mail to `wtm@bunker.afd.olivetti.com`.

Speech

Name: commdis
Resource: LISTSERV
Address: `commdis@rpitsvm.bitnet`
This is a forum providing ongoing exchange of support and ideas about speech disorders.

Stroke/CVA/TIA

Name: stroke-l
Resource: LISTSERV
Address: `stroke-l@ukcc.uky.edu`
This is for persons whose lives are affected by strokes (CVAs) or transient ischemic attacks (TIAs), and for ongoing research and rehabilitation.

Stuttering

Name: stutt-l
Resource: LISTSERV
Address: `stutt-l@templevm.bitnet`
This forum provides an exchange of information about stuttering, including research and clinical practice.

Technology

Name: l-hcap
Resource: LISTSERV
Address: `l-hcap@ndsuvm1.ndsu.edu`
A discussion list about how best to serve the needs of the disabled or handicapped with technology.

Women's Issues

Name: living
Resource: List
Address:
`living-request@qiclab.scn.rain.com`
(women only)
Living is a list for women with some sort of physical handicap.

Education

Academic Freedom

Name: alt.comp.acad-freedom.talk
Resource: USENET
Academic freedom issues related to computers.

Alumni

Name: BTHS-ENews-L
Resource: LISTSERV
Address: `LISTSERV@Cornell.edu`
For providing an open forum for students, teachers, and alumni of Brooklyn Technical High School. To subscribe, send mail to `LISTSERV@Cornell.edu` with a message body of this form: `subscribe BTHS-ENews-L <Full Name>`.

Name: drewids
Resource: List
Address:
`drewids-request@Warren.MentorG.COM`
This is the mailing list for Drew
University alumni/alumnae to chat.
To subscribe, send a mail message to
`majordomo@Warren.MentorG.com`. The first
line of the message (the subject line is
ignored) should be `subscribe drewids`
or `subscribe drewids-news`. Send other
administrative questions and requests
to the e-mail address
`drewids-approval@plts.org`.

Name: Friends of Ohio State
Resource: List
Address: `antivirus@aol.com`
(Jerry Canterbury)
Discussions to share items of interest
with alumni and other friends of
OSU.

Name: GSP-List
Resource: List
Address: `gsp-list-request@ms.uky.edu`
(David W. Rankin, Jr.) or
`gsp-list-request@ukma.BITNET` or `{uunet,`
`gatech, rutgers}!ukma!gsp-list-request`
To allow alumni (as defined by the
GSPAA) of the Kentucky Governor's
Scholars Program to participate in
intellectual discussions on various
topics, while also promoting the spirit
of community fostered by GSP.

Name: hadiko
Resource: List
Address:
`listproc@ubka.uni-karlsruhe.de`
(Patrick Dockhorn)
The HaDiKo list is a forum for current
and past members of the HaDiKo, a
student's community college in the
city of Karlsruhe, Germany.

Name: partners
Resource: List
Address: `partners-request@cs.cmu.edu`
To advise the administration of
Carnegie Mellon University, through
the Vice President of Human Re-
sources, of developments in Domestic
Partnership benefits and to make
recommendations on CMU policy
regarding benefits.

Name: UPS-alumni
Resource: List
Address:
`ups_alumni-request@stephsf.com`
(Bill England)
The mailing list has been put together
for the purpose of linking graduates
of The University of Puget Sound.

Children

Name: The Learning List
Resource: List
Address:
`Learning-Request@sea.east.sun.com`
(Rowan Hawthorne)
The Learning List is an electronic
forum for discussing child-centered
learning.

College

Name: soc.college
Resource: USENET
Discussion about college, college
activities, campus life, and so on.

College Bowl

Name: alt.college.college-bowl
Resource: USENET
Discussions of the College Bowl
competition.

General

Name: ashe-l
Resource: LISTSERV
Address: `ashe-l@mizzou1.bitnet`
Association for the Study of Higher
Education.

Name: newedu-l
Resource: LISTSERV
Address: `newedu-l@vm.usc.edu`
For the exchange of information
related to new and improved meth-
ods of education.

Gifted

Name: tag-l
Resource: LISTSERV
Address: `tag-l@ndsuvm1.ndsu.edu`
Devoted to the discussion of talented
and gifted students.

Graduate Schools

Name: soc.college.gradinfo
Resource: USENET
Information about graduate schools.

History

Resource: telnet

Address: `ukanaix.cc.ukans.edu`
User id: `history`

Home Education

Name: home-ed
Resource: List
Address: `home-ed-request@think.com`
(David Mankins)
This mailing list is for the discussion
of all aspects and methods of home
education.

Name: home-ed
Resource: List
Address: `home-ed@think.com`
A place for advocates of home
education to share and discuss ideas
and techniques. Send subscription
requests to `home-ed-request@think.com`.

Name: home-ed-politics
Resource: List
Address:
`home-ed-politics-request@mainstream.com`
(Craig Peterson)
To discuss political issues dealing
with home education.

IB

Name: IB
Resource: List
Address: `hreha@vax2.concordia.ca`
(Dr. Steve Hreha)
To provide a forum for teachers, IB
coordinators and administrators
involved with the International
Baccalaureate Diploma Program.

Law

Name: edlaw
Resource: LISTSERV
Address: `edlaw@ukcc.uky.edu`
This list is to discuss law and educa-
tion.

Law School

Name: lawaid
Resource: LISTSERV
Address: `lawaid@rutgers.edu`
Law school financial aid discussion.

Name: lawsch-l
Resource: LISTSERV
Address: `lawsch-l@auvm.bitnet`
A law school discussion list for everyone currently attending law school, teaching, or investigating the possibility of becoming a law student.

Learning

Name: altlearn
Resource: LISTSERV
Address: `altlearn@sjuvm.bitnet`
This list provides a forum for the exchange of information about alternative approaches to learning.

MBA Studies

Name: mba-l
Resource: LISTSERV
Address: `mba-l@marist.bitnet`
This discussion list is devoted to MBA student curricula.

Miscellaneous

Name: misc.education
Resource: USENET
Discussion of the educational system.

Science

Name: ascd-sci
Resource: LISTSERV
Address: `ascd-sci@psuvm.psu.edu`
This is the Alliance for Science Teaching forum.

Electronics

Cellular

Name: cellular
Resource: List
Address:
`cellular@mail-server@yngbld.gwinnett.com`
Discussion list for the cellular industry and related technologies.

Entertainment

Animation

Name: rec.arts.animation
Resource: USENET
Discussion of various kinds of animation.

Name: rec.arts.anime
Resource: USENET
Japanese animation fan discussion.

Name: rec.arts.anime.info
Resource: USENET
Announcements about Japanese animation. (Moderated)

Anime

Resource: FTP
Address: wpi.wpi.edu
Directory: `/anime/Scripts`

Name: anime-l
Resource: LISTSERV
Address: `anime-l@vtvm1.bitnet`
A discussion list for Japanese animedia and other animation news.

Audio

Name: rec.audio
Resource: USENET
High fidelity audio.

Brass

Name: brass
Resource: List
Address:
`brass-request@geomag.gly.fsu.edu`
(Ted Zateslo)
A discussion group for people
interested in brass musical perfor-
mance and related topics, especially
small musical ensembles of all kinds.

British Comedy

Name: alt.comedy.british
Resource: USENET
Discussion of British comedy in a
variety of media.

Cinema

Name: cinema-l
Resource: LISTSERV
Address: `cinema-l@auvm.bitnet`
This is a forum for discussion of all
forms of cinema.

Dylan Dog

Name: dylandog
Resource: LISTSERV
Address: `dylandog@igecuniv.bitnet`
This is the fan club list for Dylan Dog.

Film and Television

Name: screen-l
Resource: LISTSERV
Address: `screen-l@ua1vm.bitnet`
This is a list that discusses television
and film.

Film Music

Name: filmus-l
Resource: LISTSERV
Address: `filmus-l@iubvm.bitnet`
This discussion list is devoted to film
music.

Firesign Theatre

Name: alt.comedy.firesgn-thtre
Resource: USENET
Firesign Theatre in all its flaming
glory.

Gossip

Name: Cyber-Sleaze
Resource: List
Address: `request-cyber-sleaze@mtv.com`
Cyber-Sleaze is a five-day-per-week
service with all the latest dirt and
celebrity soil from the entertainment
biz. To subscribe, send mail to
`request-cyber-sleaze@mtv.com` in the
message type: `subscribe CYBER-SLEAZE`
`<Full Name>`.

Medieval

Name: perform
Resource: LISTSERV
Address: `perform@iubvm.bitnet`
This list is for everyone interested in
the medieval performing arts.

Movies

Name: amia-l
Resource: LISTSERV
Address: `amia-l@ukcc.uky.edu`
This list is frequented by the Association for Moving Image Archivists.

Name: film-l
Resource: LISTSERV
Address: `film-l@itesmvf1.bitnet`
This list is about filmmaking and reviews.

Name: horror
Resource: LISTSERV
Address: `horror@pacevm.bitnet`
This list is about horror films and fiction.

Name: Rocky Horror
Resource: List
Address: `mossap@essex.ac.uk`
(Adam Moss)
To distribute news and creative material concerning the film *The Rocky Horror Picture Show*, the stage shows, or anything else in any way connected with the *Rocky Horror* films or their stars.

Music

Resource: List
Contact `J.Arnold@bull.com` for information about subscribing to a list devoted to the music group Emerson, Lake, and Palmer.

Resource: FTP
Address: `ftp.uwp.edu`
Directory: `/pub/lyrics`

Resource: FTP
Address: `ftp.iastate.edu`
Directory: `/pub/lyrics`

Name: 4-AD-L
Resource: List
Address: `listserv@jhuvm.bitnet`
This list is for discussion of music on the 4AD Records label, which includes Cocteau Twins, Throwing Muses, Breeders, Belly, Colourbox, and many others.

Name: Accordion
Resource: List
Address: `Accordion@marie.stat.uga.edu`
For everyone interested in playing, appreciating, acquiring, or repairing all types of accordions. Send your subscription in the form of e-mail to `accordion@marie.stat.uga.edu`.

Name: Acid Jazz
Resource: List
Address:
`gregbb@uhunix.uhcc.hawaii.edu`
(Greg "Boyteen" Beuthin)
This is a manually operated mailing list, not a reflector, for the discussion of Acid Jazz, a relatively new form of dance music popular in European clubs and at raves around the world.

Name: acmr-l
Resource: LISTSERV
Address: `acmr-l@uhccvm.bitnet`
Association for Chinese Music Research network.

Name: alicefan
Resource: LISTSERV
Address: `alicefan@wkuvx1.bitnet`
This list is for all fans who want to discuss and exchange information about Alice Cooper.

Name: allman
Resource: List

Address: `allman-request@world.std.com`
(Eric Budke)
The discussion of the Allman Brothers
Band and its derivatives.

Name: allmusic
Resource: List
Address:
`allmusic@auvm.bitnet@vm1.nodak.edu`
Devoted to the discussion and
exchange of information and viewpoints about all forms of music. Send
direct subscriptions and administrative information to
`U6183%wvnvm.bitnet@vm1.nodak.edu`.

Name: alt.emusic
Resource: USENET
Discussion about ethnic, exotic,
electronic, elaborate, and similar
music.

Name: alt.exotic-music
Resource: USENET
Exotic music discussions.

Name: alt.fan.frank-zappa
Resource: USENET
Is that a Sears poncho?

Name: alt.fan.jimmy-buffett
Resource: USENET
A white sports coat and a pink
crustacean.

Name: alt.music.alternative
Resource: USENET
For groups having two or fewer
Platinum-selling albums.

Name: alt.music.bela-fleck
Resource: USENET
Bela and the Flecktones.

Name: alt.music.canada
Resource: USENET
Oh, Canada, eh?

Name: alt.music.enya
Resource: USENET
Gaelic set to spacey music.

Name: alt.music.filk
Resource: USENET
SF/fantasy-related folk music.

Name: alt.music.james-taylor
Resource: USENET
JT!

Name: alt.music.jewish
Resource: USENET
Jewish music.

Name: alt.music.progressive
Resource: USENET
Yes, Marillion, Asia, King Crimson,
and so on.

Name: alt.music.queen
Resource: USENET

Name: alt.music.rush
Resource: USENET
For Rushheads.

Name: alt.music.ska
Resource: USENET
Discussions of ska (skank) music,
bands, and the like.

Name: alt.music.tmbg
Resource: USENET
They Might Be Giants.

Name: alt.rap
Resource: USENET
For fans of rap music.

Name: alt.rock-n-roll
Resource: USENET
Counterpart to alt.sex and alt.drugs.

Name: alt.rock-n-roll.acdc
Resource: USENET
Dirty deeds done dirt cheap.

Name: alt.rock-n-roll.classic
Resource: USENET
Classic rock, both the music and its marketing.

Name: alt.rock-n-roll.hard
Resource: USENET
Music where stance is everything.

Name: alt.rock-n-roll.metal
Resource: USENET
For the headbangers on the net.

Name: alt.rock-n-roll.metal.heavy
Resource: USENET
Non-sissyboy metal bands.

Name:
alt.rock-n-roll.metal.ironmaiden
Resource: USENET
Sonic torture methods.

Name:
alt.rock-n-roll.metal.metallica
Resource: USENET
Sort of like formica with more hair.

Name:
alt.rock-n-roll.metal.progressive
Resource: USENET
Slayer teams up with Tom Cora.

Name: alt.rock-n-roll.stones
Resource: USENET
Gathering plenty of moss by now.

Name: backstreets
Resource: List
Address:
backstreets-request@virginia.edu
(Kevin Kinder)
Discussions of any and all issues likely to be of interest to people who enjoy Bruce Springsteen's music.

Name: bagpipe
Resource: List

Address:
pipes-request@sunapee.dartmouth.edu
Any topic related to bagpipes, most generally defined as any instrument where air is forced manually from a bellows or bag through drones and/or over reeds.

Name: barbershop
Resource: List
Address: barbershop@bigd.cray.com
For anyone interested in barbershop harmony and singing. Send your e-mail subscription requests to barbershop-request@bigd.cray.com.

Name: bass
Resource: List
Address:
bass-request@gsbcs.uchicago.edu
The purpose of this list is to discuss the reproduction and enjoyment of deep bass, primarily in consumer audio.

Name: Bel Canto
Resource: List
Address:
dewy-fields-request@ifi.uio.no
The Bel Canto list is open to all discussion regarding the music, lyrics, shows of the group, or the group members' solo projects—even related artists, if appropriate.

Name: Beloved
Resource: List
Address:
beloved-request@phoenix.oulu.fi
(Jyrki Sarkkinen)
This list is for the discussion of The Beloved, an English pop group with strong ambient & techno influences.

Name: Between the Lines
Resource: List
Address: `mkwong@scf.nmsu.edu`
(Myra Wong)
To share information and discuss Debbie Gibson and her music.

Name: bgrass-l
Resource: LISTSERV
Address: `bgrass-l@ukcc.uky.edu`
Bluegrass music discussion.

Name: bit.listserv.emusic-l
Resource: USENET
Electronic Music Discussion List.

Name: blues-l
Resource: LISTSERV
Address: `blues-l@brownvm.brown.edu`
Blues music list.

Name: BLUES-L
Resource: LISTSERV
Address: `LISTSERV@BROWNVM.brown.edu`
For everyone who can't get enough of the blues, there is a mailing list for blues.

Name: bolton
Resource: List
Address: `ai411@yfn.ysu.edu`
The purpose of the list is to allow Bolton fans to discuss Michael, his music, and his work.

Name: Bong (Depeche Mode)
Resource: List
Address:
`bong-request@lestat.compaq.com`
(Colin Smiley)
Bong is for the discussion of the mostly-electronic band Depeche Mode and related projects such as Recoil.

Name: brass
Resource: List
Address: `brass@geomag.gly.fsu.edu`
For persons interested in performing with brass musical instruments. Send your subscription requests to `brass-request@geomag.gly.fsu.edu`.

Name: btl
Resource: List
Address: `btl @mkwong@scf.nmsu.edu`
For fans of Debbie Gibson. Send subscription requests to `mkwong@scf.nmsu.edu`.

Name: chalkhills
Resource: List
Address:
`chalkhills-request@presto.ig.com`
(John M. Relph)
Chalkhills is a mailing list for the discussion of the music and records of XTC (the band).

Name: chorus
Resource: List
Address:
`chorus-request@psych.toronto.edu`
Lesbian and gay chorus mailing list, formed November 1991 by John Schrag (`jschrag@alias.com`) and Brian Jarvis (`jarvis@psych.toronto.edu`).

Name: concrete-blonde
Resource: List
Address:
`concrete-blonde@ferkel.ucsb.edu`
A list devoted to Concrete Blonde. Send subscriptions and related administrative information to `concrete-blonde-request@ferkel.ucsb.edu`.

Name: concrete-blonde
Resource: List
Address:
concrete-blonde-request@piggy.ucsb.edu
(Robert Earl)
Discussion of the rock group Concrete
Blonde and related artists and issues.

Name: costello
Resource: List
Address: costello@gnu.ai.mit.edu
For fans of Elvis Costello. Send your
subscriptions and administrative
information to
costello-request@gnu.ai.mit.edu.

Name: Crowes
Resource: List
Address: rstewart@unex.ucla.edu
To provide a forum for discussion
about the rock band the Black
Crowes.

Name: dead-flames
Resource: List
Address: dead-flames@virginia.edu
Gatewayed to the USENET group
rec.music.gdead. For all Deadheads!
Send your subscription requests to
dead-flames-request@virginia.edu.

Name: dead-heads
Resource: List
Address: dead-heads@virginia.edu
"Deadicated" to the discussion of
nonmusic aspects of Deadhead
culture. Send subscription requests to
dead-heads-request@virginia.edu.

Name: Deborah Harry/Blondie
              Information Service.
Resource: List
Address: gunter@yarrow.wt.uwa.oz.au
An information service on everything
and anything regarding Deborah

Harry and Blondie, including tour
information, recordings/films release
information, and so on.

Name: dire-straits
Resource: List
Address:
dire-straits-request@merrimack.edu
(Rand P. Hall)
Discussion of the musical group Dire
Straits and associated side projects.

Name: direct
Resource: List
Address:
direct-request@ctsx.celtech.com
(Keith Gregoire)
Discussion of the work of the musical
artist Vangelis.

Name: Dokken/Lynch Mob
Resource: List
Address: kydeno00@ukpr.uky.edu
(Kirsten DeNoyelles)
kydeno00@mik.uky.edu
Articles, questions, and discussions
on Dokken and Lynch Mob.

Name: Drone On…
Resource: List
Address: droneon-request@ucsd.edu
The Drone On… list is for the discussion of Spacemen 3 and resultant
bands, as well as any other droning
guitar bands that anyone wants to
bring up.

Name: Echoes
Resource: List
Address: Echoes@Fawnya.tcs.com
A discussion group devoted to the
rock band Pink Floyd. Send your
subscriptions to
echoes-request@fawnya.tcs.com.

Name: echoes
Resource: List
Address:
`echoes-request@fawnya.tcs.com`
(H. W. Neff)
Info and commentary on the musical group Pink Floyd, as well as other projects members of the group have been involved with.

Name: ecto
Resource: List
Address: `ecto-request@ns1.rutgers.edu`
(Jessica Dembski)
Information and discussion about singer/songwriter Happy Rhodes, and other music, art, books, films of common (or singular) interest.

Name: Electric Light Orchestra
Resource: List
Address:
`elo-list-request@andrew.cmu.edu`
Discussion of the music of Electric Light Orchestra and later solo efforts by band members and former members.

Name: ELP
Resource: List
Address: `J.Arnold@bull.com`
(John Arnold)
To share news, opinions, and other discussions about the musical group Emerson, Lake & Palmer and related topics.

Name: Elvis Costello
Resource: List
Address:
`costello-request@gnu.ai.mit.edu`
(Danny Hernandez)
For the discussion and dissemination of information of Declan Patrick Aloysius MacManus, better known as Elvis Costello.

Name: emusic-d
Resource: LISTSERV
Address: `emusic-d@auvm.bitnet`
This is a digest for electronic music discussion.

Name: Eno-L
Resource: List
Address:
`eno-l-request@udlapvms.pue.udlap.mx`
(Alex Rubli)
Eno-L is for the discussion of the music of Brian Eno.

Name: Erpnotes (Ozric Tentacles)
Resource: List
Address:
`erpnotes-request@toys.fubarsys.com`
(Christopher Ambler)
Erpnotes is for discussion of the English psychedelic rock/ambient band Ozric Tentacles and related spin-off projects.

Name: Escape From Noise
Resource: List
Address: `efn@wvolusia.uucp`
The Escape From Noise Digest is a (more or less) monthly compendium of articles, reviews, and other info for fans of industrial and cyberpunk music. Address requests for subscription, reader submissions, and letters to the editor to `efn@wvolusia.uucp` or `wvolusia!efn@edus.oau.org`. Back issues are available by anonymous FTP at `bradley.bradley.edu`.

Name: fegmaniax
Resource: List
Address:
`fegmaniax-request@gnu.ai.mit.edu`
Discussion, news, and information regarding that English eccentric and musician, Robyn Hitchcock.

Name: finewine
Resource: List
Address:
`finewine-request@world.std.com`
(Eric Budke)
A newsgroup dedicated to the rock
music group God Street Wine.

Name: fogelberg
Resource: List
Address: `ai411@yfn.ysu.edu`
The purpose of the list is to allow
Fogelberg fans to discuss Dan, his
music, and his work.

Name: folk_music
Resource: LISTSERV
Address: `listserv@nysernet.org`
(Alan Rowoth)
Folk_music is a moderated discussion
list dealing with the music of the
recent wave of American singer/
songwriters. To subscribe, send mail
to `<listserv@nysernet.org>` with the
request `SUBSCRIBE FOLK_MUSIC <Full`
`Name>`.

Name: freaks
Resource: List
Address: `freaks-request@bnf.com`
A list that talks about Marillion and
related rock groups. To subscribe
send a message containing: `subscribe`
`freaks <Full Name>`.

Name: Funky Music
Resource: List
Address:
`funky-music-request@hyper.lap.upenn.edu`
The Funky Music mailing list is for
discussion of funk and
funk-influenced music, including
funk, hip-hop, house, soul, r&b, and
so on.

Name: funky-music
Resource: List
Address:
`funky-music-request@athena.mit.edu`
(George Zipperlen)
The funky-music mailing list is for the
discussion of funk music, as well as
rap, hip-hop, soul, r&b, and related
varieties.

Name: fuzzy-ramblings
Resource: List
Address:
`fuzzy-ramblings-request@piggy.ucsb.edu`
(Robert Earl)
Discussion of the British girl group
Fuzzbox.

Name: grunge-l
Resource: LISTSERV
Address: `listserv@ubvm.cc.buffalo.edu`
(Jon Hilgreen)
This list is intended for the discussion
of any and all topics related to the
form of music known as "grunge
rock"—not just Seattle-based or Sub
Pop bands. To subscribe, send a
message containing the message
`subscribe grunge-l <Full Name>` to
`listserv@ubvm.cc.buffalo.edu`.

Name: Grunge-L
Resource: LISTSERV
Address: `Grunge-L@ubvm.cc.buffalo.edu`
For anyone who is a fan of the grunge
music scene.

Name: hey-joe
Resource: List
Address: `hey-joe-request@ms.uky.edu`
(Joel Abbott)
Discussion and worship of Jimi
Hendrix and his music.

Name: IDM (Intelligent Dance Music)
Resource: List
Address:
`majordomo@techno.stanford.edu`
(Brian Behlendorf & Fluid)
The IDM list is for the discussion of the form of electronic music that has been coined "Intelligent Dance Music" by a British music magazine and "Electronic Listening Music" by a label promoting the new genre.

Name: indigo
Resource: List
Address: `indigo@athena.mit.edu`
For fans and enthusiasts of the Indigo Girls. Send your subscription requests to `indigo-request@athena.mit.edu`.

Name: indigo-girls
Resource: List
Address:
`indigo-girls-request@cgrg.ohio-state.edu`
(Stephen Spencer)
Discussion of the Indigo Girls and related artists' music, tour dates, concert reviews, and so on.

Name: Introspective (Pet Shop Boys)
Resource: List
Address:
`introspective-request@ferkel.ucsb.edu`
(Jim Lick)
This list is for the discussion of the synth pop group Pet Shop Boys; list traffic tends to be chatty in nature.

Name: INXS
Resource: List
Address:
`INXS-list-request@iastate.edu`
An unmoderated forum for the discussion of the Australian rock group INXS.

Name: irtrad-l
Resource: LISTSERV
Address: `irtrad-l@irlearn.ucd.ie`
Irish traditional music list.

Name: janes-addiction
Resource: List
Address: `janes-addiction@ms.uky.edu`
For fans of Jane's Addiction. Send your subscription requests to `janes-addiction-request@ms.uky.edu`.

Name: jazz-l
Resource: LISTSERV
Address: `jazz-l@templevm.bitnet`
For jazz lovers.

Name: jpop
Resource: List
Address: `jpop@ferkel.ucsb.edu`
For fans and devotees of Japanese popular music and the related culture. Send subscription requests to `jpop-request@ferkel.ucsb.edu`.

Name: JTull
Resource: List
Address:
`jtull-request@remus.rutgers.edu`
(Dave Steiner)
A mailing list for discussions about the music group Jethro Tull, including ex-members and related artists.

Name: jump-in-the-river
Resource: List
Address:
`jump-in-the-river-request@presto.ig.com`
(Michael C. Berch)
`{apple,ames,rutgers}!bionet!ig!jump-in-the-river-request`
Jump-in-the-river is a mailing list for the discussion of the music and recordings of Sinead O'Connor, as well as related matters such as lyrics, and tour information.

Name: kiwimusic
Resource: List
Address:
kiwimusic-request@athena.mit.edu
(Katie Livingston)
Discussion of New Zealand pop bands, particularly those on the Flying Nun, Failsafe, and Xpressway labels.

Name: klarinet
Resource: LISTSERV
Address: klarinet@vccscent.bitnet
For fans and performers of the clarinet.

Name: KLF/Orb
Resource: List
Address: klf-request@asylum.sf.ca.us
(Lazlo Nibble)
The KLF/Orb mailing list is for discussion of the JAMS, Timelords, KLF, and K Foundation (who are all one and the same), The Orb, and tangentially related artists such as System 7, Fortran 5, and Andy Falconer.

Name: kosmos
Resource: List
Address:
kosmos-request@athena.mit.edu
Cool discussions involving the solo career of Paul "The Mod God" Weller.

Name: Kraftwerk
Resource: List
Address: kraftwerk-request@cs.uwp.edu
(Dave Datta)
This list is for discussion of the pioneering German techno-pop group Kraftwerk, arguably the founding fathers of electro, techno, and at least half of all dance music produced in the last 10 years.

Name: Level 42
Resource: List
Address:
level42-request@enterprise.bih.harvard.edu
To support discussions of the musical act Level 42.

Name: life-talking
Resource: List
Address:
life-talking-request@ferkel.ucsb.edu
(Jim Lick)
Discussion of the musical group Life Talking.

Name: loureed
Resource: List
Address:
loureed-request@cvi.hahnemann.edu
(Sylvia)
Mailing list for discussion of music and other items related to the 30-years-and-running career of Mr. Lou Reed, including Velvet Underground matters.

Name: Lute
Resource: List
Address: Lute@sunapee.dartmouth.edu
This discussion list focuses on playing lutes and researching lute music. Send your subscription request to lute-request@sunapee.dartmouth.edu.

Name: Maria McKee/Lone Justice
Resource: List
Address: MCKEEFAN@aol.com
(Ken Bourbeau)
A new digest for discussion of Maria McKee, Lone Justice, and related topics.

Name: Melissa Etheridge
Resource: List

Address:
Etheridge-request@krylov.cnd.mcgill.ca
The purpose of this list is to discuss
Melissa Etheridge and her music.

Name: Middle-Eastern Music
Resource: List
Address:
middle-eastern-music-request@nic.funet.fi
(Juhana Kouhia)
Discussion of the music originating
from the Middle East.

Name: miles
Resource: LISTSERV
Address: miles@hearn.bitnet
A discussion list for all fans of jazz
trumpeter Miles Davis.

Name: mla-l
Resource: LISTSERV
Address: mla-l@iubvm.bitnet
Music Library Association mailing
list.

Name: MLoL (Musical List of
            Lists)
Resource: List
Address: mlol-request@wariat.org
(John C. Rowland)
Not really a mailing list, the MLoL is
a list of music-related mailing lists.

Name: NetJam
Resource: List
Address:
netjam-request@xcf.berkeley.edu
(Craig Latta)
NetJam provides a means for people
to collaborate on musical composi-
tions, by sending Musical Instrument
Digital Interface (MIDI) and other
files (such as MAX patchers and
notated scores) to each other,
mucking about with them, and
resending them.

Name: Network-Audio-Bits
Resource: List
Address: Murph@Maine.BITNET
(Michael A. Murphy)
Network Audio Bits & Audio Software Review is a bimonthly electronic
magazine that features reviews of and
information about current rock, pop,
new age, jazz, funk, folk and other
musical genres.

Name: Numan (Gary Numan)
Resource: List
Address: numan-request@cs.uwp.edu
(Dave Datta)
This list, available as a weekly digest
only, is for the purpose of the acquisi-
tion and dissemination of info about
the electronic musician Gary Numan.

Name: OMD (Orchestral
            Manoevres In The Dark)
Resource: List
Address: omd-request@cs.uwp.edu
(Dave Datta)
The OMD list is a forum for discus-
sions about the English pop band
Orchestral Manouevres In The Dark,
who often incorporate modern dance
elements into their music.

Name: on-u
Resource: List
Address: on-u-request@connect.com.au
(Ben Golding)
The On-U Sound mailing list encour-
ages discussions related to Adrian
Sherwood's On-U Sound label and
the artists who record on it.

Name: oysters
Resource: List
Address:
`oysters-request@blowfish.taligent.com`
For discussion of the British folk-rock band The Oyster band and related topics.

Name: ph7
Resource: List
Address: `ph7-request@bnf.com`
A list that talks about Peter Hammill and related rock groups. To subscribe, send a message containing the following: `subscribe ph7 <Full Name>`.

Name: Pipes
Resource: List
Address: `Pipes@sunapee.dartmouth.edu`
Any topic related to bagpipes or related instruments. Send subscription requests to
`pipes-request@sunapee.dartmouth.edu`.

Name: piporg-l
Resource: LISTSERV
Address: `piporg-l@albnyvm1`
This list is for the discussion of pipe organs and related topics.

Name: Police
Resource: List
Address: `majordomo@xmission.com`
This mailing list is dedicated as a service to keep fans of The Police and its members Sting, Stewart Copeland, and Andy Summers, informed and connected. To subscribe, mail to `majordomo@xmission.com`; the body of the message must contain `subscribe police` for the unmoderated list or `subscribe police-digest` for the digested version.

Name: Prince
Resource: List

Address:
`prince-request@icpsr.umich.edu`
The Prince list is devoted to discussing the musician Prince, as well as related artists.

Name: Queen
Resource: List
Address: `qms-request@uiuc.edu`
(Dan Blanchard)
Discussion about the rock group Queen.

Name: Really-Deep-Thoughts
Resource: List
Address:
`really-deep-thoughts-request@gradient.cis.upenn.edu`
`rdt-request@gradient.cis.upenn.edu`
(Anthony Kosky)
Information and discussion on Tori Amos, her music, and other subjects that are relevant or of interest.

Name: rec.music.bluenote
Resource: USENET
Discussion of jazz, blues, and related types of music.

Name: rec.music.classical
Resource: USENET
Discussion of classical music.

Name:
rec.music.classical.performing
Resource: USENET
Performing classical (including early) music.

Name: rec.music.compose
Resource: USENET
Creating musical and lyrical works.

Name: rec.music.dylan
Resource: USENET
Discussion of Bob's works and music.

Name: rec.music.early
Resource: USENET
Discussion of preclassical European music.

Name: rec.music.folk
Resource: USENET
Folks discussing folk music of various sorts.

Name: rec.music.funky
Resource: USENET
Funk, rap, hip-hop, house, soul, r&b and related.

Name: rec.music.gaffa
Resource: USENET
Discussion of Kate Bush and other alternative music. (Moderated)

Name: rec.music.gdead
Resource: USENET
A group for (Grateful) Dead-heads.

Name: rec.music.indian.classical
Resource: USENET
Hindustani and Carnatic Indian classical music.

Name: rec.music.indian.misc
Resource: USENET
Discussing Indian music in general.

Name: rec.music.industrial
Resource: USENET
Discussion of all industrial-related music styles.

Name: rec.music.info
Resource: USENET
News and announcements on musical topics. (Moderated)

Name: rec.music.makers
Resource: USENET
For performers and their discussions.

Name: rec.music.makers.bass
Resource: USENET
Upright bass and bass guitar techniques and equipment.

Name: rec.music.makers.guitar
Resource: USENET
Electric and acoustic guitar techniques and equipment.

Name:
rec.music.makers.percussion
Resource: USENET
Drum and other percussion techniques and equipment.

Name: rec.music.makers.synth
Resource: USENET
Synthesizers and computer music.

Name: rec.music.misc
Resource: USENET
Music lovers' group.

Name: rec.music.newage
Resource: USENET
New Age music discussions.

Name: rec.music.phish
Resource: USENET
Discussing the musical group Phish.

Name: rmusic-l
Resource: LISTSERV
Address: `rmusic-l@gitvm1.bitnet`
A general discussion about the music industry, including concert, albums, song lyrics, performers, and anything else related to general music.

Name: rock
Resource: LISTSERV
Address: `rock@tritu.bitnet`
Rock 'n' roll music discussion list.

Name: rush
Resource: List
Address: `rush-request@syrinx.umd.edu`
Fans of the Canadian rock group Rush discuss things about the group and its music.

Name: sabbath
Resource: List
Address:
sabbath-request@fa.disney.com
(Michael Sullivan)
To discuss the rock group Black
Sabbath and, to a limited extent, its
former members.

Name: saturn
Resource: LISTSERV
Address: saturn@hearn.bitnet
For fans of the late Sun Ra and his
Arkestra.

Name: Screaming in Digital
Resource: List
Address:
queensryche-request@pilot.njin.net
Discussion of the band Queensryche
and related topics.

Name: siouxsie+
Resource: List
Address: siouxsie+@andrew.cmu.edu
A list for all fans of Siouxsie and the
Banshees. Send subscription requests
to siouxsie-request+@andrew.cmu.edu.

Name: smiths-fans
Resource: List
Address: larryn@csufres.csufresno.edu
We are a mailing list dedicated to the
music of the rock group The Smiths.

Name: sonic-life-l
Resource: LISTSERV
Address: rtv1@cornell.edu
SONIC-LIFE-L is a mailing list
dedicated to the discussion of the
music and other work of Sonic Youth.
To subscribe, send a message to
listserv@cornell.edu; the message
should contain the following: SUB
SONIC-LIFE-L <First Name> <Last Name>.

Name: Space Music
Resource: List
Address:
space-music-request@cs.uwp.edu
(Dave Datta)
The Space Music mailing list is for the
discussion of artists and their works
who primarily use electronic instruments, create "sound spaces" or
sound atmospheres that fall into
categories sometimes defined as
"floating" or "cosmic," and are
generally considered noncommercial
and demand an active listener.

Name: stormcock
Resource: LISTSERV
Address: stormcock-request@qmw.ac.uk
(Paul Davison)
For general discussion and news
concerning the music of Roy Harper,
a folk-rock musician with a con-
science. To join, send mail to
listserv@qmw.ac.uk with the following
message body: subscribe stormcock
<Full Name>.

Name: Sylvian
Resource: LISTSERV
Address: john@ucc.gu.uwa.edu.au
(John West)
This list discusses the work of Japan
and its solo members including David
Sylvian. To subscribe, send the
message SUBSCRIBE SYLVIAN <Full Name>
to LISTSERV@ucc.gu.uwa.edu.au.

Name: Synth-L
Resource: LISTSERV
Address: listserv@american.edu
(Joe McMahon)
Synth-L is the electronic music
"gearhead" list, dedicated to the
discussion of the less-esoteric aspects
of synthesis.

Name: tadream
Resource: List
Address: `tadream@vacs.uwp.wisc.edu`
This list provides a common forum for fans of the band Tangerine Dream. Send your subscription request to `tadream-request@vacs.uwp.wisc.edu`.

Name: tadream
Resource: List
Address: `tadream-request@cs.uwp.edu` (Dave Datta)
Discussion of Tangerine Dream and solo projects by members of the band, such as Edgar Froese and Christopher Franke.

Name: tears4-fears
Resource: List
Address: `tears4-fears-request@ms.uky.edu` (Joel Abbot)
Discussion of the music group Tears For Fears.

Name: The Sugarcubes
Resource: LISTSERV
Address: `glocke@morgan.ucs.mun.ca` (Gord Locke)
The blue-eyed-pop mailing list is for discussion of the now-defunct (though-not-necessarily-for-good) Icelandic band, the Sugarcubes. To subscribe to this list, send a message to `listserver@morgan.ucs.mun.ca`; the body of of the message should simply read `blue-eyed-pop <Full Name>`.

Name: TheWho
Resource: List
Address: `majordomo@cisco.com`
An unmoderated mailing list for discussion of the band The Who, its individual members, lyrics, and so on. To subscribe, e-mail to

`majordomo@cisco.com` with the following line in the body of the message (not the subject line): `subscribe thewho`.

Name: they-might-be
Resource: List
Address: `they-might-be-request@super.org`
Discussion of the musical group They Might Be Giants.

Name: dire-straits
Resource: List
Address: `Dire-Straits@Merrimack.Edu`
A discussion list for the fans of Dire Straits.

Name: top
Resource: List
Address: `top-request@cv.ruu.nl` (Ger Timmens)
Discussion of the musical group Tower of Power and associated side projects.

Name: Trumpet List
Resource: LISTSERV
Address: `listserv@acad1.dana.edu`
This unmoderated list is devoted to the subject of the trumpet. To subscribe, send the message `subscribe trumpet` to `listserv@acad1.dana.edu`.

Name: tuba-l
Resource: LISTSERV
Address: `tuba-l@vtvm2.bitnet`
This is the tuba players' mailing list.

Name: undercover
Resource: List
Address: `undercover@snowhite.cis.uoguelph.ca`
This is an open list for fans of the Rolling Stones. Send subscription requests and related administrative information to `undercover-request@snowhite.cis.uoguelph.ca`.

Name: Yello
Resource: List
Address:
`yello-request@overpass.csc.calpoly.edu`
(Cliff Tuel)
The Yello list is for discussion of the Swiss electronic band Yello.

Name: Zang Tuum Tumb
Resource: List
Address: `ztt-request@asylum.sf.ca.us`
(Lazlo Nibble)
For discussion of producer Trevor Horn's UK record label Zang Tuum Tumb and its associated artists.

Name: zeppelin
Resource: LISTSERV
Address: `zeppelin-l@cornell.edu`
For fans of the rock group Led Zeppelin.

Music Theory

Name: Music-Research
Resource: List
Address:
`Music-Research-Request@prg.oxford.ac.uk`
(Stephen Page)
The Music-Research electronic mail redistribution list provides an effective and fast means of bringing together musicologists, music analysts, computer scientists, and others working on applications of computers in music research.

Newspaper

Name: alt.fan.dave_barry
Resource: USENET
Electronic fan club for humorist Dave Barry.

Public Radio

Name: pubradio
Resource: LISTSERV
Address: `pubradio@idbsu.bitnet`
This is the public radio discussion group.

Radio

Name: alt.fan.howard-stern
Resource: USENET
Fans of the abrasive radio and TV personality.

Name: AM/FM
Resource: LISTSERV
Address: `listserv@orbital.demon.co.uk`
AM/FM is the mailing list for the AM/FM Online Edition, a monthly compilation of news stories concerning the UK radio industry. To subscribe to the list, write to `listserv@orbital.demon.co.uk` with `subscribe amfm <Full Name>` as the first line in the message body.

Reviews

Name: joe-bob
Resource: List
Address: `joe-bob-request@blkbox.com`
Dedicated to the humor, writings, TV, and movie performances, and movie reviews of the infamous Joe Bob Briggs.

Science Fiction

Name: rec.arts.sf.announce
Resource: USENET
Major announcements of the SF world. (Moderated)

Name: rec.arts.sf.misc
Resource: USENET
Science fiction lovers' newsgroup.

Name: rec.arts.sf.movies
Resource: USENET
Discussing SF motion pictures.

Name: rec.arts.sf.reviews
Resource: USENET
Reviews of science fiction/fantasy/
horror works. (Moderated)

Name: rec.arts.sf.science
Resource: USENET
Real and speculative aspects of SF
science.

Name: rec.arts.sf.tv
Resource: USENET
Discussing general television SF.

Soundtracks

Name: soundtracks
Resource: List
Address:
soundtracks-request@ifi.unizh.ch
(Michel Hafner)
Discussion about soundtracks, both
past and present, available and out of
print.

Stage Work

Name: stagecraft
Resource: List
Address:
stagecraft@jaguar.cs.utah.edu
A discussion list devoted to all
aspects of stage work in the theater.
Send subscription requests to
stagecraft-request@jaguar.cs.utah.edu.

Star Trek

Name: rec.arts.startrek.current
Resource: USENET
New *Star Trek* shows, movies, and
books.

Name: rec.arts.startrek.fandom
Resource: USENET
Star Trek conventions and memora-
bilia.

Name: rec.arts.startrek.info
Resource: USENET
Information about the universe of
Star Trek. (Moderated)

Name: rec.arts.startrek.misc
Resource: USENET
General discussions of *Star Trek*.

Name: rec.arts.startrek.tech
Resource: USENET
Star Trek's depiction of future tech-
nologies.

Television

Name: 30something
Resource: List
Address:
30something-request@fuggles.acc.virginia.edu
(Marc Rouleau)
Discussion of the TV show by the
same name, including actors, epi-
sodes, plots, characters, and so on.

Name: 90210
Resource: List
Address: 90210@ferkel.ucsb.edu
The *Beverly Hills, 90210* lover's
discussion list. Send subscription
requests and other administrative
information to
90210-request@ferkel.ucsb.edu.

Name: alt.fan.chris-elliott
Resource: USENET
Get a Life, you Letterman flunky.

Name: alt.fan.letterman
Resource: USENET
One of the Top Ten reasons to get the
alt groups.

Name: alt.fan.ren-and-stimpy
Resource: USENET
For folks who couldn't find
alt.tv.ren-n-stimpy.

Name: alt.tv.animaniacs
Resource: USENET
Steven Spielberg's *Animaniacs*!

Name: alt.tv.game-shows
Resource: USENET
Just look at these wonderful prizes.

Name: alt.tv.mash
Resource: USENET
Nothing like a good comedy about
war and dying.

Name: alt.tv.mst3k
Resource: USENET
Hey, you robots! Down in front!

Name: alt.tv.mwc
Resource: USENET
Married…With Children.

Name: alt.tv.northern-exp
Resource: USENET
For the TV show with moss growing
on it.

Name: alt.tv.prisoner
Resource: USENET
The *Prisoner* television series from
years ago.

Name: alt.tv.ren-n-stimpy
Resource: USENET
Some change from *Lassie*, eh?

Name: alt.tv.simpsons
Resource: USENET
Don't have a cow, man!

Name: alt.tv.tiny-toon
Resource: USENET
Discussion about the *Tiny 'Toon
Adventures* show.

Name: catv
Resource: List
Address: `catv@quack.sac.ca.us`
A discussion list devoted to the cable
television industry. Send your
subscription request to
`catv-request@quack.sac.ca.us`.

Name: clarissa
Resource: List
Address: `clarissa-request@tcp.com`
(Jim Lick)
Discussion of the Nickelodeon TV
show *Clarissa Explains It All*.

Name: clarissa
Resource: List
Address: `clarissa@ferkel.ucsb.edu`
Discussion of the Nickelodeon
television show *Clarissa Explains It All*.
Send your subscription requests to
`clarissa-request@ferkel.ucsb.edu`.

Name: Class96
Resource: List
Address: `Class96@dream.saigon.com`
A discussion of the Fox TV show *Class
of '96*. Send an e-mail subscription
request to
`class96-request@dream.saigon.com`.

Name: dark-shadows
Resource: List
Address:
`shadows-request@sunee.waterloo.ca`
(Bernie Roehl)

A number of international fan clubs for the series *Dark Shadows* exist, but so far there has been no newsgroup or (electronic) mailing list devoted to it. Now there is.

Name: disney-afternoon
Resource: LISTSERV
Address:
`ranger-list-request@taronga.com`
(Stephanie da Silva)
Discussion of the Disney Afternoon and other related topics.

Name: Eerie, Indiana
Resource: List
Address: `owner-eerie-indiana@sfu.ca`
(Corey Kirk)
The list is for the discussion of the critically acclaimed but short-lived TV series *Eerie, Indiana*, which originally aired on NBC in 1991-1992 and is now distributed internationally.

Name: flamingo
Resource: List
Address:
`flamingo-request@lenny.corp.sgi.com`
The list is for unmoderated discussion among fans of the series *Parker Lewis* (formerly *Parker Lewis Can't Lose*) on the Fox television network.

Name: macgyver
Resource: List
Address: `shari@cc.gatech.edu`
(Shari Feldman)
This is a forum to discuss current and previous *MacGyver* episodes.

Name: Mayberry
Resource: LISTSERV
Address: `listserv@bolis.sf-bay.org`
This mailing list is for discussion of TV shows featuring Andy Griffith,

including *The Andy Griffith Show* and *Mayberry RFD*. To subscribe, send an e-mail message to `listserv@bolis.sf-bay.org` containing the following message body: `subscribe Mayberry`.

Name: melrose-place
Resource: List
Address:
`melrose-place@ferkel.ucsb.edu`
For fans and devotees of the television show *Melrose Place*. Send subscription requests to
`melrose-place-request@ferkel.ucsb.edu`.

Name: mst3k rsk
Resource: List
Address:
`mst3k rsk@gynko.circ.upenn.edu`
For fans and mavens of the television show *Mystery Science Theater 3000* (Comedy Channel).

Name: rec.arts.tv
Resource: USENET
The boob tube, its history, and past and current shows.

Name: rec.arts.tv.soaps
Resource: USENET
Postings about soap operas.

Name: rec.arts.tv.uk
Resource: USENET
Discussions of telly shows from the UK.

Name: rec.video.cable-tv
Resource: USENET
Technical and regulatory issues of cable television.

Name: rec.video.satellite
Resource: USENET
Getting shows via satellite.

Name: SATNEWS
Resource: LISTSERV
Address: `listserv@orbital.demon.co.uk`
SATNEWS is the mailing list for Satnews, a biweekly report of events in the satellite television industry worldwide. To subscribe to the list, write to `listserv@orbital.demon.co.uk` with `subscribe satnews <Full Name>` as the first line in the message body.

Name: shadows
Resource: List
Address: `shadows@sunee.waterloo.edu`
This forum is devoted to the daily soap opera *Dark Shadows*. Send your subscriptions to `shadows-request@sunee.waterloo.edu`.

Name: shadows-updates
Resource: List
Address:
`shadows-update-request@sunee.uwaterloo.ca`
Regular synopses of the episodes of the television series *Dark Shadows*, currently being shown on the Sci-Fi cable channel.

Name: Space: 1999
Resource: List
Address:
`space-1999-request@quack.kfu.com`
The charter of the list is for discussion on almost any subject of interest to fans of the 1975-1976 TV show *Space: 1999*.

Name: strek-d
Resource: LISTSERV
Address: `strek-d@pccvm.bitnet`
This is the *Star Trek* fan club digest.

Name: strek-l
Resource: LISTSERV
Address: `strek-l@pccvm.bitnet`
This is the *Star Trek* fan club list.

Name: strfleet
Resource: LISTSERV
Address: `strfleet@pccvm.bitnet`
This is the *Starfleet* forum.

Name: trek-review-l
Resource: LISTSERV
Address: `trek-review-l@cornell.edu`
This is a forum dedicated to reviewing, rating, and giving commentary on all aspects of the *Star Trek* phenomenon.

Name: tv-l
Resource: LISTSERV
Address: `tv-l@trearn.bitnet`
General television discussions.

Name: xpress-list
Resource: LISTSERV
Address: `listserv@grot.starconn.com`
Discussion of the X*Press X*Change data service, which is available on some cable television system in the USA and Canada and on some satellite television channels.

Theater

Name: alt.cult-movies
Resource: USENET
Movies with a cult following.

Name:
alt.cult-movies.rocky-horror
Resource: USENET
Virgin!

Name: comedia
Resource: LISTSERV
Address: `comedia@arizvm1.bitnet`
This list discusses Hispanic classic theater.

Name: musicals
Resource: List

Address:
musicals-request@world.std.com
(Elizabeth Lear Newman)
This forum is intended for the general
discussion of musical theater, in
whatever form it may take, but
related nonmusical theater topics are
also welcome.

Name: rec.arts.disney
Resource: USENET
Discussion of any Disney-related
subjects.

Name: rec.arts.movies
Resource: USENET
Discussions of movies and movie
making.

Name: rec.arts.theatre
Resource: USENET
Discussion of all aspects of stage work
and theatre.

Name: stagecraft
Resource: List
Address:
stagecraft-request@jaguar.cs.utah.edu
(Brad Davis)
This list is for the discussion of all
aspects of stage work, including (but
not limited to) special effects, sound
effects, sound reinforcement, stage
management, set design and building,
lighting design, company management, hall management, hall design,
and show production.

Name: theatre
Resource: List
Address:
theatre-request@world.std.com
(Elizabeth Lear Newman)
This forum is intended for the general
discussion of theater, in whatever
form it may take.

Video

Name: rec.music.video
Resource: USENET
Discussion of music videos and music
video software.

Food

Food and Wine

Name: foodwine
Resource: LISTSERV
Address: foodwine@cmuvm.csv.cmich.edu
This is a discussion list for those who
appreciate food and wine.

Recipes

Resource: FTP
Address: GATEKEEPER.DEC.COM
(16.1.0.2)
Directory: /pub/recipes

Resource: FTP
Address: mthvax.cs.miami.edu
Directory: pub/recipes

Name: eat-l
Resource: LISTSERV
Address: eat-l@vtvm1.bitnet
Devoted to foodlore and recipe
exchange.

Name: rec.food.cooking
Resource: USENET
Food, cooking, cookbooks, and
recipes.

Name: rec.food.recipes
Resource: USENET
Recipes for interesting food and
drink. (Moderated)

Fun

Answers

Name: misc
Resource: LISTSERV
Address: `misc@trearn.bitnet`
This list provides a common area for miscellaneous questions and requests.

Fun

Resource: telnet
Address: `astro.temple.edu 12345`
Telnet to this site; it will return something different every time!

Name: oracle
Resource: List
Address: `oracle@iuvax.cs.indiana.edu`
Where to turn when you need an answer. Send your administrative mail and subscription requests to `oracle-request@iuvax.cs.indiana.edu`.

Humor

Name: alt.shenanigans
Resource: USENET
Practical jokes, pranks, randomness, and so on.

Name: rec.humor.funny
Resource: USENET
Jokes that are funny (in the moderator's opinion). (Moderated)

Name: rec.humor.oracle
Resource: USENET
Sagacious advice from the USENET Oracle. (Moderated)

Jokes

Resource: FTP
Address: `pc10868.pc.cc.cmu.edu`
An archive of the Rec.Humor and Rec.Humor.D USENET groups.

Mardi Gras

Name: mardi-gras
Resource: List
Address:
`mardi-gras@mintir.new-orleans.la.us`
For those interested in celebrating the annual festival known as Mardi Gras. Send your subscription request to `mail-server@mintir.new-orleans.la.us` with the following command in the message: `subscribe mardi-gras`.

On-This-Day

Resource: Email
Contact `geiser@pictel.com` and you'll receive a daily message containing important events in history, astronomical events, religious holidays, and so on.

Name: on-this-day
Resource: List
Address: `geiser@pictel.com`
(Wayne Geiser)
Subscribers to on-this-day receive a daily listing of interesting birthdays, events, religious holidays, astronomical events, and so on. The messages are sent out in the wee hours of the morning, so you should have it for your morning coffee. :-)

Open Discussion

Name: freetalk
Resource: LISTSERV
Address: freetalk@brownvm.brown.edu
This is an open list for free talking; all subjects are fair game.

Oracle

Name: USENET-oracle
Resource: List
Address: oracle-admin@cs.indiana.edu
(Steve Kinzler)
An active, cooperative effort for creative humor. The USENET Oracle answers any questions posed to it.

Puzzles

Name: cube-lovers
Resource: List
Address: cube-lovers@ai.ai.mit.edu
A discussion list for information about Rubik's Cube and related puzzles.

Smiley

Resource: FTP
Address: nic.funet.fi
Directory: pub/doc/fun/smiley.txt This is the ultimate smiley dictionary.

Tasteless

Name: alt.tasteless
Resource: USENET
Truly disgusting.

Thought for the Day

Name: tftd-l
Resource: LISTSERV
Address: tftd-l@tamvm1.tamu.edu
This list provides a Thought for the Day.

Weird

Name: talk.bizarre
Resource: USENET
The unusual, bizarre, curious, and often stupid.

Weird Stuff

Name: weird-l
Resource: LISTSERV
Address: weird-l@brownvm.brown.edu
The stranger the better! Know of anything disturbing, weird, bizarre? Here's where you should hang out!

Games

Backgammon

Resource: telnet
Address: ouzo.rog.rwth-aachen.de 8765
Watch or participate in online backgammon games.

Name: bkgammon
Resource: LISTSERV
Address: bkgammon@indycms.iupui.edu
This list is devoted to the discussion and exchange of backgammon strategy.

Name: rec.games.backgammon
Resource: USENET
Discussion of the game of backgammon.

Board

Name: rec.games.board
Resource: USENET
Discussion and hints on board games.

Name: rec.games.chess
Resource: USENET
Chess and computer chess.

Name: rec.games.chinese-chess
Resource: USENET
Discussion of the game of Chinese chess, Xiangqi.

Name: rec.games.diplomacy
Resource: USENET
The conquest game Diplomacy.

Name: rec.games.go
Resource: USENET
Discussion about Go.

Name: rec.games.miniatures
Resource: USENET
Tabletop wargaming.

Name: shogi-l
Resource: LISTSERV
Address:
`shogi-l@technion.technion.ac.il`
This is a discussion list for the exchange of ideas, analysis, and tournament information for Shogi, also known as Japanese chess.

Card

Name: rec.games.bridge
Resource: USENET
Hobbyists interested in bridge.

Chess

Resource: telnet
Address: `aragorn.andrew.cmu.edu 5000`
Watch or participate in chess games online.

Resource: telnet
Address: `valkyries.andrew.cmu.edu 5000`
Play or watch chess games with real people in real-time.

Name: chess-l
Resource: LISTSERV
Address: `chess-l@grearn`
This list is devoted to international chess. Strategies, analysis, tournament information, and a position ladder are available.

Name: chessnews
Resource: List
Address: `chessnews-request@tssi.com` (Michael Nolan)
The chessnews mailing list is a repeater for the USENET newsgroup rec.games.chess.

Computer

Name:
comp.sys.ibm.pc.games.announce
Resource: USENET
Announcements for all PC gamers. (Moderated)

Name:
comp.sys.ibm.pc.games.flight-sim
Resource: USENET
Flight simulators on PCs.

Name: crossfire
Resource: List

Address: crossfire-request@ifi.uio.no
(Frank Tore Johansen)
To discuss the development of the
game Crossfire.

Name: gnu.chess
Resource: USENET
Announcements about the GNU
Chess program.

Name: rec.games.corewar
Resource: USENET
The Core War computer challenge.

Name: rec.games.misc
Resource: USENET
Games and computer games.

Name: rec.games.netrek
Resource: USENET
Discussion of the X window system
game Netrek (XtrekII).

Name: rec.games.video.3do
Resource: USENET
Discussion of 3DO video game
systems.

Name: rec.games.video.advocacy
Resource: USENET
Debate on merits of various video
game systems.

Name: rec.games.video.arcade
Resource: USENET
Discussions about coin-operated
video games.

Name: rec.games.video.atari
Resource: USENET
Discussion of Atari's video game
systems.

Name: rec.games.video.classic
Resource: USENET
Older home video entertainment
systems.

Name: rec.games.video.misc
Resource: USENET
General discussion about home video
games.

Name: rec.games.video.nintendo
Resource: USENET
All Nintendo video game systems
and software.

Name: rec.games.video.sega
Resource: USENET
All Sega video game systems and
software.

Conflict Simulation

Name: consim-l
Resource: LISTSERV
Address: consim-l@ualtavm.bitnet
This list was created for those inter-
ested in conflict simulation games.

Design

Name: rec.games.design
Resource: USENET
Discussion of game design-related
issues.

Electronic

Name: alt.games.sf2
Resource: USENET
The video game Street Fighter 2.

Go

Resource: telnet
Address:
icsib18.icsi.berkeley.edu 6969
This provides a real-time connection
for you to watch or play games of Go.

Name: go-l
Resource: List
Address:

`go-l@smcvax.bitnet@vm1.nodak.edu`
For the exchange of information and strategies, as well as an opportunity to find electronic (e-mail) opponents. Send subscription requests in the form of SUBSCRIBE GO-L to

`MailServ%SmcVax.Bitnet@VM1.NoDak.Edu.`

Live Action

Name: alt.games.frp.live-action
Resource: USENET
Discussion of all forms of live-action gaming.

Miscellaneous

Name: rec.games.hack
Resource: USENET
Discussion, hints, and so on about the Hack game.

Name: rec.games.moria
Resource: USENET
Comments, hints, and info about the Moria game.

Name: rec.games.pbm
Resource: USENET
Discussion about Play by Mail games.

Pinball

Name: rec.games.pinball
Resource: USENET
Discussing pinball-related issues.

Poker

Name: ba-poker-list
Resource: List
Address: `ba-poker-request@netcom.com`
(Martin Veneroso)
Discussion of poker as it is available to residents of and visitors to the San Franciso Bay Area (broadly defined), in home games as well as in licensed card rooms.

Puzzles

Name: rec.puzzles
Resource: USENET
Puzzles, problems, and quizzes.

Name: rec.puzzles.crosswords
Resource: USENET
Making and playing gridded word puzzles.

Role-Playing

Name: adnd-l
Resource: LISTSERV
Address: `adnd-l@utarlvm1.bitnet`
This is the Advanced Dungeons & Dragons discussion list.

Name: Ars Magica
Resource: List
Address:

`ars-magica-request@soda.berkeley.edu`
A mailing list for the discussion of White Wolf's Role Playing Game, Ars Magica. Also available as a nightly digest, upon request.

Name: flashlife
Resource: List

Address: `flashlife-request@netcom.com`
(Carl Rigney)
A mailing list for GMs of Shadowrun and other cyberpunk role-playing games to discuss rules, scenarios, ask questions, make-up answers, and similar fasfax.

Name: gmast-l
Resource: LISTSERV
Address: `gmast-l@utcvm.bitnet`
This is for everyone who is or wants to be a role-playing gamemaster.

Name: MUD
Resource: List
Address: `jwisdom@gnu.ai.mit.edu`
(Joseph Wisdom)
If you are new in the MUD world, or are simply looking for new places to get into, try subscribing to Internet Games MUD-List today!

Name: Nero Ashbury
Resource: List
Address: `Lsonko@pearl.tufts.edu`
Involves Nero, a live-action medieval role-playing game with a plot line and characters who continue from one adventure to the next.

Name: rec.games.frp.advocacy
Resource: USENET
Flames and rebuttals about various role-playing systems.

Name: rec.games.frp.announce
Resource: USENET
Announcements of happenings in the role-playing world. (Moderated)

Name: rec.games.frp.cyber
Resource: USENET
Discussions of cyberpunk-related role-playing games.

Name: rec.games.frp.dnd
Resource: USENET
Fantasy role-playing with TSR's Dungeons and Dragons.

Name: rec.games.frp.live-action
Resource: USENET
Live-action role-playing games.

Name: rec.games.frp.marketplace
Resource: USENET
Role-playing game materials wanted and for sale.

Name: rec.games.frp.misc
Resource: USENET
General discussions of role-playing games.

Name: rec.games.mud.admin
Resource: USENET
Administrative issues of multiuser dungeons.

Name: rec.games.mud.announce
Resource: USENET
Informational articles about multiuser dungeons. (Moderated)

Name: rec.games.mud.diku
Resource: USENET
All about DikuMuds.

Name: rec.games.mud.misc
Resource: USENET
Various aspects of multiuser computer games.

Name: rec.games.mud.tiny
Resource: USENET
Discussion about Tiny muds, like MUSH, MUSE and MOO.

Name: rec.games.rogue
Resource: USENET
Discussion and hints about Rogue.

Name:
rec.games.roguelike.angband
Resource: USENET
The computer game Angband.

Name:
rec.games.roguelike.announce
Resource: USENET
Major info about rogue-styled games.
(Moderated)

Name: rec.games.roguelike.misc
Resource: USENET
Rogue-style dungeon games without
other groups.

Name: RuneQuest
Resource: List
Address:
RuneQuest-Request@Glorantha.Holland.Sun.COM
The RuneQuest Daily is a daily
bulletin with discussion on the
RuneQuest role-playing game and the
fantasy world of Glorantha. To
subscribe to either, send mail to the
contact address, with the text: `sub-
scribe list our@address <Full Name>` or
`subscribe digest your@address <Full
Name>`.

Name: ShadowTalk
Resource: LISTSERV
Address: `LISTSERV@HEARN.BITNET`
`LISTSERV@HEARN.nic.SURFnet.nl`
(Robert Hayden)
SHADOWTK, bitnet convention for
ShadowTalk, is a Listserv devoted to
the role-playing game Shadowrun,
which is published by FASA.

Name: stargame
Resource: LISTSERV
Address: `stargame@pccvm.bitnet`
For persons involved in the FASA
Star Trek role-playing game.

Name: The Chaosium Digest
Resource: List
Address: `appel@erzo.berkeley.edu`
A weekly digest for the discussion of
Chaosium's many games, including
Call of Cthulhu, Elric!, Elfquest, and
Pendragon.

Name: torg
Resource: List
Address:
`torg-request@cool.vortech.com`
(Clay Luther)
Torg is the mailing list dedicated to
the infiniverse of West End Game's
Torg, the Possibility Wars role-
playing game.

Name: traveller
Resource: List
Address:
`traveller-request@engrg.uwo.ca`
(James T. Perkins)
This mailing list exists to discuss the
TRAVELLER Science Fiction role-
playing game, published by Game
Designers' Workshop.

Name: ud-l
Resource: LISTSERV
Address: `ud-l@uriacc.bitnet`
This is the "ultimate dungeon list."

Name: vampire
Resource: List
Address: `vampire-request@math.ufl.edu`
There is now a mailing list dedicated
to the White Wolf role-playing game,
Vampire. To subscribe, send `sub
vampire` as the first line of a message to
`vampire-request@math.ufl.edu`.

Name: warhammer
Resource: List

Address:
`wfrp-request@morticia.cnns.unt.edu`
For the discussion of Games Workshop's Warhammer Universe, the Old World, Warhammer Fantasy Role Play, and Warhammer Fantasy Battle. To subscribe, send e-mail to the above request address and, as the first word on the subject line or any line in the text of the message, include the word `sub`.

Theory

Name: pd-games
Resource: List
Address: `pd-games-request@math.uio.no`
(Thomas Gramstad)
pd-games is a mailing list for game theory, especially Prisoner's Dilemma type of problems.

Toys

Name: alt.toys.lego
Resource: USENET
Snap 'em together.

Name: rec.toys.lego
Resource: USENET
Discussion of Lego, Duplo, and compatible toys.

Trivia

Name: rec.games.trivia
Resource: USENET
Discussion about trivia.

War

Name: CZ
Resource: List
Address: `cz-request@stsci.edu`
(Tom Comeau)
The purpose of The Convergence Zone (or CZ for short) is to discuss the Harpoon naval wargame series and related topics.

General

Kids

Name: pen-pals
Resource: List
Address:
`pen-pals-request@mainstream.com`
To provide a forum for children to correspond electronically with each other.

Problem Solving

Name: cre8tv-l
Resource: LISTSERV
Address: `cre8tv-l@psuvm.psu.edu`
This list discusses how to teach creative problem solving to engineers.

Quotations

Name: alt.quotations
Resource: USENET
Quotations, quips, sig lines, witticisms, *et al.*

Skills

Name: SkillsBank
Resource: List
Address: `sun!kass!richard`
(Richard Karasik)
A forum for people who are willing to share their skills with others.

Weird News

Name: Trepan-D
Resource: LISTSERV
Address: `listserv@brownvm.brown.edu`
Unmoderated discussion of weird news items. To subscribe, send the message SUB TREPAN-D <Full Name> to `listserv@brownvm.brown.edu`.

Name: Trepan-L
Resource: LISTSERV
Address: `listserv@brownvm.brown.edu`
Publication of weird news items. The list is moderated and submissions may be edited. To subscribe, send the message SUB TREPAN-L <Full Name> to `listserv@brownvm.brown.edu`.

Words

Name: words-l
Resource: LISTSERV
Address: `words-l@uga.cc.uga.edu`
The formal description of this list is "A discussion of the English language." In reality, the sky is the limit!

Geography

General

Name: geograph
Resource: LISTSERV
Address: `geograph@searn.sunet.se`
This is a general-purpose geography discussion list.

Mapping

Name: maps-l
Resource: LISTSERV
Address: `maps-l@uga.cc.uga.edu`
This forum is for persons interested in maps and air photo systems.

Health

12-Step Programs

Name: 12step
Resource: List
Address: `muller@camp.rutgers.edu`
(Mike Muller)
To discuss/share experiences about 12-step programs such as Alcoholics Anonymous, Overeaters Anonymous, Alanon, ACOA.

Addiction

Name: addict-l
Resource: LISTSERV
Address: `addict-l@kentvm.bitnet`
This list was formed for the academic and scholarly discussion of addictions.

Name: alcohol
Resource: LISTSERV
Address: `alcohol@lmuacad.bitnet`
This list is for alcohol and drug studies.

AIDS

Name: aids
Resource: LISTSERV
Address: `aids@wuvmd.bitnet`
Sci.med.aids newsgroup.

Name: aids
Resource: LISTSERV
Address: `aids@rutgers.edu`
This list is gatewayed to the USENET group sci.med.aids.

Name: aids
Resource: List
Address: `aids-request@cs.ucla.edu`
(Daniel R. Greening)
A distribution list for people who can't read sci.med.aids. Covers predominately medical issues of AIDS. Some discussion of political and social issues.

Name: aidsbkrv
Resource: LISTSERV
Address: `aidsbkrv@UICVM.uic.cc.edu`
This is an AIDS book review forum.

Name: info-aids
Resource: List
Address: `info-aids@rainbow.UUCP`
`(pacbell,apple,hoptoad,ucbvax}!well!rainbow!info-aids`
(Ken Davis)
A clearinghouse for information, and discussion about AIDS, including alternative treatments, political implications, and so on. Exchanges files with `AIDNEWS@RUTVM1.BITNET`.

Name: sci.med.aids
Resource: USENET
Discussions about AIDS: treatment, pathology/biology of HIV, prevention. (Moderated)

Anesthesiology

Name: anest-l
Resource: LISTSERV
Address: `anest-l@ubvm.cc.buffalo.edu`
Anesthesiology discussion list.

Brain Injuries

Name: tbi-sprt
Resource: LISTSERV
Address: `listserv@sjuvm.stjohns.edu`
Created for the exchange of information by survivors, supporters, and professionals concerned with traumatic brain injury and other neurological impairments that currently lack a forum. To subscribe to tbi-sprt, send mail to `listserv@sjuvm.bitnet` or `listserv@sjuvm.stjohns.edu`. Leave the subject line blank, and in the body of the message put the line `tbi-sprt` followed by your name as you want it to appear in the list.

Brain Tumors

Name: braintmr
Resource: LISTSERV
Address: `braintmr@mitvma.mit.edu`
This list was created to exchange brain tumor research and support information.

Cancer

Name: clan
Resource: LISTSERV
Address: `clan@frmop11.bitnet`
This is the cancer liaison and action network discussion list.

Chronic Fatigue

Name: cfs-med
Resource: LISTSERV
Address: `cfs-med@nihlist.bitnet`
This list provides a general forum to discuss chronic fatigue syndrome.

Name: cfs-news
Resource: LISTSERV
Address: `cfs-news@nihlist.bitnet`
This is the chronic fatigue syndrome newsletter discussion list.

Computers

Name: NeXT-Med
Resource: List
Address: `next-med-request@ms.uky.edu`
NeXT-Med is open to end-users and developers interested in medical solutions using NeXT computers and/or 486 systems running NeXTStep.

Crohn's Disease

Name: IBDlist
Resource: List
Address:
`IBDlist-request%mvac23@udel.edu`
(Thomas Lapp)
`...!udel!mvac23!IBDlist-request`
IBDlist is a moderated mailing list that discusses all aspects of Inflammatory Bowel Diseases, with particular emphasis on Crohn's disease and Ulcerative Colitis.

Diabetes

Name: diabetes
Resource: LISTSERV

Address: `diabetes@irlearn.ucd.ie`
This is the international research project on diabetes discussion forum.

Name: misc.health.diabetes
Resource: USENET
Discussion of diabetes management in day-to-day life.

Dietary

Name: rec.food.veg
Resource: USENET
A forum for vegetarians.

Name: VEGGIE
Resource: LISTSERV
Address: `LISTSERV@gibbs.oit.unc.edu`
If you are interested in vegetarianism, veganism, fruitarianism, macrobiotics, whole/natural foods, health/fitness, cooking, and so on, this new mailing list may be for you! To subscribe, send a message to `LISTSERV@gibbs.oit.unc.edu` with this line `SUB VEGGIE <first name> <last name>`.

Dieting

Name: diet
Resource: LISTSERV
Address: `diet@ubvm.cc.buffalo.edu`
This list is for the support and discussion of weight loss.

Drugs

Name: alt.drugs
Resource: USENET
Recreational pharmaceuticals and related flames.

Name: alt.drugs.caffeine
Resource: USENET

All about the world's most-used stimulant drug.

Name: alt.hemp
Resource: USENET
It's about knot-tying with rope. Knot!

Name: Leri-L (Leri-L Metaprogramming Mail Service)
Resource: List
Address: `leri-request@pyramid.com`
Basically, Leri is an electric commune, and is probably one of the most interesting, albeit laden by its own verbosity, mailing lists one could ever hope to be a part of.

Endometriosis

Name: WITSENDO
Resource: LISTSERV
Address:
`LISTSERV@dartcms1.dartmouth.edu`
WITSENDO is a moderated mailing list that discusses all aspects of endometriosis with particular emphasis on coping with the disease and its treatment. To subscribe to the list, send mail to `LISTSERV@DARTCMS1.BITNET` or `LISTSERV@dartcms1.dartmouth.edu` with the BODY of the mail (not subject) containing the command: `SUB WITSENDO <Full Name>`.

Fitness

Name: fit-l
Resource: LISTSERV
Address: `fit-l@etsuadmn.etsu.edu`
This is an exercise, diet, and wellness discussion list.

Free Radicals

Name: oxygen-l
Resource: LISTSERV
Address: `oxygen-l@mizzou1.bitnet`
This list discusses oxygen-free radical biology and medicine.

General Fitness

Name: misc.fitness
Resource: USENET
Physical fitness, exercise, bodybuilding, and so on.

Holistic

Name: alt.backrubs
Resource: USENET
Lower…to the right…aaaah!

Name: herb
Resource: LISTSERV
Address: `herb@trearn.bitnet`
Medicinal and aromatic plants discussion list.

Name: holistic
Resource: LISTSERV
Address: `holistic@siucvmb.bitnet`
This discussion list exchanges information about holistic medicine and practices.

Hyperactivity

Name: add-parents
Resource: List
Address:
`add-parents-request@mv.mv.com`
For providing support and information to parents of children with Attention Deficit/Hyperactivity Disorder. To subscribe, send mail to `add-parents-request@mv.mv.com`.

Hyperbaric

Name: hypbar-l
Resource: LISTSERV
Address:
`hypbar-l@technion.technion.ac.il`
This list is for hyperbaric and diving medicine research and information exchange.

Immune Disorders

Name: immune
Resource: List
Address: `immune@weber.ucsd.edu`
A discussion list for persons whose lives are affected by immune disorders. Send your subscription requests to `immune-request@weber.ucsd.edu`.

Immune System

Name: immune
Resource: List
Address:
`immune-request@weber.ucsd.edu`
(Cyndi Norman)
A support group for people with immune-system breakdowns (and their symptoms), such as Chronic Fatigue Syndrome, Lupus, Candida, Hypoglycemia, Multiple Allergies, Learning Disabilities, and so on, as well as their SOs and medical caretakers.

Ingestive Disorders

Name: ingest
Resource: LISTSERV
Address: `ingest@cuvmb.bitnet`
This list is for persons with ingestive disorders.

Laser

Name: lasmed-l
Resource: LISTSERV
Address: `lasmed-l@taunivm.tau.ac.il`
Laser medicine.

Lyme

Name: LymeNet-L
Resource: List
Address:
`listserv@Lehigh.EDU mcg2@Lehigh.EDU`
(Marc Gabriel)
The LymeNet Newsletter provides timely information on the many aspects of the Lyme disease epidemic.

Medical Imaging

Name: medimage
Resource: LISTSERV
Address: `medimage@polyvm.bitnet`
Medical imaging discussion list.

Medical Students

Name: medstu-l
Resource: LISTSERV
Address: `medstu-l@unmvma.bitnet`
This list is where medical students can exchange ideas, experiences, and general information.

Medical Testing

Name: sci.med.physics
Resource: USENET
Issues of physics in medical testing/ care.

Medicine

Name: sci.med
Resource: USENET
Medicine and its related products and regulations.

Mental

Name: alt.meditation
Resource: USENET
General discussion of meditation.

Name: alt.suicide.holiday
Resource: USENET
Talk of why suicides increase at holidays.

Name: walkers-in-darkness
Resource: LISTSERV
Address:
walkers-request@world.std.com
(David Harmon)
Walkers-in-Darkness is intended for sufferers from depression and/or bipolar disorder, and affected friends.

Mind-Brain

Name: brain-l
Resource: LISTSERV
Address: brain-l@mcgill1.bitnet
Mind-brain discussion group.

Motor Skills

Name: motordev
Resource: LISTSERV
Address: motordev@umdd.bitnet
Human motor skill development list.

Multiple Sclerosis

Name: mslist-l
Resource: LISTSERV
Address:
mslist-l@technion.technion.ac.il
This list focuses on multiple sclerosis discussion and support.

Neuroscience

Name: neuro1-l
Resource: LISTSERV
Address: neuro1-l@UICVM.uic.cc.edu
Neuroscience information forum.

Nuclear Medicine

Name: nucmed
Resource: List
Address: nucmed-request@uwovax.uwo.ca
trevorc@uwovax.uwo.ca
(Trevor Cradduck)
A discussion of Nuclear Medicine and related issues. Of particular concern is the format of digital images.

Nutrition

Name: FATFREE
Resource: List
Address:
fatfree-request@hustle.rahul.net
(Michelle R. Dick)
FATFREE, the McDougall/Ornish mailing list, is for discussion about extremely lowfat vegetarianism. To join, send email to
fatfree-request@hustle.rahul.net using one of the following subjects: ADD to join as a regular member, or ADD DIGEST to join as a digest member.

Name: nutepi
Resource: LISTSERV
Address: `nutepi@db0tui11.bitnet`
Nutritional epidemiology.

Occupational Injuries

Name: sci.med.occupational
Resource: USENET
Preventing, detecting, and treating occupational injuries.

Panic/Anxiety

Name: Panic
Resource: List
Address: `Panic-Request@gnu.ai.mit.edu`
This is a support group for panic disorders.

Smoking

Name: smoke-free
Resource: LISTSERV
Address: `maynor@ra.msstate.edu`
A support list for people recovering from addiction to cigarettes. To subscribe to the list, send the following command to `listserv@ra.msstate.edu`: `subscribe smoke-free <Full Name>`.

Transplantation

Name: brit-l
Resource: LISTSERV
Address: `brit-l@ksuvm.bitnet`
Behavioral research in transplantation.

Transplants

Name: bit.listserv.transplant
Resource: USENET
Transplant recipients list.

History

18th Century

Name: c18-l
Resource: LISTSERV
Address: `c18-l@psuvm.psu.edu`
This is an interdisciplinary list devoted to the discussion of the 18th century.

America

Name: earam-l
Resource: LISTSERV
Address: `earam-l@kentvm.bitnet`
This is the Society of Early Americanists distribution list.

China

Name: emedch-l
Resource: LISTSERV
Address: `emedch-l@uscvm.bitnet`
This list is for the discussion and exchange of information about early medieval China.

Classical

Name: sci.classics
Resource: USENET
Studying classical history, languages, art, and more.

Clothing

Name: vintage
Resource: List
Address:
`vintage-request@presto.ig.com`
Vintage clothing and costume jewelry.

Columbus

Name: nat-1492
Resource: LISTSERV
Address: `nat-1492@tamvm1.tamu.edu`
This is a moderated list for the discussion of how Christopher Columbus's voyage in 1492 has affected the world in the last 500 years.

Costumes

Name: Historic Costume
Resource: List
Address:
`h-costume-request@andrew.cmu.edu`
This list concentrates on recreating period elegance, from the Bronze age to the mid-20th Century.

England

Name: victoria
Resource: LISTSERV
Address: `victoria@iubvm.bitnet`
This list discusses all aspects of 18th century Great Britain.

General

Name: history
Resource: LISTSERV

Address: `history@psuvm.psu.edu`
A general history discussion forum.

Name: soc.history
Resource: USENET
Discussions of things historical.

Holocaust

Name: holocaus
Resource: LISTSERV
Address: `holocaus@UICVM.uic.cc.edu`
This list is devoted to the discussion of the Holocaust.

Name: Holocaust Information
Resource: LISTSERV
Address: `listserv@oneb.almanac.bc.ca`
The Holocaust Information list is devoted to Holocaust research, and to the refutation of those who deny the event. To subscribe to the list, send the following command to `listserv@oneb.almanac.bc.ca` in the form: `subscribe hlist <First Name> <Last Name>`.

Law

Name: hislaw-l
Resource: LISTSERV
Address:
`hislaw-l@ulkyvm.louisville.edu`
This list is about the history of law (feudal, common, and canon).

Medieval

Name: mediev-l
Resource: LISTSERV
Address: `mediev-l@ukanvm.cc.ukans.edu`
This list is devoted to the topic of medieval history.

Military

Name: milhst-l
Resource: LISTSERV
Address: milhst-l@ukanvm.cc.ukans.edu
This list provides a forum for those interested in military history.

Name: siege
Resource: List
Address:
siege-request@bransle.ucs.mun.ca
The siege mailing list is intended for the dicussion of pre-black powder methods of attack and defense of fortified positions. To subscribe, send mail to siege-request@bransle.ucs.mun.ca and include a single line saying:
subscribe siege <Full Name>.

Renaissance

Name: renais-l
Resource: LISTSERV
Address:
renais-l@ulkyvm.louisville.edu
This list focuses on the Renaissance.

Theoretical

Name: cliology
Resource: LISTSERV
Address: cliology@msu.bitnet
This list is devoted to the theories of history.

United Kingdom

Name: h-albion
Resource: LISTSERV
Address: h-albion@ucsbvm.bitnet
This list was created to provide a forum concerning British and Irish history.

Vietnam War

Name: vwar-l
Resource: LISTSERV
Address: vwar-l@ubvm.cc.buffalo.edu
This is the Vietnam War discussion list.

World War II

Name: wwii-l
Resource: LISTSERV
Address: wwii-l@ubvm.cc.buffalo.edu
This is the World War II discussion list.

Hobbies

Airplanes

Name: airplane-clubs
Resource: List
Address:
airplane-clubs-request@dg-rtp.dg.com
(Matthew Waugh)
This mailing list is for the discussion of all matters relating to the management and operation of groups operating aircraft.

Antennae

Name: rec.radio.amateur.antenna
Resource: USENET
Antennas: theory, techniques, and construction.

Aquariums

Name: alt.aquaria
Resource: USENET
The aquarium and related as a hobby.

Name: rec.aquaria
Resource: USENET
Keeping fish and aquaria as a hobby.

Aviation

Name: aircraft
Resource: LISTSERV
Address: `aircraft@grearn.bitnet`
Focuses on airplanes and helicopters, both new and old. Includes updates about air shows.

Name: rec.aviation.answers
Resource: USENET
Frequently asked questions about aviation. (Moderated)

Name: rec.aviation.simulators
Resource: USENET
Flight simulation on all levels.

Balloon Sculpting

Name: balloon sculpting
Resource: List
Address:
`balloon-request@ent.rochester.edu`
(Larry Moss)
This list is for the discussion of balloon sculpting.

Balloonists

Name: balloon
Resource: List
Address: `balloon-request@lut.ac.uk`
(Phil Herbert)
This is a list for balloonists of any sort, be they hot air or gas, commercial or sport.

Beer/Zymurgy

Name: beer-l
Resource: LISTSERV
Address: `beer-l@ua1vm.bitnet`
This is the homebrew digest distribution list.

Name: homebrew
Resource: List
Address:
`homebrew%hpfcmr@hplabs.hp.com`
For the discussion and sharing of information related to zymurgy (beer brewing). Send your subscription request to
`homebrew-request%hpfcmr@hplabs.hp.com.`

Bicycling

Name: bcdv
Resource: List
Address: `bike-request@bcdv.drexel.edu`
To discuss issues related to cycling in the Philadelphia greater metropolitan region, and the advocacy work of the Bicycle Coalition of the Delaware Valley.

Name: bikecommute
Resource: List
Address:
`bikecommute-request@bike2work.eng.sun.com`
We are mainly Silicon Valley folk, and the discussion centers around bicycle transportation, and the steps necessary for improved bicycling conditions in (sub)urban areas.

Name: bikepeople
Resource: List
Address: karplus@ce.ucsc.edu
(Kevin Karplus)
An area group of bicycle activists, mainly in Santa Cruz County, California, who discuss bicycle issues.

Name: rec.bicycles.misc
Resource: USENET
General discussion of bicycling.

Billiards

Name: alt.sport.pool
Resource: USENET
Knock your balls into your pockets for fun.

Birdwatching

Name: birdband
Resource: LISTSERV
Address: birdband@arizvm1.bitnet
This is the bird bander's forum.

Name: birdcntr
Resource: LISTSERV
Address: birdcntr@arizvm1.bitnet
This is the central branch of the national birding hotline cooperative.

Name: birdeast
Resource: LISTSERV
Address: birdeast@arizvm1.bitnet
This is the east branch of the national birding hotline cooperative.

Name: birdeast
Resource: LISTSERV
Address:
birdeast@arizvm1.bitnet@cornellc.cit.cornell.edu
National Birding Hotline Cooperative. This list is for the Eastern United States.

Name: birdwest
Resource: LISTSERV
Address: birdwest@arizvm1.bitnet
This is the west branch of the national birding hotline cooperative.

Name: rec.birds
Resource: USENET
Hobbyists interested in bird watching.

Boating

Name: rec.boats
Resource: USENET
Hobbyists interested in boating.

Name: rec.boats.paddle
Resource: USENET
Talk about any boats with oars, paddles, and so on.

Bonsai

Name: bonsai
Resource: LISTSERV
Address: bonsai@cms.cc.wayne.edu
This is for anyone interested in bonsai.

Name: Bonsai
Resource: List
Address: LISTSERV@CMS.CC.WAYNE.EDU
(Dan@foghorn.pass.wayne.edu)
This list has been setup to facilitate discussion of the art and craft of Bonsai and related art forms.

Name: rec.arts.bonsai
Resource: USENET
Dwarfish trees and shrubbery.

Books

Name: exlibris
Resource: LISTSERV
Address: `exlibris@rutgers.edu`
This is the forum for rare books and
special collections.

Climbing

Name: rec.climbing
Resource: USENET
Climbing techniques, competition
announcements, and so on.

Coin Collecting/Numismatics

Name: coins
Resource: List
Address:
`COINS-REQUEST@ISCSVAX.UNI.EDU`
(Daniel J. Power)
To provide a forum for discussions on
numismatic topics including U.S. and
world coins, paper money, tokens,
medals, and so on.

Name: coins
Resource: List
Address: `coins@rocky.er.usgs.gov`
Send subscription requests and other
administrative information to
`ROBERT@WHIPLASH.ER.USGS.GOV`.

Comix

Name: Comix
Resource: List
Address: `Comix@world.std.com`
Devoted to the discussion of nontra-
ditional comix. Send your subscrip-
tion requests to
`comix-request@world.std.com`.

Dollhouses

Name: dollh-l
Resource: LISTSERV
Address: `dollh-l@ferris.bitnet`
This list will be of interest to those
involved in designing, building, and
just enjoying dollhouses.

Drum & Bugle Corps

Name:
rec.arts.marching.drumcorps
Resource: USENET
Drum and bugle corps.

Equestrian

Name: horse
Resource: List
Address:
`equestrians-request@world.std.com`
(David C. Kovar)
Discussion of things equestrian.
Horse enthusiasts of all disciplines
and levels of experience are welcome.

Firearms

Name: rec.guns
Resource: USENET
Discussions about firearms. (Moder-
ated)

Flags

Name: flags
Resource: List
Address: `bottasini@cesi.it`
(Giuseppe Bottasini)
The creation of worldwide, real-time
updated database about all kind of

flags: (inter)national, (un)official, ethnical, political, religious, movements' flags.

Flying Disc

Name: rec.sport.disc
Resource: USENET
Discussion of flying-disc-based sports.

Gambling

Name: rec.gambling
Resource: USENET
Articles on games of chance and betting.

Gardening

Name: gardens
Resource: LISTSERV
Address: `gardens@ukcc.uky.edu`
This is a list devoted to the discussion of gardens and gardening.

Name: mgarden
Resource: LISTSERV
Address: `mgarden@wsuvm1.bitnet`
This is a list for master gardeners. Show off your green thumb!

Name: orchids
Resource: List
Address:
`orchids@scu.bitnet@cunyvm.cuny.edu`
For persons interested in growing orchids. Send the text `subscribe orchids` to `mailserv%scu@cunyvm.cuny.edu`.

Gem/Mineral

Name: rockhounds
Resource: List
Address:
`rockhounds-request@infodyn.com`
(Tom Corson)
To exchange ideas, collecting sites, tips, and other information of general interest to gem and mineral collectors.

Genealogy

Name: roots-l
Resource: LISTSERV
Address: `roots-l@vm1.nodak.edu`
This list is for those interested in and involved with genealogy.

Name: ROOTS-L
Resource: LISTSERV
Address: `listserv@vm1.nodak.edu`
ROOTS-L is a discussion list where those who have interest in Genealogy may communicate via e-mail messages in hopes of finding more family history information. To subscribe to the list, send e-mail to `LISTSERV@NDSUVM1` on BITNET or `listserv@vm1.nodak.edu` with the BODY of the mail containing: `SUB ROOTS-L <Full Name>`.

Name: soc.roots
Resource: USENET
Discussing genealogy and genealogical matters.

Juggling

Name: Juggling
Resource: List
Address:
`Juggling@Moocow.Cogsci.Indiana.Edu`
This list is for everyone who wants to juggle as a hobbyist or professional.

Send a message containing the command ADD to
`Juggling-Request@Moocow.Cogsci.Indiana.Edu`.

Kites

Name: Kites
Resource: List
Address: `Kites@Harvard.Harvard.Edu`
This list is for anyone who flies or makes kites. Send your subscription request to
`kites-request@harvard.harvard.edu`.

Name: kites
Resource: List
Address:
`kites-request@harvard.harvard.edu`
`harvard!kites-request` (USA/Canada/Europe)
`koscvax.keio.junet!kites-request` (Japan)
This mailing list is for people interested in making, flying, or just talking about all kinds of kites.

Lapidary

Name: jewelry
Resource: List
Address:
`jewelry-request@mishima.mn.org`
A forum for discussing jewelry and its related disciplines. To subscribe to the list, send mail to
`jewelry-request@mishima.mn.org` with `subscribe` in the `Subject:`.

Magic

Name: alt.magic
Resource: USENET
For discussion about stage magic.

Name: magic
Resource: List
Address: `magic@maillist.crd.ge.com`
Devoted to the subjects of illusion and sleight of hand, this list is for serious practitioners only. Send your request for a questionnaire to
`magic-request@mailllist.crd.ge.com`.

Name: magic
Resource: List
Address:
`magic-request@maillist.crd.ge.com`
(Bruce Barnett)
The magic mailing list is for the discussion of sleight of hand and the art of magic.

Miniatures

Name: miniatures
Resource: List
Address: `minilist-request@cs.unc.edu`
The Miniatures Digest is an archived mailing list for discussion of painting, sculpting, converting, and displaying of miniature figurines.

Model Horses

Name: model-horse
Resource: List
Address:
`model-horse-request@qiclab.scn.rain.com`
(Darci L. Chapman)
Discussion of the model horse hobby.

Nudists

Name: rec.nude
Resource: USENET
Hobbyists interested in naturist/nudist activities.

Origami

Name: origami
Resource: List
Address: origami-l-request@nstn.ns.ca
This unmoderated mailing list is for discussion of all facets of origami, the Japanese art of paper folding.

Name: origami-l
Resource: List
Address: origami-l@nstn.ns.ca
For those interested in the exchange of information related to the art of origami (paper folding). Send your subscription request to origami-l-request@nstn.ns.ca.

Outdoors

Name: rec.backcountry
Resource: USENET
Activities in the Great Outdoors.

Pen Pals

Name: penpal-l
Resource: LISTSERV
Address: penpal-l@unccvm.bitnet
This is for anyone interested in pen pals.

Photography

Name: 3d
Resource: List
Address: JHBercovitz@lbl.gov
(John Bercovitz)
Discussion of 3D (stereo) photography. General info, hints, experiences, equipment, techniques, and stereo "happenings." Anyone interested is welcome to join.

Name: photo-l
Resource: LISTSERV
Address: photo-l@buacca.bu.edu
This is a general photography forum.

Name: pinhole
Resource: List
Address: pinhole@mintir.fidonet.org
A discussion list for persons interested in all aspects of pinhole photography. Send your subscription requests to
pinhole-request@mintir.fidonet.org.

Name: rec.photo
Resource: USENET
Hobbyists interested in photography.

Postcards/Deltiology

Name: postcard
Resource: LISTSERV
Address: postcard@idbsu.bitnet
For those interested in the world's third most popular hobby!

Puzzles

Name: IAMS (Internet Amateur
            Mathematics Society)
Resource: List
Address: iams-request@quack.kfu.com
For discussion of math puzzle and problems.

Pyrotechnics

Name: rec.pyrotechnics
Resource: USENET
Fireworks, rocketry, safety, and other topics.

Quilting

Name: quiltnet
Resource: LISTSERV
Address: `quiltnet@emuvm1.bitnet`
For persons interested in quilts:
patterns, tips, mail-order houses, and
stores.

Name: rec.crafts.quilting
Resource: USENET
All about quilts and other quilted
items.

Radio

Name: FM-10
Resource: List
Address: `fm-10-request@dg-rtp.dg.com`
To talk about modifications, enhancements, and uses of the Ramsey FM-10,
other BA-1404 based FM Stereo
broadcasters; also some discussion of
the FM pirate radio.

Name: ICF-2010
Resource: List
Address: `Contact`
`icf-2010-request@cup.hp.com`
(Gary Gitzen) or `{hplabs,`
`uunet}!cup.hp.com!icf-2010-request`
This is a low-volume mutual support
group to discuss/share technical
issues, problems, solutions, performance, and modifications related to
the Sony ICF-2010 and 2001D shortwave radios.

Name: Internet Radio Journal
Resource: List
Address: `rrb@airwaves.chi.il.us`
The Internet Radio Journal is both a
repeater for the newsgroup
rec.radio.broadcasting and, on
occasion, carries independent material as well.

Name: PRL
Resource: List
Address: `brewer@ace.enet.dec.com`
(John Brewer)
The Pirate Radio SWL list is for the
distribution of questions, answers,
information, and loggings of Pirate
Radio Stations.

Name:
rec.radio.amateur.digital.misc
Resource: USENET
Packet radio and other digital radio
modes.

Name:
rec.radio.amateur.equipment
Resource: USENET
All about production amateur radio
hardware.

Name:
rec.radio.amateur.homebrew
Resource: USENET
Amateur radio construction and
experimentation.

Name: rec.radio.amateur.misc
Resource: USENET
Amateur radio practices, contests,
events, rules, and so on.

Name: rec.radio.amateur.policy
Resource: USENET
Radio use and regulation policy.

Name: rec.radio.amateur.space
Resource: USENET
Amateur radio transmissions through
space.

Name: rec.radio.broadcasting
Resource: USENET
Discussion of global domestic broad-
cast radio. (Moderated)

Name: rec.radio.cb
Resource: USENET
Citizen-band radio.

Name: rec.radio.info
Resource: USENET
Informational postings related to radio. (Moderated)

Name: rec.radio.noncomm
Resource: USENET
Topics relating to noncommercial radio.

Name: rec.radio.scanner
Resource: USENET
Utility broadcasting traffic above 30 MHz.

Name: rec.radio.shortwave
Resource: USENET
Shortwave radio enthusiasts.

Name: rec.radio.swap
Resource: USENET
Offers to trade and swap radio equipment.

Name: swl$l
Resource: LISTSERV
Address: swl$l@cuvmb.bitnet
This is the shortwave listener's list.

Radio Scanners

Name: alt.radio.scanner
Resource: USENET
Discussion of scanning radio receivers.

Radio-Controlled Models

Name: rec.models.rc
Resource: USENET
Radio-controlled models for hobbyists.

Railroad

Name: rec.models.railroad
Resource: USENET
Model railroads of all scales.

Railroading

Name: railroad
Resource: LISTSERV
Address: railroad@cunyvm.cuny.edu
This is a general list for those interested in railroading.

Recipes

Name: Kuharske Bukve
Resource: List
Address:
Kuharske-Bukve@KRPAN.ARNES.SI
(Polona Novak and Andrej Brodnik)
Kuharske.Bukve@Uni-LJ.SI
Kuharskve Bukve is a moderated mailing list published weekly; each issue brings one recipe previously tested by a member of editorial board. The recipes are in Slovene.

Remote Control

Name: remote-l
Resource: LISTSERV
Address: remote-l@suvm.bitnet
This is a discussion group for those interested in remote-control hobbies.

Roller Coasters

Name: rec.roller-coaster
Resource: USENET
Roller coasters and other amusement park rides.

Sailing

Name: yacht-l
Resource: LISTSERV
Address: `yacht-l@grearn.bitnet`
This list focuses on yachting, sailing, and amateur boat building.

SCUBA Diving

Name: rec.scuba
Resource: USENET
Hobbyists interested in SCUBA diving.

Name: scuba-d
Resource: LISTSERV
Address: `scuba-d@brownvm.brown.edu`
This is a redistribution (digest) of the scuba-l LISTSERV.

Name: scuba-l
Resource: LISTSERV
Address: `scuba-l@brownvm.brown.edu`
This list is for anyone interested in SCUBA diving.

Sewing

Name: alt.sewing
Resource: USENET
A group that is not as it seams.

Name: rec.crafts.textiles
Resource: USENET
Sewing, weaving, knitting, and other fiber arts.

Shortwave

Name: Drake-R8
Resource: List

Address: `mik@hpsesuka.pwd.hp.com`
(Mik Butler)
To discuss and share experiences, technical issues, problems, and so on related to the Drake R8 shortwave receiver.

Singing

Name: rec.music.a-cappella
Resource: USENET
Vocal music without instrumental accompaniment.

Skating

Name: rec.skate
Resource: USENET
Ice skating and roller skating.

Skydiving

Name: base-jumping
Resource: List
Address:
`base-request@lunatix.lex.ky.us`
An open discussion of fixed object skydiving. Membership is open to anyone who has made at least one base jump or skydive.

Name: rec.skydiving
Resource: USENET
Hobbyists interested in skydiving.

Smoking

Name: Pipes
Resource: List
Address: `Pipes@Paul.Rutgers.Edu`
This list is for anyone who enjoys smoking and collecting pipes and tobacco. Send your subscription requests to `pipes-request@paul.rutgers.edu`.

Name: Pipes
Resource: List
Address: `masticol@scr.siemens.com`
(Steve Masticola)
The Pipes Mailgroup provides a forum for discussing the moderate use and appreciation of fine tobacco, including cigars, pipes, quality cigarettes, pipe making and carving, snuff, collectible tobacciana, publications, and related topics.

Spelunking

Name: cavers
Resource: List
Address: `cavers-request@vlsi.bu.edu`
(John D. Sutter)
Information resource and forum for all interested in exploring caves. To join, send a note to the above address including your geographical location as well as e-mail address; details of caving experience and locations where you've caved; NSS number if you have one; and any other information that might be useful.

Sports Cards

Name: Cards
Resource: List
Address:
`cards-request@tanstaafl.uchicago.edu`
(Keane Arase)
For people interested in collection, speculation, and investing in baseball, football, basketball, hockey, and other trading cards and/or memoribilia.

Name: cards
Resource: List
Address: `cards@tanstaafl.uchicago.edu`
For persons interested in the collecting, trading, and speculating of baseball, football, and hockey cards. Send your subscription requests to `cards-request@tanstaafl.uchicago.edu`.

Stamps/Philately

Name: stamps
Resource: LISTSERV
Address: `stamps@cunyvm.cuny.edu`
This list is for those who appreciate and collect postage stamps.

Theme Parks

Name: rec.parks.theme
Resource: USENET
Entertainment theme parks.

Trading Cards

Name: sports-cards
Resource: List
Address:
`cards-request@tanstaafl.uchicago.edu`
(Keane Arase)
For people interested in collection, speculation, and investing in baseball, football, basketball, hockey, and other trading cards and/or memoribilia.

Ultralight Aircraft

Name: ultralight
Resource: List
Address: `ultralight-flight@ms.uky.edu`
For anyone interested in flying ultralight aircraft. Send your subscription request to `ultralight-flight-request@ms.uky.edu`.

VHF Radio

Name: vhf
Resource: List
Address: `vhf@w6yx.stanford.edu`
A discussion list devoted to VHF and amateur radio. Send your subscription requests to `vhf-request@w6yx.stanford.edu`.

Woodworking

Name: rec.woodworking
Resource: USENET
Hobbyists interested in woodworking.

Name: woodwork
Resource: LISTSERV
Address: `woodwork@ipfwvm.bitnet`
Anyone interested in woodworking can find a home here. All information related to tools, techniques, methods, and plans are open for discussion.

Zymurgy

Name: alt.beer
Resource: USENET
Good for what ales ya.

Name: homebrew
Resource: List
Address:
`homebrew-request%hpfcmr@hplabs.hp.com` or
`...!hplabs!hpfcmr!homebrew-request`
(Rob Gardner)
Forum on Beer, homebrewing, and related issues.

Name: JudgeNet
Resource: List
Address: `judge-request@synchro.com`
(Chuck Cox - BJCP Master Judge)
Discussion of beer judging and competition organization. Please include your name, Internet adderess, and judging rank (if any) in your subscription request.

Name: rec.crafts.brewing
Resource: USENET
The art of making beers and meads.

Human Sexuality

Bondage

Name: alt.sex.bondage
Resource: USENET
Tie me, whip me, make me read the net!

Name: alt.sex.fetish.fashion
Resource: USENET
Rubber, leather, chains, and other fetish clothing.

Name: gl-asb
Resource: List
Address: `MAJORDOMO@QUEERNET.ORG`
(Roger B.A. Klorese)
The gl-asb list is a discussion list for discussion of bondage and SM topics for gay men and lesbians. In order to

be added to the list, please send a message to one of the following addresses: `majordomo@queernet.org` `<wellconnectedsite>!unpc!majordomo` (if you support only UUCP paths) with the following content in the message: `subscribe gl-asb end`. Any administrative questions should be addressed to `gl-asb-approval@queernet.org` `<wellconnectedsite>!unpc!gl-asb-approval` (if you support only UUCP paths).

Erotica

Name: alt.binaries.pictures.erotica
Resource: USENET
Gigabytes of copyright violations.

Name:
alt.binaries.pictures.erotica.d
Resource: USENET
Discussing erotic copyright violations.

Name: rec.arts.erotica
Resource: USENET
Erotic fiction and verse. (Moderated)

Feminism

Name: FEMINIST
Resource: LISTSERV
Address: `FEMINIST@mitvma.mit.edu`
ALA Feminist Task Force discussion.

Gay/Lesbian/Bisexual Issues

Name: AUGLBC-L
Resource: LISTSERV
Address: `LISTSERV@american.edu`
(Erik G. Paul)
The American University Gay, Lesbian, and Bisexual Community is a support group for lesbian, gay,

bisexual, transgender, and supportive students. To subscribe: send a message with one line containing: SUB AUGLBC-L <Full Name> to `listserv@american.edu`.

Name: AusGBLF
Resource: List
Address:
`ausgblf-request@minyos.xx.rmit.oz.au`
Welcome to AusGBLF, an Australian based mailing list for gays, bisexuals, lesbians, and friends. The mailing list is maintained from `zglc@minyos.xx.rmit.oz.au`.

Name: ba-sappho
Resource: List
Address:
`ba-sappho-request@labrys.mti.sgi.com`
Ba-sappho is a Bay Area lesbian mailing list intended for local networking and announcements.

Name: bears
Resource: List
Address: `bears-request@spdcc.COM`
(Steve Dyer and Brian Gollum)
`...!{harvard,ima,linus,mirror}!spdcc!bears-request`
This is a mailing list in digest format for gay and bisexual men who are bears themselves and for those who enjoy the company of bears.

Name: biact-l
Resource: LISTSERV
Address: `biact-l@brownvm.brown.edu`
This is the bisexual activist list.

Name: BiFem-L
Resource: LISTSERV
Address: `LISTSERV@BROWNVM.BROWN.EDU`
(Elaine Brennan)
BiFem-L mailing list for bi women and bi-friendly women. To subscribe, send a message to

`listserv@brownvm.brown.edu` with no subject line and the following message body: `SUBSCRIBE BIFEM-L <Full Name>`.

Name: bifem-l
Resource: LISTSERV
Address: `bifem-l@Brownvm.Brown.Edu`
This is the bisexual women's discussion list.

Name: BiNet / New Jersey
Resource: List
Address: `bnnj-request@plts.org`
The Bisexual Network of New Jersey no longer exists, but this mailing list is still used for announcements (and some discussions) relevent to New Jersey bisexuals. To subscribe, send a mail message to `majordomo@plts.org`. The first line of the message (the subject line is ignored) should be `subscribe bnnj`. Other administrative questions and requests should be sent to the e-mail address `bnnj-approval@plts.org`.

Name: bisexu-l
Resource: LISTSERV
Address: `bisexu-l@brownvm.brown.edu`
This is an open forum devoted to the subject of bisexuality.

Name: Bisexu-L
Resource: LISTSERV
Address: `LISTSERV@brownvm.brown.edu` (Bill Sklar)
For discussion of issues of bisexuality. To subscribe, send the following command to `LISTSERV@brownvm.brown.edu`: `SUBSCRIBE BISEXU-L <Full Name>`.

Name: BITHRY-L
Resource: LISTSERV
Address: `LISTSERV@brownvm.brown.edu` (Elaine Brennan)
For the theoretical discussion of bisexuality and gender issues. To subscribe, send the message `SUB BITHRY-L <Full Name>` to `LISTSERV@brownvm.brown.edu`.

Name: DC-MOTSS
Resource: List
Address: `DC-MOTSS-REQUEST@vector.intercon.com`
DC-MOTSS is a social mailing list for the GLBO folks who live in the Washington Metropolitan Area— everything within approximately 50 miles of The Mall.

Name: gaynet
Resource: List
Address: `gaynet@athena.mit.edu`
A digest form list for the purpose of discussing gay and lesbian issues and concerns on college campuses. Send subscription requests to `gaynet-request@athena.mit.edu`.

Name: glb-news
Resource: LISTSERV
Address: `glb-news@brownvm.brown.edu`
A moderated, "blind" (the author's name is removed from the original message) discussion list for the exchange of information related to LesBiGay issues and news.

Name: glbpoc
Resource: List
Address: `glbpoc-request@ferkel.ucsb.edu`
glbpoc is a mailing list for lesbian, gay, and bisexual people of color. To

be added to the list, you must provide your full name and a complete Internet address.

Name: khush
Resource: List
Address:
`khush-request@husc3.harvard.edu`
Khush is a mailing list for gay, lesbian, bisexual South Asians, and their friends. To join the list, send mail to `khush-request@husc3.harvard.edu`. The first line in your mail must be of the form: `subscribe khush <Optional E-Mail Address>`. Send any questions or other administrative items to `khush-help@husc3.harvard.edu`.

Name: Labrys
Resource: List
Address:
`C._LOUISE_VIGIL.OSBU_NORTH@XEROX.COM`
Labrys is a mailing list that provides a safe space for lesbians to discuss topics of interest. All administrative requests should be sent to `C._Louise_Vigil.Osbu_North@Xerox.com`. Please include the word `labrys` in the subject line.

Name: MEDGAY-L
Resource: LISTSERV
Address: `LISTSERV@ksuvm.ksu.edu`
(Robert Clark)
This is the official list of the Society for the Study of Homosexuality in the Middle Ages, an affiliated society of the Medieval Institute of Western Michigan University. To subscribe, send a one-line message `SUB MEDGAY-L <Full Name>` to `LISTSERV@ksuvm.ksu.edu`.

Name: qn
Resource: List
Address: `qn@queernet.org`
For those involved in the activities of Queer Nation. Send your subscription request to `qn-request@queernet.org`.

Name: soc.bi
Resource: USENET
Discussions of bisexuality.

Name: soc.motss
Resource: USENET
Issues pertaining to homosexuality.

General

Name: alt.sex
Resource: USENET
Postings of a prurient nature.

Name: alt.sex.wizards
Resource: USENET
Questions for only true sex wizards.

Group

Name: triples
Resource: List
Address: `triples-request@hal.com`
(Howard A. Landman)
To discuss nonmonogamous relationships, polyfidelity, and group marriage, and the various issues that arise in that context, like jealousy, shared housing, marriage laws, sex, and so on.

Men's Studies

Name: mail-men
Resource: List

Address: `mail-men@usl.com`
This list is dedicated to the male movement. Send your subscription requests to `mail-men-request@attunix.att.com`.

Open Lifestyles

Name: alternates
Resource: List
Address:
`alternates-request@ns1.rutgers.edu`
This is a mail list for people who advocate, and/or practice an open sexual lifestyle.

QueerNet

Resource: FTP
Address: `nifty.andrew.cmu.edu`
Directory: Pub/QRD/README

Research

Name: sssstalk
Resource: LISTSERV
Address: `sssstalk@tamvm1.tamu.edu`
A discussion list for all persons involved in the research of human sexuality.

Stories

Name: alt.sex.stories.d
Resource: USENET
For those who talk about needing it now.

Transsexual/Transvestite

Name: cd-forum
Resource: List
Address: `cd-request@valis.biocad.com`
(Valerie)
To provide support/discuss/share experiences about gender-related issues; Crossdressing, Transvestism, Transsexualism, and so on.

Name: Transgen
Resource: LISTSERV
Address: `LISTSERV@brownvm.brown.edu`
Transgen is a list specifically for and about people who are transsexual, transgendered, and/or transvestites. To set TRANSGEN to post by post format, the proper command is SET TRANSGEN MAIL. To set it to digest format, the command is SET TRANSGEN DIGEST. The proper address to which to send these commands is one of the following: `LISTSERV@brownvm.brown.edu` or `LISTSERV@brownvm.bitnet`.

Internet

Access Wanted

Name: alt.internet.access.wanted
Resource: USENET
Oh. OK, how about just an MX record for now?

Answers

Name: alt.answers
Resource: USENET
As if anyone on alt has the answers. (Moderated)

Name: comp.answers
Resource: USENET
Repository for periodic USENET articles. (Moderated)

Name: misc.answers
Resource: USENET
Repository for periodic USENET articles. (Moderated)

Name: news.announce.newusers
Resource: USENET
Explanatory postings for new users. (Moderated)

Name: news.answers
Resource: USENET
Repository for periodic USENET articles. (Moderated)

Name: rec.answers
Resource: USENET
Repository for periodic USENET articles. (Moderated)

Name: sci.answers
Resource: USENET
Repository for periodic USENET articles. (Moderated)

Name: soc.answers
Resource: USENET
Repository for periodic USENET articles. (Moderated)

Name: talk.answers
Resource: USENET
Repository for periodic USENET articles. (Moderated)

Archie

Resource: telnet
Address: Use one of the following addresses: `archie.ans.net<cr>archie.au<cr>archie.doc.ic.ac.uk<cr>archie.funet.fi<cr>archie.kuis.kyoto-u.ac.jp<cr>archie.luth.se<cr>archie.ncu.edu.tw<cr>archie.nz<cr>archie.rutgers.edu<cr>archie.sogang.ac.kr<cr>archie.sura.net<cr>archie.th-darmstadt.de<cr>archie.univie.ac.at<cr>archie.unl.edu`
User id: `Archie`

BBS

Resource: telnet
Address: `bbs.oit.unc.edu`
User id: `bbs` University of North Carolina "laUNChpad" BBS

Resource: telnet
Address: `lambada.oit.unc.edu`
User id: `bbs`
This is a "freenet" site. A menu-oriented system will direct you to a public USENET feed, electronic libraries, and so on.

Name: alt.bbs.internet
Resource: USENET
BBSs that are hooked up to the Internet.

BITNET

Name: bit.admin
Resource: USENET
Newgroups Discussions.

CARL

Resource: telnet
Address: `pac.carl.org`
User id: `wais`

Resource: telnet
Address: `quake.think.com`
`(192.31.181.1)`
User id: `wais`

Name: carl-l
Resource: LISTSERV
Address: `carl-l@uhccvm`
CARL user information list.

Commercialization

Name: com-priv
Resource: List
Address: `com-priv@uu.psi.com`
An electronic list dedicated to the
commercialization of the Internet.
Send subscription requests to
`COM-PRIV-REQUEST@UU.PSI.COM`.

CompuServe Gateway

Resource: telnet
Address: HERMES.MERIT.EDU
When prompted for the system,
specify CIS. This is a telnet gateway to
CompuServe.

Culture

Name: alt.culture.internet
Resource: USENET
The culture(s) of the Internet.

Name: alt.culture.USENET
Resource: USENET
A self-referential oxymoron.

CWIS

Resource: FTP
Address: `ftp.oit.unc.edu`
Directory: `pub/docs/cwis-1`

Resource: telnet
Address: `info.rutgers.edu`
User id: `wais`

Cyberculture

Name: Fringeware
Resource: List
Address:
`fringeware-request@illuminati.io.com`
A moderated list devoted to
cyberculture and the like.

Discussion Lists

Name: List-Managers
Resource: List
Address: `Brent@GreatCircle.COM`
(Brent Chapman)
A mailing list for discussions of issues
related to managing Internet mailing
lists, including (but not limited to)
software, methods, mechanisms,
techniques, and policies.

E-Mail

Name: comp.mail.mime
Resource: USENET
Multipurpose Internet Mail Exten-
sions of RFC 1341.

Electronic Journals

Resource: FTP
Address: `ftp.eff.org`
Directory: `/pub/journals`

Freenet

Resource: telnet
Address: `yfn.ysu.edu`
User id: `visitor` This is the Youngstown Freenet/Electronic Village.

Resource: telnet
Address: `freenet.scri.fsu.edu`
User id: `visitor` This is the Tallahassee Freenet/Electronic Village.

Resource: telnet
Address: `FREENET.HSC.COLORADO.EDU`
Telnet to the electronic version of the city of Denver.

Freenets

Name: neci-discuss
Resource: List
Address:
`neci-discuss-request@pioneer.ci.net`
This is the general discussion forum of New England Community Internet, an organization dedicated to making USENET and Internet accessible to the public without barriers of economics or technical expertise. To get a daily digestified version, subscribe to `neci-digest`. To receive organizational announcements only, subscribe to `neci-announce`.

FTP

Resource: FTP
Address: `pilot.njin.net`
Retrieve the file /ftp.list.

FTPmail

Name: FTPMAIL
Resource: e-mail

Address: `FTPMAIL@decwrl.dec.com`
Send a message containing the word HELP for full instructions.

Fun

Resource: FTP
Address: `cerberus.cor.epa.gov`
Directory: `/pub/bigfun`

General

Name: `alt.politics.datahighway`
Resource: USENET
Electronic interstate infrastructure.

Name: `soc.net-people`
Resource: USENET
Announcements, requests, and so on about people on the net.

Gopher

Resource: Telnet
Address: `<cr>ux1.cso.uiuc.edu`
`(userid: gopher)`
`<cr>consultant.micro.umn.edu<cr>`
`panda.uiowa.edu<cr>gdunix.gd.chalmers.`
`se<cr>gopher.uiuc.edu<cr>gopher.unt.`
`edu<cr>tolten.puc.cl<cr>wsuaix.csc.wsu.`
`edu (Login:wsuinfo)<cr>una.hh.lib.`
`um1mich.edu<cr>harpoon.cso.uiuc.edu`
`(Login: gopher)`

Resource: FTP
Address: `liberty.uc.wlu.edu`
Directory: `/pub/lawlib` Retrieve the file `veronica.gopher.sites`.

Name: comp.infosystems.gopher
Resource: USENET
Discussion of the Gopher information service.

Hytelnet

Resource: telnet
Address: laguna.epcc.edu
User id: library

Resource: telnet
Address: info.anu.edu.au
User id: hytelnet

Resource: telnet
Address: access.usask.ca
User id: hytelnet

Resource: FTP
Address: access.usask.ca
Directory: pub/hytelnet

Name: hytel-l
Resource: LISTSERV
Address: hytel-l@kentvm.bitnet
Hytelnet updates distribution.

Indexes/How-To

Name: ann-lots
Resource: LISTSERV
Address: ann-lots@vm1.nodak.edu
Indexing forum for annotated lists of things.

Info

Resource: FTP
Address: nic.merit.edu
Directory: documents/rfc Retrieve the file rfc1394.txt.

Resource: FTP
Address: pit-manager.mit.edu
Text files of frequently asked questions, from artifical intelligence to z-faq. Over 275 subjects.

IRC

Name: alt.irc
Resource: USENET
Internet Relay Chat material.

Name: alt.irc.ircii
Resource: USENET
The IRC II client programme.

Name: alt.irc.questions
Resource: USENET
How-to questions for IRC (Internet Relay Chat).

Name: operlist
Resource: List
Address: operlist-request@eff.org
(Helen Trillian Rose)
A discussion list for everything having to do with IRC.

Link Failures

Name: linkfail
Resource: LISTSERV
Address: linkfail@uga.cc.uga.edu
This list posts "downed" network sites.

List Management

Name: list-managers
Resource: List
Address:
list-managers@greatcircle.com
A discussion group devoted to the management of mailing lists. Send the text subscribe list-managers in an e-mail message to
majordomo@greatcircle.com.

List of Lists

Resource: FTP
Address: `ftp.nisc.sri.com`
Directory: `netinfo` Retrieve
interest-groups.

List Ownership

Name: lstown-l
Resource: LISTSERV
Address: `lstown-l@searn.bitnet`
This list is for anyone involved in
creating, supporting, or moderating a
LISTSERV list.

Lists

Name: interest-groups
Resource: List
Address:
`interest-groups-request@nisc.sri.com`
There is a document, interest-groups,
that can be obtained by anonymous
`ftp` from `ftp.nisc.sri.com`. The document contains a listing of many of the
current mailing lists.

Name: new-list
Resource: LISTSERV
Address: `new-list@vm1.nodak.edu`
New list announcements are generally
made here. This is also a good place to
inquire about the existence of lists.

Mailing Lists

Name: newlists
Resource: List
Address: `Addressinfo@vm1.nodak.edu`
(Marty Hoag)

This is a mailing list "clearing house"
for new mailing lists. Subscribers will
get announcements of new lists that
are mailed to this list.

MUDs

Resource: FTP
Address: `caisr2.caisr.cwru.edu`
Directory: `/pub/mud`

Navigating

Name: k12nav-l
Resource: LISTSERV
Address: `k12nav-l@kentvm.bitnet`
This discussion list is for K-12 educa-
tors investigating Internet navigation.

Name: k12nav-n
Resource: LISTSERV
Address: `k12nav-n@kentvm.bitnet`
This is the Internet navigation course
for K-12 educators.

Name: navigate
Resource: LISTSERV
Address: `navigate@ubvm.cc.buffalo.edu`
Navigating the Internet workshop list.

Organizations

Name: comp.org.eff.talk
Resource: USENET
Discussion of EFF goals, strategies,
etc.

Project Gutenberg

Resource: FTP
Address: mrcnext.cso.uiuc.edu
Directory: /pub/etext

Resource: FTP
Address: MRCNEXT.CSO.UIUC.EDU

Name: gutnberg
Resource: LISTSERV
Address: gutnberg@vmd.cso.uiuc.edu
Project Gutenberg e-mail list.

Protocols

Name: comp.protocols.ppp
Resource: USENET
Discussion of the Internet Point to
Point Protocol.

Public Access

Resource: FTP
Address: nnsc.nsf.net
Directory: nsfnet Retrieve the file
nixpub.

Public USENET

Resource: telnet
Address: tolten.puc.cl

Resources

Resource: telnet
Address: stis.nsf.gov
User id: public

Services

Name: alt.internet.services
Resource: USENET
Not available in the uucp world, even
via e-mail.

Software

Name: news.software.anu-news
Resource: USENET
VMS B-news software from Austra-
lian National University.

Name: news.software.b
Resource: USENET
Discussion about B-news-compatible
software.

Name: news.software.nn
Resource: USENET
Discussion about the "nn" news
reader package.

Name: news.software.readers
Resource: USENET
Discussion of software used to read
network news.

USENET

Resource: FTP
Address: gator.netcom.com
Directory: /pub/profile

Resource: FTP
Address: ftp.uu.net
Directory: uunet-info

Resource: telnet
Address: nyx.cs.du.edu
User id: new

Resource: telnet
Address: quip.eecs.umich.edu 119

Resource: telnet
Address: m-net.ann-arbor.mi.us
When prompted for Which host:,
enter um-m-net. Enter g for guest.
Login: newuser

Resource: FTP
Address: pit-manager.mit.edu
Directory: pub/USENET

Resource: FTP
Address: `pit-manager.mit.edu`
`[18.172.1.27]`
Directory: `/pub/USENET/news.answers/`
`news-answers` Retrieve the file introduction.

Resource: telnet
Address: `vaxc.cc.monash.edu.au 119`

Resource: FTP
Address: `ftp.netcom.com`
Directory: `/pub/profile` Retrieve the file ftp-list.

Resource: telnet
Address: `suntan.ec.usf.edu 119`
Retrieve the file maps.

Resource: telnet
Address: `hermes.merit.edu`

Name: news.groups
Resource: USENET
Discussions and lists of newsgroups.

Name: news.lists
Resource: USENET
News-related statistics and lists.
(Moderated)

Name: news.lists.ps-maps
Resource: USENET
Maps relating to USENET traffic flows. (Moderated)

Name: news.misc
Resource: USENET
Discussions of USENET itself.

Name: news.newusers.questions
Resource: USENET
Q & A for users new to the USENET.

Name: VMEbus
Resource: List
Address: `att!houxl!mlh`
(Marc Harrison)

A user's group for the AT&T VMEbus products.

Name: vmsnet.admin
Resource: USENET
Administration of the VMSnet newsgroups.

Name:
vmsnet.announce.newusers
Resource: USENET
Orientation info for new users.
(Moderated)

USENET/Newsgroups

Name:
news.announce.newgroups
Resource: USENET
Calls for newgroups & announcements of same. (Moderated)

USENET Search

Resource: telnet
Address: `mudhoney.micro.umn.edu`

USENET-Maps

Resource: FTP
Address: `gatekeeper.dec.com`
Directory: `/pub`

Utilities

Resource: telnet
Address: `wugate.wustl.edu`
Userid: `services`

Veronica

Resource: FTP

Address: `cs.dal.ca`
Directory: `pub/comp.archives/`
`bionet.software` Retrieve the file
veronica.

WAIS

Resource: telnet
Address: `sunsite.unc.edu`
User id: `swais`

Resource: telnet
Address: `nnsc.nsf.net`
User id: `wais`

Resource: FTP
Address: `julian.uwo.ca`
Directory: `doc/wais`

Resource: FTP
Address: `think.com`
Directory: `wais`

Resource: telnet
Address: `info.funet.fi`
User id: `info`

Resource: telnet
Address: `swais.cwis.uci.edu`
User id: `swais`

Name: wais-discussion
Resource: List
Address:
`wais-discussion-request@think.com`
WAIS (Wide Area Information
Servers). An electronic publishing
project lead by Thinking Machines.

Name: wais-talk
Resource: List
Address: `wais-talk-request@think.com`
WAIS (Wide Area Information
Servers). An open list for
implementors and developers.

Whois

Resource: FTP
Address: `sipb.mit.edu`
Directory: `/pub/whois` Retrieve the file
whois-servers.list.

World Wide Web (WWW)

Resource: telnet
Address: `nxoc01.cern.ch`

Resource: telnet
Address: `ukanaix.cc.ukans.edu`
User id: `www`

Resource: FTP
Address: `info.cem.ch`
Directory: `pub/www/doc` Retrieve the file
the_www_book.

Resource: telnet
Address: `fatty.law.cornell.edu`
User id: `www`

Name: comp.infosystems.www
Resource: USENET
The World Wide Web information
system.

Languages

Chinese

Name: alt.chinese.text
Resource: USENET
Postings in Chinese; Chinese lan-
guage software.

Name: alt.chinese.text.big5
Resource: USENET
Posting in Chinese[BIG 5].

Esperanto

Name: esper-l
Resource: LISTSERV
Address:
`esper-l@trearn.bitnet@cunyvm.cuny.edu`
A discussion group about the language Esperanto.

Name: esperanto
Resource: List
Address: `esperanto-request@rand.org`
(Mike Urban)
A forum for people interested in Esperanto.

Name: esperanto
Resource: List
Address: `esperanto@lll-crg.llnl.gov`
A discussion list devoted to the language Esperanto, gatewayed to the USENET group mail.esperanto.

Name: soc.culture.esperanto
Resource: USENET

Gaelic

Name: GAELIC-L
Resource: LISTSERV
Address: `GAELIC-L@irlearn.ucd.ie`
A discussion of the Gaelic (Irish) language.

Name: GAELIC-L
Resource: LISTSERV
Address: `LISTSERV@IRLEARN.UCD.IE`
Read on for instructions in Scottish Gaelic (SG) Irish (IG) and Manx (MG).
Listserver: `LISTSERV@IRLEARN.BITNET`
`LISTSERV@IRLEARN.UCD.IE`

General

Name: linguist
Resource: LISTSERV
Address: `linguist@tamvm1.tamu.edu`
For everyone involved in linguistics research.

Iroquois

Name: iroquois
Resource: LISTSERV
Address: `iroquois@utoronto.bitnet`
For the discussion and exchange of ideas about the Iroquois language.

Japanese

Name: nihongo
Resource: LISTSERV
Address: `nihongo@mitvma.mit.edu`
This is the Japanese language discussion list.

Latin

Name: latin-l
Resource: LISTSERV
Address: `latin-l@psuvm.psu.edu`
This list is devoted to Latin and Neo-Latin.

Lojban

Name: lojban
Resource: List
Address:
`lojban-list-request@snark.thyrsus.com`
(John Cowan)
To use, discuss, and contribute to the development of the constructed human language called Lojban.

Name: lojban-list
Resource: List
Address:
`lojban-list@snark.thyrsus.com`

For supporters of Lojban. Send your subscription request to `lojban-list-request@snark.thyrsus.com`.

Natural

Name: sci.lang
Resource: USENET
Natural languages, communication, and so forth.

Older Germanic

Name: GERLINGL
Resource: LISTSERV
Address: `GERLINGL@cso.uiuc.edu`
This list discusses and researches older (to 1500) Germanic languages.

Romania

Name: romanians
Resource: List
Address: `romanians@sep.stanford.edu` (Mihai Popovici)
Mailing list for discussion, news, and information in the Romanian language.

Russian

Name: Info-Russ
Resource: List
Address: `info-russ@smarty.ece.jhu.edu` (Aleksander Kaplan)
Informal communication in Russian-speaking (or related interests) community.

Name: Sovokinform
Resource: List
Address: `burkov@drfmc.ceng.cea.fr`
CIS news, events, general information; usually in transliterated Russian.

Sign Language

Name: slling-l
Resource: LISTSERV
Address: `slling-l@yalevm.ycc.yale.edu`
This is the sign language list.

Signing

Name: SLLing-L
Resource: LISTSERV
Address: `listserv@yalevm.ycc.yale.edu`
SLLING-L (formerly ASL-LING) is for discssions of Sign Language Linguistics. `listserv@yalevm.ycc.yale.edu` is the server; `cromano@uconnvm.bitnet` (owner) and `mosko@matai.vuw.ac.nz` are the humans.

Telugu

Name: TELUGU
Resource: LISTSERV
Address: `TELUGU@vm1.nodak.edu`
Telegu (Andhra Pradesh) language and culture.

Welsh

Name: WELSH-L
Resource: LISTSERV
Address: `WELSH-L@irlearn.ucd.ie`
Welsh language bulletin board (bilingual).

Yiddish

Name: mail.yiddish
Resource: List
Address: `mail.yiddish@dave@lsuc.on.ca`
For those interested in the Yiddish language. Send your subscription request to `dave@lsuc.on.ca`.

Name: Mendele
Resource: LISTSERV
Address: Mendele@yalevm.ycc.yale.edu
For the discussion of the Yiddish language.

Legal

Criminal Justice

Name: cjust-l
Resource: LISTSERV
Address: cjust-l@cunyvm.cuny.edu
Criminal justice discussion list.

Literature

American Literature

Name: amlit-l
Resource: LISTSERV
Address: amlit-l@umcvmb.missouri.edu
Created for the exchange of ideas, opinions, and information related to American Literature.

Asimov, Isaac

Name: asimov-l
Resource: LISTSERV
Address: asimov-l@utdallas.bitnet
Discussion of Isaac Asimov's works.

Austen, Jane

Name: austen-l
Resource: LISTSERV
Address: austen-l@vm1.mcgill.ca
Jane Austen discussion list.

Bach, Richard

Name: alt.soulmates
Resource: USENET
Richard Bach and his herculean odds.

Chicano

Name: chicle
Resource: LISTSERV
Address: chicle@unmvma.bitnet
Chicano literature discussion list.

Children

Name: kidlit-l
Resource: LISTSERV
Address: kidlit-l@bingvmb.bitnet
Children and youth literature list.

Chinese Poetry

Name: chpoem-l
Resource: LISTSERV
Address: chpoem-l@ubvm.cc.buffalo.edu
Chinese poem exchange and discussion list.

Classics

Name: classics
Resource: LISTSERV
Address: classics@uwavm.bitnet
Classical Greek and Latin discussion group.

Comic Writing

Name: comicw-l
Resource: LISTSERV

Address: `comicw-l@unlvm.bitnet`
Workshop for comic writers.

Comics

Name: alt.comics.superman
Resource: USENET
No one knows it is also alt.clark.kent.

Name: cerebi
Resource: List
Address:
`cerebi-request@tomservo.b23b.ingr.com`
(Christian Walters)
About the Cerebus comic book by
Dave Sim.

Name: comics-l
Resource: LISTSERV
Address: `comics-l@unlvm.bitnet`
Comics discussion list.

Name: comix
Resource: List
Address: `comix-request@world.std.com`
(Elizabeth Lear Newman)
Intended for talking about
non-mainstream and independent
comic books.

Name: disney-comics
Resource: List
Address:
`disney-comics-request@student.docs.uu.se`
(Per Starb{ck)
Discussion of Disney comics.

Name: Gunk'l'dunk
Resource: List
Address: `jeremy@stat.washington.edu`
(Jeremy York)
A forum for discussing and promot-
ing *Tales of the Beanworld*, an unusual
black-and-white comic published by
Eclipse comics.

Name: rec.arts.comics.info
Resource: USENET
Reviews, convention information, and
other comics news. (Moderated)

Name: rec.arts.comics.misc
Resource: USENET
Comic books, graphic novels, sequen-
tial art.

Name: rec.arts.comics.strips
Resource: USENET
Discussion of short-form comics.

Name: Valiant Visions
Resource: List
Address: `CVITEK@DREW.DREW.EDU`
A forum for discussing and promot-
ing Valiant comics.

Dick, Philip K.

Name: pkd-list
Resource: List
Address: `pkd-list-request@wang.com`
The discussion of the works and life
of Philip K. Dick (1928-1982).

Dickens, Charles

Name: dickns-l
Resource: LISTSERV
Address: `dickns-l@ucsbvm.bitnet`
Charles Dickens forum.

Disney Comics

Name: Disney-Comics
Resource: List
Address:
`Disney-Comics@Student.Docs.Uu.Se`
A discussion group devoted to
Disney comics.

Electronic

Resource: telnet
Address: `bbs.oit.unc.edu`
User id: `bbs`

Name: Twilight Zone
Resource: List
Address:
`r.c.karsmakers@stud.let.ruu.nl`
Twilight Zone is a fiction-only, online magazine.

Fantasy

Name: alt.fan.douglas-adams
Resource: USENET
Author of "The Meaning of Liff" & other fine works.

Name: alt.fan.tolkien
Resource: USENET
Mortal Men doomed to die.

Name: deryni-l
Resource: List
Address:
`mail-server@mintir.new-orleans.la.us`
`elendil@mintir.new-orleans.la.us`
(Edward J. Branley)
A list for readers and fans of Katernine Kurtz' novels and other works.

Name: rec.arts.books.tolkien
Resource: USENET
The works of J.R.R. Tolkien.

Name: Tolkien-Czech
Resource: LISTSERV
Address: `TOLKIEN-request@pub.vse.cz`
The discussion, held in Czech and Slovak languages only, concerns works of J. R. R. Tolkien.

Name: TolkLang
Resource: List

Address:
`tolklang-request@lfcs.ed.ac.uk`
(Julian Bradfield)
Discussions of the linguistic aspects of J.R.R. Tolkien's works.

Fiction

Name: vampyres
Resource: LISTSERV
Address: `vampyres@guvm.bitnet`
Vampiric lore and fiction.

Finnegans Wake

Name: fwaken-l
Resource: LISTSERV
Address: `fwaken-l@irlearn.ucd.ie`
Finnegans Wake textual notes.

General

Name: rec.arts.books
Resource: USENET
Books of all genres, and the publishing industry.

Gothic

Name: GOTHIC-TALES
Resource: List
Address: `carriec@eskimo.com`
Gothic/vampire/blood stories pertaining to darkness, obscurity, and beauty.

Gothic Horror

Name: Ravenloft
Resource: List
Address:
`raven+request@drycas.club.cc.cmu.edu`

Discussion of Gothic Horror with respect to the Ravenloft Accessory to Advanced Dungeons & Dragons.

Hemingway

Name: Papa
Resource: List
Address: `dgross@polyslo.calpoly.edu`
(Dave Gross)
The life and works of Ernest Hemingway.

Interactive Fiction

Name: rec.arts.int-fiction
Resource: USENET
Discussions about interactive fiction.

King Arthur/Camelot

Name: camelot
Resource: List
Address: `camelot@castle.ed.ac.uk`
Discussion of King Arthur and the Holy Grail.

Magazines

Name: alt.zines
Resource: USENET
Small magazines, mostly noncommercial.

Name: InterText
Resource: List
Address: `intertxt@network.ucsd.edu`
(Jason Snell)
A bi-monthly fiction magazine.

Name: magazine
Resource: LISTSERV
Address: `magazine@rpitsvm.bitnet`
Magazines.

Name: rec.mag
Resource: USENET
Magazine summaries, tables of contents, and so forth.

Manga

Name: rec.arts.manga
Resource: USENET
All aspects of Japanese storytelling art form.

Medieval English

Name: chaucer
Resource: LISTSERV
Address: `chaucer@uicvm.bitnet`
Medieval English literature and culture (1100-1500).

Mystery

Name: alt.fan.holmes
Resource: USENET
Elementary, my dear Watson. Like he ever said that.

Name: dorothyl
Resource: LISTSERV
Address: `dorothyl@kentvm.Kent.Edu`
This is a mystery literature electronic conference.

Name: mystery
Resource: List
Address: `mystery-request@introl.com`
(Thomas Krueger)
A mailing list for mystery and detective fiction.

Nabokov, Vladimir

Name: nabokv-l
Resource: LISTSERV
Address: `nabokv-l@ucsbvm.bitnet`
Discusses the life and works of Vladimir Nabokov.

Online Books

Resource: FTP
Address: `wiretap.spies.com`

Poetry

Name: e-poetry
Resource: LISTSERV
Address: `e-poetry@ubvm.cc.buffalo.edu`
Electronic poetry distribution list.

Name: poet
Resource: LISTSERV
Address: `poet@gsuvm1.bitnet`
This is a works-in-progress list. You can submit your poems and receive feedback, as well as critique the work of others.

Prose

Name: rec.arts.prose
Resource: USENET
Short works of prose fiction and followup discussion.

Reviews

Name: alt.books.reviews
Resource: USENET
If you want to know how it turns out, read it!

Robin Hood

Name:
Resource: FTP
Address: `rtfm.mit.edu`
Directory: `/pub/USENET/news.answers/ books` Retrieve the file robin-hood.

Romance

Name: rra-l
Resource: LISTSERV
Address: `rra-l@kentvm.kent.edu`
For everyone interested in romance novels.

Science Fiction

Name: alt.fan.dune
Resource: USENET
Herbert's drinking buddies.

Name: alt.fan.pern
Resource: USENET
Anne McCaffery's s-f oeuvre.

Name: alt.fan.pratchett
Resource: USENET
For fans of Terry Pratchett, s-f humor writer.

Name: alt.startrek.creative
Resource: USENET
Stories and parodies related to *Star Trek.*

Name: alt.startrek.klingon
Resource: USENET
Ack! What is that thing on your head?!

Name: Milieu
Resource: List
Address:
`milieu-request@yoyo.cc.monash.edu.au`
Discussion of the works of Julian May.

Name: Quanta
Resource: List
Address: `da1n@andrew.cmu.edu`
Quanta is an electronically distributed magazine of science fiction.

Name: quanta
Resource: List
Address: `quanta@andrew.cmu.edu`
An e-magazine devoted to the science fiction genre.

Name: rec.arts.sf.written
Resource: USENET
Discussion of written science fiction and fantasy.

Name: sf-lovers
Resource: LISTSERV
Address:
`sf-lovers-request@rutgers.edu`
(Saul Jaffe)

Screenwriting

Name: scrnwrit
Resource: LISTSERV
Address: `scrnwrit@tamvm1.tamu.edu`
For people interested in screenwriting for television or movies.

Shakespeare

Name: shaksper
Resource: LISTSERV
Address: `shaksper@utoronto.bitnet`
Shakespeare electronic conference.

Technical

Name: alt.books.technical
Resource: USENET
Discussion of technical books.

Name: biz.books.technical
Resource: USENET
Technical bookstore and publisher advertising and information.

Name: misc.books.technical
Resource: USENET
Discussion of books about technical topics.

Technical Writing

Name: techwr-l
Resource: LISTSERV
Address: `techwr-l@vm1.ucc.okstate.edu`
For anyone involved in technical writing and technical communications, including documentation and specifications.

Tolkien, J.R.R.

Name: tolkien
Resource: LISTSERV
Address: `tolkien@jhuvm.bitnet`
This is for all fans who wish to discuss the literary works of J.R.R. Tolkien.

Twain, Mark

Name: twain-l
Resource: LISTSERV
Address: `twain-l@vm1.yorku.ca`
This is the Mark Twain/Samuel Clemens forum.

Weird

Name: WEIRD-L
Resource: LISTSERV

Address: `listserv@brownvm.brown.edu`
Disturbing and potentially offensive prose or poetry.

Writing

Name: misc.writing
Resource: USENET
Discussion of writing in all of its forms.

Writing/Fiction

Name: fiction
Resource: LISTSERV
Address: `fiction@psuvm.psu.edu`
Fiction writers' workshop.

Name: fiction-writers
Resource: List
Address:
`fiction-writers@studguppy@lanl.gov`

Miscellaneous

Miscellaneous

Name: misc.misc
Resource: USENET
Various discussions not fitting in any other group.

Motorcycles

BMW

Name: BMW Motorcycles
Resource: List
Address: `bmw-request@rider.cactus.org`
Talk about all years and models of BMW motorcycles.

British

Name: Brit-Iron
Resource: List
Address: `Brit-Iron@indiana.edu`
`cstringe@indiana.edu`
To provide a friendly forum for riders, owners, and admirers of British motorcycles to share information and experiences.

Building/Designing

Name: moto.chassis
Resource: List
Address: `moto.chassis@oce.orst.edu`
For persons interested in building and designing a motorcycle chassis.

General

Name: rec.motorcycles
Resource: USENET
Motorcycles and related products and laws.

Name: rec.motorcycles.dirt
Resource: USENET
Riding motorcycles and ATVs off-road.

Name: rec.motorcycles.harley
Resource: USENET
All aspects of Harley-Davidson motorcycles.

Name: Two-Strokes
Resource: List
Address:
`2strokes-request@microunity.com`
For the discussion of two-stroke motorcycle technology, maintenance, and riding.

Harley-Davidson

Name:　　Harleys
Resource: List
Address:

`harley-request@thinkage.on.ca` (Ken Dykes) `harley-request@thinkage.com`
`uunet!thinkage!harley-request`
Discussion about the bikes, politics, lifestyles, and anything else of interest to Harley-Davidson motorcycle lovers.

New England

Name:　　nedod
Resource: List
Address:

`nedod-request@mbunix.mitre.org` (automated LISTSERV)
`cookson@mbunix.mitre.org`
The discussion of events, technical issues, and just plain socializing related to motorcycling in New England.

Racing

Name:　　rec.motorcycles.racing
Resource: USENET
Discussion of all aspects of racing motorcycles.

Motorcycling

General

Name:　　wetleather
Resource: List
Address:

`wetleather-request@mom.isc-br.com`
(automated instructions)
`wetleather-owner@mom.isc-br.com`

(Carl Paukstis)
A mailing list for discussion, general chatter, chaos, ride reports, and announcements of upcoming motorcycle events in the Greater Pacific Northwest.

Parapsychology

Astrology

Name:　　astrol-l
Resource: LISTSERV
Address:　`astrol-l@brufpb.bitnet`
This is a forum for astrological discussion.

General

Name:　　psi-l
Resource: LISTSERV
Address:　`psi-l@rpitsvm.bitnet`
This is the parapsychology discussion forum.

Out-of-body Experiences

Name:　　alt.out-of-body
Resource: USENET
Out of Body Experiences.

Skepticism

Name:　　SKEPTIC
Resource: LISTSERV
Address:　`LISTSERV@JHUVM.HCF.JHU.EDU`
A mailing list devoted to critical discussion of extraordinary claims.

Skeptics

Name: skeptic
Resource: LISTSERV
Address: `skeptic@jhuvm.bitnet`
The skeptic discussion group.

UFOs

Name: ufo-l
Resource: LISTSERV
Address: `ufo-l@psuvm.psu.edu`
For everyone interested in
UFO-related phenomena.

Pets

Birds

Name: rec.pets.birds
Resource: USENET
The culture and care of indoor birds.

Cats

Name: feline-l
Resource: LISTSERV
Address: `feline-l@psuvm.psu.edu`
A discussion list created just for cat
fanciers.

Name: rec.pets.cats
Resource: USENET
Discussion about domestic cats.

Dogs

Name: canine-l
Resource: LISTSERV
Address: `canine-l@psuvm.psu.edu`
A discussion list for all dog lovers
and fanciers.

Name: golden
Resource: List
Address:
`golden-request@hobbes.ucsd.edu`
A mailing list for Golden Retriever
enthusiasts.

Name: obed
Resource: List
Address:
`obed@reepicheep.gcn.uoknor.edu`
Discussion of all aspects of training
and showing dogs.

Name: obed-l
Resource: List
Address:
`obed-l@reepicheep.gcn.uoknor.edu`
Discussion of dog obedience training
and related working dog topics.

Name: rec.pets.dogs
Resource: USENET
Any and all subjects relating to dogs
as pets.

Ferrets

Name: Ferret
Resource: List
Address: `Ferret@Ferret.ocunix.on.ca`
For anyone interested in ferrets.

Name: ferrets
Resource: List
Address:
`ferret-request@ferret.ocunix.on.ca`
(Chris Lewis)
`{utzoo,utai,uunet}!cunews!latour!ecicrl!ferret-request`
A mailing list for people who have or
are merely interested in ferrets
(*Mustela furo*).

General

Name: pets-l
Resource: LISTSERV
Address: pets-l@itesmvf1.bitnet
For the discussion of domestic animal care and education.

Horses

Name: equine-d
Resource: LISTSERV
Address: equine-d@pccvm.bitnet
A gateway digest to the USENET group rec.equestrian.

Miscellaneous

Name: rec.pets
Resource: USENET
Pets, pet care, and household animals in general.

Philosophy

Ayurveda

Name: Ayurveda
Resource: List
Address: ayurveda-request@netcom.com
A mailing list for Ayurveda, the ancient science of life originating in India.

General

Name: Miracles
Resource: List
Address: perry.sills@EBay
perrys@spiritlead.Sun.COM
Provides readings from Miracles Centers.

Name: philosop
Resource: LISTSERV
Address: philosop@vm1.yorku.ca
Philosophy discussion forum.

Holistic

Name: urantial
Resource: LISTSERV
Address: urantial@uafsysb.bitnet
An open forum for the discussion of the Urantia book.

Meta

Name: sci.philosophy.meta
Resource: USENET
Discussions within the scope of MetaPhilosophy.

Objectivism

Name: objectivism
Resource: List
Address: objectivism-request@vix.com
(Paul Vixie)
A mailing list of Objectivism.

Rand, Ayn

Name: alt.philosophy.objectivism
Resource: USENET
A product of the Ayn Rand corporation.

Name: ayn-rand
Resource: LISTSERV
Address: ayn-rand@iubvm.bitnet
A moderated list for the discussion of objectivist philosophy.

Stirner, Max

Name: Non Serviam
Resource: List
Address: `solan@math.uio.no`
(Svein Olav Nyberg)
An electronic newsletter centered on
the philosophy of Max Stirner, author
of "Der Einzige und Sein Eigentum"
("The Ego and Its Own"), and his
dialectical egoism.

Technical

Name: sci.philosophy.tech
Resource: USENET
Technical philosophy: math, science,
logic, and so on.

Politics

2nd Ammendment

Name: pro-rkba-democrats
Resource: List
Address: `donb@netcom.com`
For liberals/Democrats who support
the Second Amendment.

Civil Liberties

Name: alt.society.civil-liberty
Resource: USENET
Same as `alt.society.civil-liberties`.

Civil Rights

Name: The Frog Farm
Resource: List
Address: `schirado@lab.cc.wmich.edu`
The Frog Farm is devoted to the
discussion of claiming, exercising,

and defending rights in America,
past, present and future.

Democratic

Name: clinton
Resource: LISTSERV
Address: `clinton@marist.bitnet`
Created for the discussion of cam-
paigning for Bill Clinton's Presidency.

Disarmament

Name: disarm-d
Resource: LISTSERV
Address: `disarm-d@albnyvm1.bitnet`
Disarmament discussion monthly
digest.

Economics

Name: alt.politics.economics
Resource: USENET
War == Poverty, and other discus-
sions.

Environment

Name: ecology
Resource: LISTSERV
Address: `ecology@emuvm1.bitnet`
This list is devoted to the discussion
of politics and the environment.

Firearms/Gun Control

Name: firearms-politics
Resource: List
Address: `firearms-politics@cs.cmu.edu`
Discussion group for the exchange of
information related to the 2nd
Amendment.

Gay/Lesbian/Bisexual Issues

Name: DSA-LGB
Resource: List
Address:
`DSA-LGB-request@midway.uchicago.edu`
A mailing list for members of the Lesbian/Gay/Bisexual Commission of the Democratic Socialists of America, and for other people interested in discussing connections between sexual identity and the democratic socialist movement.

Name: FREEDOM
Resource: LISTSERV
Address: `LISTSERV@idbsu.idbsu.edu`
Mailing list of people organizing against the Idaho Citizens Alliance anti-gay ballot initiative.

General

Name: POLITICS
Resource: LISTSERV
Address: `POLITICS@ucf1vm.cc.ucf.edu`
Politics.

Law

Name: misc.legal
Resource: USENET
Legalities and the ethics of law.

Name: misc.legal.moderated
Resource: USENET
All aspects of law. (Moderated)

Libertarian

Name: alt.politics.libertarian
Resource: USENET
The Libertarian ideology.

Name: ba-liberty
Resource: List
Address:
`ba-liberty-request@shell.portal.com`
(Jeff Chan)
Announcement of local Libertarian meetings, events, activities, and so forth.

Name: ca-liberty
Resource: List
Address:
`ca-liberty-request@shell.portal.com`
(Jeff Chan)
Announcement of local libertarian meetings, events, activities, and so forth. The ca- list is for California statewide issues; the ba- list is for the San Francisco Bay Area.

Name: libernet
Resource: List
Address:
`libernet-request@dartmouth.edu`
(Barry S. Fagin)
A Libertarian mailing list.

Middle East

Name: talk.politics.mideast
Resource: USENET
Discussion and debate about Middle Eastern events.

Miscellaneous

Name: soc.politics
Resource: USENET
Political problems, systems, solutions. (Moderated)

Name: talk.politics.misc
Resource: USENET
Political discussions and ravings of all kinds.

Monarchy

Name: Counterev-L
Resource: List
Address: ae852@yfn.ysu.edu
(Jovan Weismiller)
This list is under the aegis of l'Alliance Monarchists and is dedicated to promoting the cause of traditional monarchy and the Counter Revolution.

Republican

Name: gop-l
Resource: LISTSERV
Address: gop-l@pccvm.bitnet
A discussion of the Grand Old Party.

Senate Bills

Resource: FTP
Address: gaia.ucs.orst.edu
Directory: /OLIS/Working Directory/ Senate

U.S.

Name: fairness
Resource: List
Address:
fairness-request@mainstream.com (automated - Craig Peterson)
Monitoring issues of "fairness" with respect to the government.

US Military

Name: navnews
Resource: List
Address: navnews@nctamslant.navy.mil
E-mail distribution list for the weekly Navy News Service (NAVNEWS).

US State Department

Name: travel-advisories
Resource: List
Address: travel-advisories@stolaf.edu
Travel advisories from the US State Department.

US Supreme Court Decisions

Resource: FTP
Address: po.CWRU.Edu
Directory: /hermes/ascii

US Trade Policy

Name: America
Resource: List
Address: subscribe@xamiga.linet.org
For people interested in how the United States is dealing with foreign trade policies, congressional status, and other inside information about the government that is freely distributable.

US Visas

Name: alt.visa.us
Resource: USENET
Discussion and information on visas pertaining to the US.

US White House

Name: President
Resource: e-mail
Address: President@WhiteHouse.Gov
Send a message to President Clinton!

Name: Vice.President
Resource: e-mail

Address:
`Vice.President@WhiteHouse.Gov`
Send a message to Vice President
Gore!

USA

Name: alt.politics.usa.misc
Resource: USENET
Miscellaneous USA politics.

Professional

Architecture

Name: larch-l
Resource: LISTSERV
Address: `larch-l@suvm.bitnet`
For anyone involved in landscape
architecture.

Audio

Name: rec.audio.pro
Resource: USENET
Professional audio recording and
studio engineering.

Clocks

Name: clocks
Resource: LISTSERV
Address: `clocks@suvm.bitnet`
Devoted to all aspects of clock/watch
repair, collecting, and construction.

Computers

Name: CJI
Resource: LISTSERV
Address:
`listserv@jerusalem1.datasrv.co.il`
(Jacob Richman)

Computer Jobs in Israel (CJI) is a one-
way list that will automatically send
you the monthly updated computer
jobs document.

Consultant

Name: cons-l
Resource: LISTSERV
Address: `cons-l@mcgill1.bitnet`
This is the consultant's discussion list.

Contract Labor

Name: misc.jobs.contract
Resource: USENET
Discussions about contract labor.

Dentistry

Name: dblist
Resource: LISTSERV
Address: `dblist@umab.umd.edu`
Discusses databases for dentistry.

DJs

Name: BPM
Resource: List
Address: `bpm-request@andrew.cmu.edu`
(Simon Gatrall)
This is a list for professional DJ's.

Emergency Services

Name: emerg-l
Resource: LISTSERV
Address: `emerg-l@marist.bitnet`
For the discussion and exchange of
information for those involved in
emergency services.

Exhibitionists/Projectionists

Name: exhibitionists
Resource: List
Address: `exhibitionists@jvnc.net`
For anyone in the cinema who shows movies.

Federal Government

Name: fedjobs
Resource: LISTSERV
Address:
`fedjobs@dartcms1.dartmouth.edu`
Postings of the Federal Job Openings list are distributed through this list.

Filmmakers

Name: Filmmakers
Resource: List
Address:
`Filmmakers@Grissom.Larc.nasa.gov`
For anyone interested in the film industry.

Flexible Work

Name: flexwork
Resource: LISTSERV
Address: `flexwork@psuhmc.bitnet`
A discussion list for all aspects of a flexible working environment, including telecommuting, flex-time, and other nontraditional work scenarios.

Forestry

Name: Park Rangers
Resource: List
Address: `60157903@wsuvm1.csc.wsu.edu`
(Cynthia Dorminey)
For anyone working or interested in working as a ranger (general, interpretive, etc.) for the National Park Service (U.S.A.), but rangers from state and county agencies as well as other countries are also welcome.

Human Resources

Name: hrd-l
Resource: LISTSERV
Address: `hrd-l@mizzou1.bitnet`
This is the human resource development group list.

Name: perdir-l
Resource: LISTSERV
Address: `perdir-l@ubvm.cc.buffalo.edu`
This is for everyone involved in human resources.

Indexers

Name: INDEX-L
Resource: List
Address: `skuster@bingvmb.bitnet`
(Charlotte Skuster)
Discussion of good indexing practice.

Insurance

Name: risk
Resource: LISTSERV
Address: `risk@utxvm.bitnet`
Discusses risk and insurance issues.

Janitorial

Name: janitors
Resource: LISTSERV
Address: `janitors@ukanvm.cc.ukans.edu`
For all college and university housekeeping personnel.

Jobs Available

Name: misc.jobs.offered
Resource: USENET
Announcements of positions available.

Name: misc.jobs.offered.entry
Resource: USENET
Job listings only for entry-level positions.

Journalism

Name: alt.journalism
Resource: USENET
Shop talk by journalists and journalism students.

Name: copyediting-l
Resource: LISTSERV
Address: copyediting-l@cornell.edu
For anyone involved in the copyediting process.

Librarians

Name: GAY-LIBN
Resource: LISTSERV
Address: LISTSERV@VM.USC.EDU
Gay/Lesbian/Bisexual Librarians Network.

Locksmithing

Name: alt.locksmithing
Resource: USENET
You locked your keys in *where*?

Medical

Name: medphys
Resource: List
Address:
medphys-request@radonc.duke.edu
Electronic communication among medical physicists.

Miscellaneous

Name: misc.jobs.misc
Resource: USENET
Discussion about employment, workplaces, careers.

Physical Plants

Name: erappa-l
Resource: LISTSERV
Address: erappa-l@psuvm.psu.edu
A list for the Association of Physical Plant Administrators.

Play-by-Play

Name: pbp-l
Resource: LISTSERV
Address: pbp-l@etsuadmn.etsu.edu
For all persons interested in play-by-play sportscasting.

Projectionists

Name: exhibitionists
Resource: List
Address:
exhibitionists-request@jvnc.net
Primarily for managers and projectionists.

Real Estate

Name: re-forum
Resource: LISTSERV
Address: `re-forum@utarlvm1.bitnet`
This is the real estate forum.

Resumes

Name: misc.jobs.resumes
Resource: USENET
Postings of resumes and "situation wanted" articles.

Veterinary

Name: vetinfo
Resource: LISTSERV
Address: `vetinfo@ucdcvdls.bitnet`
This list enables those in the veterinary profession to exchange information, ideas, and research information.

Name: vetmed-l
Resource: LISTSERV
Address: `vetmed-l@uga.cc.uga.edu`
Discussion and exchange of information and research for persons involved in veterinary medicine.

Writing

Name: writers
Resource: LISTSERV
Address: `writers@ndsuvm1.ndsu.edu`
Exchanging information by current and would-be professional writers.

Psychology

Aging/Geriatrics

Name: humage-l
Resource: LISTSERV
Address: `humage-l@asuacad.bitnet`
Discusses the humanistic effects of aging.

Children

Name: behavior
Resource: LISTSERV
Address: `behavior@asuacad.bitnet`
Discusses behavioral and emotional disorders in children.

Consciousness

Name: bridge-l
Resource: LISTSERV
Address: `bridge-l@ucsbvm.bitnet`
Devoted to the bridge across consciousness.

Creativity

Name: crea-cps
Resource: LISTSERV
Address: `crea-cps@hearn.bitnet`
Discussion of creativity and creative problem solving.

Drug Abuse

Name: drugabus
Resource: LISTSERV
Address: `drugabus@umab.umd.edu`
Community drug abuse education and related issues.

Family Relations

Name: famcomm
Resource: LISTSERV
Address: `famcomm@rpitsvm.bitnet`
For the discussion of marital/family and relational communication.

Industrial

Name: ioobf-l
Resource: LISTSERV
Address: `ioobf-l@uga.cc.uga.edu`
This is the industrial psychology forum.

Mind Altering Techniques

Name: Mind-L
Resource: List
Address:
`mind-l-request@asylum.sf.ca.us`
(John Romkey)
A discussion group for people interested in mind altering techniques in general, and mind machines (light & sound, TENS/CES, electromagnetic pulse, floatation) & biofeedback equipment in particular.

Support Groups

Name: 12Step
Resource: List
Address: `12Step@trwrb.dsd.trw.com`
Discusses and shares information and experiences related to 12-step programs, such as Alcoholics Anonymous and Alanon.

Thinking

Name: fnord-l
Resource: LISTSERV
Address: `fnord-l@ubvm.cc.buffalo.edu`
Discusses new ways of thinking.

Violence

Name: violen-l
Resource: LISTSERV
Address: `violen-l@bruspvm.bitnet`
Discusses all forms of violence.

Publishing

CD-ROM

Name: CDPub
Resource: List
Address: `CDPub-Info@knex.via.mind.org`
An electronic mailing list for folks engaged or interested in CR-ROM publishing in general and desktop CD-ROM recorders and publishing systems in particular.

Reference

Acronyms

Resource: telnet
Address: `info.mcc.ac.uk`

Dictionary

Resource: telnet
Address: `cs.indiana.edu 2627`

Resource: telnet
Address: `chem.ucsd.edu`
User id: `webster`

Law Libraries

Resource: telnet
Address: `liberty.uc.wlu.edu`
User id: `lawlib`

Resource: telnet
Address: `pegasus.law.columbia.edu`
User id: `pegasus`

Library

Resource: telnet
Address: `library.dartmouth.edu`
User id: `dante`

Reference

Resource: telnet
Address: `CHEM.UCSD.EDU`
User id: `webster`

Religion

Anglican

Name: anglican
Resource: LISTSERV
Address: `anglican@auvm.bitnet`
Episcopal mailing list.

Atheism

Name: alt.atheism
Resource: USENET
Godless heathens.

Name: alt.atheism.moderated
Resource: USENET
Focused godless heathens. (Moderated)

Baha'i

Name: Bahai-faith
Resource: List
Address: `Bahai-faith@oneworld.wa.com`
A peaceful, open forum for discussing the Baha'i faith.

Name: soc.religion.bahai
Resource: USENET
Discussion of the Baha'i Faith. (Moderated)

Baptist

Name: baptist
Resource: LISTSERV
Address: `baptist@ukcc.uky.edu`
Open discussion list for all things Baptist.

Buddhism

Name: buddha-l
Resource: LISTSERV
Address:
`buddha-l@ulkyvm.louisville.edu`
The Buddhist academic discussion forum.

Name: hindu-d
Resource: LISTSERV
Address: `hindu-d@arizvm1.bitnet`
The Hindu digest.

Catholicism

Name: amercath
Resource: LISTSERV
Address: `amercath@ukcc.uky.edu`
Devoted to the exchange of information about Catholicism in America.

Name: Catholic
Resource: LISTSERV
Address: `LISTSERV@american.edu` or `cms@dragon.com` (Cindy Smith)
A forum to discuss discipleship to Jesus Christ in terms of the Catholic approach to Christianity.

Name: catholic
Resource: LISTSERV
Address: `catholic@auvm`
This is an open list for all Catholics.

Name: Catholic Doctrine
Resource: List
Address:
`catholic-request@sarto.gaithersburg.md.us`
Discussions of orthodox Catholic theology by everyone under the jurisdiction of the Holy Father, John Paul II. Moderated.

Name: catholic-action
Resource: List
Address: `catholic-action@rfreeman@vpnet.chi.il.us`
A moderated list for the discussion of the Catholic religion.

Name: Catholic-action
Resource: List
Address: `rfreeman@vpnet.chi.il.us` (Richard Freeman)
A moderated list concerned with Catholic evangelism.

Cell Churches

Name: Cell Church Discussion Group
Resource: List

Address:
`cell-church-request@bible.acu.edu`
`reid@cei.com` (Jon Reid)
A list for Christians who are in cell churches or interested in learning more about cell churches.

Chrisitianity

Name: Vision
Resource: List
Address: `pruss@math.ubc.ca`
To discuss in a charitable and Christian context visions, prophecies, and spiritual gifts.

Christianity

Name: christia
Resource: LISTSERV
Address: `christia@asuacad.bitnet`
A list for discussing practical Christian life.

Name: christian
Resource: List
Address:
`ames!elroy!grian!mailjc-request`
`mailjc-request@grian.cps.altadena.ca.us`
A nonhostile environment for discussion among christians.

Name: conchr-l
Resource: LISTSERV
Address: `conchr-l@templevm.bitnet`
A conservative Christian discussion list.

Name: elenchus
Resource: LISTSERV
Address: `elenchus@acadvm1.uottawa.ca`
Dedicated to the events and literature of early Christianity.

Name: globlx-l
Resource: LISTSERV
Address: globlx-l@qucdn.bitnet
A list for the discussion of global Christianity.

Name: histec-l
Resource: LISTSERV
Address: histec-l@ukanvm.cc.ukans.edu
This list discusses the history of evangelical Christianity.

Name: mailjc
Resource: List
Address:
mailjc@grian.cps.altadena.ca.us
Open discussion of Christianity.

Computers

Name: GodlyGraphics
Resource: List
Address:
GodlyGraphics-request@acs.harding.edu
(Ron Pacheco)
A mailing list for the discussion of Christian uses of computer graphics and animations, especially using the Amiga computer.

Creationism vs. Evolution

Name: talk.origins
Resource: USENET
Evolution versus creationism (sometimes hot!).

Epsicopalian

Name: Episcopal (Anglican)
Resource: List
Address: LISTSERV@american.edu
cms@dragon.com (Cindy Smith)

This mailing list provides a nonhostile environment for discussion among Christians who are members of the Holy Catholic Church in the Anglican Communion or who are simply interested in Episcopal beliefs and practices.

Feminism

Name: femrel-l
Resource: LISTSERV
Address: femrel-l@mizzou1.bitnet
An open discussion of women, religion, and feminism.

General

Name: contents
Resource: LISTSERV
Address: contents@uottawa.bitnet
The religious studies publications journal.

General Beliefs

Name: belief-l
Resource: LISTSERV
Address: belief-l@Brownvm.Brown.Edu
The personal ideologies discussion list.

Hindu

Name: Hindu Digest
Resource: LISTSERV
Address:
listserv@arizvm1.ccit.arizona.edu
Hindu Digest is a forum to discuss various Hindu doctrines as they are applicable to day to day living.

Islam

Name: soc.religion.islam
Resource: USENET
Discussions of the Islamic faith.
(Moderated)

Judaism

Name: jewish
Resource: LISTSERV
Address:
(machine) `listserv@israel.nysernet.org`
(human) `mljewish@israel.nysernet.org`
(Avi Feldblum)
The mailing list provides a nonabusive forum for discussion of Jewish topics, with an emphasis on Jewish law, within the framework of the validity of the Halakhic system.

Name: Jewishnt
Resource: LISTSERV
Address: `Listserv@bguvm.bgu.ac.il`
(Dov Winer)
A discussion forum on all things concerning the establishment of the Global Jewish Information Network.

Name: liberal-judaism
Resource: List
Address: `faigin@aerospace.aero.org`
(Daniel Faigin)
Nonjudgemental discussions of liberal Judaism.

Mormon

Name: LDS-Net
Resource: List
Address:
`lds-net-request@andrew.cmu.edu`
A forum for members of The Church of Jesus Christ of Latter-Day Saints (Mormons).

Name: Saints-Best
Resource: List
Address:
`lds-net-request@andrew.cmu.edu`
A low-volume, heavily filtered magazine featuring a few of the best messages of interest to Latter-day Saints (Mormons) from all over the Internet.

Muslim

Name: MSA-Net
Resource: List
Address:
`msa-request@htm3.ee.queensu.ca`
(Aalim Fevens)
A mailing list to meet the communication needs of Muslim Student Associations in North America.

Old Testament

Name: ot-hebrew
Resource: List
Address: `ot-hebrew@virginia.edu`
For those interested in studying Old Testament Hebrew.

Orthodox

Name: orthodox
Resource: LISTSERV
Address: `orthodox@iubvm.bitnet`
A moderated list for discussing the Orthodox Christian Church.

Pagan

Name: alt.pagan
Resource: USENET
Discussions about paganism & religion.

Name: pagan
Resource: List
Address:
pagan-request@drycas.club.cc.cmu.edu
(Stacey Greenstein)
To discuss the religions, philosophy, and so forth of paganism.

Paganism

Name: pagan
Resource: List
Address: pagan@drycas.club.cc.cmu.edu
For those interested in pursuing paganism.

Quaker

Name: quaker-l
Resource: LISTSERV
Address: quaker-l@vmd.cso.uiuc.edu
This list is devoted to Quaker concerns.

Name: soc.religion.quaker
Resource: USENET
The Religious Society of Friends.

Scientific Study

Name: ssrel-l
Resource: LISTSERV
Address: ssrel-l@utkvm1.bitnet
This forum is for the scientific study of religion.

Scientology

Name: alt.religion.scientology
Resource: USENET

SDA

Name: SDAnet
Resource: List
Address: st0o+SDA@andrew.cmu.edu
(Steve Timm)
A list for and about Seventh-Day Adventists.

Shaker

Name: shaker
Resource: LISTSERV
Address: shaker@ukcc.uky.edu
This is the Shaker forum.

Shaman

Name: soc.religion.shamanism
Resource: USENET
Discussion of the full range of shamanic experience. (Moderated)

Unitarian

Name: UUs-L
Resource: LISTSERV
Address: uus-l@info.terraluna.org
(Automated Info Server) or
uus-lman@terraluna.org (Steve Traugott)
A global meeting place for Unitarian Universalists and anyone going our way.

Unitarians

Name: uus-l
Resource: LISTSERV
Address: uus-l@ubvm.cc.buffalo.edu
A list for Unitarian Universalists.

Science

Aeronautics

Name: aeronautics
Resource: List
Address:
aeronautics-request@rascal.ics.utexas.edu
A news-to-mail feed of the
sci.aeronautics newsgroup.

Agriculture

Name: Agmodels-l
Resource: LISTSERV
Address: jp@unl.edu (Jerome Pier)
Discussion of agricultural simulation
models of all types.

Name: beef-l
Resource: LISTSERV
Address: beef-l@wsuvm1.bitnet
For those considered to be beef
specialists, this list provides a com-
mon arena for information exchange.

Name: dairy-l
Resource: LISTSERV
Address: dairy-l@umdd.bitnet
For those involved in the dairy
industry.

Name: newcrops
Resource: LISTSERV
Address: newcrops@purccvm.cc.vm.edu
A discussion list for new crops.

Animal Behavior

Name: ethology
Resource: List
Address: saarikko@cc.helsinki.fi
(Jarmo Saarikko)
An unmoderated mailing list for the
discussion of animal behavior and
behavioral ecology.

Anthropology

Name: anthro-l
Resource: LISTSERV
Address: anthro-l@ubvm.cc.buffalo.edu
Devoted to all aspects of anthropol-
ogy research and information
exchange.

Name: sci.anthropology
Resource: USENET
All aspects of studying humankind.

Aquaculture

Name: aqua-l
Resource: LISTSERV
Address: aqua-l@vm.uoguelph.ca
This is the aquaculture discussion list.

Archaeology

Name: arch-l
Resource: LISTSERV
Address: arch-l@tamvm1.tamu.edu
This is the all-purpose archaeology
list.

Astrology

Name: alt.astrology
Resource: USENET
Twinkle, twinkle, little planet.

Astronomy

Name: alt.sci.planetary
Resource: USENET
Studies in planetary science.

Name: Earth and Sky
Resource: List
Address: Majordomo@lists.utexas.edu
This is a weekly online publication to learn more about Earth science and astronomy.

Name: sci.astro
Resource: USENET
Astronomy discussions and information.

Name: sci.astro.planetarium
Resource: USENET
Discussion of planetariums.

Aviation

Name: aviation
Resource: List
Address: aviation@mc.lcs.mit.edu
Devoted to subject matter of interest to pilots.

Name: aviation-theory
Resource: List
Address:
aviation-theory@mc.lcs.mit.edu
Devoted to the discussion of all matters related to aerospace engineering.

Bees (Apiary)

Name: bee-l
Resource: LISTSERV
Address: bee-l@albnyvm1.bitnet
A general discussion of bee biology and beekeeping.

Biology

Name: aquarium
Resource: LISTSERV

Address: aquarium@emuvm1.bitnet
For everyone who has or studies aquariums and fish.

Name: bionet.announce
Resource: USENET
Announcements of widespread interest to biologists. (Moderated)

Name: bionet.info-theory
Resource: USENET
Discussions about biological information theory.

Name: bionet.software.acedb
Resource: USENET
Discussions by users of genome DBs using ACEDB.

Name: brine-l
Resource: LISTSERV
Address: brine-l@uga.cc.uga.edu
A discussion list devoted to the topic of brine shrimp.

Name: camel-l
Resource: LISTSERV
Address: camel-l@sakfu00.bitnet
This is an open forum for all camel researchers.

Name: cturtle
Resource: LISTSERV
Address: cturtle@nervm.bitnet
For everyone who has an interest in sea turtle biology and conservation.

Name: deepsea
Resource: LISTSERV
Address: deepsea@uvvm.uvic.ca
Devoted to a discussion of all aspects of deep-sea diving and underwater science.

Name: sci.aquaria
Resource: USENET
Only scientifically-oriented postings about aquaria.

Name: sci.bio
Resource: USENET
Biology and related sciences.

Name: Wildnet
Resource: List
Address:
`zaphod!pnwc!wildnet-request@tribune.usask.ca`
`wildnet-request@tribune.usask.ca`
(Eric Woodsworth)
Computing and statistics in fisheries and wildlife biology.

Biomechanics

Name: Biomch-L
Resource: LISTSERV
Address: `listserv@nic.surfnet.nl`
(Ton van den Bogert)
Intended for members of the International, European, American, Canadian and other Societies of Biomechanics, ISEK (International Society of Electrophysiological Kinesiology), and for all others with an interest in the general field of biomechanics and human or animal movement.

Botany

Name: CP
Resource: LISTSERV
Address: `listserv@hpl-opus.hpl.hp.com`
(Rick Walker)
Topics of interest to the group include Cultivation and Propagation of CPs (Carniverous Plants).

Name: NPLC
Resource: List
Address: `tout@genesys.cps.msu.edu`
(Walid Tout)
This network is for rapid communica-

tion among researchers in the field of plant lipids.

Chemical Engineering

Name: chem-eng
Resource: List
Address: `trayms@cc.curtin.edu.au`
(Dr. Martyn Ray)
An electronic newsletter on chemical engineering.

Name: cheme-l
Resource: LISTSERV
Address: `cheme-l@psuvm.psu.edu`
A list for discussing chemical engineering.

Chemistry

Name: chem-talk
Resource: List
Address:
`...!{ames,cbosgd}!pacbell!unicom!manus`
(Dr. Manus Monroe)
Dialogue and conversation with other chemists.

Cryonics

Name: cryonics
Resource: List
Address: `cryonics`
`@kqb@whscad1.att.com`
Dedicated to the discussion and dissemination of information about cryonics.

Name: cryonics
Resource: List
Address: `...att!whscad1!kqb`
`kqb@whscad1.att.com` (Kevin Q. Brown)
This list is a forum for topics related to cryonics.

Name: sci.cryonics
Resource: USENET
Theory and practice of biostasis, suspended animation.

Dentistry

Name: amalgam
Resource: LISTSERV
Address:
amalgam@ibmvm.rus.uni-stuttgart.de
A list devoted to the exchange of information about amalgam fillings and the potential health hazards of mercury poisoning for those with silver fillings.

Dinosaurs

Name: dinosaur
Resource: List
Address: dinosaur@wichitaks.ncr.com
An open list for the discussion of dinosaurs.

Earthquakes

Name:
Resource: telnet
Address: geophys.washington.edu
User id: quake

Ecology

Name: biosph-l
Resource: LISTSERV
Address: biosph-l@ubvm.cc.buffalo.edu
This is the biosphere and ecology discussion list.

Name: sci.environment
Resource: USENET
Discussions about the environment and ecology.

Economics

Name: sci.econ
Resource: USENET
The science of economics.

Name: sci.econ.research
Resource: USENET
Research in all fields of economics. (Moderated)

Electromagnetics

Name: electromagnetics
Resource: List
Address:
EM-request@decwd.ece.uiuc.edu
Discussion of issues relating to electromagnetics.

Name: emflds-l
Resource: LISTSERV
Address: emflds-l@ubvm.cc.buffalo.edu
A list devoted to electromagnetics in medicine, science, and communications.

Electronics

Name: sci.electronics
Resource: USENET
Circuits, theory, electrons, and discussions.

Engineering

Name: racefab
Resource: List
Address:
racefab-request@pms706.pms.ford.com

To discuss racing fabrication and engineering.

Environment

Name: envbeh-l
Resource: LISTSERV
Address: `envbeh-l@polyvm.bitnet`
A forum on environment and human behavior.

Name: envst-l
Resource: LISTSERV
Address: `envst-l@brownvm.brown.edu`
The environmental studies discussion list.

Extropians

Name: Extropians
Resource: List
Address:
`extropians-request@extropy.org`
Devoted to the discussion and development of Extropian ideas.

Fraud

Name: scifraud
Resource: LISTSERV
Address: `scifraud@albnyvm1.bitnet`
This list provides an open forum for the discussion of fraud in science.

Fuller, Buckminster

Name: geodesic
Resource: LISTSERV
Address: `geodesic@ubvm.cc.buffalo.edu`
A list for the discussion of the life and science of Buckminster Fuller.

Fusion

Name: fusion
Resource: LISTSERV
Address: `fusion@vm1.nodak.edu`
Current status of and information related to the energy of the future: fusion.

Name: fusion
Resource: List
Address:
`fusion-request@zorch.sf-bay.org`
E-mail redistribution of USENET sci.physics.fusion newsgroup, for sites/users that don't have access to USENET.

Future

Name: info-futures
Resource: List
Address: `info-futures@world.std.com`
A list for persons who like to speculate about the future and what it might be like.

General

Name: sci.misc
Resource: USENET
Short-lived discussions on subjects in the sciences.

Geology

Name: geology
Resource: LISTSERV
Address: `geology@ptearn.bitnet`
Geology discussion list.

Name: sci.geo.geology
Resource: USENET
Discussion of solid earth sciences.

GPS

Name: GPS Digest
Resource: List
Address: `gps-request@esseye.si.com.`
A forum for the discussion topics related to the USAF Global Positioning System (GPS) and other satellite navigation positioning systems.

Marine Studies

Name: marine-l
Resource: LISTSERV
Address: `marine-l@uoguelph.bitnet`
Marine studies/shipboard education discussion.

Mathematics

Name: NA-net
Resource: List
Address: `na.join@na-net.ornl.gov`
Numerical analysis discussions.

Name: nmbrthry
Resource: LISTSERV
Address: `nmbrthry@ndsuvm1.ndsu.edu`
This list is devoted to number theory and related mathematics.

Name: sci.math
Resource: USENET
Mathematical discussions and pursuits.

Name: sci.math.num-analysis
Resource: USENET
Numerical analysis.

Name: sci.math.research
Resource: USENET
Discussion of current mathematical research. (Moderated)

Name: sci.op-research
Resource: USENET
Research, teaching, and application of operations research.

Mechanical Engineering

Name: mech-l
Resource: LISTSERV
Address: `mech-l@utarlvm1.bitnet`
This is the mechanical engineering discussion list.

Medieval

Name: medsci-l
Resource: LISTSERV
Address: `medsci-l@brownvm.brown.edu`
This is the medieval science discussion list.

Meteorology

Name: Meteorology Students
Resource: List
Address:
`dennis@metw3.met.fu-berlin.de`
A new mailing list for meteorology students.

Name: sci.geo.meteorology
Resource: USENET
Discussion of meteorology and related topics.

Name: weather-users
Resource: List
Address:
`weather-users-request@zorch.sf-bay.org`
Updates from the maintainer of the Weather Underground at University of Michigan.

Name: wxsat
Resource: List
Address: `wxsat-request@ssg.com`
(Richard B. Emerson)
The primary function is the distribution of NOAA status and prediction bulletins for the GOES and polar weather satellites.

Military Technology

Name: military
Resource: List
Address: `military@att.att.com`
A gateway to the USENET group sci.military for those who do not have USENET access.

Museums

Name: museum-l
Resource: LISTSERV
Address: `museum-l@unmvma.bitnet`
The museum discussion list.

New Theories

Name: alt.sci.physics.new-theories
Resource: USENET
Scientific theories you won't find in journals.

Optics

Name: optics-l
Resource: LISTSERV
Address: `optics-l@taunivm.tau.ac.il`
This is the optics newsletter.

Paleontology

Name: dinosaur
Resource: List
Address:
`dinosaur-request@donald.WichitaKS.NCR.COM`
(John Matrow)
Discussion of dinosaurs and other archosaurs.

Parapsychology

Name: psi-l
Resource: LISTSERV
Address: `psi-l@rpitsvm.bitnet`
For those interested in pursuing ESP and related phenomena.

Photosynthesis

Name: photosyn
Resource: LISTSERV
Address: `photosyn@taunivm.tau.ac.il`
Photosynthesis research list.

Physics

Name: physics
Resource: List
Address:
`physics-request@qedqcd.rye.ny.us`
(Mike Miskulin)
Current developments in theoretical and experimental physics.

Name: sci.physics
Resource: USENET
Physical laws, properties, and so forth.

Research

Name: sci.comp-aided
Resource: USENET
The use of computers as tools in scientific research.

Name: Testing-Research
Resource: List
Address:
Testing-Research-Request@cs.uiuc.edu
(Brian Marick)
A forum for testing researchers to discuss current and future research.

Research Methodologies

Name: methods
Resource: LISTSERV
Address: methods@rpitsvm.bitnet
This list discusses research methodology.

Seismology

Name: quake-l
Resource: LISTSERV
Address: quake-l@vm1.nodak.edu
Earthquake discussion list.

Name: seismd-l
Resource: LISTSERV
Address: seismd-l@bingvmb.bitnet
This is for seismological discussion.

Skepticism

Name: sci.skeptic
Resource: USENET
Skeptics discussing pseudo-science.

Soil

Name: Soils-l
Resource: LISTSERV
Address: jp@unl.edu (Jerome Pier)
A discussion of all subjects dealing with soil science.

Space

Name: sci.space
Resource: USENET
Space, space programs, space-related research, and the like.

Name: sci.space.science
Resource: USENET
Space and planetary science and related technical work. (Moderated)

Name: sci.space.shuttle
Resource: USENET
The space shuttle and the STS program.

Name: sci.space.tech
Resource: USENET
Technical and general issues related to space flight. (Moderated)

Space Studies

Name: ssi_mail
Resource: List
Address: listprocessor@link.com
A moderated list for space development topics related to Space-Studies Institute programs past, present and future.

Superconductivity

Name: sup-cond
Resource: LISTSERV

Address: `sup-cond@taunivm.tau.ac.il`
This is the superconductivity list.

Volcanoes

Name: volcano
Resource: LISTSERV
Address: `volcano@asuacad.bitnet`
For everyone interested in volcanoes.

Water

Name: aquifer
Resource: LISTSERV
Address: `aquifer@ibacsata.bitnet`
This list discusses pollution and
groundwater recharge.

Weather

Resource: telnet
Address: `downwind.sprl.umich.edu`
University of Michigan Weather
Underground

Name: met-stud
Resource: List
Address:
`met-stud@metw3.met.fu-berlin.de`
An open list for meteorology students
to meet and exchange information.

Name: wx-lsr
Resource: LISTSERV
Address: `wx-lsr@vmd.cso.uiuc.edu`
Local storm reports and related
weather information.

Name: wx-misc
Resource: LISTSERV

Address: `wx-misc@vmd.cso.uiuc.edu`
This is a miscellaneous weather
discussion list.

Name: wx-natnl
Resource: LISTSERV
Address: `wx-natnl@vmd.cso.uiuc.edu`
A list for distribution of weather
summaries for the nation and selected
cities.

Name: wx-swo
Resource: LISTSERV
Address: `wx-swo@vmd.cso.uiuc.edu`
This list distributes severe weather
outlook information.

Name: wx-talk
Resource: LISTSERV
Address: `wx-talk@vmd.cso.uiuc.edu`
This is a general weather discussion
and talk list.

Name: wx-tropl
Resource: LISTSERV
Address: `wx-tropl@vmd.cso.uiuc.edu`
This list distributes tropical storm and
hurricane information.

Name: wx-watch
Resource: LISTSERV
Address: `wx-watch@vmd.cso.uiuc.edu`
For the distribution of weather
watches and cancellations.

Name: wx-wstat
Resource: LISTSERV
Address: `wx-wstat@vmd.cso.uiuc.edu`
Weather watch status and storm
reports.

Zoology

Name: killifish
Resource: List

Address:

killie-request@mejac.palo-alto.ca.us
For people interested in killifish, (family cyprinodontidae).

Social Issues

Abuse

Name: alt.sexual.abuse.recovery
Resource: USENET
Helping others deal with traumatic experiences.

Name: recovery
Resource: List
Address: recovery@wvnvm.wvnet.edu
(Jeff Brooks)
A forum and support group for survivors of childhood sexual abuse/ incest and their SOs.

Activism

Name: activ-l
Resource: LISTSERV
Address: activ-l@mizzou1.bitnet
This is a general forum for activists to meet and exchange ideas and opinions.

Name: ACTIV-L
Resource: LISTSERV
Address:
listserv@mizzou1.missouri.edu.
Peace, empowerment, justice, and environmental issues.

Name: alt.activism
Resource: USENET
Activities for activists.

Name: HANDS

Resource: List
Address: HANDS@u.washington.edu
A list compiled by Hands Off Washington-University of Washington chapter.

Adoption

Name: adoptees
Resource: LISTSERV
Address: listserv@ucsd.edu
Discussion among adult adoptees of any topic related to adoption.

Name: adoption
Resource: List
Address: adoption-request@think.com
The list's charter is to discuss anything and everything connected with adoption.

Name: Birthmother
Resource: List
Address: nadir@acca.nmsu.edu
For any birthmother who has relinquished a child for adoption.

AIDS

Name: act-up
Resource: List
Address: act-up@world.std.com
Discussion and information exchange related to the ACTUP organization (AIDS Coalition To Unleash Power).

Alternative Publications

Name: Prog-Pubs
Resource: List
Address:
prog-pubs-request@fuggles.acc.virginia.edu
A mailing list for people interested in progressive and alternative publications and other media.

Animal Rights

Name: AR-News
Resource: List
Address: `AR-News-Request@cygnus.com`
(Ian Lance Taylor) (Chip Roberson)
A public news wire for items relating
to Animal Rights and Welfare.

Name: AR-Talk
Resource: List
Address: `AR-Talk-Request@cygnus.com`
(Chip Roberson) (Ian Lance Taylor)
An unmoderated list for the discussion of Animal Rights.

Censorship

Name: alt.censorship
Resource: USENET
Discussion about restricting speech/
press.

CoHousing

Name: COHOUSING-L
Resource: LISTSERV
Address: `listserv@uci.com`
Discussion of cohousing.

College

Name: actnow-l
Resource: LISTSERV
Address: `actnow-l@brownvm.brown.edu`
This is for anyone interested in
college activism.

Drugs

Name: talk.politics.drugs
Resource: USENET
The politics of drug issues.

Feminism

Name: soc.feminism
Resource: USENET
Discussion of feminism and feminist
issues. (Moderated)

Gay/Lesbian/Bisexual Issues

Name: ACTION-ALERT
Resource: List
Address:
`ACTION-ALERT-request@vector.intercon.com`
(Ron Buckmire) (David Casti)
A mailing list designed to provide the
LGB community a resource by which
we can respond to attacks on our
community that are occurring anywhere.

Name: amend2-discuss
Resource: List
Address: `Majordomo@cs.colorado.edu`
For people who are discussing the
implications and issues surrounding
the passing of amendment 2.

Name: amend2-info
Resource: List
Address:
Majordomo@cs.colorado.edu
For people interested in information
on the implication and issues of
amendment 2.

Name: dont-tell
Resource: List
Address:
`dont-tell-request@choice.princeton.edu`
An e-mail distribution list for people
concerned about the effects that the
new military policy known as "don't
ask/don't tell" will have at academic
institutions.

Name: eagles
Resource: List
Address: `eagles-request@flash.usc.edu`
A forum for Scouts, Scouters, and former Scouts who are gay/lesbian/bisexual to discuss how they can apply pressure to the BSA to change their homophobic policies.

Name: fl-motss
Resource: List
Address: `FL-MOTSS-REQUEST@pts.mot.com`
Discussion of LGB issues in Florida.

Name: GayNet
Resource: List
Address: `GAYNET-REQUEST@queernet.org`
(Roger B.A. Klorese)
This is a list about gay, lesbian, and bisexual concerns.

Name: LA-motss
Resource: List
Address:
`la-motss-request@flash.usc.edu`
Online social and political forum for gay, lesbian, and bisexual issues in the Los Angeles and Southern California area.

Name: LA-motss-announce
Resource: List
Address:
`la-motss-request@flash.usc.edu`
Online social and political forum for gay, lesbian, and bisexual issues in the Los Angeles and Southern California area.

Name: LAMBDA
Resource: LISTSERV
Address: `LISTSERV@UKCC.UKY.EDU`
(Jeff Jones)

This list is open to the discussion of all topics relating to gays/lesbians/bisexuals and their issues with specific focus on issues at the University of Kentucky, Lexington, and Kentucky communities.

Name: LIBFEM
Resource: List
Address: `libfem-request@math.uio.no`
(Thomas Gramstad)
The focus classical liberty and individual rights perspective as applied to feminist issues.

Name: LIS (Lesbians in Science)
Resource: List
Address: `ZITA@AC.GRIN.EDU`
The list serves as a forum for discussions, resource for professional and personal information-sharing, and social network and support group. Womyn only.

Name: moms
Resource: List
Address:
`moms-request@qiclab.scn.rain.com`
Moms is a list for lesbian mothers (women only).

Name: ne-social-motss
Resource: List
Address:
`ne-social-motss-request@plts.org`
Announcements of events and other happenings in the North East (of the continental United States) of interest to lesbians, gay men, and bisexuals.

Name: NJ-motss
Resource: List
Address: `MAJORDOMO@plts.org`
Mailing list for gay, lesbian, and bisexual issues in New Jersey.

Name: noglstp
Resource: List
Address:
noglstp-request@elroy.jpl.nasa.gov
Sponsored by the National Organization of Gay and Lesbian Scientists and Technical Professionals, Inc.

Name: oh-motss
Resource: List
Address: Address:
oh-motss-request@cps.udayton.edu
Ohio Members Of The Same Sex mailing list is for open discussion of lesbian, gay, and bisexual issues in and affecting Ohio.

Name: OUTIL (Out in Linguistics)
Resource: List
Address:
outil-request@csli.stanford.edu
(Arnold Zwicky)
The list is open to lesbian, gay, bisexual, dyke, queer, homosexual linguists and their friends.

Name: pdx-motss
Resource: List
Address:
PDX-MOTSS-REQUEST@agora.rain.com
Discussion of LGB issues in the Portland, Oregon metro area.

Name: qn
Resource: List
Address: qn-request@queernet.org
(Roger Klorese)
A mailing list for Queer Nation activists and for all interested in Queer Nation.

Name: REGAYN
Resource: List
Address:
regayn-request@csd4.csd.uwm.edu
uunet!csd4.csd.uwm.edu!regayn-request

A mail group for discussions, opinions, meetings, personal experience sharing of addictions and recovery issues for gay, lesbian, bi-sexual and transsexual people.

Name: sappho
Resource: List
Address:
sappho-request@mc.lcs.mit.edu
(Regis M. Donovan)
A forum and support group for gay and bisexual women.

Name: stonewall25
Resource: List
Address:
stonewall25-request@queernet.org
<wellconnectedsite>!unpc!stonewall25-request
A mailing list for discussion and planning of the "Stonewall 25" international gay/lesbian/bi rights march in New York City on Sunday, June 26, 1994.

Name: uk-motss
Resource: List
Address: uk-motss-request@pyra.co.uk
(Internet)
uk-motss-request@uk.co.pyra (JANet)
uk-motss-request%pyrltd.uknet
(Brain dead JANet mailers)
Mailing list for gay people in the UK or those interested in the UK gay scene/politics.

Gender

Name: gender
Resource: List
Address: ericg@indiana.edu
(Eric Garrison)
A list for discussing gender issues.

General

Name: oregon-news
Resource: List
Address:
oregon-news-request@vector.intercon.com
Mailing list of people organizing
against the Oregon Citizens' Alliance.

Gun Control

Name: ba-firearms
Resource: List
Address:
ba-firearms-request@shell.portal.com
(Jeff Chan)
Announcement and discussion of
firearms legislation and related issues.
The ba- list is for the San Francisco
Bay Area and gets all messages sent
to the ca- list.

Name: ca-firearms
Resource: List
Address:
ca-firearms-request@shell.portal.com
(Jeff Chan)
Announcement and discussion of
firearms legislation and related issues.
The ca- list is for California statewide
issues.

Name: talk.politics.guns
Resource: USENET
The politics of firearm ownership and
(mis)use.

Name: tx-firearms
Resource: List
Address:
tx-firearms-request@frontier.lonestar.org
Mailing list to keep interested parties
aware of basically anything related to
firearms in the State of Texas.

Guns

Name: firearms
Resource: List
Address: firearms-request@cs.cmu.edu
(Karl Kleinpaste)
The mailing list for sportsmen to
discuss issues of concern to them.

Headlines

Name: misc.headlines
Resource: USENET
Current interest: drug testing, terror-
ism, etc.

Human Rights

Name: hrs-l
Resource: LISTSERV
Address: hrs-l@bingvmb.bitnet
Discusses and exchanges information
about the systematic studies of
human rights.

Intellectual Property Rights

Name: misc.int-property
Resource: USENET
Discussion of intellectual property
rights.

Kids

Name: Y-RIGHTS
Resource: LISTSERV
Address: LISTSERV@SJUVM.BITNET
Discussion group on the rights of kids
and teens.

Media

Name: prog-pubs
Resource: List
Address:
prog-pubs@fuggles.acc.virginia.edu
For persons interested in alternative, progressive media.

Men

Name: men
Resource: List
Address:
mail-men-request@summit.novell.com
Mailing list discusses "men's issues." Both women and men may join.

Parental Rights

Name: free-l
Resource: LISTSERV
Address: free-l@indycms.iupui.edu
A discussion list for supporters of Fathers' Rights and Equality Exchange.

Political Science

Name: POSCIM
Resource: List
Address: UPS500@DBNRHRZ1
(Markus Schlegel)
Intended as a forum of those researching, teaching, or studying political science as well as the practicians of politics.

Race

Name: POS302-L
Resource: LISTSERV
Address: LISTSERV@ILSTU.EDU
A discussion list for the "Race, Ethnicity, and Social Inequality" seminar offered at Illinois State University in the Spring, 1994 semester.

Science Activism

Name: YSN
Resource: List
Address:
ysn-adm@zoyd.ee.washington.edu
(John Sahr)
Activism on employment issues for scientists just beginning their careers.

Women's Issues

Name: femail
Resource: List
Address:
femail-request@lucerne.eng.sun.com
(Ellen Eades)
Mailing list for discussion of issues of interest to women, in a friendly atmosphere.

Name: feminism-digest
Resource: List
Address:
feminism-digest@ncar.ucar.edu
(Cindy Tittle Moore)
This is actually a digest version of soc.feminism. It is intended for those who have difficulty getting soc.feminism.

Workplace Benefits

Name: domestic
Resource: List
Address:
`domestic-request@tattoo.mti.sgi.com`
The domestic partners mailing list exists for the discussion of workplace-related issues concerning domestic partners.

Social Organizations

College

Name: Societies
Resource: List
Address:
`societies-request@athena.mit.edu`
Discussion of Greek letter societies of all sorts, primarily those at American colleges.

Kiwanis

Name: Circle K International
Resource: List
Address: `jwolff@nyx.cs.du.edu`
(Jeffrey M. Wolff)
For members and alumni of the worldwide collegiate service organization sponsored by Kiwanis International.

Masons

Name: masonic
Resource: List
Address: `masonic@ptrei@asgard.bbn.com`
A discussion list for those involved in Freemasonry and related groups.

Name: Masonic Digest
Resource: List
Address: `ptrei@mitre.org` (Peter Trei)
A moderated forum for discussion of Free Masonry, affiliated groups, and other fraternal orders.

Mensa

Name: mensatalk
Resource: List
Address: `mensatalk-request@psg.com`
(Ed Wright)
For members (only) of Mensa.

Name: mensatalk
Resource: List
Address: `mensatalk@psg.com`
This list is open to all Mensa members.

Name: rec.org.mensa
Resource: USENET
Talking with members of the high IQ society Mensa.

SCA

Name: rec.org.sca
Resource: USENET
Society for Creative Anachronism.

Name: sca
Resource: List
Address: `sca-request@mc.lcs.mit.edu`
(Danulf Donaldson, MKA Dana Groff)
This group discusses anything relating to the Society for Creative Anachronism.

Name: sca-west
Resource: List
Address:
`sca-west-request@ecst.csuchico.edu`

For persons who have interest in the Society of Creative Anachronism members in the west.

Scouting

Name: rec.scouting
Resource: USENET
Scouting youth organizations worldwide.

Name: scouts-l
Resource: LISTSERV
Address: scouts-l@tcubvm.bitnet
This is the scouting and youth volunteer discussion forum.

Secret

Name: GRASS
Resource: List
Address:
grass-server@wharton.upenn.edu
The Generic Religions and Secret Societies mailing list is a forum for the development of religions and secret societies for use in role-playing games.

Sierra Club

Name: Sierra Club
Resource: List
Address: 931ROWE@MERLIN.NLU.EDU
(Eddie Rowe)
Discussion of environmental topics with a focus on the Sierra Club's campaigns, news and outings. A mirror of the Fidonet Sierra Club Conference (SIERRAN).

Toastmasters

Name: alt.org.toastmasters
Resource: USENET
Public speaking and Toastmasters International.

Twins

Name: twins
Resource: List
Address: owner-twins@athena.mit.edu
Even though the term *twins* is used, it is meant to represent all multiples. The purpose is to provide an open forum for the discussion of issues about twins.

Sports

Aikido

Name: Aikido-L
Resource: LISTSERV
Address: LISTSERV@PSUVM.PSU.EDU
(Gerry Santoro)
Discussion and information exchange regarding the Japanese martial art Aikido. Send subscription requests to LISTSERV@PSUVM.PSU.EDU as electronic mail with the following in the body of the mail // JOB SUBSCRIBE AIKIDO-L your-name-here // EOJ This is based on an IBM LISTSERV.

Archery

Name: alt.archery
Resource: USENET
Robin Hood had the right idea.

Balloon

Name: Balloon
Resource: List
Address: `Balloon@lut.ac.uk`
For all balloonists. Send your subscription requests and related administrative information to
`balloon-request@lut.ac.uk`.

Baseball

Resource: telnet
Address: `culine.colorado.edu 862`
Schedules online.

Name: Minor League Baseball
Resource: List
Address:
`minors-request@medraut.apple.com`
(Chuq von Rospach)
Issues affecting the minor league.

Name: San Francisco Giants
Resource: List
Address:
`giants-request@medraut.apple.com`
(Chuq Von Rospach)
Discussion, information exchange on the San Francisco Giants baseball team.

Name: seattle-mariners
Resource: List
Address:
`seattle-mariners-request@kei.com`
Discussion of the Seattle Mariners baseball club, criticism included. :)

Name: statlg-1
Resource: LISTSERV
Address: `statlg-1@brownvm.brown.edu`
Baseball (and lesser sports) discussion list.

Name: Toronto Blue Jays
Resource: List
Address: `stlouis@unixg.ubc.ca`
(Phill St-Louis)
Discussion of the Toronto Blue Jays Baseball Club.

Baseball-Toronto Blue Jays

Name: jays
Resource: List
Address: `jays@hivnet.ubc.ca`
For fanatics of the Toronto Blue Jays baseball team. Submit your subscription request to
`jays-request@hivnet.ubc.ca`.

Basketball

Resource: telnet
Address: `culine.colorado.edu 859`
Schedules online.

Bicycling

Name: bicycles
Resource: List
Address: `bicycles@bbn.com`
A discussion list for all topics related to bicycling, both recreational and racing. Send your subscription request to `bicycles-request@bbn.com`.

Name: ebikes
Resource: List
Address: `ebikes-request@panix.com`
(Danny Lieberman)
Metro NYC bicycle discussion list, unmoderated.

Name: tandem
Resource: List
Address:
`tandem-request@hobbes.ucsd.edu`

A mailing list for tandem bicycle enthusiasts.

Canoeing / Kayaking

Name: whitewater
Resource: List
Address:
`whitewater-request@gynko.circ.upenn.edu`
To discuss whitewater sports, experiences, and information.

Caving/Spelunking

Name: Cavers
Resource: List
Address: `Cavers@M2c.Org`
For anyone interested in caving. Send subscription requests to
`cavers-request@m2c.org`.

Cleveland

Name:
Resource: List
Address: `@cleveland.freenet.edu`
A general support list for all Cleveland sports activities. Contact
`aj755@cleveland.freenet.edu` for more information about subscribing.

Name: Cleveland Sports
Resource: List
Address: `aj755@cleveland.freenet.edu`
(Richard Kowicki)
This mailing list provides a forum for people to discuss their favorite Cleveland Sports teams/personalities, and it provides news and information about those teams that most out-of-towners couldn't get otherwise.

Cricket

Name: cricket
Resource: LISTSERV
Address: `cricket@ndsuvm1.ndsu.edu`
This is a redistribution of cricket information.

Drag Racing

Name: dragnet
Resource: List
Address:
`dragnet-request@chiller.compaq.com`
To discuss strip drag racing from a participant's viewpoint. (moderated)

Fencing

Name: rec.sport.fencing
Resource: USENET
All aspects of swordplay.

Figure Skating

Name: skating
Resource: LISTSERV
Address: `skating@umab.umd.edu`
For all fans of figure skating.

Fly Fishing

Name: flyfish
Resource: LISTSERV
Address: `flyfish@umab.umd.edu`
This is the fly-fishing digest.

Football

Resource: telnet
Address: `culine.colorado.edu 863`
Schedules online.

Name: coordcom
Resource: LISTSERV
Address: `coordcom@msu.bitnet`
This is a football information list.

Name: Raiders
Resource: List
Address: `raiders-request@super.org`
(Adam Fox)
This list is not moderated and all Raider fans are welcome.

Name: rec.sport.football.canadian
Resource: USENET
All about Canadian-rules football.

Name: rec.sport.football.college
Resource: USENET
US-style college football.

Name: rec.sport.football.pro
Resource: USENET
US-style professional football.

Golf

Name: golf-l
Resource: LISTSERV
Address: `golf-l@ubvm.cc.buffalo.edu`
This is the golf discussion list.

Name: rec.sport.golf
Resource: USENET
Discussion about all aspects of golfing.

Guns/Firearms

Name: firearms
Resource: List
Address: `firearms@cs.cmu.edu`
Devoted to the nonpolitical aspects of guns and firearms. Send your subscription requests to `firearms-request@cs.cmu.edu`.

Gymnastics

Resource: List
This list discusses all aspects of gymnastics. Contact `raek@athena.mit.edu`.

Name: gymn
Resource: List
Address: `owner-gymn@mit.edu`
(Robyn Kozierok)
A forum for the discussion of all aspects of the sport of gymnastics. Archive location: `ftp.cac.psu.edu`. Ftp items may be retrieved by sending email to `rachele@rice.edu`.

Hang Gliding

Name: hang-gliding
Resource: List
Address: `hang-gliding@virginia.edu`
This discussion list covers all aspects of hang gliding and ballooning.

Hang-Gliding

Name: hang-gliding
Resource: List
Address:
`hang-gliding-request@virginia.edu`
(Galen Hekhuis)
Topics covering all aspects of hang gliding and ballooning, for ultra-light and lighter-than-air enthusiasts.

Hockey

Resource: telnet
Address: `culine.colorado.edu 860`
Schedules online.

Name: ahl-news
Resource: List
Address: `ahl-news@andrew.cmu.edu`
For people interested in discussing and following the American Hockey League.

Name: Boston Bruins
Resource: List
Address:
`bruins-request@cristal.umd.edu`
(Garry Knox)
Discussion of the Boston Bruins and their farm teams.

Name: Dallas Stars
Resource: List
Address: `hamlet@u.washington.edu`
(Mitch McGowan)
Discussion of the Dallas Stars and their farms clubs.

Name: East Coast Hockey League
Resource: List
Address:
`echl-news-request@andrew.cmu.edu`
For people interested in discussing and following the East Coast Hockey League.

Name: Hartford Whalers
Resource: List
Address: `kayleigh@access.digex.net`
(Steve Gallichio)
Discussion of the Hartford Whalers hockey club and any tangential discussions that emerge.

Name: hockey-l
Resource: LISTSERV
Address: `hockey-l@maine.maine.edu`
A college hockey discussion list.

Name: HOCKEY-L
Resource: List
Address: `LISTSERV@maine.maine.edu`

Discussion of collegiate ice hockey.

Name: Los Angeles Kings
Resource: List
Address:
`kings-request@cs.stanford.edu`
Discussion on the Los Angeles Kings.

Name: New York Islanders
Resource: List
Address: `dss2k@virginia.edu`
(David Strauss)
To discuss the NYI hockey team.

Name: NHL Goalie Stats
Resource: List
Address: `dfa@triple-i.com`
Weekday reports of NHL goalie stats.

Name: OlymPuck
Resource: LISTSERV
Address: `LISTSERV@Maine.Maine.Edu`
(Charlie Slavin)
Discussion of Olympic ice hockey. To subscribe: Send mail to `LISTSERV@Maine.Maine.Edu`. The *body* of the message should contain: `SUBscribe OlymPuck your_name`

Name: olympuck
Resource: LISTSERV
Address: `olympuck@maine.maine.edu`
The Olympic ice hockey discussion list.

Name: Quebec Nordiques
Resource: List
Address:
`nords-request@badaboum.ulaval.ca`
(Danny J. Sohier)
Discusses topics concerning the National Hockey League's Quebec Nordiques.

Name: rec.sport.hockey
Resource: USENET
Discussion about ice hockey.

Name: REDWING
Resource: LISTSERV
Address: vergolin@cps.msu.edu
(David Vergolini)
Discuss and exchange information regarding The Detroit Red Wings.

Name: San Jose Sharks
Resource: List
Address:
sharks-request@medraut.apple.com
(Laurie Sefton)
Discussion, information exchange on the San Jose Sharks.

Name: St. Louis Blues
Resource: List
Address: blues@medicine.wustl.edu
(Joe Ashkar)
Information, game reports, stats, and discussion about the St. Louis Blues.

Name: The Mighty Ducks of Anaheim
Resource: List
Address: <bnc@macsch.com>
(Brian Casey)
Discussion of the Mighty Ducks of Anaheim. To subscribe/unsubscribe, send a request to
mda-request@macsch.com

Name: uk-hockey
Resource: List
Address:
uk-hockey-request@cee.hw.ac.uk
(Steve Salvini)
An open invitation to followers of hockey in the UK to join a mailing list dedicated to the discussion of (ice!) hockey in Britain.

Name: Vancouver Canucks
Resource: List
Address: boey@sfu.ca
Discussion of anything related to the Canucks.

Name: Western Hockey League
Resource: List
Address: klootzak@u.washington.edu
(Michael A. Stuyt)
Discuss matters relevant to the Western Hockey League. To subscribe, e-mail klootzak@u.washington.edu with the words "WHL SUB" in the subject line of your message.

Horse Racing

Name: Derby
Resource: List
Address: Derby@Ekrl.Com
For anything related to horse racing, including gambling and handicapping. Send subscriptions to Derby--Request@Ekrl.Com.

Hunting

Name: hunting
Resource: LISTSERV
Address: hunting@tamvm1.tamu.edu
This is a gateway to the USENET group Rec.Hunting.

Lacrosse

Name: lacros-l
Resource: LISTSERV
Address:
lacros-l@villvm.bitnet@vm1.nodak.edu
For everyone interested in lacrosse.

Management

Name: sportmgt
Resource: LISTSERV

Address: `sportmgt@unbvm1.bitnet`
For everyone who is interested in sport management.

Martial Arts

Name: aikido-l
Resource: LISTSERV
Address: `aikido-l@psuvm.psu.edu`
This is the aikido list.

Name: kokikai
Resource: LISTSERV
Address: `kokikai@psuvm.psu.edu`
This list is devoted to kokikai aikido.

Name: martial-arts
Resource: List
Address:
`martial-arts-request@dragon.cso.uiuc.edu`
(Steven Miller)
Discussion on various aspects of the martial arts.

Name: rec.martial-arts
Resource: USENET
Discussion of the various martial art forms.

Miscellaneous

Name: rec.misc
Resource: USENET
General topics about recreational/participant sports.

Name: rec.sport.misc
Resource: USENET
Spectator sports.

Mountaineering

Name: mount-l
Resource: LISTSERV

Address: `mount-l@trmetu.bitnet`
This is the mountaineering discussion list.

Nordic

Name: nordic-skiing
Resource: List
Address:
`nordic-ski-request@graphics.cornell.edu`
(Mitch Collinsworth)
Discussion of Nordic skiing sports.

Nordic Skiing

Name: nordic-ski
Resource: List
Address:
`nordic-ski@graphics.cornell.edu`
This list discusses all aspects of Nordic skiing. Send your subscription requests to
`nordic-ski-request@graphics.cornell.edu.`

Orienteering

Name: Orienteering
Resource: List
Address:
`Orienteering@Graphics.Cornell.Edu`
This list is for the purpose of exchanging information on and discussing the sport of orienteering. Send your subscription requests to
`orienteering-request@graphics.cornell.edu.`

Pac-10

Name: Pac Ten Sports
Resource: List
Address: `crs@u.washington.edu`
(Cliff Slaughterbeck)

An unmoderated mailing list dedicated to discussing sports of all types that are played competitively within the Pac Ten Athletic Conference.

Psychology

Name: sportpsy
Resource: LISTSERV
Address: sportpsy@templevm.bitnet
This list discusses exercise and sports psychology.

Running

Name: dead-runners
Resource: List
Address:
dead-runners-request@unx.sas.com
(Christopher Mark Conn)
The Dead Runners Society is a mailing list for runners who like to talk about the psychological, philosophical, and personal aspects of running.

Name: drs
Resource: LISTSERV
Address: drs@dartcms1.dartmouth.edu
This is the Dead Runners Society.

Name: rec.running
Resource: USENET
Running for enjoyment, sport, exercise, and so on.

Soccer

Name: Everton
Resource: List
Address:
everton-request@wg.estec.esa.nl
Discussion concerning Everton Football Club and anything vaguely related.

Name: france-foot
Resource: List
Address:
france-foot-request@inf.enst.fr
(Vincent Habchi) dv1khh@cs.umu.se
(Kent Hedlundh)
Discussions of the French football (soccer) scene.

Name: soccer-l
Resource: LISTSERV
Address: soccer-l@ukcc.uky.edu
This is the soccer boosters list.

Swimming

Name: swim-l
Resource: LISTSERV
Address: swim-l@uafsysb.uark.edu
For persons interested in any aspect of swimming.

Table Tennis

Name: rec.sport.table-tennis
Resource: USENET
Things related to table tennis (a.k.a. Ping Pong).

Technology

Name: sportpc
Resource: LISTSERV
Address: sportpc@unbvm1.bitnet
This list discusses the use of computers in sporting events.

Tennis

Name: rec.sport.tennis
Resource: USENET
Things related to the sport of tennis.

Training

Name: athtrn-l
Resource: LISTSERV
Address: `athtrn-l@iubvm.bitnet`
This is a discussion list for athletic trainers.

University of Nebraska

Name: huskers
Resource: List
Address: `huskers-request@tssi.com`
(Michael Nolan)
Provides coverage of University of Nebraska sports.

Volleyball

Name: ba-volleyball
Resource: List
Address:
`ba-volleyball-request@klerk.cup.hp.com`
Announcements about San Francisco Bay Area volleyball events, clinics, tournaments, and such.

Name: rec.sport.volleyball
Resource: USENET
Discussion about volleyball.

Water Skiing

Name: waterski
Resource: List
Address: `waterski-request@nda.com`
Discussion topics are open to anything of interest to water-skiers, from absolute beginners to competitors.

Weight Lifting

Name: weights
Resource: List
Address: `weights@mickey.disney.com`
Exchange of information related to all aspects of weight lifting. Send your subscription requests to
`weights-request@mickey.disney.com`.

Weight Training

Name: weights
Resource: List
Address:
`weights-request@mickey.disney.com`
(Michael Sullivan)
Discussion of all aspects of using weights in exercise.

Windsurfing

Name: Windsurfing
Resource: List
Address: `Windsurfing@gcm.com`
For everyone interested in windsurfing and boardsailing. Send your subscription requests to
`windsurfing-request@gcm.com`.

Windsurfing/Boardsailing

Name: windsurfing
Resource: List
Address: `windsurfing-request@fly.com`
Discussion forum for boardsailing enthusiasts all over the world.

Wrestling

Name: rec.sport.pro-wrestling
Resource: USENET
Discussion about professional wrestling.

Technology

Audio

Name: info-high-audio
Resource: List
Address:

`info-high-audio-request@csd4.csd.uwm.edu`
(Thomas Krueger)
Exchange of subjective comments about high-end audio equipment and modifications performed to high-end pieces.

Aviation

Name: skunk-works
Resource: List
Address:

`skunk-works-request@harbor.ecn.purdue.edu`
Discuss Lockheed special project planes and current aviation news.

Biotechnology

Name: biotech
Resource: LISTSERV
Address: `biotech@umdd.bitnet`
This is a biotechnology discussion list.

Home Satellites

Name: homesat
Resource: LISTSERV
Address: `homesat@ndsuvm1.ndsu.edu`
This list discusses home satellite technology.

Laser Printers

Name: laser-l
Resource: LISTSERV
Address: `laser-l@irlearn.ucd.ie`
This is the laser printer information distribution list.

Mass Communications

Name: masscomm
Resource: LISTSERV
Address: `masscomm@rpitsvm.bitnet`
This list discusses and exchanges information about mass communications and new or emerging technologies.

Pagers

Name: IXO
Resource: List
Address:

`ixo-request@Warren.MentorG.COM`
Discussion about pagers and software that implements the "ixo" protocol. Send a mail message to `majordomo@Warren.MentorG.com`. The first line of the message (the "Subject:" line is ignored) should be `subscribe ixo`.

Touchtone

Name: touchton
Resource: LISTSERV
Address: `touchton@sjsuvm1.sjsu.edu`
For the discussion of touchtone/voice response systems.

Video

Name: videotech
Resource: List
Address:

`videotech@wsmr-simtel20.army.mil`
Discussion and information exchange

of all video technologies. Send your subscription and related administrative information to `videotech-request@wsmr-simtel20.army.mil`.

Travel

Tourism

Name: travel-l
Resource: LISTSERV
Address:
`travel-l@trearn.bitnet@vm1.nodak.edu`
For persons interested in discussing the tourist trade.

World Issues

Afghanistan

Name: soc.culture.afghanistan
Resource: USENET
Discussion of the Afghan society.

Africa

Name: AFRICA-N
Resource: LISTSERV
Address: `frabbani@epas.utoronto.ca`
(Faraz Rabbani)
A moderated mailing list dedicated to the exchange of news and information on Africa from many sources. To subscribe, e-mail
`LISTSERV@utoronto.bitnet`, and send the following one-line message (the subject header is ignored): SUBSCRIBE
`AFRICA-N` YOUR NAME.

Arabic

Name: soc.culture.arabic
Resource: USENET
Technological and cultural issues, *not* politics.

Argentina

Name: argentina
Resource: List
Address:
`argentina-request@ois.db.toronto.edu`
(Carlos G. Mendioroz)
General discussion and information.

Arms

Name: arms-l
Resource: LISTSERV
Address: `arms-l@buacca.bu.edu`
Focuses on the exchange of information and discussion related to national armaments.

Asia

Name: cenasia
Resource: LISTSERV
Address: `cenasia@mcgill1.bitnet`
Discusses the former Soviet Republic and Central Asian politics.

Asian-American

Name: soc.culture.asian.american
Resource: USENET
Issues and discussion about Asian-Americans.

Australian

Name: soc.culture.australian
Resource: USENET
Australian culture and society.

Bangladesh

Name: soc.culture.bangladesh
Resource: USENET
Issues and discussion about
Bangladesh.

Bolivia

Name: Llajta
Resource: LISTSERV
Address:
`listserv@io.dsd.litton.com` (machine)
`reading@io.dsd.litton.com` (human)
Discussion of any and all topics
relating to Bolivia.

Bosnia

Name: BosNet
Resource: List
Address: `listproc@cu23.crl.aecl.ca`
BosNet is a group/forum run by
volunteers. Its goals are to present
and distribute information relevant to
the events in/about Republic of
Bosnia-Hercegovina (RB&H). To
subscribe, send email to
`listproc@cu23.crl.aecl.ca` with message
body `subscribe BOSNET` *Firstname*
Lastname

Name: soc.culture.bosna-herzgvna
Resource: USENET
The independent state of Bosnia and
Herzegovina.

Brazil

Name: brasil
Resource: List
Address: `bras-net-request@cs.ucla.edu`
(B. R. Araujo Neto)
Mailing list for general discussion and
information.

Bulgaria

Name: soc.culture.bulgaria
Resource: USENET
Discussing Bulgarian society.

Canada

Name: can-stud-assoc
Resource: List
Address:
`can-stud-assoc-request@unixg.ubc.ca`
Discuss issues of concern to Canadian
students.

Name: canada-l
Resource: LISTSERV
Address: `canada-l@vm1.mcgill.ca`
Exchange of ideas about Canadian
issues.

Name: soc.culture.canada
Resource: USENET
Discussions of Canada and its people.

Caribbean

Name: carecon
Resource: LISTSERV
Address: `carecon@vm1.yorku.ca`
This list discusses the Caribbean
economy.

Central America

Name: centam-l
Resource: LISTSERV
Address: centam-l@ubvm.cc.buffalo.edu
The Central America discussion list.

China

Name: china
Resource: LISTSERV
Address: china@pucc.bitnet
This forum is for Chinese studies.

Croatia

Name: Cro-News/SCYU-Digest
Resource: List
Address:
cro-news-request@medphys.ucl.ac.uk
(Nino Margetic)
This non-moderated list is the distribution point for the news coming from Croatia.

Name: Cro-Views
Resource: List
Address:
Joe@Mullara.Met.UniMelb.Edu.AU (Joe Stojsic)
An opinion service that consists of discussions relating to Croatia and other former-Yugoslav republics.

Name: Croatian-News/ Hrvatski-Vjesnik
Resource: List
Address:
Croatian-News-Request@Andrew.CMU.Edu
Hrvatski-Vjesnik-Zamolbe@Andrew.CMU.Edu
News from and related to Croatia, run by volunteers. These are actually two news distributions: one in Croatian (occasionally an article can be in some other South Slavic language) and one in English.

Cuba

Name: cuba-l
Resource: LISTSERV
Address: cuba-l@unmvma.bitnet
Cuba today. This is a bilingual list in Spanish/English for the discussion of Cuba's current state of affairs.

Diversity

Name: divers-l
Resource: LISTSERV
Address: divers-l@psuvm.psu.edu
For anyone interested in the diversity of the world's peoples.

Dominican Republic

Name: KISKEYA
Resource: LISTSERV
Address: listserv@conicit.ve
Dominican mailing list oriented towards the discussion of promoting and developing an efficient telecommunication network in the Dominican Republic and the rest of the Caribbean.

Name: SDOMINGO
Resource: LISTSERV
Address: listserv@enlace.bitnet
Discuss and exchange information about the culture and events related to the Dominican Republic.

Estonia

Name: E-List
Resource: List
Address: vilo@cs.helsinki.fi
(Jaak Vilo)
News and discussion on Estonia.

Europe

Name: soc.culture.europe
Resource: USENET
Discussing all aspects of all-European society.

France

Name: soc.culture.french
Resource: USENET
French culture, history, and related discussions.

General

Name: val-l
Resource: LISTSERV
Address: val-l@ucf1vm.cc.ucf.edu
Valentine Michael Smith's commentary.

Germany

Name: soc.culture.german
Resource: USENET
Discussions about German culture and history.

Greece

Name: soc.culture.greek
Resource: USENET
Group about Greeks.

Hong Kong

Name: soc.culture.hongkong
Resource: USENET
Discussions pertaining to Hong Kong.

Hungary

Name: HIX
Resource: List
Address: hix@cipher.pha.jhu.edu
Hollosi Information Exchange is a mail server containing information about Hungarian electronic resources.

Name: soc.culture.magyar
Resource: USENET
The Hungarian people and their culture.

Name: Szemle
Resource: List
Address:
ujsagker@vuhepx.phy.vanderbilt.edu
Discussion and distribution of news about Hungary, in digest form. Information is mainly in Hungarian. To receive the digest, write to the contact address, with Subject: KELL.

India

Name: india-d
Resource: LISTSERV
Address: india-d@utarlvm1.bitnet
India News Network.

Name: soc.culture.indian
Resource: USENET
Group for discussion about India and things Indian.

Indigenous Peoples

Name: NativeNet
Resource: List
Address: `gst@gnosys.svle.ma.us`
(Gary S. Trujillo)
Information and discussion about issues relating to indigenous people around the world, and current threats to their cultures and habitats.

International Trade

Name: International Trade andCommerce
Resource: List
Address:
`info-request@tradent.wimsey.bc.ca`
Discussions of International Trade, Commerce, and the global economy including postings of company profiles, trade leads and topics pertaining to entrepreneurial ventures.

Iran

Name: soc.culture.iranian
Resource: USENET
Discussions about Iran and things Iranian/Persian.

Israel

Name: soc.culture.jewish
Resource: USENET
Jewish culture and religion. (`cf.`
`talk.politics.mideast`)

Italy

Name: soc.culture.italian
Resource: USENET
The Italian people and their culture.

Japan

Name: soc.culture.japan
Resource: USENET
Everything Japanese, except the Japanese language.

Latin America

Name: lasnet
Resource: List
Address:
`lasnet-request@emx.utexas.edu`
(Langston James Goree VI)
Exchange of information among scholars doing research related to Latin America.

Name: soc.culture.latin-america
Resource: USENET
Topics about Latin-America.

Lebanon

Name: soc.culture.lebanon
Resource: USENET
Discussion about things Lebanese.

Macedonia

Name: Mak-News
Resource: LISTSERV
Address: `listserv@UTS.Edu.Au`
Developments in the Republic of Macedonia. Send e-mail to
`listserv@UTS.Edu.Au` with message body
`subscribe MAK-NEWS` *Firstname Lastname.*

Malaysia

Name: soc.culture.malaysia
Resource: USENET
All about Malaysian society.

Mexico

Name: soc.culture.mexican
Resource: USENET
Discussion of Mexico's society.

Middle Europe

Name: mideur-l
Resource: LISTSERV
Address: `mideur-l@ubvm.cc.buffalo.edu`
An open list for the purpose of
discussing all aspects of Middle
European politics.

Migration

Name: Migra-List
Resource: List
Address:
`migra-list-request@cc.utah.edu`
`moliva@cc.utah.edu` (Maurizio Oliva)
Mailing list on international
migration.

Native Peoples

Name: alt.native
Resource: USENET
People indigenous to an area before
modern colonization.

Name: soc.culture.native
Resource: USENET
Aboriginal people around the world.

Netherlands

Name: soc.culture.netherlands
Resource: USENET
People from the Netherlands and
Belgium.

Norway

Name: NORWEAVE
Resource: LISTSERV
Address: `LISTSERV@NKI.NO`
An e-mail service for Norwegians and
friends of Norway.

Pakistan

Name: soc.culture.pakistan
Resource: USENET
Topics of discussion about Pakistan.

Palestine

Name: soc.culture.palestine
Resource: USENET
Palestinian people, culture and
politics.

Peru

Name: Peru
Resource: List
Address: `owner-peru@cs.sfsu.edu`
(Herbert Koller)
For discussion of Peruvian culture
and other issues. This mailing list is
simply an echo site, so all posts get
bounced from that address to all the
people subscribed.

Poland

Name: Donosy
Resource: List
Address: przemek@ndcvx.cc.nd.edu
(Przemek Klosowski)
Distribution of a news bulletin from Poland. English and Polish versions are both avaialble.

Name: Pigulka
Resource: List
Address: zielinski@acfcluster.nyu.edu
(Marek Zielinski)
davep@acsu.buffalo.edu (Dave Phillips)
Digest on the net news from Poland, in English. Irregular.

Name: Spojrzenia
Resource: List
Address: krzystek@u.washington.edu
(Jerzy Krzystek)
A weekly e-journal, devoted to Polish culture, history, politics, etc. In Polish.

Serbia

Name: SII
Resource: List
Address: Owner@moumee.calstatela.edu
(Stanislav Markovic)
Serbian Information Initiative is an unmoderated network for distribution of news and discussions about the current events involving or affecting Serbs.

Name: Vizantija
Resource: List
Address: Dimitrije@buenga.bu.edu
(Dimitrije Stamenovic)
Distributes news and provides forum for discussions about the current events in ex-Yu.

Slavic

Name: Mailing-Lists
Resource: List
Address: mailing-lists@krpan.arnes.si
Information on mailing lists from South Slavic countries.

Slovenia

Name: Novice MZT
Resource: List
Address: Novice-MZT@KRPAN.ARNES.SI or
Novice.MZT@Uni-Lj.SI
The role of News of Ministry for Science and Technology of the Republic of Slovenia is to provide easy accessible news from science, development, universities, innovative activities to indviduals and institutions in research and development area.

Name: Oglasna Deska
Resource: List
Address: Oglasna-Deska@KRPAN.ARNES.SI
(Dean Mozetic and Marjeta Cedilnik)
Oglasna.Deska@Uni-LJ.SI
Oglasna Deska (bulletin board) is transcripts taken from SLON, which is a nickname for Decnet connecting several computers in Slovenia.

Name: Pisma Bralcev
Resource: List
Address: Pisma-Bralcev@KRPAN.ARNES.SI
(Andrej Brodnik and Srecko Vidmar)
Pisma.Bralcev@Uni-LJ.SI
Pisma bralcev is an edited (not moderated) mailing list that provides the possibility of publishing readers' opinions, questions, inquiries for help, answers, etc.

Name: RokPress
Resource: List
Address: IBenko@Maveric0.UWaterloo.CA
(Igor Benko) or RokPress@KRPAN.ARNES.SI
or RokPress@Uni-LJ.SI
RokPress is a moderated mailing list,
intended primarily for news from
Slovenia.

Spain

Name: espana-l
Resource: LISTSERV
Address: espana-l@albnyvm1.bitnet
A discussion list dedicated to Spain
and its people.

Sri Lanka

Name: Sri Lanka Net (SLNet)
Resource: List
Address: pkd@fed.frb.gov,
slnetad@ganu.colorado.edu
A moderated mailing list that carries
news and other articles about Sri
Lanka.

Name: soc.culture.sri-lanka
Resource: USENET
Things and people from Sri Lanka.

Tibet

Name: CTN News
Resource: List
Address: ctn-editors@utcc.utoronto.ca
A list covering news on Tibet.

Turkey

Name: soc.culture.turkish
Resource: USENET
Discussion about things Turkish.

UK

Name: uklegal
Resource: List
Address: lsg001@uk.ac.coventry.cck
The objective of the mailing group is
to consider and discuss matters of a
legal nature relating to English and to
some respects Scottish law. People
may join the group by mailing
lsg001@uk.ac.coventry.cck. People
should put the word uklegal as the
header and put their e-mail address
on the next line.

Uruguay

Name: uruguay
Resource: List
Address:
uruguay-request@db.toronto.edu
(Mariano Consens)
A mailing list for general discussions
and information on topics related to
Uruguay.

USA

Name: neworl-dig
Resource: List
Address:
mail-server@mintir.new-orleans.la.us
elendil@mintir.new-orleans.la.us

(Edward J. Branley)
This is a digest version of the New
Orleans mailing list
(`new-orleans@mintir.new-orleans.la.us`).
To subscribe, send a message to
`mail-server@mintir.new-orleans.la.us`,
with SUBSCRIBE NEW-ORLEANS in the body.

Yugoslavia

Name: Jugo
Resource: List
Address: `Dimitrije@buenga.bu.edu`
(Dimitrije Stamenovic)
Distributes news and provides forum
for discussions about the current
events in ex-Yu.

Name: Vreme
Resource: List
Address: `p00981@psilink.com`
VREME carries "Vreme News Digest"
(selected articles from "Vreme"
translated to English), the major
independent newspaper in Yugosla-
via and "neighboring countries".

Name: Vreme News Digest
Resource: List
Address: `Dimitrije@BuEnga.Bu.Edu`
(Dimitrije Stamenovic)
Vreme News Digest is an
English-language newsletter pub-
lished by the Vreme News Digest
Agency (VNDA) from Belgrade.

INDEX

Eudora™ by QUALCOMM is really nifty e-mail. Just ask the tens of thousands of Internauts who use it to zip around cyber-space on a daily basis.

Eliminating special bridges or gateways on your corporate LANs enables your Mac and PC users to communicate like they never have before.

When they heard their favorite e-mail was going to get a new lease on life, sad little emoticons got smiley again.

Why did we take the world's most popular freeware and start charging $65 a pop for it?

The 100,000-plus current users saw red when they heard Eudora e-mail might die of neglect. They wanted it revived, with better documentation, customer support and new features. (100,000 people usually get what they want.)

$65 now could save you thousands later. By using TCP/IP protocols, Eudora by QUALCOMM e-mail plugs right into the Internet. Which is to say, right into the world.

You can use it to tell Hillary just what you think about healthcare in America. Try president@whitehouse.gov.

If you want truly robust software, you've got to feed it and pump it up with new features. That takes money.

Incredibly, some LAN administrators just didn't care if Eudora died. One can only wonder where their heads were when the world turned to open systems.

Eudora by QUALCOMM. Or should we say Eudora (saved) by QUALCOMM? Anyway, it's the best-connected e-mail in the world. Call us at 1-800-2-Eudora; fax: 619-587-8276; e-mail: eudora-sales@qualcomm.com; and we'll send you the complete scoop.

QUALCOMM

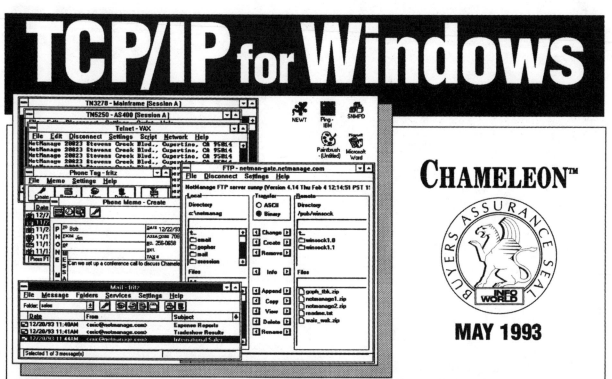

Add to Your Sams Library Today with the Best Books for Programming, Operating Systems, and New Technologies

The easiest way to order is to pick up the phone and call

1-800-428-5331

between 9:00 a.m. and 5:00 p.m. EST.

For faster service please have your credit card available.

ISBN	Quantity	Description of Item	Unit Cost	Total Cost
0-672-30466-X		Internet Unleashed	$39.95	
0-672-30326-4		Absolute Beginner's Guide to Networking	$19.95	
0-672-30457-0		Learning UNIX	$39.95	
0-672-30464-3		Teach Yourself UNIX in a Week	$28.00	
0-672-30382-5		Understanding Local Area Networks, Fourth Edition	$26.95	
0-672-30206-3		Networking Windows, NetWare Edition	$24.95	
0-672-30209-8		NetWare Unleashed	$45.00	
0-672-30026-5		Do-It-Yourself Networking with LANtastic	$24.95	
0-672-30173-3		Enterprise-Wide Networking	$39.95	
0-672-30170-9		NetWare LAN Management Toolkit	$34.95	
0-672-30243-8		LAN Desktop Guide to E-mail with cc:Mail	$27.95	
0-672-30005-2		Understanding Data Communications, Third Edition	$24.95	
0-672-30119-9		International Telecommunications	$39.95	
❏ 3 ½" Disk		Shipping and Handling: See information below.		
❏ 5 ¼" Disk		TOTAL		

Shipping and Handling: $4.00 for the first book, and $1.75 for each additional book. Floppy disk: add $1.75 for shipping and handling. If you need to have it NOW, we can ship product to you in 24 hours for an additional charge of approximately $18.00, and you will receive your item overnight or in two days. Overseas shipping and handling adds $2.00 per book and $8.00 for up to three disks. Prices are subject to change. Call for availability and pricing information on latest editions.

201 West 103rd Street, Indianapolis, Indiana 46290

1-800-428-5331 — Orders   1-800-835-3202 — FAX   1-800-858-7674 — Customer Service

Macintosh Disk Offer

If you're a Macintosh user, you can receive a Macintosh disk with a variety of Internet programs, utilities, and reference files.

- ⚓ *Eudora* Mailreader.
- ⚓ *Fetch* FTP Client.
- ⚓ *TurboGopher* Gopher client.
- ⚓ *UUEncode/UUDecode* program for sending and receiving binary files as e-mail.
- ⚓ *Archiving utilities* for uncompressing BinHex, StuffIt, Zip, CompactPro, and other types of files.
- ⚓ Online directories of Internet resources.

To order the disk, complete this form and mail it with your check or money order to:

Sales Department
Navigating the Internet **Disk Offer**
201 West 103rd Street
Indianapolis, IN 46290-1097

Enclose a money order or check for $5 (add $4 for international orders).

Name _____

Company (for company address) _____

Street _____

City _____

State _____ ZIP or Postal Code _____

Country (outside USA) _____

ISBN # 0-672-30485-6D

SPECIAL
Internet Access Time Offer

The Chameleon Sampler software that's included with this book contains configuration files for accessing a number of popular service providers. These providers have agreed to give readers of this book a special offer of up to one month free Internet Access when you sign up with their service.

Contact each provider for specific details of their special offer and information on their services. Be sure to mention this book when you call.

The provider may require you to send the original (or a copy) of this page.

CERFNet

Voice number: (800) 876-2373 or (619) 455-3900

NetCom

Voice Number: (800) 501-8649 or (408) 554-8649

Portal

Voice Number: (408) 973-9111

PSINet

Voice Number: (703) 620-6651

UUNet's AlterNet

Voice Number: (703) 204-8000

THE
NAVIGATING THE INTERNET DISK

This disk contains a special collection of PC Windows software for connecting with and navigating the Internet.

- *Chameleon Sampler*, from NetManage—TCP/IP software for SLIP connections to the Internet, plus a suite of valuable Internet tools, including FTP, Telnet, and E-mail.
- *HGopher*—a Windows Gopher+ client for exploring the resources of the Internet.
- *UUCode*—for UUencoding and UUdecoding binary files.
- Online directories of Internet mailing lists, Newsgroups, and ListServe lists.
- A text search program for the directories.

> **Navigator's Note:** Macintosh users can get a disk of Mac Internet programs and tools—see the disk offer page near the back of the book.

Installing the Disk

Insert the disk in your floppy disk drive and follow these steps to install the software. You must have at least 4 megabytes of free space on your hard drive.

1. From Windows File Manager or Program Manager, choose **File** + **R**un from the menu.
2. Type `<drive>INSTALL` and press Enter. `<drive>` is the letter of the drive that contains the installation disk. For example, if the disk is in drive B:, type `B:INSTALL` and press Enter.
3. Choose **F**ull Install to install all the software; choose **C**ustom Install to install only some of the software.

Follow the on-screen instructions in the installation program. The files are installed to a directory named C:\NAVIGATE, unless you change this name at the beginning of the install program.

When the installation is complete, the file NAVINTER.TXT will be displayed for you to read. This file contains information on the files and programs that were installed. A Program Manager group named *Navigating the Internet* will be created by the installation program.

> **Navigator's Note:** The Chameleon Sampler software must still be installed after the main installation is complete. Go to the *Navigating the Internet* Program Manager group and double-click the Install Chameleon Sampler icon. See Appendix G for more information.